Praise for PassPorter®

It's the first and only book that covers Disney cruises in detail. And what splendid detail! Jennifer and Dave tell you everything you need and want to know, from embarkation to debarkation. Even if you don't currently have a Disney cruise planned, this is great armchair reading. It certainly took me back to happy thoughts of my last Disney cruise and made me want to plan the next one!

— Mary Waring
MouseSavers.com

I LOVE all the details in PassPorter! It really helps me to prepare and set my expectations.

— Michelle Bryant
in North Carolina

I always find great nuggets of information that you can't find anywhere else. In addition, the highlighting of new information is great for repeat readers!

— Carrianne Basler
in Wisconsin

Easy read, well laid out, simple and quick to find the information I needed, and fits into my day travel bag!

— Sherisse White in
Alberta, Canada

PassPorter books have all the information you could possibly need to know about fully enjoying a Disney cruise!

— Valerie Pfenning
in Nebraska

The independent and objective information was well researched and very well organized.

— Eric Platt
in Pennsylvania

I love how informative PassPorter is! I just love it!

— Monique Craft
in Kentucky

What's New and Unique

New In This Edition:

- ✓ **Latest information on the new ships**—the new Disney Dream and Disney Fantasy have now joined the Disney fleet! Learn all about the new staterooms, eateries, activities, and more!
- ✓ **Coverage of all the recent changes** aboard and at Castaway Cay, including the new kids club policies, and more!
- ✓ **More information** on "tween" activities (ages 11–13) onboard.
- ✓ **Coverage of all current ports of call**, including Adriatic, Greece, Jamaica, and Alaska!
- ✓ **Listings of the many new shore excursions** along with detailed descriptions and extra information, plus updated details for all existing excursions in all ports.
- ✓ **Sneak peek at new itineraries** for 2014.

Unique Features and Information:

- ✓ **Comprehensive yet concise information** is packed into our pages—PassPorter is information-rich and padding-free!
- ✓ **Blending of personal experience** and photographs from your authors and the collective wisdom of tens of thousands of readers means a guidebook that's full of heart and soul.
- ✓ **Well-organized chapters and pages** make it easy to find what you need. We edit our information carefully so that sections always begin at the top of a page.
- ✓ **Extensive index** to make it easier to find things.
- ✓ **Worksheets** to jot notes and make travel arrangements
- ✓ **Reader tips** that highlight practical and helpful ideas from vacationers like you.
- ✓ **Magical memories** from your authors and fellow travelers to convey the spirit and wonder of Disney cruising.
- ✓ **Expert peer reviewers** to ensure accuracy and thoroughness.
- ✓ **Changes highlighted** with a light gray background to mark significant changes since our last edition.
- ✓ **Cruise Journal** for you to keep notes on your adventure.

Disney Magic/Wonder Deck Plans

Note: These plans do not reflect changes (see page 37) coming to the Magic in late 2013.

Tip: Once you know your stateroom number, note it on this page and highlight the section of the ship where it is located in the profile map to the left.

Our stateroom number: ______________

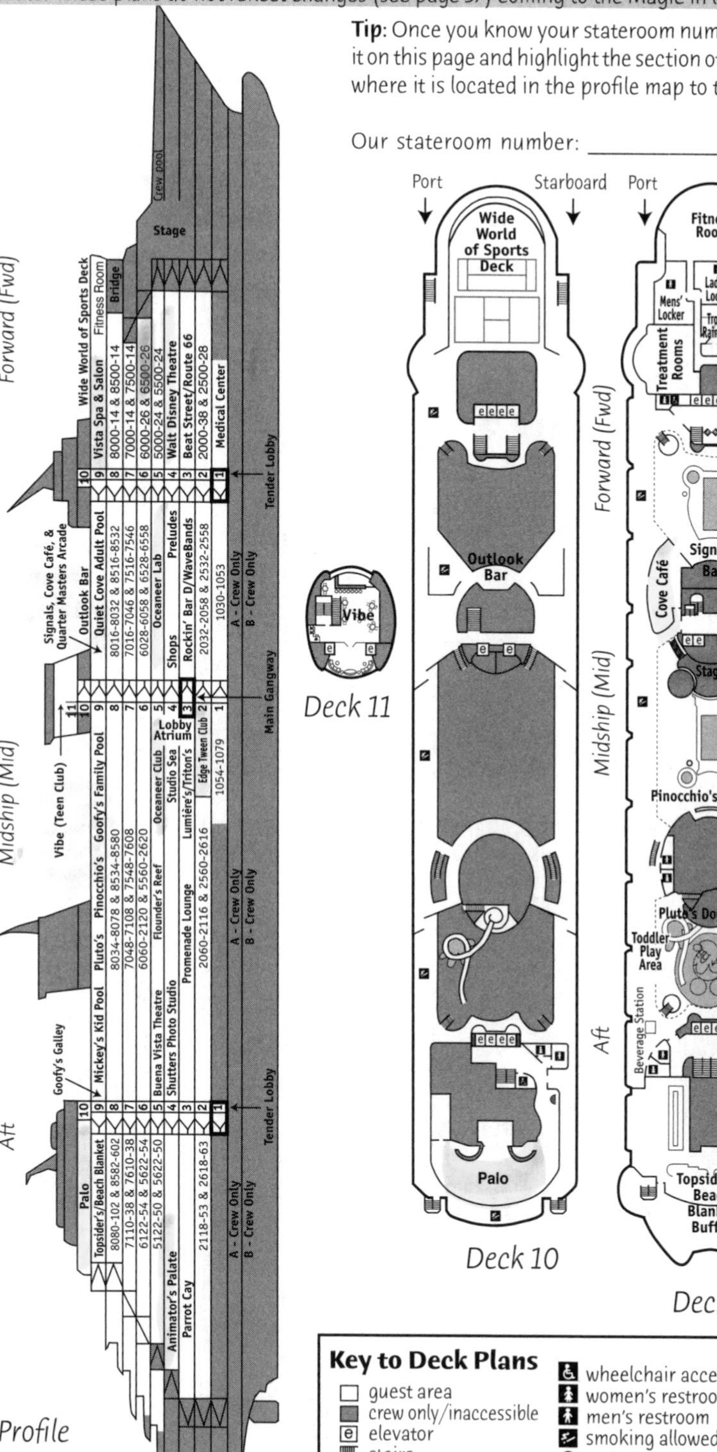

Disney Magic/Wonder Decks 8, 7, 6, and 5

Get These Deck Plans Online!
Owners of this guide have free access to more detailed, color versions of all our deck plans—you can even zoom in closer! Access requires an Internet connection for downloading the files. Visit http://www.passporter.com/dcl/deckplans.htm

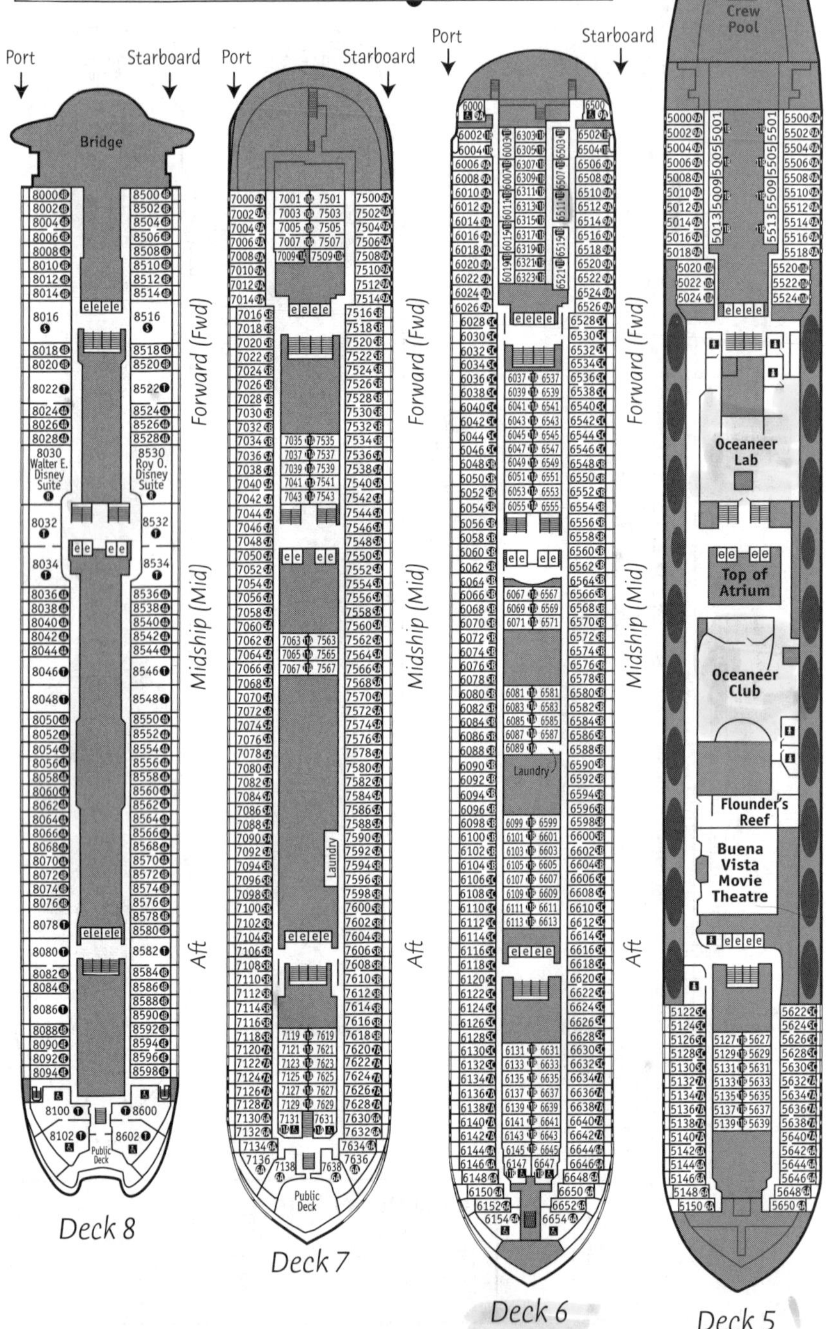

Disney Magic/Wonder Decks 4, 3, 2, and 1

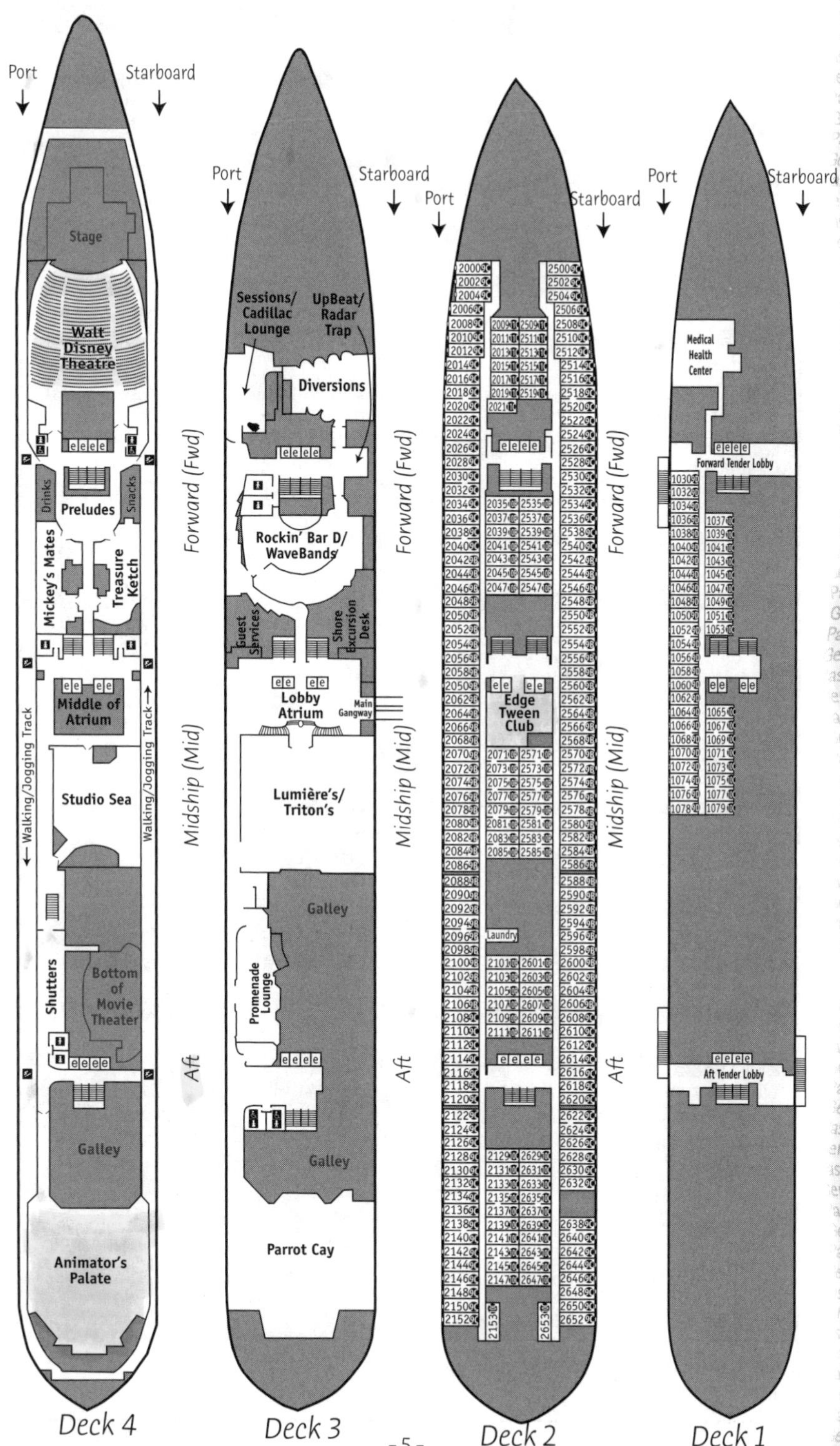

Disney Magic (M)/Wonder (W) Directory

Note: This list does not reflect changes (see page 37) coming to the Magic in late 2013.

Location	Deck	Page
Adult pool	9 Fwd	3
Adult cafe	9 Mid	3
Adult district	3 Fwd	5
Adult restaurant	10 Aft	3
Aerobics studio	9 Fwd	3
Animator's Palate	4 Aft	5
Assembly stations	4	5
Atrium (Lobby)	3-5 Mid	5,4
Arcade	9 Mid	3
Bars	3,4,9,10,11	5,4,3
Beach Blanket Buffet (W)	9 Aft	3
Beat Street (M)	3 Fwd	5
Beverage station	9 Aft	3
Buena Vista Theatre	5 Aft	4
Buffet restaurant	9 Aft	3
Cadillac Lounge (W)	3 Fwd	5
Casual dining	9	3
Children's clubs	5 Mid	4
Children's pool	9 Aft	3
Cove Café	9 Mid	3
Dance club	3 Fwd	5
Deck parties	9 Mid	3
Diversions	3 Fwd	5
Duty-free shop	3 Fwd	5
Edge (tween club)	2 Mid	5
Family nightclub	4 Mid	5
Family pool	9 Mid	3
Fast food	9	3
Fitness center	9 Fwd	3
Flounder's Reef	5 Mid	4
Fruit station	9 Aft	3
Goofy's Family Pool	9 Mid	3
Goofy's Galley	9 Aft	3
Guest Services	3 Mid	5
Hair salon	9 Fwd	3
Hot tubs	9	3
Ice cream station	9 Aft	3
Internet Cafe	3 Aft	5
Kids pool	9 Aft	3
Kids clubs	5 Mid	4
Laundry rooms	2,6,7 Mid	5,4
Liquor shop	3 Fwd	5
Lobby (Atrium)	3 Mid	5
Lounges	3,4,9,10,11	5,3
Lumière's (M)	3 Mid	5
Medical Center	1 Fwd	5
Mickey's kids' pool	9 Aft	3
Mickey's Mates	4 Mid	5
Movie theater	5 Aft	4
Nightclubs	3 Fwd	5
Nursery	5 Mid	4
Oceaneer Club & Lab	5 Mid	4
Outdoor movies	9 Mid	3
Outlook Bar/Lounge	10 Mid	3
Palo	10 Aft	3
Parrot Cay	3 Aft	5
Photo studio	4 Aft	5
Piano lounge	3 Fwd	5
Ping-Pong tables	9	3
Pinocchio's Pizzeria	9 Mid	3
Pluto's Dog House	9 Aft	3
Pools	9	3
Preludes Bar	4 Fwd	5
Promenade Lounge	3 Aft	5
Pub (Diversions)	3 Fwd	5
Quarter Masters arcade	9 Mid	3
Quiet Cove adult pool	9 Fwd	3
Radar Trap duty free (W)	3 Fwd	5
Restrooms	3,4,5,9,10	5,4,3
Rockin' Bar D (M)	3 Fwd	5
Route 66 (W)	3 Fwd	5
Salon	9 Fwd	3
Sessions lounge (M)	3 Fwd	5
Shore excursion desk	3 Mid	5
Shuffleboard	4	5
Shutters photo studio	4 Aft	5
Shops	4 Mid	5
Sickbay	1 Fwd	5
Signals	9 Mid	3
Snack bars	9	3
Spa (Vista Spa)	9 Fwd	3
Sports deck	10 Fwd	3
Teen club	11 Mid	3
Tender lobbies	1 Fwd & Aft	5
Theater (movies)	5 Aft	4
Theater (stage shows)	4 Fwd	5
Toddler water play area	9 Aft	3
Topsider's Buffet (M)	9 Aft	3
Treasure Ketch	4 Mid	5
Triton's (W)	3 Mid	5
Tween club	2 Mid	5
UpBeat duty free (M)	3 Fwd	5
Vibe (teen club)	11 Mid	3
Vista Spa & Salon	9 Fwd	3
Walt Disney Theatre	4 Fwd	5
Waterslide	9 Aft	3
Whirlpools	9	3
WaveBands (W)	3 Fwd	5
Wide World of Sports Deck	10 Fwd	3

Fwd, Mid, or Aft? These common abbreviations are for the Forward (front), Midship (middle), and Aft (rear) of the ship. Refer to the labels on our deck plans.

Disney Dream/Fantasy Deck Plans

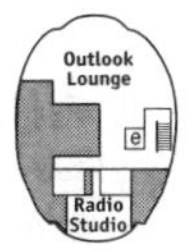

Deck 14

Tip: Once you know your stateroom number, note it on this page and highlight the section of the ship where it is located in the profile map to the left.

Our stateroom number: ___________________

Port
Starboard

Sun Deck
Satellite Falls (Fantasy only)
Concierge Sun Deck
Currents
Edge Tween Club
Funnel Vision
Goofy's Sports Deck
Golf Sim
Golf Sim
Goofy Golf Course

Deck 13

12002
12000
12502
Spa Treatment Rooms
Concierge Lounge
Wading Pool (Fantasy)
Sun Deck
Sun Deck
Sun Deck
Sun Deck
Aqua Duck Loading
AquaLab (Fantasy only)
Waves Bar
Remy
Palo
Meridian Lounge

Deck 12

Senses Spa Treatment Salons
Couple's Villa
Couple's Villa
Mens' Locker
Ladies' Locker
Chill Spa
Rainforest Room
Fitness Area
Senses Spa & Salon
Quiet Cove Adult Pool
Cove Cafe
Eye Scream/Frozone
Flo's Cafe
Whozit's & Whatzit's
Deck Stage
Donald's Pool
Mickey's Pool
Mickey Slide
Nemo's Reef
Arr-cade
Cabanas

Deck 11

Laundry

Deck 10

Disney Dream/Fantasy Decks 9, 8, 7, and 6

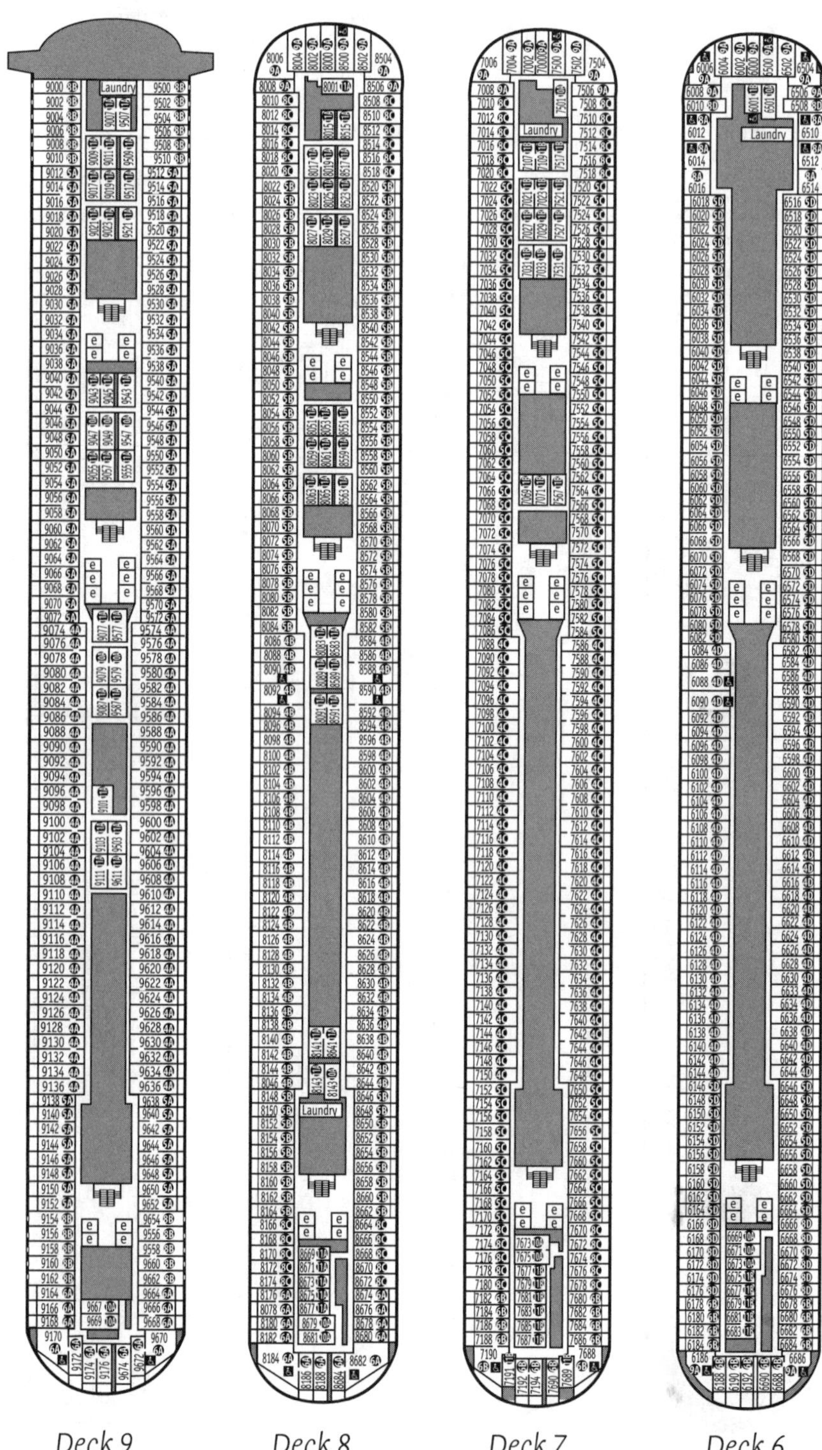

Disney Dream/Fantasy Decks 5, 4, 3, 2, and 1

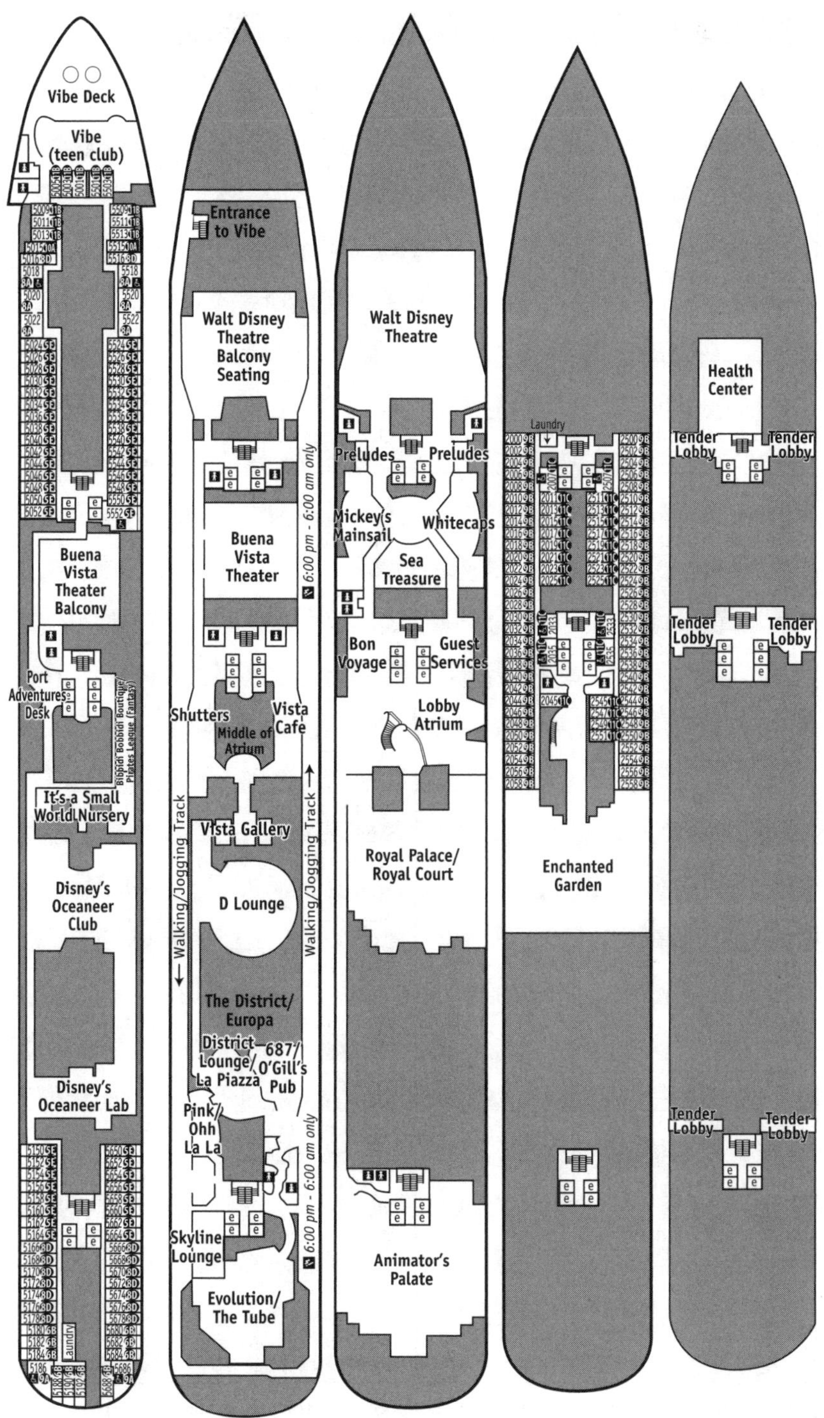

Disney Dream/Fantasy Directory

(D) = Disney Dream; (F) = Disney Fantasy

Location	Deck	Page
687 (D) / O'Gills (F)	4 Aft	9
Adult pool	11 Fwd	7
Adult cafe	11 Fwd	7
Adult district	4 Aft	9
Adult restaurants	12 Aft	7
Animator's Palate	3 Aft	9
AquaDuck entrance	12 Mid	7
Assembly stations	4	9
Atrium (Lobby)	3-5 Mid	9
Arcade	11 Mid	7
Bars	3,4,11,12,13	
Beverage stations	11 Mid	7
Bon Voyage desk	3 Mid	9
Buena Vista Theatre	4 Mid	9
Buffet restaurant	11 Aft	7
Cabanas restaurant	11 Aft	7
Casual dining	11	7
Children's clubs	5 Mid	9
Children's pool	11 Mid	7
Chill Spa (teens)	11 Fwd	7
Coaster (water)	12 Mid	7
Concierge Lounge	12 Fwd	7
Conference rooms	5 Mid	9
Cove Café	11 Mid	7
Currents Bar	13 Fwd	7
Dance club	4 Aft	9
Deck parties	11 Mid	7
D Lounge	4 Mid	9
The District (D)	4 Aft	9
District Lounge (D) / La Piazza (F)	4 Aft	9
Donald's Family Pool	11 Mid	7
Duty-free shops	3 Fwd	5
Edge Tween Club	13 Mid	7
Enchanted Garden	2 Mid	9
Evolution (D) / Tube (F)	4 Aft	9
Eye Scream/Frozone	11 Mid	7
Family nightclub	3 Mid	9
Family pool	11 Mid	7
Fast food	11	7
Fitness center	11 Fwd	7
Flo's Cafe	11 Mid	7
Funnel Vision Stage	11 Mid	7
Goofy's Sports Deck	13 Aft	7
Guest Services	3 Mid	9
Hair salon (Senses)	11 Fwd	7
Hot tubs	11	7
Ice cream station	11 Mid	7
It's a Small World Nursery	5 Mid	9
Kids pool	11 Mid	7
Kids clubs	5 Mid	9
Laundry rooms	2,5–10	7-9
Liquor shop	3 Fwd	9
Lobby (Atrium)	3 Mid	9
Lounges	3,4,11,12,13	7,9
Medical Center	1 Fwd	9
Meridian	12 Aft	7
Mickey's kids' pool	11 Mid	7
Mickey's Mainsail shop	3 Fwd	9
Mickey slide	11 Mid	7
Midship Detective Agency	5 Mid	9
Movie theater	4 Fwd	9
Nightclubs	4 Aft	9
Nemo's Reef	11 Mid	7
Nursery	5 Mid	9
Oceaneer Club & Lab	5 Mid	9
Outdoor movies	11 Mid	7
Palo	12 Aft	7
Photo studio	4 Mid	9
Pink (D) / Ooh La La (F)	4 Aft	9
Pools	11	7
Preludes Bar	3 Fwd	9
Quiet Cove adult pool	11 Fwd	7
Remy	12 Aft	7
Restrooms	2,3,4,5,11,12,13	
Royal Palace/Royal Court	3 Mid	9
Salon	11 Fwd	7
Sea Treasure shop	3 Fwd	9
Senses Spa & Salon	11 Fwd	7
Shore excursion desk	4 Mid	9
Shuffleboard	4	9
Shutters photo studio	4 Mid	9
Shops	3 Fwd	9
Sickbay	1 Fwd	9
Skyline Lounge	4 Aft	9
Snack bars	11, 3 Fwd	9
Spa (Senses Spa)	11 Fwd	7
Sports deck	13 Aft	7
Tender lobbies	1	9
Theater (movies)	4 Fwd	9
Theater (stage shows)	3,4 Fwd	9
Toddler water play area	11 Mid	7
Vibe teen club	5 Fwd	9
Vista Café	4 Mid	9
Vista Gallery	4 Mid	9
Walt Disney Theatre	3,4 Fwd	9
Waterslides	11 & 12	7
Waves bar	12 Mid	7
Whirlpools	11	7
Whitecaps shop	3 Fwd	9
Whozits & Whatzits	11 Mid	7

Fwd, Mid, or Aft? These common abbreviations are for the Forward (front), Midship (middle), and Aft (rear) of the ship. Refer to the labels on our deck plans.

PassPorter's® Disney Cruise Line® and Its Ports of Call

11th Edition

The take-along travel guide and planner

Dave Marx
and
Jennifer Marx

PassPorter Travel Press

An imprint of MediaMarx, Inc.
P.O. Box 3880, Ann Arbor, Michigan 48106
877-WAYFARER
http://www.passporter.com

PassPorter's® Disney Cruise Line® and Its Ports of Call (Eleventh Edition)
by Dave Marx and Jennifer Marx

P.O. Box 3880, Ann Arbor, Michigan 48106
877-WAYFARER or 877-929-3273 (toll-free)
Visit us on the World Wide Web at http://www.passporter.com

Special Sales: PassPorter Travel Press publications are available at special discounts for bulk purchases for sales premiums or promotions. Special editions, including personalized covers and excerpts of existing guides, can be created in large quantities. For information, write to Special Sales, P.O. Box 3880, Ann Arbor, Michigan, 48106.

Distributed by Publishers Group West

ISBN-10: 1-58771-120-6
ISBN-13: 978-1-58771-120-6

10 9 8 7 6 5 4 3 2 1

Printed in the United States of America

About the Authors

Dave Marx may be considered a Renaissance Man, a jack-of-all-trades, or a dilettante, depending on how you look at things. He took a 20-year hiatus between his early journalism training and the start of his full-time writing career. Beyond co-authoring more than 40 books with Jennifer, he's been a radio writer/producer; recording engineer; motion picture music editor; broadcast engineer supervisor; whitewater safety and rescue instructor; developer of online publishing courses; and newsletter editor and promotions chief for an online forum. He discovered the Walt Disney World Resort in March 1997 and first cruised in October 1999. He's since cruised 16 more times, including his award cruise for being a Million-Point Winner at the retired "Who Wants to Be a Millionaire—Play It!" attraction at Walt Disney World. His most recent cruise was aboard the new Disney Fantasy in March 2012. Dave lives in Ann Arbor, Michigan.

Name: Dave Marx
Date of birth: 04/07/55
Residence: Ann Arbor, MI
Signature: Dave Marx

Name: Jennifer Marx
Date of birth: 10/09/68
Residence: Ann Arbor, MI
Signature: Jennifer Marx

Jennifer Marx grew up in Michigan, where you can stand anywhere within the state and be less than six miles from a lake, river, or stream. Her shipboard experiences include two weeks aboard a sailboat as a crew member and nine months working aboard the sternwheeler "Michigan" on Lake Biwa, Japan. Her first Disney Cruise Line adventure was for three nights in October 1999. A four-night cruise followed in May 2001. She had the good fortune to be aboard the Panama Canal crossing (eastbound) in August 2005. Her most recent cruise was aboard the Disney Fantasy for Magical Inaugural Preview Cruise. Jennifer is the author of more than 60 books, including the guide that started it all: *PassPorter's Walt Disney World*. Jennifer makes her home in the university town of Ann Arbor, Michigan with her amazing son, Alexander (see below).

About the Contributor

Alexander Marx is our nine-year-old "Kid Contributor." He's had the good fortune to be have cruised nine times in his young life, with his first cruise at just five months old. He's experienced cruise life at every stage of his development—as an infant, toddler, preschooler, and now as a school-age child. He adds his comments throughout the book to help other kids know what to expect when cruising and to make sure they don't miss out on the "really cool stuff." Look for the special KidTip tag to find his notes!

PassPorter Peer Reviewers

What's behind our smiling faces? A team of amazingly talented individuals with years of collective experience traveling and cruising. These folks combed through our manuscript checking for omissions, errors, and ways we could improve this guidebook for you. In many cases, our peer reviewers have reviewed multiple editions of this guidebook to ensure accuracy and readability for you! Many thanks to our peer reviewers!

Dianne Cook is a PassPorter Forums Guide and has been a Disney Vacation Club member since 1994. She and her husband along with their two college age sons have been on the Disney Magic, the Disney Wonder, and the Disney Dream—and they cruised on the Disney Fantasy to the Western Caribbean in 2012.

Bernie Edwards served on the 2010, 2011, and 2012 Walt Disney World Moms Panel, and on the 2013 Disney Parks Moms Panel. Bernie, his wife Laura, and their two sons, Christopher and Thomas, all love cruising with Disney and it is their favorite Disney vacations these days. The whole family is looking forward to their next cruise which will be on the Dream.

Cam Matthews is a PassPorter Guide and a Disney Vacation Club member. For their 25th wedding anniversary, husband Luke treated her and their daughter Stefanie to their first Disney cruise for four nights on the Disney Wonder. Cam is also a peer reviewer for *PassPorter's Walt Disney World Resort*.

Cheryl Pendry is the author of *PassPorter's Walt Disney World for British Holidaymakers* and co-author of *PassPorter's Disney Vacation Club Guide*. She and her husband Mark have taken a number of Disney cruises around the Caribbean, Mediterranean, and Alaska, and have cruised on have cruised on all four Disney ships. They are looking forward to cruising to new ports of call in the Eastern Mediterranean on the Magic in 2014.

Terri Sellers is a Disney Vacation Club member, PassPorter Guide, and avid Disney vacation fan. She recently completed her eighth Disney cruise on the Disney Fantasy with her husband Chris. She and Chris love dining at Disney restaurants and being pampered at Disney Spas on the cruise ships and in the resorts. They are looking forward to their next Disney cruise.

Don Willis is a retired government appraiser living in Northern California. He has enjoyed three Disney Cruises and tries to visit Walt Disney World annually. He is a Guide for several forums on the PassPorter message boards and is also a peer review for *PassPorter's Walt Disney World Resort*.

Acknowledgments

Oceans of thanks to our readers, who've contributed loads of tips and stories since the debut of the first PassPorter more than 14 years ago in 1999. A special thanks to those who contributed to this edition:

Mary Waring, Michelle Bryant, Carrianne Basler, Sherisse White, Valerie Pfenning, Eric Platt, Monique Craft (page 1); Sharon Diehl (page 38); Allison Hickman (page 178); Mary Albright (page 178); Christine Krueger (page 178); Renea Govekar, Glenn Laterre (page 214); Jody Williams (page 178); Cindy Seaburn, Kathleen David-Bajar (page 472); and our photo contributors Cheryl Pendry, Sabine Rautenberg, Terri Sellers, Kenny Jenkins, Mike Powell, Judy Vosecky, and Gail F. May you each receive a new memory for every reader your words touch.

PassPorter would not be where it is today without the support of the Internet community. Our thanks to the friendly folks below and to all those we didn't have room to include!

- AllEars®.net (http://www.allears.net). Thanks, Deb!
- CruiseCritic.com (http://cruisecritic.com). Thanks, Laura!
- MEI-Travel and Mouse Fan Travel (http://www.mei-travel.com). Thanks, Beci!
- MouseEarVacations.com (http://www.mouseearvacations.com). Thanks, Jami!
- MousePlanet (http://www.mouseplanet.com). Thanks, Mark, Alex, and Mike!
- MouseSavers.com (http://www.mousesavers.com). Thanks, Mary!
- The Platinum Castaway Club (http://www.castawayclub.com). Thanks, Barb & Tony!
- Unofficial Disney Information Station (http://www.wdwinfo.com). Thanks, Pete!

A special thank you to the Guides (moderators) of our own message boards: Tiffany Bendes, Tanya Blissman, Sandra Bostwick, Dyan Chaplin, Michelle Clark, Dianne Cook, Pam Dorr, Lesley Duncan, Dawn Erickson, Marisa Garber-Brown, Rob Gatto, Debbie Hendrickson, LauraBelle Hime, Linda Holland, Christina Holland-Radvon, Kelly Hughes, Claudine Jamba, Ann Johnson, Deb Kendall, Robin Krening-Capra, Susan Kulick, Marcie LaCava, Denise Lang, Jodi Leeper, Eileen Lloyd, Keri Madeira, Heather Macdonald, Janine Marshall, Cam Matthews, Yvonne Mitchell, Sarah Mudd, Bill Myers, Rebecca Oberg, Allison Palmer-Gleicher, Cheryl Pendry, Susan Rannestad, Sabine Rautenberg, Terri Sellers, Ann Smith, Marie St. Martin, Mindy Stanton, Marnie Urmaza, Sara Varney, Susan Wagner, Suzi Waters, Don Willis, and the 62,000+ readers in our amazing community at http://www.passporterboards.com/forums.

A heartfelt thank you to our family and friends for their patience while we were away on research trips or cloistered at our computers, and for their support of our dream: Allison Cerel Marx; Alexander Marx; Carolyn Tody; Fred and Adele Marx; Kim, Chad, Megan and Natalie Larner; Dan, Jeannie, Kayleigh, Melanie, and Nina Marx; Gale Cerel; Jeanne and David Beroza; Robert, Sharon, and Nicole Larner; Gregory A. Reese; Tracy DeGarmo and Jeff Skevington; Gordon Watson and Marianne Couch; and Marta Metcalf. In loving memory of Dave's mother, Adele Marx, who last cruised with Disney on the Dream in February 2011.

Printer: Edwards Brothers Malloy in Ann Arbor, Michigan

Newsletter Editor and Online Coordinator: Sara Varney
Special thank yous to Ernie Sabella, Phil Adelman, Jeff Howell, Fred Marx, Paul McGill, Jonathan Frontado, and the Disney crew members.

Last but not least, we thank Walter Elias Disney for his dream.

Contents

Jennifer poses by a porthole

© MediaMarx, Inc.

List of Maps, Worksheets, and Charts

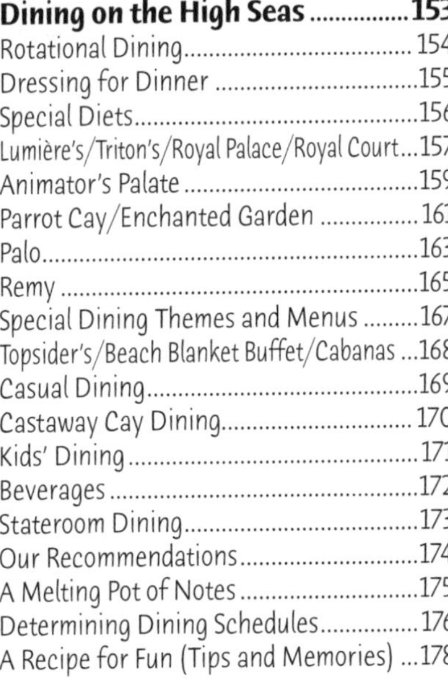

Dave anticipates a fine meal at Palo

Goofin' around at the Mickey Pool

Bonus Features...

Bon Voyage!

You're about to embark on a marvelous voyage aboard one of the most beautiful and celebrated cruise lines in the world. You couldn't have made a better choice—the Disney Cruise Line will surprise and delight you with its stunning architecture, legendary service, and fun-for-the-whole-family activities. Boy, we wish we could go with you!

Our original travel guide, *PassPorter's Walt Disney World*, contains the basic information for the Disney Cruise Line. Even so, our readers sent in many requests to add more details on the cruises. Our answer is this guide, which is chock-a-block with information on virtually every aspect of cruising with Disney. We designed it to stand alone or work with our Disney World guidebook and/or the PassPorter travel planning system. Everything you need to know to plan and enjoy a magical cruise is within these pages!

You're holding the eleventh edition of the first guidebook dedicated to the Disney Cruise Line! As always, we include in-depth coverage of scheduled "special itinerary" ports along with Disney's regular stops. Changes and updates aboard the Disney Cruise Line since our last edition are highlighted in gray, too! The Disney Cruise Line is constantly evolving, which makes this travel guide a perpetual work in progress. Please tell us what you like and where we've missed the boat so we can improve our next edition!

This field guide is the embodiment of not just our knowledge and experience, but that of our fellow cruisers and PassPorter readers as well. In essence, this is a cruise guide by cruisers, for cruisers. We share what we like and don't like, and you may find some differing opinions just within the pages of this guide. Reader opinion plays a big part of our shore excursion reviews in chapter 6. And our expert reviewers shared their own opinions and experiences to enrich our information.

Use this field guide for planning before you embark, and then keep it handy onboard during your voyage. We hope you find this field guide a useful companion on your adventure!

Jennifer and Dave

We'd love to hear from you! Visit us on the Internet (http://www.passporter.com) or drop us a postcard from Castaway Cay!

P.S. This edition was last revised in June 2013. To check for new revisions or view our latest online update list, visit us on the Internet at this address: http://www.passporter.com/dcl

Preparing to Cast Off

Cruising doesn't just refer to the time you're onboard—it's a state of mind. To help you get into the spirit of the adventure that awaits, try out our favorite ways to build excitement for a Disney cruise. You may discover they help you "cruise" through the planning process without a hitch!

Check Out the Literature
A trip to your local travel agent will reward you with the free Disney Cruise Line Vacations booklet—it's in full color and crammed with photos. You can also request one at 888-325-2500 or at http://www.disneycruise.com. The Disney web site is also a great source for photos, excursions, etc.

Watch the DVD
Request your free Disney Cruise Line DVD by calling 888-325-2500 or on the web at http://www.disneycruise.com. It arrives in about 3-4 weeks. The DVD offers a fun peek at the ship and ports.

Network With Other Cruisers
Fans of Disney cruises are scattered far and wide—chances are you know someone who has been on a Disney cruise. If not, come join us on the Internet, where many Disney cruisers congregate to share tips. See page 36 for links to popular gathering places, including PassPorter.com.

Tune In to TV
Watch the Travel Channel and the Discovery Channel for specials about cruises and the Caribbean. Or have fun with reruns of "The Love Boat."

FROM CASTAWAY CAY

Being on Castaway Cay and hearing all this great music reminds us that there's nothing like steel drums to conjure up visions of cruising through the Caribbean. Find some Caribbean-style music and play it as you plan. We guarantee it'll get you in the mood. If you have access to iTunes, try the Reggae/Island radio stations.

Your authors,
Jennifer and Dave

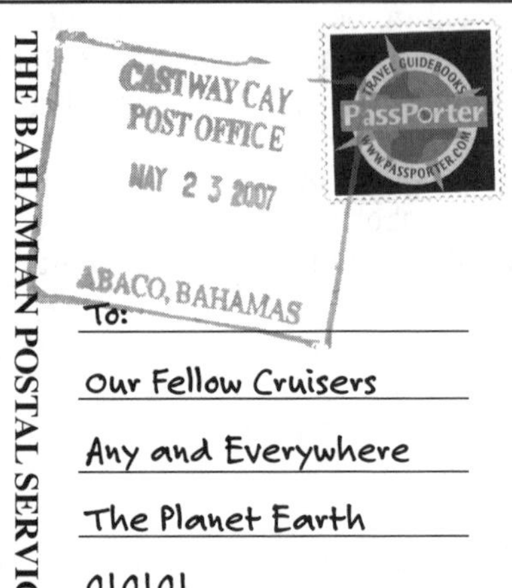

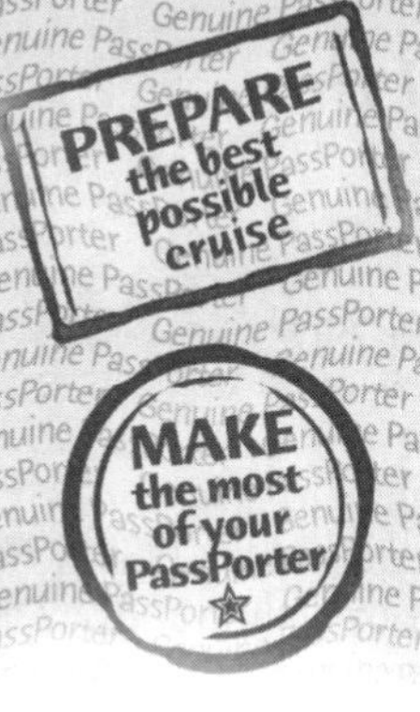

Getting Your Feet Wet

So, you've decided to take a Disney cruise! Disney cruises attract many first-time cruisers. If you're among them, welcome to the world of cruising! If you're a cruise veteran, welcome back!

Now that you've decided to cruise, you're likely to have one of two reactions. You may feel overwhelmed by the complexity that looms ahead. Or you may be lulled into a sense of complacency, sure that all the details will be taken care of. We understand—before our early cruises, we wavered between these two reactions ourselves. It wasn't until we learned more about the Disney cruises that we received a welcome splash of cold water. Thanks to a boatload of knowledge and the experience of other cruisers, we were able to dispel that feeling of drifting into uncharted waters.

We figure you don't want a splash of cold water in your face, so instead we offer this chapter as a friendly introduction to the world of cruising with Disney. We filled the chapter with highlights and histories, as well as facts and figures. You can read the chapter straight through or jump to the sections that interest you. We've included articles on the Disney Cruise Line, cruising in general, and hints for first-time cruisers. And to help you make important decisions, we also provide comparisons with other cruise lines and Walt Disney World, fleet facts, the differences between the four ships, budgeting, money-saving ideas, and the best places to find more information. We wrap up the chapter with tips and memories.

Before you delve deeper, we want to share a secret. Yes, it's true that you could plunk down your money and just show up. But you wouldn't be getting your money's worth—not by a long shot. Planning is the secret to any successful vacation. Not only do you learn the tips and tricks, but you get to start your cruise early through anticipation. By the end of this guide, you'll know more than the vast majority of your shipmates. You'll know the way to get those coveted reservations. You'll know the way to pack and what to bring. You'll even know your way around the ship before you board it. In short, you'll be cruising your way ... straight out of those uncharted waters and into the true "magic" and "wonder" of a "dream" cruise of "fantasy."

The Disney Cruise Line

The Disney Cruise Line is more than just another cruise. Disney designed its ships to be **innovative**, offering unique facilities and programs, each with Disney's hallmark, first-class service.

The **history of the Disney Cruise Line** began in November 1985, when Premier Cruise Lines became the official cruise line of Walt Disney World Resort. Premier's "Big Red Boat" offered Disney characters and packages that included stays at the Walt Disney World Resort. When the ten-year contract with Premier was up, Disney set off on its own with an ambitious goal: To become the best cruise line in the world. Disney commissioned the Fincantieri Shipyard (in Venice, Italy) to build two 350-million-dollar liners reminiscent of the grand, trans-Atlantic liners of the early 20th century. A private island was developed into the delightful Castaway Cay, a stop on most Florida-based itineraries. On July 30, 1998, the Disney Magic set sail on her maiden voyage. The magnificent new ship boasted a classic, streamlined silhouette, twin funnels, and well-appointed interiors. The Disney Magic sailed from her dedicated, art deco-inspired cruise terminal in Port Canaveral, Florida on three- and four-night cruises to the Bahamas. The Disney Wonder set sail for the first time on August 15, 1999. Seven-night itineraries to the Eastern Caribbean on the Disney Magic were added in 2000, leaving the shorter cruises to the Wonder. In 2002, 7-night Western Caribbean cruises were added. The Disney Magic sailed the Mexican Riviera in 2005 and 2008, the Mediterranean in 2007, and went back to Europe in summer 2010, with a bevy of itineraries in both the Mediterranean and Baltic. In 2010 the Wonder added five-night itineraries, with visits to Nassau, Castaway Cay, plus either a second day at Castaway Cay or a stop in Key West, Florida. Both ships have received upgrades over the years, enhancing their comforts, and are scheduled for additional upgrades in 2013 and 2014.

The cruise line took a **big leap forward in 2011-2012**, with the addition of two brand-new ships built by Meyer Werft Shipyards in Papenburg, Germany. The Disney Dream entered regular service on January 26, 2011 from its home port of Port Canaveral, Florida. It took over the Wonder's historic assignment, the 3- and 4-night Bahamas itineraries. The Disney Wonder then moved to Los Angeles, offering Mexican Riviera itineraries. In spring 2011, Disney visited Alaska for the first time, with 7-night itineraries sailing from Vancouver, British Columbia during the spring and summer. In March 2012, Disney's fourth ship—the Disney Fantasy—entered service and offers 7-night Caribbean cruises. The 2012 schedule had cruises departing from Port Canaveral, New York, Seattle, Galveston, and Miami. What lies ahead? See page 37 for a discussion of the future.

The **Disney Magic** and the **Disney Wonder** (the "Magic Class" ships) are almost identical vessels, with only a few minor differences (see page 31). The ships' hulls are painted dark blue-black, white, yellow, and red (Mickey's colors) with elegant gold scrollwork that cleverly reveals the silhouettes of classic Disney characters. As you board, you are greeted by friendly crew members in the three-story lobby atrium, distinguished by sweeping staircases and a bronze statue (Mickey on the Magic, Ariel on the Wonder). Warm woods, polished metal railings, and nautical touches embrace passengers in elegance. Subtle Disney touches are abundant, from character silhouettes along the staircases to valuable Disney prints and artwork on the walls. Every area of the ship is decorated and themed.

© Disney

The Disney Magic and the Disney Wonder

The **Disney Dream** began service on January 26, 2011 and The **Disney Fantasy** entered service on March 31, 2012 (the "Dream Class" ships). Both are almost identical vessels, about 50% larger than the Magic and Wonder. Their appearance and features echo and expand upon the now-classic design of the Magic Class, and several exciting new features have been added. The new ships carry approximately 50% more passengers, with a comparable increase in the number of staterooms and the overall size of the vessels (including two additional passenger decks). Stateroom size is roughly 2%–3% smaller than that of the Magic Class, but the design manages to maintain the features Disney cruise passengers love, including the split bathroom. All ships are a delight to the senses.

© MediaMarx, Inc.

The Disney Dream

Disney Cruise Line introduced a new category of shore excursions in 2010, or as they're now called, **"Port Adventures."** Along with the bulk of the excursions, which continue to be produced and provided by outside excursion operators, Disney has begun to collaborate with tour operators to add distinctively "Disney" family-oriented experiences, with several including the presence of Disney characters. Imagine, if you will, a glittering, princess-studded Royal Ball at the Catherine Palace in St. Petersburg, Russia. In other cases, ship's counselors will accompany the kids on kids-only excursions.

Introducing the Dream and Fantasy

The new Disney Dream and Disney Fantasy ships are similar in many ways to the older Disney Magic and Disney Wonder. **Most changes are evolutionary, not revolutionary.** Most public facilities are 50% larger, reflecting the ship's size. The decor on the Disney Dream is Art Deco, like the Magic; the statue in the Atrium Lobby depicts Admiral Donald Duck, and Sorcerer Mickey decorates the stern. The Fantasy's decor is Art Nouveau, like the Wonder; Minnie Mouse graces the lobby, and Dumbo dangles from the stern.

So what's new? The Walt Disney and Buena Vista Theatres each moved down one deck, and both added balconies. The adult entertainment district (The District on the Dream, Europa on the Fantasy), moved from deck 3 forward to 4 aft, and added two more lounges. The Promenade Lounge on deck 3 disappeared, with a small new bar, Bon Voyage, within the Atrium Lobby on deck 3, and Vista Cafe overlooking the lobby on deck 4. Shutters Photo Studio now also overlooks the lobby from deck 4.

What about the **main dining rooms**? Animators Palate (with an enhanced "show") moved from deck 4 to 3. Enchanted Garden, replacing Parrot Cay, is down on deck 2 and has a small "show" of its own, a formal garden/conservatory motif that transforms from day to night. Royal Palace/Royal Court, the most formal regular dining room, is on deck 3 adjacent to the lobby. Adults-only Remy joins Palo, on deck 12, as a second extra-cost dining choice, paired with Meridian Lounge next door. Deck 11 hosts the pools, Flo's Cafe quick service food counters, and Cabanas casual dining. Cabanas has multiple serving stations offering a variety of cuisines.

There are still **three swimming pools**, but Donald now "owns" the family pool. Toddlers have a much bigger, shaded and glass-enclosed water play area by the Mickey Pool. Goofy's Sports Deck occupies deck 13, with Goofy mini golf added to the old standbys. AquaDuck, a 765-foot "water coaster" starts on deck 16 and splashes down on deck 12 (see page 200).

The **children's programs** echo recent changes (see page 194), but "tweens" age 11–13 got the forward funnel ("Edge"), and teens age 14–17 moved to "Vibe" on deck 5, with its own outdoor deck. The Peter Pan-themed Oceaneer's Club (ages 3–10) also added areas themed on Toy Story, Monster's Inc., Finding Nemo, and Pixie Hollow; and "Turtle Talk with Crush" (an interactive audiovisual experience) shows on a 103-inch video screen. The Oceaneer's Lab features Stitch on its interactive screen. Video technology is used widely, with "Living Art" that comes to life in the public areas, including the Skyline Lounge with glittering, penthouse views of great cities.

New stateroom categories are the Family Oceanview Stateroom with Porthole that sleeps up to 5, and Concierge Family Oceanview Stateroom with Verandah. Concierge and suite guests have a lounge on deck 12 and a private sun deck. Inside Staterooms gain a "virtual porthole," a video screen with a live, outdoor view. Verandah partitions on connecting staterooms can open, for a double-wide experience.

Our Disney Dream & Fantasy Cruises

We were fortunate to sail on the Disney Dream's Christening Cruise in 2011. Jennifer then followed that up with the four-night Disney Dream Maiden Voyage less than a week later, and Dave sailed again on the Disney Dream in February 2011. Then, in March 2012 we were aboard for a 3-night Preview Cruise on the Disney Fantasy. We've gone over every bit of the ships in detail—we ***know*** the Disney Dream-class ships!

The Disney Dream Christening was an exciting, two-day whirlwind. Not only was there a new ship to experience, but the ship was loaded with Disney Cruise Line managers and Disney Imagineers, on hand to brief the assembled media. Jennifer and our six-year-old son, Alexander, focused on the family/kids experience, while Dave took guided tours, explored on his own, and interviewed the assembled experts. Dave's immediate impression was that the Dream is far more ship than Disney conveyed in advance. The technological innovations, many unheralded, dazzled and entertained, and the ship's design and décor surpassed his dreams. He was expecting a bigger version of the Disney Magic and Wonder, and what he found was a ship in a league of its own.

It began when Dave stepped on board into the Atrium Lobby, a space easily twice the size of the lobbies on the Magic and Wonder, with all the elegance of a very grand, fairytale ballroom. Dining room décor, too, is more elegant and distinctive. Kid-only and adult-only areas are dramatically expanded and upgraded, and the recreation decks bring more fun and the luxury that comes with space. Concierge accommodations are more elegant, comfortable and protected, the spa more extensive and pampering. Even the elevators are greatly improved, in quantity and size. Overall, the increased space in the ship's public areas enhances the cruise experience in every way. Size only becomes a liability on the stateroom decks, with hallways of seemingly infinite length. Entertainment, perhaps, shows the smallest boost. How much better could Disney do? The theaters are, naturally, larger, and the stage shows as wonderful as ever. Little additions are appreciated, like the live musical groups who perform in the Atrium Lobby and by the adult pool. The ship herself has become more entertaining, and on a constant basis. The interactive Enchanted Artwork on display around the ship, Virtual Portholes in the inside staterooms, huge video screens posing as windows into the sea and overlooking great cities, and the subtle integration of Disney storytelling into even the smallest detail have made this a ship we love to explore.

The Disney Dream Maiden Voyage, the first cruise with paying passengers, was quite an experience. Jennifer was one of the 3,000 or so passengers who ponied up more than double the price of a regular cruise for the privilege of being aboard. And she, too, found a great many things to like about the Disney Dream and only a few that needed improvement. She absolutely loves the beds in the staterooms—these are some of the most comfortable beds she's ever experienced, on land or sea. Plus, the beds are now elevated so she could easily store all her suitcases underneath. Another thing she really enjoyed was the round tub in her Family Oceanview Stateroom, a huge improvement over the rectangular tubs found in most other stateroom categories. She also really enjoys the stage shows in the gorgeous Walt Disney Theatre, particularly "Believe"—do not miss this show! There's still room for improvement in the dining—service was spotty and the "shows" in Animator's Palate and Enchanted Garden could be tweaked to better enhance the dining experience. She has no doubt that both will improve over time, though!

Our Disney Dream Cruises (continued)

Dave's impressions were reinforced on a second, four-night cruise that he shared with his parents. He snagged one of only 150 inside staterooms, which are now, amazingly, coveted spaces onboard thanks to the Virtual Portholes that deliver both a view to the outside world and a bit of Disney whimsy. On this adults-only cruise he experienced the ship in greater detail, and basked in her adults-only culinary delights. Palo is a dining experience most cruisers are likely to enjoy, elegant but accessible. Remy, however, with its high price tag and French "tasting menu," may best be enjoyed by those who identify with food critic Anton Ego in the Disney-Pixar film Ratatouille, "...I don't just like food, I loooove it.," (as does Dave). While Dave and Jennifer agree on most things, he had much more consistent (and excellent) dining room service, and was delighted by the "show" in Animator's Palate.

The Disney Fantasy, though in most ways identical to the Dream, has unique delights of her own. It starts right in the Art Nouveau-styled Atrium Lobby, a style we tend to prefer to the Dream's Art Deco. Designed for 7-night cruises, the Fantasy has features suited to longer voyages. Our son, Alexander, was delighted with his Pirate Night makeover at Pirates League (which at all other times is Bibbidi Bobbidi Boutique, a Princess makeover salon)! Longer voyages include several days at sea, so the recreation decks have more places to get wet, taking some pressure off the main pools and drawing guests to under-utilized sun decks. We saw two of the four new shows produced for the Walt Disney Theatre, and another new show in Animator's Palate dining room. The theater shows, Disney's Aladdin—A Musical Spectacular, and Disney's Wishes, are certainly up to the cruise line's standards. Aladdin, is, of course, a classic, and Wishes is like Disney Dreams in theme, but with a High School Musical/Glee spin. Animation Magic made its debut in Animator's Palate, melding classic Disney animation with some amazing technology. Imagine our excitement when characters drawn by both Alexander and Jennifer were "animated" by Sorcerer Mickey at the end of our meal! The adult entertainment district has a different theme on each Disney ship. We find the Fantasy's theme, Europa, the most appealing of the lot, especially the London subway-themed night club.

The Disney Dream and Fantasy are magnificent vessels, beautiful on the inside and out. To learn more about our experiences, visit http://www.passporter.com/disney-dream and http://www.passporter.com/disney-fantasy where you'll find 50+ videos, 500+ photos, and several articles all about these new ships!

My Cruises on Mickey's New Boats by Alexander

I really really really REALLY liked the Disney Dream and Fantasy. My favorite thing to do was the Midship Detective Agency because I got to explore the ship and solve a mystery! I didn't have time to finish the puppy mystery on the Dream, so I made sure I finished the new Muppet mystery on the Fantasy! I also like swimming in Mickey's pool and playing in the water fountains in Nemo's Reef. The Aqua Lab on the Fantasy is really cool, too. The kids club was super awesome—I spent most of my time in the Oceaneer Lab. I got to do crafts and we even made cupcakes one night. Castaway Cay is my favorite "pirate island" and I found buried treasure on it every time I've visited. I think other kids would really love Mickey's new boats!

Alexander at Nemo's Reef

Why Cruise?

Cruising is something very special. Imagine yourself on a big—really big—beautiful ship. A low hum of excitement fills the air. The ship's whistle sounds smartly (Where have you heard that tune before?) and the ship begins to glide out of her berth. The ship is yours—deck upon deck of dining rooms, lounges, theaters, and staterooms.

People cruise with Disney for many reasons. Some love everything Disney, some want to be pampered, others enjoy the onboard activities, and still others want to visit foreign ports. Some families love the together-time they can have onboard, while other families appreciate the many activities for different ages. Adults love the peace of the adults-only areas, the gourmet tastes at Palo, and the evening fun in the adults-only club district. Teens love having their own hangout and meeting fellow teens. Kids love the Oceaneer Club/Lab and the pools. What about us? Our first Disney cruise was to experience Disney's "next new thing." What brought us back again and again? Pure relaxation! A vacation to Disney World is wonderful, but very intense. On the cruise, we take a deep breath and slow down. We disembark refreshed and renewed, ready to tackle anything.

Jennifer blows bubbles during the sailaway deck party

Cruising Myths

Here are some oft-quoted reasons why some people don't cruise—each is a common myth that we're happy to dispel. *Myth #1: It's too expensive.* Actually, cruising costs the same as a land-based vacation—a Disney Cruise is equivalent to a comparable stay at the Walt Disney World Resort. *Myth #2: I'll be bored.* If anything, there's too much to do! You'll find it hard to choose between activities, and you'll probably disembark with a list of things you wish you'd had time to do. *Myth #3: I'll get seasick.* Most people don't, but there's a chance you could be one of the unlucky few. But if you follow our tips on page 463, you should be just fine. *Myth #4: Cruises are too formal.* Hey, this is a Disney cruise! Casual clothing is the norm onboard (most of the time). Yes, the cruise is luxurious, but you won't feel out of place. *Myth #5: The Disney Cruise is for kids (or people with kids).* Kids love the Disney Cruise, but so do adults (we cruised many times sans kids). There are plenty of adult activities and areas. *Myth #6: I'll feel claustrophobic or unsteady on my feet.* Disney ships' staterooms are 20-25% larger than most other lines, and the ships have stabilizers to minimize rolling.

First-Time Cruisers

Are you going on your first cruise and wondering what to expect?

You're not alone—many of your fellow cruisers will also be on their first cruise. We remember our first cruise well—we had only "The Love Boat" reruns and stories from friends and family to rely upon. We fretted over getting seasick, which wasn't a problem at all. We worried there wouldn't be enough to do, but in fact there was too much—a cruise is quite overwhelming (especially for first-timers) and we wished we had more time. We were even concerned we'd feel like "poor relations" mingling with wealthier cruisers, but we fit right in.

Life aboard a Disney cruise ship is unlike most land-based vacations, unless perhaps you live the lifestyle of the rich and famous. Even if you're staying in budget lodgings, you'll receive the same level of luxurious, personal service as the deluxe guests. Your stateroom attendant will keep your room ship-shape (cleaning twice a day), see to your special needs, and turn down the bed every night (perhaps leaving a cute animal made from towels). You may form a personal relationship with your dining room team, who'll attend you at every shipboard dinner (apart from Palo and Remy).

And you'll eat! **Nearly all food and soft drinks onboard are included** in your Disney cruise—meals, snacks, room service, more snacks—so order anything you want, even if it's "seconds" or two different entrées.

The **ship hums with activity**, from sunup to the wee hours. Parties, live shows, children's programs, recreational activities, first-run movies, seminars, and guest lectures ... nearly everything is included in the price of your cruise, as is the right to do "none of the above."

Some say that modern cruise ships are "floating hotels," but "traveling resort" is a better description. Each day brings new vistas and often a new port. No matter how distracted you may be by onboard activities, the subtle vibration and motion of the ship whispers that your **luxurious little world** is going somewhere. Unlike long road trips or jet flights, your life doesn't go into an uncomfortable state of suspended animation while en route to your destination. Getting there can be far more than half the fun!

Our **advice to first-time cruisers** is two-fold: Learn as much as you can about cruising, and then leave your expectations at home. Keep an open mind and be willing to try new things. You can rest assured that Disney has taken the needs of first-time cruisers into mind and considered your needs even before you realize you have them.

What's Included in a Disney Cruise?

Shipboard Accommodations: Up to 20%–25% larger rooms than other ships—from 169 sq. ft. to 304 sq. ft. for non-suite staterooms.

Shipboard Meals: Three full-service dining room meals daily (breakfast, lunch, and dinner). Alternatives for breakfast, lunch, and dinner, such as buffets, quick-service, and room service, are also included. Let's not forget the snacks (soft-serve ice cream, fruit, hot dogs, sandwiches, pizza), afternoon cookies, evening hors d'oeurves, and at least one late-night dessert buffet. The seven-night and longer cruises serve up even more late-night munchies. Soft drinks (Coke, Diet Coke, Caffeine-Free Diet Coke, Sprite, Diet Sprite, Hi-C pink lemonade, and Hi-C fruit punch), milk, coffee, tea (Twinings hot and fresh or Nestea iced), hot cocoa, water, and ice are always free at meals and at the Beverage Station (deck 9/11), but are not free through room service or at the bars. Lunch (with soda) at Castaway Cay is also included.

Shipboard Entertainment and Activities: Disney offers a wide variety of entertainment, including live stage shows, first-run movies, deck parties, live bands, dancing, nightclubs, karaoke, trivia games, bingo, Disney character meet and greets, seminars, tours, and social gatherings.

Sports and Recreation: Three pools, four whirlpool tubs, fitness center, aerobics studio, walking/jogging track, Ping-Pong, shuffleboard, basketball, and the Wide World of Sports deck (with mini-golf on the Dream Class).

Kids' Activities: Participation in kids' programs is included for ages 3–17, with activities and areas for varying age groups. Kids' shore excursions (other than Castaway Cay programming) are not included, however.

Ports of Call: Stops at all ports on the itinerary are included, as is transportation to the shore by tender (small boat), if necessary. Port charges are included in the price quote, unlike some other cruises.

What Isn't Included?

Your airfare may or may not be included in your cruise package—check when making your reservation. This goes for insurance and ground transfers between the airport to the ship as well. Accommodations, meals, and park passes for any time you spend at Walt Disney World are not included, unless you book an add-on package that specifically includes these. Other extras: alcoholic beverages, specialty beverages (i.e., smoothies), soft drinks (at a bar or from room service), Internet, bingo games, spa and beauty treatments, Palo meals ($20/adult), Remy meals ($75), childcare for kids under 3, arcade games, onboard or off-ship shopping, photos, formalwear rental, shore excursions, meals off-ship (except Castaway Cay), medical treatment, laundry services (including the self-service washers and dryers, though you can use the iron and ironing board freely), parking at the cruise terminal, and gratuities.

Introduction Reservations Staterooms Dining Activities Ports of Call Magic Index

How Do They Measure Up?

Despite today's age of the mega-ship, the Disney vessels are still among the **most spacious ships afloat**. Staterooms are 25% larger on average than those found on non-Disney ships. Other unique aspects of the Disney Cruise Line include split bathrooms (in most stateroom categories 10 and up), a cruiser-friendly dining system (different dining rooms, same servers), half a deck designed just for kids (with programs for specific age groups), areas reserved just for adults (pool, restaurant, Cove Café, spa, beach on Castaway Cay, and an entertainment district that's reserved just for adults after 9:00 pm), a visit to Castaway Cay (Disney's private island), Disney's famous characters, and that Disney magic!

Experienced cruisers may miss having a casino or a library aboard. The sentiment seems to be that the Disney Cruise Line offers the best family cruise afloat, but that it lacks enough activities for adults without children. We disagree (especially after several "drydock" upgrades)—we've sailed without kids and never lack adult activities. The generous adults-only areas deliver welcome isolation and surpass other "family" cruise lines. Some cruisers have also reported that the Disney Cruise Line is too, well, "Disney." Let's face it: If you don't like Disney, you may not like this cruise either. But these aren't theme parks. The quality service and elegant surroundings could easily outweigh any negative associations you have with Mickey Mouse.

Safety and **cleanliness** is a big deal on cruise ships, and all international ships are inspected by the U.S. Centers for Disease Control (CDC) on a regular basis. The Disney ships were most recently inspected between October 2012 and May 2013. All four ships passed—the Dream Class ships received scores of 100/100; the Magic Class ships both received 92–96/100. To view the latest results, visit: http://www.cdc.gov/nceh/vsp.

If you've been to the Walt Disney World Resort and wonder how a Disney cruise compares to a **resort vacation**, it is really quite different. The cruise feels more laid-back yet formal at the same time. The excitement (and stress) of dashing from attraction to attraction is gone, and you may feel like you're missing "something" that you can't identify. On the upside, everything is within walking distance, the food is "free," and rain isn't the same party-pooper it is at the theme parks. You'll take things a bit slower on the cruise (although there's still plenty to do), all the while feeling pampered by the gorgeous setting and excellent service. Walt Disney World and the Disney cruise do share many perks, however: single key-card access for rooms and purchases, Disney character greetings, and that "red carpet" guest service. Don't expect to find "Walt Disney World on water." You'll discover the Disney Cruise Line has its own unique charm.

Fleet Facts and Differences

(Does not reflect changes coming to the Magic in late 2013)

Fact	Magic	Wonder	Dream	Fantasy
Home port:	Varies	Varies	Port Canaveral	Port Canaveral
Country of Registry	The Bahamas			
Year launched	1998	1999	2011	2012
Radio call signs	C6PT7	C6QM8	C6YR6	C6ZL6
Captains	Captain Tom Forberg, Captain Henry Andersson, Captain John Barwis, Captain Gus Verhulst, Captain Thord Haugen, and Captain Marco Nogara			
Crews	950 crew members		1,458 crew members	
Guests	2,400 (1,750 at double occupancy)		4,000 (2,500 at double occupancy)	
Space Ratio	48.3 (at double occupancy)		51 (at double occupancy)	
Tonnage (volume)	83,000		130,000	
Length	964 ft./294 m. (longer than Titanic!)		1,115 ft./340 m.	
Beam (width)	106 ft./32.25 m.		121 ft./36 m.	
Draft (depth below)	25.3 ft./7.7 m.		27 ft./8 m.	
Speed	21.5 knots or 25 mph/40 kph		22 knots or 25 mph/40 kph	
Systems	Five 16-cylinder diesel engines, two 19-megawatt GE propulsion motors, three bow and two stern thrusters, and one pair of fin stabilizers		Three 12-cylinder and two 14-cylinder MAN V48/60CR diesel engines, plus 2 x 19 MW Converteam Motors, stabilizers	
Passenger Decks	11		13	
Lifeboats	20 (150 persons each) + rafts		16 (270 persons each) + rafts	
Staterooms	877 (252 inside, 625 outside)		1250 (150 inside, 1,100 outside)	
Theatres	2 (975 seats and 268 seats)		2 (1,340 seats and 399 seats)	
Restaurants	4 (138 in Palo, 442 in rest)		5 (176 in Palo, 96 at Remy, 697 in rest)	
Buffets/Snack Bars	4 (294 seats inside, 332 outside)		6	
Lounges	8		12	
Pools/splash zones	4 (one pool is for crew only)/1 zone		3 pools/2 zones	3/5 zones
Shops	4		5	
Decor	Art Deco	Art Nouveau	Art Deco	Art Nouveau
Bow Decoration	Sorcerer Mickey	Steamboat Willie	Captain Mickey	Sorcerer Mickey
Stern Decoration	Boatswain Goofy	Donald and Huey	Sorcerer Mickey	Dumbo
Atrium Statue	Helmsman Mickey	Ariel	Donald Duck	Minnie
Grand Dining Room	Lumière's	Triton's	Royal Palace	Royal Court
Casual Dining	Topsider's	Beach Blanket	Cabanas	Cabanas
Adults District	Beat Street	Route 66	The District	Europa
Dance Club	Rockin' Bar D	WaveBands	Evolution	The Tube
Piano Bar	Sessions	Cadillac Lounge	District Lounge	La Piazza
Teen Club	The Stack	Aloft	Vibe	Vibe
Navigator's Verandah	Round porthole	Oblong porthole	n/a	n/a

Can I Afford It?

Cruises were once reserved for wealthy globetrotters. These days, cruises are **more affordable**, but not always "inexpensive." Disney Cruise Line's popularity and "demand-based" pricing keep pushing rates up. Still, a seven-night Disney cruise can be comparable in price to a seven-night land vacation at Walt Disney World. To determine what you can afford, make a budget (see below). Budgeting not only keeps you from spending too much, it encourages you to seek out ways to save money. With a little research, you can often get **more for less**. To get an idea of what an actual cruise costs, check out our recent cruise expenses at the bottom of the page.

A **cruise package** may include ground transportation, airfare, insurance, lodging at Walt Disney World or your port of embarkation; theme park admission, and other extras. This may seem convenient, but planning each aspect of your cruise yourself often saves you more money. Learn about cruise packages on page 38.

Your **cruise expenses** fall into six categories: planning, transportation, lodging, cruise passage, port activities, and extras. How you budget for each depends upon the total amount you have available to spend and your priorities. Planning, transportation, lodging, and cruise passage are the easiest to factor ahead of time as costs are fixed. The final two—port activities and extras—are harder to control and can quickly add-up, but we provide sample costs throughout this field guide to help you estimate.

Begin your budget with the **worksheet** on the next page (use pencil at the start). Enter the minimum you prefer to spend and the most you can afford in the topmost row. Set as many of these ranges as possible before you delve into the other chapters of this book. Your excitement may grow as you read more, but it is doubtful your bank account will.

As you uncover costs and ways to save money, return to your worksheet and **update it**. Your budget is a work in progress—try to be flexible within your minimums and maximums. As plans crystallize, write the amount you expect (and can afford) in the Goals column. If you are using PassPockets (see page 489), **transfer the amounts** from the Goals column to the back of each PassPocket when you are satisfied with your budget.

Our Recent Cruise Expenses
(2 adults, 1 child)

Round-trip airfare: $960
Rental mini-van: $50
7-night cruise (cat. 6): $3517
Port activities: $220
Souvenirs: $49
Beverages: $35
Phone/Internet: $300
Gratuities: $85

TOTAL: $5216

Budget Worksheet

Electronic, interactive worksheet available– see page 492

As you work through this field guide, use this worksheet to identify your resources, record estimated costs, and create a budget. We provide prices and estimates throughout the book.

	Minimum		Maximum		Goals	
Total Projected Expenses	$		$		$	
Planning:						
Phone calls/faxes:						
Guides/magazines:						
Transportation: *(to/from)*						
Travel/airline tickets:						
Rental car:						
Fuel/maintenance:						
Ground transfer/shuttle:						
Town car/taxi:						
Wheelchair/ECV:						
Parking:						
Lodging: *(pre-/post-cruise)*						
Resort/hotel/motel:						
Meals/extras:						
Cruise Passage:						
Cruise:						
Protection plan/insurance:						
Port Activities:	Per Port	Total	Per Port	Total	Per Port	Total
Excursions:						
Meals:						
Attractions:						
Rentals:						
Transportation/taxis:						
Extras:						
Souvenirs/photos:						
Beverages:						
Resortwear/accessories:						
Palo/Remy/formal wear:						
Spa treatments:						
Childcare (nursery):						
Phone/Internet/stamps:						
Gratuities/duties:						
Other:						
Total Budgeted Expenses	$		$		$	

Money-Saving Ideas and Programs

The Disney Cruise Line enjoys great popularity, so discounts can be scarce. Here are the ways we've found to save money on your cruise:

Reserve Early to Get Early Booking Savings

Reserve early enough and you could save approximately $100–$890 per stateroom (7-night cruises) or $30–$650 per stateroom (3- and 4-night cruises). Staterooms at this discount are limited, however. To get the best early booking savings, reserve your cruise as soon as dates are announced (generally up to 18 months in advance).

Go à la Carte

Disney emphasizes the Add-On Package, combining a stay at the Walt Disney World Resort with a cruise. This is appealing to many vacationers, but it can be pricier than making your own arrangements as you can usually find better deals on hotel rooms at Walt Disney World.

Find Promotions and Discounts

As with most cruise lines, Disney uses demand-based pricing. Unlike most cruise lines, this means prices generally rise as a cruise date approaches. The last-minute specials common with other lines are less common at Disney. That said, deals and specials are available, if you're alert. There have been "kids sail free" promotions lately, but with kids' fares low to begin with, an early booking may be better than waiting for this deal. Visit http://www.disneycruise.com to learn more. Also visit MouseSavers.com (http://www.mousesavers.com), which summarizes available discounts, and http://www.themouseforless.com.

Use a Travel Agent

Larger travel agencies sometimes pre-book blocks of staterooms, locking in discounts for you to snag later on. Check with agents before booking on your own (see page 1 for a list). Travel agents are very good at finding the best prices, too! Mouse Fan Travel (http://www.mousefantravel.com) and MouseEarVacations.com (http://www.mouseearvacations.com) have saved us considerable money on our cruises (yes, we find travel agents quite helpful!), and other agencies can do the same.

Watch for Onboard Credits

Wouldn't it be nice to have an extra $50 sitting in your onboard account? Keep an eye out for onboard credit specials. Currently, guests who use their Disney Visa card receive a $50 credit. Credits are sometimes offered when you book onboard (see next page) and through some travel agents. Credits for repeat cruisers have been replaced by in-stateroom gifts.

Move to Florida

We're not serious about moving, but if you're already a Florida resident you may get discounts up to 50% off select cruises (limited staterooms). Call Disney at 888-325-2500 to inquire about Florida resident discounts, or check http://www.mousesavers.com. Proof of residency is required.

Book Your Next Cruise Onboard

On your next Disney cruise, check the *Personal Navigator* or the Cruise Sales Desk on Deck 4 for onboard specials. Not only can booking onboard offer great prices (10% less than land-based prices recently), but sometimes onboard credits, too. Two catches: The best rates are often for cruises sailing the same time next year, and you must reserve before you disembark. If you see a deal, grab it—you can change or cancel your reservation later if necessary (you can resechedule once without penalty); just call Disney at 888-325-2500. Tip: You can give the reservationist your travel agent's information when booking onboard or transfer your booking to your travel agent when you return home (must transfer within 30 days of booking).

Stay Off-Site Before Your Cruise

If you're like us and prefer to arrive at least a day ahead of your cruise, look for an inexpensive hotel or motel. In-airport hotels can be pricey—to save money, see page 36. Lodging is described beginning on page 37. It can sometimes be less expensive to fly in a day early, so always investigate.

Compare Local Transportation Costs

Depending on your party size, it can be less expensive to rent a car to drive from the airport to the port and back again. On the other hand, transportation companies such as Quicksilver Tours & Transportation may offer price plus convenience. Explore your options starting on page 31.

Special Tips for Special People

- ✔ **Infants and kids** 12 and under are less expensive than adults, but only if there are two adults along as well (the first two stateroom guests always pay full adult fare). The third and fourth adults in a stateroom also cruise at a lower price. See page 62.
- ✔ **AAA and Costco** members can get rates and make reservations through these companies and often get excellent deals. AAA members: Ask about your local AAA chapter's "Disney Month" for extra savings and goodies, and be sure to inquire about any extras (such as an onboard credit) with your AAA Disney package.
- ✔ **Disney Vacation Club** members may be eligible for exclusive cruises at good rates. Check with this program or the Disney Cruise Line for details.
- ✔ **Canadian residents** may get special rates on select cruises. Contact the Disney Cruise Line or a travel agent.
- ✔ **Military personnel** may be eligible for some last-minute rates, similar to those offered to Florida residents. Call the Disney Cruise Line or a travel agent for more details.
- ✔ **Repeat cruisers** are automatically members of the Castaway Club and receive special perks, including some great deals (see page 470 for more details).

Porthole to More Cruising Information

While this field guide could serve as your single source, we recommend you gather as much information as possible. Each of the sources described below offers its own unique porthole into the world of Disney cruising.

Official Disney Information—Definitely get the free booklet and DVD we mention on page 20, and visit the web site (http://www.disneycruise.com). Any other brochures you can get from your travel agent will be helpful, too. Disney also sends cruise documentation (more about this on page 20) that contains some basic information.

Books—Disney published an official guidebook, *Birnbaum's Disney Cruise Line*, starting in 2004, but we were disappointed to find little detail beyond what's available at the Disney Cruise Line's web site—the shore excursion reviews are insightful, however. And while virtually all Walt Disney World Resort guidebooks mention the Disney Cruise Line, most only give it a few pages. The two with the most information are *Fodor's Walt Disney World with Kids* by Kim Wright Wiley and *The Unofficial Guide to Walt Disney World* by Bob Sehlinger (Wiley). Both have about 10 pages on the topic. Several other PassPorter publications contain information on Disney Cruise Line: *PassPorter's Cruise Clues* is an e-book filled with cruise tips, packing lists, and cruise line comparisons (see page 490), *PassPorter's Disney Weddings & Honeymoons* is another book with solid information on getting married or honeymooning onboard a Disney cruise ship (see page 491), and *PassPorter's Disney Vacation Club* covers cruising on points (see page 491).

Magical Disney Cruise Guide—This excellent, free online guide offers a detailed overview of Disney cruising, including reviews. http://www.allears.net/cruise/cruise.htm.

Web Sites—Some of the best sources of information are the official and unofficial sites for the Disney Cruise Line. Here are our picks:

Disney Cruise Line Official Site—http://www.disneycruise.com
Disney Cruise Line Official News Site—http://www.disneycruisenews.com
PassPorter.com (that's us!)—http://www.passporter.com/dcl
PassPorterBoards.com (advice from fellow cruisers)—http://www.passporterboards.com
Platinum Castaway Club—http://www.castawayclub.com
DIS—http://www.wdwinfo.com (click "Disney Cruise Line") and http://www.disboards.com
Walt Disney World Mom's Panel - http://disneyworldforum.disney.go.com/
AllEars.net—http://www.allears.net/cruise/cruise.htm
epinions.com—http://www.epinions.com (search on the ship names)

These are excellent sites on general cruising:
CruiseCritic—http://www.cruisecritic.com
About.com—http://cruises.about.com
CruiseMates—http://cruisemates.com
AvidCruiser—http://avidcruiser.com
Tom's Port Guides— http://www.tomsportguides.com

The Future of the Disney Cruise Line

In many ways, the future of the Disney Cruise Line arrived in January 2011, when the Disney Dream entered service, ending Disney's 12-year stretch as a two-ship cruise line. This fabulous new vessel (see page 25), and her sister-ship, the Disney Fantasy (which entered service in March 2012) have raised the bar for the cruise line and the cruise industry as a whole, topping several influential polls along the way.

With passenger capacity 2 1/2 times what it was in 2010, the line's immediate challenge is to fill all four ships with happy passengers. Exciting new ships are a big help, but the real trick is to keep the older ships in high demand. Their future includes upgraded facilities, and visits to new destinations and home ports—the line visited 9-18 ports annually between 2004-2009, 31-37 ports in 2010-2013, and will call at 53 ports in 2014! We doubt the cruise line will declare "permanent" home ports for the Magic Class ships any time soon, if ever. Cruise ships can lift anchor in search of greener pastures (or bluer seas), returning only if the grass grows back. We saw this recently when the cruise line established a "permanent" base in Los Angeles, just in time for the collapse of tourism to Mexico. Goodbye, LA, hello Miami! Except for summer season all four ships now ply the Caribbean/Bahamas region. In 2013 that means departures from Port Canaveral, Miami, and Galveston. In 2014 Galveston is off the schedule, replaced by more departures from Port Canaveral and Miami, and several from San Juan, Puerto Rico. The line is also playing with the mix between longer and shorter cruises. In 2013, Disney will have 145 sailings of 6 or more nights, and 153 3-5-night cruises. In 2014, there are 95 6-15-night sailings and 189 3-5-night cruises. That's essentially a return to the tried-and-true Walt Disney World-plus-cruise vacation. Will they be able to fill 2.4 times as many staterooms for Port Canaveral-based 3- and 4-night cruises as they did in 2010?

Though there are rumors of new ships that could debut by 2017, we don't think that's likely. Walt Disney Parks and Resorts has a history of slow, careful expansion, and tends to build later, rather than sooner, when business grows.

Features from the new ships are coming to the older ships, debuting on the Magic in October 2013 and (probably) on the Wonder in late 2014. The Oceaneer Club and Oceaneer Lab kids clubs get a total re-do to echo their new siblings, as will the nursery. The kids' Mickey Pool will be replaced by AquaLab and a grander slide, and the tots get an upgraded splash zone. AquaDunk will be the all-new thrill slide for bigger cruisers. Grownups get a re-made nightclub district and the spa gets a facelift, more space, and a teen spa. The pool deck buffet expands and morphs into Cabanas, addressing chronic space issues. Animator's Palate gets a revised show and decor, plus a second show, "Animation Magic," which is already featured on the Disney Fantasy. Parrot Cay dining room re-feathers into Carioca's, and Palo gets redecorated. The atrium lobby will be renewed, the family nightclub becomes D Lounge, staterooms will be refreshed, gaining the same queen beds found on the new ships, and the suites will be redecorated. Plus, a "ducktail" will extend the ship's stern at the waterline, to enhance stability. Sorry, no Virtual Portholes for the inside staterooms, and no word yet about Enchanted Art/Mickey's Midship Detective Agency.

Whatever happens, you can be sure **we'll be keeping an eagle eye on developments**, and reporting on them between guidebook editions at the PassPorter.com web site and free weekly newsletter (subscribe at http://www.passporter.com/news.htm).

Cruise Reviews You Can Use

Cruiser reviews and reports are one of the absolute best ways to evaluate and get acquainted with the Disney Cruise Line before you embark. With that in mind, we've collected several tips and memories from our own experiences. Enjoy!

- If you have access to the **Internet**, make it a point to get online and explore the web sites listed throughout this field guide. PassPorter's readers post many interesting, detailed trip reports on their cruises at http://www.passporterboards.com/forums/sharing-your-adventure-disney-cruise-reports. We also recommend you visit MousePlanet's Trip Reports web site, which offers a nice collection of cruise reports at http://www.mouseplanet.com/dtp/trip.rpt.

- Want to **find other like-minded travelers** to hang out with on your cruise? The PassPorter message board has a forum expressly for the purpose of meeting up with fellow cruisers! Come visit and tell us about your plans at: http://www.passporter.com/cruisers

- One of the first "guides" to Disney Cruise Line was a free online publication by Mickey Morgan, the "Magical Disney Cruise Guide." You can still find this **informative online guide** at AllEarsNet. Read it at http://www.allears.net/cruise/cruise.htm.

Magical Memory

- *"We love to 'dream' about and plan our next cruise right after booking. We hold countdown parties every 100 days. This last time we actually had 500+ days to countdown but it went very quickly with the anticipation of our 100-day parties. We planned out each party with a character theme, food theme, and then an activity or craft item we'd use on the ship. Here's an example: 300 party was Chip and Dale, we ate peanut butter desserts and decorated magnetic memo boards for our stateroom doors to keep in touch. Other activities included: making T-shirts for our group, decorating over-the-door shoe holders for our bathroom items (dollar store find), making magnetic fun foam door banners with a catchy phrase and 'who we are' (example: 'There's no traffic when you travel on the Magic' - Diehls from Pennsylvania). We have also used the time to plan excursions, make packing lists, and just talk about the food we look forward to eating again! Our final party will be a Bon Voyage theme and we will wear our Caribbean attire or newly-made T-shirts, eat a dessert buffet, and then make some special luggage tags so our luggage is easily noticed at pick-up! Have fun dreaming and the time will go by quickly!"*

...as told by Disney cruiser Sharon Diehl

DISCOVER the best times to cruise with Disney

Plotting Your Course

FIND many ways to get to the port

PACK just what you need to bring on the cruise

By now, we're certain you're hooked on the idea of a Disney cruise vacation. The time has come, the Walrus said, to turn those Disney dreams into a voyage filled with "wonder," "magic," "dreams," and "fantasies."

Every journey starts with the first step, and this vacation is no exception. That step, of course, is planning. Planning is the keel upon which the rest of your cruise is built. This chapter is filled with the principal planning steps you'll need to take, plus a cargo of savvy advice and a chartroom filled with maps, charts, and worksheets to help keep you on course.

Some of you may be embarking on a cruise and/or leaving the United States for the very first time. While you may be visiting cozy, nearby ports, you'll encounter some subtle and not-so-subtle differences between cruise preparations and land journeys. Start your planning as far ahead as possible. Not only can you save some money, but you may need that head start to obtain the proper identity documents.

So just how do you plot the course that takes you from your front door to the gangway of your Disney cruise ship? In this chapter, we'll chart the many steps in the journey, from selecting your cruise itinerary and sail dates to steering your way around tropical storms. You'll be able to pick your way through the turbulent waters of cruise rates and packages and safely reserve your snug stateroom.

Your ship's captain will ably plot your course on the high seas, but you'll need your own map and compass to get to Port Canaveral or other port of embarkation. We cover the many highways and byways that form your journey-before-the-journey, including fair lodgings at the port itself.

Finally, it's Embarkation Day! We make sure you aren't waylaid enroute to the cruise terminal, that your important identity papers are all in order, and that your trunks and sea bags are packed!

Choosing Your Itinerary

Disney Cruise Line offers **an ever-expanding choice of itineraries and ports of embarkation**. In **2013** alone, you can choose from 2-, 3-, 4-, 5, 7, and 8-night Bahamas cruises (some from Miami or Galveston), 5-, 6-, 7- and 8-night Eastern and Western Caribbean cruises (some departing from Galveston, others from Miami), -4, -7, and -12-night Mediterranean cruises (including new itineraries visiting Venice or Greece), 7-night Alaskan cruises departing from Vancouver, and repositioning cruises between Miami and Los Angeles, Los Angeles and Galveston, and Port Canaveral and Barcelona. Your choice of itineraries may be solely based on price or length, particularly if you combine your cruise with a stay at Walt Disney World (see page 59).

3-Night Bahamas Cruise Itinerary (Port Canaveral, Disney Dream, Disney Magic): A short and affordable cruise, with three nights at sea and two ports of call: Nassau and Castaway Cay. Actual time spent afloat: about 68 hours (almost three days). This cruise whizzes by, and you may feel like it's over before it's barely begun. On the flip side, this is a great cruise on which to get your feet wet if you're new to cruising. If you plan to stay at the Walt Disney World Resort before your cruise, the 3-night cruise works best for this as it falls at the end of the week. The Disney Magic sails this same itinerary from Miami on December 27 and 30, 2013.

3-Night Itinerary:
Thursday: Set sail
Friday: Nassau
Saturday: Castaway Cay
Sunday: Return to port

4-Night Bahamas Cruise Itineraries (Port Canaveral and Miami, Disney Dream, Disney Wonder, Disney Magic): Like the 3-night, the 4-night stops at Nassau and Castaway Cay. The extra day is spent at sea. Miami-based cruises substitute Key West for the day at sea. Actual time spent afloat: about 92 hours (almost four days). If cruising is your focus, you'll be happier with a 4-night cruise than a 3-night—the extra night is more relaxing and it gives you a greater chance of dining at Palo or Remy. If the Captain has to bypass Castaway Cay due to weather, he can try again the next day.

4-Night Itinerary:
Day 1: Set sail
Day 2: Nassau
Day 3: Castaway Cay
Day 4: At sea
Day 5: Return to port

2-Night and 5-Night Bahamas Itineraries (Miami, Disney Magic): Two special cruises depart Miami in fall 2013, a 2-night "cruise to nowhere," and a 5-night "double-dip" that visits Nassau and makes two stops at Castaway Cay.

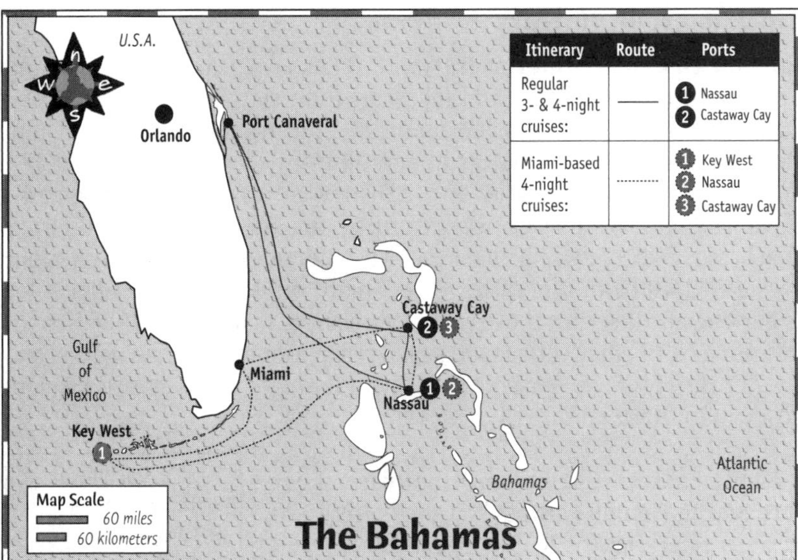

7-Night Bahamas Itinerary (Galveston, Disney Wonder): With departures in fall 2013, the Disney Wonder will visit Key West, Nassau, and Castaway Cay, and spend three relaxing days at sea.

8-Night Bahamas Itinerary (Galveston, Disney Magic): Sailing in spring 2013, the Disney Magic will visit Key West, Port Canaveral/Walt Disney World, and Castaway Cay, and spend 4 restful days at sea. The very long day (18.5 hours) in Port Canaveral includes ground transportation and Park Hopper admission to Walt Disney World Resort in Orlando. If you'd rather, you can spend the day in and around Port Canaveral, visiting the beach or Kennedy Space Center (not included).

8-Nt. Bahamas:
Day One: Set sail
Day Two: At sea
Day Three: At sea
Day Four: Nassau
Day Five: Castaway Cay
Day Six: Port Canaveral
Day Seven: At sea
Day Eight: At sea
Day Nine: Return to Port

© Cheryl Pendry (26661)

The view of the Atlantis Resort in the Bahamas, as seen from the deck of the ship

Choosing Your Itinerary *(continued)*

Caribbean Cruise Itineraries: For 2013 Disney Cruise Line is offering a wider variety of Caribbean itineraries than ever, though most of the variation is in cruise length and departure port, rather than ports visited. **Port Canaveral** offers its traditional line-up of 7-Night Eastern and Western Caribbean itineraries on the Disney Fantasy. **Galveston** hosts 4-, 6-, and 7-Night Western Caribbean cruises, including a 7-Night itinerary that brings Disney to Jamaica for the first time, while **Miami** offers 5-night Western Caribbean itineraries. The 7-night cruise is a great choice for experienced cruisers or those who really want to relax. Cruisers on 7-night itineraries also enjoy formal and semi-formal evenings, theme nights, and a wider variety of onboard activities. Night for night, the 7-night is no more costly than shorter cruises.

7-Night Eastern Caribbean Itineraries (Port Canaveral, Disney Fantasy): Disney offers two Eastern itineraries for 2013. Between January and April, cruisers visit St. Thomas, San Juan Puerto Rico, and Castaway Cay. From May onward, the Fantasy visits St. Maarten, St. Thomas, and Castaway Cay. Both itineraries feature three days at sea. Actual time spent afloat: 164 hours.

7-Nt. E. Caribbean 'A':
Saturday: Set sail
Sunday: At sea
Monday: At sea
Tuesday: St. Maarten
Wednesday: St. Thomas
Thursday: At sea
Friday: Castaway Cay
Saturday: Return to port

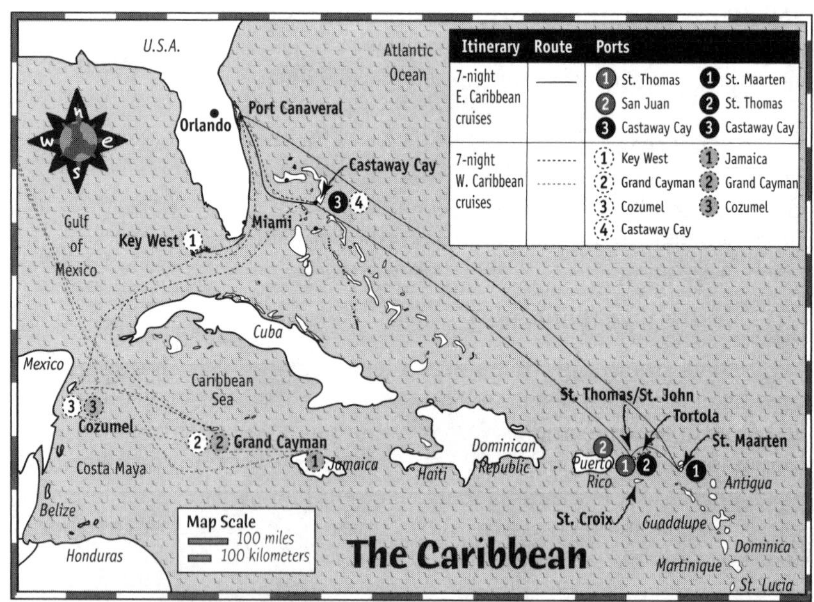

This map depicts the itineraries and routes in the Caribbean that occur most frequently.

4-Night Western Caribbean (Galveston, Disney Magic): Available January through April 2013, this sampler-length cruise visits just one port, Cozumel, and includes two restful days at sea. Actual time spent afloat: 92 hours.

5-Nt. W. Caribbean 'B':
Day 1: Set sail
Day 2: At sea
Day 3: Grand Cayman
Day 4: Cozumel
Day 5: At sea
Day 6: Return to port

5-Night Western Caribbean Itineraries (Miami, Disney Wonder, Disney Magic): This cruise comes in two "flavors:" One itinerary, available in early and late 2013, visits Cozumel and Grand Cayman. The other, available January-March, visits Cozumel and Castaway Cay. Both include two days at sea. Actual time spent afloat: 116 hours.

6-Night Western Caribbean Itinerary (Galveston, Disney Magic, Disney Wonder): Available January-April 2013, plus one holiday sailing in December, this itinerary spends just two days in port (Cozumel and Grand Cayman), and spends three days at sea. Actual time spent afloat: 140 hours.

7-Night Western Caribbean Itinerary (Port Canaveral, Disney Fantasy): Available throughout 2013, this cruise visits Grand Cayman, Costa Maya, Cozumel, and Castaway Cay, and spends two days at sea. Actual time spent afloat: 164 hours.

7-Nt. W. Caribbean Port Canaveral:
Saturday: Set sail
Sunday: Key West
Monday: At sea
Tuesday: Grand Cayman
Wednesday: Cozumel
Thursday: At sea
Friday: Castaway Cay
Saturday: Return to port

7-Night Western Caribbean Itinerary (Galveston, Disney Wonder): This cruise includes Disney's first-ever visit to Jamaica. Sailing in November and December 2013, the ship visits Falmouth (Jamaica), Grand Cayman, and Cozumel, and spends three days at sea. Actual time spent afloat: 164 hours.

© Julie Rudinski (2206)

A glorious view of St. Thomas in the Caribbean

Choosing Your Itinerary *(continued)*

2013 Mediterranean Itineraries: 2013 brings the Disney Disney Magic back to the Mediterranean, with 12 cruises departing from Barcelona, Spain. Four itineraries are on the schedule, with two of those visiting ports in the Adriatic and Eastern Mediterranean for the first time. Most sailings will be either 4- or 7-nights, which presumably brings the Disney experience within reach of more European cruisers (historically, few of Disney's European itineraries were less than 10 nights long).

4-Night Mediterranean Itinerary: Disney brings the "sampler cruise" to Europe for the first time, with an itinerary that pays calls at just two ports, Villefranche (Monte Carlo/Cannes/Nice) and Palma Mallorca, plus one day at sea. Actual time spent afloat: 92 hours

4-Nt. Mediterranean:
Tuesday: Set sail
Wednesday: Villefranche
Thursday: At Sea
Friday: Palma Mallorca
Saturday: Return to port

7-Nt. Mediterranean:
Saturday: Set sail
Sunday: At Sea
Monday: Villefranche
Tuesday: La Spezia
Wed.: Civitavecchia
Thursday: Naples
Friday: At sea
Saturday: Return to port

7-Night Mediterranean Itinerary: Departing Barcelona on six Saturdays in June and August, these work week-friendly cruises visit four popular ports: Villefranche (Monte Carlo/Cannes/Nice), La Spezia (Florence/Pisa), Civitavecchia (Rome), and Naples (Pompeii/Capri), and spend two days at sea. Actual time afloat: 164 hours.

12-Night Eastern Mediterranean Itinerary: In another first, Disney Cruise Line will visit Eastern Mediterranean ports, with two sailings making first-ever visits to Piraeus (Athens), Kusadasi (Ephesus Turkey) and the Greek isle of Mykonos. The cruise also calls at Villefranche, La Spezia, Civitavecchia, and Valletta, and includes four days at sea. Actual time afloat: 284 hours.

12-Night Eastern Mediterranean:
Saturday: Set sail
Sunday: Villefranche
Monday: La Spezia
Tuesday: Civitavecchia
Wednesday: At sea
Thursday: At sea
Friday: Piraeus
Saturday: Kusadasi
Sunday:
Monday: At sea
Tuesday: Valleta
Wednesday: At sea
Thursday: Return to port

12-Night Adriatic/Mediterranean Itinerary: For the first time since she was launched, the Disney Magic returns to Venice, docking just four miles from the shipyard where she was built, and affording cruisers one-and-a-half days in that port. She'll also pay a first-time visit to Dubrovnik, Croatia. Like the 7-night itinerary, visits to Villefranche, La Spezia, Civitavecchia, and Naples are on the agenda, plus a stop in Valletta, Malta and three days at sea. Actual time afloat: 284 hours

12-Night Adriatic/Mediterranean:
Saturday: Set sail
Sunday: Villefranche
Monday: La Spezia
Tuesday: Civitavecchia
Wednesday: Naples
Thursday: At sea
Friday: Venice
Saturday: Venice
Sunday:Dubrovnik
Monday: At sea
Tuesday: Valleta
Wednesday: At sea
Thursday: Return to port

© MediaMarx, Inc.

Walking along the promenade in Nice, France.

Introduction Reservations Staterooms Dining Activities Ports of Call Magic Index

Choosing Your Itinerary *(continued)*

Alaskan Itinerary: The Disney Wonder returns to Alaska for the 2013 summer season, departing Mondays on 7-night voyages from Vancouver, Canada. Cruisers will journey the famed Inside Passage north to the Alaskan Panhandle, delivering nearly non-stop vistas of mountains, glaciers, forests, and fjords. After a scenic first day at sea, the ship cruises the Tracy Arm Fjord, visits historic Skagway, Juneau, and Ketchikan. Actual time afloat: 164 hours.

7-Night Alaskan:
Monday: Set sail
Tuesday: At sea
Wednesday: Tracy Arm
Thursday: Skagway
Friday: Juneau
Saturday: Ketchikan
Sunday: At Sea
Monday: Return to port

2013 Repositioning Cruises: If a cruise ship has to move from one home port to another, there's almost always a repositioning cruise on the agenda. These cruises are especially popular with veteran cruisers who appreciate the many days at sea and bargain rates that are common on these voyages. In 2013 Disney Cruise Line offers five "repos:" three 14-day long trips, and two of more modest length (rather than cruise between Alaska and the Caribbean in one voyage, Disney has made it a two-leg journey).

Panama Canal Repositioning Itineraries: With the Wonder spending most of the year in the Caribbean, the 2013 Alaska season requires two passages through the Panama Canal. The first 14-night voyage departs Miami on May 6, 2013, and stops at Castaway Cay, Cartagena Colombia, Puerto Vallarta, and Cabo San Lucas en route to Los Angeles. The return trip departs Los Angeles on September 14, substitutes Cozumel for Castaway Cay, and ends in Galveston, Texas. Total time afloat 332 hours.

Glacial ice slowly slides past an Alaskan hillside

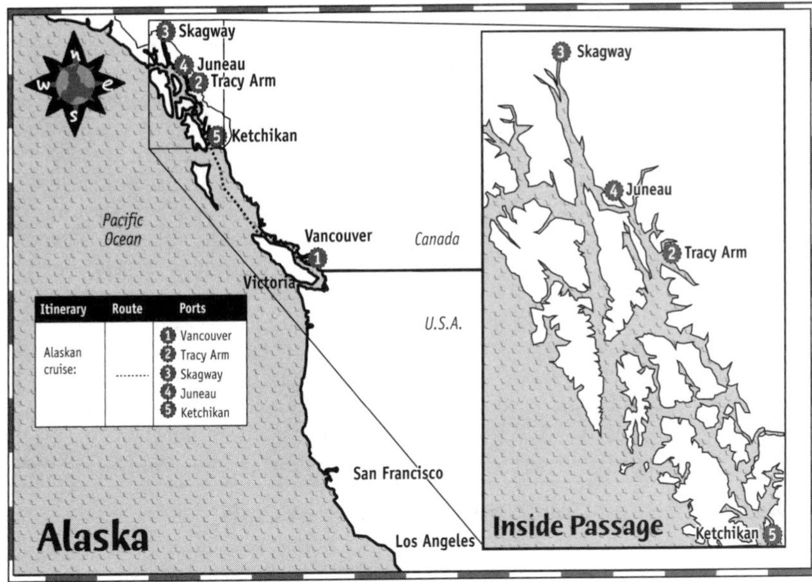

Itinerary	Route	Ports
Alaskan cruise:	....	1 Vancouver 2 Tracy Arm 3 Skagway 4 Juneau 5 Ketchikan

Alaska Repositioning Itineraries: On May 20, 2013 the Wonder departs Los Angeles for Vancouver, Canada on a 7-night cruise that stops overnight in San Francisco and spends a full day in Victoria BC., plus three days at sea. Actual time afloat: 164 hours. On September 9, 2013, the Wonder departs Vancouver on a 5-night cruise with a one-day visit to San Francisco, and three days at sea. Total time afloat 116 hours.

14-Night Eastbound Transatlantic Repositioning: The Disney Magic departs Galveston, Texas on May 18, 2013, bound across the Atlantic to Barcelona, Spain. Along the way, she'll make just three stops: Castaway Cay, Funchal (Madiera) Portugal, and Gibraltar. That means 10 restful days at sea! Total time afloat 332 hours.

Won't there be a westbound repo after the Mediterranean season? Following the last 7-night Mediterranean cruise in 2013, the Magic heads to a European shipyard for a major overhaul, and the crew will continue the work as she crosses the Atlantic, headed for Miami. See page 37 for details on the changes to the Magic.

The mountains of British Columbia from the Inside Passage

Choosing Your Itinerary *(continued)*

Do Itineraries Ever Change?

Occasionally, itinerary changes occur after you've made a booking. Your cruise contract does allow for these changes, as the cruise line must adapt to changing circumstances. If the change happens before you sail, Disney Cruise Line will contact you about your options. Occasionally, itineraries are modified immediately before or during your cruise, but it is rare. Most last-minute itinerary changes are due to bad weather, and usually other ports are substituted. Castaway Cay is the port most often bypassed due to weather (as it is the most frequently visited), but even that is uncommon, most often because seas are too rough to allow safe docking. Changes may also occur when Disney feels a port is unsafe. Most recently, that meant dropping Mazatlán, Mexico and substituting a second day in Cabo San Lucas on the former Mexican Riviera Itinereries. If you have plans at a port of call that cannot be modified (e.g., a wedding), you shouldn't count on a cruise to get you there—you're best off flying in and leaving the cruise for another time.

Does This Book Cover the 2014 Ports of Call?

Our policy is to have each yearly edition cover the ports that are visited that year, to keep the size and price of the book manageable. Thus, this 2013 edition covers only ports on the 2013 schedule (other than brief mentions and a weather page). Full port descriptions, maps, and excursion listings for the 2014 ports will appear in the 12th edition of this guide. You can expect in-depth coverage and our suggestions for shore excursions, plus detailed home port guides for San Diego, San Juan, and Venice. Of course, many ports visited in 2013 will also be visited in 2014, so you may find this edition has all you need to know for 2014, too.

Playing at Castaway Cay during our Bahamas cruise on the Disney Dream

December Holiday Itineraries: Like land-based resorts, cruise ships are especially popular during the Christmas-New Year season, and cruise lines adjust their schedules to suit the needs of families enjoying their holiday vacations. Though Disney Cruise Line has been known to offer special holiday itineraries during this period, the 2013 schedule promotes just one "holiday cruise." For that, the Disney Wonder departs Galveston Texas for a 6-night Western Caribbean cruise departing December 21 visiting Grand Cayman and Cozumel. The only special feature is that the normal 6-night cruise schedule has been modified so that Christmas Day is spent at sea. Though not promoted as holiday cruises, the Wonder follows that with three, 4-night Western Caribbean cruises to Cozumel and back. For Christmas, the Magic will be on a 5-night cruise from Miami that visits Castaway Cay and Cozumel, and she follows that with two, 3-night cruises stopping at Castaway Cay and Nassau that are unique on the Miami schedule. The Disney Dream and Disney Fantasy will undoubtedly celebrate the holidays, but they'll be on their regular schedules. More details on the 2014 fall cruising season are on the next page.

Port of Embarkation: It's good to be within driving distance of the port! The cost of airfare can make or break your ability to cruise. With more ships at its disposal, the cruise line has begun sailing from more U.S. and international ports. It pays to look at the schedule, and see if Disney Cruise Line is coming to a port near you. You may not be able to visit the destination of your dreams, but any cruise is better than no cruise, or at least, we think so.

Three Nights or Four for a First-Time Cruise?

To get your feet wet cruising, the 3-night Bahamas itinerary seems attractive. However, we recommend four nights if you can swing it. There's so much to do on board, and the normal urge is to try to do it all. That can be exhausting on a 3-night cruise, especially since it doesn't include a day at sea, which maximizes the opportunity to enjoy the ship. On a 3-night cruise you may also feel that, as soon as you've unpacked, it's time to pack up again. If you plan to add a first-time visit to Walt Disney World, we consider four days in the parks the minimum, for a combined eight night-vacation. See page 62 for theme park add-on packages.

Adventures by Disney

If you're eager for other destinations with that "Disney touch," whether as an add-on to a cruise, theme park vacation, or just for its own sake, look into Adventures by Disney (ABD). These are special, immersive guided tours—designed and led by Disney cast members—to popular destinations on every continent but Antarctica. These tours are for adults and kids ages 4 and older. In 2013, ABD's cruise-specific offerings focus on Europe, with a 3-night pre-cruise Barcelona-based add-on tour,and 7- and 12-night "on-board experiences" that use the Disney ships as home base for escorted tours (see page 62). For more details and rates, visit http://www.adventuresbydisney.com.

Sneak Peek at 2014 Ports of Call

One could say that Disney Cruise Line's theme for 2014 is, "Variety!" The schedule has 42 different itineraries, though just 11 Bahamas and Caribbean routes account for 75% of all sailings. On the other hand, 20 itineraries will sail only once, and a fair number of those are just small variations on other, more frequent trips. The cruise line sets a new record for itself, visiting 54 ports (in 2013, that was 37 ports), though 13 of those ports will be visited just once. At the other extreme, Castaway Cay will host 238 stops, and thanks to operating two home ports in Florida, more than 150 cruises are 3- to 5-night Bahamas itineraries. 15 ports are either first-time visits, or haven't been called-at by the cruise line in at least 5 years. Cruises will depart for the first time from San Juan PR, San Diego, and Venice, but there will be just one Galveston departure, at the beginning of the year. The Disney Magic will spend her second straight summer in the Mediterranean, with the highlights undoubtedly the two 9-night cruises that begin and end in Venice, and the three 12-night cruises. The cruise line officially offers a Southern Caribbean itinerary for the first time, though four of the five ports of call have been visited in the past. There are two twists to the line's Alaskan schedule. The first cruise from Vancouver will be a 9-night itinerary that adds a first-time visit to Sitka to the regular line-up of Alaskan ports. The other twist is that the four repositioning cruises will begin or end in San Diego, rather than Los Angeles. Want short and sweet? There are two, 2-night cruises on the schedule, one from San Diego (with no stops) on May 17 , the other departs Miami on October 20 bound for Castaway Cay.

2014 Repositioning Itineraries

When a cruise line has to move a ship from one home port to another, it's called a repositioning (or repo), and often promises a **long, relaxing voyage with many sea days**, typically at a lower cost per-day than regular itineraries. There are six repos in 2014: May 2, the Wonder departs Miami for San Diego via the Panama Canal (15 nights), and on May 19 she leaves San Diego for Vancouver (5 nights). Also on May 19, the Magic departs Port Canaveral, headed for Barcelona (12 nights). September 6 the Magic heads back across the Atlantic to San Juan (14 nights). On September 8, the Wonder departs Vancouver, destination San Diego(4 nights), and she departs San Diego on September 12, bound for Port Canaveral via the Panama Canal.

© MediaMarx, Inc.

Lions Gate Bridge in Vancouver

Sneak Peek at 2014 Ports of Call (continued)

2014 European Cruises (Disney Magic)

The Disney Magic's summer includes first-ever departures from Venice, Italy.

4-night Mediterranean Itinerary (home port: Barcelona,Spain) August 7-11
Ports: Palma, Mallorca (Spain), Ibiza, Spain; 1 day at sea

5-night Mediterranean Itinerary (home port: Barcelona,Spain) August 11-16
Ports: Villefranche, France (Monte Carlo and French Riviera); La Spezia, Italy (Florence & Pisa); Civitavecchia, Italy (Rome); 1 day at sea

7-night Mediterranean Itinerary (home port: Barcelona,Spain) May 31-June 7, June 7-14, August 16-23, August 23-30, August 30-September 6
Ports: Villefranche, France (Monte Carlo and French Riviera); La Spezia, Italy (Florence & Pisa); Civitavecchia, Italy (Rome); Naples, Italy (Pompeii); 2 days at sea

9-night Mediterranean Itinerary (home port: Venice, Italy) June 26-July 5, July 5-14
Ports: Katakolon, Greece (Olympia); Pireaus, Greece (Athens); Kusadasi, Turkey (Ephesus); Rhodes, Greece; Mykonos, Greece; 2 days at sea

12-night Mediterranean itinerary A (home port: Barcelona,Spain) July 26–August 7
Ports: Villefranche, France (Monte Carlo and French Riviera); La Spezia, Italy (Florence & Pisa); Civitavecchia, Italy (Rome); Piraeus, Greece (Athens); Kusadasi, Turkey (Ephesus); Mykonos, Greece; Valletta, Malta; 4 days at sea

12-night Mediterranean itinerary C (home port: Barcelona,Spain) June 14–26
Ports: Villefranche, France (Monte Carlo and French Riviera); La Spezia, Italy (Florence & Pisa); Civitavecchia, Italy (Rome); Naples, Italy (Pompeii); Catania, Italy (Sicily); Corfu, Greece; Dubrovnik, Croatia; ends in Venice, Italy (overnight); 3 days at sea

12-night Mediterranean itinerary D (home port: Venice, Italy)July 14–26
Ports: Piraeus, Greece (Athens); Kusadasi, Turkey (Ephesus); Rhodes, Heraklion (Crete), Mykonos, and Santorini, Greece; Valletta, Malta; ends in Barcelona, Spain; 4 days at sea

2014 Alaskan Cruises (Disney Wonder)

Disney Cruise Line spends the summer in Alaska for the fourth straight year.

7-night Alaskan Itinerary (home port: Vancouver, Canada) *May-September*
Ports: Tracy Arm (by sea only), Skagway, Juneau, and Ketchikan, Alaska; 2 days at sea

9-night Alaskan Itinerary (home port: Vancouver, Canada)May 24-June 2
Ports: Sitka, Tracy Arm (by sea only), Skagway, Juneau, and Ketchikan, Alaska; 3 days at sea

2014 Miami Cruises (Disney Wonder)

The Disney Wonder sails from Miami January-May.

2-night Bahamas Itinerary October 20-22 *Ports: Castaway Cay*

3-night Bahamas Itinerary January 2-6 *Ports: Nassau, Key West*

4-night Bahamas Itineraries
Ports: Key West, Nassau, Castaway Cay (January-April, November-December)
Ports: Castaway Cay, Key West; 1 day at sea (October 22-26, November 5-9)
Ports: Nassau, Castaway Cay; 1 day at sea (December 26-30)

5-night Bahamas Itinerary *December 30, 2014-January 4, 2015*
Ports: Castaway Cay, Nassau, Key West; 1 day at sea

5-night Western Caribbean itineraries
Ports: Cozumel, Mexico; Castaway Cay; 2 days at sea (January-April, October-December)
Ports: Grand Cayman;Cozumel, Mexico; 2 days at sea (January-April, October-December)

2014 Southern Caribbean Cruise (Disney Magic)

The Disney Magic sails from San Juan, Puerto Rico for four weeks in early fall.

7-night Southern Caribbean itinerary *(departures September 20 & 27, October 4 & 11)*
Ports: Antigua, St. Lucia, Grenada, Barbados, St. Kitts; 1 day at sea

Itinerary Comparison Chart

Wondering about the specific differences between the various cruise itineraries? Below is a chart of the **differences only** between the most common (and popular) Port Canaveral-based itineraries. As you read through the book, you can assume that any feature mentioned applies to all cruise itineraries unless we specifically state otherwise.

Feature	3-Night	4-Night	7-Night E. Caribbean	7-Night W. Caribbean
Ports of call	2	2	3	4
Sea days	0	1	3	2
Embarkation day	Thursday	Sunday	Saturday	Saturday
Debarkation day	Sunday	Thursday	Saturday	Saturday
Hours afloat	68	92	164	164
Special dinner menus		1	4	4
Character breakfast			✔	✔
Champagne brunch		✔	✔	✔
Tea with Wendy			✔	✔
Dessert buffets	1	1	2	2
Formal nights			1	1
Semi-formal nights			1	1
Dress-up nights	1	1		
Stage shows	3	3	3	3
Variety shows		1	3	3
Adult seminars		✔	✔	✔

As you might imagine, the 7-night cruise offers more activities than the 3- or 4-night cruises—there are more days to fill, after all! Activities differ from cruise to cruise, but here's a list of some of the extra activities that have been offered on the 7-night cruises in the past:

- ✔ Intro to Internet session
- ✔ Dance lessons
- ✔ Family & Adult Talent Show
- ✔ Cruisin' for Trivia
- ✔ Family Fun Kite Making
- ✔ Family Magic Quest
- ✔ Mickey 200 Race
- ✔ Ping-Pong tournament
- ✔ Champagne art auction
- ✔ Mixology demonstrations
- ✔ Ice carving demonstrations
- ✔ Artist-led workshops

See chapter 5, "Playing and Relaxing Onboard," starting on page 36 for many more details on the various activities aboard.

Selecting Your Sail Dates

Once you've selected an itinerary, it's time to choose a sail date. The cruise line has doubled its fleet, so you have more choices than ever before. Deciding when to go involves many factors: your schedules, plans, price, itinerary availability, and weather. Let's go over each of these in detail:

Your Schedules—It's better to book as far ahead as possible, so check now with your employer/school for available vacation dates.

Your Plans—Do you want to go to Walt Disney World or spend time visiting the port of embarkation? If so, select a sail date that works in tandem with your vacation dates and plans—see the "To Visit Disney Parks or Not?" topic on page 59 for tips. Most cruisers prefer a weekend departure or return, but a mid-week departure can open up days for pre/post-cruise activities.

Your Location—You can save a bundle on airfare if your port of embarkation is within driving distance.

Price—The Disney Cruise Line has rate trends that correspond to demand (check out our rate trends chart on page 61). In general, cruising is more affordable in January, and September through early December (excluding Thanksgiving). Early spring, summer, and major holidays are the most expensive times to cruise. See page 60 for more pricing details.

Caribbean Itinerary Availability—The various cruise itineraries depart and return on particular days of the week (see chart opposite for Port Canaveral-based departures), which may be important to your vacation schedule. Also, the 7-night Port Canaveral-based cruises alternate between the Eastern Caribbean and Western Caribbean. For specific dates of future cruises, visit http://www.disneycruise.com, or check your Disney Cruise Line booklet.

When do we like to sail? We're fond of May—great weather, decent rates!

Are Any Dates Unavailable?

Typically, yes. Ships do fill up near certain dates—such as Christmas and New Year's Eve. And some dates may be reserved for members of a certain group, such as the Disney Vacation Club members-only cruises. There are two DVC cruises on the Disney Dream in 2013, a 3-night cruise took place January 10-13, and a four-nighter is September 29-October 3. Also, the ships go into drydock for maintenance. The next scheduled drydock is for the Magic on Sep. 7-Oct. 19, 2013. The Wonder will be in drydock Oct. 10-Nov. 15, 2014. A quick call to the Disney Cruise Line, or itinerary search at the cruise line web site can tell you if your preferred dates are available.

Weather

Weather conditions along your voyage vary greatly by location and season. Below you'll find weather charts for all of the Disney Cruise Line's home ports as well as nearly all ports of call (and if a port is missing, you can be sure we've included nearby ones with very similar weather). The first number is the lowest average temperature for that season, followed by the highest average temperature, and, when available, the third number is the average precipitation in inches. Please note that for the purposes of this chart, spring is March–May, summer is June–August, fall is September–November, and winter is December–February.

Home Ports	Spring	Summer	Fall	Winter
Port Canaveral	66°F/78°F (2")	76°F/87°F (4.4")	72°F/82°F (4.9")	55°F/69°F (2.2")
San Pedro, CA	53°F/89°F (0")	70°F/99°F (1.7")	64°F/93°F (1.1")	48°F/78°F (.7")
Galveston, TX	65°F/74°F (2.6")	79°F/87°F (3.8")	68°F/78°F (2.9")	48°F/59°F (3.8")
Miami, FL	68°F/83°F (3")	76°F/89°F (8.8")	72°F/85°F (7")	60°F/76°F (2")
Barcelona, Spain	47°F/62°F (10")	66°F/81°F (6")	54°F/70°F (10")	40°F/55°F (8")
Dover, England	43°F/53°F (1.4")	57°F/69°F (2")	49°F/58°F (2.5")	37°F/44°F (2")
Seattle, WA	43°F/58°F (2.2")	56°F/74°F (.7")	48°F/60°F (3")	36°F/45°F (5.1")
Vancouver, WA	41°F/61°F (2.7")	54°F/79°F (.6")	43°F/64 (3.2")	33°F/49°F (5.8")
New York, NY	43°F/60°F (3.6")	68°F/84°F (4.2")	50°F/65°F (3.7")	26°F/38°F
Bahamas	**Spring**	**Summer**	**Fall**	**Winter**
Nassau	69°F/81°F (2.6")	77°F/89°F (6")	74°F/85°F (7")	64°F/77°F (2")
Grand Bahama	69°F/81°F (2")	79°F/88°F (8")	73°F/84°F (3.4")	64°F/74°F (2.3")
Castaway Cay	69°F/81°F (2.6")	77°F/89°F (6")	74°F/85°F (7")	64°F/77°F (2")
W. Caribbean	**Spring**	**Summer**	**Fall**	**Winter**
Key West, FL	72°F/82°F (1.9")	79°F/90°F (5")	76°F/85°F (4.7")	65°F/75°F (2.2")
Costa Maya	75°F/87°F (1.3")	76°F/89°F (2.9")	73°F/87°F (6.2")	70°F/82°F (3.2")
Grand Cayman	77°F/84°F (1.9")	81°F/87°F (7")	79°F/85°F (9.3")	74°F/80°F (2.3")
Cozumel	72°F/87°F (6.8")	74°F/87°F (5.7")	73°F/86°F (14")	68°F/82°F (3.8")

E. Caribbean	Spring	Summer	Fall	Winter
St. Thomas	74°F/87°F (2.7")	78°F/90°F (2.6")	77°F/88°F (6")	72°F/85°F (2")
St. Maarten	74°F/83°F	77°F/86°F	77°F/86°F	72°F/82°F
Tortola	73°F/84°F	77°F/87°F	75°F/86°F	71°F/82°F
St. Croix	74°F/86°F (2")	78°F/88°F (3")	76°F/88°F (5.6")	72°F/84°F (2.1")
San Juan, PR	73°F/86°F (4")	77°F/86°F (4.8")	76°F/88°F (5.6")	71°F/83°F (3.4")
Curaçao	78°F/87°F (1")	79°F/89°F (1.3")	79°F/88°F (3.2")	76°F/84°F (2")
Aruba	78°F/87°F	79°F/88°F	80°F/89°F	76°F/85°F
Cartagena	78°F/86°F (1")	79°F/87°F (3.4")	78°F/86°F (8.8")	75°F/85°F (.2")
St. Lucia	78°F/84°F	80°F/85°F	79°F/86°F	76°F/82°F
Barbados	76°F/84°F (2.1")	78°F/85°F (5.1")	78°F/85°F (6.7")	74°F/82°F (2.5")
St. Kitts	76°F/83°F	79°F/87°F	78°F/87°F	75°F/81°F
Antigua	75°F/83°F	79°F/87°F	77°F/86°F	73°F/81°F
W. Mediterranean	**Spring**	**Summer**	**Fall**	**Winter**
Palermo	55°F/64°F	74°F/83°F	66°F/74°F	51°F/59°F
Valletta, Malta	54°F/65°F (1")	71°F/86°F (.1")	64°F/75°F (3.1")	49°F/59°F (3.5")
Naples	48°F/64°F (3")	66°F/85°F (.9")	55°F/71°F (5.2")	40°F/54°F (3.8")
Civitavecchia	54°F/58°F	72°F/78°F	62°F/67°F	47°F/52°F
La Spezia	53°F/62°F	71°F/82°F	57°F/68°F	41°F/51°F
Ajaccio, Corsica	45°F/62°F (2.1")	62°F/81°F (.3")	53°F/71°F (3.6")	39°F/56°F (2.9")
Villefranche	52°F/57°F	70°F/75°F	60°F/65°F	46°F/51°F
Palma, Mallorca	45°F/65°F (1.4")	64°F/86°F (.3")	54°F/73°F (3")	39°F/58°F (1.6")
Olbia, Sardinia	48°F/63°F	67°F/85°F	57°F/72°F	43°F/56°F
Tunis	51°F/68°F (1.5")	69°F/90°F (.1")	61°F/78°F (2.2")	46°F/60°F (2.4")
Marseille	47°F/63°F (1.8")	66°F/84°F (.6")	52°F/68°F (3.7")	37°F/51°F (1.9")

Weather *(continued)*

E. Mediterranean	Spring	Summer	Fall	Winter
Piraeus (Athens)	52°F/66°F (.9")	67°F/83°F (.2")	60°F/73°F (2.1")	44°F/55°F (1.9")
Kusadasi (Ephesus)	48°F/66°F (1.9")	64°F/86°F (.1")	53°F/73°F (1.6")	39°F/55°F (6.3")
Mykonos	56°F/65°F	73°F/79°F	64°F/70°F	50°F/57°F
Venice	46°F/61°F (2.9")	65°F/81°F (2.7")	50°F/64°F (3")	33°F/43°F (2.2")
Dubrovnik	50°F/62°F	69°F/82°F	56°F/69°F	41°F/52°F
Alaska	**Spring**	**Summer**	**Fall**	**Winter**
Skagway	40°F/58°F (1.2")	49°F/65°F (1.2")	26°F/36°F (4.2"0	17°F/27°F (2.2")
Juneau	32°F/47°F (2.8")	48°F/64°F (4.2")	37°F/47°F (7.7")	18°F/29°F (4.2")
Ketchikan	41°F/57°F (9.9")	52°F/65°F (5.9")	34°F/43°F (23")	28°F/36°F (15")
Tracy Arm	36°F/56°F (9.3")	48°F/62°F (9.3")	27°F/35°F (28")	21°F/29°F (17")
Victoria	40°F/56°F (1.7")	51°F/71°F (.7")	42°F/58°F (3.1")	33°F/44°F (5.4")
Maritime Canada & New England	**Spring**	**Summer**	**Fall**	**Winter**
Halifax	32°F/47°F	57°F/73°F	40°F/54°F	14°F/29°F
Saint John	30°F/59°F (4.4")	53°F/72°F (3.9")	40°F/53°F (4.7")	32°F/50°F (5.5")
Mexican Riviera	**Spring**	**Summer**	**Fall**	**Winter**
Ensenada	50°F/70°F (.4")	64°F/78°F (0")	55°F/75°F (.8")	45°F/68°F (1.4")
Cabo San Lucas	60°F/84°F (.1")	73°F/92°F (0")	71°F/90°F (1.3")	55°F/78°F (.6")
Mazatlán	61°F/84°F	77°F/90°F	73°F/89°F	57°F/80°F
Puerto Vallarta	65°F/86°F (.3")	76°F/93°F (14")	74°F/93°F (4.7")	62°F/84°F (1")
Manzanillo	69°F/82°F	78°F/88°F	77°F/88°F	68°F/83°F
Panama City	78°F/87°F	77°F/87°F	76°F/85°F	76°F/89°F
Acapulco	73°F/87°F (.1")	77°F/90°F (9.6")	77°F/89°F (5.5")	72°F/87°F (.6")
West Coast	**Spring**	**Summer**	**Fall**	**Winter**
San Diego	55°F/68°F (1.9")	65°F/76°F (0")	60°F/74°F (.4")	48°F/65°F (2.2")
San Francisco	50°F/63°F (1.4")	54°F/66°F (.2")	54°F/69°F (1.1")	46°F/57°F (4.4")

Eastern Atlantic	Spring	Summer	Fall	Winter
Madiera	48°F/75°F	37°F/60°F	44°F/75°F	55°F/87°F
Gibraltar	56°F/66°F (2.6")	68°F/81°F (0")	62°F/71°F (3")	52°F/61°F (4.8")
Cadiz	55°F/66°F (2.2")	68°F/80°F (0")	61°F/71°F (2.7")	52°F/60°F (4.2")
Lisbon	51°F/65°F	63°F/82°F	57°F/70°F	45°F/57°F
Vigo	44°F/58°F (6.8")	58°F/75°F (1.6")	51°F/64°F (8.9")	41°F/52°F (8.5")
Cherbourg	42°F/51°F (2.2")	55°F/66°F (1.7")	49°F/57°F (3.9")	28°F/45°F (3.5")
Tenerife, Canary Islands	61°F/72°F	69°F/81°F	69°F/79°F	60°F/70°F
Baltic	**Spring**	**Summer**	**Fall**	**Winter**
Oslo	34°F/49°F	55°F/71°F	38°F/49°F	20°F/31°F
Warnemünde/ Berlin	39°F/49°F	58°F/68°F	45°F/54°F	30°F/37°F
Copenhagen	36°F/49°F (1.6")	55°F/69°F (2.6")	44°F/53°F (2.1")	20°F/37°F (1.7")
St. Petersburg	33°F/46°F (1.2")	56°F/70°F (2.6")	37°F/45°F (2")	15°F/24°F (1.1")
Helsinki	31°F/45°F (1.5")	53°F/70°F (2.4")	36°F/46°F (2.7")	16°F/26°F (1.8")
Tallinn	33°F/45°F (1.3")	55°F/68°F (2.6")	28°F/47°F (2.3")	21°F/47°F (1.3")
Stockholm	31°F/47°F	54°F/70°F	38°F/48°F	22°F/31°F
Hawaii	**Spring**	**Summer**	**Fall**	**Winter**
Kahului, Maui	66°F/82°F (1.4")	71°F/87°F (.3")	69°F/87°F (1.1")	63°F/80°F (3.8")
Honolulu, Oahu	69°F/82°F (1.3")	73°F/87°F (.6")	72°F/86°F (2")	66°F/80°F (3.4")
Hilo, Hawaii	65°F/80°F (13.5")	69°F/83°F (10")	68°F/83°F (9.8")	63°F/79°F (9.2")
Nawiliwili, Kauai	68°F/79°F (2.8")	73°F/84°F (2")	72°F/83°F (2.3")	65°F/78°F (5")
Theme Parks	**Spring**	**Summer**	**Fall**	**Winter**
Walt Disney World	60°F/83°F (3.1")	72°F/92°F (7.7")	65°F/84°F (4")	50°F/73°F (2.2")
Disneyland (CA)	50°F/73°F (1")	61°F/84°F (0")	55°F/79°F (.5")	43°F/68°F (2.8")
Disneyland Paris	40°F/58°F (1.7")	55°F/75°F (2.2")	45°F/59°F (2.2")	32°F/42°F (2.7")

Hurricanes

Following historic hurricane seasons in recent years, we can't blame you for thinking long and hard on whether a major storm will affect your vacation. However, we were at sea for three and a half weeks during the now-legendary 2005 season, and the **impact was far less than you might expect**. In the Eastern Pacific, a storm near Baja, California forced the Disney Magic to bypass Cabo San Lucas, and we visited Manzanillo instead. The rest of our two-week Panama Canal journey was smooth sailing, although farther north, Hurricane Katrina was doing its worst. On a Western Caribbean cruise in June, our ship changed the order of its port visits and dashed to dodge a storm near Cuba. Other cruisers didn't do as well. Port Canaveral closed for several days, with embarkation/debarkation delayed and relocated to Fort Lauderdale (Disney bused cruisers there and back). Another time, the Disney Magic and Wonder huddled together in Galveston, Texas, dodging a storm. Most important is that the passengers and ships were kept safe. Modern mariners have plenty of warning about storms and are quite adept at keeping their passengers safe. We all hope for risk-free journeys, but it helps to prepare yourself mentally for the chance that all may not go as planned. When compared to the dangers of bygone eras, we're way far ahead of the game. One thing we won't do is dissuade you from taking a hurricane-season cruise. After unexpectedly cold, icy, soggy, or scorching vacations on land, there's something to be said for a trip where you can lift anchor and head for fair weather. We'd rather be "stuck" on a cruise ship with all its facilities than be holed up in a motel room playing endless hands of cards, even if the ship's deck heaves occasionally.

Unfortunately, we have **more stormy weather in our future**. Atlantic hurricanes follow roughly 25-year cycles of above- and below-average activity, and we're about halfway through an up cycle. The National Weather Service releases its annual Atlantic storm outlook in May, with an update in August (see http://www.nhc.noaa.gov).

There's not much you can do to **prepare for a stormy voyage**. Try out seasickness medication in advance if you're susceptible and bring it with you (see page 463). Vacation insurance may add peace of mind, but insurance is typically more useful for your journey to and from the cruise ship than for the voyage itself. Disney Cruise Line has to put passenger safety first, and the company is not obligated to "make good" weather-related changes, but they have an admirable record of delivering passenger satisfaction, even in such difficult cases.

To Visit Disney Parks, or Not?

Perhaps a Disney Add-On Package (see page 62) tempts you to make a rare (or first) visit to nearby Walt Disney World in Florida, or you just can't resist the urge to visit "The Mouse" whenever you're nearby. Whatever your reason, you're not alone—many of your fellow cruisers will also visit the parks on their trip. If you're just not quite sure yet, let's weigh the pros and cons:

Reasons to Visit the Mouse House:

- ✔ You love Disney parks and can't be nearby without a visit.
- ✔ You've never been, and this is a great opportunity.
- ✔ You're not sure you'll feel the "Disney magic" if you skip the parks.

Reasons to Just Cruise:

- ✔ You want a laid-back, really relaxing vacation.
- ✔ You've been there, done that, and don't need to go back yet.
- ✔ You don't have the time or money.

If you do **decide to go** to Walt Disney World, you'll need to choose between a Disney Cruise Line add-on package and arranging it yourself. We always make our own arrangements—we can save money and enjoy greater flexibility. You also can't grab hotel-only or cruise-only discounts that are often available, and the popular Disney Dining Plan is not offered with the add-on package. You can't beat the add-on for convenience—you'll be ushered everywhere with a minimum of fuss. How long? We prefer at least four full days at Walt Disney World. We refer you to our *PassPorter's Walt Disney World* guidebook for loads of details. Our various e-books about Walt Disney World, such as *Disney 500*, add invaluable details you can't often find elsewhere. You can pick up our guidebooks at most bookstores, online at http://www.passporter.com, and at 877-929-3273.

Should you visit Disney parks **before or after** you cruise? If you're new to Disney's parks, visit the parks first—a theme park vacation can be an intense experience, and the cruise will be a relaxing break. Parks fans may prefer visiting the parks after the cruise, as "dessert."

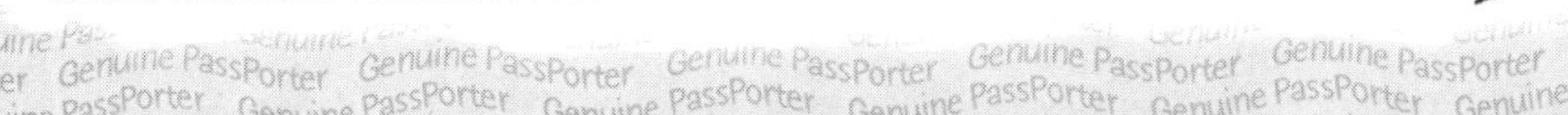

Cruise Rates

While we can't give you exact prices, we can give you rate ranges for various itineraries and stateroom categories. The rates below are based on our own research of 2013–2014 rates—we feel these are realistic numbers, but we can virtually guarantee that you'll get different rates when you do your own research. Use these as **guidelines only**. Actual rates are based on demand and fluctuate during the year. To get actual rate quotes, call the Disney Cruise Line, visit http://www.disneycruise.com, or talk to your travel agent. The rates below are for **two adult fares** with taxes and early booking savings, but do not include air, insurance, or ground transfers.

Typical Cruise Rate Ranges (for two adults in one stateroom)

Category	3-Night Bahamas	4-Night Bahamas	7-Night Pt. Canav.	6-Night Galveston
	Low to High	*Low to High*	*Low to High*	*Low to High*
R	$6,537–7,698	$9,237–12,421	$16,614–23,279	$8,971–12,567
S	n/a	n/a	n/a	$7,851–10,998
T	$3,597–5,895	$4,775–8,717	$7,436–13,417	$5,821–8,854
V	$2,073–3,165	$2,725–4,212	$4,196–8,107	n/a
4	$1,419–2,529	$1,853–3,693	$3,235–7,743	$3,413–7,981
5	$1,299–2,379	$1,693–3,493	$3,205–7,463	$2,993–6,762
6	$1,257–2,209	$1,637–3,293	$3,055–6,764	$2,797–6,561
7	$1,239–1,875	$1,613–2,543	$2,774–4,563	$2,727–6,541
8	$1,192–2,205	$1,549–2,205	$2,591–4,857	n/a
9	$1,149–2,077	$1,493–2,077	$2,493–4,129	$2,363–5,526
10	$1,143–1,981	$1,485–1,981	$2,479–4,087	$2,181–4,818
11	$1,108–1,949	$1,437–1,943	$2,395–3,905	$1,971–4,609
3rd & 4th Guest: Kids Under 3	$243–449	$272–410	$322–864	$246–450
3rd & 4th Guest: Kids 3–12	$443–844	$500–825	$644–1,651	$492–894
3rd & 4th Guest: Ages 13 & up	$459–922	$615–1,046	$693–1,917	$564–1,134

- ✔ Each stateroom booked must include at least one adult, and no more than 3–5 total guests may occupy a stateroom, depending on occupancy limits. If your party size is greater than five, you'll need to book a category R or S suite on the Magic or Wonder, or more than one stateroom. Most staterooms and suites on the Dream and Fantasy have connecting doors.
- ✔ Staterooms with just one adult and one child are charged the price of two adults.
- ✔ Guests cruising alone (one adult in a room) are charged roughly 87% of the above rates.
- ✔ Wondering about categories R, S, T, and V? Disney reclassified staterooms in 2011. (See page 124).
- ✔ Note: Women who are past their 24th week of pregnancy and infants under 12 weeks cannot sail with the Disney Cruise Line.

Confused by all those cruise rate ranges? We feel the same way. So we **researched every regular cruise rate for the past decade** at early booking discounts. We then graphed the minimum rates per night (for two adults in a category 6 stateroom) into the chart below. This chart gives you a very useful overview of the historical rate trends. Rates for higher categories follow the same basic trends as category 6, so you can use this chart to pinpoint seasons for the best rates. Keep in mind, however, that these rates can and do change at any time. Don't take the numbers in this chart at face value—concentrate on the trends instead. Also note that this chart does not take into account seasonal discounts that may be offered. You may want to compare this to the chart starting on page 54 to pick the best compromise between great cruise rates and great weather (we're partial to May ourselves).

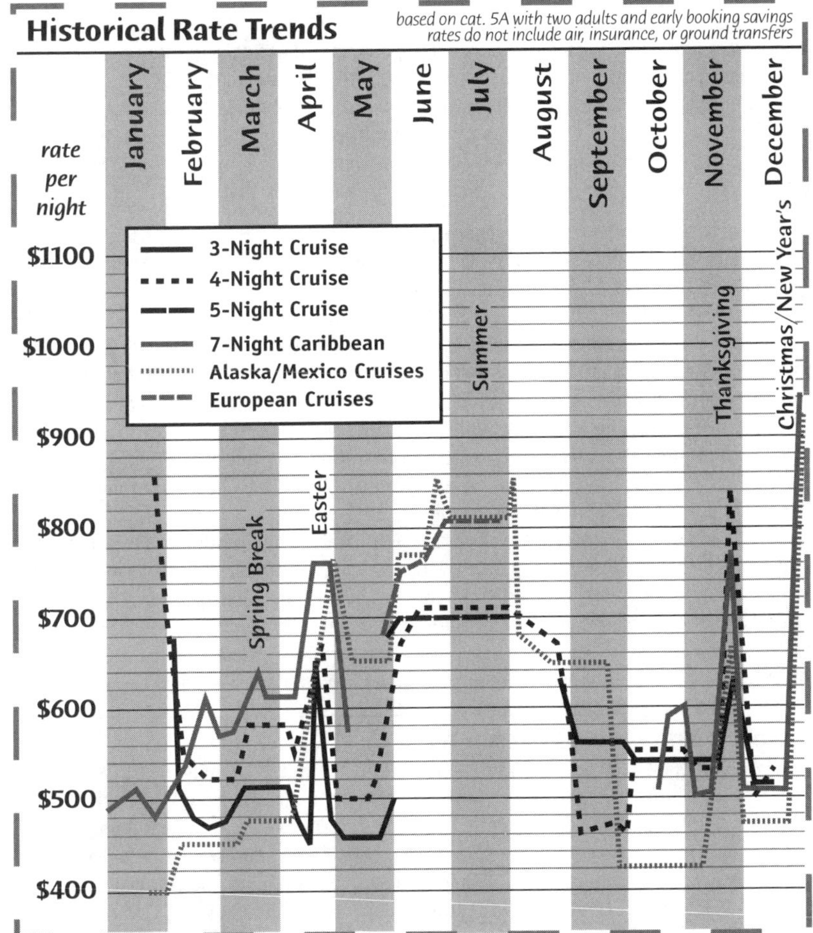

Note: Lines above correspond to actual itineraries, and thus may not continue across the graph.

Cruise Add-Ons

If you're looking to add a little more magic to your cruise or add a pre- or post-cruise stay to your cruise, there are add-ons designed to help you get the most out of it. Below are the basic packages offered at press time. Please call the Disney Cruise Line for specific packages and prices.

Pre- or Post-Cruise Add-On Stays are available through the cruise line for most itineraries, and can include ground transportation. Stays at Walt Disney World can be reserved at any Disney-owned resort, with ground transportation and theme park admission as optional extras (Walt Disney World's popular Disney Dining Plan is not available through Disney Cruise Line—if that's a "must" for you, book your Walt Disney World stay separately). Rates vary by hotel and date, but don't expect discounts.

Wedding at Sea, **Vow Renewal at Sea**, and **Commitment at Sea** Whether for a wedding, vow renewal, or commitment, ceremonies onboard the ship start at $2,500 for up to eight guests and the happy couple (additional guests extra). Ceremonies on Castaway Cay start at $3,500 (available only for cruises that visit that island, of course). Weddings and/or vow renewals are available on all Disney ships. See page 491 for more information, as well as details on *PassPorter's Disney Weddings & Honeymoons guidebook*.

Cruise Packages by Adventures by Disney add all the features of an escorted tour to cruises on the Disney Cruise line. In 2013 the Disney Magic is home base for the **Mediterranean Magic** packages, available on all 7- and 12-night cruises. Adventures by Disney provides enhanced on-board activities and deluxe excursions in every port of call (meals included), and Adventure Guides are on hand throughout the cruise. Group size is limited. Special on-board activities may include welcome and farewell receptions, and a private animation class. This package is available on all 7- and 12-night departures from June 1 to August 31, 2013. A 3-night **pre-cruise package** is available for 2013's Mediterranean itineraries, featuring welcome and farewell meals, and escorted touring in and around Barcelona. Check with Disney Cruise Line for availability. These Adventures have to be booked through Disney Cruise Line or a travel agent (not through Adventures by Disney), and can't be booked or priced online—you'll have to speak to an agent. For cruise vacation descriptions, visit http://abd.disney.go.com. Pre-cruise packages, when available, are described on the Disney Cruise Line web site. The prices for the cruise tour packages are a flat amount that's added to the cost of the selected stateroom, and include gratuities for your stateroom host/hostess, dining room servers, and independent tour guides. Gratuities for your Adventures by Disney tour escort are not included ($6-$9 per guest per day recommended).

Walt Disney World Packages

When you book your stay at Walt Disney World separately from your cruise, you can take advantage of a number of other packages. The Magic Your Way packages start with the basics (accommodations plus Magic Your Way base tickets) and add on dining plans, recreation plans, and premium Magic Your Way tickets. Magic Your Way packages start at about $330/person. To learn more about the available packages for Walt Disney World vacations, call the Walt Disney Travel Company at 407-934-7639, ask your travel agent, or visit http://www.disneyworld.com.

Reserving Your Cruise

Once you know when, how, and where you want to cruise, it's time to **make reservations**. You can call the Disney Cruise Line directly, book online at DisneyCruise.com (all categories), or use a travel agent (see sidebar at bottom). There are pros and cons to all. Dealing directly with Disney may give you more control over stateroom selection, while travel agents may offer better deals. Disney Vacation Club (DVC) members who want to cruise on points (see sidebar on page 64) should contact DVC Member Services.

Before you make your reservations, **use the worksheet** on page 69 to jot down your preferred sailing dates along with alternates. Even a small change in your travel dates can open the door to a great deal. Be familiar with all stateroom categories (see chapter 3) in your price range, too.

To make reservations, call **888-325-2500**, 8:00 am to 10:00 pm Eastern Time (weekdays) and 9:00 am to 8:00 pm ET (weekends). From outside the U.S., call +1-800-511-9444 or +1-407-566-6921. Representatives offer help in English, Spanish, Japanese, French, Portuguese, and German. Castaway Club members have a special phone number (see page 470). You can also reserve at http://www.disneycruise.com and at cruise-related sites—see below.

Call Disney Cruise Reservations as far in advance as possible. Ask for any **special deals or packages** for your dates—Disney generally doesn't volunteer this information. If you have a Disney Visa or are a Disney Vacation Club member, Florida resident, or Department of Defense personnel, ask about discounts. If your dates aren't available, check alternates.

Shopping Around

You can also make reservations through various travel reservation sites or travel agents specializing in Disney Cruise reservations (in alphabetical order):

Travel Reservation Sites
http://www.cruise.com
http://www.cruise411.com
http://www.sevenseastravel.com
http://www.expedia.com
http://www.orbitz.com
http://www.travelocity.com
http://www.vacationstogo.com

Travel Agents
http://www.aaa.com
http://www.costco.com
http://www.dreamsunlimitedtravel.com
http://www.earstoyoutravel.com
http://www.mouseearvacations.com
http://www.mousefantravel.com
http://www.themagicforless.com

Get Your Passports Together Now

Your cruise takes you to foreign ports, so you must have proper ID. Passports (or other compliant travel documents) are most likely required, depending upon your itinerary. It can take months to obtain passports if you haven't already done that, so get started now! See page 68 for more details.

Reserving Your Cruise *(continued)*

Make any **special requests**, such as a handicap-accessible room or the need for special meals, at the time of reservation (Disney's online reservation system now includes an option for selecting accessible staterooms). If you have a particular stateroom or deck in mind (see chapter 3), make sure to tell the reservations agent at the time of booking. You can also select your stateroom when reserving online.

You will be asked if you want the **Vacation Protection Plan**, and the cruise line agents automatically include it in their quote. This insurance plan covers trip cancellations, travel delays, emergency medical/dental, emergency medical transportation/assistance, and baggage delay, loss, theft, or damage. The insurance plan price is based on the total price of your cruise vacation—typical prices range from $59–$189 or more per person for the first and second individuals in your stateroom (additional guests are a bit lower). If your flight could be affected by weather, seriously consider insurance. Note that Disney's policy only covers those parts of the vacation you book with Disney Cruise Line. If you book pre-/post-cruise travel separately, use an insurance policy other than Disney's—air travel delays can cause you to miss your cruise departure, so be sure that's covered! Also note that the Protection Plan does not cover some pre-existing medical conditions. If you don't want this insurance, ask to have it removed from your quote.

Save on **vacation insurance** by booking it yourself—visit http://www.insuremytrip.com or call your insurance agent. But don't delay—most companies will waive preexisting medical conditions only if you buy insurance within 7–14 days after making your trip deposit. Trip interruption/cancellation coverage is great for circumstances beyond your control, but it doesn't help if you simply change your mind. If the cruise is only part of your vacation, make sure your policy covers the entire trip. Policies vary, so shop carefully. You may already have life, medical, theft, and car rental protection in your regular policies (be sure you're covered overseas). Credit cards, AAA, and/or other memberships may also include useful coverage. Airlines already cover lost baggage—make sure your policy exceeds their limits. Seniors and travelers with preexisting conditions should seriously consider insurance—the costs of evacuation, overseas medical care, and travel/lodging for a companion while you're under treatment are very high.

Disney Vacation Club Members

Members of Disney's innovative time-share program, the Disney Vacation Club (DVC) who purchased their points directly from Disney, can pay a fee to use their points for cruises. Contact Disney Vacation Club directly at 800-800-9100 or visit http://www.disneyvacationclub.com to get point charts and details on reserving cruises. Note that you can use a combination of points and cash (or credit) for a cruise. Reservations with points can be made up to 24 months in advance. We've heard mixed reports from guests who use DVC points to cruise—some feel it works out well, while others feel the cruise requires too many points. Disney Vacation Club members booking cruises without points may also be entitled to an onboard credit—inquire at time of reservation.

You may also be asked if you want **airfare**. In general, we've found it is less expensive to book our own airfare, but you may prefer to leave the flight details up to Disney. At times Disney's fares are lower, so it still pays to comparison shop. The biggest drawback to using the Disney Air Program is that they decide which flight you'll take, and you may arrive later than you prefer or have tight ground transfers. If you do use Disney Air, ground transfers are automatically included in your package (see below). All Disney cruisers flying on participating airlines can take advantage of Disney's Onboard Airline Check-In program (see page 73).

Ground transfers are automatic for those using the Disney Air Program and an option for those arranging their own flights. Disney roundtrip ground transfers are available to/from the airport to the cruise terminal and/or between Walt Disney World or Disneyland and the cruise terminal. Price per guest is $70 (Caribbean and Bahamas), $59 (Mediterranean), and $49 (Alaskan). The ground transfers include baggage handling. For cruisers arriving at Orlando Intl. Airport, your bags go directly from the plane to your ship (provided you're flying in on the day of your cruise and you affix the Disney-supplied labels prior to checking your bags with your airline). One-way transfers between the cruise terminal and the airport or Walt Disney World. See page 82. If you're traveling between the airport and Walt Disney World (and staying at a Disney resort hotel), those transfers are free of charge as part of Disney's Magical Express program (see below).

A **deposit** equal to 20% of your cruise fare including taxes and fees is required to confirm your reservation, for all stateroom categories. Reservations are held for 1-7 days without confirmation (24 hours for cruises within the final payment window, three days for popular holiday cruises, and seven days for all other cruises), and then they are deleted if no deposit is received. Pay your deposit by 10:00 pm ET on the necessary day (or by 8:00 pm if the necessary day is a Saturday or Sunday)—you can do it over the phone with Visa, MasterCard, Discover, JCB, Diner's Club, or American Express. Record deposits on the worksheet on page 67.

Disney's Magical Express

Disney offers its resort guests free bus transportation between Orlando International Airport (MCO) and Disney's resort hotels. Guests arriving at MCO can bypass baggage claim and head right to the bus loading area—as long as they've affixed special luggage tags back home, their luggage will be gathered right off the plane and delivered to their resort room. Provided their airline participates in the program (see list on page 73), guests headed back to the airport can do their airline check-in (including baggage) right at their hotel. Reservations must be made at least one day in advance, but try to do it at least two weeks in advance to allow time to receive your luggage tags and instruction booklet in the mail. If you're staying at a Disney resort hotel before or after your cruise, inquire at 866-599-0951. If you're on a Disney Cruise Line add-on package, Disney's Magical Express is already built in—ask your reservation agent for details.

Reserving Your Cruise *(continued)*

Once your cruise is confirmed, Disney mails a **confirmation** of your reservation. Payment is due in full 90 days (stateroom categories R,S,T, & V) or 75 days (categories 4–12) prior to sailing. If you need to cancel, reservations can be canceled for full credit up to 75 days (categories 4–12) prior to your vacation. The deposit is nonrefundable for categories R, S, T & V. If you cancel 74–45 days (categories 4–12) (89-45 days for cruises that embark/debark in a non-U.S. port)) prior to your vacation, you lose your deposit. If you cancel 44–30 days prior, you lose 50% of the vacation price. If you cancel 29-15 days prior, you lose 75% of the vacation price. There is no refund if you cancel 14 days or less prior to your vacation (all categories). There is a $35/person fee for document reissue and name/air changes within 30 days of your vacation. You can avoid those penalties if you reschedule your cruise. There is a $50/person fee if you change your sail dates 0–59 days prior to your cruise, in addition to the document reissue fee (if applicable). Insurance may help with these penalties.

Your **cruise documents** are mailed to you 10–14 days before sailing. Read everything in your cruise document package and fill out the mandatory embark/departure form, cruise contract, immigration form(s), and payment authorization before you leave home. Note: You can fill out this paperwork for your cruise at http://www.disneycruise.com, but **be sure to print it out and bring it with you**. Three additional forms may also have to be filled out: the flight modification form (to change flights when you're using Disney Air), Medical Information Form (to notify Disney of a pre-existing medical condition or special need), and the Minor Authorization Form (if you are traveling with a child of whom you are not the parent or legal guardian)—these forms are available online. Luggage tags are included with each cruise booklet and should be placed on your bags before you arrive. Included with your cruise document package is the "Ship and Shore Vacation Guides," a collection of mini-guides covering a checklist of action items, shore excursions, quick tips, onboard gifts, "Setting Sail" (a brief guide to the cruise), and Disney's Vacation Plan (insurance). Your cruise documents are required to board, and you should have them with you (or in your carry-on) on the day of departure. Don't make the mistake of putting them in a suitcase that gets checked through.

Once your cruise is reserved, you may be eager to **meet other families** sailing with you on the same cruise. You can do this in advance of your cruise by posting your own sail dates on Disney Cruise Line message boards such as our own PassPorter Message Boards (http://www.passporterboards.com) or at CruiseCritic (http://www.cruisecritic.com). You can use these resources to plan get-togethers, find companions for your table in the dining rooms, or find playmates for your kids. You'd be surprised at how many of your fellow cruisers are online and eager to make friends!

➢

Cruise Reservation Worksheet

see page 492

Use this worksheet to jot down preferences, scribble information during phone calls, and keep all your discoveries together. Don't worry about being neat—just be thorough! Circle the cruise you finally select to avoid any confusion.

Cruise length (nights): 2 3 4 5 6 7 8 9 10 11 12 13 14 15 __ *nights*

Departure date: ____________ Alternate: ____________

Return date: ____________ Alternate: ____________

We prefer to stay in category: ________ Alternates: ________

Discounts: *Disney Visa* *Disney Vacation Club* *Castaway Club* *AAA* *Seasonal* *Floridian* *Canadian* *DoD* *Other:* ____________

Dates	Itinerary	Category	Rates	Insurance	Total

Reservation number: ____________

Confirm reservation by this date: ____________

Deposit due by: ____________ Deposit paid on: ____________

Balance due by: ____________ Balance paid on: ____________

Do we need to order passports/birth certificates? ____________

Introduction | Reservations | Staterooms | Dining | Activities | Ports of Call | Magic | Index

Have Your Passports Ready

Do you need a passport? Despite the final passport regulations that went into effect in 2008 (and were supposed to settle the issue once and for all), the answer is still, "maybe." While the answer is "yes" for nearly all air, land, and sea entry into the U.S. as of June 1, 2009, the regulations carved out a "**closed-loop itinerary" exception for cruise travelers**.

For the foreseeable future, adult U.S. citizen cruise ship passengers departing from and returning to the same U.S. port **can still present government-issued photo ID plus a certified birth certificate** (with a raised seal or multiple colors) to re-enter the country. Be sure to bring original or official documents; no copies will be accepted. Children 16 and under only need birth certificates or other proof of U.S. citizenship such as a naturalization certificate or citizenship card. This applies, for example, to all Disney cruises that depart from and return to Port Canaveral, Miami, and Galveston. It would not apply to repositioning itineraries, since the cruise ends in a different port, and any cruise that begins and/or ends in a non-U.S. port. Other valid identity documents for a closed-loop itinerary would (of course) include a conventional passport "book," the Passport Card, and the Enhanced Driver's Licenses issued by some states (see below).

Despite this, we **strongly encourage you to have a full passport book**, and Disney Cruise Line "strongly encourages Guests of all ages have a valid U.S. passport for all cruises," (DCL does not voice an opinion on the issue of Passport Book vs. Passport Card). Photo ID-plus-birth certificate, Passport Cards, and Enhanced Drivers Licenses cannot be used for re-entry by air (for example, if you must cut your cruise short in an emergency and return home by air), or for international travel outside North America and the Caribbean. If you choose to spend any money on a passport, you'll have the maximum flexibility for future travel by paying the higher price for a passport book, since Passport Cards can't be used for international air travel. Why apply and pay twice?

Compliant Travel Documents—These are the main accepted travel documents for U.S. citizens entering the U.S. by land or sea:

> **U.S. Passport Book**—This is the traditional passport booklet, available by filling out an application. See our information on applying for a passport on the next page.
>
> **U.S. Passport Card**—The highly touted Passport Card (a credit card-sized alternate passport) is only valid for land and sea travel between the United States, Canada, Mexico, the Caribbean, and Bermuda. It is not valid for air travel or for other destinations. The PASS Card is cheaper than a passport, but its limited use makes it a false economy. If you feel it meets your needs, get details at http://travel.state.gov.
>
> **Enhanced Driver's License**—Some states offer an "Enhanced Driver's License" that is the legal equivalent of a Passport Card. We expect that most border states will offer it, and currently Arizona, California, Michigan, New Mexico, New York, Texas, Vermont and Washington have or will have them. Check with your state for details/availability.

Disney Cruise Line asks that all guests with passports **supply their passport numbers** at least 75 days prior to departure. If you have applied for passports but fear you may not receive them in time, discuss the situation with a Disney Cruise Line representative prior to the 75-day deadline.

Getting a Passport Book

Passport book applications are accepted at **more than 9,000 locations in the United States**, including many post offices, county clerks' offices, and city halls. For a full listing, including hours of operation, visit http://travel.state.gov or call 877-487-2778. The same site also provides application forms and full information on the application process.

It typically takes **6-8 weeks to receive a passport book** after you file the application, so apply for your passport book(s) no later than 135 days (four months) prior to sailing, or pay extra to expedite your application. See below for details on getting a rush passport.

New applications for everyone including infants must be made in person, but passport book renewals can be made by mail provided the current passport book is undamaged, your name hasn't changed (or you can legally document the change), the passport book is no more than 15 years old, and you were 16 years or older when it was issued.

Are you in a rush? **Expedited passport book applications** can be processed for an extra fee. If you apply through a regular passport "acceptance facility," you can get your passport book within two weeks—pay an extra $60 with each application, plus overnight shipping. If you are traveling within two weeks, urgent passport applications can be processed at 14 Passport Agencies in the U.S., by appointment only. Services such as USBirthCertificate.net (http://www.usbirthcertificate.net) can do it for you, provided you first visit a local passport acceptance facility to handle the preliminaries.

Important: You need a **birth certificate or other birth/naturalization record** before you can apply for your passport, so you may need even more time! While there are services (such as USBirthCertificate.net) that can obtain a domestic birth certificate in as little as 2-3 days, if you were born outside the U.S., the process may take weeks or even months.

Budget **$135 for a "standard" adult passport book application**, $120 for each child under 16. Expedited (two-week) processing adds $60 to each application, plus next-day shipping costs. Passport renewals are $110. Duplicate/replacement birth certificate fees vary by state, but cost about $5-$15. Naturally, the help of a passport/birth certificate service adds even more to the price—typically an extra $100/passport, $50/birth certificate.

Passport Timeline

My Cruise Date:	
Subtract 135 days from cruise date:	Passport application (regular) due:
Subtract 90 days from cruise date:	Passport application (expedited) due:
Subtract 75 days from cruise date:	Passport # to Disney Cruise Line due:
Need birth certificates, too? Subtract 15 days from the passport application due date (for those born in the U.S.), 120 days (for those born outside the U.S.):	

Passport Worksheet

Name	Passport Number	Completed Application	Proof of Citizenship	Proof of Identity	Passport Photos (2)	Fees

Getting to Florida

By Car, Van, Truck, or Motorcycle

Many vacationers arrive in Florida in their own vehicle. It's hard to beat the **slowly rising sense of excitement** as you draw closer or the freedom of having your own wheels once you arrive (helpful when you're combining your cruise with a land vacation). Driving may also eliminate any concerns you or family members may have with air travel. And driving can be less expensive than air travel, especially with large families. On the downside, you may spend long hours or even days on the road, which cuts deeply into your vacation time. And you'll need to park your car while you're cruising, which is pricey (see page 87). Drivers from outside the U.S. may have heard that a new Florida law was introduced requiring drivers from other countries to have an International Driving Permit as well as their driver's license. This law was repealed by the Florida governor in April 2013.

We suggest you carefully **map your course** ahead of time. One way is with a AAA TripTik—a strip map that guides you to your destination. Only AAA members (see page 35) can get a printed TripTik, but TripTik Online is available free at your regional AAA web site. Other trip-routing web site are http://www.mapquest.com and http://maps.google.com. If you're driving I-75, we recommend *Along Interstate-75* by Dave Hunter (Mile Oak Publishing, http://www.i75online.com). I-95 drivers will benefit from the *Drive I-95* guide by Stan and Sandra Posner (Travelsmart, http://www.drivei95.com) or http://www.i95exitguide.com. For navigating the Sunshine State, look for Dave Hunter's *Along Florida's Expressways*.

If you live more than 500 miles away, **spread out your drive** over more than one day, allotting one day for every 500 miles. If your journey spans more than a day, decide in advance where to stop each night and make reservations. If possible, arrive a day ahead of your cruise departure day for a more relaxing start to the cruise (see page 84 for lodging in Cape Canaveral). Compare the price of driving versus flying, too.

By Train

The train is a uniquely relaxing way to travel. **Amtrak** serves the Orlando area daily with both **passenger trains** and an Auto Train, which carries your family and your car. The **Auto Train** runs between suburban Washington, D.C. and suburban Orlando (Sanford, FL). The Auto Train is also available one-way, and in many seasons, one direction is less expensive than the other. Late arrivals are the norm, so allow extra time. Keep in mind that you may need to take a taxi or town car from the train station, or you can rent a car from the nearby Hertz office. Call Amtrak at 800-USA-RAIL or visit them at http://www.amtrak.com.

By Bus

Greyhound serves Melbourne, Orlando, and Kissimmee. Buses take longer to reach a destination than cars driving the same route. Fares are lowest if you live within ten hours of Central Florida. For fares and tickets, call Greyhound at 800-231-2222 or visit them at http://www.greyhound.com.

By Airplane

Air travel is the fastest way for many vacationers, but we recommend you fly in at least a day before in the event there are flight delays. You have two choices: use the Disney Air Program, which adds airfare to your package–ask about this when you book your cruise–or book your own flight. It's often less expensive and more flexible to book your own flight–Disney Air Program arrival and departure times aren't always optimal, but check both options. To find an **affordable flight**, be flexible on the day and time–fares can differ greatly depending on when you fly and how long you stay. Second, take advantage of the many fare sales available–to learn about sales, sign up for fare alerts at airline web sites or travel sites such as Travelocity (http://www.travelocity.com), Expedia (http://www.expedia.com), Orbitz (http://www.orbitz.com), and Kayak.com (http://www.kayak.com). Third, try alternate airports and airlines (including low-fare airlines like Southwest and jetBlue). Fourth, be persistent. When you find a good deal, be ready to reserve immediately - it may not last - but understand that most cheap flights are non-refundable and charge a substantial fee to make a change. Research fares on your **airline's web site** rather than by phone–you may have more flight options. Priceline.com (http://www.priceline.com) is an option–you can name your own price, but your choices may be limited. For **ground transportation**, see page 79.

Our Top 10 Flying Tips, Reminders, and Warnings

1. Visit http://www.tsa.gov for travel security news and updates and check the status of your flight before departing for the airport. Use online check-in if it is offered by your airline (most now offer it).
2. Many airlines now charge for baggage and seat selection–factor-in the cost.
3. Pick up a meal and drinks for the flight after you pass through security, as most domestic flights have discontinued meal service.
4. Pack sharp or dangerous items in checked luggage (or just leave them at home). This includes pocket knives and sport sticks. Cigarette lighters, scissors with blades under 4", and nail clippers are allowed. For details, visit http://www.tsa.gov. Call the Disney Cruise Line to confirm any questionable objects.
5. Remember the **3-1-1 rule** for liquids/gels in carry-ons: They must be in **3 oz. or less** bottle(s), all in **1 quart-sized, clear, zip-top bag**, and **1 bag per person**, placed in screening bin. Limit your carry-ons to one bag and one personal item (e.g., purse).
6. Keep your luggage unlocked for inspections, or it may be damaged.
7. Plan to arrive at the airport at least two hours prior to departure.
8. Curbside check-in may be available (fee may apply), but you may need to obtain a boarding pass from your airline's customer service desk anyway.
9. E-ticket holders need a confirmation or boarding pass. Get it from your airline's web site, from Disney's Onboard Check-In Desk (see page 73), or Lobby Concierge at Walt Disney World.
10. Keep your ID handy. We carry ours in PassHolder Pouches (see our web site).

Getting Around the Orlando International Airport

Most cruise-bound passengers will arrive in the Orlando International Airport, a large, sprawling hub and one of the better airports we've flown into. Your plane docks at one of the **satellite terminals** (see map on next page). Follow the signs to the automated **shuttle** to the main terminal—there you'll find **baggage claim** and ground transportation. Once you reach the main terminal, follow signs down to baggage claim (Level 2). If you're using Disney ground transportation for either the cruise or a pre-cruise visit to Walt Disney World (and you affixed your Disney-supplied luggage tags before your flight departed), you can skip baggage claim and head directly to the Disney's Magical Express check-in desk on "B" side, Level 1 (note: luggage delivery service is only available between 5:00 am and 10:00 pm—if your plan lands outside those times, you should collect your own luggage). Shuttles, town cars, taxis, and rental cars are also found on Level 1 (take the elevators opposite the baggage carousels). Each transportation company has its own ticket booth, so keep your eyes open. If you get lost, look for signs that can get you back on track.

Disney's Magical Express check-in desk on level 1, side B

Need to **meet up at the airport**? It's best to meet your party at their baggage claim area as you won't be allowed past security without a valid boarding pass. The trick here is knowing which airline and baggage claim area. Use the map and airline list on the next page, or call the airport directly at 407-825-2001. Be careful when differentiating between the side A and side B baggage claim. Also note that gates 1–29 and 100–129 use side A, while gates 30–99 use side B. Check the arrival/departure boards in the terminal for flight status, too! Other terminal meeting spots are the Disney Stores (see stars on map on next page) and/or the **airport restaurants**, especially for long waits. Be sure to exchange cell phone numbers, too.

For **more details** on the Orlando International Airport, call 407-825-2001 or visit http://www.orlandoairports.net. Air travelers can be paged at 407-825-2000.

Upon your return to the Orlando International Airport for your flight back home, be sure to give yourself ample time to check in (if you didn't use Disney's Onboard Airline Check-In Program—see sidebar below) and get through security. The security checkpoint can be lengthy during peak travel times, so we suggest you go directly to security when you arrive at the airport. Small eateries and convenience stores are located in the satellite terminals, where you'll wait for your flight after passing security. There are also InMotion DVD rental kiosks at the terminals for gates 30–59, gates 60–99 , and gates 100-129 (as well as an InMotion store in the main terminal itself)—see http://www.inmotionpictures.com for details.

Aero Mexico, Air Canada, Air Transat, Alaska Airlines, American Airlines, Avianca, CanJet, Caribbean, Copa, Edelweiss, GOL, Interjet, JetBlue, MiamiAir, SunWing, Taca, West Jet, vivaaerobus, and Whitejets use Gates 1-29; Aer Lingus, BahamasAir, Continental, Frontier, Spirit, Sun Country, United, and US Airways use Gates 30–59; Air France, British Airways, Delta, Lufthansa, TAM, and Virgin Atlantic use Gates 60-99; and AirTran, Southwest, and Virgin America use Gates 100–129.

Disney's Onboard Airline Check-In Program

All Disney cruisers can take advantage of Disney's Onboard Airline Check-In Program to get your return boarding passes and luggage transferred from ship to plane, whether or not you purchased Disney ground transfers and/or Disney Air. What's the catch? Your flight must come through the Orlando International Airport, you must be flying on one of the participating airlines (currently AirTran, Alaska, American, Continental, Delta, JetBlue, Southwest, US Airways, and United), and you must be flying home directly after your cruise. If you qualify, you can register for onboard airline check-in at the cruise terminal or at a Disney Cruise Line hospitality desk at your Disney resort before your cruise. There is also a form in your cruise documents, which you can then turn in at the cruise terminal or Disney resort. If you use this program, your boarding pass will be delivered to your stateroom on the day prior to disembarkation. And your luggage is trucked to the airport and loaded onto your plane for you!

Getting Around the Orlando Sanford Airport

Travelers flying to Orlando **from Europe or via group charter** may arrive at the smaller Orlando Sanford International Airport (FSB), located about 18 miles northeast of Orlando and 67 miles from Port Canaveral. Airlines with scheduled service into Sanford include Allegiant Air, ArkeFly, Direct Air, Icelandair, Iceland Express, SST Air, and Vision Airlines, as well as three international charter services with flights from the United Kingdom and Ireland (Monarch, Thomas Cook, and Thomson Airways).

Alamo/National, Avis, Budget, Dollar, Enterprise, Hertz, and Thrifty all operate **in-terminal car rental desks**. Accessible Mini-Van Rentals has an off-site rental office. Several services provide bus/van service from Sanford to Orlando-area attractions and Port Canaveral. Mears Transportation no longer offers regular bus/shuttle service to/from Sanford.

International passengers arrive and depart from Terminal A, while domestic travelers use Terminal B. A Welcome Center is located across the street from Terminal A and is home to ground transportation services.

Dining options here include the Royal Palm Lounge (terminal A) and basic food courts (terminals A & B).

For more details on the Orlando Sanford International Airport, phone 407-322-7771 or visit http://www.orlandosanfordairport.com. If you plan to rent a car at the airport and drive to Port Canaveral, use a map routing service such as MapQuest.com before you leave home to get directions (the airport is located at 1 Red Cleveland Blvd., Sanford, FL 32773).

Travel Worksheet

Electronic, interactive worksheet available—see page 492

Use this worksheet to jot down preferences, scribble information during phone calls, and keep all your discoveries together. Don't worry about being neat—just be thorough! Circle the names and numbers once you decide to go with them to avoid confusion.

Arrival date: ____________ Alternate: ____________

Return date: ____________ Alternate: ____________

We plan to travel by: ❑ Car/Van ❑ Airplane ❑ Train ❑ Bus ❑ Tour ❑ Other: ____________

For Drivers:

Miles to get to port: ______ ÷ 500 = ____ days on the road

We need to stay at a motel on: ____________

Tune-up scheduled for: ____________

Rental car info: ____________

____

For Riders:

Train/bus phone numbers: ____________

Ride preferences: ____________

Ride availabilities: ____________

Reserved ride times and numbers: ____________

Routes: ____________

For Tour-Takers:

Tour company phone numbers: ____________

Tour preferences: ____________

Tour availabilities: ____________

Reserved tour times and numbers: ____________

Routes: ____________

For Fliers:

Airline phone numbers: ______________________________

Flight preferences: ______________________________

Flight availabilities: ______________________________

____

____

____

Reserved flight times and numbers: ______________________________

____

For Ground Transportation:

Town car/shuttle/rental car phone numbers: ______________________________

____

Town car/shuttle/rental car reservations: ______________________________

____

Package ground transportation details: ______________________________

____

Additional Notes:

Reminder: Don't forget to confirm holds or cancel reservations (whenever possible) within the allotted time frame.

Lodging Near Orlando Intl. Airport

If you fly into Orlando a day ahead of time but arrive too late in the day to make the trek to Port Canaveral, consider bunking near the airport the night before. We describe several hotels near the airport below—even one hotel that's actually in the airport itself! Here are the details:

Hyatt Regency Orlando $188+ 0 mi./0 km. from airport

You can't beat the convenience of staying right in the airport at this Hyatt, but you will pay for the privilege. This six-story hotel is built right into the main terminal at the Orlando International Airport, offering 445 sound-proof, luxurious rooms at a whopping 400 sq. ft. each. While we haven't had the opportunity to stay here, a walk around the hotel spaces gives the impression of a very upscale business hotel. Standard room amenities include two double "Grand Beds," oversized work desk with dataport, armchairs, cable TV, balcony (not all rooms), iHome clock radio, refrigerator, coffeemaker, hair dryer, iron and ironing board, daily newspaper, voice mail, and free wireless Internet—there are no in-room safes. Hotel amenities include baggage retrieval/delivery around the airport (fee), room service, arcade, beauty salon, heated outdoor pool, sundeck with a runway view, 24-hour fitness room, and access to the airport shopping mall. The Hyatt has three restaurants: Hemispheres serves breakfast buffets and elegant dinners on the top two floors; McCoy's Bar and Grill is a casual eatery serving American food, and Hiro's Sushi Bar. The Lobby South lounge offers drinks and appetizers. Check-in: 4:00 pm; check-out: 12:00 pm. The hotel was built in 1992 and renovated in 2000. Visit http://orlandoairport.hyatt.com or call 407-825-1234. Address: 9300 Jeff Fuqua Boulevard, Orlando, FL 32827. Note that when you purchase air travel through Disney Cruise Line and they fly you in the night before your cruise, this appears to be the hotel that Disney puts you up at most frequently (but no guarantees, of course!).

Orlando Airport Marriott $149+ 2.5 mi./4 km. from airport

© MediaMarx, Inc.
A standard room

We enjoyed a night at this Marriott before a Disney cruise in May 2003 and found it both convenient and affordable (we got a great rate here via Priceline.com—see sidebar on next page). The Marriott is a mere 5 minutes from the Orlando Airport via a 24-hour complimentary shuttle (available by using a courtesy phone in the terminal). The 484 renovated rooms at this 10-story business hotel offer two double beds, work desk with dataport, 27-in. cable TV, two-line speakerphone, coffeemaker, hair dryer, iron and ironing board, in-room safe, daily newspaper, voice mail, and wireless high-speed Internet access (fee)—there are no balconies. Hotel amenities include room service, arcade, indoor/outdoor heated pool, hot tub, sauna, fitness center, tennis courts, and basketball court. Dining options include LUXE, serving casual American food for breakfast, lunch, and dinner. Fidalgo Bay Café offers light fare at breakfast, lunch, and dinner. A pool bar, The Landings, serves drinks and sandwiches seasonally. The hotel was built in 1983 and renovated in 2007. Check-in time: 3:00 pm; check-out time: 12:00 pm. Visit http://marriott.com/property/propertypage/MCOAP or call 407-851-9000 or 800-380-6751. Address: 7499 Augusta National Drive, Orlando, FL 32833. See our detailed review of this hotel, complete with photos, at http://www.passporter.com/articles/orlandoairportmarriott.asp. We would stay here again without hesitation.

☐ Sheraton Suites $143+ 2.5 mi./4 km. from airport

This all-suite, three-story hotel offers 150 suites at affordable rates. Suite amenities include a living room with sofa bed, work desk, two-line phones with dataports, 37" HD TV, armchair, and kitchenette area with fridge, coffeemaker, and microwave, private bedroom with French doors, pillowtop beds, another HD TV, marble bathroom with hair dryer, iron and ironing board, voice mail, and wireless Internet access (fee)—there are no in-room safes, but there are balconies in some rooms. Hotel amenities include room service, a heated indoor/outdoor pool, sundeck, hot tub, and fitness room. The on-site restaurant, Mahogany Grille, offers a breakfast buffet plus lunch and dinner. Several restaurants—Chili's, Tony Roma's, and Bennigan's—are within walking distance. A free, 24-hour shuttle is available between the airport and hotel—use the courtesy phone in the terminal to request it. Check-in time: 3:00 pm; check-out time: 12:00 pm. Visit http://www.sheratonorlandoairport.com or call 407-240-5555 or 800-325-3535. Address: 7550 Augusta National Drive, Orlando, FL 32833.

☐ La Quinta Inn & Suites North $89+ 3 mi./5 km. from airport

This five-story, 148-room motel offers clean rooms, free breakfasts, and free high-speed Internet access in all rooms. Room amenities include two double beds (or one king bed), 25-in. cable TV, dataport phone, coffeemaker, hair dryer, iron and ironing board, voice mail, free local calls, and newspaper—there are no balconies or in-room safes. There are also five suites with a separate living room, sofa bed, microwave, and refrigerator. Motel amenities include an outdoor heated swimming pool, hot tub, sundeck, and fitness center. No on-site restaurant, but a TGIFriday's is adjacent and Tony Roma's, Cracker Barrel, Bennigan's, and Chili's are within walking distance. This motel was built in 1998. A free airport shuttle is available from 5:00 am to 11:00 pm daily. Check-in time: 3:00 pm; check-out time: 12:00 pm. Visit http://www.laquinta.com or call 407-240-5000. Address: 7160 N. Frontage Rd., Orlando, FL 32812

☐ Hyatt Place Airport NW $145+ 3 mi./5 km. from airport

Enjoy a 480 sq. ft. suite in this six-story hotel renovated in 2009 (formerly Amerisuites). Each suite has two double beds (or one king bed), sofa bed, 42" TV, two phones with dataport, desk, free high-speed Internet, wet bar, coffeemaker, refrigerator, microwave, hair dryer, iron and ironing board. The living and sleeping areas are separated by half walls. Hotel amenities include an outdoor heated pool and fitness center. Complimentary continental breakfast, 24-hour "Guest Kitchen" food service. TGIFriday's, Tony Roma's, Cracker Barrel, Bennigan's, and Chili's are nearby. A free, 24-hour shuttle serves the airport and destinations within a 3-mile radius of the hotel. Check-in time: 3:00 pm; check-out time: 11:00 am. Visit http://www.hyattplace.com or call 407-816-7800. Address: 5435 Forbes Place, Orlando, FL 32812

Priceline.com

We've had great success with Priceline.com (http://www.priceline.com), where you can bid on hotel rates in particular areas. Before one of our cruise trips, we got the Marriott Orlando Airport (see previous page) through Priceline.com for about $35. If you do decide to try Priceline.com, read the directions thoroughly, and keep in mind that once your bid is accepted, you can't cancel. We recommend you visit BiddingForTravel.com (http://www.biddingfortravel.com) for Priceline.com advice and tips. Note that as of December 2011, each of the hotels we describe in the Lodging Near Orlando Intl. Airport section is a potential hotel available via Priceline.com. Not sure about Priceline.com? Another place to try for hotel deals is Hotwire.com at http://www.hotwire.com.

Want to stay near or at Walt Disney World before or after your cruise? For Disney resorts and hotels nearby, we recommend you pick up a copy of PassPorter's Walt Disney World guidebook (see page 489)—it goes into great detail on Walt Disney World lodging.

➤

Getting to Port Canaveral

Port Canaveral, Florida, is Disney's main home port. Situated in the city of Cape Canaveral, it's easily accessible from anywhere in Central Florida.

From the Orlando International Airport
Port Canaveral is about one hour (45 mi./72 km.) east of the airport. You have four options: transfer, town car/limo, taxi, or rental car.

Disney Cruise Line Ground Transfer—If you're sailing the day you arrive at the airport and you've booked ground transfers, a Disney Cruise Line representative meets you at the airport and directs you to a motorcoach. Check your cruise documents for transfer details. If you're not on a package, you can purchase these transfers for $70/person roundtrip—inquire at 800-395-9374, extension 1. If you're departing in the next day or so, just fill out the Transfer Purchase Option in your cruise documents and hand it over at the Disney's Magical Express counter on the first floor of the airport (a $70/person charge will appear on your shipboard account). For more details on motorcoaches, see page 82.

Note: Mears Transportation no longer provides shuttle transportation to Port Canaveral (no doubt because they operate the Disney Cruise motorcoaches).

© MediaMarx, Inc.
Dave relaxes in a limo on the way to the port

Town Car/Limo—A luxurious alternative is a town car or limo, through a company like Quicksilver (888-468-6939) or Happy Limo (888-394-4277). The driver meets you in baggage claim, helps you with your luggage, and drives you to the port. Cost is around $210 plus tip for a town car ($230 for a van) round-trip to and from the port.

Taxi—At approximately $110 one-way, it's not the best value, though a minivan taxi has its points. You can get taxis at the airport on level 1.

Rental Car—This option works well if you'll be spending time elsewhere before you cruise and need the wheels (thus, this is usually our preference). It can also be less expensive than the other options, but you must spend time for pickup/dropoff. For our tips on choosing the best rental car company for your needs, see the next page.

Getting to Port Canaveral

(continued)

Rental Cars *(continued)*

All the major car rental companies serve Orlando International Airport, but we favor Avis, Budget, Dollar, Enterprise, Hertz, and Thrifty because they have on-airport rental offices and offer a complimentary shuttle between their Port Canaveral office and the cruise terminal. For the best deal, forget brand loyalty; any of these agencies can deliver the winning rate on a given day and/or with the right discount code(s). Check http://www.mousesavers.com/rentalcar.html for current discount codes—be sure to try all codes that apply! Your airline or online booking site may offer a good bundle rate with your airfare or hotel. Many companies, frequent flier programs, and organizations have special codes. Though two one-way rentals are often cheapest, a discounted weekly round-trip rate may beat the cost of one-day rentals plus parking. For more rental car tips, see http://www.passporter.com/rentalcars.asp.

Company	Price[1]	Dist.	Key Information
Avis	$76	4 miles *P3F*[2]	Reserve: http://www.avis.com 800-331-1212. Local address: 6650 N. Atlantic Ave., Cape Canaveral; local phone: 321-783-3643.
Budget	$64	3 miles *CC5*[2]	Reserve: http://www.budget.com 800-527-0700. Local address: 8401 Astronaut Blvd., Port Canaveral; local phone: 321-951-4813.
Hertz	$66	2 miles *COIC10*[2]	Reserve: http://www.hertz.com 800-654-3131. Local address: 8963 Astronaut Blvd.; Port Canaveral; local phone: 321-783-7771.
Dollar	$37	*2 miles* *C011*[2]	Reserve: http://www.dollar.com 866-957-0018. 6799 N. Atlantic Ave., Cape Canaveral; local phone 321-799-2945
Enterprise[3]	$89	*4 miles*	Reserve: http://www.enterprise.com 800-261-7331. Local address: 6211 N. Atlantic Ave., Cape Canaveral; local phone 321-866-0324
Thrifty	$37	*4 miles* *MU2*[2]	Reserve: http://www.thrifty.com 866-957-0058. Local address: 6799 N. Atlantic Ave., Cape Canaveral; local phone 321-783-2600

[1] Base rate of a one-day, one-way intermediate-class rental Fri. March 1 to March 2, 2013, priced on January 28, 2013.
[2] Company's office code in Port Canaveral—use it when checking rates!
[3] Reserve as a round-trip, no charge or advance notice to drop-of at either MCO or port.

....➤

Getting to Port Canaveral

(continued)

Driving directions from the Orlando airport: Follow airport signs to the "North Exit" and take the Beachline Expressway (528) east 43 mi. (69 km.) to Cape Canaveral. You'll need $3.00 in bills/coins for tolls, round trip.

From Orlando and Walt Disney World—You have four options: ground transfer, town car/limo, rental car, and your own car. Disney offers ground transfers, and Quicksilver and Happy Limo offer town cars/limos/vans to Port Canaveral (see page 82). If you're driving, take the Greenway (SR-417) to exit 26, and then take the Beach Line (SR-528) to Port Canaveral. Allow at least one hour and $5.50 for tolls. See directions below to the terminal.

From I-75—Take I-75 south to Florida's Turnpike. Take the turnpike south to exit 254 and take the Beachline Expressway (528) east 50 mi. (80 km.) to Port Canaveral. Expect $7.50 in tolls. See directions below to terminal.

From I-95—Take I-95 to exit 205 East and take the Beachline Expressway (528) east 12 mi. (19 km.) to Port Canaveral.

From Port Canaveral to the Disney Cruise Line Terminal—As you drive east on the Beachline Expressway (528), you'll cross two bridges (see if you can spot your ship when you're atop these bridges). After the second bridge, take the Route 401 exit to the "A" cruise terminals and follow the signs to the Disney Cruise Line Terminal (detailed on page 87).

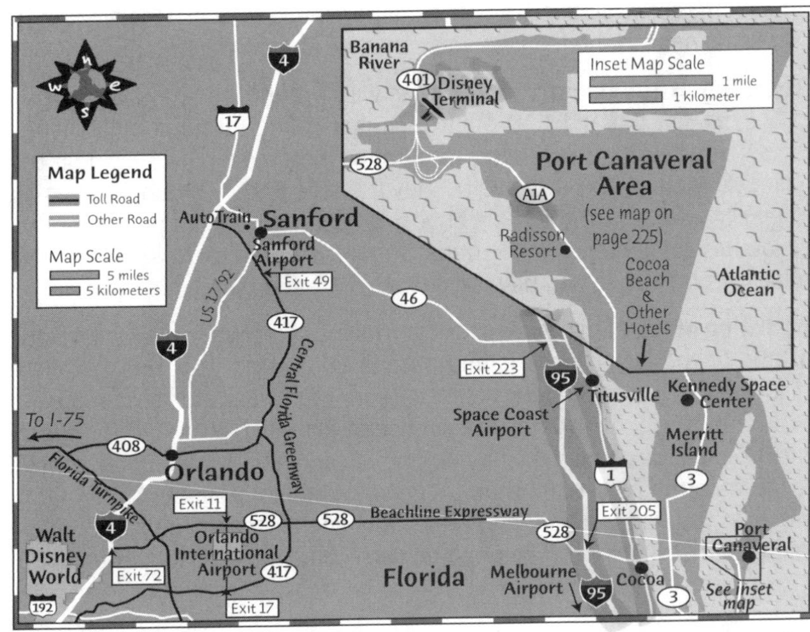

Disney Cruise Line Motorcoach (Ground Transfers)

Passengers on a Disney vacation package and those who've booked ground transfers separately (see page 65) may ride in a Disney Cruise Line motorcoach. These handicap-accessible **deluxe buses** are all decked out with classic round portholes. On board, the cushy seats recline and there's even a restroom in the back. On the way to Port Canaveral, you're treated to a delightful video that heightens your anticipation. On the way back, you may watch a Disney movie on the overhead monitors.

© MediaMarx, Inc.

Disney Cruise Line Motorcoach

There are some **downsides** to the ground transfers. There's no guarantee you'll get a Disney Cruise Line motorcoach just because you purchased the transfers. Once, when we used the transfers, we rode in the motorcoach on the way to Port Canaveral from the airport, but on the way back to the Walt Disney World Resort, we were squeezed into a drab Mears shuttle van instead. This is more likely to happen if you're going to the Walt Disney World Resort after your cruise than if your trip starts at Walt Disney World. Another downside is that you usually need to wait to board the bus. This could mean you may feel rushed when you arrive at the airport. And check-in may go slower, since you're in the midst of a large group of people who've arrived with you. You'll need to decide which is more important: convenience (take the bus) or speed (use another method). Tip: Sit as near to the front as you can to be among the first off.

Boarding at the airport: Passengers with ground transfers who arrive between 9:00 am and 1:30 pm will be met in the terminal by a Disney representative and told where to board the motorcoach (usually near the Disney's Magical Express desk on level 1, side B). Cruise check-in is no longer available at the airport check-in desk. Your luggage (if properly tagged) is conveniently intercepted and transported to the ship. The first buses depart for Port Canaveral betwen 9:30 and 10:30 am.

Boarding at Walt Disney World: If you have a pre-cruise Add-On Package at one of the Disney hotels and purchased ground transfers, you'll be instructed to leave your luggage inside your room near the door for pickup on the morning of your cruise. Between about 12:00 and 2:00 pm (a pickup time is assigned the day before you depart), you meet in a central location in the resort and then proceed to the motorcoach. Note that in the past you had the option of departing from Disney's Animal Kingdom theme park on the morning of your cruise, but that is no longer possible.

Introduction Reservations Staterooms Dining Activities Ports of Call Magic Index

Ground Transportation Worksheet

Use this worksheet to research, record, and plan your transportation to and from Port Canaveral or the Port of Los Angeles.

Method	Price	Details	Reservation #
Disney Cruise Line Transfers: *800-395-9374*			
Town Car/Limo/Van **Orlando:** *Quicksilver Tours:* *888-468-6939* *Happy Limo:* *888-394-4277* **Los Angeles:** *SuperShuttle:* 800-258-3266 *Primetime Shuttle:* 800-733-8267 *LAX Shuttle & Limo:* 877-529-7433			
Rental Car: *Avis:* *800-331-1212* *Budget:* *800-527-0700* *Hertz:* *800-654-3131*	*(don't forget tolls)*		

Scheduling Pick-Up and Departure Times
Allow 90 minutes to get to **Port Canaveral from either Orlando Airport or Walt Disney World**. If you have an early arrival time (chosen during online check-in), use a pickup/departure time of 9:30 am or 10:00 am. Depart no later than 1:30 pm so you reach Port Canaveral by 3:00 pm at the latest. **From LAX or Disneyland to Port of Los Angeles**, allow 45-60 minutes. For your return trip, the earliest you can expect to disembark the ship is 7:45 am to 8:30 am (and yes, you can still do the sit-down breakfast). It takes about 15 to 20 minutes to collect your bags and go through customs. Thus your pickup/departure time could be set between 8:00 am and 9:15 am. We do not recommend a flight departure before 12:30 pm from Orlando, or Noon from Los Angeles.

Lodging Near Port Canaveral

You may want to take advantage of the visit to the "Space Coast" to squeeze in a trip to Kennedy Space Center or a day at the beach. Or perhaps you want to arrive in advance to avoid stress on the morning of your cruise. While there are many motels and hotels in the area, we've stayed at five (Radisson, Quality Suites, Ron Jon, Motel 6, and Residence Inn), all of which we recommend. We also detail one other hotel. To see the location of each, check the map on page 225.

Radisson Resort at the Port $128+ 2.7 mi./4.3 km. to port

This 284-room luxury resort is one of the closest lodgings to the Disney Cruise Line terminal and is quite popular with cruisers. While it is not an oceanfront hotel, it does feature a themed pool (see photo below), wading pool, hot tub, tennis court, fitness center, room service, and 1- and 2-bedroom suites in addition to its standard, Caribbean-themed rooms (see photo at left). All rooms have ceiling fans, TVs, coffeemakers, hair dryers, voice mail, and free wireless Internet access. Suites add another TV and phone line, whirlpool tub, microwave, refrigerator, and walk-in showers. An on-site restaurant, Flamingos, is open from 6:30 am to 10:00 pm daily and serves American food, with a seafood buffet on Saturday nights and a champagne brunch on Sundays. Check-in time: 3:00 pm; check-out time: 12:00 pm. One notable feature is the complimentary shuttle between the hotel and the port, and Kennedy Space Center. (Reserve your cruise day shuttle up to two weeks in advance–ask at check-in and you may get a late pickup or none at all.) Special cruise package includes parking while you cruise. Promotional rates are often available on the Internet for less than $100, but pay attention to the cancellation details, as you may have to pay a $25 fee to cancel. Visit http://www.radisson.com/capecanaveralfl or call 321-784-0000. Address: 8701 Astronaut Boulevard, Cape Canaveral, FL 32920

© MediaMarx, Inc.

Our standard, king bed room at the Radisson

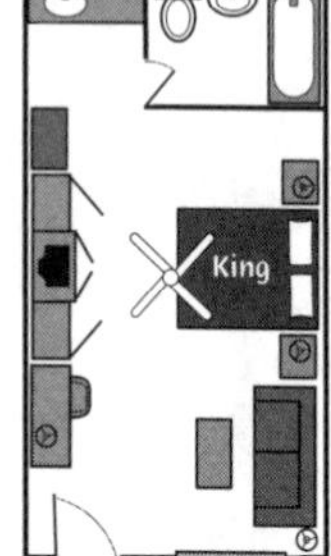

Typical floor plan

© MediaMarx, Inc.

The beautiful, themed pool, complete with a waterfall and perching lioness and eagle

Cocoa Beach Suites — $99+ — 6.1 mi./9.8 km. to port

Quality Suites

© MediaMarx, Inc.

This small, all-suite hotel (formerly Quality Suites) offers 48 spacious rooms and low rates. The two-room suites offer a living room with a queen sofa bed, TV, phone, kitchenette with sink, microwave, refrigerator, and coffeepot, and in the bedroom, a queen bed (no double beds available), another TV, phone, and a desk. All rooms have hair dryers, irons, and high-speed Internet access (free). There's no on-site restaurant, but a Taco Bell and Waffle House are next door. This hotel has no pool, but guests have pool access at the nearby Four Points and the Radisson; it does have a large whirlpool, and the ocean is 300 feet away. Ron Jon Surf Shop is one block away. Free shuttle to the port with most rates—make a reservation at the desk the day before. Cruise parking packages are available, but you'll need to drive to and park at the Radisson. Check-in time: 3:00 pm; check-out time: 12:00 pm. For details, visit http://www.qualitysuitescocoabeach.com or call 321-783-6868.

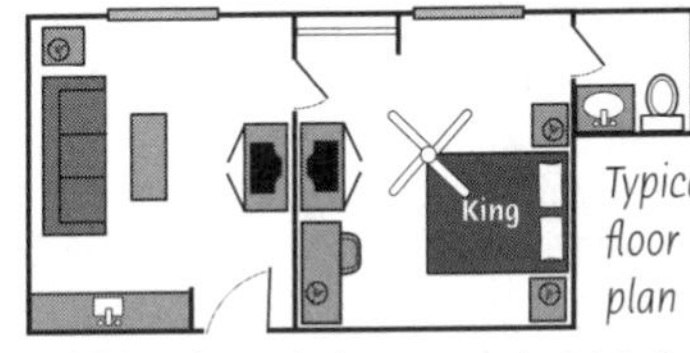

Typical floor plan

Suite living room

© MediaMarx, Inc.

Motel 6 Cocoa Beach — $60+ — 6.1 mi./9.8 km. to port

The Motel 6 in Cocoa Beach has the lowest published rates in the area. The clean motel features an outdoor swimming pool, cable TV, and a laundry room. WiFi $3/day. While there is no restaurant on-site, a Waffle House is within walking distance. This motel is also close to tourist attractions such as Ron Jon Surf Shop, and it's only one block from the beach. No shuttle is available to the port; expect to pay about $11 to $15 for a taxi. Check-in time: 2:00 pm; check-out time: 12:00 pm. Visit http://www.motel6.com or call 321-783-3103. Address: 3701 N. Atlantic Avenue, Cocoa Beach, FL 32931

© MediaMarx, Inc.

Motel 6 room

Resort on Cocoa Beach — $180+ — 7.2 mi./11.6 km. to port

Resort on Cocoa Beach

© MediaMarx, Inc.

A gorgeous, 8-story beach resort within reasonable distance of the port. The 147-suite resort features two-bedroom "condominiums" which sleep six with one king bed, two queen beds, and a sleeper sofa. Features include balconies, two bathrooms, full kitchens, two phone lines, two TVs, DVD player, whirlpool tub, washer/dryer, and high-speed Internet access (no extra fee). Resort amenities include beach access, outdoor pool with kid's water play area, sauna, hot tub, fitness center, playground, tennis and basketball courts, a 50-seat movie theater, and a drop-in childcare center. This is a true resort! An on-site Mexican restaurant, Azteca Two, is open 11:00 am to 10:00 pm weekdays, 4:00 pm to 10:30 pm weekends. No shuttle to the port; expect to pay about $11 to $15 for a taxi. Check-in time: 4:00 pm; check-out time: 10:00 am. Visit http://www.theresortoncocoabeach.com or call 866-469-8222. Address: 1600 N. Atlantic Avenue, Cocoa Beach, FL 32931

Lodging Near Port Canaveral *(continued)*

☐ Holiday Inn Express $145+ 4.7 mi./7.5 km. to port

Holiday Inn Express

© MediaMarx, Inc.

This hotel opened in late 2000, offering 60 guest rooms in a variety of family-friendly configurations. Beyond standard queen bed and king bed rooms, Holiday Inn Express offers one-bedroom suites (some with Jacuzzi), and a 2-bedroom VIP suite (Family Suites and Romantic Suites are no longer available). All rooms have a microwave, refrigerator, coffeemaker, free wireless Internet access, hair dryer, iron and ironing board, and free newspaper delivery. A free buffet breakfast is provided each morning. Amenities include a covered outdoor pool, whirlpool, and a fitness center, plus it is just two blocks from the beach. There is no on-site restaurant, but Durango Steakhouse, Florida Seafood, and The Omelet Station are nearby. Park & Cruise Package includes parking and transportation for two to the cruise terminal ($10 each additional passenger). Check-in time: 3:00 pm; check-out: 11:00 am. For details, visit http://www.hiexpress.com or call 321-868-2525 (local) or 800-465-4329 (toll-free). Address: 5575 N. Atlantic, Cocoa Beach, FL 32931

☐ Residence Inn $139+ 1.9 mi./3 km. to port

This all-suite hotel opened in 2006 and has proved popular with cruisers—we've stayed here several times and love it! Each of the 150 suites has separate living and dining areas, as well as fully-equipped kitchens. Rooms come with either two queen-size beds or one king bed, plus a sofa bed. Among its amenities are complimentary high-speed Internet access, free hot breakfasts, free happy hour (Mondays–Thursdays), free parking (fee for cruise parking), and a $6 round-trip port shuttle (departs at 10:00 or 10:30 am—signup when you check-in). Check-in time: 3:00 pm; check-out: 12:00 pm. For details, visit http://www.residenceinn.com/mlbri or call 321-323-1100 (local) or 800-331-3131 (toll-free). Address: 8959 Astronaut Blvd., Cape Canaveral, FL 32920

© MediaMarx, Inc.

Residence Inn dining area and living room

☐ Ron Jon Cape Caribe Resort $156+ 3.2 mi./5.2 km. to port

Anyone can rent the studios (up to 4 people), one-bedroom (6 people), two-bedroom (8–10 people), and three-bedroom villas (12 people) at this lovely resort. All villas have a sitting or living room, refrigerator, microwave, coffeemaker, and complimentary WiFi Internet. The one- and two-bedroom villas add a patio/balcony and full kitchen. Two-bedroom villas also have a whirlpool tub (our one-bedroom villa had only a shower, no tub at all). Resort amenities include a "water park" with large heated pool, 248-ft. water slide, lazy river, and beach, plus an on-site restaurant, fitness center, children's play center, movie theater, miniature golf, and organized activities. This resort is 600 yards (about 3 blocks) from the beach, but it does provide a shuttle to the beach. Guests receive a discount at Ron Jon Surf Shop in Cocoa Beach. You can arrange for a shuttle to the cruise terminal through the concierge for an additional fee, or expect to pay about $9 to $12 for a taxi. We loved our one-bedroom villa here in December 2004—we found it bright, cheery, very spacious, clean, and full of amenities. Check-in time: 4:00 pm; check-out time: 10:00 am. Visit http://www.ronjonresort.com or call 888-933-3030 or 321-799-4900. Address: 1000 Shorewood Drive, Cape Canaveral, FL 32920

© MediaMarx, Inc.

Ron Jon living room and kitchen

The Disney Cruise Line Terminal

Not content to use an existing, plain-Jane terminal for its cruise line, Disney had a **beautiful terminal** built in Port Canaveral to its specifications for $27 million. The Disney Cruise Line Terminal (terminal #8) is distinguished by its 90-foot glass tower and art deco design. The terminal opens at 11:00 am on cruise days for embarking passengers.

The cruise terminal

A gated, fenced parking lot and a 1,000-space parking garage with elevated walkway to the terminal are available–prices are based on length of cruise; $60/3-nt, $75/4-nt., $90/5-nt., and $120/7-nt. Over 20 ft. long costs $12-15/day extra. Preferred parking by the terminal is available for $20 extra per cruise. Online parking reservations are available at http://portcanaveral.com/cruising/parking.php–choose terminal 8. You **pay when you depart** with cash, U.S. traveler's checks, Visa, or MasterCard. The Canaveral Port Authority operates the parking and we know of no discounts. If you do not drop off your luggage curbside (see below), you can take it to one of the drop-off sites in the parking lot. It may be cheaper to arrange two one-way car rentals than to park a rental here. Off-site parking (with shuttle) is about $7–$8 per day, http://parkcruise.com, http://cruiseparkingofportcanaveral.com, and http://www.executiveparkingportcanaveral.com.

Security at the terminal is tight. Have photo IDs for everyone in the car handy when you drive up. Guests and luggage may be dropped off at the terminal curbside or the parking lot. A porter **collects all luggage** (tip $1 to $2/bag) except your carry-ons before you enter the terminal–luggage is scanned and delivered to your stateroom later, so be sure to attach those luggage tags. Security scans your carry-ons when you reach the second floor of the terminal (up the escalators or across the bridge from the parking garage). In the main hall, look down at the gorgeous, 13,000 sq. ft. terrazzo tile Bahamas map.

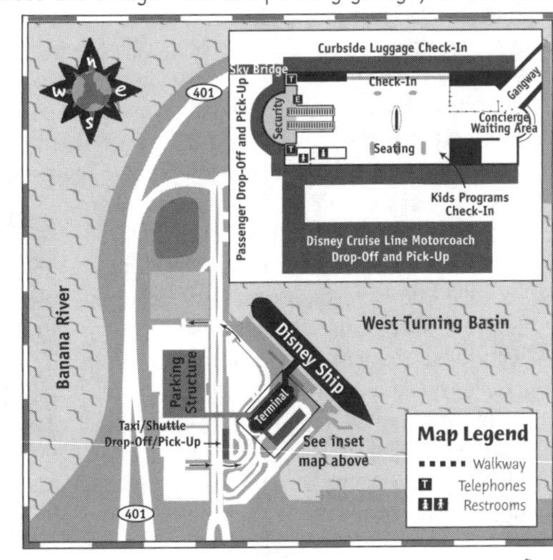

Plan to arrive at your predesignated "arrival time" (selected during online check-in). Ships are scheduled to leave at 5:00 pm, but they may leave earlier when weather dictates. All passengers must be onboard by 3:45 pm.

Street Address: 9150 Christopher Columbus Drive, Port Canaveral, FL 32920

Phone: 321-868-1400

Introduction
Reservations
Staterooms
Dining
Activities
Ports of Call
Magic
Index

Check-In and Embarkation at Port Canaveral

Be sure to **complete Online Check-In ahead of time** at http://www.disneycruise.com, where you can enter important information for your party and choose a port arrival time. Each arrival time has a limited number of spaces, so you should check-in online as soon as possible in order to have the largest selection. Note that Concierge and Platinum Castaway Club members do not need to worry about arrival times—they may arrive at any time. Additionally, if you purchased Disney air or ground transportation, you do not select an arrival time (one is chosen for you automatically). You get advance access to Online Check-In up to 75 days (first-time cruisers), 90 days (Silver Castaway Club members), 105 days (Gold Castaway Club members), or 120 days (Platinum Castaway Club members and Concierge guests).

If you can't get online, be sure to **fill out the cruise forms before arrival**, which you can find in your Travel Booklet (which comes in your cruise document package—see page 66). Note that immigration forms may not be included in your cruise documents—you can complete those online.

When you arrive at the Port Canaveral cruise terminal, have your cruise travel booklets and passports (see page 68) handy (be sure to bring **original or official documents**). A cast member may first check to ensure your cruise documents are together. You then proceed to the **check-in counters** (28 in total) which are lined up along the left-hand side. If you are a member of the Castaway Club (see page 470) or a Concierge guest, you may be directed to special counters. A separate area at the far end of the terminal is a special check-in area for Concierge and Castaway Club Platinum members, and the Concierge Lounge.

Your Key to the World Card and Money

It's your stateroom key, ship boarding pass, and shipboard charge card—no wonder Disney calls it your Key to the World. Everyone will have his or her own card—be sure to sign them as soon as you get them, and keep them safe. Disney ships are a cash-free society—everything you buy onboard and at Castaway Cay (except stamps) must be charged to that card. Stash your wallet in your room safe, grab your Key to the World Card, and travel ultra-light. At check-in, you'll need to make a deposit of at least $500 toward your on-board spending using a credit card (any of those listed on page 65 work), traveler's checks, cash, and/or Disney Gift Cards. You can even put a different credit card on each person's room key (great for friends traveling together). Disney charges your credit card whenever your shipboard account reaches its limit. If you deposited cash or cash-equivalent, you'll be called down to the Guest Services desk (Purser) to replenish the account. Cruising with kids? You can give them full charging privileges, deny them any charge privileges, or place a limited amount of cash on their account. Whatever you decide, you can make changes later at the Guest Services desk on deck 3 midship.

A Key to the World card (Castaway Club member version)

Check-in takes about 10 minutes (you may spend more time in line). Once your forms are filed, your identification is verified, and your security photo is taken (if you already have a photo from a previous cruise, they may not take a new one), each member of your party will get a **Key to the World card**, which is your ID, charge card and room key for the duration of the cruise (see bottom of previous page). Keep this card with you at all times.

Non-U.S. citizens (including alien residents of the U.S.) may have special check-in counters—look for the signs as you approach the counters. You will need to present your passport with any necessary visas at check-in to ensure that you can reenter the U.S. upon the ship's return. (Canadian citizens must also present a passport, according to Canada's Passport Office at http://www.ppt.gc.ca.) If you live in a country that participates in the U.S. Visa Waiver Program (see http://travel.state.gov) and plan to be in the U.S. for 90 days or less, you don't need a visa, but you do need to present proof of return transport and a signed visa waiver arrival/departure form (I-94W form) that you get from your airline. For more information on visas, check with the U.S. consulate or embassy in your country (see http://usembassy.state.gov). Non-U.S. citizens may have to surrender their passports at check-in; if this is necessary, they will be returned upon disembarkation—see page 468. Generally, though, passports are not surrendered at check-in and are instead handed back to be kept in the passenger's care for the entire duration of the cruise. Regardless, you should bring extra forms of photo identification, which you can use when you leave and reenter the ship at most ports of call.

Embarkation usually begins between noon and 1:00 pm, and continues until all guests are onboard. Upon arriving at the terminal, you will receive a boarding number and may board when your number is called; there is no need to wait in line. While you're waiting you can relax on cushy sofas, watch Disney cartoons, and read whatever papers you received at check-in (usually the daily schedule, the *Personal Navigator*, or cruise summary sheet). While you wait, Captain Mickey, Donald, or other characters may appear for photos and autographs. If you haven't already, you may also be able to sign up your kids for Oceaneer Club/Lab—look for a sign-up desk. Be sure to visit the 20-foot-long model of the Disney Magic in the middle of the terminal. You'll also find a small coffee kiosk and can look for more than 50 images of Mickey (both obvious and hidden) in and around the terminal! See the terminal map on page 87 to get your bearings before you arrive. **Be sure to arrive at the terminal by 3:45 pm. If you arrive later, you will be denied boarding.**

© MediaMarx, Inc.

Inside the Disney Cruise Line Terminal

When it's **your turn to board**, you'll walk through the 16 ft. (5 m.) high Mickey-shaped embarkation portal (see photo) and present your Key to the World card, which is swiped through a card reader and handed back to you. Just before you reach the ship, photographers will arrange your party for the first of many ships' photo opportunities (and the only one that is not optional). Then proceed on up the gangway to the magic, wonder, dream, and fantasy that await you.

Getting to Miami

Disney Cruise Line offered its first itineraries from Miami, Florida in December 2012, and at this writing has cruises scheduled through May 2014. A vacation destination since Henry Flagler's Florida East Coast Railroad arrived in 1896, Miami has been a **legendary vacation escape** for generations of North and South Americans fleeing winter's chill. Disney's Miami cruise schedule (September-May) means many cruisers may be tempted to extend their warm weather getaway with a few extra days in and around Miami, or elsewhere in Florida. Air, highway, and rail connections are all convenient to this, the Southeast's greatest metropolis.

Air travel is the top choice for visitors from outside the region, with two major airports within a 25-mile drive of the port. Use the tips on page 71 for booking the best airfare to the Miami area. **Miami International Airport (MIA)**,is a bustling, modern facility, which has replaced both of its main terminals within the past 5 years. Just 8 miles west of downtown Miami and the port, it serves over 105,000 passengers daily, year-round. For airport information: http://www.miami-airport.com or call 800-825-5642. Airport address: 2100 NW 42nd Ave., Miami, Fl 33142. **Fort Lauderdale-Hollywood International Airport (FLL)** is a fine alternative, especially when the airfare is right. 64,000 travelers pass through there daily. The airport is next to I-95, just a 25-mile drive to the port, and ground transportation to Miami is very competitively-priced. http://www.broward.org/airport or call 866-435-9355. Airport address: 100 Terminal Drive, Fort Lauderdale, FL 33315

If you plan to drive to Miami, I-75, the Florida Turnpike, and I-95 are your likely routes. Orlando is 3.5 hours to the north, Key West is about the same distance south, Tampa about 4.5 hours to the northwest, and Atlanta, Georgia 10 hours to the north. Of course, all but Key West are closer to Port Canaveral, if driving time is the only factor.

Without rail travel Miami may have never made it onto the map. Amtrak's Silver Meteor and Silver Star each trace the historic route once daily between New York City and Miami, and if you don't stop to see the many sights and cities along the way, the entire trip takes 28-31 hours. Amtrak's daily Auto Train will transport you and your car between Lorton, Virgina and Sanford, Florida (near Orlando). http://www.amtrak.com or call 800-USA-RAIL. Florida East Coast Railroad, the modern successor to Henry Flagler's railway, has proposed re-entering the passenger rail business (today it carries only freight), with service between Orlando and Miami to take three hours, starting as soon as 2014.

Miami - Orlando "Open Jaw" Itineraries

It usually makes more sense to cruise from Port Canaveral if your heart is set on a visit to Walt Disney World, but visitors from overseas may want to include both Miami and Orlando in their Florida vacations. For others, it might be a matter of a better cruise schedule and/or fare. "Open jaw" itineraries, where you arrive at one airport and depart from another, may be little different in cost than a conventional round-trip. Closing the jaw may best be done by rental car—one-way rentals within Florida rarely cost extra, and the two cities are just 3.5 hours away. That's about the same time you'd spend flying when you consider the time spent pre-flight at the airport, plus the rental cost is likely to beat the airfare by a large margin.

Getting to PortMiami

From the Airports and Highways

With two nearby airports, and a short drive from I-95, PortMiami, the world's busiest cruise port, is very easy to reach.

Disney Ground Transfer—Available to/from MIA and the cruise terminal. Just add it onto your cruise reservation. The cruise line is still gauging demand for service between FLL and the port, so contact the cruise line. For more details, see page 82. The cruise line also offers several shore excursions on debarkation day that include airport transfers.

Shuttle Van—Airport-authorized shared-ride shuttle service is available **from MIA** through SuperShuttle for $16 for the first passenger and $5 for each additional rider, round-trip. http://www.supershuttle.com 800-258-3826. **At FLL**, Go Airport Shuttle provides the same service for $27/passenger, round-trip (gratuity included). http://www.go-airportshuttle.com 800-244-8252. Both companies offer private vans, town cars, and limos as well.

Sedan/Town Car, or Limo—PortMiami maintains a list of over 250 ground transportation companies, and the airport web sites have similar lists. Super Shuttle/ExecuCar (see above) offers round-trip private sedan service from MIA for $75. Go Airport Shuttle and Executive Car Service (see above) offers round-trip private sedan service from FLL for $86, tip included.

Taking a Taxi—Taxis between MIA and the port are $24 flat rate, one-way. Zoned, flat-rate fares to other spots are also offered at the airport. Metered fares are $2.50 for the first 1/6 mile, $0.40 for each additional 1/6th, with a $2 surcharge for trips to MIA or PortMiami plus a $1 fuel surcharge on all trips. Trips to/from nearby hotels are in the $8-$16 range.

Rental Car—There are no on-site rental car offices at the port. Avis/Budget, Dollar, Hertz, Vanguard and Amigo's currently have permits to provide shuttle service to/from their offices, but others may offer the same service. While rentals are good for a pre- or post-cruise stay, other choices are more convenient for direct airport-to-cruise transportation.

Long-term cruise parking structures and surface lots are operated by PortMiami. Rates are $20/day, $7/hour for short-term parking, and vehicles over 20 feet are $20 extra per day. Parking for the disabled is free, see the port's web site for details http://www.miamidade.gov/portmiami/parking-transportation.asp#parking.

Driving directions from the north (including FLL Airport): Take I-95 southbound to Exit 3B-NW 8th St./Port of Miami. Turn left onto NE 5th St., which becomes Port Blvd. Follow the signs to the cruise terminals.

Driving directions from the south: Take I-95 northbound to Exit 2A-NW 2nd St. Go north three blocks and turn right onto NE 5th St., which becomes Port Blvd. Follow the signs to the cruise terminals.

Driving directions from MIA Airport: Exit the airport on NW 21st St eastbound. Turn south (right) onto NW 37th Ave. to Florida 836 (Dolphin Expressway - $1.25 toll) which becomes I-395 eastbound. After 4 miles take Exit 2B southbound onto Biscayne Blvd., then exit left onto Port Blvd. Follow the signs to the cruise terminals.

Note: A new tunnel is under construction, linking the port to I-395. When it opens in mid-2014, that will become the preferred route to the port from the airport and I-95, though the current routes will remain in service, too. http://www.portofmiamitunnel.com

Lodging in Miami

The Greater Miami area boasts more than 400 hotels within 25 miles of the port, and for a resort area encompassing over 70 miles of beachfront, that 25 miles barely gets us to Fort Lauderdale. Palm Beach is 65 miles away. If you're driving and just need a place to rest your head, bargains are easy to come by near highway exits north of the city. Flying in the day before your cruise? Downtown Miami is your best bet, with most hotels just a couple of miles from the cruise terminal, though better overnight deals are had at the airport-area hotels. For a longer visit, Miami Beach and points north add the beachfront that Downtown lacks. In any case, if you're cruising January-April, be prepared for peak season rates.

☐ Holiday Inn Port of Miami — $143+ — 1.7 mi/2.7 km to port

Across the street from Bayside Market and Bayfront Park, very close to the port, and moderately priced. Rooms can be hard to get—book early. Standard rooms sleep 2-4, rooms with sofa beds sleep up to 5. Amenities are basic (outdoor pool, free WiFi), but kids eat free at Marinas Bar and Grill. Renovated in 2012. Parking $12. Check-in: 3:00 pm; check-out: 11:00 am. http://www.holidayinn.com, 305-371-4400. 340 Biscayne Blvd., Miami, FL 33132

☐ Hampton Inn Miami-Airport S. — $161+ — 8.7 mi/14 km to port

A good, affordable choice for a near-airport stay. Standard rooms sleep 2-4, suites sleep up to 6. Free airport shuttle 5:00 am-1:00 am Free breakfast and "breakfast bags," outdoor pool and whirlpool, free WiFi. Self-parking free during stay. Check-in time: 3:00 pm; check-out time: 12:00 pm. http://www.hamptoninnmiamiairport.com, 305-262-5400. 777 NW 57th Ave, Miami, FL 33126

☐ DoubleTree Grand Hotel Biscayne Bay — $228+ — 2.4 mi/3.9 km to port

This bayfront hotel with bay, park, or garden views offers regular guestrooms and 1- and 2-bedroom condos, many with balconies. All feature luxury bedding, 47" TV, mini-fridge, WiFi, and marble-lined bathrooms.Four restaurants, outdoor pool and hot tub, and fitness center. Valet parking $29. Park n' Cruise package available. Check-in: 3:00 pm; check-out: 12:00 pm. http://doubletree3.hilton.com, 305-372-0313. 1717 Bayshore Dr., Miami, FL 33132

☐ JW Marriott Marquis — $310+ — 3.1 mi/5 km to port

One of Miami's best-regarded luxury hotels can also deliver value rates. 492+ sq. ft. rooms boast a 52" TV, computer, espresso machine, and huge marble bathrooms with separate tub and shower. City, partial and full water views. Three restaurants, including db Bistro Moderne by Daniel Boulud; day spa, fitness center, and outdoor pool with a view. Check-in: 4:00 pm; check-out: 11:00 am. http://www.marriott.com, 888-717-8850. 255 Biscayne Blvd. Way, Miami, FL 33131

☐ EPIC, a Kimpton Hotel — $339+ — 3 mi/4.8 km to port

This luxury boutique hotel rises above the Miami River near Biscayne Bay, 475 sq. ft. guestrooms come with city or water views, and all have balconies,luxury bedding, computer, 42" TV, and double-sink baths with separate tub and shower. Evening wine hour, day spa, Area 31 restaurant and lounge, ZUMA Japanese restaurant, rooftop pool. Check-in: 3:00 pm; check-out: 12:00 pm. http://www.epichotel.com, 305-424-5226. 270 Biscayne Blvd. Way, Miami, FL 33131

Check-In and Embarkation at the Port of Miami

PortMiami is the world's largest and busiest jumping-off spot for cruise ships. The seaport, both cruise and cargo, occupies Dodge Island, in Biscayne Bay east of downtown Miami. The port is just south of famed MacArthur Causeway, which links Miami Beach to the mainland (a drive along the causeway delivers stupendous views of the docked cruise ships).There are seven berths dedicated to the cruise trade, with up to six ships "parallel parked" alongside a one mile-long wharf, the bow of one ship a mere 150 feet from the stern of the next. It can be quite a sight! The Disney ships normally berth at Terminal F, though other berth assignments are possible. Electronic signboards will guide you to the correct terminal.

Terminal F is one of the port's mid-sized terminals. Curbside drop-off and pick-up is just outside the terminal's street-level entrance, and porters will be on hand to help with luggage. Parking structures are a short walk away, by Terminals E and G.

While Terminals D and E have been recently rebuilt to handle today's super-ships, and provide extensive passenger comforts, Terminal F is older, with just basic services inside. As this terminal is shared with other cruise lines, there's no significant "Disney" experience within the terminal.

The terminal opens for check-in at 11:00 am. Have your cruise travel booklets and passports (see page 68) handy. Be sure to bring **original or official documents**. The check-in/embarkation procedure moves quickly, especially if you **fill out the cruise forms before arrival**, which you can do online. Your cruise documents booklet (see page 66) also has the forms to be completed in advance.

Wheelchair, scooter, and medical rentals are supplied by Special Needs at Sea—contact them at http://www.specialneedsatsea.com or at 800-513-4515. Reserve in advance.

Disembarking cruisers head down to the ground level for **bagage claim and customs clearance**. On-board airline check-in with luggage delivery should be offered.

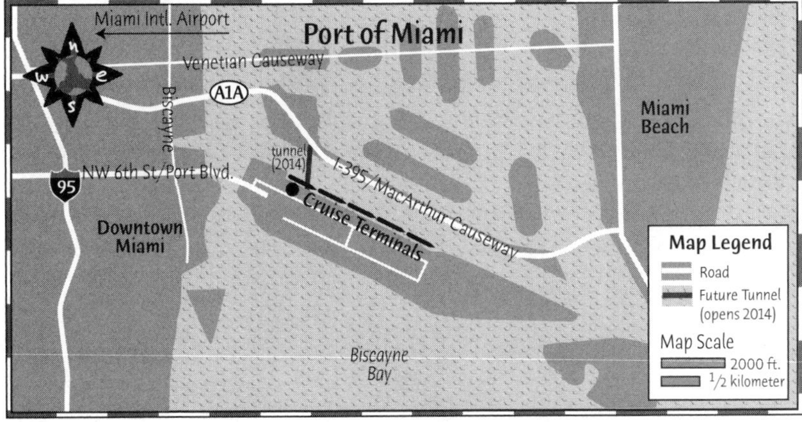

Sailing from Galveston? This part's just for you!

Getting to Galveston

Once the Gulf Coast's busiest port and second only to New York at that time, Galveston, Texas rests on a barrier island 50 miles south of Houston. Today, nearly all land and air routes to Galveston pass through Houston.

Air travel is the main choice for visitors from outside the region. Though private flights can use Galveston's own Scholes International Airport, all commercial flights use either **Houston's William P. Hobby (HOU)** or **George Bush Intercontinental (IAH)** airports. Though HOU is 30 miles and 40 minutes closer to Galvaeston than IAH, your choice of airline will determine which airport you'll use. Only American and Delta serve both airports. **Hobby (HOU)**, a 42-mile, 50-minute drive to Galveston on the south side of Houston, serves only domestic routes. The merged Southwest/AirTran carries over 90% of Hobby's passengers. **Bush Intercontinental (IAH)**, a 72-mile, 90 minute drive to Galveston on Houston's north side, is dominated by the merged United/Continental, which carries 86% of all that airport's passengers. IAH also handles all international flights. Use the tips on page 71 for booking the best airfare to Houston. Visit http://www.fly2houston.com for information about both airports.

If you choose to **drive**, out-of-state cities within an 8-hour drive include Mobile, New Orleans, Little Rock, and Oklahoma City, along with most of East, Central and South Texas. Most routes will take you through Houston. Check traffic conditions as you approach the city. KTRH 740AM has local traffic reports. **When Houston-bound traffic is heavy**, avoid the city center by using one of the beltways, I-610 or the Sam Houston Parkway (Loop/Beltway 8). I-610 is the inside loop, about 5 miles outside the city's center. Sam Houston Parkway is about 12 miles out, and is a toll road for most of its distance. The parkway's northeast section requires an EZ-Tag toll device—cash is not collected. In that segment, vehicles without EZ-Tag use the frontage road that parallels the highway. I-45 is the primary route if you're coming from the north. **I-10 is the region's main east-west route**. Both pass through the heart of Houston. Travelers from points east can avoid Houston by exiting I-10 for SR 146 South. Then exit onto I-45 South. **As you approach Galveston on I-45**, you'll cross the Galveston Causeway. Exit immediately for Exit 1C Harborside Blvd. Turn left onto Harborside. The cruise terminal is 4.75 miles ahead.

Rail travel is possible, but not perfect. Amtrak's Sunset Limited stops in Houston on its thrice-weekly journeys between New Orleans and Los Angeles, and a connecting bus extends service to Galveston. The Texas Eagle runs from Chicago to Los Angeles via Dallas, with a connecting bus to Galveston via Longview Texas (a 5-hour plus bus ride). New Orleans is a transfer point between the Sunset Limited and such storied routes as the City of New Orleans from Chicago, and the Crescent, which originates in New York and makes its way to The Big Easy via Washington D.C., Charlotte, and Atlanta. For details, visit http://www.amtrak.com or phone 800-USA-RAIL.

Getting to Galveston Cruise Terminal

From the Airports

The Port of Galveston is 50 min. (42 mi./67.5 km.) south of Houston Hobby Airport (HOU) and 90 min. (72 mi./116 km.) south of George Bush Intercontinental Airport (IAH). Disney ground transfer, shuttle van, car service, taxi, and rental car are all options.

Disney Ground Transfer—Available to/from both airports and the cruise terminal. Just add it onto your cruise reservation. For more details, see page 82.

Shuttle Van—SuperShuttle (http://www.supershuttle.com, 800-258-3826) is the official ground transportation provider at the airports, but they don't offer shared ride service to Galveston. A 10-person van can be reserved for $100 (HOU) or $145 (IAH) one-way. Galveston Limousine (http://www.galvestonlimousineservice.com, 800-640-4826) offers scheduled shared-ride service $45 adult/$20 ages 3-10 one-way (HOU), and $55 adult/$26 ages 3-10 (IAH). Reservations are strongly recommended.

Sedan, Town Car, or Limo—SuperShuttle's ExecuCar (http://www.supershuttle.com, 800-258-3826) offers 3-passenger town cars and 5-passenger luxury SUVs between the airports and Galveston. $90 or $110 (HOU), $125 or $145 (IAH), one-way. Galveston Limousine (http://www.galvestonlimousineservice.com, 800-640-4826) and Action Limousines (http://www.actionlimo.com, 800-0736-5466) both offer town cars, limos, luxury SUVs, and mini-bus charters. Contact them for rates.

Taking a Taxi—Taxis are available as you exit the airport terminals. Cabs are metered, and cost around $110 (HOU) or $180 (IAH) including time stuck in traffic and tip.

Rental Car—This is a challenging port for a one-way car rental. Many major agencies have offices at the airports, but of those agencies, only Enterprise has an office in Galveston, at 5919 Broadway St., over 4 miles from the pier. Pick-up/drop-off at the pier is not provided due to port regulations. Hertz has an agency on the mainland, but pickup/dropoff service is possible at several hotels. For other agencies, a round-trip rental will be required, with the added expense of long-term parking during the cruise (see below). At HOU you'll find rental desks near baggage claim, and shuttles take you to the rental offices. At IAH, all agencies use a consolidated rental facility. A single fleet of shuttles serve all the agencies.

Driving directions from George Bush Intercontinental Airport (IAH): Exit the airport via John F. Kennedy Blvd., exit left for Beltway 8 East/US-59. Go 2 miles and exit onto US-59 South. Go 14 miles and exit onto I-45 South. Go 43 miles and take Exit 1C Harborside Blvd. Turn left onto Harborside Blvd. and drive 4.75 miles to the cruise terminal.

Long-term cruise parking is supplied by the Port of Galveston and several independently-run lots. In most cases you should drop-off passengers and luggage at the terminal, and then park (shuttles are provided). All offer about $5 off if you pre-pay. For a 7-night cruise, the pre-paid rate at the Port of Galveston's outdoor lots is $65. Limited, indoor parking is available when you arrive, first-come, first-served (pre-payment will be applied to the fee) (http://www.portofgalveston.com/index.aspx?NID=92, 409-766-6100). Galveston Park N Cruise (http://www.galvestonparkncruise.com 866-479-7275) is just across the street from the terminal (no shuttle required) and offers outdoor ($50 pre-paid) and indoor ($65 pre-paid) parking. Lighthouse Parking charges outdoor rates ($50 pre-paid), but the spaces are sheltered by car ports (http://www.lighthouseparking.org 877-915-4448.) If you're staying overnight, many hotels offer free or low-cost cruise parking.

Lodging in Galveston

Galveston is a historic, seaside resort offering a choice of beachfront and downtown lodgings. While we do not cover Bed and Breakfasts, those are also an option. A stay in Houston, either near the airports or in town, is also a possibility, but beyond the scope of this guide. We'd like to thank Teresa Cory and Siriann Cuhel at Fairy Godmother Travel for their assistance with this section.

☐ Harbor House at Pier 21 — $80+ — .02 mi/.04 km to port

Next-door to the cruise terminal and convenient to the Strand District, this converted warehouse offers casual, nautically-themed harbor-view rooms. Free WiFi, microwave, fridge, coffeemaker, complimentary Continental breakfast. Parking $10/day. Cruise parking for guests is $30, or free at sister-resort Hotel Galvez. Check-in: 4:00 pm; check-out: 12:00 pm. http://www.harborhousepier21.com 800-874-3721. 28 Pier 21, Galveston, TX, 77550

☐ Hotel Galvez — $125+ — 1.4 mi/2.25 km to port

Built in 1911, the beachfront "Queen of the Gulf" has been lovingly restored to period elegance. Rooms offer ocean or city views, pillowtop beds, robes, and free WiFi. Heated outdoor pool with swim-up bar, day spa. Bernardo's Restaurant and limited room service. Free shuttle to attractions. Cruise package includes valet parking and shuttle. Check-in: 4:00 pm; check-out: 12:00 pm. http://www.wyndham.com/hotels/GLSHG/main.wnt, 409-765-7721. 2024 Seawall Blvd., Galveston, TX, 77550

☐ Holiday Inn - On the Beach — $85+ — 3.44 mi/5.54 km to port

Our pick for best value, plus a great beachfront location! The rooms are clean and comfortable, and all have ocean views. Kids program. Kids under 12 eat free at Jetty Restaurant. Free WiFi, coffeemaker, microwave, fridge, outdoor pool, free shuttle to pier, free cruise parking. Part of the San Luis Resort complex. Check-in: 4:00 pm; check-out: 12:00 pm. http://www.holidayinn.com, 409-740-5300. 5002 Seawall Blvd., Galveston, TX 77551

☐ San Luis Resort — $169+ — 3.54 mi/5.7 km to port

The Holiday Inn's AAA 4-Diamond cousin next door, with large standard rooms, all with ocean view and balcony, and extra-luxurious club level rooms. Theme pool with swim-up bar. Kids program. 7 on-site and nearby restaurants including Rainforest Cafe. Day spa. Free shuttle to pier (reserve at check-in), free cruise parking. Check-in: 3:00 pm; check-out: 11:00 am. http://www.sanluisresort.com, 800-445-0990. 5222 Seawall Blvd., Galveston, TX 77551

☐ Moody Gardens Hotel — $179+ — 6.0 mi/9.65 km to port

It's not quite a Disney resort, but... Moody Gardens and Schlitterbahn are next door, plus kids program, golf, outdoor pool, lazy river (seasonal), and day spa. 500 sq. ft. rooms with free WiFi, turn-down, robes, 37" TV, HBO. Kids eat free at Terrace Restaurant. Shearn's for fine dining, 24-hour room service. Free cruise shuttle, cruise parking $20. Check-in: 4:00 pm; check-out: 12:00 pm. http://www.moodygardenshotel.com, 409-741-8484. Seven Hope Blvd., Galveston, TX 77554

Check-In and Embarkation at the Port of Galveston

The Port of Galveston is on the north shore of Galveston Island, between the island and the mainland. The cruise terminals are in the midst of the busy commercial port, with the silos of a grain export terminal immediately to the west, and floating oil rigs under repair in the shipyard on the far side of the Galveston Ship Channel. Immediately to the terminal's east, however is tourism-focused Pier 21, offering maritime museums, tour boats, restaurants and lodging. The Strand District is also close at hand. You could drop off your luggage at the terminal early in the day, then spend a couple of hours seeing the sights before boarding.

Arrival: Port authorities recommend that drivers **drop-off passengers and luggage at the terminal before parking**. Vehicles enter the terminal area at 22nd Street and Harborside Drive (Rt. 275). If you plan to use the Port of Galveston parking lots, you'll be directed to the appropriate lot as you exit the terminal area. There may also be limited luggage drop-off in the parking lots. Some of the port's parking lot shuttles are equipped to carry luggage, some are not.

Check-in will begin at 11:00 am, but boarding doesn't start until around Noon. Cruise line personnel will distribute boarding group numbers as you enter the terminal. Have your cruise travel booklets and official ID (see page 68) handy as you enter the terminal. As these are closed-loop itineraries visiting the Caribbean, U.S. citizens need only government-issued photo ID (ages 18 and up) and proof of citizenship such as a certified birth certificate (all ages). Passports, however are still best. Be sure to bring **original or official documents**.

Food and beverages can be found inside the cruise terminal.

Should you need a wheelchair or electric scooter throughout the cruise (but are not traveling with it), rentals can be arranged through Special Needs at Sea (http://www.specialneedsatsea.com, 800-513-4515) and Scootaround (http://www.scootaround.com, 888-441-7575). Reserve in advance.

Going on a West Coast cruise? This part's just for you!

Getting to California

If you opt to **drive** to California, or from points within California, our best advice is to get a good map. Drivers unfamiliar with Southern California laws and freeways should visit **California Driving: A Survival Guide** at http://www.caldrive.com. This web site provides an excellent introduction to the "car culture" of California.

Air travel is the best way for many to get to Southern California—and it's a great way to strengthen the air travel industry and the U.S. economy. Use the tips on page 71 for booking the best airfare to California. There are five airports you could fly into—Los Angeles International (LAX), nearby Long Beach (LGB), John Wayne/Orange County (SNA), Bob Hope/Burbank (BUR), and Ontario (ONT), the most distant from the port. The vast majority of travelers use LAX, however, so we focus on that.

The granddaddy of California airports, **Los Angeles International Airport** is the world's third busiest airport. It's located about 30 miles from Disneyland and 20 miles from the Port of Los Angeles. When you arrive, your plane docks at one of nine terminals (see map below). From there, follow signs to baggage claim. Most ground transportation, including rental cars and shuttles, is located on the Lower/Arrival Level.

For **more details** on the Los Angeles International Airport, call 310-646-5252 or visit http://www.lawa.org and click the "LAX" tab. The airport address: 1 World Way, Los Angeles, CA 90045.

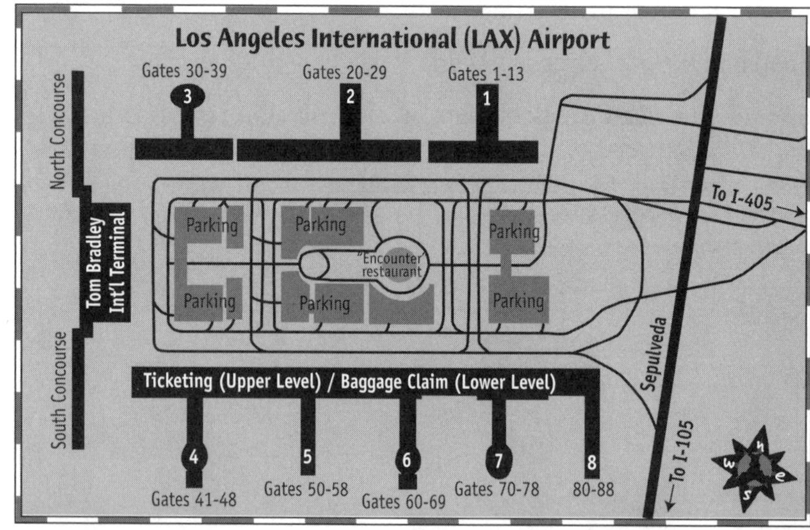

Getting to the Port of Los Angeles

From the Los Angeles International Airport

The Port of Los Angeles is about 30-60 min. (20 mi./32 km.) south of the airport. You have five options: Disney ground transfer, shuttle, town car/limo, taxi, or rental car.

Taking a Disney Ground Transfer—Available to/from the airport, cruise terminal, and Disneyland. Just add it onto your cruise reservation. For more details, see page 82.

Using a Shared-Ride Van Service or Shuttle—SuperShuttle (714-517-6600 or 800-BLUE-VAN, http://www.supershuttle.com) and Prime Time Shuttle (310-342-7200 or 800-RED-VANS, http://www.primetimeshuttle.com) will take you nearly anywhere in the greater Los Angeles area. From LAX, follow the signs to the Lower/Arrival Level island and request a pickup under the Shared-Ride Vans sign. From other locations, call or go online to make reservations at least 24 hours in advance—upon arrival, you may also need to use a courtesy phone to request pickup. A one-way fare from LAX to the port is $17/person (SuperShuttle) or $16/person (Prime Time Shuttle). Kids ride free under age 3 (on SuperShuttle) and under age 2 (on Prime Time Shuttle). Parents take note: If you're traveling with a child under 6 years of age or under 60 lbs. (27 kg.), you must bring an approved child safety seat to use on the shuttle. What about hotel shuttles? Generally speaking, hotels near the port are just too far away from airports to offer shuttles. If you're staying in a hotel within 5-10 miles of an airport, inquire with that hotel directly.

Using a Car Service, Town Car, or Limo—Both SuperShuttle and Prime Time Shuttle offer car services, though they're pricey— $83-$87 (tip incl.) for a one-way trip from LAX to the port for up to three adults. We've found better rates through LAX Shuttle and Limo (877-529-7433, http://www.laxshuttlelimo.com) which offers a $58/one-way fare (without tip) for up to four adults. Reservations are required.

Taking a Taxi—This is not our favored method of transportation, as these metered rides deliver less value than town cars—figure about $62 plus tip for a one-way fare from LAX to the port. For parties of four to six, a taxi mini-van can be very economical, however. From LAX, follow the signs to the Lower/Arrival Level and look for a yellow taxi sign.

Rental Car—Enterprise has an office in downtown San Pedro and offers free shuttle service to the cruise terminal. Other agencies are about five miles away in Long Beach, and you'll need a taxi to get to/from the ship (allow $15-$20). Drop off your companions at the ship before dropping off the rental, as the cabs can't carry much baggage.

Driving directions from LAX Airport: Follow signs to the San Diego Freeway (I-405) South, take it to the Harbor Freeway (I-110), then go south on the Harbor Freeway to the "CA 47-Terminal Island" exit. Merge right to the Harbor Blvd. exit. Proceed straight through the Harbor Blvd. intersection and turn right into the World Cruise Center parking lot.

Driving directions from the Disneyland Resort: Take I-5 north, then CA-91 west to Harbor Freeway (I-110), then south on the Harbor Freeway to the "CA 47-Terminal Island" exit. Merge right to the Harbor Blvd. exit. Proceed straight through the Harbor Blvd. intersection and turn right into the World Cruise Center parking lot.

Lodging Near the Port of Los Angeles

You may find it most convenient to stay near the port the night before your cruise. These are the San Pedro hotels near the cruise terminals.

San Pedro Inn & Suites $105+ .5 mi/1 km to port

Formerly a Clarion Inn, this faux Victorian building houses 60 guest rooms with 10 foot ceilings. Rooms have two queen beds or one king bed with pillowtop mattresses, 25 in. cable TV, refrigerator, coffeemaker, hair dryer, iron and ironing board, newspaper, voice mail, and free high-speed Internet. The hotel has an outdoor heated pool, hot tub, and fitness center. Free continental breakfast is included, but the restaurant is closed at other times. The hotel was built in 1986 and renovated in early 2012. Free shuttle to the World Cruise Center. Fly & Cruise packages are available with transfers from the airport to the pier—call or check their web site for details. Good advance rates are available at their web site. Check-in time: 3:00 pm; check-out time: 12:00 pm. Visit http://www.sanpedroinnandsuites.com or call 310-514-1414. Address: 111 S. Gaffey Street, San Pedro, CA 90731

Sunrise Hotel San Pedro $79+ .5 mi/1 km to port

From all accounts this hotel won't win awards for amenities or style, but it is convenient and reasonably priced. The 110-room, three-story hotel has been recently renovated. Rooms have two queen beds (or one king bed), cable TV, refrigerator/minibar, coffeemaker, free high-speed Internet access, free local calls, hair dryer, iron and ironing board, and voice mail—there are no balconies, but the windows do open. Complimentary newspapers and continental breakfast are provided each morning in the lobby. There is an outdoor heated swimming pool and hot tub. The hotel has no restaurant, but the Grinders eatery is adjacent. The Ports o' Call Village across the street has restaurants and shops, too. A complimentary shuttle is available to the World Cruise Center, which is just four blocks away. Park & Cruise packages are available. Check-in time: 3:00 pm; check-out time: 12:00 pm. Visit http://www.sunrisesanpedro.com. or call 310-548-1080 Address: 525 S. Harbor Blvd., San Pedro, CA 90731

Doubletree Hotel San Pedro $127+ 2.5 mi/4 km to port

Located at the Cabrillo Marina, this three-story hotel offers 226 rooms and suites, a short walk from the beach. Rooms come equipped with two queen beds (or one king bed), high-speed Internet access (fee), two-line phones, cable TV, minibar, coffeemaker, hair dryer, iron and ironing board, and newspaper delivery. Hotel amenities include an outdoor heated pool, hot tub, tennis court, and fitness center. Deals may be had via Priceline.com (see page 78). Park and cruise packages are available—inquire with hotel. A free shuttle is available to the World Cruise Center, plus a complimentary van service within a five-mile radius. Check-in time: 3:00 pm; check-out time: 12:00 pm. Visit http://www.doubletreesanpedro.com or call 310-514-3344. Address: 2800 Via Cabrillo, San Pedro, CA 90731

Crowne Plaza Los Angeles Harbor $172+ .6 mi/1 km to port

The 244 rooms and 56 suites at this attractive hotel offer two queen beds (or one king bed), cable TV, desk, dataport, refrigerator, coffeemaker, hair dryer, iron and ironing board, voice mail, and wireless Internet access (fee). Hotel amenities include an outdoor heated pool, hot tub, arcade, and fitness center. Blu Restaurant is open all day until 10:00 pm, room service until 11:00 pm. Cruise packages are available—inquire with hotel. A free shuttle is available to the World Cruise Center. Good deals may be found on Priceline.com. Check-in time: 3:00 pm; check-out time: 12:00 pm. Visit http://www.crowneplaza.com or call 310-519-8200. Address: 601 S. Palos Verdes Street, San Pedro, CA 90731

The Queen Mary

$129+ 7.5 mi/12 km to port

Want to stay somewhere really interesting? On the night before our 2005 repositioning cruise, we stayed on the Queen Mary, just across the harbor from the World Cruise Center! The Queen Mary is the original "grandest ocean liner ever built," playing hostess to the rich and famous during the 1930s. The ship is now permanently moored and operates as a museum and hotel within very reasonable driving distance of the Wonder's berth in San Pedro. There is even a Disney connection with the Queen Mary, as Disney owned her and planned to build a major waterfront attraction around her. Disney's plans changed, but that fact simply added to the mystique. The "hotel" is comprised of the ship's original 365 staterooms, which span three decks. Each historic stateroom is unique, and many include original rich wood paneling, lovely Art Deco built-ins, and small portholes (outside cabins only). Five classes of staterooms are available: deluxe staterooms, family staterooms (with an extra bed), standard stateroom (double bed), inside stateroom (one queen or two twin beds for the budget-minded), mini suites (two rooms, queen bed and sleep sofa), and full suites (several rooms, original wood paneling, and originally occupied by nobility and heads of state). Staterooms were recently updated, and amenities include air conditioning, pillow-top mattresses, room service, 32"HDTV, CD/iPod clock radios, and high-speed Internet access (fee). Accommodations include a self-guided tour of the ship, too. On the ship you'll find six restaurants: Sir Winston's is an elegant, reservations-required restaurant serving dinner only; Chelsea Chowder House is an award-winning seafood restaurant; The Promenade Cafe serves a diner-style menu at breakfast, lunch, and dinner; a festive Sunday brunch is held in the Grand Salon (the ship's original first-class dining room), Hollywood Deli, and Starboard Bakery. The Observation Bar is the original Art Deco, first class lounge with an impressive view, and the Starboard Lounge is open Fridays-Sundays. Dining with the Spirits is a Saturday night dining event at Winston's, that includes a visit to paranormal "hot spots" not normally open to the public. Hotel services include a business center, fitness rooms, and The Queen Mary Spa. Numerous boutiques are also available, as are several museum-like attractions and tours. Of particular interest to some is the reported paranormal activity onboard, which we think is part of the ship's charm. There's even a "Haunted Encounters" admission package for $28/adults ($16/kids age 5-11, $25/seniors and military). We really enjoyed our night on the Queen Mary, but we wouldn't classify it as a five- or even four-star hotel. It's a bit rundown in places—our bathroom had peeling wallpaper, for example. In all honesty, we didn't mind this—we felt this obvious wear made the whole experience seem more authentic. Parking is $15/day. Check-in time: 4:00 pm; check-out time: 12:00 pm. Visit http://www.queenmary.com, e-mail reservations@queenmary.com, or call 877-342-0742. Address: 1126 Queen's Highway, Long Beach, CA 90802

© MediaMarx, Inc.

Strolling the deck on the Queen Mary

© MediaMarx, Inc.

Our deluxe stateroom on the Queen Mary

The World Cruise Center

The Disney Wonder sails out of the **World Cruise Center** at the Port of Los Angeles in San Pedro. (Don't confuse this with the port at Long Beach—they are two entirely different ports.) The World Cruise Center is the **busiest cruise port on the West Coast**—you may remember it as the home port of "The Love Boat" TV series. It's located at berths 91–93 and encompasses two terminal buildings. More information is available online at http://www.portoflosangeles.org and http://www.pcsterminals.com.

The Disney Wonder docks at **berth 93** at the World Cruise Center. The recently remodeled terminal that serves this berth is spacious, providing plenty of seating and several large flat-screen TVs. This is the larger of the two cruise terminals at World Cruise Center.

If you're driving, a gated, fenced lot with 2,560 **parking spaces** is available for $12 per 24-hour period (or $1/hour for the first ten hours). You can pay with cash, U.S. traveler's checks, and major credit cards. Parking Concepts (310-547-4357) operates the parking, and we know of no discounts. Lots 1 and 2 are closest to the terminal. Lots 6, 7, and 8 are further away, but courtesy shuttles (which are not wheelchair accessible) are available to and from the cruise terminals.

Security checks photo IDs for everyone in your car when you drive up. Porters are on hand to **collect all luggage** (tip $1 to $2/bag) except your carry-ons before you enter the terminal—luggage is scanned and delivered to your stateroom later, so be sure to attach those luggage tags you received with your cruise documents. Security scans your carry-ons before you enter the terminal.

Plan to arrive before 12:00 pm. Guests must board before 4:00 pm.

Address: 425 S. Palos Verdes St., Berth 93, San Pedro, CA 90731

Telephone: 310-514-4049

© MediaMarx, Inc.

The Disney Magic berthed at the World Cruise Center terminal in San Pedro, California

Check-In and Embarkation at the Port of Los Angeles

The World Cruise Center in Los Angeles, unlike the Disney Cruise Line Terminal in Port Canaveral, is shared with other cruise lines. While the facilities can't be Disney-specific, the procedures are consistent with the cruise line's familiar approach. Be sure to review our in-depth coverage of Port Canaveral procedures on page 88.

The check-in/embarkation procedure is remarkably smooth, especially if you **fill out the cruise forms before arrival**, which you can do online. Forms also come with your cruise document package(see page 66).

When you arrive, a cast member may first check to ensure your cruise documents are together. You then proceed to the **check-in counters**. Check-in generally begins around 10:30 am or 11:00 am. If you are a member of the Castaway Club (see page 470) or staying in a suite, you may be directed to special counters.

Have your cruise travel booklets and passports (see page 68) handy. Be sure to bring **original or official documents**. Immigration forms may not be included in your cruise documents, but you can complete those online.

Check-in takes about 10 minutes (you may spend more time in line). Once your forms are filed, you'll each get a **Key to the World card**, which is your ID, charge card ,and room key for the duration of the cruise (see page 88). Keep this card with you at all times.

Pulling up at the World Cruise Center

Getting to Vancouver

Vancouver, British Columbia is on the North American mainland, about 140 miles north of Seattle, Washington. The city hosted the 2010 Winter Olympics, and is a **top tourist destination** in its own right—its transportation and tourism infrastructure is in tip-top condition. You can arrive conveniently by air, road, or rail, and easily spend a few extra days here seeing the sights.

Air travel is the prime choice for visitors from outside the region. Vancouver and the Alaskan cruise itineraries draw large numbers of visitors from Australia, China, Great Britain, Japan, and New Zealand, as well as Canada and the US. Use the tips on page 71 for booking the best airfare to Vancouver. **Vancouver International Airport (YVR)** is Canada's second-busiest airport, welcoming about 45,000 passengers daily. It's about 9 miles/14.5 km from the Canada Place cruise terminal, on Sea Island just south of the city. Visit http://www.yvr.ca or call 604-207-7077. Airport address: 3211 Grant McConachie Way, Richmond, BC, Canada.The far smaller **Coal Harbour Airport (CXH)** is just a short walk from Canada Place, for those who can arrive by seaplane. **Seattle-Tacoma International Airport (SEA)** can also be practical. From there, Quick Coach bus (http://www.quickcoach.com, 800-665-2122), rail, car rental, and commuter planes are all possible.

If you opt to **drive from the States**, I-5 gets you there. Allow 2 ½ hours from Seattle. I-5 becomes Provincial Route 99 at the border and follows Seymour Street in Downtown Vancouver. Take Seymour St. to its end at Cordova St., turn left, then right two blocks later at Howe St., which takes you straight to the cruise terminal entrance (just drive down the ramp). It doesn't get much easier! By bus, Quick Coach (above) offers shuttles from downtown Seattle, and Cantrail (http://www.cantrail.com, 877-940-5561) has service between Seattle's Amtrak station and Vancouver's Pacific Central Station.

Rail travel is a prime, very scenic choice. Amtrak's Cascades Line provides a gorgeous ride along the Pacific Coast from Eugene, Oregon through Portland and Seattle, and the Coast Starlight Line runs from Los Angeles. For details, visit http://www.amtrakcascades.com or phone 800-USA-RAIL.The rail trip through the Canadian Rockies is legendary, with the deluxe Rocky Mountaineer from Calgary to Vancouver via Banff delivering a spectacular pre- or post-cruise two-day rail tour (We loved it!) Visit http://www.rockymountaineer.com or phone 877-460-3200 for rates. VIA Rail Canada (http://www.viarail.ca, 888 VIA-RAIL), offers regular service originating in Toronto, following a more northerly route through the Rockies via Edmonton, Alberta. The trip from Toronto takes 3.5 days. All these trains take you to Vancouver's Pacific Central Station, with direct SkyTrain light rail service to Canada Place.

Jennifer in Vancouver

Getting to Canada Place Terminal

From the Vancouver International Airport

The Port of Vancouver is 15-30 min. (9 mi./14.5 km.) north of the airport. You have many options: Disney ground transfer, SkyTrain, shuttle van, car service, taxi, or rental car.

Disney Ground Transfer—Available to/from the airport, cruise terminal, and pre- or post-cruise hotels. Just add it onto your cruise reservation. For more details, see page 82. For travelers to/from the US going directly between the cruise terminal and airport, transfers have the unique benefit of US Direct service—expedited customs procedures, baggage handling direct from aircraft to ship, and on-board airline check-in for most US-bound airlines.

SkyTrain—The Vancouver metro area has excellent rail, bus, and ferry service under the umbrella of Translink (http://www.translink.ca, 604-953-3333). The Canada Line SkyTrain route, completed in 2009, provides direct service from YVR to Canada Place, with the station right outside the air terminal. Many hotels are within several blocks of a Canada Line stop. Fares are paid by zone, and a ticket can be used to transfer to any combination of SkyTrain routes, city buses, and the SeaBus ferry. The modern Canada Line stations (elevated and subway) have automated fare machines, and even airline check-in kiosks. A regular adult fare between airport and pier is $3.75 (two zones), and a DayPass saves a lot if you're staying in town. Hold onto your tickets. While there's no turnstile (honor system), you must show your ticket if asked.

Shuttle Van—Aeroshuttle (http://aeroshuttleyvr.ca, 877-921-9021) provides scheduled, walk-up van service to many Vancouver hotels, including those at Canada Place. No reservations are taken, pay with cash or credit card. Vans are found right at the exit of the air terminal. Service runs from approximately 7:30am until 8:00pm. Fares are $25 roundtrip for adults, $15 ages 2-12, plus tax.

Sedan, Town Car, or Limo—Aerocar (http://www.aerocar.ca, 888-821-0021) provides walk-up service in a wide range of vehicles at YVR. One-way, walk-up sedan service is $52 to Canada Place, $43 to other downtown locations (plus tax). Call to book cruise terminal and hotel pick-ups. Meet and Greet service, limos, large-capacity vehicles, and other services are available at higher rates.

Taking a Taxi—Taxis are available as you exit the airport terminal. Cabs are metered, and rates average $30-$32 to downtown Vancouver and Canada Place.

Rental Car—Many rental agencies have facilities at the airport and near Canada Place. However, we don't recommend a rental except in support of a pre- or post-cruise stay. Other alternatives are much more practical for direct airport-to-cruise transportation.

Driving directions from YVR Airport: Exit the airport on Grant McConachie Way. Merge onto Marine Drive in the direction of Granville St./BC 99. Head north on Granville Street/ BC 99, which becomes Seymour St. downtown. Take Seymour to its end at Cordova St., turn left, go two blocks to Howe St., turn right, and Canada Place is at the end of the block.

Long-term cruise parking at the cruise terminal is available from VinciPark (http://www.vinciparkcanadaplace.ca, 866-856-8080) at $23 per day, but availability is limited. A reservation form is available at their web site. CruisePark (http://www.cruisepark.com, 800-665-0050) is nearby, charges $120 per week (tax included), accepts oversized vehicles, and provides shuttle service to the cruise terminal. Reservations are also recommended.

Introduction Reservations Staterooms Dining Activities Ports of Call Magic Index

Lodging in Vancouver

Vancouver overflows with comfortable, recently-renovated lodging, thanks in part to the recent Olympics. Downtown luxury is easy to find, and deals are, too, though not at the upscale Fairmont chain, which Disney offers as cruise add-ons. We've stayed at the three non-Fairmonts on this page. Coast Hotels offer good value and locations, but were not reviewed.

☐ Fairmont Waterfront — $485+ — .02 mi/.04 km to port

Just across from the cruise terminal, it doesn't get much more convenient (or expensive) than this. The very comfortable guestrooms have expansive city or harbor views, and average 400 sq. ft. Heron's Restaurant features herbs and honey from the hotel's rooftop garden. Available as a DCL add-on. Check-in: 3:00 pm; check-out: 12:00 pm. Visit http://www.fairmont.com or phone 800-257-7544. 900 Canada Place Way, Vancouver, BC, V6C3L5

☐ Fairmont Pacific Rim — $364+ — .17 mi/.27 km to port

Second-most convenient for cruisers, this deluxe hotel opened in 2010, and is diagonally across the street from the Canada Place cruise terminal. Rooms have 42-inch TVs, and the views of the city or harbor are even more spectacular. Features a day spa, rooftop pool, and extensive dining options. Available as DCL add-on. Check-in time: 3:00 pm; check-out time: 12:00 pm. http://www.fairmont.com, 800-257-7544. 1038 Canada Place, Vancouver, BC, V6C0B9

☐ Fairmont Vancouver Airport — $258+ — 9 mi/14.5 km to port

Fairmont's in-airport deluxe hotel is convenient for those who need one night pre- or post-cruise and prefer to stay at the airport. However, with Vancouver's great downtown, we suggest staying in-town since the airport's still close by. 411 sq. ft. rooms with expansive views. Day spa and on-site dining. Available as a DCL add-on. Check-in: 3:00 pm; check-out: 12:00 pm. http://www.fairmont.com, 800-257-7544. 3111 Grant McConachie Way, Vancouver, BC, V7B0A6

☐ Moda Hotel — $148+ — .8 mi/1.2 km to port

Modern, boutique style in a restored 1908 building. A good choice for the Robson St. theater and shopping district, and two long blocks from a Canada Line station. The rooms are comfortable and nicely appointed, but views are pure city side street. Chic, on-site restaurants and wine bar. Check-in: 3:00 pm; check-out: 12:00 pm. http://www.modahotel.ca, 877-683-5522. 900 Seymour St., Vancouver, BC, V6B3L9

☐ Lonsdale Quay Hotel — $131+ — 2.25 mi/3.6 km to port

Comfortable, boutique hotel in a small mall next to the SeaBus ferry dock. A perfect spot for exploring North Vancouver's natural wonders (great bus service from the ferry), yet Canada Place is just a short ferry ride away. On-site day spa, with restaurants nearby. A tad over-priced at rack rate, but deals can be had. Check-in: 3:00 pm; check-out: 11:00 am. http://www.lonsdalequayhotel.com, 800-836-6111. 123 Carrie Cates Ct, N. Vancouver, BC V7M3K7

☐ Ramada Limited Downtown — $133+ — .4 mi/.66 km to port

Budget lodging this close to the port is rare. While neat and clean, the rooms in this renovated 1913 hotel are tiny. The neighborhood is a bit rundown, but you're just blocks from Gastown, Chinatown, and Canada Place, and the Canada Line station is within 4 blocks. If you can deal with "a bit edgy," this may suit you. Check-in: 3:00 pm; check-out: 12:00 pm. http://www.ramadalimited.org, 888-389-5888. 435 West Pender St., Vancouver, BC, V7B0A6

Check-In and Embarkation at the Port of Vancouver

Canada Place is a **vibrant waterfront area** filled with hotels, restaurants, offices, and the Vancouver Convention Center. On the pier above the cruise terminal are the convention center, the Pan Pacific Hotel, an IMAX theater, and a pedestrian promenade where folks view the cruise ships and wave to the passengers. You can walk down a ramp and right into the terminal from the street, take an elevator from the hotel lobby, or be dropped-off inside the terminal by bus or car. Baggage can be dropped off curbside. This is not a comfy terminal if you want to sit down and wait, but you can deposit your luggage and stroll Canada Place before you board.

Vancouver's cruise terminal is **shared with other cruise lines**. In 2013, a Monday departure, you will be mingling with passengers from one other ship (when several ships sail on the same day, things can be quite chaotic). Alaska-bound passengers clear U.S. Customs before boarding, and check-in follows Customs.

Be alert when you **queue-up for Customs and check-in**. There may be several lines separating passengers by cruise ship, nationality, and /or customs status. While you stand in line you may shuffle past souvenir and gift kiosks offering typical travel goods plus an Alaskan itinerary specialty, binoculars - you'll be viewing whales and other wildlife from the ship. Buy these in advance, on the ship, or in your first port of call, as you won't have time here to shop wisely. The queue area also houses Care Vacations (http://www.cruiseshipassist.com, 877-478-7827), a wheelchair/ECV/ medical equipment rental company. Book in advance!

Once you clear the customs area, the check-in/embarkation procedure moves quickly, especially if you **fill out the cruise forms before arrival**, which you can do online. Check your Travel Booklet (which comes in your cruise document package—see page 66) for the forms to be completed in advance.

The check-in queue begins to gather around 10:30 or 11:00 am, but Customs and check-in won't begin until the ship is ready to board, at around Noon. Have your cruise travel booklets and passports (see page 68) handy. Be sure to bring **original or official documents**. Immigration forms may not be included in your cruise documents, but you can complete those online or in-terminal.

Going on the Mediterranean cruise? This part's just for you!

Getting to Barcelona

Air travel is the only way for many to get to Barcelona. Use the tips on page 71 for booking the best transatlantic flight.

Flights to Barcelona from the U.S. are **expensive**. We couldn't find a flight from Detroit (our major hub) for anything under $1300/person, thanks in part to the hefty taxes. Several East coast airports do offer flights for about $200-$500 less, if that is an option for you. Note that we didn't find the best rates many months in advance, but rather 4–8 weeks before. To search multiple travel sites at a time, try http://www.kayak.com. Also look into Disney Air (see page 65) to see if it's a better fit for you—for our Mediterranean scouting cruise, we used Royal Caribbean's air program and saved a bit of money (and headaches). Travelers coming from elsewhere in Europe should investigate easyJet (http://www.easyjet.com), which has excellent fares for flights to/from Barcelona.

Most likely, you'll fly into **Barcelona Airport/Aeroport de Barcelona (BCN)**—also known as El Prat de Llobregat—but it's possible your flight may have a connection in another city, such as Munich. If you do connect through another airport, you can get more information on airports and their terminals at http://www.airwise.com/airports/europe/.

Barcelona Airport is located 40 minutes from the port, making it very convenient for cruisers. Of the more than 35 airlines that fly into this modern airport, popular lines include US Airways (this is what we took on our visit), Iberia, KLM, United, and Delta. When you arrive, your plane docks at one of the three terminals (see map below), though most international flights arrive in Terminal A. From there, follow signs to baggage claim. Taxi stops are positioned opposite each terminal.

For **more details** on the Barcelona Airport, call +34-932-983-838 or visit http://www.aena.es, click "English," then select Barcelona from the "Choose airport..." drop-down menu. Airport address: Edificio Bloque Tecnico, 08820 El Prat de Llobregat, Spain.

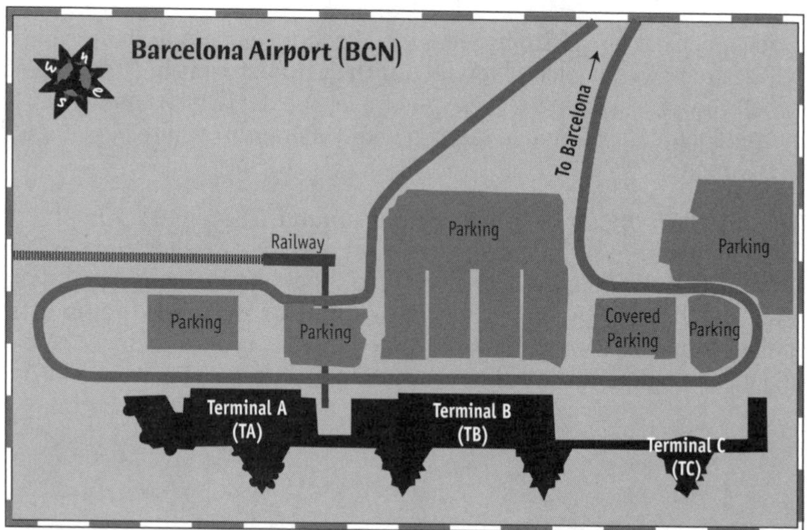

Getting to the Port of Barcelona

The Disney Magic berths at the Port of Barcelona while it cruises the Mediterranean in the summer of 2013. The Port of Barcelona is about 40 min. (11 mi./18 km.) south of the airport. You have five options: Disney ground transfer, public transportation, town car/limo, taxi, or rental car.

Disney Ground Transfer—Available to/from the airport and the cruise terminal. Just add it to your cruise reservation. If you take this option, Disney will give you more information on where to get your ground transfer. Most likely, you'll just need to look for a representative bearing a "Disney Cruise Line" sign after you exit the international terminal. We took advantage of ground transfers on our scouting trip, and they were efficient and comfortable—in fact, because our flight arrived very early in the morning (8:00 am), we received a complimentary Barcelona city tour before we arrived at the port around 11:15 am.

Taxi—This is your best mode of transportation if you aren't doing a ground transfer. Barcelona taxis are plentiful, clean, and reliable; they are black with yellow doors—green lights indicate they are available for hire. Figure about €25-30 for a one-way fare from the airport to the port (estimate 40 min. for the trip). Exchange rate at press time is €1=$1.36. Luggage is €.90/bag. Taxis at the airport work on a queue system—just follow the signs to the taxi stop outside the terminal and wait in line for an available taxi. If you have special needs or need a taxi adapted for disabled passengers, you can call +34 93 420 80 88.

Black-and-yellow Barcelona taxis at the airport

Public Transportation—While it is possible to take public transportation from the airport to the port, it isn't easy—plan on several changes and some walking. We strongly discourage you from using this method—you'll have to contend with pickpockets while juggling your luggage. If you want to check out public transportation options, see http://www.tmb.net.

Town Cars/Limousines—If you'd like to arrive in style, consider a town car or limousine. Barcelona Airport Transfers (http://www.barcelonaairporttransfers.com, +34 605 32 72 73) offers one-way transports to the port in a Mercedes for about €95. The Golden Wheels limousine service also comes highly recommended—visit their site at http://www.thegoldenwheels.com or phone +34 93 364 44 33.

Rental Car—Several rental car ("car hire") companies are available at the airport, namely Hertz, Avis, National Atesa, Sixt, and Europcar. But unless you're planning to stay in Barcelona several days, want to go out of town, and have a sense of adventure, we don't recommend you rent a car. Barcelona roads are congested and difficult to drive. Besides, a rental car really won't get you from the airport to the port, as you'd still need to return to the airport to return the car. Nonetheless, here are the driving directions to the port: Exit the airport, take the road to Barcelona city (see map on previous page), then take the Ronda Litoral Highway, exiting at "Puerto." Upon exiting, turn right and follow the "Puerto" signs.

Lodging Near the Port of Barcelona

You may find it convenient to stay near the port the night before your cruise, or even for a few nights before/after your cruise to explore the city of Barcelona (as we did). You can reserve on your own, or book a pre-/post-cruise stay hotel package (from one to three nights) through Disney Cruise Line. Note that children staying in your room incur an extra cost. These are the five hotels available through Disney for pre-/post-cruise stays (we've even evaluated one firsthand for you—the AC Barcelona):

AC Barcelona Forum $229+ 4.7 mi./7.5 km. to port

This sleek, modern hotel is located near the convention center, in the new shopping district, Diagonal Mar, about 40 minutes (14 km.) from the airport, 2.5 miles from the center of downtown, near a Metro stop, and only 300 meters from the Mediterranean. Built in 2004, the 368-room, 22-story hotel has many modern amenities and panoramic views of the sea. Rooms have twin beds (in our case, they were pushed together to make one king bed), air conditioning, cable TV, phone, CD/radio stereo, free minibar with soft drinks), high-speed Internet access (€12/24-hour period), hair dryer, designer bath toiletries, and bidets. Each room is decorated with dark wood floors and lots of glass—the windows even open. Hotel services include complimentary newspapers, a fitness center, outdoor pool, Turkish bath, solarium, sauna, and massage room. WiFi is available in public areas—there's also a public Internet area with laptops available (but you must still pay the Internet access fee mentioned above). The hotel has an excellent restaurant open for breakfast, lunch, and dinner that serves traditional Mediterranean cuisine; 24-hour room service is also offered. A complimentary hot breakfast buffet was included in our room rate—the food was delicious and selection is excellent. We enjoyed our room overlooking the city on the 11th floor, but we didn't feel the room was child-friendly—too much glass, including the bathroom door! Otherwise the room was spacious for a European hotel, service was good, and we loved breakfast—we recommend this hotel. Check out the 13th floor observation deck for glorious views. Check-in time is 3:00 pm; check-out time is 12:00 pm. For details, visit http://www.marriott.com, U.S. reservations: 888-236-2427 local: +34 93 489 82 00. Address: 278 Passeig Taulat, Barcelona, 08019.

Our room (#1116) at AC Barcelona Forum

Pullman Barcelona (AB) Skipper — $251+ — 2.6 mi./4.2 km to port

This contemporary-styled 241 room, 6-story hotel is just 50 meters from Barceloneta beach, and within moderate walking distance of Port Vell, Las Ramblas, the Gothic Quarter, and other downtown sights. The hotel boasts two pools, one at ground level (unheated), and another on the rooftop (heated), a fitness center, and day spa, plus great jogging on the nearby beachfront boardwalk. Restaurant Syrah serves Catalan/Mediterranean fare at lunch and dinner. Rooms have city or waterfront views, free Internet, flat screen TVs with cable, DVD players, safes, mini-bar, iron, bathrobes, bathroom with separate tub and shower, and 24-hour room service. A Metro stop is just a block away. Check-in time is 2:00 pm; check-out time is 12:00 pm. For details, visit http://www.pullman-barcelona-skipper.com, call 93 221 65 65, or e-mail h7341@accor.com. Address 10 Av. del Litoral, Barcelona, 08005

Rennaissance Barcelona — $279+ — 3 mi./4.8 km. to port

Formerly the AC Diplomatic and recently renovated, this member of the Marriott chain is within moderate walking distance of many attractions including the Gothic Quarter, Las Ramblas and shopping on Passeig de Gracia. This 11-story, 211 room hotel includes a fitness center, outdoor pool, free wireless Internet and newspapers (in lobby), rooftop terrace, CRU Steakhouse, and CUIT Bar and Lounge serves breakfast, lunch and dinner. Rooms sport dark wood floors and furniture, and amenities include complimentary mini-bar, cable TV, marble bathroom, designer toiletries, bathrobes, iron, wireless Internet (fee), and 24-hour room service. Check-in time: 3:00 pm; check-out time: 12:00 pm. Visit http://www.marriott.com, U.S. reservations: 888-236-2427 local: +34 93 272 38 10. Address: 122 Pau Claris, Barcelona 08009

Hilton Diagonal Mar — $214+ — 4.7 mi./7.5 km. to port

This unusually shaped, 23-story high-rise hotel is located on the main thoroughfare of Diagonal Mar, within a block of Hotel AC Barcelona (previous page). Each of the 433 guest rooms offers spacious accommodations (323 sq. ft.), views of the city or sea, 28-in. flat-screen TV with cable, reading chair, desk, multi-line phones, mini-bars, high-speed Internet access (fee), bathrooms with three-jet "monsoon" showers, bidets, and complimentary Crabtree & Evelyn toiletries. Hotel features include an outdoor swimming pool, pool bar, fitness center, and business center. There is an on-site restaurant, Indigo, that serves breakfast, lunch, and dinner, as well as a lobby bar, a pool bar, and 24-hour room service. Additional eateries are nearby (including a Starbucks). Breakfast may be complimentary with some packages (if it isn't included, the price is €20). The beach is a three-minute walk away. Check-in time: 3:00 pm; check-out time: 12:00 pm. Visit http://www.hilton.com, e-mail res.diagonalmar@hilton.com, or call +34 93 507 07 07. Address: 262-264 Passeig del Taulat, Barcelona 08019

Le Méridien Barcelona — $443+ — 2.25 mi./3.6 km. to port

Nothing can be more convenient than this five-star hotel right on Barcelona's famed Las Ramblas, within walking distance of the Gothic Quarter, Placa Catalunya, museums, theaters, shopping, and the waterfront. The hotel boasts of its famous clientele, but we'll guess you won't meet them. CentOnze Restaurant melds French and Catalan influences. There's complimentary WiFi in public areas and free newspapers in the lobby, but the hotel is surprisingly light on recreational amenities—no pool, no fitness room (free access to off-premises facility), but there is a day spa. The 233 rooms (including 40 suites) offer cable TV, Internet access (fee), coffeemaker, 24-hour room service, iron, trouser press, rainforest shower, bathrobe and slippers, and a TV in the bathroom. Note the courtyard-view rooms have showers, not baths. Check-in time: 3:00 pm; check-out time: 12:00 pm. Visit http://www.lemeridienbarcelona.es,, U.S. reservations 800-543-4300 local: +34 93 318 6200. Address: La Rambla 111, Barcelona 08002

Port of Barcelona

While the Disney Magic is in the Mediterranean, she sails out of the Port of Barcelona (*Port de Barcelona*), which is also known as *Port Vell*. Barcelona's port is the **busiest Mediterranean port**. The port area used to be a bit rundown and seedy, but it was rebuilt in time for the 1992 Summer Olympics, which were held not far from the port. More information is available at the port's official web site at http://www.portdebarcelona.es.

The Disney Magic is scheduled to dock at **Moll D'Adossat Terminal D** at the port. [Our Mediterranean scouting cruise (see next page) used Terminal B.] The cruise check-in buildings that serve each of these terminals are of recent construction—the one we used was particularly good with plenty of check-in stations, chairs to wait upon, and even a few shops to browse.

Porters will be on hand to **collect all luggage** (tip €1 -2/bag) except your carry-ons before you enter the terminal—luggage is scanned and delivered to your stateroom later, so be sure to attach those luggage tags you received with your cruise documents. Security scans your carry-ons before you enter the terminal, and you will need to pass through a metal detector.

Check-in and Embarkation begin at 10:30 am. **Plan to arrive** before 3:00 pm - All Aboard time is 4:00 pm (though the preliminary port schedule shows the ship leaving later in the evening).

Tip: To see a detailed aerial view of the port, download the free Google Earth program at http://earth.google.com. (The cruise pier is the long jetty running parallel to the shoreline, just east of Montjuic.)

© MediaMarx, Inc.

Terminal B on Moll D'Adossat

© MediaMarx, Inc.

Inside the modern and spacious terminal

Our European Cruise Experiences

Like many other die-hard Disney Cruise Line fans, we jumped at the chance to book the inaugural Mediterranean cruises in 2007. When the fever abated, we realized we had a much bigger problem on our hands: How were we going to write authoritatively about all those amazing ports of call? There was only one answer: Get to Europe ... and fast! We thought of visiting each port by air or rail, but we wouldn't be experiencing the cities and ports from our readers' perspective. If our readers were going to do Rome in a day, so would we! So, we booked a cruise on Royal Caribbean that hit most of the same ports as Disney's itineraries. Here are some key lessons learned:

Lost Luggage—This seems to be far more common on flights to Europe. Dave's suitcase went to Lisbon for a couple of days before it found him again in Villefranche. Another couple on our flight lost everything, and all four parties at Dave's lunch table in Florence reported at least one lost item. Distribute each traveler's clothing between several bags, just in case. If a bag doesn't show up on the carousel in Barcelona's Terminal A, search out the Iberia lost luggage desk. The staff handles lost luggage for most airlines. File a report with Disney once you board the ship, too, with the incident number given to you by the airline.

Shore Excursions—We're convinced that for most ports, a shore excursion is the best choice for the majority of cruisers. It may feel like "If this is Tuesday it must be Rome," but the time you save by never getting lost and never having to wait in line for an admission ticket is golden. Many of Dave's full-day excursions came with wireless headsets, which meant he could wander a short distance from the tour group but still hear everything and keep track of the group's movements. Jennifer's half-day excursions were hit-or-miss. The more overwhelming ports—such as Rome—are best served by full-day excursions.

Shopping—Even though most excursions include shopping stops, they leave little time for indecision or comparison shopping. If something strikes your fancy, get it—you probably won't get another chance. Be prepared for just a little buyer's remorse, especially on big-ticket items. Have a plan, have a budget, have a recipient list, and do your best to stick to it.

Money—You'll want Euros for most in-port purchases. Onboard the Disney Magic, you'll be dealing in U.S. currency. Get Euros from your hometown bank to save time and money.

Security—We cover this in each port section, but we can't say it enough: Be careful. Dave lost his wallet on our trip. Was his pocket picked? It's easy to blame, harder to prove. You're most vulnerable when you're distracted, as travelers will undoubtedly be from time to time.

Customs—Thanks to the European Union umbrella, there will be no passport or customs inspections in most ports of call, much like in the Caribbean. Customs clearances take place at the airport. And regardless of what convolutions U.S. law may be going through, you will need a passport for these trips. Period. See pages 70–71.

Read our **in-depth report** at http://www.passporter.com/dcl/mediterranean.asp.

Packing for Your Cruise

Some folks hear "cruise" and start packing enough clothes for an around-the-world tour. If you tend to overpack, a cruise is the best place to do it. Guests on land/sea vacations or with ground transfers may only need to handle their bags at the very start and end of their trip. But if you're combining your cruise with a stay near your port of embarkation without Disney's help, you'll appreciate having **less luggage**. The Disney Cruise Line limits each guest to two suitcases and one carry-on. Need help packing light? Visit http://www.travelite.org.

When you arrive at the terminal, luggage is collected and you won't see it again until later that day, when it's delivered to your stateroom (usually between 2:00 pm and 6:00 pm). Be sure you have your travel documents in hand before handing your bags to the porter. Pack a **separate carry-on** (no larger than 22" x 14"/56 x 36 cm.) with your ID, cruise documents, prescriptions, and a swimsuit. Keep this bag light as you may be carrying it around for a few hours. You'll also need this carry-on for your last night, when you place the rest of your luggage outside your stateroom by 11:00 pm for collection.

A word about your **personal documentation**: We strongly recommend that U.S. citizens obtain and use passport books. There is a special exception for "closed loop" cruise itineraries, but that doesn't cover you if you must fly home unexpectedly. For more information and tips on passports and other compliant travel documents, see page 68.

When your cruise documentation arrives, you'll find two **luggage tags** for each individual, with your ship, name, stateroom, and departure date. Read your cruise documentation to find out if you should tag your luggage before or after you arrive at the terminal. In general, if you're not on an add-on package or haven't booked Disney ground transfers, don't tag your luggage until you arrive at the cruise terminal. You wouldn't want your bags collected prematurely. Don't forget to ID every piece of luggage with your own tags, too.

Deciding what **clothing** to pack depends a bit on what time of year you're cruising and your itinerary (see page 54). Cruises in the cooler months require a few more jackets and sweaters, while you'll want to be ready with raingear in the summer, especially if you're headed to Alaska. Pack nice clothing for dinner (see page 116) regardless of your itinerary. Guests on the 7-night and longer itineraries will want to add more dress clothing for the formal and semi-formal evenings (see page 458). Everyone may want to consider pirate or tropical garb for the Pirates in the Caribbean evening. Guests on shorter cruises can get by with just one nice outfit.

Packing Tips

There's no need to over-pack. Unlike some other cruise lines, self-service **laundry rooms** are available onboard, as is valet laundry service.

The air-conditioned public rooms on the ships can be **chilly**, as are the winds on deck. Bring sweaters or jackets.

Pack comfortable **shoes** with non-slip rubber soles for walking around on deck and on shore. You'll also appreciate sandals and water shoes.

While room service is free, delivery is not immediate. If you need snacks on hand, bring packaged **snacks** like crackers or granola bars. You can bring your own bottled water, beer, wine, and/or spirits, but they must be carried on by hand or in your carry-on (these liquids no longer allowed in checked luggage). Disney prohibits personal coolers onboard unless they are for medications, baby foods, or dietary needs. Ice buckets are provided in the staterooms, as are small coolers.

The health-conscious may want to consider a well-stocked **medicine kit**, as trips to the onboard infirmary cost you. Beyond the usual items, consider anti-nausea aids (see page 463), antidiarrheal aids, sunblock, sunburn gel, and "Safe Sea," a sunblock that helps protect against the stinging of most jellyfish, sea lice, coral, and sea anemone (see http://www.nidaria.com).

Two-way radios with extra subchannels can be used for keeping in touch onboard, but the Wave phones provided in your stateroom will work better (see page 147). Use radios only if you need more devices than the two complimentary Wave Phones provided in your room.

You can bring your own **stroller** or just borrow one at Guest Services ($200 security deposit on room account) and/or at Castaway Cay (no deposit). Wheelchairs can also be borrowed free of charge. In all cases, the supply is limited, so if you know you'll need one, we recommend that you rent.

Unlike many other cruises, you can bring your own **alcohol** onboard in your carry-on to save money on drinks. Beer and wine are the best items to bring; you can usually buy hard liquor for great prices on the islands. Note: You may not bring opened bottles ashore with you at the end of the cruise, and beverages are not allowed in checked luggage.

Worried about **lost or delayed luggage**? Don't pack all your items in one bag. Instead, split items between bags. Couples can pack half their things in their suitcases and half in their partner's suitcases to be safe.

Knives, pocket tools, and other **potential weapons** are prohibited onboard. All luggage is inspected, and confiscated items are held until you return to port. This can seriously delay luggage delivery, too. For a full list of prohibited items, go to http://www.disneycruise.com and view the FAQ.

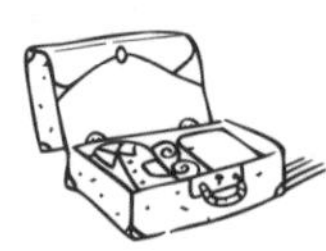

Packing List

Electronic, interactive worksheet available–see page 492

Packing for a cruise is fun when you feel confident you're packing the right things. Over the years, we've compiled a packing list for a great cruise vacation. Just note the quantity you plan to bring and check them off as you pack. Consider packing items in **bold** in your cruise carry-on (some items may not be appropriate for your airplane carry-on due to security restrictions).

The Essentials

❑ Casual, nice clothing for daytime and late-night wear
___ *Shorts* ___ *Long pants* ___ *Shirts* ___ *Skirts/dresses*
___ *Underwear (lots!)* ___ *Socks* ___ *Pajamas* ___ *Robes*

❑ Jackets/sweaters (lightweight in warm months, cozy fleece for Alaska)
___ ***Jackets*** ___ *Sweatshirts* ___ *Sweaters* ___ *Vests*

❑ Formal and semi-formal clothing for special evenings
___ *Suits and ties* ___ *Dresses* ___ *Jewelry* ___ *Tropical dress*

❑ Comfortable, well-broken-in shoes, sandals, and dress shoes
___ *Walking shoes* ___ *Sandals* ___ *Dress shoes* ___ ________

❑ Swim wear and gear (regular towels are provided)
___ ***Suits/trunks*** ___ ***Cover-ups*** ___ *Water shoes* ___ *Goggles*

❑ Sun protection (the Caribbean sun can be brutal)
___ ***Sunblock*** ___ ***Lip balm*** ___ ***Sunburn relief*** ___ ***Sunglasses***
___ ***Hats w/brims*** ___ ***Caps*** ___ ***Visors*** ___ ________

❑ Rain gear (for your port excursions, and a "must" for Alaska)
___ *Raincoat* ___ *Poncho* ___ *Umbrella* ___ ________

❑ Comfortable bags with padded straps to carry items in port
___ *Backpacks* ___ *Waist packs* ___ *Shoulder bags* ___ ***Camera bag***

❑ Toiletries (in a bag or bathroom kit to keep them organized)
___ ***Brush/comb*** ___ ***Toothbrush*** ___ ***Toothpaste*** ___ *Dental floss*
___ *Favorite soap, shampoo, conditioner* ___ *Deodorant* ___ *Baby wipes*
___ ***Anti-nausea aids*** *and* ***pain relievers*** ___ ***Band aids*** ___ ***First aid kit***
___ ***Prescriptions*** *(in original containers)* ___ *Vitamins* ___ ***Fem. hygiene***
___ ***Makeup*** ___ *Hairspray* ___ *Cotton swabs* ___ *Curling iron*
___ *Razors* ___ *Shaving cream* ___ *Nail clippers* ___ ***Spare glasses***
___ *Lens solution* ___ *Safety pins* ___ *Bug repellent* ___ *Insect sting kit*
___ *Mending kit* ___ *Small scissors* ___ ***Ear plugs*** ___ ________

❑ Camera/camcorder and more film than you think you need
___ ***Cameras*** ___ ***Camcorder*** ___ ***Batteries*** ___ ***Memory cards***

❑ Money in various forms and various places
___ ***Charge cards*** ___ ***Traveler's checks*** ___ ***Bank cards*** ___ ***Cash***

❑ Personal identification, passes, and membership cards
___ ***Driver's license*** ___ ***Passports*** ___ ***Compliant travel documents***
___ ***AAA card*** ___ ***Travel perks cards*** ___ ***Discount cards*** ___ *Air miles card*
___ ***Other IDs*** ___ ***Insurance cards*** ___ ***Calling cards*** ___ *SCUBA cert.*

Tip: Label everything with your name, phone, and stateroom to help reunite you with your stuff if lost. Every bag should have this information on a tag as well as on a slip of paper inside it.

For Your Carry-On

- ❑ **PassPorter**, **cruise documentation**, **ground/air confirmations**, **passports or other compliant travel documents**, and a **pen/pencil**!
  Remember not to pack any sharp or potentially dangerous items in your carry-on.
- ❑ **Camera** and/or **camcorder**, along with **film/memory/tapes** and **batteries**
- ❑ Any **prescription medicines**, **important toiletries**, **sunblock**, **sunglasses**, **hats**
- ❑ **Change of clothes**, including **swimwear** and **dress clothes** for dinner
- ❑ **Snacks**, water bottle, juice boxes, **gum**, **books**, **toys**, **games**
- ❑ **PassHolder Pouch** for passports, IDs, cash, etc. (see http://www.passporter.com)

For Families

- ❑ **Snacks** and **juice boxes**
- ❑ **Books**, **toys**, and **games**
- ❑ Familiar items from home
- ❑ Stroller and accessories
- ❑ **Autograph books** and **fat pens**

For Couples

- ❑ **Champagne** for your send-off
- ❑ Wine and favorite adult beverages
- ❑ Portable CD player, speakers, and CDs
- ❑ Good beach novels
- ❑ Massage oil

For Connected Travelers

- ❑ **iPad/iTouch/iPod/MP3 player**
- ❑ Laptop, cables, extension cord
- ❑ Chargers
- ❑ GPS system or compass
- ❑ Security cable with lock
- ❑ **Cell phones** and/or **two-way radios**

For Heat-Sensitive Travelers

- ❑ **Personal fan/water misters**
- ❑ **Water bottles**
- ❑ Loose, breezy clothing
- ❑ **Hats** with wide brims
- ❑ **Elastics** to keep long hair off neck
- ❑ **Sweatbands**

Everyone Should Consider

- ❑ **Penlight** or flashlight (for reading/writing in dark places)
- ❑ Battery-operated alarm with illuminated face and nightlight (or just open the closet)
- ❑ Earplugs, sound machine, or white-noise generator (for noisy staterooms)
- ❑ **Water bottles** and personal **fans/water misters**
- ❑ Plastic storage bags that seal (large and small) and plastic cutlery for snacks
- ❑ Address book, envelopes, and stamps (with numeric denominations)
- ❑ Laundry detergent/tablets, dryer sheets, stain stick, and wrinkle remover
- ❑ **Binoculars** and a **soft-sided, insulated tote** for going ashore
- ❑ Currency exchange calculator or card (if you'll be doing a lot of shopping)
- ❑ Collapsible bag or suitcase inside another suitcase to hold souvenirs on your return
- ❑ **Small bills and coins** for tipping and quarters for laundry
- ❑ Photo mailers or large envelope with cardboard inserts (for safeguarding photos)
- ❑ **Highlighters** (multiple colors for each person to mark activities in your *Personal Navigator*)
- ❑ Closet organizer (the kind used to hold shoes) to store small items and avoid clutter
- ❑ **Sticky notes** (to leave your cabinmates messages)
- ❑ Plenty of **batteries** (and don't forget the charger if you're using rechargeables)
- ❑ An electrical power strip if you'll need extra outlets for lots of chargers
- ❑ Something to carry your small items, such as a **PassHolder Pouch** or evening bag

Your Personal Packing List

- ❑ ____________________
- ❑ ____________________
- ❑ ____________________
- ❑ ____________________
- ❑ ____________________
- ❑ ____________________

Adventuring!

Here are our tried-and-true cruise traveling tips:

- Any travel delay can sink your plans, so don't let the ship sail without you. Plan to **fly (or drive) in the day/night before** you sail to have a stress-free, early start to your vacation. There are many hotels near the airport that offer shuttle service, and good deals can be had by shopping on http://www.priceline.com or the hotel web sites in the weeks before you cruise. In the morning, you can take the hotel's shuttle back to the airport and catch Disney's ground transfer to the port. Or give yourself a full day in port—many hotels offer shuttles (free or low cost) to the cruise terminal.
- "Be certain to **call your credit card companies** to let them know you will be leaving the country before you depart for your Disney cruise vacation, even if it's only the three-night cruise to the Bahamas! We have traveled out of the country many times before and have always called prior to leaving but for some reason we failed to call when we took our cruise to the Bahamas. We tried to use our Disney Visa credit card to pay for some pictures in Nassau and were denied, but we thought it was a connection problem. On the last day of our cruise we went to use our Rewards card and it, too, was denied. We tried calling Chase but they were closed (apparently they aren't staffed on Sundays). We then tried using our Disney credit card—that was denied as well. We ended up using another card but it was annoying to know that we not only didn't get to use the points we'd accumulated but that we weren't going to get any points for what we'd just spent! If someone was really relying on using either points or a certain credit card, it could be more than just annoying—it could really cause problems." – *contributed by Disney vacationer Allison Hickman*

Magical Memory

- *"The Disney Dream's christening was an unforgettable event. Disney's invited guests arrived in Orlando a day early to party in the Magic Kingdom. The feeling of anticipation the next morning as we rode to the port on the Disney Cruise Line bus was even greater than usual, and when we arrived at the cruise terminal we were ushered to a huge grandstand (room for 5,000) alongside the pier, with the Dream standing some distance away, in the harbor. The stage was a good 150 feet wide, with Spectracolor video screens as its backdrop. There were musical production numbers, a stage overflowing with performers, speeches, a military band, an army of Disney characters.. and when it came time to smash the traditional bottle of champagne a barge arrived carrying a 20-foot tall bottle. A helicopter flew in, hooked the bottle, and carried it away to "smash" against the ship, triggering a cascade of fireworks! Who else but Disney would put on a show like this?"*

  ...as told by author Dave Marx

Staying in Style in a Stateroom

VIEW each stateroom's layout

EXPLORE your stateroom in detail with info and maps

Style is, indeed, the operative word for Disney Cruise Line staterooms. Every stateroom, regardless of its price, category, or location, is resplendent with warm, natural woods, luxurious fabrics, nautical touches, and dramatic lighting. Disney's **distinctive design** delivers stateroom interiors with more storage space and the innovative split bathrooms available in categories 10 and up. Staterooms on Disney ships have the "luxury of space"—they are substantially larger (up to 25%) than those on many other ships. Ocean views and private verandahs are in generous supply. 73% of the staterooms on the Magic Class ships and 88% of those on the Dream Class have an ocean view, while 44% of all rooms on the Magic Class and 79% of those on the Dream Class have private verandahs. Many cruise industry insiders consider Disney Cruise Line staterooms to be among the best afloat. You'll actually enjoy being in your stateroom!

Every stateroom has a **generous queen-size pillow-top bed**, ample closet space, shower/tub combination (or roll-in showers in the handicap-accessible rooms), hair dryer, desk/vanity, phone with voice mail, portable "Wave Phones," safe, flat screen color TV, small cooler, individual climate controls, and room service. Most staterooms also have a sitting area with a desk/dressing table and a sofa that converts into a twin bed, and most also have a pull-down single berth. A curtain separates the sleeping area from the sitting area. Staterooms sleep 2–7 guests (Magic Class) or 2–5 guests (Dream Class), though most sleep 3–4. Staterooms are located on decks 1–2 and 5–8 (Magic Class) and decks 2 and 5–12 (Dream Class), all of which are above the waterline.

Choosing your stateroom is one of the first things you'll do after you decide to cruise, so we put this chapter before dining and playing. We recommend you **read this chapter along with chapter 2** before you make reservations. Different stateroom categories offer different amenities, and some rooms and decks have an added benefit or two. The ship will be your home away from home for several days. Stateroom changes and upgrades are rarely available once you board.

....➢

Selecting Your Stateroom

You'll need to select a category when you make your reservation, so it pays to know as much as possible about each category in advance. You have **11 main stateroom categories** plus many sub-categories to choose from. Nine categories are found on all four ships, while category 8 is unique to the Dream Class, and category S is unique to the Magic Class.

The most obvious difference between categories is **price**. Category R is the priciest, while category 11C is the least expensive. Price may be your only concern, and if so, we encourage you to check the current cruise category rates at http://www.disneycruise.com. You can also find typical rates on page 60. Sub-categories (5A, 5B, 5C, etc.) rank staterooms within a category, with letter A ranked as the most attractive (and most expensive) by the cruise line. You may find that B, C, or even E will suit your needs quite nicely, depending on your feelings about being on a higher deck, or fore, aft, or midship. We think many of these distinctions offer little benefit on today's ships.

Beyond price, we can combine the stateroom **categories** into four groups: suites with verandahs (R, S, & T), outside staterooms with verandahs (4–7, V), outside staterooms with portholes (8–9), and inside staterooms (10–11). We devote one overview page to each of these four groups, plus four to six pages of delightful detail for each category.

The Disney Cruise Line may offer different "categories," but old-fashioned "classes" are a relic of the past. If you choose a category 11C stateroom, you won't be made to feel like you have lower status than any other passenger. You will have **access to all facilities** on your ship(except those reserved for concierge level guests) and dine in the same style, regardless of your category. We booked our first cruise in an old category 12 (now 11C) and never once felt funny about it. (We were later upgraded to category 9, which we loved. For more on upgrades, see page 149.)

Another deciding factor may simply be **availability**. This is particularly true of the highest and lowest category (and sub-category) staterooms, which are in shorter supply or lower-priced. Research availability before you choose a date, by looking up your desired sail date(s) at the cruise line web site, or speaking to a Disney reservations agent. To learn how to check specific stateroom availability, see page 132. Note that you may be offered a "guaranteed category" (GTY, VGT, OGT, IGT) rather than a specific room. This tends to happen when most of the staterooms in a category are booked. GTY means you're guaranteed a room in that category *or higher*, but all regular terms and conditions apply. VGT, OGT, and IGT guarantee a verandah, outside, or inside room, respectively, but special restrictions apply.

➢

What's the Difference?

Staterooms are organized into different categories, and decoding category descriptions is fairly straightforward.

Outside stateroom, of course, is a room with a view, located on the outer hull of the ship. Outside staterooms always have a view through a glass porthole or verandah.

Inside staterooms do not have a view—they're usually away from the outer hull in the central core of the deck.

Oceanview stateroom describes an outside room with a window or portholes.

Verandah staterooms, of course, are outside and have a private balcony. The next few terms are harder to decode.

Standard staterooms on Disney Cruise Line have an all-in-one bathroom with tub, vanity, and toilet. Standard rooms are also smaller than Deluxe staterooms by about 30 sq. ft., but much of that difference can be chalked off to the Deluxe's "split bathroom"—space in the living/sleeping area is comparable.

Deluxe refers to staterooms with the cruise line's distinctive split bathroom—tub and vanity in one room, toilet and a second vanity in another room.

Family refers to larger staterooms that sleep up to five. They have approximately 35 sq. ft/3.25 sq. m. more floor space than Deluxe staterooms, and most have an additional single-sized fold-out bed.

Concierge refers to the extra service and amenities that accompany all suites. On the Dream Class ships a limited number of Family Staterooms with Verandah on decks 11 and 12 offer concierge service and access to that ship's concierge lounge and sundeck.

Connecting rooms are adjacent staterooms with an internal connecting door.

Adjacent staterooms are simply next to each other, but without a connecting door.

How do staterooms differ on the Magic, Wonder, Dream, and Fantasy? There are currently no discernible differences between staterooms on sister ships Disney Magic and Disney Wonder. This will change in late 2013, after the Magic leaves drydock. Decor will be refreshed (particularly in the suites) and queen beds will be replaced with the style found on the newer ships. Staterooms on sister ships Dream and Fantasy are the same on both ships. But there are differences between the Magic Class and Dream Class—the biggest difference is probably that oceanview family staterooms exist on the Dream Class, but not on the Magic Class. There are also small details that differ—decor is slightly different, an extra cupboard is above the chest of drawers on the Dream Class, there is no steamer trunk on the Dream Class, and the suites are significantly different. Most Family staterooms on the Dream Class have a circular bathtub. For a detailed discussion of our experience with the staterooms on Disney's newest ships, see the next page.

Disney Dream Class Staterooms

On our cruises aboard the Disney Dream and Fantasy, we were fortunate enough to stay in four different staterooms and personally tour every other type of stateroom! Here's what we thought:

The **biggest stateroom changes** are on the "suite" decks (11 and 12). The two Royal Suites (Walter E. Disney and Roy E. Disney suites) have just one bedroom, but gain hot tubs on the verandahs and the location and layout of those suites is quite different. There are no two-bedroom suites (Category S on the Magic and Wonder)—if you need this, you'll need to add a connecting Family stateroom. A concierge lounge and private sun deck are also new on these ships. Even sweeter, the suites are no longer beneath the pool deck, so they ought to be even quieter.

© MediaMarx, Inc.

Outdoor hot tub in a Royal Suite

© MediaMarx, Inc.

A virtual porthole on the Dream

The most heralded change has been the addition of "**virtual portholes**" to inside staterooms, with real-time, high definition video views outdoors that correspond to the stateroom's location on the ship (port/starboard/fore/aft). Friends from Disney animated films also pop onscreen from time to time. (The Magic and Wonder may gain these at some point in the future, but not in 2013.)

Nearly all Family staterooms on the Dream Class have a large round tub, and its shape is echoed by a curved wall in the living area. The Dream Class also introduces a new stateroom category, Deluxe Family Outside Stateroom (Category 8), which offers the same interior space and layout as the familiar Deluxe Family Staterooms with Verandah, but at a more affordable price (In 2011, all Category 8 staterooms on the Magic Class were re-assigned to Category 9). The Dream Class doesn't offer a Navigator's Verandah comparable to those on the older ships—Category 7 indicates a regular verandah with a partially obstructed view. Some staterooms on decks 6-8 have a bow view, and more staterooms face astern.

Parties that book adjoining verandah staterooms can ask their stateroom host/hostess to open a door in the partition between the verandahs.

© MediaMarx, Inc.

A Dream stateroom facing the bow (#8504)

© MediaMarx, Inc.

Overhead mural on the Dream

Partway through 2011, the cruise line re-classified some staterooms due to variations in their verandahs. Rooms with oversized verandahs moved up a full category. Rooms with undersized verandahs or obstructed views moved down. Of special note are the category 4E rooms on deck 5. While now considered Deluxe Family Staterooms, they have the interior dimensions and features of category 5–10 rooms, but have a double-depth verandah.

Stateroom **interior design** for the Dream Class is very similar to that of the Magic Class, but with new artwork, woodwork, and other minor changes. Speaking of artwork, if the pull-down berth is opened for the evening, an overhead mural of Peter Pan and Tinker Bell is revealed to the lucky person in the upper bunk. Storage space is even more plentiful. The coffee table in the sitting area has been replaced by a storage hassock, and the chest of drawers near the closet now has overhead shelving. Under-bed height has been increased for the queen bed to store larger luggage, but that bed can't be split into two twins. Wall-mounted bedside shelves and lamps clear up some floor space, and the vertical "steamer trunk" found on the Magic Class ships is gone, replaced by making another cabinet taller. Also, the vast majority of staterooms have connecting doors, and for connecting verandah staterooms, a door now connects the verandahs, to create a double-width space.

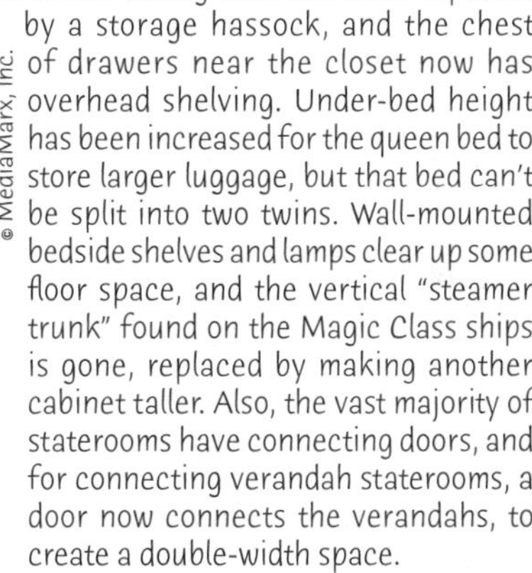

© MediaMarx, Inc.

Hassock with storage

Much more information on the new staterooms on the Disney Dream Class, including photos and videos, is available on our web site at http://www.passporter.com/disney-dream.

Outside or Inside Stateroom?

There's no easy answer to this question. Each choice affects your cruise experience, but not necessarily in the ways you may think. First off, no matter where you sleep, it won't affect your status with fellow cruisers or staff—everyone receives the same quality of service. What does change is how much time you're likely to spend in your stateroom. Verandahs encourage folks to stay in their staterooms, while inside rooms help push you out the door to enjoy the rest of the ship. With a ship full of attractive public spaces, there's nothing wrong with spending less time in your room. And a cheaper room can mean having more to spend on once-in-a-lifetime shore excursions, the deluxe wine package, or shopping in port. But then there are those magical, early morning moments in your bathrobe on the verandah while everyone else is asleep, reading a good novel and sipping room service coffee. We haven't made your choice any easier, have we? Maybe you can compromise with a picture-window-sized porthole?

The Great Stateroom Reclassification
(Magic Class Only)

To maintain consistency between the older Magic Class ships and the new Dream Class, Disney Cruise Line **reclassified all staterooms** on the Magic and Wonder effective with the 2011 cruising season. In part, this meant adding sub-categories to each major category, and in one case, it meant eliminating an entire category on the Magic Class (category 8). While all the ships now use the new classifications, we're keeping this chart in this edition for past cruisers who are not familiar with these changes.

Old Cat.	Old Deck(s)	Stateroom Type	New Cat.	New Deck (s)
1	8	Royal Suite (Roy O. & Walter E. Disney Suites)	R	8
2	8	2-Bedroom Suite	S	8
3	8	1-Bedroom Suite	T	8
4	8	Deluxe Family Stateroom with Verandah	4A	8 mid
4	8	Deluxe Family Stateroom with Verandah	4B	8 fwd & aft
4	8	Deluxe Family Stateroom with Verandah	4E	8 far aft
5	7	Deluxe Stateroom with Verandah	5A	7 mid
5	7	Deluxe Stateroom with Verandah	5B	7 fwd & aft
5	7	Deluxe Stateroom with Verandah	6A	7 far aft
6	6	Deluxe Stateroom with Verandah	5B	6 mid
6	6	Deluxe Stateroom with Verandah	5C	6 fwd & aft
6	5	Deluxe Stateroom with Verandah	5C	5 aft
6	6 & 5 far aft	Deluxe Stateroom with Verandah	6A	6 & 5 far aft
7	7, 6, & 5 aft	Deluxe with Navigator's Verandah	7A	7, 6, & 5 aft
8	7, 6, & 5 fwd	Deluxe Oceanview Stateroom	9A	7, 6, & 5 fwd
9	2	Deluxe Oceanview Stateroom	9B	2 mid
9	2	Deluxe Oceanview Stateroom	9C	2 fwd & aft
9	1	Deluxe Oceanview Stateroom	9D	1 mid
10	7 & 5 fwd	Deluxe Inside Stateroom	10A	7 & 5 fwd
10	2	Deluxe Inside Stateroom	10B	2 mid
10	2	Deluxe Inside Stateroom	10C	2 aft
10	1	Deluxe Inside Stateroom	10C	1 mid
11	7	Standard Inside Stateroom	11A	7
11	6	Standard Inside Stateroom	11A	6 mid
11	6	Standard Inside Stateroom	11B	6 fwd & aft
11	5	Standard Inside Stateroom	11B	5 fwd & aft
12	2	Standard Inside Stateroom	11C	2 fwd

Staterooms Side-by-Side

Charms and Delights	Issues and Drawbacks
Outside Stateroom Suites With Verandahs (categories R, S, & T)	
Huge staterooms, two with room for up to 7 people (Magic Class) or 5 (Dream Class). Total separation of sleeping and sitting areas. DVD and CD players, duvets, pillow choices, walk-in closets, wet bars, and some whirlpool tubs. Extra-large verandahs. Concierge, 120-day advance activity reservations, and expanded room service.	Very expensive, and deals are almost never offered. Very popular and are booked far in advance. There are only 22 suites (deck 8 on Magic Class; decks 11 & 12 on Dream Class). Most cat. T suites have a pull-down bed in the master bedroom. Can be noisy when crew is cleaning deck 9 above (Magic Class). Non-refundable deposit.
Outside Staterooms With Verandahs (categories 4-7, V)	
Verandahs! It's like having a private deck to watch waves or gaze at passing islands. And the wall-to-wall glass adds light and a sense of extra space. Located on decks 5 and up, close to all activities. Categories 4 and V are larger and sleep 4-5; the others sleep 3-4. Staterooms are 214-256 sq. ft. excluding balcony. Category V includes Concierge benefits.	Still on the pricey side, and may be out of range for many vacationers. Sitting and sleeping areas are in the same room. Category 5-7 layouts and interior square areas are identical to category 9. Wind and/or bad weather can make the verandah unusable. Category 7 on the Magic Class sleeps only 3. Category 4E (Dream Class) sleeps only 4.
Outside Staterooms With Portholes (categories 8-9)	
Portholes! Some natural sunlight and the ability to see where you are. These rooms are also more affordable than verandah rooms. Most sleep 4. All have split bathrooms. Portholes on decks 2 and up are picture-window-sized. Category 8 on the Dream Class is the larger, Family configuration, 241 sq. ft., sleeps 4-5. Category 9 on the Magic Class is 214 sq. ft. Category 9 on the Dream Class is 204 sq. ft.	No verandahs. Category 9 rooms on deck 1 (Magic Class) are harder to reach. Category 9 rooms on deck 2 are good on all ships. While the Dream Class category 8 & 9B, 9C, and 9D staterooms are on higher decks, they're located far forward or far aft (though 9C & 9D have views forward, which are nice). Sitting and sleeping areas are in the same room.
Inside Staterooms (categories 10-11)	
The least expensive staterooms available. Some rooms sleep up to 4. Category 10 has the same square footage as category 9. Some category 10-11 staterooms are on decks 5-7 (5-9, Dream Class). Six staterooms in category 10A on the Magic Class have an obstructed porthole (bonus!). Same access to the ship as higher categories. Staterooms on the Dream Class include the "virtual porthole."	No daylight, making the rooms seem smaller and dark. Smaller room size (169-184 sq. ft.) for category 11. Category 11C rooms sleep no more than 3. All staterooms in category 11C are on deck 2, and there are few staterooms in this category (making them harder to get). Category 11 doesn't have split bathrooms (see explanation on page 141).

Outside Concierge Stateroom Suites
(categories R, S, and T)

The best of the ship's staterooms, these suites (all on the highest passenger decks) offer many luxuries. All feature extra-large verandahs, DVD and CD players, dining areas, wet bars, walk-in closets, special pillows, robes and slippers, marble bathrooms, plus concierge and expanded room service.

AMENITIES

Concierge guests may get **perks** like priority boarding, a separate waiting area in the terminal, a special planning meeting once you're aboard, a private party with the Captain, personalized stationery, and some special surprise gifts. You may be able to request water and soda delivery for your room. All suites come with **concierge service**. You can make reservations for Palo, Remy, childcare, the spa, and shore excursions in advance of most other guests, and the concierge staff will help with other special requests. You can borrow from a library of CDs, DVDs, and games (board and electronic)—check the concierge book in your stateroom for a list. The crew often adds goodies, such as a fruit basket or cookies. Royal Suite guests also get **expanded room service**, meaning you can order a full breakfast in the mornings (same menu as Lumiere's/Triton's/Royal Palace/Royal Court—see page 158) and a full dinner from most restaurants during dinner hours—menus are available from concierge, or check our menus in chapter 4. Suite guests can also book massages in their staterooms or on their verandahs. The Dream Class adds a Concierge Lounge on deck 12 with snacks, drinks (including cocktails before dinner), magazines, and TVs, a private Concierge sun deck with cooling misters on deck 13, and a private entrance to Senses Spa.

TIPS & NOTES

The suites are **extremely popular**; if you do not book one far in advance, expect to be put on a waiting list.

Suite decor on the Magic will be refreshed, debuting in October 2013.

Concierge guests get online **priority booking** for excursions, spa treatments, Palo, Remy, kids' programming, and nursery up to 120 days in advance (see page 183). If you have not booked in advance, plan to meet with the concierge staff on your first afternoon.

Suites guests have a **choice of pillows**: a hypo-allergenic, feather, and/or therapeutic memory foam pillow.

Concierge guests have **gold Key to the World cards**.

Note that deposits for suites are **non-refundable**.

Category R Staterooms (Magic Class)

(Walter E. and Roy O. Disney Royal Suites)

The two **category R suites**, known as the Walter E. Disney Suite and the Roy O. Disney Suite, are the height of cruising. **On the Magic and Wonder** the suites measure 813 sq. ft. (interior) and sleep up to 7 guests. They offer 2 bedrooms, 2 ½ baths including a master bath with whirlpool tub and separate shower, a media library with a queen-sized pull-down bed, a dining area, and butler's pantry. When the libary's sliding doors are open, half the suite is available for entertaining guests, in an area four times the width of a standard stateroom. The quadruple-width verandah is the depth of a standard verandah, perhaps the least party-friendly feature of the suite. Both suites are located on deck 8, midship.

© MediaMarx, Inc.

Entryway

© MediaMarx, Inc.

Pantry

© MediaMarx, Inc.

A view from the media library into the bedroom on the Disney Magic

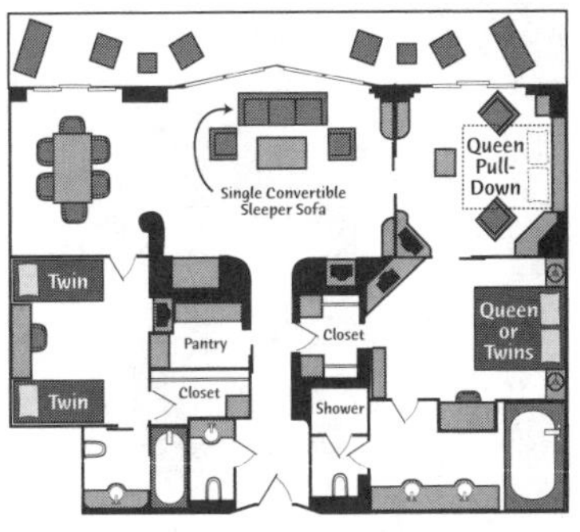

Disney Magic Class category R

Category R Staterooms (Dream Class)

(Walter E. and Roy O. Disney Royal Suites)

On the Disney Dream and Fantasy, the Walter E. Disney and Roy O. Disney Suites are found at the forward end of deck 12. The 898 sq. ft. (interior) suites sleep up to five, with two guests in a master bedroom with queen bed and up to three more guests on one single and one double pull-down bed in the living room. The suite has two bathrooms, with a whirlpool tub and separate shower in the master bath, plus a butler's pantry. Both the bedroom and living room feature 42-inch TVs, and another video screen is embedded in the master bathroom mirror. The wedge-shaped living room offers panoramic views through a curved window wall,and the expansive teak-decked verandah includes a whirlpool spa. These suites can connect to adjoining category T and V staterooms, allowing for a substantially larger travel party.

Bedroom in the Royal Suite on the Disney Dream

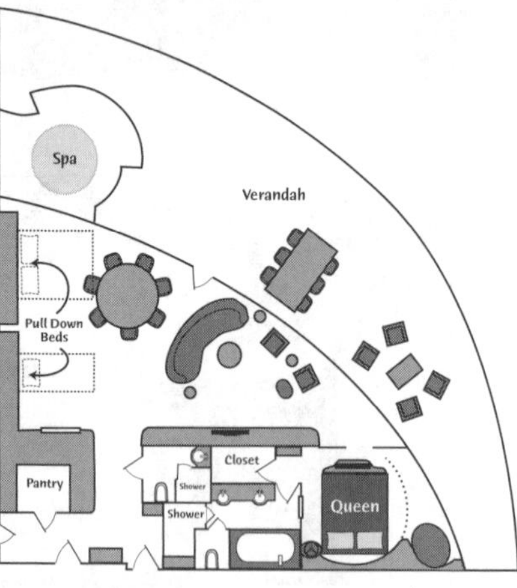

Disney Dream category R suite

The living room in the Royal Suite

Category S Staterooms (Magic Class Only)
(Two-Bedroom Suite–sleeps 7 guests)

The **category S** suites, available only on the Magic Class, offer 783 sq. ft. of interior space. They have two bedrooms, 2½ baths, a whirlpool tub, and a triple-wide verandah. There are just two of these suites onboard, and each sleeps up to seven.

Tip: Connecting rooms are great for larger groups. Many of the category T suites have connecting doors to a category T or 4 or V, which holds four to five more guests. Alas, the category R and S suites on the Magic Class vessels do not have connecting staterooms. All suites on the Dream Class have connecting doors to either another suite or a Concierge Family Stateroom.

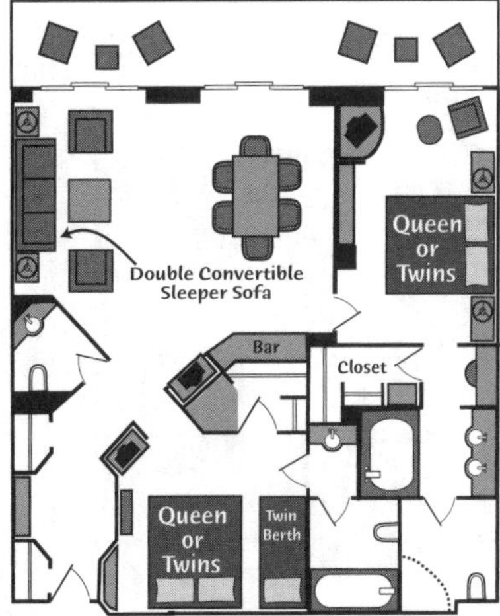

© MediaMarx, Inc.

The triple-wide verandah of a cat. S suite

© MediaMarx, Inc.

A category S bedroom

© MediaMarx, Inc.

The entertainment center

Category T Staterooms (Magic Class)
(One Bedroom Suite–sleeps 4-5 guests)

The 18 suites in **category T** (506 sq. ft.) on the **Magic Class** ships are twice the width of a standard stateroom, and sleep 4-5 guests. The bedroom features a queen bed and a master bath with whirlpool tub and separate shower. The living room includes a dining table, wet bar, a double-size convertible sofa and bath with shower. Most suites also have a fold-down twin bed in the bedroom. Four suites (8032, 8034, 8532, and 8534) have a slightly different layout–the room is triple-width but less deep,and features the pull-down twin bed in the living room. These are under the Goofy Pool, however, and are noisier. Suites 8100, 8102, 8600, and 8602 are handicap-accessible and have deeper verandahs. Decor will be refreshed on the Magic, debuting in late October 2013.

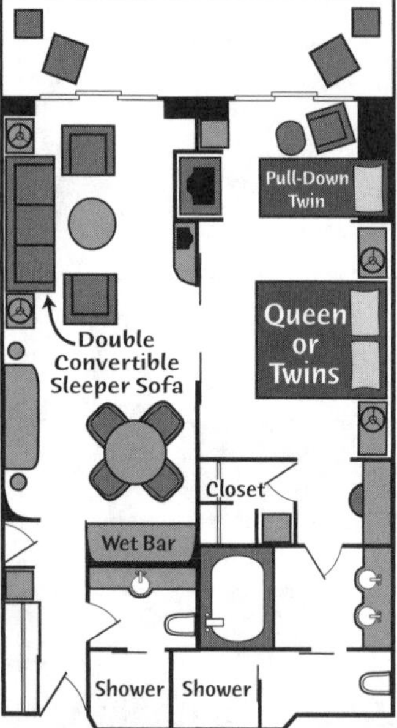

© MediaMarx, Inc.

Bedroom of a category T stateroom on the Magic

© MediaMarx, Inc.

Dave relaxes in the living room of stateroom 8034 on the Disney Magic

Category T Staterooms (Dream Class) (One Bedroom Suite–sleeps 4-5 guests)

The 19 suites in **category T** (536 sq. ft.) on the **Dream Class** ships sleep 4-5, with a queen bed in the master bedroom, and a full-size sleep sofa and twin Murphy bed in the living room. The master bath features a whirlpool tub and separate shower, while the second bath comes with a shower only. Both the bedroom and living room feature 42-inch TVs, and another video screen is embedded in the master bathroom mirror. The living/dining room runs the width of the suite and opens onto a double-width verandah. Most verandahs are extra-deep, but eight (12614, 12620, 12624, 12626, 12514, 12520, 12524, and 12526) have standard-depth verandahs. All suites connect to an adjoining category V room (see page 133) with one exception: stateroom 12000, which faces the bow and can connect with either or both of the Royal Suites. Category T suites sleep four to five guests.

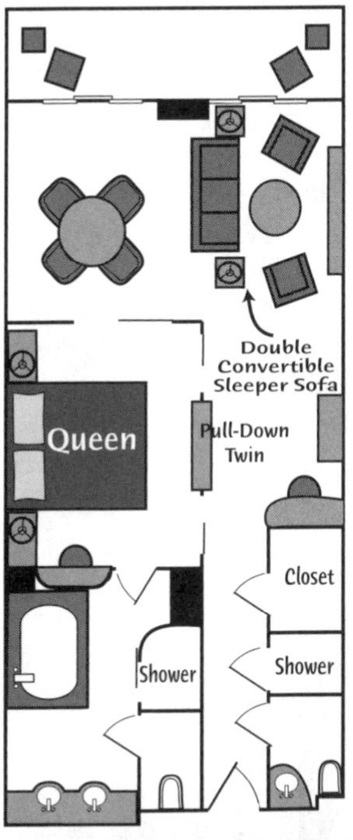

© MediaMarx, Inc.

A category T bedroom on the Disney Dream

Outside Staterooms With Verandahs

(categories V, 4, 5, 6, and 7)

Welcome to the luxury of a private verandah at just a fraction of the cost of a suite! Staterooms with verandahs (categories V and 4–7) comprise the largest percentage of the ship's staterooms at a whopping 42%–69%. All have split baths (see page 131) and are on decks 5–8 or 5–12.

AMENITIES

The main amenity in categories V, 4–7 is the verandah (balcony). Not only does the verandah offer fresh air and a gorgeous view, but it extends the space of your stateroom. The option to sit outside and enjoy a sunset or read while someone else watches TV or sleeps inside is a huge bonus. Verandahs in categories V, 4–6 are open to the air, covered, and have privacy dividers. Category 7 staterooms (same size as categories 5 and 6) have either a slightly obstructed view or a Navigator's Verandah, which offers more privacy by hiding the verandah behind a large, glassless "porthole" (see photos on page 137). All verandahs have exterior lighting that is controlled by an on/off switch inside the stateroom. All can sleep at least three guests, and most category V and 4 rooms sleep up to five guests. Category V rooms (Dream Class) are on decks 11 and 12 and have Concierge benefits and richer decor.

© MediaMarx, Inc.

Verandah with plexiglass railing

© MediaMarx, Inc.

Verandah with metal railing

Most verandahs have a clear, plexiglass-covered outer wall (shown in the first photo). Others have a solid, metal wall (as shown in the second photo). There are fans of both styles, though we personally prefer the clear walls.

Which Staterooms Are Available for My Cruise?

Most guests let Disney or their travel agent select their stateroom. If you'd rather have a specific stateroom, find out which staterooms are available by calling Disney (888-325-2500). If you have Internet access, get online and visit Disney Cruise Line (http://www.disneycruise.com) or Travelocity.com (http://www.travelocity.com)—follow the directions to choose your cruise, then continue through the windows to check rates and to see any availabilities. If you have your heart set on a particular stateroom, call Disney or check the Internet to find a cruise with that room available. When you make your reservations, indicate the exact stateroom you want. Confirm that the stateroom you requested is printed in your travel booklet when it arrives.

Category V and 4 Staterooms

(Deluxe Family Stateroom with Verandah–sleeps 4–5)

Categories V and 4 are the Deluxe Family Staterooms, which sleep four or five guests (250–256 sq. ft.). Category V staterooms are only available on the Dream Class ships. **Category 4** rooms have a queen-sized bed, convertible twin sofa bed, pull-down twin berth, and a pull-down twin Murphy bed for the fifth guest. Access to the verandah is limited when you have the Murphy bed pulled down. **The Magic Class** has 80 category 4 rooms, all on deck 8. Avoid staterooms directly below the Goofy Pool (8036–8044 and 8536–8544) due to noise. Staterooms 8092–8094 and 8596–8698 have a solid railing, rather than a plexiglass railing.

Magic/Wonder

© Paul McGill

A category 4 stateroom (8544 on Magic)

© MediaMarx

Desk/vanity area in category 4 (Dream)

© Paul McGill

Another view of category 4 (Magic)

Category V and 4 Staterooms *(continued)*

(Deluxe Family Stateroom with Verandah—sleeps 4–5)

Deluxe Family Staterooms on the **Dream Class ships** have one extra distinction—most have a round bathtub. The presence of that tub is accentuated by a curved wall in the living area. **The 20 category V staterooms**, all on the Dream Class ships, are on decks 11 and 12, the concierge level, and include concierge privileges. The rooms are decorated in elegant, Art Deco style, with high-gloss wood finishes, dark teakwood accents, a tan, dark blue, aquamarine, and dark brown color palette, and extra touches like terry robes and slippers, and a valet kit. As in all concierge level rooms, a second, 42" wall-mounted TV faces the queen bed. The interior layout of these rooms is comparable to category 4, with the distinctive circular tub, but the convertible sofa is a double, rather than a twin, and there is no Murphy bed. These differences free-up floor space and give the room a more spacious feeling than category 4. All deck 11 rooms have extra-deep verandahs, as do 12008, 12010, 125008 and 125010 on deck 12. Stateroom 11000 is larger and handicap-accessible. **There are 361 Category 4 staterooms on the Dream Class ships**, a dramatic increase from the Magic Class, which makes them much easier to get. Even parties of 2, 3, or 4 are now booking them for the sake of extra floor space. Especially noteworthy are the **44 category 4E staterooms**, all on deck 5. **These rooms are different in several ways** from other category 4 staterooms. They debuted on the Dream as category 5 staterooms, but the cruise line soon re-classified them to 4E. What's so special? The verandahs are the same width but double the depth of typical verandahs. The interior space and layout is the same as a category 5 room, sleeping 3-4 in a queen-sized bed, convertible twin sofa bed, and a pull-down twin berth. These rooms also have a rectangular tub, rather than the round tub seen in other category V and 4 rooms.

Dream/Fantasy

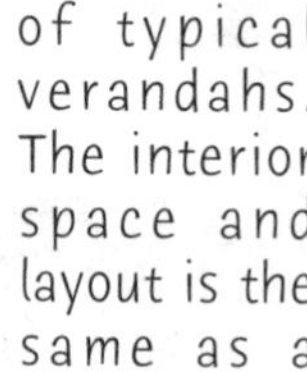

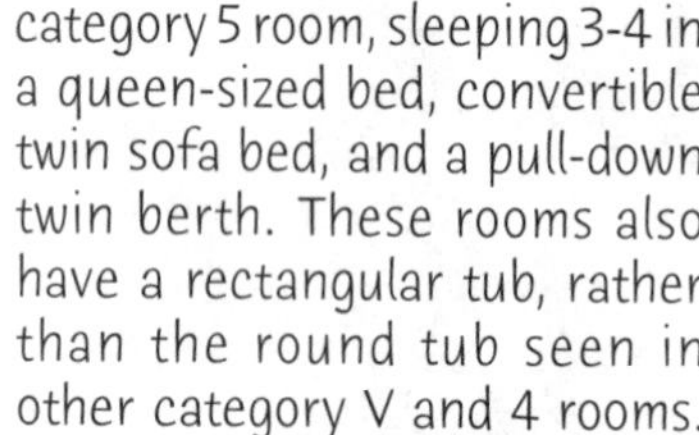

A category V stateroom with wall-mounted large-screen TV.

© MediaMarx, Inc.

Category 5 & 6 Staterooms

(Deluxe Stateroom With Verandah–sleeps 3-4 guests)

Categories 5 and 6 are the Deluxe Staterooms With Verandahs, the most plentiful categories on board. These staterooms are identical to category 4 in most ways (see previous pages) except they sleep one less guest and are smaller (214/204 sq. ft. interior), as they need floor space for one less bed. **On the Dream Class ships**, the bathrooms have rectangular, rather than the round tubs found in classes V and 4. **The Magic and Wonder's** 114 category 5 staterooms are located on deck 7, mostly midship and aft. Staterooms to the aft have quick access to a secluded public deck. Staterooms 7130-7138 and 7630-7638 have a solid, four-foot metal railing (as opposed to the plexiglass railing), but the verandahs may be deeper. Avoid 7590 as it is across from a laundry room. The 138 **category 6** staterooms are situated on decks 5 and 6. We recommend deck 6 for its slightly larger verandahs. Avoid 6588 as it is across from a laundry room. Staterooms 5142-5150, 5642-5650, 6144-6154, and 6644-6654 have a solid railing. **The 443 category 5 and 30 category 6 staterooms on the Dream Class ships** are on decks 5-10. Category 5E staterooms in the very aft (facing back) on these ships have extra-deep verandahs. Aft-facing "solid wall" verandahs on these ships actually have clear plexiglass above an 18" solid lower wall, so the impact on views is minimal.

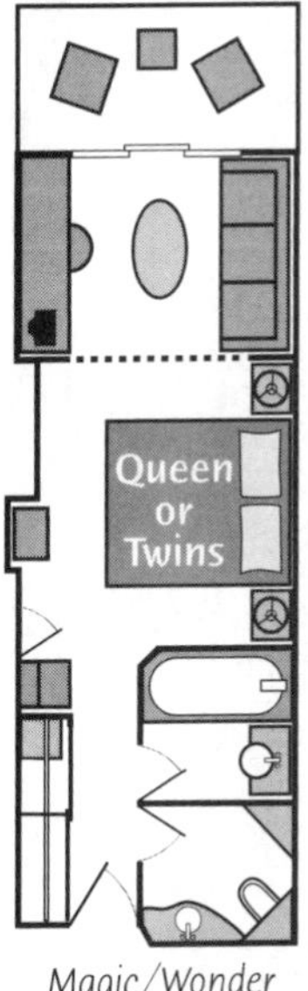

Magic/Wonder

Verandah at sunset

Stateroom entry way

A category 6 stateroom on the Disney Dream

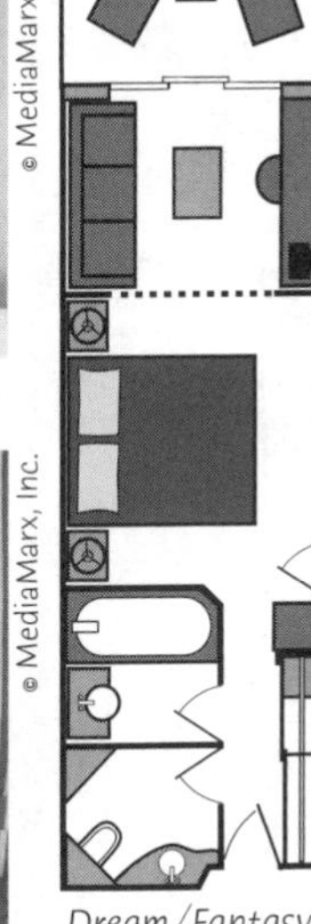
Dream/Fantasy

Category 7 Staterooms (Magic Class)
(Navigator's Verandah—sleeps 3 guests)

There are only 30 **category 7** staterooms (214 sq. ft. interior) on the Magic and Wonder, of which 26 have Navigator's Verandahs (enclosed verandah with open-air porthole). All are located on the quietest decks: 5, 6, and 7. We recommend deck 7 for its easy access to the public deck to the aft. Note that the verandahs on deck 5 are a bit shallower at 42" (106 cm.) than those on upper decks at about 48" (122 cm.). Four of the category 7 staterooms (#6134, #6634, #7120, and #7620) were originally category 5 and 6 staterooms—they have plexiglass railings and partially obstructed views due to the hull design, and their verandahs aren't enclosed like the other category 7 rooms.

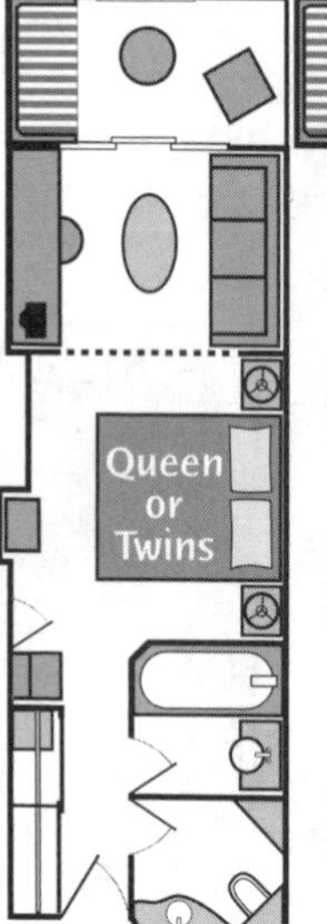

Note that the Navigator's Verandah on the Disney Wonder sports a larger porthole, while the Magic's is a bit smaller. Both have a built-in, padded bench, a chair, and a small table.

© MediaMarx, Inc.

Our category 7 stateroom was cozy and comfortable

© MediaMarx, Inc.

The enclosed navigator's verandah

© MediaMarx, Inc.

Dave loves the built-in bench

Introduction Reservations Staterooms Dining Activities Ports of Call Magic Index

Category 7 Staterooms (Dream Class)
(Obstructed-View Verandah—sleeps 3-4 guests)

When the Dream was launched, the ship had no Category 7 staterooms. Partway through 2011, the cruise line re-classified more than 80 staterooms on each Dream Class ship. 26 former Category 5 and 6 rooms on decks 5-9 are now Category 7A. While referred to as Navigator's Verandah/ Obstructed View, obstructed view is more appropriate. While the verandahs are full width and depth, with plexiglass-covered railings, either the left- or right-hand end of the verandah is hidden behind metalwork, creating a sheltered alcove. We stayed in one of these rooms (#7022) for the Dream's Christening. In all regards but this one, these are identical to Category 5 and 6 rooms. While the exact amount of obstruction varies, the photos below are representative.

© MediaMarx, Inc.

© MediaMarx, Inc.

Looking out an obstructed-view verandah

Seating in an obstructed-view verandah

The Dream Class Stateroom Re-Categorization of 2011

As soon as cruisers began to explore the Disney Dream and compare notes about their staterooms, certain rooms were clearly noteworthy for their differences. While this will always be true of handicap-accessible rooms, in the other cases, the differences had to do with verandahs and views. Those differences included the rooms with oversized-verandahs on deck 5, and most aft-facing verandahs are also extra-large. These quickly became highly sought-after—extra space at no extra charge. In other cases, the verandahs left something to be desired. Two of the aft-facing verandahs (#5188 and #5688) are seriously under-sized. Other verandahs have partially-obstructed views. The cruise line responded by bumping some rooms up into newly-created categories 4E and 5E, and others down into category 7A (see above). Finally, bow-facing category 9A rooms were moved into brand-new categories 9C and 9D. These rooms have a sloping front wall, which affects headroom when near that wall and affects the view from the porthole. These changes allowed the cruise line to charge rates that are more in line with the value delivered.

Outside Staterooms With Portholes

(categories 8 and 9)

Affordable elegance is yours if you choose a porthole over a verandah. These rooms make up only 27% of the staterooms onboard the Magic Class ships. They're located on decks 1, 2, 5, 6, and 7. On the Dream Class that's been reduced to 16% of all staterooms, and they're are found on decks 2, 5, 6, 7, 8, and 9.

AMENITIES

Beginning in 2011, category 8 became an all-new classification, called the Deluxe Outside Family Stateroom, and the category 8 staterooms on the Magic Class ships are now in category 9A. Most (but not all) staterooms in these categories feature the split bathroom (see page 141), and the sitting area is in the far rear of the stateroom, by the porthole(s). The natural light is a real bonus over inside staterooms, especially for kids who tend to rely more heavily on outside light for their sleep/wake cycle.

© MediaMarx, Inc.

Baby Alexander enjoys our category 9 stateroom

On the Magic class the portholes on deck 1 differ from those on the higher decks (see photos, below). We prefer the larger porthole (wouldn't you?).

© MediaMarx, Inc.

Deck 1 portholes (Magic Class only)

© MediaMarx, Inc.

Deck 2 and up porthole

(Category 8 on the Magic Class is now category 9A.)

Category 8 Staterooms (Dream Class only)
(Deluxe Family Oceanview Stateroom, sleep 4-5)

The **Disney Dream and Fantasy add only one new stateroom layout** to the Disney fleet, and this is it. You no longer have to pay verandah pricing to have space for a family of five (or additional elbow room for smaller families). The room interiors are roughly equivalent to the Deluxe Family Staterooms with Verandah, only without the verandah.

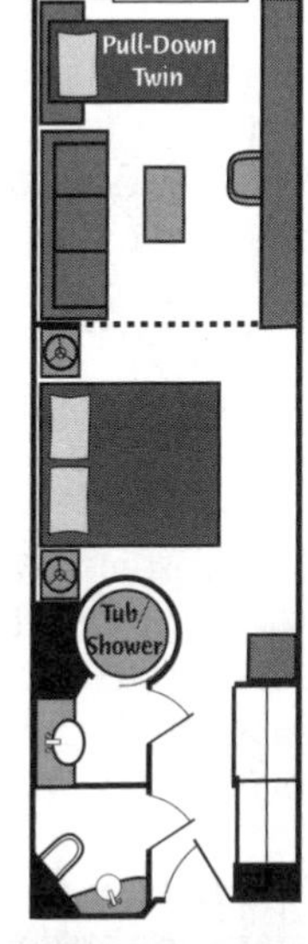

There are 109 category 8 staterooms (sub-categories 8A-8D) on the Dream Class ships. Interior area is 241 sq. ft., 15 sq. ft. less than the otherwise comparable category 4 Deluxe Family Stateroom with Verandah (see page 133), and 38 sq. ft. larger than category 9 Deluxe Oceanview Staterooms (see page 140). The rooms have the same circular tub and fold-down single bed as categories 4 and V. The 12 category 8A staterooms are located near the bow on decks 5 and 6, and have a different layout, wider and less deep (roughly square). Of those, six are handicap-accessible (5018, 5518, 6012, 6014, 6510, 6512). 22 category 8B rooms are found on deck 9 near the extreme front and rear of the ship. 45 category 8C rooms are found in the same locations on decks 7 and 8. 30 category 8D rooms are in about the same locations on deck 6, but mostly aft on deck 5 (5016 and 5516 are forward).

© MediaMarx, Inc.

Fold-down bed, berth bed, and couch bed

© MediaMarx, Inc.

3.5-ft. diameter round tub and shower

Category 9 Staterooms

(Deluxe Oceanview Staterooms, sleep 2-4)

Category 9 staterooms have the same interior layout and space as categories 5 and 6, but with a window instead of a verandah. **There are 60 category 9A staterooms on the Magic Class ships**, scattered among decks 5-7 forward. Staterooms on deck 5 are convenient to the kid's clubs. The fact that these staterooms are directly over the Walt Disney Theatre shouldn't be a problem—you aren't likely to be in your room during a show. Staterooms on decks 6 and 7 are excellent, by all accounts. Note that two category 9A rooms are handicap-accessible (#6000 and #6500). Category 9B, 9C, 9D staterooms are found on decks 1 and 2 on the Magic Class. We don't recommend deck 1 as it only has access to the forward and midship elevators and stairs. Additionally, staterooms #1030-1037 are fairly noisy on port days. Perhaps more importantly, the outside staterooms on deck 1 have two small portholes, rather than the one large porthole found on the other decks. We liked 1044 (deck 1) well enough, but we much prefer the staterooms we've had on deck 2. On deck 2 some staterooms are better than others. Due to fairly constant noise and vibration, we recommend you avoid: 2000-2004, 2036-2044, 2078-2096, 2114-2129, 2140-2152, 2500-2508, 2586-2600, 2626, and 2630-2653. Our family stayed in rooms 2610-2616 on one cruise and we loved them—quiet and convenient (near the aft elevators and stairs).

The Dream Class has 91 category 9 staterooms. The 10 category 9A rooms are on decks 5-8. Of those, 5186, 5686, 6186, and 6686 are oversize and handicap-accessible. The 60 category 9B staterooms are all on deck 2, have somewhat smaller windows, and have access to only the forward and midship elevators. The 21 category 9C and 9D rooms are on decks 6-8, have distinctive views of the bow, and sloping front walls. Six of those are oversized, corner rooms: 6006, 6504, 7006, 7504, 8006, and 8506. 5 are handicap-accessible: 6006, 6500, 6504, 7500 and 8500.

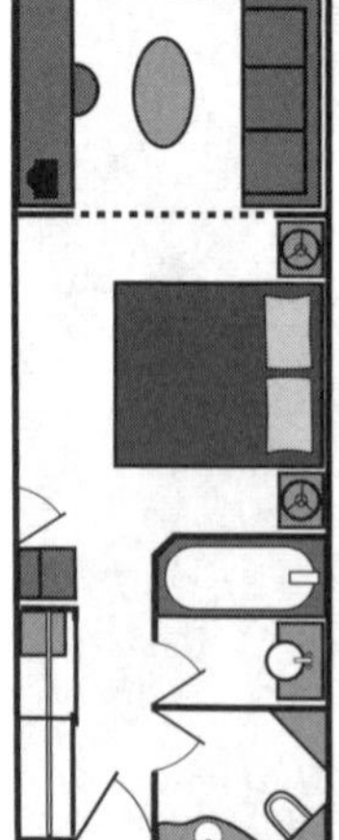

© MediaMarx, Inc.

Relaxing in our category 9A stateroom with a porthole (7514)

Inside Staterooms

(categories 10 and 11)

Resplendent with the same luxurious decor found in the other staterooms, inside staterooms are smaller and more affordable versions of the higher categories. Inside staterooms make up 29%/12% of the staterooms onboard and are located on decks 1, 2, 5, 6, and 7/2, 5, 6, 7, 8, 9, and 10.

AMENITIES

Inside staterooms come in two layouts. Category 10 is the Deluxe Inside Stateroom and is 214/200 sq. ft. with a split bath (see below). Category 11 is the Standard Inside Staterooms at 184/169 sq. ft. (Category 12 staterooms were reclassified to 11C in 2011). Beyond the size and the split bath, there's little difference. All categories put the sitting area before the sleeping area, because without a window there's no benefit to having the sitting area at the farthest end of the stateroom. Two notable differences between category 10 and 11 on the Magic Class is the orientation of the bed (see room layout diagrams on following pages) and that none of the staterooms in category 11 offer connecting rooms. The Dream Class add the new "virtual porthole" built into the queen bed's headboard (see next page for more details on this innovation). Connecting rooms are plentiful in category 11 on the Dream Class ships.

The split bathroom found in category 10 (as well as V and 4–9) is convenient for families.

© MediaMarx, Inc.

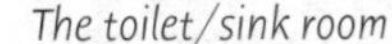

The toilet/sink room

© MediaMarx, Inc.

The shower/tub/sink room

The one-room bathroom in category 11 is much more compact. We show two views: a regular bathroom and a handicapped bathroom.

© MediaMarx, Inc.

A category 11 bathroom

© MediaMarx, Inc.

A cat. 11 handicapped bathroom

Category 10 Staterooms

(Deluxe Inside Stateroom–sleeps 3-4 guests)

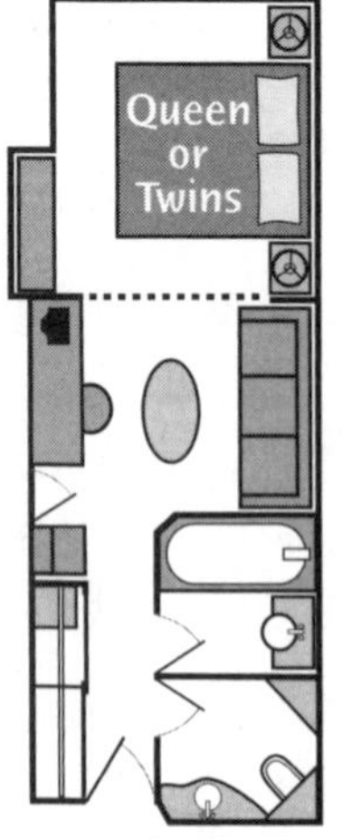

Magic Class

On the Magic Class ships, the 96 category 10 staterooms are found on decks 1, 2, 5, and 7. The staterooms on deck 1 are our least favorite because the corridor doesn't run the entire length of the deck making it harder to reach the aft of the ship. Many of the staterooms on deck 2 are immediately below noisy places. To avoid noises from above, try for odd-numbered staterooms between 2071-2075, 2571-2575, 2101-2111, 2601-2611, 2629-2635, and 2129-2135. We also recommend the staterooms on deck 7. You should also note that almost half of the category 10 staterooms have connecting rooms. If you need only one stateroom, our advice is to avoid these connecting rooms. Many cruisers have reported that the connecting doors do not dampen noise well. Try to swing a category 10 on deck 5 (5020, 5022, 5024, 5520, 5522, or 5524) with a partially obstructed, "secret" porthole–see the next page for details. All category 10 staterooms sleep up to four guests.

On the Dream Class vessels, 19 category 10 rooms fill various odd spaces on decks 5-9. With so few available, they're hard to come by and may be candidates for free upgrades.

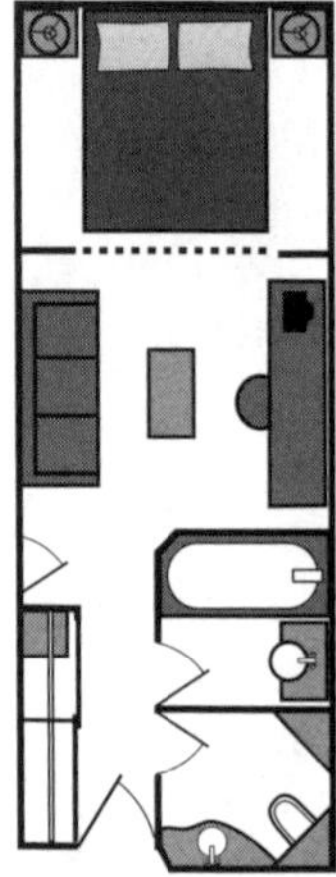

Dream Class

All inside staterooms on the Dream Class ships have nifty "virtual portholes" with real-time, high definition video views outdoors that correspond to the stateroom's location on the ship (port/starboard) and occasional visits by a wide variety of animated friends from Disney feature films and shorts. Porthole animations are preceded by a bit of animated pixie dust and occur once every 30 minutes. View our video of a porthole at http://www.passporter.com/disney-dream.

© MediaMarx, Inc.

A "virtual porthole" in stateroom #8643.

(Available only on Magic Class ships)

Special Category 10A Staterooms

("Secret Porthole"–sleeps 4 guests)

Six of the category 10A staterooms on the Magic Class ships have a different layout–and a porthole! Now before you get too excited, the porthole has an obstructed view (see photo below), but most cruisers are delighted with these "secret porthole rooms." We've included the layout for these special staterooms below as well. These six special category 10A staterooms are all located on deck 5 (5020, 5022, 5024, 5520, 5522, or 5524), and all sleep up to four guests.

Getting one of these special category 10A staterooms can be difficult. You can simply try checking with Disney Cruise Line or your travel agent to see if one of these staterooms is available for your cruise (use the stateroom numbers noted above). You can also use the Internet to find out which staterooms are still available for your cruise–then if you find that one of these coveted secret porthole staterooms is available, book that cruise before someone else books it. See page 132 to learn how to determine which staterooms are still available for your cruise.

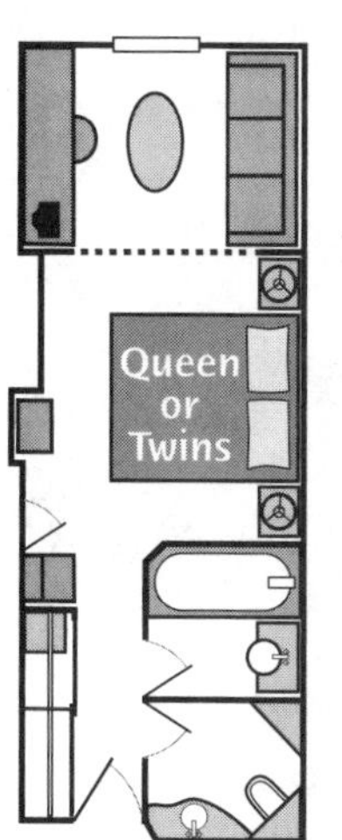

If you're considering a "secret porthole" stateroom but aren't sure how you feel about the obstructed view, we refer you to the excellent Platinum Castaway Club web site (http://www.castawayclub.com), which has photos of each of the six "secret portholes" so you can judge for yourself. Just click on the "Secret Porthole Rooms" link in the left column to get the photos and a list of pros and cons to help you make your decision.

© MediaMarx, Inc.

A "secret porthole" stateroom (#5024)

© MediaMarx, Inc.

Another view of this category

Category 11 Staterooms

(Standard Inside Stateroom–sleeps 3-4 guests)

The Magic Class has 147 Category 11 A and 11B staterooms on decks 5, 6, and 7. There are 18 category 11B rooms on decks 5 and 6 with an alternate, "sideways" layout–some cruisers find them a touch roomier. While staterooms 6002, 6004, 6502, and 6504 are located on the ship's outer hull, they have no portholes. The 13 Category 11C staterooms are on deck 2 forward. All sleep no more than 3 guests, but you may be able to book them for 4 guests and get an automatic upgrade. Due to their low price and scarcity, demand is high and upgrades are common (to clear space for last-minute bargain hunters). These rooms are conveniently close to the forward elevators and stairs, but they are also noisier, being directly below Beat Street/Route 66. Request another category for less noise. **The Dream Class has 104 Category 11A and 11B rooms** on decks 5-10. Rooms 7191 and 7689 are on the ship's outer hull, but have no portholes. All 27 Category 11C rooms are on deck 2.

© MediaMarx, Inc.

A handicap-accessible, category 11 inside stateroom (6647)

© MediaMarx, Inc.

Another view of stateroom 6647, a handicap-accessible category 11 room

Category 11 is the only inside category to offer **handicap-accessible rooms** (see photos above). On the Magic Class: 6147, 6647, 7131, and 7631. On the Dream Class: 6001, 2007, 2033, 2035, 2507, 2533, and 2535.

© MediaMarx, Inc.

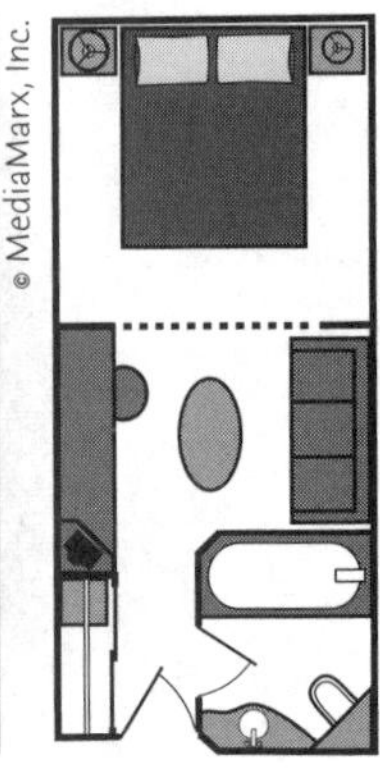

A standard category 11 inside stateroom

Stateroom Amenities and Services

Bathrooms—All staterooms have their own bathrooms, while categories V and 4–10 have innovative split bathrooms with a sink/toilet in one small room, and a second sink plus tub/shower in another room—see page 141. Plush bath towels and bath sheets are provided. We love the split bathrooms—it makes getting ready much easier. Note that the light switches are located outside the bathrooms—remember to turn them on before you enter!

Beds—Every room has a Sealy Posturepedic Premium Plush Euro-top bed with 600 thread-count Egyptian cotton sheets made by Frette. On the Magic Class, the comfy queen-size beds can be unlocked and separated into two single beds by your stateroom host/hostess if needed (beds on the Dream Class cannot be separated, and the Magic will have the same beds as the Dream Class starting in late October 2013). Most staterooms also have a twin-size, convertible sofa (72"/183 cm. long). Categories V and T have a double-size convertible sofa instead. Many rooms have a pull-down, twin-size upper berth (72"/183 cm. long with a weight limit of 220 lbs./100 kg.) with safety rails. Category 4 has an extra twin-size fold-out bed.

Closets—Every stateroom has a roomy closet with a clothes rod, a dozen or so hangers, a set of drawers, a safe, your life jackets, and an overhead light (that turns on automatically when you open the closet). If you don't have enough hangers, ask your stateroom host/hostess for more.

Cribs—Portable, "pack-n-play" cribs are available, as are bed safety rails—request when reserving. High chairs are also provided in the dining areas.

© MediaMarx, Inc.

A pack-n-play crib in a stateroom

© MediaMarx, Inc.

Electrical Control—On the Dream Class ships, you'll find a silver panel just inside your stateroom—this controls electricity in your room. Insert a card into the top slot to keep your electricity on. You do not need to use your Key to the World card—any card-sized object will do. We don't recommend you use your Key to the World card because as soon as that card is removed, the lights in the room go out—and this can be very inconvenient if you're left in the dark when your husband takes his card on the way out to get a soda!

Electrical Outlets—Staterooms are outfitted with four standard U.S. 110v, three-pronged electrical outlets: two near the desk/vanity, plus two behind the TV (Magic Class) or under the clock (Dream Class). Two special outlets—one in each bathroom—are marked "for shavers only" and have a standard U.S. 110v, two-pronged outlet along with a European 220v outlet (20 watts/20VA max.). You can't plug your hair dryer into the bathroom outlets, but electric toothbrushes should be OK. On the Magic Class, there's no outlet near the bed, so bring an extension cord or power strip if necessary.

Hair Dryers—On the Magic Class built-in hair dryers are attached to the wall of the bathroom in each stateroom. On the Dream Class, a portable, handheld hair dryer is in a bag hanging from the back of your bathroom drawer, or possibly in your desk drawer—you can only plug it in at the desk. If you are particular about drying your hair, consider bringing your own.

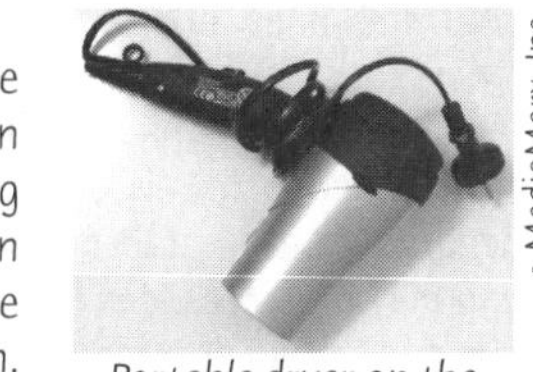
© MediaMarx, Inc.

Portable dryer on the Dream Class

Introduction Reservations Staterooms Dining Activities Ports of Call Magic Index

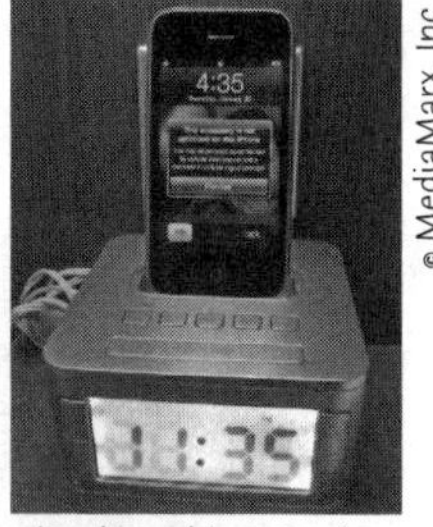

© MediaMarx, Inc.

iPod Docking Station

Internet Access—Wireless Internet access is available in staterooms onboard (though we find the reception to be weak/spotty in some staterooms), as well as in many public areas. For details, see page 151.

iPod Docking Station—On the Dream Class, there is an iPod player/clock/alarm near the bed. The player will charge and play music from both iPods and iPhones. To hear music from its speakers, use the Mode button to put it into iPod mode.

Laundry—Self-service laundries are available on all ships, as is valet laundry service, dry cleaning, and pressing. The three laundry rooms onboard the Magic Class are located across the hall from staterooms 2096, 6588, and 7590, while the seven laundry rooms on the Dream Class are across the hall from staterooms 2002, 5190, 6510, 7014, 8150, 9500, and 10572. Each laundry room has several stacked washer/dryers ($2.00 each), two irons and boards (no charge), detergent vending machine ($1.00), and table. Washers and dryers take about 45 minutes for each cycle. Estimate $5.00 for a full load of laundry. Machines have a card reader, so you must swipe your Key to the World card (no coins accepted). If you plan to do laundry, pack some detergent or Purex sheets and a mesh bag to tote your items. Plan to visit in the mornings—afternoons are very busy. We do not recommend you bring your own iron or steamer as their use is prohibited in the staterooms for safety reasons.

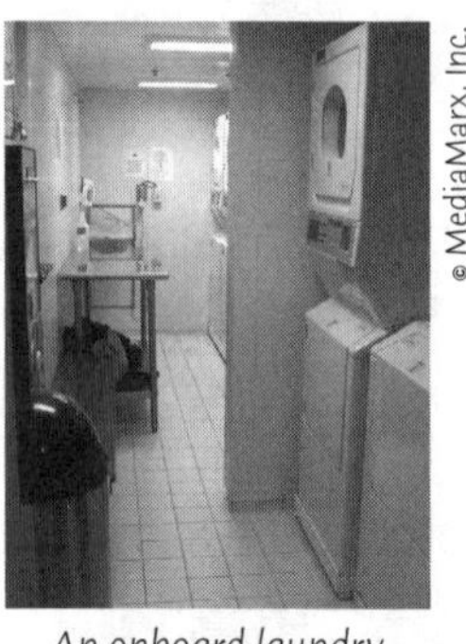
© MediaMarx, Inc.

An onboard laundry (the iron is in the back)

Lights—The staterooms are well illuminated, but it can get pitch black in your room when you turn off the lights (especially the staterooms without a porthole). If you need it, bring a nightlight, leave the bathroom light on, or open your closet door a crack to trigger its automatic light. Tip: On the Dream Class, look for a switch at the desk for a nightlight above the sitting area.

Luggage—Once you've unpacked, you can store your empty luggage in the closet, or slide it under the bed. The clearance is 9" (Magic Class) or 13" (Dream Class). Lift up the bed and put the luggage underneath if you can't slide it, or ask your stateroom host/hostess if they can store your luggage (this is usually not an option). You'll have plenty of drawers handy when you unpack your belongings—there is a lot of storage in your stateroom!

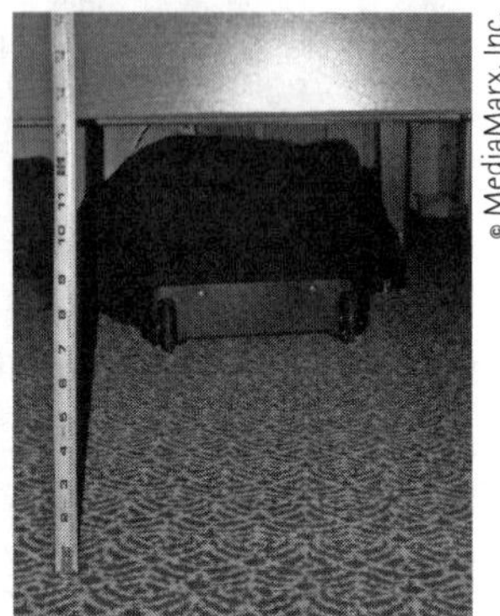
© MediaMarx, Inc.

Underbed space on the Dream/Fantasy

Messages—There is a variety of ways to leave and retrieve messages. First, the phone system allows you to call staterooms directly (dial 7 + the stateroom number) and leave voice mail messages. To check and retrieve your messages, just pick up the phone and press the "Messages" button. If you have messages, the light on your phone will blink until you listen to them. See page 150 for more details on the voice mail system. For a lower-tech message system, a decorative sea creature ornament outside your stateroom door serves as a message holder—you may find messages from crew members or fellow passengers. Third, we recommend you pack a pad of sticky notes—these are handy for messages to your roommates!

Phones—All staterooms have regular, in-room phones, in addition to new, portable "Wave Phones" (see below for details on those). For the most part, you'll use your stateroom phone to call other staterooms, room service, guest services, and other places on the ship. You can call locations off the ship for $6.95/minute at ship-to-shore rates (Disney uses SeaMobile—http://www.seamobile.com). You cannot call toll-free numbers from your stateroom phone, nor can you use calling cards. If someone needs to reach you while you're on the cruise, they can call toll-free 888-DCATSEA (callers from outside the United States can call +1-732-335-3281). Regardless of which number your caller uses, they will be prompted for a major credit card number. Your caller's card will be charged $6.95 for each minute the call is connected. A less expensive option may be to use your cell phone in your stateroom—see page 151 for details. Another possibility is to use your cell phone when in port and when sailing past islands with cell service (you'll need international roaming) or use a pay phone in port (bring calling cards). Castaway Cay has no pay phones, but it does have cellular coverage.

Portable "Wave Phones"—which look and feel like cell phones—are provided so you can stay in touch with your party while you're on the ship. You can send and receive calls and texts on these phones, but you can only use them to contact other Wave Phones or other phones on the ship. Each stateroom comes with two Wave Phones for complimentary use during the cruise. Additional Wave Phones can be rented for $3.50 per day per phone. The Wave Phones work most everywhere on the ship—even on Castaway Cay, but not in other ports. If you have children in the kids' clubs, the counselors will use your Wave Phone to contact you (rather than the old pager system). Note that you must sign a damage waiver prior to their use (at check-in) and you'll be charged $250 per phone for loss or damage. You may opt out of using these phones and have the service disconnected in your stateroom by contacting Guest Services. If you choose to carry the Wave Phone around with you, we recommend you not keep them in a pants pocket—we've heard reports of them slipping out easily. They do, however, fit neatly in a PassHolder Pouch—you can slip them in the large velcro pocket or slide them snugly into the small pocket on the back (see page 493 for details on the pouch.)

Wave Phones

Refrigerator—While it may be best described as a beverage cooler, there is a small refrigerator in the sitting area of your stateroom. It's cool enough to chill your drinks (roughly 55° F/13° C). It is large enough (8"d x 12"w x 16.5"h, or 20.3 cm. x 30.5 cm. x 50 cm. on the Magic Class and 5"d x 12.5"w x 18"h, or 12.5 cm. x 31.75 cm. x 45.7 cm. on the Dream Class) to store several bottles of water, cans of soda/beer, and a bottle of wine or champagne. It seems to work best when it's 3/4 full. There's also an ice bucket in the room, and you may request ice for it. Proper refrigerators can be requested to store medication.

A stateroom refrigerator on the Magic/Wonder

Room Service—Free room service is available 24 hours a day for most of your cruise. For details, see page 173. When your food arrives, guests on the Magic Class ships can raise their coffee table (it adjusts with a lever like an office chair), and use it as a dining table. Guests on the Dream Class ships can put their food on the desk or the top of the hassock.

Stateroom Amenities and Services *(continued)*

Safes—Every stateroom has its own safe in the closet—on the Magic Class they are roughly shoebox-sized (9"d x 6.5"h x 14"w, or 22.9 cm. x 16.5 cm. x 35.6 cm.), and on the Dream Class they are 14.5"d x 6"h x 12"w (37 cm. x 15 cm. x 30.5 cm.). The safes have a keypad that requires that you set and use a chosen four-digit code—pick something easy, but don't use 1-2-3-4 for the sake of security!

Smoking—Smoking is allowed on stateroom verandahs, but not in staterooms. Guests who are found smoking in staterooms will be charged a $250 stateroom recovery fee, which covers a deep cleaning to replace filters, extract carpet, and clean fabrics.

Special Needs—Handicap-accessible, barrier-free rooms (16 total available in categories S, 5, 6, 8, and 11 on the Magic Class, 37 total in categories V, T, 4, 5, 6, 8, 9, and 11 on the Dream Class) are larger—see photos on page 144. Special features include open bed frames, ramped bathroom thresholds, fold-down shower seats, rails, emergency call buttons, and lowered bars. To reserve a handicap-accessible stateroom, call Disney and request the special medical form. Guests with young kids may request bed railings, pack-and-play cribs, and high chairs from the stateroom host/hostess. Strollers are available on a first-come, first-served basis from Guest Services, as are wheelchairs for emergencies. If you need a wheelchair while onboard or in ports, bring your own, or if sailing from Port Canaveral, rent one through Brevard Medical Equipment with delivery and pickup right at the ship (call 866-416-7383 or visit http://www.brevardmedicalequip.com). Beach wheelchairs are available on a first-come basis at Castaway Cay.

Stateroom Door—All staterooms have a white, metal door with a magnetic or touch-style key card lock and an inside deadbolt. Many cruisers like to decorate their door with magnets (and only magnets—no tape or stickers allowed). It may be helpful to know that the standard door is 72" (six feet) tall and 27" wide, and the circular room number plaque is $7^1/_2$" in diameter.

Stateroom Host/Hostess—This crew member attends to all of your stateroom needs. Your stateroom host/hostess will tidy your stateroom once during the day and again in the evening while you're at dinner (turndown), but does not bring ice unless you request it. If you want ice, look for a small card from your stateroom host/hostess, tick the appropriate checkbox to request ice, and leave the card out in plain sight. See page 467 for tipping.

Television—All staterooms in categories 4–11 have 22" flat-screen TVs mounted on a swivel arm. Categories R, S, T, and V have multiple TVs, including at least one 42" flat screen. A printed channel listing with movie schedules is provided (see page 202 for a typical listing). Channels may change as you sail, especially when you're in port—expect to see some international networks show up on a channel or two. Special channels offer cruise details, such as "What's Afloat" and onboard shows. Recordings of special talks on golf, shore excursions, shopping, and debarkation are also shown. Check channel 13 to trace your voyage's progress and channel 12 for bridge reports and views, including the current time, weather conditions, etc. On the Dream Class you can also view your onboard photo portfolio and your room charges.

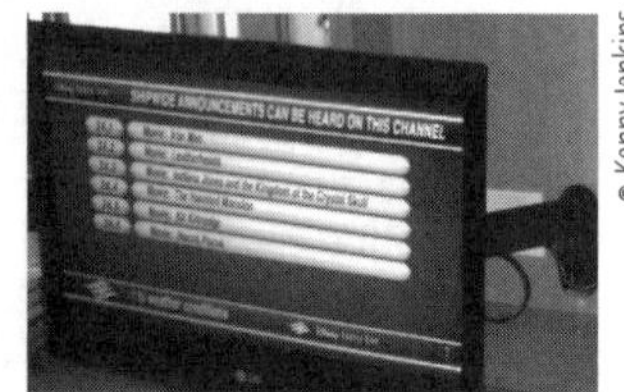

© Kenny Jenkins

Flat-screen TV

Temperature—Every stateroom has individual climate controls. The thermostat is normally located near the bed, high on the wall. If you get cold at night, there is an extra blanket—it's usually stored in a cupboard by the TV. Consider bringing a small, portable fan, especially if you are staying in an inside stateroom. The staterooms can get very humid and warm when several people take showers in quick succession.

© MediaMarx, Inc.
The generously sized toiletries

Toiletries—Your stateroom is stocked with H2O Plus Spa products, including Sea Marine Revitalizing Shampoo, Marine Collagen Conditioner, and Hydrating Body Butter, (all in 2.0-oz. size containers) plus Spa Facial Bar Soap (1.5 oz). Bath soap, tissues, and toilet paper are also provided. The concierge suites offer upgraded toiletries, including H2O Sea Salt Body Wash and Solar Relief Gel. For details on the products, see http://www.h2Oplus.com.

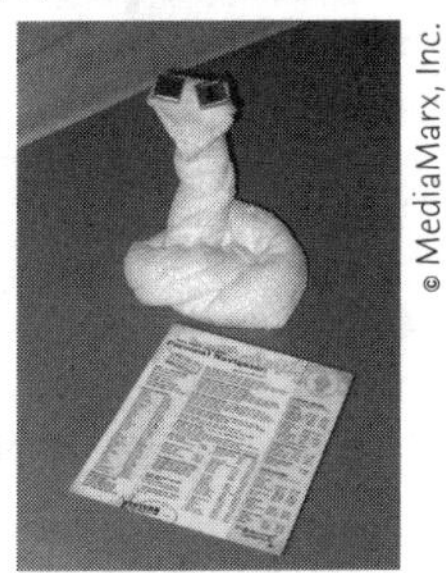
© MediaMarx, Inc.
A towel "snake"

Towel Animal—Don't be surprised to see a towel imaginatively folded and twisted into the shape of an animal on your bed at the end of the day. Disney's stateroom hosts and hostesses regularly create these "magical touches" for guests to discover in their staterooms. And if you have some props lying around, such as sunglasses, hats, or stuffed animals, your towel animal may become even more embellished. (Towel animal creation is up to the host or hostess, and there may be some that can't make them.) If towel animals interest you, look to see if a towel animal class is being offered in your *Personal Navigator*.

Will I Get a Free Upgrade?

Who wouldn't want a free upgrade to a "better" stateroom? It's the kind of perk that everyone wants, and plenty of cruisers look for ways to improve their chances of winning this particular lottery. Unfortunately, in all our time cruising, we've never discovered a foolproof system. And since upgrades are so unpredictable, our most important advice is this: Never, never book a room you won't be happy to spend your cruise in, should a hoped-for upgrade never materialize.

- Most upgrades occur well in advance of your cruise, as Disney tries to maximize occupancy. In fact, those upgrades often go completely unheralded. Watch your online reservation info, and look closely at your cruise documents when they arrive—if those stateroom numbers don't match your earlier reservation documents, check a deck plan—you've probably been upgraded! Other cruisers have been delighted to learn they've been upgraded when they check in at the terminal. You may be able to purchase an upgrade at check-in, too—just ask.
- Disney sometimes offers "guaranteed" ("GTY") staterooms—you're guaranteed to receive a stateroom in a particular or better category, but you won't be able to reserve a specific stateroom number or location. In exchange for giving the cruise line the flexibility to locate you wherever they please, you may get an upgrade.
- Disney may want to create vacancies in the lower-priced categories, which tend to sell better at the last minute than the higher-priced rooms. If someone is going to get that vacant verandah stateroom at a bargain price, it'll be someone who booked well in advance. Some folks intentionally "under-book" in the lowest categories in hopes of an upgrade, but again, be sure you'll be happy in a Cat. 11C stateroom.
- On longer cruises, there's higher demand for verandah staterooms and less for inside staterooms, so your chances of an upgrade from inside to outside may be quite low. If they need to "clear space" at all, the upgrade may go from verandah to suite.
- Off-season travelers may hope for an upgrade because there will be more vacancies aboard, but on the flip side, if Disney doesn't have to move you to make room for someone else, then you won't be going anywhere.
- With the new sub-category system, we think it's more likely you'll move up a sub-category within the same category than bump up a full category.

Introduction | Reservations | Staterooms | Dining | Activities | Ports of Call | Magic | Index

Stateroom Amenities and Services *(continued)*

Verandahs—All staterooms in categories 7 and up have a private verandah. A heavy, sliding glass door opens to reveal a deck as wide as your stateroom. Dividers offer privacy from your neighbors and the deck overhead protects you from most of the elements. The sliding door has a child-resistant latch that can be difficult to open at first—the trick is to grasp the handle and pull hard without turning. Turn the handle horizontally to lock the sliding door. Two plastic/fabric chairs and a small table are on most verandahs, along with an ashtray and two deck lights (the light switch is inside the stateroom, somewhat concealed by the curtains). The deck can be slippery, and the railing can be sticky from salty, moist air. Most verandahs have a clear plexiglass-and-metal railing that you can see through, while some staterooms in the aft have a solid railing—see photos on page 132. If you leave your verandah door open, your room can get warm and muggy quickly if you're in a hot climate. Parents should always supervise children when they're on the verandah. **When our son was three years old, he was able to climb up onto the arm of a deck chair within seconds—it's a very good thing we were right there to get him down!** If you are concerned about kids climbing on the deck furniture, you may ask to have it removed.

Voice Mail—As previously mentioned on page 147, each stateroom has its own voice mail. A red light on your phone will blink when you have a message—to check your message(s), just pick up the phone and press the "Messages" button. You can also personalize your outgoing message by following the prompts when you click "Messages." If you are on the phone when a call comes in, the voice mail system still takes your caller's message. We use the voice mail system quite a bit to stay in touch with one another—it's easy to pick up a "house phone" anywhere on board to leave a message with details on where we are and what we're doing. You may prefer to use Wave phones to reach people directly, rather than leave voice mail (see page 147).

Wake-Up Calls—A clock is provided in your stateroom, but the one on the Magic Class ships does not have a lighted dial or numbers. You may prefer to set wake-up calls from your stateroom phone. Try it at least once—Mickey Mouse himself calls you! Alternatives to the wake-up call service are to bring your own alarm clock, set the alarm on a portable electronic device you may have brought with you (such as a laptop, iPod, or iPhone), or preorder room service for breakfast (a crew member may even give you a reminder call before delivery).

Fitting In

If you're bringing a lot of stuff, or just packing a lot of people into your stateroom, where do you put all your stuff? We suggest you unpack everything you'll use into the available drawers and cupboards. Use all the hangers in your closet, too. Put your suitcases under the bed, along with anything you don't need on a daily basis. The hassock on the Dream Class opens for storage, too. Need more space? Take the blanket out of the cupboard by the TV or the hassock, and drape it across the sofa. You may be able to squeeze a few things on the top shelf in the closet, but don't move the life jackets. We store dirty laundry in our empty suitcases. Bulky items like car seats may fit in the space under the desk. After this, you can get creative by bringing and hanging organizer bags in the closet or on the back of the bathroom door (but be careful they do not cause damage to the door; if they do, you may be assessed a fine). We also recommend suction cup hooks for hanging light items on the back of the stateroom door and in the bathrooms (no self-adhesive hooks!). Strollers can be challenging—we suggest you bring an umbrella stroller that will fit in the closet when not in use. You may or may not be able to leave a stroller in the hallway—it depends on where your stateroom is located and if there's space available.

Staying Connected in Your Stateroom

Disney Cruise Line offers stateroom wireless Internet access and cell phone usage. We've used both and can offer tips for you to get the most out of your money and time.

Stateroom Wireless (WiFi) Internet Access–All staterooms have wireless (WiFi) access. Alas, we find the service to be spotty or sluggish, especially during peak usage times (late afternoon and evening). If you need the best connection, you'll still want to go out to one of the public "hot spots" (we recommend deck 4 or deck 5 midship)–see page 204 for details. But if you tend to check your mail late at night before bed, stateroom Internet access is extremely convenient. As to which staterooms have the best access, it's hard to say without testing each one. On our most recent cruises on the Magic Class ships, we had spotty service in our staterooms (both on deck 6). When our reception was bad, we walked down to deck 5 midship, where it was quite strong. In a pinch, we were able to position the laptop closer to the stateroom door for improved service.

© MediaMarx, Inc.

Our laptop connected!

Stateroom Cell Phone Usage–Disney has enabled cell phone usage in your stateroom (this is different from the Wave Phones–see page 147 for details). Once your ship is 8–10 miles out to sea, the Wireless Maritime Services (WMS) kick in and allow personal cell phone usage, but only in your stateroom. This "Cellular at Sea" service is available for most major cell phone carriers (such as AT&T, Verizon Wireless, Sprint, T-Mobile, Alltel, etc.), and your carrier bills you directly. No cell phone charges will appear from Disney on your cruise bill. If you plan to use your cell phone at sea, call your provider before leaving to check on rates and find out what is needed (such as international roaming). Don't assume that your cell phone won't work without international roaming turned on, however. To avoid unexpected charges, turn off your cell phone and other wireless devices while you're on your cruise, or use "airplane mode." We tested the service on a recent cruise and discovered that we were able to make a call from our stateroom without having turned on international roaming. When we checked our bill upon returning home, AT&T had charged us $2.50/minute. The charge appeared on our bill immediately, but be aware that these special usage charges can take up to 90 days to appear on a bill. Note that these cellular services are disabled while in a port, but you may be able to make cell phone calls using the port's cellular networks anyway. Look for a brochure in your stateroom that explains the current Cellular at Sea service in detail.

I Cruise, iPhone

Yes, we have iPhones... and we successfully used them on our last ten cruises! If you have one of these extremely handy devices, you should know that you probably don't need to specifically enable international roaming to send and receive cell calls while at sea. Thus, put your iPhone in "Airplane Mode" to avoid problems such as incoming calls, e-mail auto-checks, or weather checks. On the other hand, you can use Disney's WiFi network on your iPhone if you wish–you can leave it in Airplane Mode, turn on WiFi, locate the "MTN-DSI" network and connect to it (don't connect to the crew network–that will cause login problems later), then go to Safari and log in as you would if you were on a laptop. When you're done, turn off WiFi to prevent unwanted charges. More tips at http://www.passporter.com/iphone.asp.

Rocking to Sleep

Sleeping on a moving vessel can be a magical experience. Make more magic in your stateroom with these tips:

- Bring something from home to **personalize your stateroom**, like a photo in a frame, a bouquet of silk flowers, or a radio or CD player. You can also decorate your stateroom door (see page 460).
- **Make every bit of space count!** After you unpack, stash your empty luggage under the bed and use one (or more) suitcases for your dirty laundry and another for souvenirs.
- Consider bringing a **clear shoe organizer** and hanging it up in your closet or on the back of your bathroom door, being careful it does not damage the door, of course. It keeps all those little items that can clutter your stateroom organized.
- The Disney Dream Class staterooms have many **light switches**. One controls a night light, which is a very nice addition. And if you have an inside room with a Virtual Porthole, there's a switch by the bed for that, too—no need to close a blackout curtain!
- "There are minimal outlets in the staterooms and with all the technology most travelers bring along these days, it helps to pack a **lightweight powerstrip**. We found one with three outlets plus a USB outlet, perfect for charging our iPods. I've really never had a need for more than three items plugged in at once, so this worked out great on our cruise." – contributed by an anonymous Disney cruiser
- "Have family, want space, but not the cost of two adjoining veranda cabins? **Book one verandah stateroom** and the inside stateroom across the hallway. You have separate sleeping areas, but are close enough that people can pop in and out and share the space." – contributed by Disney cruiser Mary Albright

Magical Memories

- *"The Royal Suites on the Dream and Fantasy are remarkable for their generous outdoor space. While the verandahs on the older ships are just long, narrow balconies, the new suites' huge deck areas and curved window walls suggest luxurious homes high in the Hollywood Hills, overlooking the city. You could host the kind of indoor/outdoor cocktail party you see only in the movies!"*

...as told by author Dave Marx

Dining on the High Seas

DECIDE how and when to dress for dinner

EXPLORE the various restaurant menus

Cruises are famous for food—buffet breakfasts, brunches, snacks, pool-side lunches, high tea, elegant dinners, dessert buffets, and room service! You won't be disappointed by the food on the Disney Cruise Line. Sure, there's plenty of it—we like to say, "If you're hungry, you're not trying hard enough." More important, in our opinion, is the quality of the food. As restaurant critics, we pay attention to food—presentation, preparation, quality, and taste. We would grade virtually every dish we tried during our cruises as a B or B+, and dining on the new Disney ships has bumped things up another notch. There were some disappointments, sure, but in general, we've been very happy cruisers with no rumblies in our tummies.

In all fairness, we have heard a few complaints about the food from other cruisers. Some feel there should be even more food offered, like on some other cruise lines. (Our poor waistlines!) Others feel the food options are too exotic for their tastes (and Disney has since added some simpler choices to the menus). Yet others say the food isn't as "gourmet" as some European lines. Vegetarian and sugar-free dessert options were considered lackluster, but Disney has made dramatic improvements there, too. Most cruisers, however, rave about the food onboard.

Dining options abound during your cruise. On the **Magic Class**: **Breakfast**—Topsider's/Beach Blanket Buffet, Lumière's/Triton's, Parrot Cay, or Palo Brunch. **Lunch**—Topsider's/Beach Blanket Buffet, Pluto's Dog House, Pinocchio's Pizzeria, Lumière's/Triton's, or Parrot Cay. **Snacks**—Goofy's Galley, Pluto's Dog House, or Pinocchio's Pizzeria. **Dinner**—Lumière's/Triton's, Animator's Palate, Parrot Cay, or Palo. Topsider's/Beach Blanket Buffet may also be open for dinner. (Dining options change on the Disney Magic, debuting in late October 2013.) On the **Dream Class**: **Breakfast**—Cabanas, Royal Palace/Royal Court, Enchanted Garden, or Palo Brunch. **Lunch**—Cabanas, Flo's Cafè, Royal Palace/Royal Court, or Enchanted Garden. **Snacks**—Flo's Cafè. **Dinner**—Royal Palace/Royal Court, Enchanted Garden, Animator's Palate, Palo, or Remy. Cabanas may also be open. On **all ships**, room service is always an option, and theme dinners and dessert buffets are held on special nights. Whew! Read on to learn about Disney's innovative dining rotations and your delicious choices. Bon appetit!

Introduction | Reservations | Staterooms | Dining | Activities | Ports of Call | Magic | Index

Rotational Dining

Unlike other ships that stick you in one dining room throughout your cruise, the Disney ships offer **three uniquely themed dining rooms** for all. Your family rotates together through these dining rooms during your cruise, enjoying a different menu each evening. Best of all, your tablemates and servers rotate with you. You can bypass the regular rotation and choose an adults-only restaurant, one of several snack counters, or room service—a buffet restaurant may also be open. You'll find it hard to do them all!

You learn your **dining room rotation** on your first day—look for a set of "tickets" in your stateroom indicating which dining rooms your party is assigned to for dinner on each day. The tickets are not required to dine, but they do help the servers direct you to your table. Your dining rotation is also printed in code on your Key to the World card (i.e., "PTA," "APPT," or "LAPLAPL"), like the one on page 88. This code indicates your rotation: L,T, or R= Lumière's/Triton's/Royal Palace/Royal Court, A = Animator's Palate, and P or E = Parrot Cay/Enchanted Garden. Your rotation is occasionally based on the ages of guests in your party. Rotation dining only applies to dinner, and breakfast on debarkation day. Breakfast and lunch are open seating—dine where you wish (see page 161). (Tip: Some readers report that Disney told them their dining rotation when they phoned and asked.)

There are **two dinner seatings**: main (first) seating and late (second) seating. Your seating is noted in your cruise documents. Main seating is typically 5:45 or 6:00 pm, and late seating is at 8:15 pm. Dinner lasts from 1 ½ to 2 hours. Guests with main seating watch the evening show after dinner, while guests with late seating see the early show. If you have a seating preference (see page 175 for tips), have it noted on your reservation prior to cruising. Parties with younger kids tend to get assigned the main seating, though with so many families on board, that's not a sure thing. Families on second seating with children 3–12 can use **Dine and Play** (see page 171).

Your **assigned table number** is also printed on your dinner tickets and your Key to the World card, and you'll have the same table number at dinner in all three of the main dining rooms. Table assignments are affected by factors like age and association (i.e., Disney Vacation Club members may be seated together); your stateroom category does not affect your table assignment. You can be seated with your traveling companions—call the cruise line well ahead of your cruise with your request. Table sizes range from four to twenty guests, but most tables seat eight. To switch to another table, check your *Personal Navigator* for a Dining Assignment Change session (held on your first afternoon) or see your head server.

Dressing for Dinner

"How should I dress for dinner?" If we had a nickel for everyone who asks! Whether you itch to **relive the elegance of days gone by**, or can't stand the thought of being bound into a "penguin suit," you'll find a happy welcome on your Disney cruise. Different itineraries call for slightly different wardrobes, as we describe below, and once you're aboard, you can also refer to your Personal Navigator for the evening's suggested dress.

In keeping with its **guest-friendly policies**, Disney doesn't strictly enforce dress codes. They rarely deny guests access to a dining room, though they do ask that you wear shoes and shirts and refrain from wearing bathing attire in the main dining rooms. You should also refrain from wearing shorts at dinner, though jeans are okay everywhere but at Palo, Remy, and on formal night.

Three-, Four, and Five-Night Itineraries—At dinner in the main, "rotational" dining rooms, men wear casual, open-collared shirts (such as polo or camp shirts) and slacks (such as khakis), and women wear a blouse and skirt or casual dress. The exception is the "Dress-Up Night" (third night of the three- and five-night cruise and second night of the four-night cruise), for which dressier attire is suggested. For "Dress-Up Night" and Palo, upscale casual dress (or nicer) is appropriate—men's jackets are commonly worn, but not required. At Remy, jackets are required for men, and the ladies are expected to don dresses or pantsuits.

Seven-Night and longer Itineraries—Suggested dress for longer itineraries follows a similar pattern, but adds one Formal Night, and Semi-Formal Night replaces Dress-Up Night (though suggested dress is the same for either). A second Formal or Semi-Formal Night is possible on the longest itineraries—see page 458 for details and tips on formal nights.

All Itineraries—On one evening, Disney suggests Pirate or casual dress for its Pirates IN the Caribbean night (see page 167). Many find it easiest to dress in a tropical shirt or dress. A fair number get into the spirit of the occasion and bring pirate accessories or even full costumes from home or the parks, or buy them onboard.

Disney requests that guests dress for dinner as it sets a **special atmosphere** in the evenings. The Disney vessels are elegant ships—dressing for dinner shows respect for the occasion, the atmosphere, and your fellow guests. We understand that some guests aren't comfortable in a jacket or suit, and that's okay, too—you'll see a wide range of dress, even on Formal Night. Don't want to change out of those shorts? Fast food is available on deck 9/11 (see page 168). Topsider's Buffet/Beach Blanket Buffet/Cabanas (deck 9/11 aft) may also be open for dinner for those guests who don't wish to get dressed up.

Special Diets

Guests with **special dietary requirements** of virtually any type (i.e., kosher, low-sodium, allergies, etc.) are accommodated. When you make your reservation, let the representative know about any requirements. The representative notes the information with your reservation and may instruct you to meet with the Food/Beverage team after you board—they are usually available in Rockin' Bar D/WaveBands/D Lounge from 1:00 pm to 3:30 pm on your first day—check your *Personal Navigator*. The Food/Beverage team gets details from you and passes it on to your servers. We recommend you remind your server of your requests at your first meal. Jennifer is lactose-intolerant and requests soy milk with her meals—the attention to her request is impressive and she is always offered soy milk.

While Disney excels at these special, pre-cruise requests, we found it **more difficult to get a special dish or variant** ordered at meal time. For example, it generally isn't possible to order a dish from the menu and have sauces or dressings kept on the side. This is because the dishes are prepared *en masse* in the kitchen. However, you can order a plain salad or simple entrée (vegetarian, grilled chicken, etc.). If it's not already on the menu, ask your server. We note the vegetarian items in the menus later in the chapter. Kosher is only available in the table-service restaurants and you should request it before the cruise to ensure availability.

Will I Gain Weight on My Cruise?

Short answer: No, you don't have to gain weight on your Disney cruise! Long answer: Cruises are renowned for their ability to add inches to your waistline. All that scrumptious, "free" food can send your diet overboard. But if you're determined to maintain your weight and healthy eating habits, it's not at all difficult to do. Your authors successfully maintain their weight on cruises while still enjoying treats. The first key is **moderation**. Eat well—don't restrict yourself too severely and don't overeat. Not only is it okay to sample a little of everything, it's a good idea—if you deny yourself, you'll likely break down halfway through your cruise and eat everything in sight. Remember that just because the food is included with your cruise doesn't mean you have to overindulge. If the temptation seems too great, grab some of the delicious fruit available at Goofy's Galley/Flo's Café (deck 9/11). If you just can't resist that chocolate ice cream cone, order one, eat half, and ditch the rest. You'll also find that buffet meals may actually be easier for you—there are more food choices. The second key to maintaining your weight is **activity**. Most of you will be more active than usual on your cruise—swimming, snorkeling, biking, and walking around the ports. Take advantage of every opportunity to move your body! You can walk a mile every morning around deck 4 (it takes three laps on the Magic/Wonder; 2.5 laps on the Dream/Fantasy), take the stairs instead of the elevator, and enjoy free exercise classes at the Vista/Senses Spa (deck 9/11 forward). Check your *Personal Navigator* for a session at the spa that shows you how to lose weight on your cruise, too.

For more tips, surf to: http://www.passporter.com/wdw/healthyeating.htm

Lumière's/Triton's/Royal Palace/Royal Court

Have you ever yearned to dine elegantly in a gorgeous, grand dining room aboard a majestic ocean liner? This is your chance. On the Disney Magic, the grandest dining room is known as Lumière's; on the Disney Wonder, it's called Triton's, on the Disney Dream, Royal Palace, and on the Disney Fantasy, Royal Court. All are located next to the ships' breathtaking lobby atrium on deck 3 midship and serve breakfast, lunch, and dinner. Breakfast and lunch have open seating—just show up when and where you like.

Decor—Lumière's (Magic) has a decidedly French flair, just like its namesake, the saucy candelabra in Disney's *Beauty and the Beast*. Rose-petal chandeliers, inlaid marble floors, and graceful columns set the mood for elegance and romance. Large portholes look out to the sea on one side of the restaurant. A mural depicting a waltzing Beauty and her Beast adorns the back wall. Look for the glass domes suspended from the ceiling—inside each is Beast's red rose. **Triton's (Wonder)** takes you "under the sea" with Ariel's father from Disney's *The Little Mermaid*. The Art Nouveau-inspired dining room is decorated in soft colors with blue glass-and-iron "lilypads" floating on the ceiling. A breathtaking Italian glass mosaic of Triton and Ariel graces the back wall. The lighting changes during the dinner, casting an "under the sea" effect. **Royal Palace (Dream)** is an elegant dining room with French accents influenced by Disney's Cinderella. Servers wear the formal, military-style dress seen at Cinderella's Royal Ball. Paintings of the Disney Princesses line the walls, and the many decorative accents, from chair-back carvings to marble-inlaid floors refer to Snow White, Cinderella, Sleeping Beauty, and Beauty and the Beast. **Royal Court (Fantasy)** is quite similar to Royal Palace, although the principal princess portraits (say that three times fast) are Venetian glass mosaics, and the overall color scheme is brighter, with less dark wood, more gold accents, and Art Nouveau touches.

Dinner Dress—Unless the evening is formal, semi-formal/dress-up, or "pirate" (see 155 and 458), dress is cruise casual: nice slacks and collared shirts for men and dresses/pantsuits for women. No shorts, please.

Our Review—The elegant setting is the restaurants' best feature. These are the only restaurants offering full table service at breakfast (Magic and Wonder) and lunch (all ships). The table service breakfast here is good, but service is slow. Lunch is enjoyable, but portions may seem small. Breakfast and lunch selections are limited compared to the buffets. The extra elegance at dinner is a treat, and the Continental-style meals are finely prepared. Our favorite rotational dining rooms on the Magic and Wonder. Jennifer and Dave's rating: 8/10.

Royal Palace on the Disney Dream

➤

Lumière's/Triton's/Royal Palace/Royal Court Sample Menus

While we can't predict exactly what you'll be offered, we can share menu highlights from past cruises. Menus vary somewhat from ship to ship, so not all items will be on your menu. We've underlined those menu items we and our fellow cruisers have enjoyed and recommend that you try.

Breakfast (a la carte Magic Class, buffet Dream Class) a la carte choices: **chilled juices** (orange, grapefruit, cranberry, prune, V-8, apple, tomato); **fresh fruit** (grapefruit, melon, banana, fruit cocktail); **yogurt** (fruit and plain yogurt, assorted low-fat yogurt); **hot cereal** (oatmeal, Cream of Wheat); **cold cereal** (Corn Flakes, Raisin Bran, Rice Krispies, Frosted Flakes, low-fat granola, Froot Loops); **Muesli** (mixture of toasted whole grain flakes, oatmeal, raisins, berries, yogurt, milk, and honey); **lox and bagel** (served with cream cheese); **pastries** (Danish pastries, muffins, croissants, bagels, donuts, English muffins, toast–white, wheat, or rye); **chef's selection** (scrambled eggs, bacon, grilled sausage, oven-roasted potatoes or hash browns); **eggs Benedict**; **eggs to order** (scrambled, fried, poached, or boiled–with oven-roasted potatoes and your choice of breakfast meat: grilled sausage, grilled ham, or bacon); **omelets** (Denver, ham and cheese, plain, Egg Beaters–with potatoes or hash browns); **hot off the griddle** (buttermilk pancakes, blueberry pancakes, French toast, waffles); **beverages** (coffee–regular or decaffeinated, assorted teas, hot chocolate, milk–whole, low-fat, skim, or chocolate).

Lunch *(menu changes daily)*
starters (shrimp cocktail, chips and salsa, roasted vegetable tart, hummus "chickpea" dip, curried pumpkin soup, Roquette salad, or sesame seed tuna); **main courses** (mushroom risotto, classic Reuben sandwich, barbecue pork ribs, traditional American meatloaf, broiled filet of tilapia, grilled chicken, or traditional hamburger); **desserts** (banana cream pie, hot apple 'n' pineapple crunch, double chocolate cake, key lime pie, or chef's sugar-free dessert).

Dinner *(first rotational visit only)*
appetizers (ratatouille, bacon and mushroom tart, spinach soufflé, duck confit, escargot); **soups and salads** (tomato and basil soup, onion soup, cauliflower cream soup, avocado citrus salad, mixed garden salad); **main courses** (grilled beef tenderloin and lobster medallions, seared sea bass, braised lamb shank, roasted duck breast, rack of lamb, roasted wild boar tenderloin, three-cheese lobster ravioli, grilled chicken breast, or vegetarian selections–mushroom-stuffed ravioli and grilled tofu with roasted vegetables); **desserts** (brioche and pannetone pudding, Grand Marnier soufflé, crème brûlée, chocolate mousse; trio of crème brûlée, peanut butter mousse and mango cheesecake, ice cream sundae, or sugar-free dessert–seasonal fruits, chocolate cheesecake, or sugar-free ice cream).

Tip: No matter where you dine, you'll find simpler and healthier choices on each menu, like grilled steak, roasted chicken breast, and baked salmon.

Dessert Buffets
You've saved room for dessert, right? On select nights of your cruise (any length), a fruit and dessert spread of monumental proportions may be laid out for your gastronomic pleasure. Check your *Personal Navigator* for days, times, and locations. Typically, this is held on Pirates IN the Caribbean Night from 10:45 to 11:15 or 11:30 pm on deck 9 by the Goofy Pool (Magic Class) or on deck 11 in Cabanas (Dream Class). Generally, this has replaced the Midnight Gala Dessert Buffet held in one of the rotational dining rooms, but that may still appear on some itineraries.

In late October 2013 a renewed Animator's Palate debuts on the Disney Magic, with HD video screens and two shows: a new take on the classic show, "Drawn to Magic," and "Animation Magic," as seen on the Disney Fantasy.

Animator's Palate

Disney's true colors shine in this imaginative restaurant that regales you with a show. Animator's Palate—which serves dinner only—is located on deck 4 aft (Magic Class) and deck 3 aft (Dream Class).

Decor—On the **Magic Class ships**, entering this large, windowless restaurant is like walking into a black-and-white sketchpad, the walls covered in line drawings of classic Disney characters. Where's all the color? As each course is served, color is added to the walls and ceilings, and the drawings come to life in full intensity in time to a wonderful musical score. The "show" is limited to your first or second visit; on subsequent evenings, there's no "show" (that's a good time to visit Palo or Remy). On the **Dream Class ships**, you enter an animator's studio, with wooden display cases and large video screens lining the walls. Reference drawings abound, and the shelves are filled with the animators' personal tchotchkes. On the Dream the show is, "Undersea Magic" featuring Crush from Disney/Pixar's *Finding Nemo*, who chats with the guests! On the Fantasy, due to her longer itineraries, there are two different shows. On your first rotational visit you're treated to "Undersea Magic" with Crush. On your second rotational visit, "Animation Magic," hosted by Sorcerer Mickey, honors classic Disney animation. Guests are invited to sketch characters before the meal, and at dinner's end, their sketches come to life as part of the show. During dinner a delightful "remix" style animation montage sets the mood.

Dress—Unless the evening is formal, semi-formal/dress-up, or "pirate" (see page 155 and 458), dress is resort casual. Polo and camp shirts are fine, but please don't wear shorts.

Our Review—Animator's Palate is a fun place for all ages. The "shows" are breathtaking and food is enjoyable, with Italian or Pacific Rim flavors that offer enough choices to please most palates. Service is fine, though on the Magic and Wonder you may feel rushed or stymied as servers have to keep pace with the show. When you arrive at the table, try to pick a seat with a view of one of the video screens on the walls. Jennifer and Dave's rating: 7.5/10.

Animator's Palate on the Disney Dream

Dining Room Etiquette

Don't worry—thanks to Disney's family atmosphere, there's no finicky, starched-up rule of etiquette here. Just remember to arrive on time for dinner, greet your tablemates and servers with a smile, place your napkin in your lap, and have your meal and beverage orders ready for your servers. If the elegant table confuses you, keep in mind that your bread plate is always on the left, your glasses are always on the right, utensils are used from the outside in, and wine glasses are held by the stem for white wine and by the base for red wine. When you get up from the table before you've finished eating, place your napkin on your chair to indicate you will be returning again. At the end of your meal, place your unfolded napkin on the table.

Animator's Palate Sample Menu

Dinner at Animator's Palate *(for your first rotational visit only)*

Appetizers (tuna tartare, mushroom risotto, black truffle pasta pursiettes, roma tomato and portobello mushrooms on polenta cake); **soups and salads** (chilled gazpacho, butternut squash soup, confetti tomato salad, smoked salmon and trout); **main courses** (penne Alfredo with turkey and prosciutto, grilled black cod, trio of veal, lemon-thyme marinated chicken, Asian-marinated beef short ribs, five-spiced fish, roasted chicken breast, salmon fillet, or vegetarian selection–potato and pea samosas, black bean chipotle cakes, stir-fry vegetables); **desserts** (strawberry sable, cranberry and orange cheesecake, lemon mousse, dessert sampler trio, dense chocolate cake, ice cream sundae, or sugar-free dessert–seasonal fruits, chilled lemon souffle̊).

An Armchair Galley Tour

Ever wonder how they prepare so much food for so many people? Adults on itineraries with at-sea days (four-night and up) usually have the opportunity to take a free galley (kitchen) tour. The 30-minute, adults-only walking tour starts in Lumière's/Triton's/Royal Palace/Royal Court, walks through the galley, and ends up on the other side at Parrot Cay/Animator's Palate. If you don't have the opportunity to experience this glimpse into the ship's inner workings, here's our armchair version:

The Disney Cruise Line galleys are big, immaculately clean, stainless steel kitchens that gleam with organization. There are six/seven galleys –three main banqueting kitchens, a crew kitchen, Topsider's/Beach Blanket Buffet/Cabanas, Palo, and Remy. In these galleys are at least 9 chefs, 120 cooks, 88 stewards, 12 provision masters, and 150 servers and assistant servers. Galleys are inspected constantly for cleanliness, safety, and food safety–the Captain himself performs inspections. Disney has a shopping list of 30,000 food items for each cruise! With more than 8,000 cups of coffee and more than 5,000 eggs served every day (and roughly 50% more on the Dream Class ships), you can imagine the size of that grocery bill! Most of the food for your voyage is brought on in your embarkation port, though longer cruises may restock at intermediate ports.

The first things you see upon entering the galley are the beverage dispensers–this is how your servers get your drink refills so quickly. Then comes the kids' food station–it's separated from other food prep areas to allow servers to get kids' meals out to the hungry munchkins as soon as possible.

Next we come to the hot food preparation areas of the galley. Did you know that nothing is prepared ahead of time (with the exception of some veggies)? There's a butcher room with four cooks and a fish room with two cooks below decks where the meats are prepared and portioned. The meats are then sent up to the galley to be seasoned and cooked based on each guest's preferences. Once cooked, the plates are cleaned and garnished based on photographs of how each dish should appear, and below each photograph is a list of the dish's ingredients, allowing the servers to spot potential allergens for guests. The servers then come in to pick up the various plates they "ordered" earlier, covering each dish with a warming lid to keep it toasty during its trip to your table. It's quite a production that goes on behind the scenes.

Beyond the hot food prep areas is the pastry prep area. There are four pastry chefs onboard. There's even a 24-hour bakery below decks that keeps churning out fresh baked goods throughout your cruise. And the tour comes to a sweet ending with chocolate chip cookies for everyone!

A pastry chef at work

➤

In late October 2013 Parrot Cay on the Disney Magic becomes Rio de Janeiro-inspired Carioca's. Like Enchanted Garden, the all-new decor will change moods between the daytime buffet and the full service dinner, and the buffet line will be hidden.

Parrot Cay/Enchanted Garden

Parrot Cay (pronounced "key") is the Magic Class' Caribbean-styled dining room on deck 3 aft, serves a Caribbean grill-inspired menu. **Enchanted Garden**, the Dream Class' conservatory garden-inspired dining room on deck 2 mid, offers international cuisine with French and Asian accents. The restaurants serve buffet breakfast and lunch with open seating, plus full service, rotational dinner.

© MediaMarx, Inc.

Enchanted Garden

Decor—The first thing you may notice at **Parrot Cay** is the cacophony of colors and sounds, with the sounds of parrots and parrot chandeliers that evoke the Enchanted Tiki Room, and lush tropical greens and oranges on the walls and floors. Large portholes line two sides of the restaurant, affording beautiful views. **Enchanted Garden** evokes an airy, Belle Époque garden conservatory on the grounds of France's Palace of Versailles, and delivers a subtle "show" where the lighting changes from day to night during dinner.

Dinner Dress—Unless the evening is formal, semi-formal/dress-up, or "pirate" (see page 155 and 458), dress is resort casual. No shorts at dinner.

Our Reviews—Parrot Cay's grillhouse-inspired dinner menu is very satisfying, with some stand-out items, and the daytime buffets are fresh, appealing, and generous. Alas, Parrot Cay is the noisiest dining room. Our rating: 7/10. (This is often the restaurant we skip for Palo.) Dinner at **Enchanted Garden** is excellent, with French-inspired cuisine in a restful setting. The daytime buffet selections are limited, but very satisfying. Our rating: 8/10

Open Seating at Breakfast and Lunch

Breakfast and lunch are usually open seating, meaning you dine where and when you please, and you don't sit at your assigned table—you are seated by a crew member. If you'd like your regular servers at breakfast or lunch, just ask to be seated at their table (if it's available and if they're on duty). Better yet, ask your servers at dinner where they are serving the following day and follow them to that restaurant.

Parrot Cay/Enchanted Garden Sample Menus

Buffet Breakfast

You can usually find fresh fruit, cereals (hot and cold), yogurt, smoked salmon, assorted pastries, scrambled eggs, bacon, link sausage, ham, hash browns, pancakes, waffles, or French toast. A made-to-order omelet station is often available.

Character Breakfast *(seven-night cruises, Magic class only; seating at 8:00 or 8:15 am for main seating guests and 9:30 or 9:45 am for those with late seating)*

Special Goofy combination plate for children (scrambled eggs, chocolate pancake, Mickey waffle, and Canadian bacon); **chilled juices** (orange, grapefruit, and cranberry); **fresh fruit and yogurt** (sliced fruit, grapefruit, plain and fruit yogurt, and low-fat yogurt); **cereals** (Cream of Wheat, Corn Flakes, Raisin Bran, KO's, Rice Krispie, and Frosted Flakes); **lox and bagel** (served with cream cheese); **pastries** (Danish pastries, muffins, croissants, donuts, and toast–white, wheat, or rye); **express breakfast** (scrambled eggs, bacon, link sausage, and hash browns); **breakfast classics** (scrambled or fried eggs served with hash browns and your choice of bacon, link sausage, or ham); **omelets** (plain or ham and cheese–served with hash browns, Egg Beaters available); **hot off the griddle** (buttermilk pancakes or blueberry pancakes); **beverages** (coffee–regular or decaf, assorted teas, hot chocolate, milk–whole, low-fat, skim, or chocolate); **preserves** (assorted jellies, jams, and marmalades).

Lunch Buffet

The buffet on the seven-night cruises changes daily: day one–welcome aboard buffet; day two–Italian buffet; day three–Asian buffet; day four–American buffet; day five–South of the Border buffet; and day six–seafood buffet. On the Disney Dream, brunch is served until 11:30 am on day two and, on the four-night itinerary, the Oriental buffet is served on the at-sea day. The menu that is offered at Cookie's BBQ on Castaway Cay is also offered at Enchanted Garden onboard the ship (all suitable itineraries).

Dinner *(for your first rotational visit only)*

Appetizers (grilled squash and mozzarella stack with tomato, spicy chicken tenderloins, baked crab Martinique, ahi tuna and avocado tower, lobster ravioli); **soups and salads** (cold cream of mango and papaya soup, cream of asparagus soup, West Indies romaine salad, baby spinach salad); **main courses** (grilled rib-eye of beef, mixed grill, pan-seared grouper, Caribbean roast chicken, caramelized sea scallops, braised Jerk-seasoned pork chop, NY strip steak with herb butter, baked salmon, or vegetarian selections–pearl barley cakes over sautéed vegetables or glazed portobello mushrooms); **desserts** (crème brûlée cheesecake, banana bread pudding, lemon meringue pie, chocolate s'more vanilla cake, sampler trio, Sacher torte, steamed lemon pudding, or sugar-free dessert–piña colada bread pudding, cheesecake, chocolate mousse, or sugar-free ice cream)

Character Breakfast (Magic Class only)

Seven-night and up cruisers have a special treat–an invitation to a character breakfast in Parrot Cay (see menu above). Typically Mickey, Minnie, Goofy, Pluto, Chip, and Dale show up in tropical garb. The characters put on a show for you and walk through the aisles, but please note that the characters do not *usually* visit tables to greet guests. Expect lots of energy, napkin-waving, character dancing, and loud music. This character meal reminds us of Chef Mickey's at the Contemporary in Walt Disney World. Character breakfasts are offered at two seatings (guests with earlier seating at dinner will have the earlier seating at breakfast). Character breakfasts usually take place on days at sea. Your server may present your tickets on the evening before, or they may be left in your stateroom–bring them with you to breakfast. Character breakfasts are not offered on the Dream Class ships at this time, reportedly because of the number of tables that would have to be visited in those large dining rooms.

As part of the Disney Magic's overhaul in late 2013, the decor at Palo will be refreshed.

Palo

Palo is an optional, adults-only restaurant on all ships, offering Northern Italian cuisine, an intimate setting, and phenomenal service. Guests must secure reservations to dine here and and there is a $20 per-person service charge for either dinner or brunch. Palo has its own servers, so be prepared to part with your regular servers. Palo is on deck 10 (Magic Class) or 12 aft (Dream Class) and serves dinner nightly from 6:00 pm until 9:00 or 10:00 pm. A wine tasting seminar may also be offered here (see page 209), as well as a champagne brunch (four-night and up cruises)—see page 164. High Tea was discontinued in August 2012, in favor of a second brunch seating.

Reservations—Reservations for all Palo meals can and should be made in advance at http://www.disneycruise.com once your cruise is paid in full. Reservations can be made as early as 75 days in advance by first-time Disney cruisers, 120 days for categories R-V, and 90/105/120 days for Castaway Club members (see page 470). Online reservations open at midnight Eastern Time, and go very fast! Disney holds some reservations at each of those intervals and on board, so everyone at least stands a chance. Only one online dinner and one brunch reservation per stateroom is allowed. You may also make reservations and changes on your first afternoon aboard—check the *Personal Navigator* for the time and place. Dispatch one member of your party, as soon as you can after you board—reservations go quickly. Arm your representative with a list of suitable days and times (use our worksheet on page 177). If you can't get reservations, get on the wait list and check for cancellations. Concierge guests (cat. R-V) can ask their concierge to make reservations for them. Reservations can be canceled without penalty up until 2:00 pm on the day of the meal. No-shows and last-minute cancellations will have the full $20 per person charged to their room.

Decor—Palo's most striking feature is its sweeping ocean views—we have fond memories of a meal served just as the sun set. Warm wood paneling, Venetian glass, and smaller tables (yes, you can get a table for two here!) make this one of the most romantic spots onboard. An exhibition kitchen and wine displays set the stage for a special dining experience. There's also a private room area called "The Captain's Table" tucked in the corner for groups. The Dream Class adds an outdoor dining deck (weather permitting) and a live pianist, and one side of the dining room offers raised, padded banquettes.

Dress—Dress shirts or jackets for men; dresses or pantsuits for women. Formalwear is welcome. No jeans, swimwear, or tank tops (these restrictions are enforced).

Gratuities—$5 of the service charge is divided amongst the staff, but we recommend an additional tip in line with your estimation of the value of the meal. Note that a 15% auto-gratuity is already added to all alcoholic beverage purchases.

Our Review—We simply adore Palo! The servers are friendly, engaging, and incredibly attentive. The restaurant is quiet and mellow, and the atmosphere elegant but relaxed. The best part of dining at Palo, however, is the food—it's simply outstanding, as items are made or finished to order. We also highly recommend Palo brunch. Jennifer and Dave's rating: 9/10.

Palo on the Disney Dream

Palo Sample Menus

Dinner at Palo *($20/person service charge; menu doesn't change; daily specials)* **Starters and salads** (sautéed eggplant, mozzarella and plum tomatoes, warm shrimp salad, grilled portobello and polenta, fried calamari, tuna carpaccio, arugula salad; **soup** (Tuscan white bean or traditional fish and seafood soup); **main courses** (pan-seared turbot, grilled tuna, halibut al cartoccio, grilled sea scallops, rack of lamb, chicken braciolo, beef tenderloin, osso buco, penne arrabbiata, lobster ravioli, pumpkin and broccoli gnocchi, bigoli alla contadina, seafood risotto, mushroom risotto, vegetable and bean casserole); **desserts** (tiramisu, panna cotta, chocolate soufflé with vanilla bean sauce, sweet pizza, chocolate amaretto torte, pineapple and almond ravioli, assorted gelato). Palo's excellent pizzas are no longer on the dinner menu, but it never hurts to ask.

Champagne Brunch *($20/person) –offered on cruises with at-sea days, including the 4-night cruise. A second brunch seating was added in mid-2012 to allow more guests to enjoy this hard-to-reserve meal. High Tea was discontinued in order to make that possible.* Buffet of assorted traditional breakfast and lunch items: **breakfast items** (cereals, breakfast breads, Danish pastries, specialty eggs, and pancakes); **lunch items** (shrimp, grilled marinated vegetables, Alaskan King Crab legs, smoked salmon & mixed greens, selection of cheeses and meats, pizzas, and garlic roasted tenderloin); and **desserts** (fresh fruit and berries, tiramisu, lemon meringue pie, and cappuccino mousse). One glass of champagne is complimentary, as is fresh-squeezed orange juice. (Tip: If you don't drink, ask for sparkling juice.) Champagne specialty drinks are available for $5.25.

© Cheryl Pendry

Palo Champagne Brunch Offerings

Beverages at Dinner *(all restaurants)*

Don't be surprised if your server learns your drink preferences. We are always impressed when our server remembers what we like after our first dinner. Complimentary beverages include soda (fountain drinks), iced tea, juice, milk, coffee, tea, and tap water. Sparkling water (Perrier or San Pellegrino) is $3.50 for a large bottle. A full bar and wine list is available. If you need suggestions, each menu has a selection of specialty drinks/apéritifs ($4.75) and featured wines ($5.25-$9+/glass). Each menu also features a themed drink, such as Lumière's French Flag (grenadine, créme de cacao, and blue curaçao), Animator's Palate's Black and White (Kahlúa and layered cream), and Parrot Cay's Island Kiss (Amaretto, Bailey's, and créme de cacao). Specialty drinks are also available without alcohol—just ask your server. If you're a wine drinker, you may be interested in the wine package—see page 172.

Remy

The Disney Dream Class ships add a second optional, adults-only restaurant, Remy, which presents French-style cuisine in very elegant style. Remy shares deck 12 aft (including the view) with Palo and adults-only Meridian Lounge. While inspired by the lead character in the Disney*Pixar animated film, *Ratatouille*, in all other regards, nothing about this restaurant is "Mickey Mouse" (well, Remy's a rat, if you didn't know). The food, service, and wine list is exquisite, the surroundings are enchanting, and if you look very closely, you can find Remy portrayed in the decor and even the fine china.

Overview: Remy out-does Palo on all criteria, as it should, as Remy's prix fixe cover charge is nearly four times Palo's ($75). Disney chose a star-studded lineup of kitchen talent to create the menu at Remy–Chef Arnaud Lallement of l'Assiette Champenoise, a Michelin two-star restaurant near Reims, France, and Chef Scott Hunnel of Victoria and Albert's at Walt Disney World's Grand Floridian Resort. Both also brought along their pastry chefs. Disney Cruise Line Executive Chef Patrick Albert oversees the restaurant. Wine service has a special focus, with over 130 vintages on the regular list, plus extra-special "Vault" wines costing as much as $2,800. Diners may meet with the sommelier pre-dinner to plan their evening's wine service. A simpler choice is the $99 per-person wine pairing–five glasses of wine, one matched to each course. Note that dinner here can be an all-evening affair, so don't count on being able to catch the evening's live show.

Reservations–Due to its small seating capacity (80 in the main dining room, 8 at the Chef's Table, and 8 in the Wine Room), Remy is a very hard reservation to get. Reservations can and should be made in advance once your cruise is paid in full, at http://www.disneycruise.com. Reservations can be made 2 to 75 days in advance for first-time Disney cruisers, from 2 to 90/105/120 days in advance for Castaway Club members (see page 470), and from 2 to 120 days in advance for concierge guests in stateroom categories R-V. Note that online reservations open at midnight Eastern Time and reservations can go in a flash. Only one online Remy reservation per stateroom is allowed. See the Palo reservations information on page 163 to learn more. Concierge guests (cat. R-V) can ask their concierge to make reservations for them. Reservations for the Chef's Table and Wine Room are available via the online reservation system. Reservations can be cancelled without penalty up until 2:00 pm on the day of the meal. No-shows and last-minute cancellations will have $75 per person charged to their room.

Decor– Remy evokes Belle Époque Paris, the age of Art Nouveau at the turn of the 20th century. Tables are set with Frette linens, Riedel crystal, and Christofle silver. The main dining room is done in soft greens, rich golds, and dark wood, with blown glass lampshades, carved flower-and-vine fretwork in the seat backs, and other elegant touches. Look closely, and you may find some "hidden Remys." The Chef's Table dining room has a more formal approach inspired by the movie, with maroon upholstery and drapes, burl walnut wainscoting, gold accents, and crystal chandeliers. Murals depict Parisian scenes and the movie's kitchen. The glass-walled Wine Room has more than 900 bottles on display!

Dress–Jackets for men (tie optional); dresses or pantsuits for women. Formalwear is welcome. No jeans, shorts, capris, sandals, flip-flops, or tennis shoes.

Remy (continued)

Our Review—Remy blows Palo out of the water. It is by far one of the finest dining experiences most of us can have at sea and in most places ashore. While $75 may seem steep (one of the most expensive extra-fee meals in the cruise industry), you'd pay $125 for a meal of equivalent style and quality at Victoria and Albert's at Walt Disney World's Grand Floridian Resort. Add drinks and tip, and $150 per person is a minimum budget (we'd rather spend it here over three hours than in an hour at the spa). Dinner at Remy may be too highfalutin' for some, and it truly isn't for everyone. While we can recommend Palo to just about anyone, thanks to its better-known Italian cuisine and relatively informal atmosphere, Remy is an experience most enjoyed by those who will be comfortable with or are eager to try French haute cuisine, formal service, and high prices. The service is indeed formal, but it's very warm, discrete, and never condescending. As everywhere else in the Disney realm, everyone is a welcome guest. While the motto in *Ratatouille* is, "Anyone can cook," at Remy, anyone can dine, and dine exceedingly well! Dinner begins with an off-menu "amuse bouche," a tiny bite to, literally, amuse the mouth, plus a complimentary champagne cocktail. In keeping with the restaurant's theme, that's followed by, again off-menu, the chef's elegant variation on ratatouille. Your choice of two, five-course tasting menus (or your a la carte selections) then kick in, interrupted at times by a sorbet to cleanse the palate, and a fabulous cheese cart (oh, that cheese cart!). *After* dessert come irresistible house-made candies; nougats, lollipops, caramels, canneles, chocolates, pet de nonne, and tiny lemon curd tarts, and when you return to your stateroom you'll find a small box of chocolates. Even the "worst" dish we sampled (and we've managed to cover most of the menu, thanks to our companions) was very good, most were excellent, and several stood out as sublime. Our favorite? The lobster with vanilla, bisque and lobster roe foam. The lobster meat was gently poached to optimum tenderness, the vanilla enhanced the lobster's sweetness, and the seafood bisque napped the bottom of the plate for a savory contrast. The veal, pigeon, and turbot (see below) were also stand-outs, and the Declinaison Tomate revealed new dimensions for that too-well-known fruit. Our dessert favorite was the richly caramelized poached pear, which far exceeded its simple description. Wine service is excellent, with too many ways to blow the budget on great vintages. Fortunately, there are more than 20 excellent wines available by the glass. If the $99, five-glass wine pairing seems a bit too much, you can do nearly as well selecting two or three glasses on your own. We find this approach more appealing than sharing full bottles that may not complement every diner's meal.

The Menus—Remy offers two set menus plus a la carte selections. All items on the set menus are also available a la carte. Menu items may change! **Saveur menu by Chef Arnaud Lallement**: Langoustines Royale (lobster with Caesar sauce); Declinaison Tomate (tomato prepared five ways); Turbot Cotier (turbot with gnocchi and yellow wine sauce); Pigeonneau (pigeon pie with foie gras, spinach, and tomato); and chocolate praline fondant with chocolate sorbet and hot chocolate foam. **Gout menu by Chef Scott Hunnel**: smoked bison with fennel salad and blood oranges; lobster with vanilla, bisque, and lobster roe foam; wild loup de mer (sea bass) with cannellini bean sauce, artichokes and Iberian ham; Australian Wagyu beef with garlic-potato puree and petit carrots; and vanilla poached pear. Additional a la carte choices are a trio of veal—tenderloin, braised shank (osso buco), and sweetbreads; Alaskan King crab; John Dory (fish) with chorizo foam, and Cochon Cul Noir (trio of black pork loin, pork trotter stew, and glazed ham).

About Ratatouille: This film from Disney/Pixar Animation, ranks as one of the greatest films about great food. Set in Paris, it stars a French rat (Remy) with unquenchable culinary taste, ambitions, and talent. A rat in a restaurant?? Nearly every human character objects to the idea, too, but Remy manages to win over those who count (except the health inspector) when they finally understand that, "Anyone can cook!" The film's passion for great food, great restaurants, and the personalities they attract has put this film (along with *Julie & Julia* and *Babette's Feast*) onto most foodie's favorite films list. If you never "got" fancy French cuisine, watching Ratatouille may whet your appetite for a dinner at Remy.

Special Dining Themes and Menus

All cruises offer at least one dining theme night simultaneously in the three main dining rooms, and the longer cruises add several more. These theme nights have their own menus and take place on different nights, depending upon your cruise length and destination. For tips on figuring out which night of your cruise you can expect these themed dinners, see page 176. Here are the menus for each theme night:

Pirates IN the Caribbean *(theme night all cruises; menu on 4+ night cruises)*
This theme night is enjoyed by all Disney cruisers, and all but the three-night cruises have a special menu (guests on the three-night cruises have their regular rotational menu). The special menu is presented on a rolled "treasure map" that you can keep as a souvenir. For more information, see page 201: **appetizers** (Black Beard's jumbo crab cake, pirate's golden "pot stickers," buccaneer's sun-ripened pineapple, or pearls of the Caribbean); **soups and salads** (chilled-to-the-bone honeydew melon and mango soup, Caribbean-style conch chowder, jerk chicken salad, or Mr. Smee's Bib Lettuce); **main courses** (treasure-of-the-seas grilled shrimp and seared scallops, Captain Swann's red snapper, Jack Sparrow's barbecue beef short ribs, Castaway chicken breast, Captain Hook's macadamia-dusted mahi mahi, The Dutchmen's roasted sirloin of beef, roasted chicken breast, baked salmon, or vegetarian selections–black-eyed pea and quinoa croquettes or Tiger Lily's stuffed savory pancakes); **desserts** (shiver-me-timbers white chocolate cheesecake, floating island of tropical fruit treasures, walk the triple-layered chocolate gangplank cake, baba rum Barbosa, The Calypso ice cream sundae, or no-sugar-added desserts–mango mousse cake or coconut rice pudding).

Prince and Princess *(most 7+ night cruises)*
appetizers (marinated sliced salmon, roasted tomatoes with goat cheese, scallops au gratin, cheese soufflé); **soups and salads** (potato and sausage soup, garden consommé, radicchio and endive Caesar salad, mixed greens with apples, walnuts, and blue cheese); **main courses** (fillet of turbot, smoked salmon salad, parma ham wrapped chicken breast, rack of lamb, beef Wellington, roasted chicken breast, baked salmon, vegetarian selections–sesame tofu steak, lasagna or mushroom pasta); **desserts** (chilled chocolate soufflé, lemon cheesecake, banana bread pudding, ice cream sundae, or no-sugar-added desserts–strawberries and cream, tiramisu, sugar-free ice cream).

Captain's Gala *(all 7+ night cruises)*
appetizers (oysters Rockefeller, sautéed shrimp, grilled vegetables and beef prosciutto, or fresh fruit cocktail); **soups and salads** (wild forest mushroom soup, chilled tomato consommé, garden fresh salad, or Californian mixed salad leaves); **main courses** (baked lobster tail, sesame seared tuna loin, steamed sole, pan-seared venison medallions, fettuccine with parmesan chicken, panko-breaded stuffed pork, baked salmon, roasted chicken breast, or vegetarian selection–gingered soba noodles or blue cheese and asparagus risotto); **desserts** (amaretto cheesecake, chocolate lava cake, banana crème brûlée, dessert sampler trio, ice cream sundae, or no-sugar-added desserts).

Til We Meet Again or **See Ya' Real Soon** *(all 7+ night cruises)*
appetizers (spinach artichoke dip, chilled tuna roll with caviar, seafood medley, or chicken satays); **soups and salads** (crawfish and lobster bisque, chilled potato leek soup, romaine salad, Florida citrus and baby spinach, or bib lettuce); **main courses** (grilled beef tenderloin, roasted Cornish hen, garlic and rosemary-marinated sirloin of lamb, seafood linguini pasta, roasted salmon, rib-eye steak, roasted chicken breast, baked salmon, or vegetarian selections–vegetable strudel or portobello moussaka); **desserts** (chocolate decadence, celebration cake, deep-dish apple-cranberry pie, baked Alaska, dessert sampler, or no-sugar-added desserts).

....→

Topsiders will have a dramatic upgrade during the Disney Magic's late 2013 overhaul. Walls will be bumped out aft and starboard to add more indoor seating and reduce crowding. The name changes to Cabanas, with Finding Nemo-inspired decor as on the Dream Class ships.

Topsider's/Beach Blanket Buffet/ Cabanas

This casual buffet restaurant on the pool deck (deck 9 on the Magic Class, or 11 aft on the Dream Class) is a pleasing alternative to the formal dining rooms. Choices are plentiful and varied, with daily themes such as seafood, Italian, Mexican, and Asian. The welcome aboard buffet (first afternoon) offers peel-and-eat shrimp and crab claws. Salad and dessert buffets are expansive, and kid-friendly food is always offered. Breakfast offerings are excellent, with hot and cold selections, omelet bar, and a cereal bar. It's usually open for breakfast (7:30 am to 10:30 am) and lunch (noon to 2:00 pm). Early-morning pastries, table service dinner (check for times), and a late-night buffet are often offered. Drinks include soda, water, fruit punch, iced tea, coffee, milk, and juice.

Decor—Topsider's (Magic) is nautically themed, with bright signal flags, teakwood tables, and glass etchings of maritime scenes. Beach Blanket Buffet (Wonder) has a surf's-up feel, with colorful surfboard, beach towel, and beach ball decorations. Cabanas (Dream Class) goes for an Australian beach style, and has a "boardwalk" with 16 food court-style serving stations offering a wide range of specialties. Large, mosaic tile murals depict undersea life from *Finding Nemo*, and various characters from that movie can be found around the room. All buffets offer indoor and outdoor seating, with and without shade. Seating space on the Dream Class is far more generous, which is a welcome improvement over the older ships.

Dress—Cruise casual. You can wear shorts and tank tops for breakfast and lunch, something a bit nicer preferred at dinner. For the sake of other guests, however, do cover up that swimsuit.

Dinner—Dinner works differently than breakfast and lunch—you go to the buffet for your appetizers, but your drinks and other courses are brought to you by servers. Main courses include some main dining room specialties. Typically available all but the first and last nights of your cruise.

Our Review—This is an excellent choice for a fast yet satisfying breakfast. On the Magic Class ships we generally prefer the other restaurants for lunch, especially on embarkation day (better food, better service, and alcohol can be purchased), but on the Dream and Fantasy, this is our first choice for breakfast and lunch, thanks to the wider menu, improved layout, and vastly improved seating arrangements. When we've stopped by for a casual dinner, we've always been pleased. It's a great place to feed kids before they go to the nursery or kid's club. Jennifer and Dave's rating: 6/10 (Magic Class), 8/10 (Dream Class).

Seating area at Cabanas on the Dream Class ships

The Disney Magic's late 2013 make-over brings changes to the deck 9 casual dining, too. Pluto's Dog House will become Pete's Boiler Bites, and Goofy's Galley becomes Daisy's De-Lites. We expect their locations also will change a bit, due to the kids pool makeover.

Casual Dining

Need to grab a bite on your way to a movie? Want to avoid the dining room at dinner? Casual dining is your ticket. Disney offers several quick-service options throughout the ship at various times during the day, all at no extra charge. All times noted below are based on previous cruises.

☐ Flo's Cafe (Dream Class) — Deck 11 Mid

Flo's is home to Luigi's Pizza, Doc's Grill, and Fillmore's Favorites, all inspired by the Disney-Pixar film, Cars. Essentially the same menu as offered at Pluto's Dog House, Goofy's Galley, and Pinocccchio's Pizzeria on the Magic and Wonder (see below). Nearby, Frozone Treats offers smoothies, and Eye Scream serves ice cream with toppings. By Donald's Pool.

☐ Pluto's Dog House (Magic Class) — Deck 9 Aft

Your not-so-basic burger stand. The menu includes burgers, hot dogs, veggie burgers, chicken sandwiches, tacos, bratwurst, chicken tenders, and fish burgers. All are served with fries. A toppings bar offers standard bun veggies (lettuce, tomatoes, onions, pickles) and condiments. Pluto's may also offer an express breakfast or treats like cheese fries and nachos on select days. Patio tables nearby. Hours vary—usually open from lunch until 8:00 pm or midnight.

☐ Goofy's Galley (Magic Class) — Deck 9 Aft

Bakery cases display the daily offerings, which usually include salads, fresh fruit, deli sandwiches, paninis, pasta, wraps, ice cream, and cookies. You may even be able to order a special-request sandwich. Self-service ice cream is available from two machines offering vanilla, chocolate, and vanilla/chocolate swirl. Sprinkles, cherries, chocolate topping, and other toppings may also be available. In the morning (7:00 am to 9:30 or 10:00 am), you'll find a selection of pastries, cereal, fruit, yogurt, and milk. Open daily from 10:30 am to 6:00 or 7:00 pm (ice cream may be available until 11:00 pm).

☐ Pinocchio's Pizzeria (Magic Class) — Deck 9 Mid

Pizza, pizza, pizza! Get your slice in traditional cheese or pepperoni. Special pizzas like veggie and Hawaiian may also be served at times. Beverages also available here. Generally open from 11:00 am to 6:00 pm, then again from 10:00 pm to midnight. Seating is at patio tables. (Tip: You can order more pizza types from room service—see page 173).

© MediaMarx, Inc.

☐ Outlook Bar/Lounge — Deck 10/14

Chicken wings, panini sandwiches and similar items are offered here around lunchtime on select days. Check your Personal Navigator or stop up for a visit.

☐ Beverage Station — Deck 9/11 Aft/Mid

Breakfast pastries are available early mornings (6:30-7:30 am). Cookies may also be served on select afternoons—look on the counters to the aft of the beverage station. Complimentary beverages, including soda, are available 24 hours/day—for more details, see page 172.

Snacks and desserts are liberally sprinkled in other places, too. You'll find snacks in the Cove Café and Promenade Lounge, Vista Café, and the adult entertainment district from 10:00 pm to midnight. Special buffets are available as noted on page 158.

Castaway Cay Dining

© MediaMarx, Inc.

Jennifer's nieces, Megan and Natalie, discuss the nutritional merits of hot dogs vs. burgers at Cookie's BBQ on Castaway Cay

All Bahamian, most Caribbean, and some repositioning itineraries visit Disney's private island, Castaway Cay, and you'll be happy to learn your food is included in the price of your cruise! The main places to eat are **Cookie's BBQ**, located directly across from the family beach and **Cookie's Too**, which opened in 2010 by the far end of the expanded family beach (see island map on page 245). Both serve from 11:30 am to 2:00 pm and offer burgers, BBQ ribs, grilled chicken sandwiches, lobster burgers, hot dogs, potato salad, fruit, frozen yogurt, and big chocolate chip cookies. Food is served buffet-style. Plenty of covered seating is nearby (see photo above). Soft drinks are provided, or purchase alcoholic beverages across the way at the Conched Out Bar and the Sand Bar.

Adults 18 and over can eat at the **Castaway Cay Air Bar-B-Q** (see photo below) located at Serenity Bay, the adults-only beach, from about 11:30 am to 2:00 pm. Offerings include burgers, salmon, grilled chicken breasts, steak sandwiches, lobster burgers, pork ribs, potato salad, fresh fruit, and fat-free frozen yogurt. Soft drinks are provided, and alcoholic beverages are at the Air Bar nearby. A dozen shaded tables are nearby, or take your tray to the beach.

© MediaMarx, Inc.

Relax at the Castaway Cay Air Bar-B-Q at Serenity Bay

In addition to the three bars already mentioned, there's a fourth—the Heads Up Bar—at the far end of the jetty that divides the expanded family beach. All bars close around 3:30–4:00 pm.

Tip: If you choose not to visit Castaway Cay, a buffet is served in Parrot Cay or Cabanas, usually from about 12:00 pm to 1:30 pm.

Kids' Dining

We don't know about your kids, but our son Alexander usually won't touch pepper-seared grouper or seafood Creole with a ten-foot pole. Alexander and many other kids prefer the kids' menus available at each table-service restaurant (and adults can order from these menus, too!). The **menus vary slightly** and are kid-friendly. Here is a typical menu:

appetizers (chicken noodle soup or honeydew melon boat); **main courses** (Mickey's macaroni and cheese, Minnie's mini burger, crusty cheese pizza, chicken strips, Mickey pasta, roasted chicken, or vegetable croquettes); **desserts** (Mickey ice cream bar, chocolate pudding, caramel custard, or assorted ice cream); **drinks** (milk–whole, low-fat, skim, or chocolate; soda, juice, water). Smoothies are $3.50 each.

And, yes, the menus come with **kid-pleasin' activities**, like word searches and connect-the-dots. Crayons are also provided with meals.

© MediaMarx, Inc.

Alexander discovers that kids are pampered during meals, too

If you are the lucky parent of children who will try anything, rest assured that your **kids can dine from the adult menu**, too. The adult fruit plates were our son's favorite as a toddler.

Kid-friendly items are **offered elsewhere** outside of the restaurants, too. The snack bars and buffet on deck 9/11 also serve plenty of kid favorites like pizza, burgers, and hot dogs. KidTip: *"Don't be afraid to try a bite of something new! Mickey's food is good."*

If your child is checked into **Oceaneer's Club and Lab** at dinnertime (a good idea if you want a quiet meal), crew members take kids up to the pool deck buffet around the start of the first dinner seating.

Dine and Play (for ages 3–10) is a help at the late dinner seating. Give your server a heads-up when you arrive. Your child's meal will be expedited, and about 45 minutes later childrens program counselors arrive to escort the kids to Oceaneer's Club and Oceaneer's Lab.

While lunch and dinner are provided for kids checked into Oceaneer's at mealtimes, **no snacks** are made available. You can check them out and take them to get a snack.

Younger children may find it **hard to sit through a meal** in a table-service restaurant. If you ask your server, you can have your child's meal served at the same time as your appetizers to curb their impatience. And the servers are typically great at entertaining the kids. Of course, you may prefer to do casual dining or room service on some nights.

Babies in **Flounder's Reef/It's a Small World** are given apple juice and crackers, as appropriate for their ages—you may also bring food for them. The dining rooms don't have pre-made baby food—you may want to bring a small food grinder to make your own. Infant formula (Similac and Isomil) is available in the ship's shop, but supplies are limited—consider using Babies Travel Lite (see page 452). Disposable bottles are also sold on board. Whole milk is available at no charge from room service and from the beverage station on deck 9/11 aft/mid.

Beverages

Your food onboard is included in your fare, but **some drinks are not free**. Sure, you can get tap water, coffee, tea, milk, and juice with your meals and at select locations onboard. Sodas (fountain drinks) are also available for free everywhere except bars and room service. But bottled water, specialty drinks, smoothies, and alcohol come at a price (but not a high price).

✔ **Soda**—Disney offers complimentary soda at all meals, at the Beverage Station (deck 9/11 aft/11 mid), and on Castaway Cay. Selection is limited to Coke, Diet Coke, Caffeine-Free Diet Coke, Sprite, Diet Sprite, pink lemonade, fruit punch, ginger ale (not available everywhere). Soda purchased at bars and from room service costs about $1.50 each.

✔ **Beers** range from about $3.25 to $4.00 and include tap beers (Bud, Miller Lite, Heineken), canned beers (Bud, Bud Lite, Coors Light, Icehouse, Miller Draft, Miller Lite, Beck's, Guinness, Heineken), and bottled beers (Amstell Light, Bass, Corona). Mixed drinks are $3.00 to $9.00 each (most about $6.00), wine is $4.25 and up, and smoothies are $3.50.

✔ A 15% **gratuity is automatically added** to all beverage purchases. There's no need to give another tip, even though there is a space provided for it on your receipt.

✔ **Bring Your Own**—Many guests opt to "BYOB." Bring bottled water, beer, wine, and/or liquor and stow it in your carry-on luggage. If you run out, pick up more at a port. Unlike other cruise lines, there are no restrictions on bringing beverages aboard so long as they are hand-carried in a day bag (hard-sided coolers are not allowed). You can only take home one liter of alcohol duty-free per person and it must be unopened. (Warning: Don't expect to restock at the onboard liquor shop—you won't get your booze until the night before you disembark.) The stateroom refrigerators keep your beverages chilled, but you'll have to ask your stateroom host/hostess for ice (see page 148). If you bring your own wine to dinner, expect to pay $23 per bottle ($20 corkage fee + 15% gratuity)—ouch! You may bring a glass of poured wine to the dinner table.

✔ **Beer Mug**—Check the lounges for a 22 oz. refillable, glass beer mug. Cost is $16.95/mug. Get 22 oz. refills at the 16 oz. price ($3.75). You'd need 10 to 12 refills to break even.

✔ **Beverage Station**—Visit the beverage station on deck 9 aft/11 aft/mid for complimentary soda, water, coffee, hot tea, iced tea, hot cocoa, whole milk, fruit punch, and lemonade—available 24 hours a day. Orange juice may also be available in the mornings.

✔ **Topsider's Buffet/Beach Blanket Buffet/Cabanas**—Soda, fruit punch, and iced tea are included at lunch or dinner. Hot tea, coffee, and juice are available at breakfast. If you want soda at breakfast or hot tea at lunch, the Beverage Station is nearby.

✔ **Wine Package**—Commit to a bottle of wine for each night of your cruise and save up to 25%. You choose your wine from a list at each dinner. The Classic package is about $28 for each night of your cruise, and the Premium package is about $43/night. If you don't finish an entire bottle, take it back to your room or ask your assistant server to store it 'til your next meal. Unopened bottles may be taken home, and count toward your customs allowance.

✔ **Fairy Tale Cuvée**—This champagne—available in the dining rooms—was created for Disney by Iron Horse Vineyard. Taittinger produced a special champagne for both the Dream's and Fantasy's inaugurals, available in those ships' duty-free shops.

✔ **Drinks Come to You**—Servers on Castaway Cay and at the Walt Disney Theatre bring specialty drinks around on trays for purchase so you don't have to get up for them.

Stateroom Dining
(Room Service)

There are no other three words that say "luxury" more than "Hello, Room Service!" It's a sinful extravagance for the filthy rich and people too pooped or love-struck to creep from their rooms. But why feel guilty, when **the cost of room service is included** in the price of your cruise? You want real luxury? Keep your stateroom stocked with oversized chocolate chip cookies, fruit, and cheese from room service throughout your cruise!

Room service is available **24 hours/day** (though it's closed the morning of disembarkation for most guests). Service is quick and punctual—food usually arrives in 20 to 30 minutes. You'll find room service menus in your stateroom, and we've included sample menus at the bottom of this page—please note that menu items and beverage prices may change. Food and basic drinks (coffee, tea, milk, juice) are free, but all other beverages carry an extra charge.

To place an order for room service, fill out the breakfast menu in your stateroom and hang it on your door handle, or simply **press the dining button on your stateroom phone** and relay the items you want. You can also specify a time for delivery if you are ordering in advance, as with the breakfast menu. Coffee drinkers may find it convenient to order a pot of coffee before going to bed and request to have it delivered at a particular time in the morning (its arrival works as a wake-up call). Don't forget to tip your room service steward on delivery. They don't get automatic tips for the food, just the drinks. $1–$2/person is fine.

Tip: Guests going on all-day excursions have been known to order a couple of sandwiches, have them delivered before departing, keep them cool in the refrigerator, and pack them in resealable bags for a midday snack. Be aware that the Disney Cruise Line does not encourage this, it **may be illegal to bring food ashore** in some ports, and you are not allowed to bring cooked/opened food back onboard. We do not recommend it.

KidTip: *"Ask your grown-ups for chocolate chip cookies before bed... they're awesome!"*

Breakfast Menu (7:00 am to 10:00 am) Note: Guests in suites may order full breakfasts (see page 126). ***Juices*** *(orange, apple, grapefruit);* ***Cold Cereal****, served with whole or skim milk (Corn Flakes, Raisin Bran, Rice Krispies, Froot Loops, KO's, Frosted Flakes, low-fat granola);* ***Breads and Pastries*** *(Danish pastries, fruit and bran muffins, croissants, donuts, toast, English muffins, bagel);* ***Condiments*** *(selection of jams and honey, butter, margarine);* ***Beverages*** *(whole milk, skim milk, chocolate milk, 100% Colombian Coffee, 100% Colombian Decaffeinated Coffee, selection of teas); and* ***Cocktails****–$4.25 (Mimosa, Screwdriver, Bloody Mary)*

All-Day Menu Note: Guests in the Royal suites may order from the dining room menus (see page 126). ***Appetizers*** *(southwestern Caesar salad, blackened chicken quesadilla salad, Mexican tortilla soup, chicken noodle soup, All Hands on Deck—a special selection of international cheeses served with crackers, and fresh fruit bowl);* ***Sandwiches*** *(BLT, ham/turkey & cheese, grilled zucchini, portobello mushrooms, and aioli on focaccia; tuna salad, chicken fajita wrap, and steak sandwich);* ***All-American Fare*** *(cheeseburger with fries and cole slaw, hot dog with fries, and macaroni & cheese);* ***Chef's Specialities*** *(Mexican fiesta pizza, vegetarian delight pizza, pepperoni pizza, and meat or veggie lasagna);* ***Desserts*** *(daily cake selection, extra large chocolate chip cookies, and oatmeal raisin cookies);* ***Beverage Packages*** *(6 domestic beers for $18.75, 6 imported beers for $22.50, 3 imported and 3 domestic beers for $21, 6 Coca Cola or other sodas or 6 bottled waters for $9.00. 24 bottled waters for $35). Milk is free.*

Our Recommendations

Your first hours on board can be very chaotic, and it's tough to arrange a proper family meal. We suggest you split up and **grab quick bites** whenever you can—the buffets close long before the ship sets sail.

Are you uncomfortable about wearing a jacket or a suit? Even on Formal Nights, **a nice shirt and slacks will be fine**, just about everywhere.

Presuming you love **Disney music** (a fair guess, we think), the soundtrack in most dining rooms takes your meal to a high "sea." You don't get a 16-piece, live, be-tuxed orchestra, but the prerecorded scores are a feast for the ears. This is especially true at Animator's Palate on the Magic and Wonder, where the visual extravaganza is choreographed to the music.

You can't keep Dave away from **smoked salmon**, even under "lox and cay." Alas, Disney's smoked salmon is not quite the stuff of dream cruises. It's fine on a bagel with cream cheese, but it's not that firm-but-buttery/velvety, smoky-sweet stuff of his dreams. The salmon at Palo's brunch is a bit better (as is their fresh-squeezed OJ!).

We love **seafood** (especially Dave), and you'll notice that many of our choices in this chapter (all those dishes we've underlined) are seafood-based. We know there are many of you who don't share our love for it, so please rest assured that virtually all the dishes are good—it's just that we've tried the seafood the most often.

The **seating and traffic flow** for the deck 9 buffet on the Magic and Wonder is quite chaotic. It's far better, though, when you enter those buffets using the right-hand doors (port). The indoor seating on that side is also more spacious and relaxing. When the weather's right, we prefer the outdoor tables aft—they're a glorious relief from the indoor chaos. We prefer Parrot Cay for lunch, which we find more relaxed.

Eating outdoors on deck 9 aft

Get to Know Your Dining Room Servers

If you've never had the chance to bond with a good server, try it! Great servers resemble stage actors—they come alive for a good audience. Be generous with your attention and thanks throughout the cruise—don't save it all for the tip. From the start, help them understand your tastes and interests. Listen attentively when they describe dishes, ask for their recommendations (they know what's good), and ask questions while ordering—you may save them several trips to the kitchen. If something disappoints you, break the news gently—but don't suffer in silence, either. Your server likes happy guests, and you'll be even happier with a happy server. You have three crew members on your dinner service staff, all of whom should be tipped at cruise end (see page 467). Your Head Server oversees many tables, supervises your special needs (and celebrations), and should visit your table once per meal. Your Server guides you through your meal, takes your orders, and (hopefully) pampers you beyond belief. Your quiet Assistant Server helps keep your food coming, serves wine and other beverages, and clears the table.

A Melting Pot of Notes

If you're thinking of **bringing any food onboard**, please note that it is against U.S. Public Health regulations to bring aboard any food that is cooked or partially cooked or packaged food that has already been opened. Unopened, commercially packaged foods are fine.

It's a good idea to **pack a change of clothes** for your first night's dinner in your carry-on. While it doesn't happen often, checked luggage may arrive in your stateroom too late to allow an unhurried change for an early dinner seating.

Even parents with **young children may appreciate the late seating**—the kids will be more alert for the early show, and you can use Dine and Play (see notes on page 171).

Trying to decide between the **earlier or later seating?** The earlier seating is most popular with families and young children. The earlier seating is also preferred by those who like to get to sleep earlier. Early seating takes about 1 ½ hours to complete your meal, while late seating can take as long as 2 hours. As you might have guessed, the later seating is comprised of mostly adults and some older children. The later seating gives you more time on your port days, as you don't need to rush back for an early dinner. Keep in mind that guests with late seating see the show before dinner, so you and/or the kids may want a snack before the show. We prefer the late seating ourselves.

Just can't **finish your meal**? Ask your server if you can take it back to your room. Most servers are happy to accommodate you. Don't be shy about asking for another dish or for seconds, either.

Jennifer's brother-in-law, Chad, enjoys two main entrees

If you are **seated with other guests**, which is likely if you aren't traveling in a large group, enjoy their company and swap tales of your adventures! Most cruisers find it more enjoyable to share a table!

On the **third night** of the four-night cruises, guests return to the restaurant where they dined on the previous night of their cruise. Regardless of what restaurant you're in, you will enjoy the "Pirates IN the Caribbean" menu (see page 167) on this evening.

Not sure what evening to **experience Palo?** We think Parrot Cay is the least interesting dining room on the Magic and Wonder, so that's the evening we prefer for Palo. Be careful, however, that you don't overlook "Pirates IN the Caribbean" theme night (see next page). The decision on the Dream and Fantasy is not so easy, as all dining rooms are worthwhile.

If you want to try **Palo or Remy more than once**, don't bother asking your friends or family members to add you to their reservation—Disney cross-references reservations and limits all cruisers to just one reservation. If you really want to do those restaurants more than once, get on their waiting list once you're aboard and cross your fingers!

Breakfast on disembarkation day is in the same restaurant you were assigned to the evening before (so if you ate in Palo or Remy, you need to go the restaurant you would have eaten in if you hadn't gone to Palo or Remy). A special "Welcome Home" menu is served—it's virtually identical to the Character Breakfast menu (page 162).

KidTip: *"To see your food before you pick it, go to the buffet restaurant! It's my favorite!"*

Determining Dining Schedules

Before you read any further, know this: You don't have to figure out your dining schedule ahead of time. If you want to just kick back and relax, all you need to pay attention to is the dining "tickets" left in your stateroom on your embarkation day and the Personal Navigators (the daily schedules left in your stateroom every evening). This approach may make it difficult to plan which night to dine at Palo or Remy, however. If you want to have a good idea of the what, where, when of your dinners, then read on!

At press time, these are the dining schedules for the various regularly scheduled cruises. If you're on a special cruise, check the bottom of this page. It's important to remember, however, that Disney can and does change these schedules at the drop of a hat. Always, always check your *Personal Navigators* to determine what's really going on for your cruise.

3-Night Cruise Dining Schedule

Day 1	Day 2	Day 3
regular rotation menu *(Casual Attire)*	Regular rotation menu *(Pirate/Casual Attire)*	regular rotation menu *(Optional Dress-Up Attire)*

4-Night Cruise Dining Schedule

Day 1	Day 2	Day 3	Day 4
regular rotation menu *(Casual Attire)*	regular rotation menu *(Optional Dress-Up Attire)*	Pirates IN the Caribbean (same restaurant as day 2) *(Pirate/Casual Attire)*	regular rotation menu *(Optional Dress-Up Attire)* Palo Brunch

7-Night Eastern Caribbean Cruise Dining Schedule

Day 1	Day 2	Day 3	Day 4	Day 5	Day 6	Day 7
regular rotation menu *(Casual Attire)*	regular rotation menu *(Formal Attire)*	regular rotation menu *(Casual Attire)*	Pirates IN the Caribbean *(Casual/ Pirate Attire)*	Prince and Princess menu *(Casual Attire)*	Captain's Gala *(Semi-Formal Attire)*	Sea Ya' Real Soon *(Casual Attire)*
	Palo Brunch	Palo Brunch			Palo Brunch	

7-Night Western Caribbean Cruise Dining Schedule

Day 1	Day 2	Day 3	Day 4	Day 5	Day 6	Day 7
regular rotation menu *(Casual Attire)*	regular rotation menu *(Formal Attire)*	regular rotation menu *(Casual Attire)*	Pirates IN the Caribbean *(Pirate Attire)*	Prince and Princess menu *(Casual Attire)*	Captain's Gala *(Semi-Formal Attire)*	Sea Ya' Real Soon *(Casual Attire)*
	Palo Brunch	Palo Brunch			Palo Brunch	

Note: The character breakfast on the 7-night cruises (Magic Class only) is on day 2 if your dining rotation starts with Animator's Palate, day 3 if you start with Lumière's/Triton's, and day 6 if you start with Parrot Cay.

Longer specialty cruises historically have two formal attire evenings (day 3 and day 7) and one semi-formal attire evening (day 9), but schedules vary greatly based on ports.

Introduction
Reservations
Staterooms
Dining
Activities
Ports of Call
Magic
Index

Dining Worksheet

Use this worksheet to note your dining preferences and be sure to keep it with you on your first day aboard.

Fill in/circle the following:
We have the **main seating** / **late seating** *(circle the appropriate choice—if you're not sure of your seating, call the Disney Cruise Line and inquire)*

Our Anticipated Dining Rotation: While this rule doesn't work for everyone, in general you can anticipate the following rotations if the occupants of your stateroom include:
All adults—day 1: **Lumière's/Triton's/Royal Palace/Royal Court**, day 2: Animator's Palate, day 3: Parrot Cay/Enchanted Garden, etc.
Young kids—day 1: **Animator's Palate**, day 2: Parrot Cay/Enchanted Garden, day 3: Lumière's/Triton's/Royal Palace/Royal Court, etc.
Older kids—day 1: **Parrot Cay/Enchanted Garden**, day 2: Lumière's/Triton's/Royal Palace/Royal Court, day 3: Animator's Palate, etc.
Note: The exception to the above rotation rule is on 4-night cruises, which repeat the second night's restaurant on the third night, then continue on. *See page 176 for details.*

Now write in the restaurants you anticipate being assigned to on each day. You may also want to add ports or other notes such as formal/semi-formal nights.

Day 1	Day 2	Day 3	Day 4	Day 5	Day 6	Day 7
Day 8	**Day 9**	**Day 10**	**Day 11**	**Day 12**	**Day 13**	**Day 14**

Now pencil in your first and second preferences for a dinner at Palo or Remy, keeping in mind which restaurants/meals you really want to try and which you are less interested in. Guests on the seven-night cruise: Add your preferences for the champagne brunch, if that interests you. (Note: High Tea was discontinued in August 2012, in favor of a second brunch seating.) Also note your preferences below for easy reference:

My first Palo/Remy preference is for ______________ at __________________ pm
My second Palo/Remy preference is for __________ _at __________________ pm

My Palo brunch preference is for ________________

You can fill in this worksheet before you leave for your cruise or once you're aboard and are confident about your dining rotation—just be sure to bring this worksheet with you!

A Recipe for Fun

Make the most of your dining experience with these delicious tips:

- Can't decide between the lamb and the sole? Tell your server you'd like to **try both dishes**! You can also order multiple appetizers and desserts if you wish. But take our advice and don't say you want "nothing" for dessert—that's just what you may get (you'll see!).
- How do you **choose between five full-service restaurants** on a three-night cruise? If you can't bear to miss the pleasures of all three regular rotational dining rooms *and* Palo or Remy, plan to visit your regular dining room before or after your Palo or Remy dinner for appetizers or dessert, or visit at breakfast or lunch (note that Animator's Palate is only open for dinner).
- For easy **room service tipping**, bring an envelope full of $1 bills and leave it by the door in your stateroom. We do not recommend coins.
- Picky eater? Ask your server to **mix and match menu items** so you can get just the meal you want.
- If you've **brought your own wine** or picked up a bottle at a port, you can request a "wine opener" (corkscrew) from room service.
- "While room service will deliver food to your stateroom free of charge, they won't bring soft drinks without an extra cost. So the last time we cruised, we brought some empty, clean 16-oz. plastic **soda bottles** with us. Fill them up at the free Beverage Station and take them back to your stateroom to stow in the mini-fridge. They don't stay real cold, but cool enough. And while they do lose some 'fizz,' when it's late and a Diet Coke is the only thing you want and it seems like a million miles to the beverage station ... it's great!"

  – contributed by Disney cruiser Christine Krueger

Magical Memory

- *"My parents and I took a four-night cruise on the Dream in February 2011 to celebrate Mom's recent 80th birthday and their upcoming 60th wedding anniversary. I managed to snag reservations for Palo brunch, Palo dinner that same evening, and Remy the following evening! To say we wined and dined in style would be an understatement, and the looks of delight and satisfaction on the faces of the people who introduced me to the pleasures of fine dining so many years ago will be with me a very long time."*

  ...as told by author Dave Marx

Playing and Relaxing Onboard

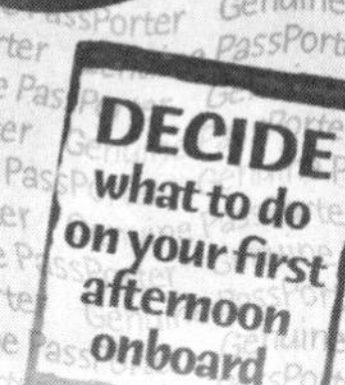

DISCOVER
activities for
kids, teens,
and adults

Cruise ships are often called floating hotels, but "mobile resort" is much closer to the truth. Like the legendary "Borscht Belt" hotels of New York's Catskill Mountains, the Disney cruise offers a bewildering array of entertainment, recreation, and enrichment opportunities from sunup way into the wee hours.

The Disney Cruise Line has become legendary for its pacesetting children's and teens' programs, and it may seem like an ocean-going summer camp. With the kids' programs open all day and well into the night, even Mom and Dad get a vacation.

Despite their emphasis on family travel, the Disney cruises are a summer camp for all ages, boasting a full range of adult-oriented activities. The single most obvious omission is a gambling casino—you'll have to be satisfied with onboard bingo and in-port casinos.

Leave time for relaxation as well as playing. On a cruise, it's just as easy to overplay as it is to overeat. You'll be tempted to fill every available hour with shipboard fun, but you'll have a far more enjoyable cruise by picking only the most tempting morsels. If you shop 'til you drop in port and play 'til you plotz (collapse) onboard, you'll be one very weary vacationer.

We start this chapter with an introduction to the *Personal Navigator*, your cruise's daily gazette. Then it's time to prep you for your first day onboard. There's a lot to do, and it's particularly hectic for first-time cruisers. From there, we move on to describe shipboard activities for families, teens, kids, and adults—this is where you learn about the famous kids' program and adult entertainment offerings. Next, in-depth details are in order—the swimming pools, deck parties, films, stateroom TV, live entertainment, surfing (the World Wide Web), the spa, and lounges all get their moment in the limelight. Finally, now that you're completely exhausted, we help you kick back and relax, and share some insider tips. Shuffleboard, anyone?

Your Personal Navigator

We hope this field guide has become your "first mate." If so, we predict the *Personal Navigator* will seem like your very own "cruise director." The *Personal Navigator* is a folded, 4-page sheet that **lists the day's activities**. A new *Personal Navigator* is placed in your stateroom each evening. While we don't have room to print the full text of *Personal Navigators* here, you can get a peek at previous editions of *Personal Navigators* at http://www.castawayclub.com—this site maintains collections from previous cruisers, and they'll give you an excellent idea of what to expect.

The first time you see a *Personal Navigator*, you may feel overwhelmed. Here's a **capsule review** of what you'll find in the daily Personal Navigator:

Page 1—Date, important times, day's destination, suggested dress, day's highlights
Page 2—Daily schedule grid for all ages: character appearances, entertainment, activities
Page 3—(Magic & Wonder) Descriptions of the day's activities for all ages
Page 3—(Dream & Fantasy) Continuation of Page 2 schedule grid
Page 4—More things to do, shopping deals, featured Port Adventures, detailed operating hours, and important reminders

We highly recommend you keep **highlighters** handy (a different color for each person) to mark appealing activities. Finding activities in your *Personal Navigator* later can be tricky—on some days, there are more than 80-200 activities listed! Obviously, you can't do everything, and that's where this chapter comes in—we introduce many of the activities here, so you'll be better informed when it comes to deciding among all of your choices.

We find that life is much easier when we each have a copy of the *Personal Navigator* with us at all times. Only one copy is left in your stateroom, so stop at Guest Services (deck 3 mid) and **pick up more copies**. (The kids', pre-teen, and teen schedules are now integrated into the regular *Navigator*.) How do you keep it with you if you don't have pockets? We fold it and tuck it into a PassHolder Pouch, which also holds our Key to the World card and other small items. See page 459 for a photo of a PassHolder Pouch—you can order one at http://www.passporter.com.

In addition to the *Personal Navigator*, you may receive a highlights sheet covering the entire cruise, a listing of movie showtimes and TV channels, plus a daily onboard shopping flyer. **Port and shopping guides** are distributed when you visit a port—they contain historical overviews, maps, shopping and dining ideas, basic information, and hours.

Note: The Personal Navigator's format changes every couple of years, so don't be surprised if your copy looks different than those pictured here.

Anatomy of a Personal Navigator

To help you get the most out of your *Personal Navigators* once you're aboard your ship, here is a recent sample with the notes on the general location of important information on the **first and second pages**. Please keep in mind this is a sample only—the format of your Personal Navigators may be similar, but they will have different information and activities

First Page

The **day's show** or other major event. Check here for times!

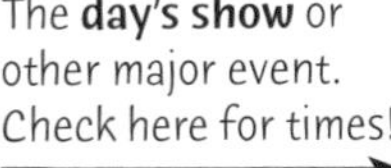

Glance here for the **day, date, and sunrise/sunset times**. On port days, "Ashore" and "All Aboard" times are noted.

The day's major **"don't-miss" events** and other essential information.

Another daily highlighted event that you may not want to miss!

The day's deals in the onboard stores, spa, and lounges.

A quick overview of the **dinner options**.

Important **phone numbers**.

First Page Tips:

✔ Upcoming events that require registration or sign-up may appear along with the day's highlighted events, such as a Galley Tour or a Family Talent Show.

✔ On port days, travel safety tips are listed on the first page, along with the ship's agent in the port of call.

✔ The evening's suggested attire (formal, semi-formal, dress-up, or cruise casual) is listed near the top page.

Anatomy of a Personal Navigator *(continued)*

The *Personal Navigator's* second and third pages contains grids which list the day's **entertainment schedule**. The grids are reminiscent of a *TV Guide* schedule, with one grid each for morning, afternoon, and evening activities. The columns across the top of each grid give specific start and end times for each activity. The rows organize the activities into types (family, adult, kids, teens, special, character, movies, etc.), making it easy to find the sort of activity that appeals to you. Refer to pages 3 and/or 4 (not shown here) for activity descriptions.

Second Page

The top third of the page is devoted to **morning activities**. On embarkation day, this space is a Ship Directory.

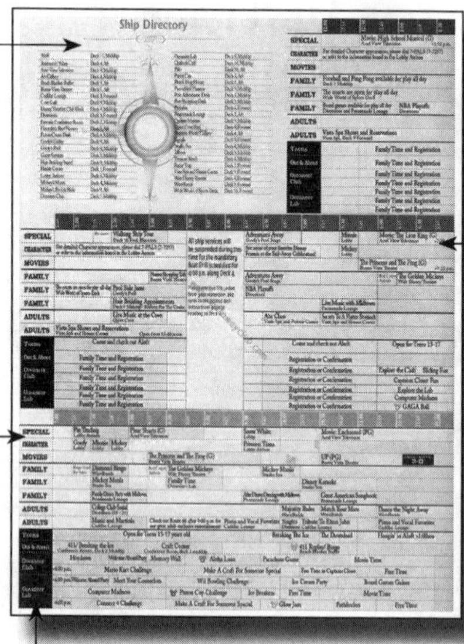

The middle third of the page lists the **afternoon activities**. This grid can be very dense (and hard to read) on at-sea days—read it carefully.

Evening activities occupy the bottom third of the page. If an event lasts longer than the last time on the grid, a small notation appears to indicate its ending time.

If you feel overwhelmed, note the **activity categories** in the left-most column and concentrate on activities that appeal to you. The "Special" category is for the day's highlights and don't-miss events. The "Character" category refers to character appearances throughout the ship.

Back Page Tips:

- ✔ The Navigator's type size can be quite small. If you find small type hard to read, consider bringing a magnifying glass or ask Guest Services if they can print it in a larger size.
- ✔ The activities are generally listed in order of popularity—highlighted events are at the top and age-specific activities are at the bottom.
- ✔ When you find an event that interests you, be sure to cross-reference the other events in the same column (and hence, same time) so you don't overlook something important.
- ✔ Parents, note that the kids' activities are listed in these grids, making it easy to see what your kids may be interested in or where they already are.

Your First Day Aboard

At last! Are you excited? Many cruisers report feeling overwhelmed and even a little nervous on their first afternoon. The good news is that your first day aboard can be far more relaxing. The Disney Cruise Line web site (http://www.disneycruise.com) lets you make Palo, Remy, Vista/Senses Spa, Flounder's Reef/It's a Small World childcare, and shore excursion reservations online—you can even preregister the kids for the Oceaneer Club and Lab. Reservations can be made online once your fare is paid in full; from 3 to 75 days in advance for first-time Disney cruisers, up to 90-120 days (depending on membership level) for Castaway Club members, and up to 120 days for guests in stateroom categories R, S, T and V. Look for the "My Disney Cruise" links on the web site. Note that online bookings are limited to one Palo and Remy reservation per meal type and no more than 8–10 hours per child in Flounder's Reef/It's a Small World nurseries. Some Spa treatments (such as haircare and the Rainforest) are not listed. Additional reservations may be available after boarding.

To give you an idea of what to expect on your first afternoon onboard, we've made up a **sample "touring plan**." You probably won't want to do everything in our touring plan, *and if you make reservations in advance whenever possible, you probably won't have to*. And remember that times/locations may differ. Modify it as needed and use the worksheet on page 185 to record your own plans!

As soon as you can—Smile for the photographer, walk the gangway, and board the ship. Go to the pool deck buffet (deck 9/11 aft) or Parrot Cay/Enchanted Garden (deck 3/2 aft) for a buffet lunch. Relax and enjoy before activities pick up.
12:00 pm (or so)—Send one adult from your party for Palo and Remy reservations, if you didn't reserve in advance (check your *Personal Navigator* for exact time and place).
12:00 pm (or so)—Send one adult to get spa bookings (including massages on Castaway Cay), if not done in advance. Send another person to your stateroom (usually ready at 1:00-1:30 pm). This is also the time to confirm any special requests you made (visit Guest Relations).
Tip: If you've got kids, they may be getting antsy by now. Let them explore your stateroom, or, if they're old enough, introduce them to the pools and meet up with them later.
1:30 pm—Go to Flounder's Reef/It's a Small World Nursery (deck 5) for reservations.
1:30 pm—Send someone to the Shore Excursions Desk (deck 3/5 midship) to fill out/drop off order forms, if not reserved in advance. (Decide which excursions you'd like in advance.)
Lunch—Take a deep breath and slow down. If you haven't eaten or visited your stateroom yet, do so now. The buffets and snack bars typically close at 3:30 pm, so don't miss it!
2:30 pm—Make dining assignment changes or special dietary requests, if needed.
2:45 pm—Take kids ages 3–12 to Oceaneer Club/Lab (deck 5 midship), if not preregistered.
3:15 pm—Return to your stateroom and get acquainted with it. If you're in need of anything (extra pillows, bed safety rail), request it from your stateroom host/hostess.
3:45 pm—Make sure everyone meets back in the room for the mandatory assembly drill.
4:00 pm—Get life jackets (if instructed) and go to your assembly station (see next page).
4:15 or 4:30 pm—After returning to your room, go up to deck 9/11 midship and have fun at the sailaway deck party, and/or explore the ship until it is time to get ready for dinner or the evening's show.
5:45/6:00 pm—Enjoy dinner (main seating) or the stage show at 6:15 pm (late seating).
6:00 pm—The kids, pre-teen, and teen program areas are now officially open. If you haven't yet registered your children, do this now.
8:15 pm—Enjoy dinner (late seating) or the stage show at 8:30 pm (early seating).

Whew! What a day! Rest assured that it all gets much, much easier from this point forward.

Introduction | Reservations | Staterooms | Dining | Activities | Ports of Call | Magic | Index

Introduction
Reservations
Staterooms
Dining
Activities
Ports of Call
Magic
Index

First Day Tips

Having a plan is the key to staying on course and feeling good. Here are a few helpful tips for your first day:

Check and double-check your ***Personal Navigator*** as soon as you get it (either at check-in or when you visit your stateroom). Places and times often change, and new activities and opportunities may be available.

Don't forget to eat! It can be hard to sit down together for one big family meal on your first afternoon. It's okay to split up and/or get **nibbles and bites** here and there.

Of course, you can always **kick back and do nothing** on your first day but eat, drink, be merry, and attend the safety drill—pre-book reservations at the cruise line web site! Or you can try to get those Palo, Remy, excursion, and spa reservations later—you may get lucky with cancellations. If someone in your family just wants to relax once they're onboard, arrange to go your separate ways on this first afternoon—you'll all be much happier.

Want to see the nursery, kids, tweens, and teen clubs? Today's Open House is your chance!

Lucky guests with **concierge service** only need to attend one meeting to make the various reservations. You'll be told when and where to meet.

Mandatory Safety Drills

It's inevitable that just as you're settling in or about to leave your stateroom for an exploration of the ship, a disembodied voice from the bridge announces the mandatory safety drill. But thanks to this guide, you now know that the drill happens at 4:00 pm on departure day, and all ship services are suspended from 3:30 to 4:15 or 4:30 pm. You'll find bright-orange life jackets on the top shelf of your stateroom closet (if you need a different size, such as an infant jacket, ask your stateroom host/hostess). The life jackets have a water-activated light and a whistle—please remind your kids not to blow the whistles. Your Assembly Station location is mapped on the back of your stateroom door. Assembly stations are all on deck 4, but may be outside on deck or inside. If you forget your assembly station designation, it's printed on your life jacket (see the "M" on Dave's jacket in the photo). When you hear the loud emergency signal, walk to the assembly station—your attendance is mandatory. Note that you no longer need to take your life vests with you as you did in the past. Be sure to bring your Key to the World card(s) with you, but leave cameras and other things behind. Crew members in the hallways will direct you to your assembly station (disabled guests should ask crew members for special instructions on attending drills). Once there, a crew member takes attendance and displays the correct way to wear and use the life jacket. If you miss the drill, you'll receive a sternly worded letter indicating where and when to meet to go over the assembly procedures—don't miss it! When the drill is over, the captain releases everyone back to their staterooms. The drill lasts from 15 to 30 minutes. If required to wear a life jacket, keep it on until you return to your stateroom.

"Hey, these life jackets aren't half bad!"

First Things First Worksheet

Electronic, interactive worksheet available–see page 492

Use this worksheet to plan those crucial activities that occur during your first day aboard. The chart below includes times (spanning the time period with the most important activities) and two columns each for activities and decks/locations. You may wish to list activities for other members of your party in the second column to coordinate and organize your day, or use the second column for notes or alternate activities.

Time	Activity	Deck	Activity	Deck
10:00 am				
10:15 am				
10:30 am				
10:45 am				
11:00 am				
11:15 am				
11:30 am				
11:45 am				
12:00 pm				
12:15 pm				
12:30 pm				
12:45 pm				
1:00 pm				
1:15 pm				
1:30 pm				
1:45 pm				
2:00 pm				
2:15 pm				
2:30 pm				
2:45 pm				
3:00 pm				
3:15 pm				
3:30 pm				
3:45 pm				
4:00 pm	Mandatory Boat Drill ↓	Deck 4	Mandatory Boat Drill ↓	Deck 4
4:15 pm				
4:30 pm				
4:45 pm				
5:00 pm				
5:15 pm				
5:30 pm				
5:45 pm				
6:00 pm				
6:15 pm				
6:30 pm				
6:45 pm				
7:00 pm				
7:15 pm				
7:30 pm				
7:45 pm				
8:00 pm				
8:30 pm				

Activities for Families

When Walt Disney was asked why he created Disneyland, he replied, "I felt that there should be something built where the parents and the children could have fun together." And that's exactly what Disney does for cruising. Family activities outnumber all other activities onboard, helping families have a great time when they're together. By "family" we mean groups of all ages, including all-adult families! Here's a list of what you can expect:

Deck Parties—Celebrate with music and dancing on deck 9/11 midship (see page 201).

Stage Shows—Disney puts on a different stage show each night of your cruise, and all shows are designed to please both adults and kids. See page 203 for more information.

Movies—Most of the movies playing in the Buena Vista Theatre and at the big outdoor screen over the Goofy/Donald Pool are rated G or PG, making them ideal for families. Special matinees may be held in the huge Walt Disney Theatre, too! See page 202 for movie details.

Studio Sea/D Lounge—This "family nightclub" (deck 4 midship) is a working TV studio. The club hosts family dance parties, family karaoke, theme parties, Tea with Wendy (see page 466), and game shows like Mickey Mania (Disney trivia) and A Pirate's Life For Me (see next page). Game shows are oriented toward families with young children, and generally contestant teams include both a parent and a child. Note that in the late evening, Studio Sea may be reserved for teens only.

D Lounge on the Disney Dream

Cabaret Shows—Shows for all ages may be held in the adult night club in the early evening. See page 198 for details.

Promenade Lounge/Vista Café—We think of these as the "family" lounges—where families can relax together here in the afternoon and early evening. Watch for many family-friendly events, hosted in the Promenade Lounge. Located on deck 3 aft/4 mid.

Oceaneer Club/Lab—At special times, families can explore these areas together.

Swimming—Families can swim together in the Goofy/Donald Pool (deck 9/11 midship), where pool games are also occasionally held. See page 200 for more on the pools. Ride tandem on AquaDuck on the Dream Class ships.

Games—Board games, shuffleboard, Ping-Pong, mini-golf (Dream Class), and basketball. Sport tournaments are held on the sports deck (10 forward/13 aft).

Pin Trading—Trading cloisonné pins is a very popular activity for kids and adults alike! Attend one of the trading sessions in the Atrium Lobby or trade casually with other cruisers and crew members. See page 211.

Character Meet & Greets—Plenty of opportunities for kids (or kids-at-heart) to get autographs and for parents to get photos. See page 466 for more information.

➤

"Port Adventures"—Most of Disney's shore excursions are great for families with kids ages 12 and up, and a good number of these work for families with kids ages six and up. Quite a few are open to all ages, as well. See chapter 6 for all the details.

Special Events—Try your hand at drawing Disney characters, or compete in a talent show or the "Mickey 200" veggie race—check your *Personal Navigator*.

Tip: Check the entertainment grid in your *Personal Navigator* for the Family, Out and About, Mouse-ter Class, and Disney Download rows—these list the family-oriented events for the day. Also, there's usually some family-oriented entertainment between dinner and the show, such as the cabaret shows and game shows. Here is a sample of activities taken from recent *Personal Navigators* (keep in mind that not all these activities may be available on your cruise):

- ✔ A Pirate's Life For Me (a game show inspired by *Pirates of the Caribbean*)
- ✔ Pictionary or Scattergories—test your skills against the crew members'
- ✔ Fun in the Sun Pool Party
- ✔ Family Dance Parties in Studio Sea/D Lounge
- ✔ Disney and Family Team Trivia
- ✔ Karaoke and Talent Show—show-off time!
- ✔ Mr. Toad's Wild Race (limited to 16 teams)
- ✔ Who Wants to be a Mouseketeer?
- ✔ Anyone Can Cook
- ✔ Animal Towel Folding
- ✔ Pirate Dance Class
- ✔ Family Golf Putting/Mini-Golf Contest
- ✔ Walk the Plank Game Show
- ✔ Ping-Pong Tournament

Dancing together during a deck party

Families That Play Together Don't Always Have to Stay Together

One of the wonderful benefits of a cruise is that each member of your family can do entirely different things, all while staying within the general vicinity of one another—a cruise ship is not nearly as big as Walt Disney World. With all the activities on your cruise, you're going to want to go in different directions at times... and you should feel free to do it! It only makes the time you spend together that much more valuable. When we sail together, we often split up—one may go to the pool with Alexander, the other to the spa—and we agree on a time and place to meet again. With larger families, including extended families, you can do your own thing in small groups while still feeling like you're "together." The key to making this work is to communicate and set meeting places/times for the next group get-together. The portable **Wave Phones** are a big help with this. Rent extras to keep everyone in the loop, and they can also be reached from any house phone. Some families bring two-way radios, but the ship's metal bulkheads can interfere with reception. A much simpler way to stay in touch is to leave notes in your stateroom—or if you're staying in multiple staterooms, leaving them on one another's doors or voice mail (there are house phones everywhere). You can keep tabs with a notepad—everyone in your family/group signs in each time they pass through the stateroom. On our group cruises, we make up our own versions of *Personal Navigators* and slip them under each other's stateroom doors. During the cruise, folks are able to add new events/times/places to the list by noting them on a magnetic whiteboard on our stateroom door. Sometimes it's as simple as picking up a phone somewhere on the ship (they're everywhere) and letting a family member know where you are (live or via voice mail). So feel free to go your separate ways—just be sure to save some special time to spend together as a family, too!

Activities for Teens

Teens are perhaps the hardest to please onboard, given their widely varying interests and levels of maturity. Some are perfectly happy to swim all day or play in the arcade. Others prefer to hang out with the adults. Still others want to socialize with other teens and party. If your teen prefers more family-oriented activities, we refer you to the previous page. Read on for Disney's teen-oriented places and events:

Note: Disney defines a teen as a 14- to 17-year-old. Older teens (18 and 19) are considered adults (although drinking age is still 21 and up).

Personal Navigators—Teens may have their own version of the daily schedule in the teen club (see below). The teen version lists teen activities for the day and what's coming up.

Vibe Teens Club—A teens-only (ages 14–17) hangout is located on all ships, but with some differences. Vibe on the Magic Class ships is located on deck 11 midship, inside the ship's aft stack! On the Magic, Vibe has huge windows dominating the large dance floor, flanked by chairs, tables, and a bar. On the Wonder, Vibe has more of a big-city loft feel to it, with lots of comfy couches, brick walls, and a big table. Both clubs serve smoothies and non-alcoholic drinks at their bars. Tucked in the corner are three Internet terminals (same rates apply—see page 204). Flat-panel screens are scattered throughout the clubs, offering a playlist of music videos that are shown on state-of-the-art TVs (including one giant-screen TV). In the back behind glass doors is an intimate little area with more comfy chairs, video screens, and a great view. Both clubs schedule plenty of parties, games, trivia, and karaoke during the cruise—the *Personal Navigators* list activities and times. The teen-only clubs also serve as an assembly spot for teen activities elsewhere on the ship, such as group events at the pool, group lunches, or a dance at Studio Sea. **On the Dream Class ships**, Vibe is found on deck 5 forward. It has a boldly-colored, modern look, with dramatically curved walls and furnishings.There are large indoor areas with spaces dedicated to lounging, dancing, watching movies, playing video games, and surfing the web. Several video game stations are in oval alcoves set in the walls, the player reclining like an astronaut, looking up at the video display. Other areas, for group video play, use wall-size screens. The bar serves complimentary smoothies. The teens also have an adjoining, exclusive outdoor sundeck with space for sunning, deck games, and cooling off in small pools and mist fountains. Access to Vibe is by special key card, which replaces the teens' Key to the World cards.

Allie at Vibe on the Disney Wonder

Vibe's outdoor sundeck on the Dream

Arcade—Quarter Masters/Arr-cade is a favorite teen hangout located on deck 9 mid/11 aft. There are also a few video arcade games on deck 10 midship on the Magic and Wonder, just below Vibe. See page 192.

Wide World of Sports Deck/Goofy's Sports Deck—Shoot some hoops on deck 10 forward. The Dream and Fantasy add mini-golf, golf simulators, and more, on 13 aft.

Internet Cafe/Vista Café—Sure, there are Internet terminals in the teen clubs, but sometimes it's just more convenient to come down to deck 3/4. See pages 204–205.

Spa—**Vista Spa** (Magic Class) is normally off-limits to anyone under 18, teens may be able to sign up for treatments on port days. $69/hour. **Chill Spa** (Dream Class) is a teens-only spa inside Senses Spa. See page 206. Chill Spa comes to the Disney Magic in late 2013.

Buena Vista Theatre—Teens love free movies! See page 202 for details.

Teen Parties—Dance parties are held either in Vibe or in Studio Sea.

Hot Tubs ("spas") at Goofy's Pool—Teens' favorite aquatic "hot spot" on the Magic Class ships. On the Dream Class, Vibe's own pools are a favorite.

Teen Shore Excursions—Special teen-only excursions are available at certain ports, such as the "Wild Side" on Castaway Cay. See chapter 6 for details.

Teen Hideout—On Castaway Cay, teens have their own area, with an open-air pavilion and organized activities. (The former Teen Beach is now part of the Family Beach).

Other Teen Activities—Here is a sample of activities taken from recent teen *Personal Navigators* (keep in mind that not all these activities may be available on your cruise):

- ✔ Mickey Mania
- ✔ Homecoming Night Party, Party in Paradise
- ✔ Pump It Up—Weight training
- ✔ Gotcha!—A day-long game of elimination
- ✔ Pirate's Life for Me Karaoke
- ✔ Teen-created activity schedule (one day on most cruises)
- ✔ Animation Antics—Learn to draw your favorite Disney characters
- ✔ H20 Splashdown in the family pool
- ✔ Mario Kart, DJ Hero, and Guitar Hero Challenges
- ✔ Video Scavenger Hunt

Tip: Even if you're not sure about all these activities, we highly recommend teens visit the club on the first evening to meet other teens and see what it's all about. This first evening is when many onboard friendships are formed.

Note to Parents of Teens

Teens have virtually the run of the ship, and aside from the times they're with you, in Vibe, or at a structured teen activity, they're not chaperoned. Teens may make friends with others from around the country and the world—their new friends' values may be incompatible with your own standards. It's a good idea to know where they are and who they're with, and agree on time(s) when they should check-in with you and/or return to the stateroom (some teen activities go late into the night). Talk before you go and remind them that being on vacation is not an excuse to throw out rules about drinking, drugs, or dating. U.S. Customs does not take drug possession lightly and penalties can be severe in other countries, too. Note also that any underage person caught with alcohol on the ship is fined $250 and could get up to three days of "stateroom arrest."

Activities for Tweens

Tweens (ages 11-13) have been **emerging from the shadows** in Disney's youth programming. For most of the cruise line's history, young people of middle-school age were divided between the kid's program (Oceaneer's Lab) and the teen program. This often led to family concerns as to whether the teen program would be too "old," and the Oceaneer Lab too "young" for kids in the tween years. The first significant change came when Ocean Quest opened on the Disney Magic, a dedicated space that embraced both young teens and older kid's program participants. After the cruise line unveiled its plans for **Edge**, a tween club on its new ships, a conference room on the Wonder was also converted to tween space. Now, the Disney Magic and Wonder offer dedicated programming for 11-13 year-olds in Edge, on Deck 2 midship (formerly Ocean Quest on the Magic, and a conference room on the Wonder). On the Dream Class ships, Edge is located on deck 13 in the forward stack, roughly the same space occupied by teens on the Magic Class. Read on for Disney Cruise Line's tween-oriented places and events:

Personal Navigators—Tweens may have their own version of the daily schedule in the tween club (see below). There is a dedicated row on the regular Navigator's schedule grid for Edge, and the Out and About row on the grid is also tween-friendly.

Edge (tweens club)—This tweens-only hangout is available on all ships. On the Magic, the tweens now "own" the former Ocean Quest on deck 2 midship. Formerly open to kids 8-14, the space is now dedicated to the tweens program. The club's centerpiece is a virtual ship's bridge, a very fun—albeit scaled down—replica of the real thing, complete with a traditional captain's chair and LCD viewscreens with live video feeds. The space also features computer and video game stations, movies on several plasma screen TVs, arts and crafts, and a sitting area with books, magazines, and board games. Edge on the Wonder is in the same space on deck 2 midship with similar facilities, lacking only the Ocean Quest ship simulator. On the Dream Class, **Edge** follows in the tradition of the *teen* clubs on the Magic Class. Located in the forward stack on deck 13, the loft-styled club includes an illuminated dance floor, an 18 foot-wide video wall, computers for game play, an onboard social media computer app open only to Edge program participants, green screens for video karaoke and other "become part of the picture" experiences, and even DVD "burners" for sharing their videotaped fun. Portholes and large picture windows invite daylight and give views of Donald's Pool and riders whizzing by on the AquaDuck water coaster. All clubs schedule plenty of parties, games, trivia, and karaoke during the cruise—the *Personal Navigators* list activities and times. On one day of the cruise, the tweens create their own activity schedule. The tweens-only clubs also serve as an assembly spot for tween activities elsewhere on the ship, such as group events at the pool, group lunches, or a dance at Studio Sea/D Lounge. On Castaway Cay most organized tween activities are centered on the In Da Shade game pavilion and the Sports Beach.

Edge on the Dream

Arcade—Quarter Masters/Arrcade is a favorite tween hangout located on deck 9 mid/11 aft. There are also a few video arcade games on deck 10 midship on the Magic and Wonder, just below the teens-only club. See page 192.

Mini golf on the Disney Dream

Wide World of Sports Deck/Goofy's Sports Deck—Shoot some hoops or play volleyball on deck 10 forward (Magic Class). The Dream Class adds mini-golf, virtual sports games, and more, on 13 aft .

Internet Café/Vista Café—Internet terminals. Need we say more? See pages 204–205.

Buena Vista Theatre—Tweens love free movies! See page 202 for details.

Tween Parties—On special evenings, tweens have dance parties in Edge or Studio Sea.

Swimming—Tweens are among the most enthusiastic users of the family pool on deck 9/11, and the family beach at Castaway Cay.

AquaDuck—The Dream Class' 765-foot long "water coaster" is a big draw for tweens (48" minimum height). See page 200. **Aqua Lab** (Fantasy only) is a fountain/splash play zone on deck 12 aft, with all sorts of contraptions for getting sprayed and soused.

In Da Shade—The game pavilion on Castaway Cay, with table tennis, basketball hoops, and other group activities, is a regular part of the tween activities on the island.

Other Tween Activities—Here is a sample of activities taken from recent *Personal Navigators* (keep in mind that not all these activities may be available on your cruise):

- ✔ Brains & Brawns Challenge
- ✔ Marshmallow Madness
- ✔ All Sorts of Sports
- ✔ Wonderful World of Magic
- ✔ Late Night Movie
- ✔ Anyone Can Cook
- ✔ Masquerade Ball
- ✔ Disney Animation: Illusion of Life - Cartoon Physics
- ✔ Goofy World Records
- ✔ Ice Cream Social
- ✔ Search for Atlantis
- ✔ Jewelry Making & Girls Chill
- ✔ DDR and Wii Fit Challenges
- ✔ Gender Wars

Note: Tween program participants are free to come and go from the program areas and activities at will.

Tip: Even if you're not sure about all these activities, we highly recommend tweens visit the club on the first evening to meet other tweens and see what it's all about. This first evening is when many onboard friendships are formed.

Activities for Kids

A whopping 15,000 sq. ft. (1,394 sq. m.) are devoted to activities just for kids on the Magic Class ships, and there's nearly twice as much space on the Disney Dream Class vessels. Naturally, there are a lot of kid-oriented activities on these ships. What else would you expect from Disney?

Oceaneer Club/Lab–A fantastic program for kids ages 3–10, with activities available daily from 9:00 am to midnight or 1:00 am. We highly recommend you encourage your kids to give these programs a try on the first day aboard. See pages 194–196 for more information.

FriendSHIP Rocks Show (Magic Class)–Kids registered for the Oceaneer Club/Lab on seven-night and longer cruises have the opportunity to appear in a special show on the last day or second to last day of the cruise (usually around 5:00 pm). All participants get to sing on stage with Mickey and receive a souvenir (such as a T-shirt). Held in the Walt Disney Theatre.

Swimming–We dare you to keep them out of the water! See page 200 for details.

Arcade–Located on deck 9 midship/11 aft, Quarter Masters/Arr-cade is a small arcade offering video games, air hockey, and a prize "claw" game (there are no award tickets or prize redemption). Most games are 50 cents to $1 each and you must use an arcade card to play. An "arcade debit card teller" machine dispenses $10 arcade cards–purchase with your Key to the World card, and cards can be bought at Guest Services. (Note: Keep arcade cards separate from your Key to the World card as they'll de-magnetize if they come into contact.) Worried about your kids racking up huge charges for arcade cards? Disable the charging privileges on their Key to the World cards at Guest Services and purchase arcade cards for them. Hours: 8:00 am to midnight (last game at 11:50 pm).

Games–In addition to the arcade, there are often pool games and Ping-Pong on deck 9/11, board games in the Oceaneer Club/Lab, basketball on deck 10/13, and shuffleboard on deck 4. There is no charge for these games.

Movies and Shows–Most of the movies playing are kid-friendly! And the stage shows in the Walt Disney Theatre are well-liked by kids. See page 203 for details.

Sports–The sports deck on deck 10 forward/13 aft is just the thing for young sports fans.

Deck Parties–The deck parties are very popular with kids! See page 201 for details.

Snacks–The opportunity to eat ice cream and hot dogs without forking over money is a real treat for kids! We don't think it's a coincidence that quick-service hot dogs, burgers, pizza, ice cream, and fruit are right by the kids and family pools. See page 168 for details.

Character Meet & Greets–Disney friends come out for autographs and photos many times during your cruise. For details, see page 466.

Bibbidi Bobbidi Boutique–Popular at Disney's theme parks, this salon (so far, only on the Disney Fantasy, deck 5 midship) offers fairy-dusted make-overs for the little princesses of the family, including hair, makeup, nails, and accessories. Prices run from $50-$595, with add-ons including full costumes and photo packages. On Pirates Night, the boutique morphs into Pirates League, offering buccaneer make-overs for all ages. Pirate make-overs for all ages start at $35, including bandanas, eye patches, swords, beards, and the like. The full make-over for kids ($100) adds wardrobe items like tunics, sashes, and hats.

Midship Detective Agency—These self-paced, detective-themed, interactive adventures on the Dream Class ships take kids (and adults) sleuthing all over the ship. Hold your game card in front of an Enchanted Artwork, to unlock an entirely different experience. Game cards and "crime scene maps" are distributed on deck 5 midship. The Fantasy adds "The Case of the Stolen Show" with the Muppets, to the line-up.

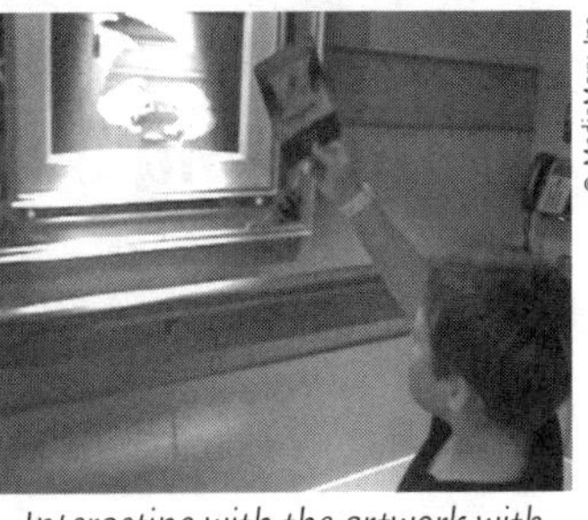

Interacting with the artwork with the Midship Detective Agency

Castaway Cay—Kid's program activities move to Scuttle's Cove at Castaway Cay, with an all-day schedule of activities for kids 3-10.

Wondering about letting your **kids roam free** onboard? It depends on their age and maturity. A general guideline is that kids 8–9 may be given some onboard freedom, while kids 10 and up can move about independently. These are in line with Disney's policies at the Oceaneer Club and Lab. If you let your kids loose, set down ground rules, such as no playing in elevators and keep in touch. Set meeting times for meals, shows, and family activities.

Pagers are no longer issued to the parents of kids program participants. The portable Wave Phones that are supplied in each stateroom are now used for this purpose.

Disney Cruise Line has phased-in the use of **electronic wristbands** for kids program participants. "Radio frequency identification" allows older children to check in and out by **tapping a sensor** with tag-embedded wristbands (shown in photo on page 195).

Kids Clubs on the Disney Dream Class Ships

The Dream Class brings several innovations and additions to the Oceaneer Club and Oceaneer Lab kids clubs (see next page), and the space dedicated to the clubs has increased dramatically, far more than the 50% that would be proportional to the increase in the ships' size. Both clubs sport 103-inch-wide video screens for movies and "live," interactive visits from animated characters, just like "Turtle Talk with Crush" at Disney's theme parks. The number of concurrent activities has also increased, to keep group sizes within reasonable bounds.

Activities for Toddlers

While the rate for your toddler to cruise with you is a great deal, the variety of toddler-friendly activities onboard isn't quite as favorable. We've spent more than five weeks onboard with a toddler (our son Alexander), and here's what we found to do: Go "swimming" in the water play area; Mickey's Splash Zone on the Magic Class (see page 200), or Nemo's Reef on the Dream Class. Take your toddler to Oceaneer Club (see page 194) to play or even participate in activities—toddlers are welcome (during Open House sessions only) as long as a parent remains with the child. Watch a movie (see page 202)—you may want to sit in the back of the theater near the aisle for easy escapes, however. Go for supervised treks down the hallways and up and down staircases—our son Alexander learned to walk independently while exploring the ship this way. Participate in activities listed on the Family "track." While not all will be suitable, many are designed to accommodate toddlers (with their parents, of course). Your toddler may or may not sit through stage shows or enjoy Flounder's Reef/It's a Small World Nursery, but both are worth trying. Keep your eyes on the *Personal Navigator*, though. Recently, a "Little Ones" row has begun to appear on the schedule on some at-sea days, with activities like *Jack Jack's Diaper Dash* in the Atrium Lobby, *Toddler Time* in the Oceaneer Club, and *Wake Up With Disney Jr.* in D Lounge.

The Oceaneer Club and Lab on the Magic change completely in late 2013. New zones in the Club will be Andy's Room, Pixie Hollow, Marvel Avenger's Academy, and Mickey Mouse Club. The Lab will be pirate-themed, with an animation workshop and buccaneer navigation sims.

Playing at Oceaneer Club/Lab

Oceaneer Club and Oceaneer Lab are special areas on deck 5 midship **designed just for kids**.

The clubs are open to potty-trained kids ages 3 to 12. The Club is designed for younger children and the Lab is intended mostly for the older kids, and each facility's decor reflects that age orientation. The kids can participate in any activity offered in either the Club or Lab, so siblings, relatives, and friends no longer have to worry about being separated by age. The *Daily Navigator* lists activities by location (Club or Lab), rather than age group, with up to five activities in progress at any time. The lack of specific age limits does not mean all activities are appropriate or intended for all ages. Each programming track appeals to a different age group. Participation in the Club and Lab is included in your cruise fare.

The Club and Lab provide fun, **age-appropriate activities** throughout the day and late into the evening. Some kids spend virtually their entire cruise in these areas, while others drop in now and then. Some prefer to spend their time with their families or just playing with other kids elsewhere. Typically, the kids that visit the Club and Lab on their first evening (when friendships are being formed) are more likely to enjoy the experience.

To participate in the Club and Lab, you may **preregister in advance online** (see page 183). Preregistering online means you can skip the Club open house on embarkation day—just pick up your child(ren)'s wristbands in the cruise terminal before you board. If you don't pre-register, drop by the Club and Lab on your first afternoon to take a look around and register your kid(s). To register, you'll need to fill out a participation form indicating name(s), birthday(s), age(s), special considerations (such as allergies, fears, and/or any special needs), and give your authorization for first aid if necessary. While there are maximum occupancy limits for the Club and Lab, Disney Cruise Line is very careful about booking and ratios—it's extremely rare that the Club and Lab fill up.

Once registered, your kids may **partake of Club/Lab activities as often as desired**—there's no need to sign up for blocks of time, no reservations for activities, and no worries. Kids ages 3 to 7 must have their parents sign them in when they enter the Club and the parents must return to sign them out later. Parents of kids 8 to 9 can indicate whether their kids can sign themselves in and out of the Lab or if the parents must sign them in and out. Ten-year-olds can sign themselves in and out by default. Wave Phones (page 147) are used for contacting parents. Each child gets a wristband—they should keep the wristband on for the duration of the cruise. Name tags are applied to children upon each visit. Parents are welcome to drop in and observe at any time.

The **Oceaneer Club on the Magic** (see photo to right) is a fanciful, Neverland-themed playroom with a pirate ship to climb and computers to play. It's also equipped with a dress-up room, and a stage. It's a big hit with the younger crowd.

© MediaMarx, Inc.

Alexander was captivated by the treasure chest TV at the Oceaneer Club

© MediaMarx, Inc.

Pixie Hollow at the Oceaneer Club on the Dream

On the Wonder, the Club offers more hands-on, interactive activities, as well as additional PlayStation and computer stations. Jennifer's niece Megan fell in love with it at first glance. Our son Alexander now enjoys playing here, too! **On the Dream Class**, activity areas include Andy's Room, Monster's Academy, Pixie Hollow, and Explorer Pod. Magic PlayFloor hosts interactive games and activities on a touch-sensitive surface, above 28 video screens –kids' movements control the game play.

The **Oceaneer Lab on the Magic Class ships** looks just like it sounds—a kids' lab! It has lots of tables and cupboards, along with computer game stations, activity stations, and board games. Allie's visit here (at age 9) is one of her best memories of the cruise—she loved making "Flubber"! **On the Dream Class**, the Lab houses The Animator's Studio, Wheel House, Craft Studio, and Sound Studio. Two large workshops located between the Club and Lab provide space for art, science, and cooking activities.

Study your ***Personal Navigator***—you'll find a great number of group activities planned, including games, crafts, movies, dancing, and theme parties . Here is a sample of activities taken from recent *Personal Navigators* (keep in mind that not all of these activities may be available on your cruise):

Sample Activities for Oceaneer Club (mostly for younger kids)

✔ Nemo's Coral Reef Adventures—Join Nemo for a magical puppet show!
✔ Do-Si-Do with Snow White—Learn the "Dance of the Seven Little Dwarves"
✔ So You Want To Be a Pirate?—Learn how to play pirate with Captain Hook!
✔ Pluto's PJ Party

Sample Activities for Oceaneer Lab (mostly for older kids)

✔ Ratatouille Cooking School
✔ Professor Goo's Magical Experiments—Make your own Flubber!
✔ Goofy Files—Enter the invisible world of forensics and crack a case
✔ Animation Cels

© MediaMarx, Inc.

Fanciful climbing toys at Oceaneer Club

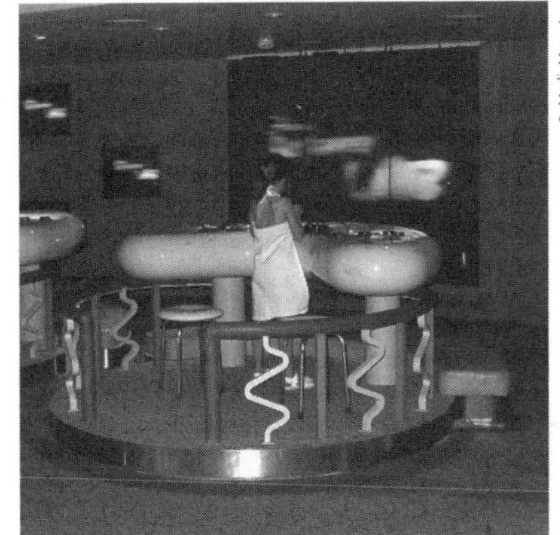
© MediaMarx, Inc.

A huge video game station at Oceaneer Lab

Oceaneer Club and Lab *(continued)*

Tips and Notes

The **first organized activities** on your first night aboard typically start at 6:00 pm or 7:00 pm (the afternoon is an Open House). Parents are welcome to accompany their children, to help them acclimate to the new surroundings.

Trained **counselors** keep kids active and safe. The counselor-to-kid ratio is 1:15 (ages 3 to 4) and 1:25 (ages 5 to 12). Counselors are mostly female, college grads, and from English-speaking countries (Canada and the United Kingdom are most likely). Be assured that counselors are trained in how to evacuate children in the event of an emergency.

If your kids are checked in during **mealtimes**, they'll generally be taken up as a group to Topsider's/Beach Blanket Buffet/Cabanas for a trip through a special kid-friendly buffet. At times, younger children may remain in the Club for meals, at the discretion of the counselors. Other than that, no food or drink (other than a water fountain) is provided.

Families with late seating dinner can use **Dine and Play**, which may help Mom and Dad have a more relaxing and leisurely dinner. Notify your server at the start of the meal, and dinner will be expedited for those children 3–12 who will be participating. 45 minutes into dinner, kids program counselors arrive in the dining room to escort the kids to their evening fun, and everyone else can continue with their meals.

If your child is very **recently potty-trained**, have a special talk with them before leaving them alone at the Club. All that first-day excitement may give them upset tummies, and they may not know what to do without you there to help. Show them where the toilet is, explain to them that they will need to use the toilet by themselves (the crew members cannot help them nor will they regularly prompt them to use the toilet), and remind them that they can ask a counselor to contact you if they have a problem. Rest assured that the toilets and sinks are kid-sized and kid height. If a child has an accident, you will be paged and they may be asked not to revisit for 24 to 48 hours in the event their accident was the result of an illness. Pull-up diapers are not allowed unless you are dropping off your child in their pajamas in the evening hours, as it is understood that young children may sleep in pull-up type diapers at night and will probably be sleeping when you pick them up.

Do you have a **toddler under three** who is already potty-trained? If so, the counselors may allow your child to join the Oceaneer Club on a trial basis. Your child must be fully potty-trained, however, from deciding when to go, finding the toilet, closing the door, removing clothing, going potty, wiping, redressing, and washing up. If you have a fully potty-trained child, and you feel your child is ready for this type of environment, talk to the counselors and politely inquire if your child can be accommodated.

Kids may stay in the Club and Lab while you go **play in port**. Just be sure to let the counselors know where you are, and be aware that your Wave Phone won't work when you leave the ship. Also check that the Club/Lab opens early enough for your shore excursion meeting time—typical morning start time in the Club and Lab is 9:00 am.

If a child gets **sleepy** while at the Club, they can nap on a sleep mat, which is usually placed near the check-in desk or in a quiet corner. If kids are still in the Club around 10:00 pm, counselors will bring out sleep mats to rest on while watching movies.

Watch for fun activities, like this cupcake decorating activity on the Dream

Activities for Adults

Kids, keep out—this page is just for grown-ups! Disney may be family-focused, but rest assured Disney hasn't forgotten your adult needs. There are **plenty of adult-oriented and adult-only activities** onboard, including an entire entertainment district (see next page). If you're worried you'll be bored, it's unlikely—we never have enough time to do what we want, with or without kids. Here's a list of specifically adult-oriented activities:

Bingo—Bingo is the only gambling onboard and attracts mostly adults. (Kids often attend and play, but you must be 18 or older to claim any winnings.) Bingo is held at least once a day in Rockin' Bar D/WaveBands/Promenade Lounge/D Lounge or Buena Vista Theatre. A special "Snowball" jackpot rolls over each day until won. Cards are currently about $19 for a single pack (3 cards, one per game) and $29 for a value pack (6 cards, two per game). Electronic card pads ($49–$99/session) "play" for you, and can provide more cards at a better value. Your odds of winning are higher earlier in the cruise, when fewer people are playing. Prizes (cash and gifts) are awarded daily at each game. Yeah, baby!

Dance Lessons—Learn the basics of ballroom dancing—check your *Personal Navigator*.

Beer, Margarita, Tequila, and Wine Tastings—There are beer and margarita tastings in Diversions/687/O'Gill's Pub (check your *Navigator*). There's also a wine tasting seminar (about $15) in which only adults can participate. Make reservations at Guest Services.

Captain's Receptions—Meet the captain at various functions, including receptions and Disney Navigator Series seminars (see page 209).

Sports—Shoot hoops or play volleyball on the sports deck (deck 10 fwd/13 aft), sharpen up your game in the golf simulator (Dream Class), play shuffleboard or run laps on deck 4, or try your hand at Ping-Pong (deck 9/11 mid). And don't forget the exercise classes in the Vista/Senses Spa (see pages 206–208).

Pin Trading—Bring along your pins and trade with others. Special pin trading sessions are generally held in the Atrium Lobby—check your *Personal Navigator*.

Games—Play chess or backgammon in Diversions/687/O'Gill's Pub or Scrabble in Sessions/Cadillac Lounge. Look for pool games at the Quiet Cove pool. Check your *Personal Navigator*.

Auction/Art Sale at Sea—Fun to bid or just watch others bid! See page 211 for details.

Cocktail Hours—Held in the Atrium (deck 3 midship) or in the adult entertainment district's lounges. Alas, the beverages—alcoholic or not—aren't complimentary, with the possible exception of the Captain's Reception.

Seminars and Tours—Get the low-down on shopping, shore excursions, and debarkation procedures with talks held in the Buena Vista Theatre (note that these talks are available on your stateroom TV if you can't make it). And on the 7-night and longer cruises, adults can learn the art of entertaining, get behind-the-scenes peeks, and more. See page 209.

You'll also enjoy these **adult-only places**: Palo and Remy restaurants (see pages 163–166), Vista/Senses Spa (see page 206–208), the Quiet Cove pool (see page 200), the Cove Café (see page 199), Signals/Cove bar (deck 9/11 forward), the adult entertainment district (see next page), and Serenity Bay Beach on Castaway Cay (see page 246). And while it's not adults-only, the Buena Vista movie theater in the late evenings may show a PG-13 film (see page 202).

Tip: Check your *Personal Navigator's* grid for the "Adult" rows for adult activities.

As part of the Disney Magic's overhaul in late 2013, Beat Street becomes After Hours, with Fathoms night club, Keys piano lounge, and O'Gill's sports pub.

Adult Entertainment District
(Beat Street/Route 66/The District/Europa)

After all those adults-only activities, you may want an adults-only place to wind down the day, too. Beat Street (Magic) and Route 66 (Wonder), both on deck 3 forward, and The District (Dream) and Europa (Fantasy) on deck 4 aft, are exclusively for adults 18 and older after 9:00 pm.

The names and decor of the clubs and lounges may differ on the four ships, but they offer comparable venues. On all ships you can expect to find a dance club; a relaxing, adult lounge (three lounges on the Dream and Fantasy); a pub; and the ship's duty-free liquor shop (Magic Class only). Here is a description of each club:

Dance Club—Rockin' Bar D (Magic), WaveBands (Wonder), Evolution (Dream), and The Tube (Fantasy) are the ships' largest clubs, offering Top 40 and Golden Oldies dance music, DJs, and karaoke hours. Cabaret acts featuring entertainers from the stage shows may also take place. Typically, a special event is held each evening around 10:30 pm or 11:00 pm, such as the Match Your Mate game show, Krazy Karaoke, Rock Star, One Hit Wonders, and so on. Guests are selected from the dance floor to participate in some shows—if you want to be picked, get up and be wild! A DJ or live band generally precedes and follows these events, with the Dream Class' schedule especially disco-heavy. Look for fun dance parties like "Disco Legends" (70s music) and "Livin' Large" (new music). Hours are usually from 7:30 pm to 2:00 am. Smoking is not allowed in any part of this club.

Dave gets drafted to play one of the Village People during 70s Disco Night

Smoking Onboard

Unlike most other cruise lines, Disney restricts smoking to limited areas on the ships, and enforces their rules. Smoking is allowed only on stateroom verandahs and certain outdoor deck areas (starboard/right side only). The Mickey Pool area is all non-smoking. Smoking is not allowed in the lounges, dance club, and indoor bars. Smoking is not allowed in any of the staterooms, and a $250 stateroom cleaning fee may be assessed for evidence of smoking. We've had no problems with smoke on our cruises. And smokers report that the accessibility of smoking areas meets their needs, though it is sometimes tough to find an ashtray (try deck 10/12). You can purchase cigarettes ($16/carton) in the liquor shop on deck 3 forward. For those interested in Cuban cigars, you can buy them in virtually all of the Caribbean ports except Key West. At the time of writing, cigar smoking was allowed only in the usual open-air guest areas (decks 9, 10, and stateroom verandahs). Sometimes there is a cigar night on the deck outside Cove Café or Meridian Lounge (Dream Class). Keep in mind that you cannot bring Cuban cigars back into the U.S., so smoke 'em while you can.

Introduction | Reservations | Staterooms | Dining | Activities | Ports of Call | Magic | Index

Skyline on the Disney Dream

Adult Lounge—This lounge is always adults-only most of the time. On the Magic, it's called Sessions and it has a jazzy feel. On the Wonder, it's Cadillac Lounge and has a vintage auto theme. On the Dream, it's the District Lounge, and on the Fantasy, it's Italian plaza-themed La Piazza, complete with a Vespa motor scooter. Younger people are welcome until 9:00 pm. Relax in low, comfy chairs, listen to live music, and get mellow. This is a perfect spot for pre-dinner or pre-show drinks and romantic interludes. Hours are usually from 4:30 pm to midnight or 1:00 am. Smoking is not permitted in any part of this club. The Dream Class ships each have two more lounges in The District/Europa; Skyline, on both ships, is lined with floor to ceiling video screens to evoke the view from an elegant penthouse (this is Dave's favorite "hang"). Every 15 minutes the scene changes to another great city. Pink (Dream) and Ooh La La (Fantasy) are quiet, moderately-lit lounges, especially popular with the ladies. Pink has a "bubbly" theme intended to evoke the inside of a glass of champagne, and Ooh La La has a Parisienne boudoir feel.

Diversions/687/O'Gill's Pub— This all-purpose pub and sports bar is a clubby room filled with comfy chairs. Warm wood tones create a relaxing atmosphere, as do chess/backgammon tables and a small selection of books and magazines. What can you do here besides drink, play, and relax? Check your *Personal Navigator* for sporting event broadcasts (shown on the numerous televisions in the back), beer tastings and trivia, and a British Pub Night. Smoking is not allowed in any part of this venue.

Beverages are served at all clubs, and each club has its specialties, such as champagne at Pink and beers in the pubs. See page 172 for details on availability and prices. Snacks may be available out in the hallway and in the pub after about10:00 pm. There's duty-free liquor for sale in the shops (see page 457), but purchases cannot be consumed onboard.

Cove Café

A cozy adults-only area is available on all ships: Cove Café on deck 9 or 11, beside the adults-only pool. Cove Café is a comfy coffeehouse, lined with books and magazines and filled with light from huge portholes and sliding glass doors. A large-screen TV shows news and sporting events, and several music listening stations are available. The area immediately outside the café has comfortable padded lounge chairs. Wireless Internet access is available, both inside and immediately outside, and "café laptops" may be available for a fee. An extensive specialty coffee menu is available—expect to pay $2.00 for espresso, $2.50 for cappuccino and café mocha, and $4.75 for coffee drinks laced with liquors. Teas ($3.75) are also available, as is champagne, wine, port, martinis, and a full bar. Light snacks such as pastries and sandwiches are available, too. Open until midnight.

Cove Café on the Disney Wonder

Coming to the Magic in late 2013: Mickey's Pool will be totally re-made into AquaLab, with a longer slide, splash play areas, and wading pool. Tots get an enhanced Nephews' Splash Zone, and cruisers 48"/122 cm and up can plunge 37 feet down the AquaDunk thrill slide.

Swimming in the Pools

Cruise ship pools aren't exactly sized for Olympic competition, but while your ship's three pools are best described as "cozy," it doesn't stop them from being some of the busiest places onboard. What makes Disney's pools especially nice is that they're fresh water, not salt; that kids, families, and adults each get their own pool; and that they have a little extra magic.

Quiet Cove Adult Pool—is on deck 9/11 forward. This is one of the many areas on the ship where adults can go for child-free relaxation. Pool depth is 48" (122 cm). Adjacent are two whirlpools, Vista/Senses Spa, Cove Café, and the Signals/Cove bar (with swim-up access on the Dream and Fantasy). Deluxe lounge chairs with comfy cushions are arranged on the teak deck, and live musicians may be on hand. The Fantasy also features **Satellite Falls**, a fountain and wading pool on the adults-only sun deck on deck 13 forward.

On Deck 9/11 midship is **Goofy's/Donald's Family Pool**, one of the busiest spots on board. Alongside the family pool are two whirlpools, an open shower, quick-service dining (see page 169), and a stage where the crew and Disney characters join the guests for the deck parties (see next page). A hideaway deck is pulled out to cover the pool during parties. The Ariel View/Funnel Vision video screen overlooks this pool. Pool depth is 48" (122 cm).

The sight to see is **Mickey's Kid's Pool**. True to Disney style, a regular wading pool and slide is transformed into Mickey Mouse. His face is the main part of the pool with a depth of 18" (46 cm). Mickey's ears (with a depth of 11"/28 cm) are for the very little ones (Magic Class). This is a very busy place on sea days. The centerpiece of Mickey's Pool is the water slide supported by Mickey's gloved hand. To use the slide, kids must be from ages 4 to 14 and between 32"/38" and 64" tall (81 to 162 cm). The slide is staffed by crew members, but there are no lifeguards. Health regulations require that kids be potty-trained—swim diapers are not allowed in the pools. Kids in swim diapers can use the adjoining, 385-sq. ft. **Mickey Splash Zone** with interactive fountains (Magic Class) or 1,500-sq.-ft., glass-enclosed and fully-shaded **Nemo's Reef** on the Dream Class. Quick-service dining (see page 169) is nearby. Note: On the Dream Class, the Mickey and Donald pools are **next to each other**, making it much easier to watch all your kids!

© MediaMarx, Inc.

Mickey Pool and AquaDuck on the Disney Dream

The Dream Class features **AquaDuck**, a 765-foot long "water coaster" that starts high in the aft stack and gradually descends to splash-down on deck 12. Riders sit atop inflatable rafts, and high-speed water jets push them along. To ride solo, riders must be at least age 7 and 54"/137 cm tall. Tandem riders must be over 42"/107cm, and under age 7 they must ride with someone 14 or older. Lines can be very long. Try riding on port days or after 6:00 pm. The Fantasy adds **AquaLab**, a splash play zone for older kids, on deck 12 aft.

Typical **pool hours** are from 6:00 am to 10:00 pm for Mickey's Pool and 6:00 am to midnight for the other pools. The Family pool closes during deck parties and other events that use the retractable deck. Mickey's slide is usually only open 9:00 am to 6:30 pm.

Living It Up at Deck Parties

Every Disney cruise, regardless of its length, has at least one of Disney's famous deck parties. These high-energy parties are held on and around the family pool on deck 9/11 midship. No, you don't have to dance on water—the pool is covered by a large, retractable dance floor during the parties. You can expect to be entertained by some or all of the following: a live band, DJ, dancers, pirates, fireworks, a dessert buffet, big video screen, and "party animals" (Disney characters). Here are descriptions:

Bon Voyage Sailaway Celebration—Every cruise begins with this celebration, held as your ship pulls away from the dock. This is probably the first time you'll meet your cruise director, who is joined by Disney characters and either a live band or a DJ. As the ship gets underway, the ship's whistle plays a familiar Disney melody. We highly recommend this party—it really gets you in the mood (see the photo on page 27). Tip: Celebrate your sailaway by bringing bubbles to blow or a small flag to wave! (Party typically starts at 4:15 pm or 4:30 pm and lasts for about 30–60 minutes.)

Pirates IN the Caribbean Night—Ahoy, ye landlubbers! This fun deck party is offered to all Disney cruisers, regardless of cruise length. On the three- and four-night cruises, it's held on your second to last evening; on the seven-night cruises, it's held on day 4 or 5 (see page 176 for schedule). Kid-focused activities may start as early as 7:30 pm, either on deck or in Studio Sea/D Lounge. The main party starts around 9:45 pm on the Magic Class, 10:30 pm on the Dream Class, after the Pirate-themed dinner earlier that evening (see page 167). Expect lots of infectious music, dancing, and visits from Disney characters (watch out for Captain Hook!). You're treated to a Pirate buffet with desserts and "pirate fare" such as chili, fajitas, and turkey legs. Pirates invade the party, and weather or local laws permitting, it's all topped off by fireworks! Night owls can watch a Pirates of the Caribbean movie afterwards, on the outdoor screen. This is a not-to-be-missed experience. Pirate or Caribbean dress is encouraged (we dress up and love it!). Pirate gear is available on board, or bring your own. The Fantasy offers pirate make-overs in Pirate's League (see page 192).

Pirates on Deck!

The **music** at the deck parties is quite loud and is geared toward older kids, teens, and young adults. If you don't want to be in the thick of things, you may enjoy watching from deck 10/12 midship. We recommend you visit deck 10/12 during the sailaway party—it's the best place to enjoy the party while watching the ship pull away (see sidebar below).

Note: In inclement weather, the deck parties are held in the Atrium Lobby (deck 3 mid).

Sailing Away From Your Ship's Home Port

One of the most exciting experiences of your cruise is when your ship pulls away from the pier for the first time and makes her way down the channel with an escort of security boats, headed for the ocean. Make time to go up to deck 10/12 around 5:00 pm to watch the scenery slide by to port or starboard, and watch your ship's forward progress from deck 10/13 forward. Look at the terminal in Port Canaveral as you pull away—crew members don huge Mickey gloves and wave the ship off.

Introduction | Reservations | Staterooms | Dining | Activities | Ports of Call | Magic | Index

Watching Movies and TV

The Walt Disney Company all started with a mouse projected on a movie screen, and its cruise line takes those beginnings seriously. From the sumptuous **Buena Vista movie theater** on deck 5 aft/4 & 5 midship with its 268/360 stadium-style seats and two-story screen, to the giant 24-by-14-foot outdoor screen on decks 9 & 10/11 & 12, and the free, round-the-clock Disney movie channels or on-demand video on your stateroom TV, you'll never lack free filmed entertainment on a Disney cruise.

Of course, you'll see Disney animated classics and first-run films from Disney's motion picture divisions. You can also see popular, non-Disney movies a few months after release. Headline films, including Disney premieres (same day they premiere on land), may be shown in the larger Walt Disney Theatre. Disney Digital 3-D is installed on all ships and you can expect at least one 3-D film during your cruise. Films are mostly rated G and PG (with some PG-13 and a rare R in the Buena Vista Theatre only) and are shown at age-appropriate times. Movies are free, and they start as early as 9:30 am—the last show usually starts between 10:00 pm and 11:00 pm. Check your *Personal Navigator* or the theater for a **list of movies** during your cruise. Matinees on at-sea days are popular—arrive early for a good seat. Wondering what will be playing when you cruise? About a week before you cruise, you can call 888-325-2500, choose the "reservations" option, then ask the representative. Tip: If you like to snack during your movies, a stand outside the theater sells packaged snacks, popcorn, and beverages. To save money, order from room service or take a detour up to deck 9/11's snack counters.

Buena Vista Theatre

The **big-screen outdoor movies on the Ariel View Television/Funnel Vision** (see page 27) are always rated G or PG and shows a wide variety of Disney favorites. The large, bright screen is affixed to the stack above Goofy's/Donald's Pool (deck 9/11 midship). Films play in afternoons and evenings, but there are generally just one or two movies daily.

Your **stateroom TV** has plenty to watch, too... more than 50 channels on the Magic Class, or a huge selection of on-demand entertainment on the Dream Class, and it is all free! Below are examples from the channel guide (channels and stations may vary). Use the TV for Disney background music. Check your stateroom for a printed movie listing. Expect about a dozen highlighted features, plus many Disney and Pixar classics. On the Magic Class, the "all movies, all the time" channels (241-264) each start a new movie every three hours, on a staggered schedule. Tip: You may be able to watch recordings of the live stage shows on your TV—look between 6:30 pm and 10:30 pm on show nights.

202 Entertain. Guide	207 CNN Headline News	221 Safety	261-262 Dis Animation
203 View from Bridge	208 CNN	222 Port Adventures	263 Disney*Pixar
204 Bridge Report	211 Disney Channel	223 Ports/Shopping	264 Dis Live Action
205 BBC World	214-217 ESPN	233 Theatre Shows	265 Sitcoms
206 ABC	218 Special Events	241-256 Feature Films	266 ABC Series

Enjoying the Shows

Depend on the world's greatest entertainment company to deliver the **best live shows** on the seven seas. Disney turned to Broadway and Hollywood for inspiration (rather than Las Vegas), and delivers shows that the whole family enjoys. Live shows are presented in the Walt Disney Theatre on deck 4/3 & 4 forward, a 975/1,340-seat showplace. State-of-the-art staging, sound, and lighting systems (there are nearly 400 stage lights!) and a very talented cast combine to entertain you.

On all of the cruise itineraries, you can expect to see three elaborately-produced stage shows. Cruises of 4 nights or longer may include a movie screening. The 7+-night cruises add the *Welcome Aboard Variety Show*, an entertainer (such as a juggler or magician), and the *Farewell Variety Show*. Shows are held **twice nightly** at roughly the same times as the dinner seatings (see page 154), so if you have the early seating, you'll see the "late" show (and vice versa). Shows are 50 to 55 minutes long. Arrive about 15 to 30 minutes before showtime to get a good seat. Disney doesn't allow videotaping, flash photography, or the saving of seats in the theater. Preludes (just outside the theater) sells beverages and snacks, or bring your own. Smoothies and beverages are sold in the theater before the show.

Toy Story-The Musical (Wonder)–follows the heartwarming storyline of the first Toy Story movie. The stage adaptation features eight new songs.

Twice Charmed–An Original Twist on the Cinderella Story (Magic)–What would happen if an Evil Fairy Godfather turned back time to stop Cinderella from wearing the glass slipper?

The Golden Mickeys (Wonder and Dream)–This delightful, Hollywood-style award show includes favorite musical scenes from Disney films, just as you might see at the Oscars.

Villains Tonight (Magic and Dream)– Hades, Pain, and Panic (who "starred" in the cruise line's *Hercules the Muse-ical*) are on hand to drive the plot forward, while an incredible lineup of Disney villains make their musically evil way across the stage.

Disney Dreams (Magic and Wonder)–Every Disney fan will be misty-eyed by the end of this "bedtime story!" Anne-Marie is visited in her dreams by characters from her favorite Disney stories. It's the most popular show aboard, so be prepared for a full house and arrive early. Check your *Personal Navigator* for an extra performance in the afternoon.

Disney's Believe (Dream and Fantasy)–A no-nonsense dad learns to believe in magic with the help of his daughter and Aladdin's Genie, featuring scenes from beloved Disney classics.

Disney's Wishes (Fantasy)–A trio of high school friends contemplate adult life at a last fling at Disneyland. Beloved Disney characters and music bring them insight.

Disney's Aladdin-A Musical Spectacular (Fantasy)–The beloved Disney film comes to life, "Street Rat," Genie, Princess Jasmine, Magic Carpet, and all!

Variety and Cabaret Shows (Magic, Wonder, Fantasy)–Featuring guest performers who do a short sampling of the shows they'll perform later in the night clubs.

Welcome and Farewell Shows (Magic, Wonder, Fantasy)–The 7-night and longer itineraries include special shows to kick-off and wrap-up a memorable voyage. The Magic Class shows feature variety acts, the Fantasy presents more elaborate productions.

Surfing the Internet

While it isn't as fun as a message in a bottle, the Internet is an easy, quick way to keep in touch with family, friends, and clients while you're cruising. Internet access is available on all ships as wireless access (WiFi) in most areas of the ships, and at computer terminals on the Magic Class ships.

Terminal Access—On the Magic Class, computer terminals are available to guests in one or two locations onboard: the Internet Cafe (main location, open to everyone), and the Cove Café (Disney Magic only). On the Dream Class, there are no terminals, but laptops may be borrowed (first come, first served, limited quantities) from the Cove Café at no charge ($200 deposit is required). Regular internet connection fees then apply. The Internet Cafe (Magic Class, aft end of the Promenade Lounge on deck 3 midship) is open 24 hours a day and boasts about 8 terminals (flat panel screens, keyboards, mice, headphones, and video cameras). All terminals are installed with web browsers. Your e-mail provider may offer a web-based interface to check your e-mail—inquire about this before you leave home and bring any necessary web site addresses, login names, and passwords with you (see worksheet on the next page). Note that if you can access your e-mail through the web, you avoid the CruisEmail rates noted later (see Pricing on the next page)—just be sure not to send e-mail through the "E-Mail" option on the terminal and use the web instead. Note that if you log in to any e-mail, message boards, or other sites that require a login name and password, be sure to log off before you leave the terminal. If you do not, the next person who uses those same sites could find themselves able to access your account or post under your user name. SeaMobile (http://www.seamobile.com) provides reliable Internet access. If you have questions once you are onboard, you can check with one of the Internet Cafe managers, who are on duty during the day and early evening. There may be a printer available near terminals (Magic Class) for an additional per-page fee—inquire with the manager on duty. Note that the Internet Cafe is not always open the morning of disembarkation.

Wireless Access—Wireless Internet access is available in public spaces in many locations on the ship. To use it, you'll need to bring your own WiFi-equipped laptop and power cables. Once onboard, look for the Wireless Internet information sheet at the Internet Cafe or from Guest Services (deck 3). Next go to a wireless "hot spot" on the ship— the hot spots include most public areas including lounges, guest staterooms, and the open deck areas on decks 9 and 10/11-13. While wireless access reaches to staterooms (see page 151), signal strength may not always be ideal. When we can't get a good signal in our stateroom, we like to use our laptop while sitting in the comfortable chairs on deck 4 or 5, overlooking the atrium, or in the Cove Café. Connecting with a variety of mobile devices (including iPhones and iPads) has been smooth sailing. Instructions for both PC and Mac users are provided on the information sheet from Guest Services. Note that printing is not available with wireless access. Note: VOIP (Voice Over Internet Protocol) services, such as Skype or FaceTime, had been blocked on the Disney ships, but cruisers are currently reporting that they are working (albeit slowly, of course).

Pricing—Alas, Internet usage is not free. Expect to pay 75 cents a minute for access (either terminal access or wireless access, which you can use interchangeably). If you

➢

expect to surf for more than an hour total, you can pre-purchase your minutes for less. For cruises shorter than 7 nights, Internet packages are 50 min./$27.50, 100 min./$40 and 250 min/$75. For cruises of 7-nights or more, packages are 100 min./$55, 250 min./$100, and 500 min./$150. Your minutes can be used for both terminal access and wireless access. Alas, there is no longer an unlimited minutes package offered. Everyone in your stateroom can use your minutes, but only one person can be logged in at a time. Note that you are "on the meter" from the moment you log in until you log off. It's very important that you specifically log off as directed when you use wireless access, or you may continue spending your minutes! All Internet usage fees are automatically billed to your onboard account. Parents who don't want their kids to use the Internet can contact Guest Services to disable their Internet accounts. Note that no credit is given for unused time plan minutes. If you feel you have fewer purchased minutes remaining than you expected and suspect an error, visit Guest Services (deck 3) to discuss it. Note that printing from terminals (Magic Class only) is available at 25 cents per page.

Logging In—Expect to enter a login name—it's typically the first initial and last name of the person under whose name the cruise reservation was made, plus the stateroom number (e.g., jmarx2612). Passwords are also required, and may initially be the birthdate of the person who made the cruise reservation.

Access—If you've pre-purchased a block of minutes, only one member of your family/group can be online at any one time. Note that if another family member is online somewhere else, you won't be able to get online until they log off. While there are computers in the Oceaneer Club and Lab, the kids can not surf the Internet from them.

Off-Board Internet Access—There are cafes with Internet terminals offering lower rates in various ports of call. In Nassau, "Tikal Tees & Tokens" has Internet access at 10 cents/min. In St. Maarten, there's an Internet Cafe at the end of the pier for 20 cents a minute. In St. Thomas, "Soapy's Station" in front of the Havensight Mall offers access at 10 cents/min. In Key West, check out the "Internet Isle Cafe" on 118 Duval Street for 25 cents/min. In Cozumel, the "C@fe Internet" near Ave. 10 and Calle 1 has access at 10 cents/min. You can usually find Internet Cafes very near the pier—just browse or ask around.

Web Site Addresses—E-mail your favorite web site addresses to yourself before you cruise or visit http://www.passporter.com/dcl/porthole.htm once onboard for helpful links.

My E-Mail: ______________________________

Account	Login Name	Password	Notes

Tip: Use some system to disguise your passwords here, just in case your PassPorter is seen by someone else.

Even the spa gets a makeover during the Magic's late 2013 overhaul! Vista Spa is re-branded Senses Spa, expands by 725 sq. ft., gets a redesigned reception area, a larger salon, and adds teeth-whitening services, a men's barber shop, and a teen spa.

Rejuvenating at the Spa

The Vista Spa & Salon (Magic Class, deck 9) and Senses Spa and Salon (Dream Class, decks 11 and 12) offer world-class spa treatments, a hair salon, an aerobics studio, and a fitness room. The large spa is **for adults** (with the exception of special teen days on the Magic Class ships and Chill Spa for teens on the Dream Class). The expansive spa on the Magic Class ships measures 10,700 sq. ft., and on the Dream Class, 16,000 sq. ft. Like most cruise ship spas, the facility is operated by Steiner (http://www.steinerleisure.com) and the spa staff tends to be female and young. The spa is typically open from 8:00 am to 10:00 pm. Most spa reservations can be made in advance online (see page 183).

If the spa interests you, we recommend you visit during the **open house** on your first afternoon (check your *Personal Navigator*). This is also the best time to reserve spa treatments, if you haven't booked online. Reservations must be canceled at least 24 hours in advance to avoid a 50% fee.

The **hair salon** offers a variety of services—reservations are necessary, can only be made on board, and they fill up quickly for formal and semi-formal evenings. The hair stylists specialize in European styles and all the basics. Prices: blow dry ($32 to $48); woman's hair cut with wash, cut, and style—$56 to $75 (depends on length); man's cut and style—$30 to $42; highlights/lowlights—$85 to $105; and permanent color (full head)—$90 to $112. You can also get nail services: Manicures are $44 to $50, pedicures are $60 to $70 and acrylics (full set) are $82. Waxing services run from $29 to $85. The Dream Class ships offer a separate men's barber shop.

The **aerobics studio** is where many of the fitness classes and seminars are held. Activities are listed in the *Personal Navigator* as well as on a schedule available in the spa. Expect complimentary hair consultations, metabolism seminars, fatburner aerobics, detoxification seminars, skin care clinics, introduction to Pilates, de-stress techniques, Step Magic, and cardio kickbox. You are encouraged to sign up in advance for the free classes and seminars, which last about 30 to 45 minutes each. Group personal training may be offered on your cruise for $82/50 minutes. Or get a Body Composition Analysis to measure your body's metabolic rate, water, fat, and lean tissue—the price is $33. Registration is required for the personal training sessions and body composition analysis.

The **fitness room** offers a panoramic vista, overlooking the ship's bow on the Magic Class ships, and views to the starboard side on the Dream Class. On all ships, the fitness room offers guests the use of free weights, Cybex weight machines, treadmills, stair-steppers, ab-rollers, and stationary bikes. iPods with preloaded music are available for use during workouts. No fees or reservations are needed to use the fitness room, though there may be a waitlist for a treadmill during peak times. The fitness room is more crowded on at-sea days. Open from 7:00 am to 8:00 pm.

Men's and women's locker rooms are available with restrooms, delightful showers, saunas, steam rooms, and lockers. Some people prefer the showers at the spa to the showers in their staterooms—there's more room, the water pressure's better, and the showerhead is luxurious. Feel free to use the locker rooms whenever you need them—lockers have electronic locks and robes are provided in the locker rooms, and both may be used free of charge.

Introduction Reservations Staterooms Dining Activities Ports of Call Magic Index

Spa Treatments are given in one of 12/17 private treatment rooms or in the private "spa villas." A variety of treatments are available at prices ranging from $26 to $288. We've underlined the spa treatments we've tried and would do again! A menu of treatments is available in the spa, but here's a sneak peek: Spa Taster (massage and facial for $109/50 min. total or $242 for couples massage); Aroma Seaweed Massage ($188/75 min.); Ionithermie Super-Detox ($188/120 min.); Aroma Stone Massage ($188/75 min.); Elemis Oxydermy Facial ($169); Elemis Pro Collagen Facial ($145/50 min.); Elemis Absolut Spa Ritual ($249/100 min.); Lime & Ginger Salt Glow with half-body massage ($151); Go-Smile Teeth Whitening ($149/30 min.); and Cabana Massage at Castaway Cay (see next page). Let's not forget the Tropical Rainforest, the Couples Rasul Ritual, and the Spa Villas—read on for more details!

Tropical Rainforest—An innovative, relaxing "thermal suite" with a dry sauna, a chamomile-essence sauna, a eucalyptus steam room, and special showers that spray water overhead and on the sides. The main room has four/10 heated, tiled loungers (see photo)—loll about on one then cool off in a fog shower. Jennifer loves this! The lounger area on the Dream Class has big picture windows and two hot tubs right outside. The Tropical Rainforest is open from 8:00 am to 10:00 pm. It's very popular and can host upwards of two dozen people—co-ed—at any one time. Quietest times are on the first day of the cruise and on port days. On busy days, the wait for a tiled lounger can be frustrating. Swimsuits are required. Cost is $15/day (not available on all cruises). Length-of-cruise passes are $42-$145. Rainforest day passes can be hard to get onboard—buy in advance at http://disneycruise.disney.go.com/gifts-and-amenities.

Jennifer relaxes in a heated lounge chair in the Tropical Rainforest

Couple Rasul Ritual (Magic Class)—This unique treatment is inspired by Ottoman cleansing rituals. You are escorted to a tile-lined suite with a sitting area, steam room, and shower. Exfoliating mud is in a small bowl—smear the mud on yourself or on each other and relax in the steam room to absorb the minerals and trace elements. Afterward, shower off and apply lotions and scrubs. This is very popular with couples. We loved it ourselves! Be warned that it does get very hot. Bring some bottled water. Cost is $89 for 50 minutes.

Relaxation Room (Dream Class)—Wind down before your treatment in this very restful space, with cushy loungers, dim lighting, and complimentary tea service.

Chill Spa for teens (Dream Class)—A mini-spa with two treatment rooms is tucked inside Senses Spa, and it's just for teens ages 13-17! Treatments run the gamut; massages ($89 solo, $195 mother and daughter or father and son), exfoliating Surfers Scrub ($65), facials ($94), manicures and pedicures ($29-$65), and hair styling ($32-$107). Parents must accompany teens when making reservations, and sign a release form.

Tip: Walk (or jog) all around the perimeter of deck 4—the "promenade" deck. One lap around deck 4 is 0.33/ 0.4 miles (535/644 m.); 3/2.5 laps is one mile (1.6 km). Note that the jogging direction is counter-clockwise to avoid collisions. Want to walk with others? Check your *Personal Navigator* for instructor-led "Walk a Mile" morning sessions.

Rejuvenating at the Spa *(continued)*

Spa Villas—For the ultimate in indulgence, consider the singles and couples spa "villas" with special spa treatments. The villas are private, Mediterranean-themed treatment rooms with their own verandahs, complete with whirlpool tubs, open-air showers, and luxurious lounge "beds." All spa treatments in the villas include a tea ceremony, a bathing ritual of your choice, and a foot cleansing ceremony—and you can spring for a bottle of champagne and strawberries or add an extra spa treatment. Treatments available in the single villas (for one person) include Alone Time (50-min. spa treatment of your choice—$199/105 min.); Body Purifying (100-min. body wrap with full body massage and dry float bed—$245/155 min.); and Sensory Awakening (facial and deep tissue massage—$295/155 min.). Treatments in the couples villas include Romantic Hideaway (50-min. spa treatment of your choice—$449/120 min.); Couples Choice (75-min. spa treatment of your choice—$475/130 min.); and Ultimate Indulgence (facial and deep tissue massage—$589/130 min.). If you do the math, you'll see that each of these treatments has 55–70 minutes of extra time included so you can enjoy your spa villa's amenities in privacy, though we should note that this extra time is not in one uninterrupted block but rather a bit before your treatment and the rest after. And if you need more privacy than the open-air verandah provides (remember, that is where your whirlpool tub and shower are located), there are two curtains you can use—one offers privacy for the shower, the other offers privacy for the tub. These curtains may not provide complete protection when it's windy or when in port (just something for the shy to keep in mind), though we didn't have difficulties in our Spa Villa experience. We absolutely adored our Spa Villa and found it infinitely relaxing and luxurious. We highly recommend it!

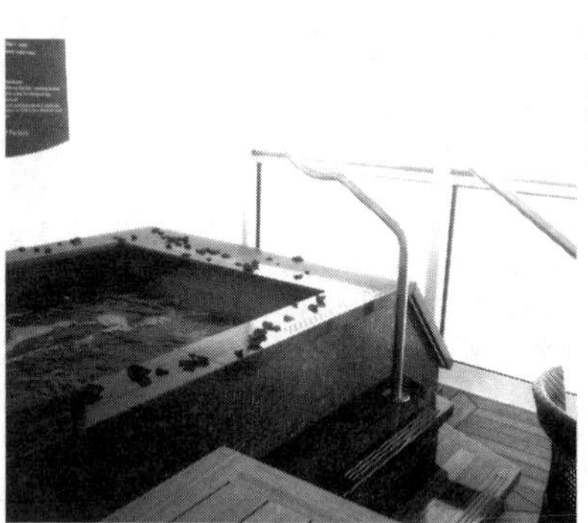

Spa villas have their own whirlpool tub!

Special Treatments—Check your *Personal Navigator* or visit the spa to learn about special treatments offered during your cruise. We've seen Teen Days for hair and nails, Pamper Package, and a Mid-Cruise Booster Package. The Pamper Package is a 50 minute massage and 25 minute facial in a private room, plus a trip to the Tropical Rainforest where you can enjoy champagne and sweets. Cost is $150.

Cabana Massages—Get a private or couples massage in one of the delightful, open-air cabanas on Castaway Cay. Note that the treatments in the cabanas are a bit more expensive than the same ones on the ship. Prices are $147 for a single massage and $294 for a couples massage (choose from Full Body, Pro-Collagen Facial, or Reflexology Combo). Reserve early as they book up quickly. We recommend you avoid the first or second appointment of the day, just in case the ship docks late. Also, keep in mind that the oils they massage into your skin can make your skin more likely to burn later in that Castaway Cay sunshine—bring hats and coverups as well as extra sunscreen. Also see page 248.

Spa Products—The spa personnel may push their spa products during treatments, which is uncomfortable for some guests. The products are Elemis (http://www.elemis.com) and are good, but pricey. If you don't want to buy a product, just say "no thank you" and be firm. You could also indicate on your health form that you don't want to purchase products.

Tipping—It's customary to tip 15%, though really good service may deserve 20%. 10% is fine for treatments like the Rasul Ritual that require minimal staff time or treatments like the spa villas that have extra private time. Just write the amount you wish to tip on your bill and it will be charged to your onboard account.

Learning Through Seminars

We keep saying that nobody has to be bored, even on a long cruise, and here's more proof! Disney produces a full schedule of shipboard tours, seminars, and programs for guests 18 and older. You don't even have to register or pay extra in most cases.

Disney's Art of Entertaining—These presentations showcase a senior chef who prepares a dish, allowing you to sample it. They also include tips on place setting, decorating, and napkin folding. Some have wine sampling. Programs include Great Expectations: The Appetizer, Dazzling Desserts, and Signature Entrée. Available on 7-night and longer itineraries only.

Galley Tour—Enjoy an adults-only guided tour of the kitchens on deck 3. Available on all ships, but may only be offered as a Castaway Club perk. See page 160 for more details.

Disney Behind the Scenes—Presentations by a Disney historian, actor, or artist (either a special guest or regular crew member), usually presented in the Buena Vista Theatre. These presentations vary in length and by topic but they are all entertaining and well worth the time. Past programs have included a Stage Works Tour (meet the stage production crew members and go up on the stage to take a look around at the set and props); Costuming Tour (see and even wear some of the costumes used in the show); and a Q&A session with the Walt Disney Theatre cast (hear stories and get answers to questions).

Innovations: Theme Parks & Resorts—A fairly recent addition to some 7-night cruises, this presentation offers an inside look at the design and technology behind Disney's famous theme parks and hotels.

Hands-on Activities—Adults-only lessons in animation and origami are recent offerings, typically held in Animators Palate.

Disney's Navigator Series—Programs include Art of the Theme Ship Tour, a look at the ship's design and decor from the Imagineer's point of view, and Captain's Corner, a Q&A session with the senior staff covering just about everything involving the cruise and the ship—it's very impressive, informative, and fun. Available on 7-night and longer itineraries only.

Wine Tasting Seminar—This is a good place to mention the wine tasting seminar held on all cruises in either Palo or one of the lounges. For $15/adult (21 and up only), the Cellar Master introduces you to wine types, gives you tips on identifying wines, and shows you how to properly taste a wine. Seminar includes tastings of four to six wines. You may also receive a commemorative pin for attending the seminar. (Pin traders take note!) Reservations are required—stop by Guest Services to make reservations. Available on all ships.

Beer Tasting—Check your *Personal Navigator* for a beer tasting session held in Diversions/687/O'Gill's Pub (deck 3 forward/4 aft).

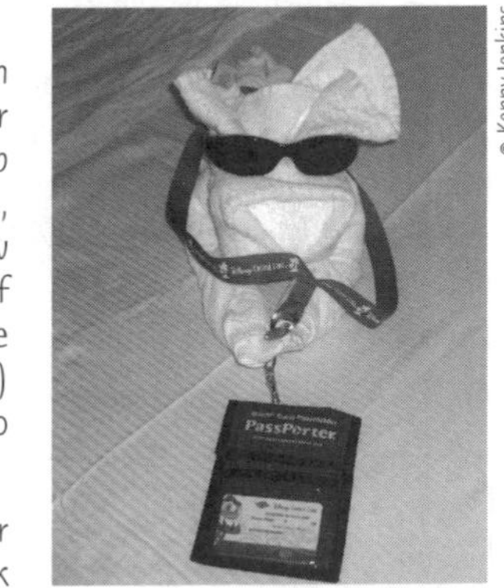

© Kenny Jenkins

A towel pig with a pouch!

Towel Animal Folding—Find out how to make those cute animals they leave in your stateroom each night—check your *Personal Navigator* for time and place.

Kicking Back and Relaxing

This chapter would not be complete without a few words on how to get the most out of your "down time" on the cruise. You know—relax, bum around, sunbathe, or whatever. This is one of the benefits of cruising, after all!

Relaxing on Deck—Looking for the best place to loll about in a deck chair? Deck 9/11 is great if you want to be near the pools or people-watch, but it gets very crowded. Try the deck aft of Topsider's/Beach Blanket Buffet after dinner—almost no one goes there. Deck 10/12 has lots of sun. Deck 7 aft has a secluded and quiet deck (Magic Class only), while the Dream Class has a large, quiet sun deck on 13 forward and cushy, round couches near the adult pool. Deck 4 has very comfy, padded deck loungers and lots of shade (see photo below). The lounge chairs on other decks are made of plastic and metal and recline in several positions, including completely flat. Disney asks that you not reserve the lounge chairs, so don't drape a towel over a chair to use later. If you see loungers being saved with towels, don't be shy about using them. There are also tables and chairs on deck 9/11 that are mostly in the shade and protected by windows, but decks 4 and 10/12 can get very windy. Alas, only the larger verandahs at the very aft of the ship are large enough for lounge chairs, but regular deck chairs are on each verandah.

Sunbathing—Sun worshippers typically prefer deck 10/12, plus deck 13 forward on the Dream Class. Deck 7 aft works well, too, on the Magic Class. Decks 4 and 9/11 are typically too shady. Don't forget sunscreen—the sun at sea is harsh.

Reading—With all the things to do onboard, you might not think to bring a book. But if you enjoy reading, you'll absolutely adore reading in a deck chair on your verandah, on deck 4 (our personal favorite), or deck 7 aft. Cove Café (page 199) has a small lending library, too!

Strolling—Haven't you always dreamed of perambulating about a deck? Deck 4, the Promenade Deck, circles the ship (3/2.5 laps = 1 mile). Decks 9/11 can be too crowded. Deck 10/12 are better, but they can be very windy.

Napping—There's nothing like a good nap, especially while cruising. It's something about the lulling effect of the waves. Your stateroom is a great choice, but you may also catch some zzz's on the deck 4 promenade.

People-Watching—It's hard to find a spot where you can't people-watch! Deck 9/11 and deck 4 overlooking the atrium are particularly good spots, though.

Spa—The Tropical Rainforest in the Vista/Senses Spa (see page 207) is a relaxing spot to spend time.

Shopping—Why not? See page 457.

Relaxing on deck 4

> **Lost & Found**
> Did you leave your half-finished book on your lounge chair before heading to lunch? Report it to Guest Services on deck 3 midship. If you discover you left something behind after disembarking, check with Lost & Found in the terminal or call Disney Cruise Line after returning home. Don't forget to ID all your important items—just in case!

Overlooked Attractions Aboard

Disney is renowned for its attention to detail, and the Disney Cruise Line is no exception. There are any number of smaller, overlooked attractions and activities that may interest you. Here's a list of our favorites:

Pin Trading—This popular activity started at the parks and migrated to the cruises! You can buy all sorts of enamel, cloisonné-style pins on the cruise to trade with others. Or bring pins from the parks or from home. Crew members wearing pin trading lanyards must accept any Disney pin in trade (look for the Disney name on the back of the pin). Check your *Personal Navigator* for trading sessions. The daily shopping supplement highlights the featured pin for the day (see page 457 for shopping).

Vista Gallery—All ships have a dedicated art gallery on deck 4 midship, operated by Disney and offering high-end Disney art and collectibles for sale. Among the more interesting items on offer for the Dream Class ships are pieces of cut steel from the ships' construction. Thomas Kincaide works may also be on display, and Silent Auctions may also be offered. For a time, the cruise line hosted Art Auctions at Sea, conducted by outside art galleries, but those have been discontinued.

Off-The-Beaten-Path —A thorough exploration of the ships reveals fascinating little nooks and crannies. Explore hallways, elevator lobbies, and staircases for art. **Magic Class**: Check out deck 6 behind the midship elevators—you can walk through for a closer look at the mural. **Dream Class**: The Midship Detective Agency scavenger hunt game, while seemingly "kids stuff," is a challenge for adults, and takes you on a tour of many public areas of the ship (see page 193). On the Fantasy, the Muppets-themed hunt will bring you to a Muppet-sized stateroom door! The views from deck 13 forward are great!

Captain's Photo Sessions and Signings—It's always good to meet the Captain! If you're willing to wait in line, you can usually get a handshake and a photo with the Captain. And let's not forget that the Captain's signature is a great souvenir! The Captain typically appears at one of the shops on deck 4/3. Check your *Personal Navigator* for times and places.

© MediaMarx, Inc.

Pirate Alexander discovers deck 7 on the Disney Wonder!

Religious Services

Seven-night cruisers can attend an interdenominational service in the Buena Vista Theatre on Sunday at 8:30 am. Erev Shabbat (Jewish Sabbath Eve) services are held on Friday at the appropriate time. Or attend services in Cape Canaveral on Sunday—see http://www.marinersguide.com/regions/florida/capecanaveral/churches.html. Western Caribbean cruisers who stop in Key West on Sunday can attend services—see http://www.marinersguide.com/regions/florida/keywest/churches.html.

Overlooked Attractions *(continued)*

Lounges—There are many quiet spots where you can relax with a tropical drink or a glass of wine. Besides the lounges we described on pages 198–199, you'll find Preludes/Hollywood and Wine (deck 4/3 forward), open for pre-show and afterglow drinks—all ages welcome; Signals/Cove Bar (deck 9/11 forward) is next to the adult pool so it's limited to ages 18 & up—it's typically open until 7:00 pm; Outlook Lounge (deck 10 fwd/14 mid) overlooks the sea and is removed from the hustle of the lower decks (indoors on Wonder and Dream). Promenade Lounge/Vista Café (deck 3/4 midship) are family-friendly lounges convenient to the Lobby Atrium, usually open to midnight.

Guest Entertainer Workshops—Seven-night and up cruises have entertainers onboard for the variety shows, and sometimes these entertainers give demonstrations and/or workshops in magic, ventriloquism, juggling, etc. Check your *Personal Navigator*.

Coffee or Lunch With the Crew—Have a chat with crew members and learn about life onboard. Various sessions may be offered for different ages and interest groups.

© MediaMarx, Inc.

This throne on the Dream makes a great photo op!

Treasure Hunts—We just love hunting for "treasure," those little-known bits of trivia and hidden details throughout the ships. You may even have the opportunity do a scavenger hunt on Castaway Cay (see page 249). And you can certainly make your own treasure hunts to challenge your friends and family, and we have hosted treasure hunts during our past group cruises. And if that's not enough, the Dream Class' "Enchanted Art" (see below) is also the focus of self-paced, detective-themed, interactive adventures, Mickey's Midship Detective Agency (see page 193).

Photo Surfing—You'll have your photo taken by Disney's professional photographers many times. Kids in particular are in lots of shots. Even if you don't want to buy, it's fun to stop by Shutters and "surf" the photos on display. And if you find a dreadful print of yourselves that you'd rather make disappear, drop it in one of the containers for unwanted photos. Be sure to check out the touch-screen photo kiosks near Shutters and elsewhere—these self-serve terminals let you edit your photos and apply fun borders!

Art Browsing—If you enjoy art, take a stroll around the ship to appreciate the various prints, paintings, and sculptures that fill the Disney ships. Stairways contain a good share of the artwork onboard but are often overlooked because many people prefer elevators. The lobbies and dining rooms on the Dream and Fantasy abound with art worth seeking out, including some fabulous mosaics. The Dream Class ships also feature **Enchanted Art**, framed images that come to life when you approach. Revisit them often, as the art on display may change. Imagineers have told us that, in the future, the Enchanted Art may even recognize you, to keep delivering new experiences!

Hair Braiding—For that authentic "I've been to the islands" look, how about cornrows or braids, ladies? Get the "look" early in the cruise from the braiders up by the pools on deck 9/11. Hair braiding is also available on Castaway Cay—see page 248.

Dolphin Spotting—Did you know dolphins sometimes frolic in the waters around the ship? The best time to spot dolphins is within the first hour of leaving a port, particularly as you're leaving Port Canaveral, Galveston, and West Coast ports. For optimum spotting, you'll want to be looking over either the port or starboard side of the ship, toward the bow. Dolphins like to hitch rides on the bow waves of moving ships. We recommend the big windows on deck 3 or outside on deck 4 for the best views, but deck 10/12 also offers good views. Taking pleasure in spotting dolphins is an old tradition—Ancient Greek sailors considered dolphin escorts a good omen for a smooth voyage.

Talent Show/Karaoke—If you've got an exhibitionist streak, you may enjoy the opportunity to show your stuff in a talent show or karaoke session. Guest talent shows aren't available on all cruises, but we have recently spotted them on the 7-night and longer cruises—they are typically held in the adult nightclub on the last day of the cruise. Look for an announcement in the *Personal Navigator* regarding sign-ups. Crew talent shows are hilarious—if you spot one of these in your *Personal Navigator*, make it a point to attend. Karaoke is much more common and is available for most age groups. Of course, watching other people perform can be almost as much fun as doing it yourself! Studio D on the Dream Class ships is home to frequent karaoke sessions.

Meeting Internet Friends—You may have friends on your voyage and not even know it. If you're a member of an Internet community, just let others know when you're sailing and try to arrange a "meet" or two while you're onboard. Three good places to hook up with fellow cruisers are PassPorter's message boards (http://www.passporterboards.com), DIS (http://www.disboards.com), and Cruise Critic (http://www.cruisecritic.com).

Learning More—Want to know the latest inside scoop on Disney Cruise Line? The single best place to pick up tidbits is at the Navigator's Series Captain's Corner session (see page 209) where the Captain answers cruiser questions. Beyond this, chatting with crew members can yield interesting news, but you'll need to take their unofficial buzz with a grain of sea salt.

'Til We Meet Again—On the last night of your cruise, the Disney characters and Walt Disney Theatre performers put on a sweet little show along the grand staircase in the lobby atrium. The characters "meet and greet" after the show so you can get that last "kiss goodnight." It's typically held at 10:15 pm, but check your *Personal Navigator*.

Restroom Tours—No, we're not joking! Public restrooms throughout the ships sport heavily-themed designs, from elegant to whimsical. Especially noteworthy are the restrooms in the Dream Class ships' adult entertainment districts.

Stuck in Your Stateroom?

Caring for a young one? Feeling queasy? It's not uncommon to be "stuck" in your stateroom for a while and unable to get out to enjoy all these wonderful activities. If you find yourself in this predicament, the stateroom TV is your obvious means of entertainment—note that many onboard talks and even some shows are recorded and later broadcast on the TV during your cruise. If you can't stomach all-TV-all-the-time, reading material is available for purchase in the shops. Cove Café also has a supply of magazines and books that you can borrow. If you have a verandah, spend as much time outdoors as you can—it'll vastly improve your mood. Here are some other ideas: take a bath at sea • listen to music on the TV (several of the channels play music non-stop) • request a Mickey Bar from room service • try your hand at folding a towel animal • record a personal greeting on your stateroom phone • decorate your stateroom door • use the Disney Cruise stationery in the desk drawer to write letters or keep a journal. Most importantly, keep this in mind: If you had to get stuck in a room somewhere, a pleasant stateroom is a good place to get stuck.

Playing Your Way

If you've read this chapter, you know just how much there is to do aboard a Disney ship. Here are some tips to help you make the most of it all:

- To help you **navigate the ship**, remember this general rule: We had Fun in the Forward (front of ship) and we Ate in the Aft (back). Also, remember that port means left, and both are four-letter words!
- Keep in mind that there is **way more to do** on the ship than you can fit in—even on days you visit ports. So don't expect or try to cram in every activity, or you'll be disappointed in the end.
- Get a **Midship Detective Agency game map** (see page 193), even if you don't want to play the games. It'll lead you to nearly every piece of Enchanted Art on board. What's missing? You may want to check out the Vista Gallery!
- "When traveling to your Disney Cruise, either wear or carry your **swimsuit with you** on embarkation day. That way if you are onboard before your rooms are ready, you can hit the pools and AquaDuck and have tons of fun! – contributed by Disney cruiser Renea Govekar

Magical Memories

- *"The Skyline Lounge on the Dream Class ships is one of my favorite places to hang out. The nighttime cityscapes would be enchanting, even if you couldn't see traffic circulating around the Arc de Triomphe in Paris, or jets landing in Hong Kong, but the fact that they do ... wow! You'd think Disney dispatched video cameramen to capture these cities in motion. Not quite. They're still photos brought to life through computer-generated animation! And when the scene changes every 15 minutes, the posters on the wall and the background music change, too."*

  ...as told by author Dave Marx

- *"On my Disney Dream cruise, I could not sleep because I was so excited. So for two nights I walked the ship at 4:00 am and I found I was the ONLY PAYING GUEST out and about on the Dream at that time of the night. Anywhere I wanted to relax ,it was mine for my enjoyment! I went to Meridian in the aft and watched the sea below me and then watched the sun come up. All my pictures have no guests in them and I could go into many areas that would normally be full of people and take full view pictures like the pool deck empty or close-ups of the smallest detail. The cleaning crew was so nice and took time to talk with me since they rarely see paying guests. You would not believe how much they clean this new ship. I would say around 6:00 am the joggers start to come out, so 3:00 to 6:00 am is the perfect time to walk the decks if you want to feel like you have the whole ship to yourself!*

  ...as told by Disney cruiser Glenn Laterre

LEARN the basics of having fun in port

GE[T] where yo[u] want to go easily

Putting Into Port

DECIDE what ports to visit and which excursions to do

DISCOVER the ports and attractions of the Caribbean

Land, ho! For many, the promise of visiting new places is the big appeal of cruising. The Caribbean, Mediterranean, and Alaska are a world away from what most of us are familiar with, and the lure of exotic lands is great. This chapter was written with your needs in mind. We hope to help you determine which ports you'd most like to visit (and hence which cruise itinerary to choose) and what you can do while you're in each port.

Most every port on the 2013 Disney cruise itineraries—including the home port of Port Canaveral, the private island of Castaway Cay, and the special itinerary ports—is represented by a "port guide." Each port guide is two to eight pages long and includes general information (time zone, currency, climate, etc.), ambiance, history, transportation, safety, walking tour, layout, attractions, sports, beaches, and shopping. In addition, we add one of our own maps of the port and a detailed listing of the shore excursions offered through Disney, or our recommended shore activities. These port guides are by no means comprehensive. (That would require an entire book for each port.) Rather, they focus on what's possible and practical during the short hours you'll have in port and should give an excellent overview.

For those of you who've "been there and done that" or simply don't want to venture off the ship, feel free to stay onboard while the ship is in port. Disney offers plenty of activities onboard during port days, and you'll enjoy the slower pace and quieter atmosphere of the ship. Do note that the onboard shops will be closed while you're in port, and some places (like the nursery) will have shorter operating hours.

On all four-night and longer itineraries, you'll have a day (or two, or more—see pages 40–49) when you visit no ports at all. These are called "at-sea" days, and most passengers adore them. The crew offers more stuff to do onboard than usual, and the ship hums with activity. Plus, there's just something special about "being underway" during the day, instead of at night as is more typical on port days.

sland Daze

whole world to explore off-ship. Each of the
ands (even Port Canaveral, which is on a barrier
ngs to do and explore. Here are the details:

, you can **get off the ship** at each port (guests under 18 will need to be with an
dult or have the permission of a responsible adult to go alone) and there is no additional fee to simply visit the ports—Disney folds the port fees into your cruise price. It does cost extra to book "Port Adventures" (shore excursions, see next page), and if you plan to eat ashore anywhere other than Castaway Cay, that cost is also your responsibility.

It's fun to watch as the **port slides into view**. Check your *Personal Navigator* for the arrival/departure times and observe from deck 4, deck 10/12, or from your verandah.

© MediaMarx, Inc.

Allie watches the ship come into port

While the ship and Castaway Cay have a cashless system, you'll need to **bring cash, major credit cards, and/or traveler's checks** to pay for anything at the other ports. You will also want to have small bills to tip excursion operators, too. Note that there is no ATM (cash machine) on the ship, but there are ATMs at the ports (except Castaway Cay). Keep in mind, however, that ATMs will give you cash in the local currency—this can be good if you're planning to use it immediately, but a drawback if you are left with extra or don't understand the local currency-to-dollar rates well enough. If you're looking for U.S. currency from an ATM, you'll generally only find it at ports that use the U.S. dollar as their main currency—check for this in the small chart at the bottom of the first page of each port description in this chapter.

Some of the ports attract merchants aggressively **hawking their wares or services** near the dock. If this makes you uncomfortable, avoid eye contact and keep walking. Most travelers find that hawkers will respect a polite, but firm, "No thank you."

Some guests like to bring **drinks and snacks** with them during their time onshore (see page 173). Be aware that you can't bring open containers of food back on the ship.

Changing facilities may not always be handy for those **planning to swim** or get wet. We suggest you "underdress" your swimsuit (wear it under your clothing) before going ashore.

Some guests **never get off the ship** at the ports, preferring to stay onboard and enjoy the ship's amenities. We've done this ourselves on non-research cruises. The decision to stay onboard or explore the port is a personal one, however, and no one way is right for everyone. If this is your first visit to a port, we suggest you at least get off and look around for an hour, or book a shore excursion. If you decide you like it, you can explore more!

Disney **does not guarantee** that you'll visit all ports on an itinerary. Bad weather or rough seas can prevent docking, and you may spend the day at sea or at an alternate port instead. Although you will not receive a refund of cruise fare if this happens, you will not be charged for the canceled Disney shore excursions, either. In addition, you may have port charges for the port you missed refunded to your stateroom account. In any case, Disney will do what they can to make your extra onboard time fun.

Shore Excursions (Port Adventures)

Disney offers many "Port Adventures" (shore excursions) at each port-of-call, and some ports of embarkation (home ports). These activities incur an additional, per-person fee, anywhere from $6 for Castaway Cay float rentals to $2,899 for a private, chartered boat. In most cases, the excursions are not run by Disney but by outside companies. The good news is that if you book one of these excursions through Disney, virtually all details are taken care of for you. All you need to do is reserve the shore excursion, pay the fees, and show up at the designated meeting point to go ashore.

A **variety of shore excursions** are available, from sightseeing, walking tours, and beach visits to snorkeling, scuba diving, and kayaking. Check the last few pages of each port guide in this chapter for a list of the shore excursions offered at the time of writing. You'll also receive a shore excursion guide from Disney via e-mail, and you can check http://www.disneycruise.com (click "Ports of Call") for a list of the excursions and prices. Note that the excursion details, times, and prices given in this guidebook may change.

Once you've read this chapter carefully, choose and **reserve your excursions in advance**. Some excursions are popular and get booked quickly. To make advance reservations from 2 to 75 days before your cruise (up to 90, 105, or 120 days for Castaway Club members and 120 days for Concierge guests), reserve at http://www.disneycruise.com or call 877-566-0968 (see page 183 for more details). (Note: You cannot make reservations until your cruise is paid in full.) You can also e-mail excursion requests to dcl.shore.excursion@disneycruise.com, or fill out the form that comes with your cruise documentation and fax to 407-566-7031. You can alter/cancel your shore excursion requests any time up to two days prior to sailing. After that time, all excursion reservations are considered final and cannot be changed or refunded. If you do not pre-reserve shore excursions, you can visit the Shore Excursion Desk (deck 3/5 mid) to check availability and reserve excursions. Use the worksheet on page 449.

When you pre-reserve your excursions, fees are billed to your onboard account once you're aboard, and your **excursion tickets** are waiting in your stateroom upon arrival. If you book excursions onboard, you'll receive your tickets in your room the night before the excursion. When you get your tickets, check the time and meeting location printed on it. With each ticket is an excursion waiver form, which you should fill out and sign ahead of time.

On the day of your excursion, bring both the ticket(s) and the signed waiver(s) to the **meeting location** at the assigned time, where they are collected. You'll receive a color-coded sticker to wear, identifying yourself as a member of the excursion group. When ready, a crew member leads the group off the ship and to the excursion.

You can sometimes book the same or similar excursions for less if you **do it on your own**. The excursion operators are locally known and most have web sites—CruiseCritic.com is a great place to read reviews, too. You may have to find your own transportation to and from the excursion (be sure to ask), but in return you'll have more flexibility. Weigh these benefits against the peace of mind you'll have when booking through Disney. We offer tips to do an excursion "On Your Own" at the end of most excursion descriptions in this chapter. Then why book with Disney Cruise Line? First, it's simple and easy. Second, cruise lines book blocks of excursion tickets, sometimes entire excursions—so you might have trouble getting a ticket on your own. Third, if a Disney excursion is delayed, they'll hold the ship for you—do it yourself, and the ship may sail without you.

➤

Understanding the Shore Excursion Description Charts

We describe many of Disney's shore excursions with our custom-designed, at-a-glance charts. Each chart includes a description, tips, restrictions, typical meeting times, our reviews (when available), cruiser reviews in summary form (when available), information on how to do the excursion on your own, a reader rating, and more! We've organized this array of information into a consistent format so you can find what you need quickly. Below is a key to our charts, along with notes and details.

Key to the Excursion Chart:

Reader Rating[2] Icons[3]

1 Excursion Name [Disney's Code Number] Rating: #

Description offering an overview of the excursion, what to expect (without giving too much away, of course), historical background, trivia and "secrets," our recommendations and review (if we've experienced it), tips on getting the most out of the excursion, height/age restrictions, typical meeting times, things you should and shouldn't bring with you, a summary of cruiser reviews we've received, and contact information if you want to do the excursion (or something similar to it) "On Your Own"—note that doing it on your own will often be with a different tour operator, however.

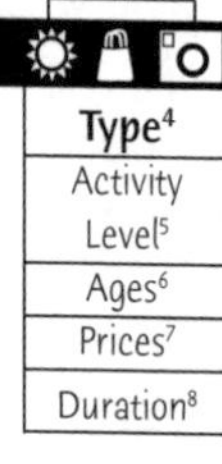

[1] Each chart has an empty **checkbox** in the upper left corner—use it to check off the excursions you want to take (before you go) or those you've taken (after you return).

[2] When available, we note a reader rating from a scale of 0 (bad) to 10 (excellent). These ratings are compiled from the shore excursion reviews we receive (see sidebar below).

[3] Icons indicate what you should (or can) bring along. The sun icon suggests plenty of sunscreen and a hat. The bag icon means you can bring a totebag or backpack along on the excursion. And the camera icon indicates you can bring a camera or camcorder.

[4] The type of activity you can expect on the excursion, such as Sports, Beach, or Tour.

[5] The physical activity level, such as "Leisurely" (a mild level of activity), "Active" (a moderate level of activity), and "Very active" (a whole lot of activity).

[6] The age requirements for the excursion. Some excursions are for "All ages," while others are for certain ages and up. A few are for teens only.

[7] Prices for adults (and kids, if available). Kids prices are for kids up to 9. Most tours that do not involve a boat transfer will allow kids under 3 to go free. Prices subject to change.

[8] The approximate duration of the excursion. If we offer a range, it's more likely that the excursion will take the maximum time noted, in our experience.

About Our Cruiser Reviews

Excerpts from our cruiser reviews, when available, are summarized in each shore excursion description. These reviews are submitted by cruisers via an online form. Excursions without ratings mean we haven't received enough reviews from cruisers. To submit your own review, visit us at http://www.passporter.com/dcl and click the "Shore Excursion Survey" link. We'd love to hear from you!

All Ashore! All Aboard!

If you decide to take a shore excursion or simply explore the port on your own, you'll need to get off the ship and onto the shore. Here's how:

To find out what time you can **go ashore** at a given port, look for the "All Ashore" time in your *Personal Navigator*—we also give typical times in each of our port guides. This time is typically the earliest you can disembark in the port. (You don't have to go ashore if you prefer to stay onboard.) Ports that put more limitations on disembarking (such as Grand Cayman) may require that guests not on shore excursions meet in the Walt Disney Theatre before going ashore. If this is necessary, the details will be in your *Personal Navigator*.

At most ports, the ship **pulls up right alongside the dock** and guests step out right onto the pier. When this isn't possible, guests must be ferried ashore in "tenders." Boarding a tender isn't difficult—you simply step off the ship and onto the tender and enjoy the ride to the shore. If the seas are rough, you are more likely to feel the effects while on the tender. At the time of writing, the only regular port that always requires tenders is Grand Cayman—other ports may require tenders if Disney cannot secure a berth or if rough seas inhibit docking.

Before you go ashore, pack a day bag with bottled water, sunscreen, hat, raingear, a watch, and any other necessities you may need. You may also want to "underdress" your bathing suit so you don't need to find changing facilities in the port. And make sure everyone has their Key to the World card and, for those over 18, photo ID. (If you lose your Key to the World card, go to Guest Services on deck 3 midship.)

To go ashore, follow the signs in the passageways to locate the specific "**tender lobby**" from which you'll disembark. There are two/three of these, located on deck 1 (see pages 5 and 9). Note that there are no passageways connecting the lobbies, so you'll need to take the proper elevator or stairs to deck 1 to reach the correct lobby—the signs won't lead you wrong. If you booked a shore excursion through Disney, you'll disembark with the other guests going on the shore excursion as a group. See page 217 for more details.

Once you're in the tender lobby, have your **Key to the World card** (and photo ID) in your hand so the crew may swipe your card and allow you to disembark. Guests under 18 must have an adult accompany them to the gangway to go ashore anywhere other than Castaway Cay. Once you're cleared to go ashore, simply step out onto the dock or into the tender. On Castaway Cay, watch for a crew member handing out towels for use ashore (towels are bath-size, not beach-size). If they run out of towels at the gangway, the crew members will invite you to take towels from the pool areas on deck 9/11.

While you're onshore, **keep an eye on the time**—you don't want to miss the boat! The "All Aboard" time is noted in your *Personal Navigator*. If you are late, the ship won't wait for you and it is your responsibility to get to the next port to reboard the ship. The exception to this rule is for guests on one of Disney's own shore excursions—if their excursion makes you late, Disney will normally hold the ship's departure for you.

Reboarding is simple. Just return to the dock area, present your Key to the World card (and photo ID) to security personnel to enter the dock, show your ID again to the Disney crew to either board the ship or board the tender (which then takes you to the ship). You will need to put your belongings through a security scanner once you're onboard and have your Key to the World card scanned again (so Disney knows you're back on the ship). Don't bring restricted items onboard, such as opened food and black coral.

Shopping Ashore

For some cruisers, shopping is a major reason to visit an exotic port of call. Not only can you find things you can't get at home, but prices on certain luxury items can be remarkably good.

If you plan to shop on shore, pick up the **Shopping in Paradise** port guide at the gangway. It lists recommended stores at which to shop, though keep in mind that these stores are included because they have an advertising relationship with the publishers of the shopping guide. The good news is that if you purchase from one of those listed stores, you'll receive a 60-day guarantee on repair or replacement of an unsatisfactory item (but the guarantee doesn't help if you change your mind about an item). Regardless of this guarantee, you should always ask about return policies before you make a purchase. If you have questions, a knowledgeable crew member is stationed at the gangway or at the Shore Excursion Desk on deck 3/5 midship. If you need to make a claim after you return from a cruise (and within 60 days of purchasing the item), you must contact the merchant directly and send a copy of your correspondence along with the store name, date of purchase, copy of receipt, and a written description of the claim to Onboard Media, 1691 Michigan Ave., Miami Beach, FL 33139. For more information, visit http://www.onboard.com or call 800-396-2999.

Live presentations on shore excursions and shopping are held during the cruise (freebies may be given out to lucky attendees at the shopping presentation) and later broadcast on your stateroom TV. Check the *Personal Navigator* for times. Stop by the Shore Excursion Desk on deck 3/5 midship for port and shopping information and excursion brochures (see examples at http://www.castawayclub.com). Desk hours are listed in the *Personal Navigator*, too.

Certain luxury items can be had for less in **particular ports**. Here's where your fellow cruisers have found good deals:

Alcohol: St. Thomas
Cigars: Everywhere but Key West
Cosmetics: St. Thomas, St. Maarten
Jewelry: St. Thomas, St. Maarten (Philipsburg), Grand Cayman, Cozumel
Perfume: St. Martin (Marigot)
Quirky/Artsy stuff: Key West
Silver jewelry: Cozumel
T-shirts: Key West (though all ports sell t-shirts, of course)
Watches: St. Maarten (Philipsburg), St. Thomas

Here are some **smart shopping tips** for great deals and quality merchandise:

- Be prepared. Know what you're looking for before you venture out. And be familiar with the typical prices of the items you're interested in so you know whether or not you're getting a good price.
- If you want to deal but aren't successful at initiating it, walk out of the store—this usually gets the clerk's attention.
- If you're shopping for jewlery, ask to go out in the sun to look at it—you may notice flaws in the sunlight that you could not see in the store.
- Check out other stores with similar goods before you buy. And before you leave the store, ask the clerk to write down the item you are interested in along with the price on the back of the shop's card in the event you decide to return.
- Don't settle for something you don't really like.

Port Canaveral and Cocoa Beach
(Bahamas/Caribbean Itineraries–Home Port)

© MediaMarx, Inc.

Cocoa Beach at sunrise

Far more than just a place to park a cruise ship, Port Canaveral offers an exciting extension to your Disney cruise vacation. This is Florida's Space Coast, home to the Kennedy Space Center, 72 miles (116 km.) of prime Atlantic beachfront, the Merritt Island National Wildlife Refuge, ecotourism, water sports, sportfishing, etc. Do you have an extra week?

AMBIENCE

Thundering rockets, crashing surf, and the total peace of an empty beach come together in the Port Canaveral area. You won't find built-up beach resorts like Daytona or Fort Lauderdale here, though crowds do rise for launches. There are just a relative handful of hotels and beachfront condos—so quiet that this is where endangered sea turtles choose to nest! Whether you unwind here prior to your cruise or wind up your vacation with a visit to the astronauts, this can easily be one of the best ports you ever visit.

GETTING AROUND

You'll either want to drive your own car or rent a car to get around (taxis are not abundant). A list of area transportation companies is at http://www.portcanaveral.com/cruising/groundtransport.php. The Space Coast region stretches from Titusville in the north to Melbourne in the south (see map on page 225). I-95 runs north/south on the mainland, paralleled by U.S. 1 for local driving. Many attractions are on the barrier islands to the east, across the Banana and Indian Rivers, and the Intercoastal Waterway. SR A1A is the principal route for beach access. Commercial airlines serve Melbourne International Airport and Orlando International. Port Canaveral is just south of Kennedy Space Center, and Cocoa Beach is immediately south of Port Canaveral, roughly halfway between Titusville and Melbourne. See chapter 2 for full details on travel to and from Port Canaveral and the Disney Cruise Terminal.

FACTS

Size: 72 mi. long (116 km.) x 15 mi. wide (24 km.) (Brevard County, Florida)	
Temperatures: Highs: 72°F (22°C) to 91°F (33°C); lows: 50°F (10°C) to 73°F (23°C)	
Population: 476,000 (Brevard)	**Busy Season:** Mid-February to April
Language: English	**Money**: U.S. Dollar
Time Zone: Eastern (DST observed)	**Transportation:** Cars and taxis
Phones: Dial 911 for emergencies, local pay phone calls = 50 cents	

Exploring Kennedy Space Center and the Astronaut Hall of Fame

KENNEDY SPACE CENTER

It just wouldn't be the Space Coast without the **Kennedy Space Center** (KSC), located 12 miles from Cocoa Beach. The huge gantries and Vehicle Assembly Building dominate the horizon for miles around. Those aren't high-rise condos along the beach; they're the historic launch towers of Cape Canaveral!

The very fun Shuttle Launch Experience simulator ride at Kennedy Space Center

You can easily **spend two days** at the KSC Visitor Complex exploring the history and future of the U.S. space program. The Shuttle Launch Experience simulator, two IMAX theaters, Shuttle Atlantis (opens July 2013), live talks with astronauts, hands-on exhibits, historic spacecraft, and the sobering Astronaut Memorial make the **main visitor complex** an all-day experience. The complex also has a kid's play area and souvenir shops. Eateries include the Orbit Café, G-Force Grill, and Moon Rock Café (at the Apollo/Saturn V center). Board a bus to tour the working Space Center (allow three more hours). The bus stops at the huge **Apollo/Saturn V interpretive center**, displaying a Saturn V rocket, an Apollo command module, and Lunar Module, plus several theaters, Apollo Launch Control, a snack bar, and a shop. Visit the **Launch Complex 39** observation gantry, a four-story launch tower affording sweeping views and even more interpretive exhibits.

ASTRONAUT HALL OF FAME

View historic spacecraft and memorabilia, and experience astronaut-training simulators at the **Astronaut Hall of Fame** in nearby Titusville, which is part of the KSC Visitor Complex. Here you can learn about past NASA astronauts and take a ride in various flight simulators to find out just what it is like to be an astronaut. Mission:SPACE fans take note: The G-Force Trainer is a longer, faster cousin of the simulator ride at Epcot—and at four times the force of gravity (4 Gs), it's not for the faint of heart! Almost half of the Hall of Fame is dedicated to hands-on experiences, and all exhibits and motion simulators are included in the price of admission. The Hall of Fame is a nine-mile drive from Kennedy Space Center, but it's worth the trip and good for at least an afternoon's enjoyment.

Exploring Kennedy Space Center and the Astronaut Hall of Fame

ADMISSION

Admission to KSC and the Astronaut Hall of Fame: $50/adult and $40/child age 3–11. Hall of Fame admission can be used on a different day (must be used within seven days of first use). Add a tour of either the Vehicle Assembly Building, Launch Control Center, or Launch Pad 39-A for an extra $25/$19. These KSC Up-Close Tours were available at press time, but have changed in the past, and may change in the future." These tours include an expert guide to bring you into areas omitted from the regular tour. The tours last about three hours, and they're well worth it! Tickets for the Astronaut Hall of Fame alone are $27/$23. Also available on most days is a chance to **Lunch With an Astronaut**. These meals add $30/adult, $16/child age 3–11 to the price of admission.

Another program is the **Astronaut Training Experience (ATX)**, an in-depth, immersion program that includes motion simulators, exclusive tours, firsthand experiences with veteran NASA astronauts, gear, and lunch. The ATX Core program is a half-day adventure for guests 14 and older—cost is $145. The ATX Family program is a half-day adventure for ages 7 and up—cost is $145 per participant. Guests under 18 must be accompanied by an adult. Some simulators have height/weight restrictions. Reservations required—reserve online or call 866-737-5235.

While the shuttle program has ended, the shuttle Atlantis goes on **permanent exhibit** here in July 2013, and unmanned launches continue. For launch viewing info, visit http://www.kennedyspacecenter.com/events-launches.aspx.

DIRECTIONS

Directions to Kennedy Space Center: From Cocoa Beach/Port Canaveral, take SR 528 west to SR 3 north, and follow the signs for the Visitor Complex. From the mainland, take I-95 or US 1 to Titusville, then take SR 407 east. Visit http://www.kennedyspacecenter.com or call 321-449-4444 for **more information**. Tickets are available on-site and online. Open every day but Christmas. Normal hours: 9:00 am–6:00 pm. The last tour bus departs at 2:45 pm.

Directions to the Astronaut Hall of Fame: From Kennedy Space Center, take SR 405 west across the Indian River and follow signs to the Astronaut Hall of Fame. From Cocoa Beach/Port Canaveral, take SR 528 to US 1 (Titusville exit), then turn right onto Vectorspace Blvd. From the mainland, take I-95 or US 1 to Titusville, get off at SR 405, and follow signs. Normal hours: 9:00 am–7:00 pm.

Exploring Port Canaveral and Cocoa Beach

PLAYING

Some of Florida's **best beaches** line the Space Coast. Cocoa Beach offers miles of soft, white sand and rolling surf. Beach access is easy, with public access points every few blocks. There's metered parking at the public accesses, or walk from the nearby motels. Cocoa Beach Pier at 401 Meade Ave. offers a variety of on-pier restaurants. For a back-to-nature experience, Canaveral National Seashore's **Playalinda Beach** is just north of the Kennedy Space Center boundary line. The long, gorgeous beach is protected by a tall sand dune and has great views of the Kennedy Space Center gantries. The park opens at 6:00 am and closes at 6:00 pm winters, 8:00 pm in the summer. Camping on the beach is no longer allowed. Park fee is $5/car, or use your National Parks pass. Take I-95 to Titusville exit 220 then SR 406 east to the park. For additional information, call 321-267-1110 or visit http://www.nps.gov/cana.

Endangered species such as bald eagles, manatees, and sea turtles call this area home. **Merritt Island National Wildlife Refuge**, just north of the Space Center, offers hiking trails and incredible wildlife viewing. On your way in, stop by the Wildlife Refuge Visitor Center for information and some museum-style exhibits featuring the wildlife—there's also a delightful boardwalk over a freshwater pond in the back. The seven-mile Black Point Wildlife Drive ($5/car fee) offers views of many kinds of birds, alligators, river otters, bobcats, and snakes. We visited the wildlife refuge just before sunset one December and were treated to beautiful panoramas and the sight of many birds roosting for the evening. A special manatee viewing platform is located at the northeast side of Haulover Canal. Located on the road to Playalinda Beach (see above). Call 321-861-0667 or visit http://fws.gov/merrittisland.

© MediaMarx, Inc.

Black Point Wildlife Drive

This is the biggest **sea turtle nesting area** in the U.S. Nesting season runs April–August. Turtle encounters are organized at Canaveral National Seashore, Melbourne, and Sebastian Inlet. Call the Sea Turtle Preservation Society at 321-676-1701. More ecotourism opportunities exist, including kayak tours, airboat rides, and guided nature encounters. For listings, visit http://www.space-coast.com, or call 877-572-3224.

Dining in Port Canaveral and Cocoa Beach

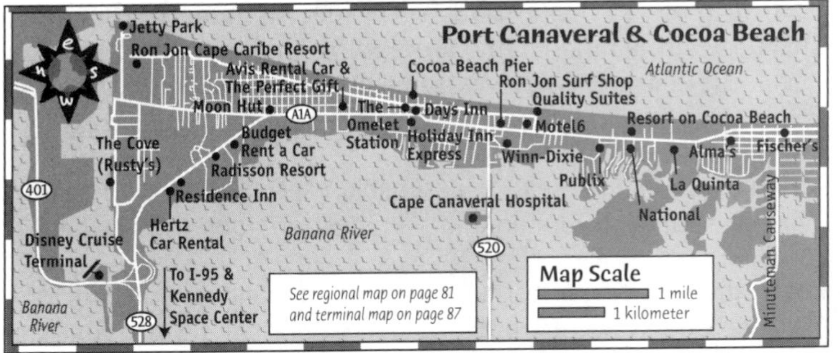

Looking for a place to eat? There are plenty of **chain restaurants**—in Port Canaveral, you'll find a 24-hour McDonald's and a Subway, and in Cocoa Beach, there's a Wendy's, Taco Bell, Denny's, International House of Pancakes (IHOP), Blimpie Subs, a Waffle House, and The Omelet Station. Over on Merritt Island, you'll also find Applebee's, Chili's, Outback Steakhouse, Olive Garden, Red Lobster, and Hooters. If you're looking for something nicer and more "local," here are the restaurants we've tried:

Grill's Seafood Deck & Tiki Bar—A fun spot right on the harbor—the menu is equally fun and the food is great. http://www.visitgrills.com. 505 Glen Cheek Dr., Cape Canaveral • 321-868-2226
Zachary's—A basic diner, serving satisfying American and Greek food. http://zacharysrestaurant.com. 8799 Astronaut Blvd., Cape Canaveral • 321-784-9007
Rusty's Seafood & Oyster Bar—Overlooking the port and harbor, this scenic restaurant serves quality seafood. http://www.rustysseafood.com. 628 Glen Cheek Dr., Cape Canaveral • 321-783-2033

Several other area restauants are getting good buzz, but we can't vouch for them personally: Fishlips is Rusty's and Grill's neighbor in the Cove area at 610 Glen Cheek Dr., Cape Canaveral. Maine'ly Lobster is a casual, low-priced spot for steamed lobster, lobster rolls, and fried fish, at 210 N. Orlando Ave., Cocoa Beach. Also in Cocoa Beach are Brano's Italian Grill at 3680 N. Atlantic Ave, and Slow and Low Barbecue at 306 N. Orlando Ave. Simply Delicious Café and Bakery, 125 N. Orlando Avenue, Cocoa Beach is a favorite breakfast stop for many NASA employees.

Playing in Port Canaveral and Cocoa Beach

ACTIVITIES

Fishing (both saltwater and freshwater) is huge in this area. Charters and fishing camps are easy to find, harder to choose. Check out Coastal Angler Magazine at 888-800-9794 or visit them at http://coastalanglermagazine.com/magazines/2011/brevard.

Lodging rates in this area are reasonable, especially in the off-season (May–December). Our lodging suggestions begin on page 84.

Port Canaveral Tips: For seafood, boating, and fishing charters, visit **The Cove**, a waterfront development a stone's throw from the cruise terminals. We had great meals and sunset views at Rusty's and Grill's (see previous page). To get there, exit SR 528 one exit east of the cruise terminals, turn left on George J. King Blvd., turn left on Dave Nisbet Dr., and take it to Glen Cheek Dr. • **Jetty Park** is a perfect spot to watch space launches, fish, camp, or watch the cruise ships—to get there, exit SR 528 one exit east of the cruise terminals, turn left (northeast) on George J. King Blvd., and follow it to Jetty Park.

Cocoa Beach Tips: No trip to the Space Coast is complete without a visit to **Ron Jon Surf Shop** on SR A1A, souvenir T-shirt capital of Central Florida. This large, very pleasant store does sell serious water sports gear, but most visitors exit with swimwear, T-shirts, and other outdoor apparel. And it's open 24 hours! • Route A1A in Cocoa Beach varies between pleasant neighborhoods and somewhat seedy sections filled with cheap eats and budget motels. For the most part, though, it's very nice, and the beach is just a few blocks to the east (see photo on page 221). • Aging sitcom fans might want to follow A1A south and look for "I Dream of Jeannie Lane," in Lori Wilson Park. • The Air Force Space and Missile Museum, at the Cape Canveral Air Force Station, offers another look at the U.S. space program, and admission is free. The History Center is open to all, Tuesdays - Sundays. It's 1.3 miles beyond the cruise terminals on SR 401. The museum's other exhibits are in restricted areas, but can be visited on free tours at 8:30 am on most Wednesdays and Thursdays (reservations encouraged). See http://www.afspacemuseum.org.

Web Cams: Several web cams offer a sneak peek. Try http://www.twopalms.com or http://bestwesterncocoabeach.com/webcam.htm.

Nearby: Melbourne is home to a wonderful planetarium, live theater productions, Montreal Expos Spring Training, and the Brevard Zoo. Call 877-572-3224 or visit http://www.space-coast.com.

A Day Ashore in Port Canaveral and Walt Disney World

Though Disney cruisers often begin or end their vacation at Walt Disney World, some itineraries include a visit to Orlando's Mouse House during a mid-cruise stop in Port Canaveral. This started with 8-night cruises from New York in Summer 2012, and continued with select 8-night itineraries from Galveston in early 2013. A one-day visit to Walt Disney World is included in the cruise fare, including bus transportation and theme park admission, though you do have to pay for your meals ashore. If you'd rather do something else, the cruise line offers excursions in the Port Canaveral area, including visits to the Kennedy Space Center, beaches, active sports, and nature experiences. We describe many of these activities on the previous pages. All ashore time is 6:15 am, all aboard is a late 12:45 am. As you'll be entering the U.S. from the Bahamas, you will need passports or other approved ID when you disembark (see page 68). We recommend that you not rent a car or hire a town car to visit Walt Disney World, although it's practical for exploring the Port Canaveral area.

Walt Disney World has four major theme parks: Magic Kingdom, Epcot, Disney's Hollywood Studios, and Disney's Animal Kingdom. **Magic Kingdom** was the first Disney park in Florida, modeled on the original Disneyland in California. Fabled Main Street U.S.A., Adventureland, Frontierland, Liberty Square, Fantasyland, and Tomorrowland are arrayed around Cinderella Castle, the park's crown jewel. **Epcot** is the ultimate world's fair, showcasing a future where technology improves our lives and the coutries of the world live in peace. **Disney's Hollywood Studios** celebrates the Hollywood of yesterday and today with live shows, peeks at the filmmaking arts, and the Tower of Terror. **Disney's Animal Kingdom** is, according to the ads, "Nahtazu" (not a zoo, get it?), but it's all about nature, both real and mythical. Explore an African savannah, encounter the Yeti in his mountain lair, and rescue dinosaurs from extinction. **Together, the four parks offer over 125 rides, shows, and other attractions, and 60 eateries**. There's no way to cover all that here. We encourage you to **use a guidebook** to plan and make the most of your day, particularly the flagship of PassPorter's "fleet," *PassPorter's Walt Disney World* (see page 489).

© runnerrae

Cinderella Castle at the Magic Kingdom

Tips for Your One-Day Walt Disney World Visit

Don't sleep in, there's so much to do! We expect the first cruise line buses to depart for Walt Disney World at 7:30 am, and it pays to be on them. The last bus back to Port Canaveral departs Magic Kingdom at 11:00 pm, and you can depart from Epcot or Disney's Hollywood Studios as late as 10:00 pm. The last bus from Disney's Animal Kingdom departs at 8:00 pm. Travel time each way is about 60-90 minutes. **Reservations for the free buses** are best made online, using the PortAdventure reservation system (see page 217). Choose both departure times and destination and pick-up parks.

Your **park tickets** (encoded on your Key to the World card) have park-hopping privileges—you can visit all four major parks if you wish. Each "hop" takes a half-hour by free Disney bus, boat, or monorail, so keep park hopping to a minimum. For the most bang, plan a one-park day at either Magic Kingdom or Epcot, as they offer the most and are open the longest. A two-park strategy: Visit either Disney's Hollywood Studios or Disney's Animal Kingdom early in the day, then enjoy Magic Kingdom or Epcot into the evening. Another fun choice is to visit both Magic Kingdom and Epcot, as you'll travel by monorail!

Prepare at least **a basic plan for your day**. List "must-do" attractions, and decide on meal options. Work your way around the park systematically. **Use FASTPASS**, Disney's ride reservation system, which can save hours of standing on line. Select attractions have FASTPASS ticket machines near their entrance. Insert your Key to the World card, and receive a ticket with a one-hour, pre-appointed Return Time. You can have just one or two FASTPASSes at a time, so choose wisely. Plan to get at least one FASTPASS soon after you arrive at the park.

End your day with a blast! There's time to enjoy the IllumiNations fireworks and light show at Epcot, or watch Mickey battle the Villains in Fantasmic! at Disney's Hollywood Studios—both typically start at 9:00 pm. Wishes fireworks at Magic Kingdom typically starts at 10:00 pm.

While quick-service food abounds in the parks, **for a nice, table service meal** (and there are some great choices), make reservations up to 180 days in advance at DisneyWorld.com, or phone 407-WDW-DINE. Epcot has the best (and most) dining choices.

The first buses leave Walt Disney World at 3:30 pm, and we know, there's free dinner on the ship, but you'll miss the fireworks, and a whole lot more, if you return to the ship so early. Your next day is at sea, so plan to sleep in and recover from your (very) long day in the parks.

Miami, Florida

(Bahamas/Carribbean Itineraries–Home Port)

© Cliff Muller

The Port of Miami

It's hard to say, "Miami," without conjuring strong images; winter escapes to **oceanfront hotels** (well, that's Miami Beach, but...), a glittering downtown skyline made famous by TV dramas, vibrant Latino culture, distinctive Art Deco and modern architecture, palm trees and flamingos, and the wilds of the nearby Everglades.

AMBIENCE

Miami has a Lifestyles of the Rich and Famous image where residents moor powerboats behind palatial homes and vacationers laze on the beach, but "suburban sprawl" describes most of the region. This is the fourth largest metro area in the U.S., a 110-mile long, 15-mile wide strip **hugging the Atlantic coast** from Jupiter in the north to Homestead in the south. Famous for Little Havana and Little Haiti, Miami is a magnet for both visitors and immigrants from throughout Latin America and the Caribbean. Downtown Miami is a center of international banking, a glittering mix of highrise offices and hotels. Miami and Fort Lauderdale are the world's #1 and #2 cruise ports, serving 7.5 million passengers annually.

HISTORY

The Miami area barely tickles the history books before the early 1800s, when the first permanent non-native settlement rose on the **banks of the Miami River**. The population was less than 1,000 when local landowner Julia Tuttle persuaded Henry Flagler to extend his railroad south from West Palm Beach, his recently-built resort for the wealthy, and build another hotel. By 1898 the tracks were literally laid for the area's dramatic growth. Real estate boom and bust followed, and distinctive Art Deco buildings rose in the 1930s. Cuban immigration began in earnest after the 1959 Cuban revolution, turning the Riverside neighborhood into Little Havana.

FACTS

Size: City: 55 sq. mi. (143 sq. km.) Metro:6,137 sq. mi. (15,890 sq. km.)	
Climate: Tropical Monsoon	**Temperatures**: 60°F (15°C) to 91°F (33°C)
Population: 408,568/5,564,635	**Busy Season**: Year-round
Language: English	**Money**: U.S. Dollar ($)
Time Zone: Eastern	**Transportation**: car, bus, rail, people mover
Phones (city): Area codes 305, 786 dial 911 for emergencies	

Making the Most of Miami

GETTING THERE

The Disney cruise ships dock at **PortMiami**, the world's busiest cruise port. Located on Dodge Island in Biscayne Bay, the port has seven passenger terminals, and there are days when ships are berthed at every one. The port is within blocks of downtown Miami, MacArthur Causeway (which links Miami and Miami Beach), and I-95. There is no lodging, dining, or attractions at the port, but Downtown is a short taxi ride away. Embarking passengers are dropped off in front of the terminals. Disembarking passengers will find taxis and shuttles waiting as they leave the terminal.

GETTING AROUND

Greater Miami has extensive mass transit, including the **free MetroMover** that circulates through Downtown and nearby Brickell, Metrorail "subway," and Metrobus, all operated by Miami-Dade Transit http://www.miamidade.gov/transit. **Metrorail and most Metrobus fares** are $2, $5 buys a one-day pass. Trains only accept fare cards, which can be purchased online and at Metrorail stations. Buses take fare cards or exact cash, but bus-to-bus transfers are only free with a fare card. **The Route 119/Route S bus** connects Downtown and Miami Beach. **Taxis** are metered ($2.50 per pickup, $0.40 per 1/6 mile) and charge flat-rate fares between major destinations. Each cab should have a fare map. Taxi stands are plentiful at the airport, cruise port, downtown, and in Miami Beach. Elsewhere, call for a pickup (they're not supposed to respond to hails). Miami-Dade Taxi (305-551-1111), Yellow Cab (305-777-7777.) Still, **many visitors drive**, especially since car rental rates are often low. Most streets are laid out on a predictable grid. Biscayne Blvd. connects Downtown's waterfront hotels and attractions. The Miami Parking Authority parking locator is a big help downtown: http://www.miamiparking.com. **I-95** is the north-south backbone of the region. **Florida's Turnpike** also runs north-south, its tolls help assure lower traffic. Dolphin Expressway (toll) heads west to the airport from Downtown. A half-dozen major causeways connect Miami Beach, Key Biscayne, and other islands to the mainland.

SAFETY

When it comes to **crime rate**, Miami ranks quite poorly among U.S. cities. New York, Los Angeles, and Chicago all come out ahead. That said, crime rates in tourist areas are more moderate, and overall crime rates have dropped by around 33% compared to 10 years ago. Typical urban precautions are advised: remain alert to those around you, keep flashy objects out of sight and don't bring valuables to the beach, stick to high-traffic areas at night, keep men's wallets in front pockets, and purse straps diagonally across the chest.

Touring Greater Miami

Near the Cruise Terminal: You can't get closer than **Bayside Marketplace** and adjacent **Bayfront Park**, where Port Blvd. and Biscayne Blvd. meet. The Marketplace hosts over 110 shops and eateries, and is the jumping-off spot for **bus tours and harbor cruises** (see next page). The landmark Freedom Tower is two blocks north on Biscayne Blvd., and the free **Metromover** is less than a block away. Watson Island, on the west end of MacArthur Causeway, hosts The **Miami Children's Museum** ($16 ages 1 and up, http://www.miamichildrensmuseum.org) and **Jungle Island** (formerly Parrot Jungle) ($33/$25 ages 3-1, http://www.jungleisland.com).

Miami: Three miles from Downtown, **Vizcaya Museum & Gardens** preserves a palatial, Italian-style estate, with furnishings and art from the 15th through 19th centuries and a 10-acre formal garden. Price is $15/$6 ages 6-12. Located at 3251 S. Miami Ave., Coconut Grove. http://www.vizcayamuseum.org. Just west of Downtown, centered on SW 8th St., is **Little Havana**, famed spot for food and shopping from all of Latin America. Versailles Restaurant, 3555 SW 8th, is a long-time favorite and Cuba Tobacco Cigar Co. at 1528 SW 8th offers a glimpse of the cigar-roller's craft.

Miami Beach: This 9-mile, hotel-studded barrier island starts just north of the port. Ocean Drive follows the oceanfront, and the 10-block strip north of 5th St. is wall-to-wall sidewalk cafes on one side, and **Lumus Park Beach** on the other, is the heart of South Beach and the eastern edge of the **Art Deco District**. The **Art Deco Welcome Center** is mid-way, at Ocean and 10th St. Most of the action is within a few blocks of the Atlantic, between Ocean Dr. and Washington Ave. Tree-shaded **Lincoln Road Mall**, is an eight-block shopping and dining promenade between 16th St. and 17th St. **Espanola Way** is a delightful, Mediterranean-styled area packed with cafes and boutiques, one block north of 14th St., off Washington.

© Phillip Pessar

Charming Espanola Way

More Attractions in Greater Miami

The cruise line offers one **post-cruise shore excursion**, *Hop On Hop Off Miami City Tour With Airport Transfer*. $49/$29 ages 3-9, (onboard bookings only). This is just $10 more than Big Bus Tours' regular 24-hour tour(see below)! Luggage is stored while you tour, then collect your baggage and board a shuttle to the airport (MIA or FLL). Shuttles to MIA depart hourly from 11:45 am to 4:45 pm, and FLL-bound trips depart at Noon and 2:00 pm.

Nature lovers have a lot to love here, and fishing, biking, kayaking, sailboarding, and stand-up paddle boarding are top picks for the active. **Everglades National Park** ($10 per vehicle fee) protects 1.5 million acres of "The River of Grass." The park's Shark Valley Visitor Center is 36 miles due west of Downtown, on Tamiami Trail (aka US 41/SW 8th St). From there, Shark Valley Tram Tours can take you on a 15-mile trail deep into the 'glades. $20/$12.75 ages 3-12. Or rent bikes to ride the same route at $8.50/hr. http://www.nps.gov/ever , http://www.sharkvalleytramtours.com The road to Shark Valley passes **Gator Park** and **Everglades Safari Park**, offering airboat rides, wildlife shows, food, and gifts. 95% of **Biscayne National Park** is underwater. Snorkel, scuba, canoe, and kayak are top activities. The park's Convoy Point visitor center includes a museum and exhibits, and the park concessionaire offers glass-bottom boat, snorkel, and scuba tours, plus canoe and kayak rentals http://www.nps.gov/bisc, http://www.biscayneunderwater.com. **Oleta River State Park** rents canoes, kayaks, and bikes and is a great place to use them, with 10 miles of bike trails, and a mangrove forest for paddlers to explore. $6 per vehicle fee. 3400 NE 163 St., N. Miami. **Fairchild Tropical Botanic Garden's** world-class collection of tropical trees and plants is a must-see for the botanically-inclined. $25/$12 ages 6-17 http://www.fairchildgarden.org. **Zoo Miami** is home to 2000 animals in 65 exhibits. $16/$12 ages 3-12. 12400 SW 152 St. **Zoological Wildlife Foundation** is a highly-regarded, for profit, exotic-animal petting zoo. Their by-appointment animal encounters begin at $70/$35 ages 4-17. 305-969-3696 http://zoologicalwildlifefoundation.com.

Deals and Tours: **Go Miami Card** provides admission to 35 attractions and tours. Passes can be bought for up to 7 days of use, and multi-day passes can be used any time within two weeks of the first use (similar to Walt Disney World's multi-day passes). Attractions include Vizcaya, bus tours to the Keys and Everglades, the Miami Zoo, Gator Park, boat and airboat rides, museums, bike rentals... and if you're driving to/from the north, even Kennedy Space Center and the Daytona Speedway tour! $65-$130/$55-$180 ages 3-12. Discounts at the web site: http://www.smartdestinations.com.**Hop-on/hop-off bus tours**: Tour Miami and Miami Beach at your own pace, leaving the bus for the sights you want to visit. Another bus will be along every 15-30 minutes when you're done. **Big Bus Tours** operates two routes, one through Miami, the other for Miami Beach, and you can ride both for the same price. Each lasts 90 minutes if you stay on board. A 24-hour ticket is $39/$29 ages 5-15. Add a second day for $10, and add a harbor cruise for $20. Tickets are available at each of the 20 stops and online: http://www.bigbustours.com **City Sightseeing** runs a comparable service, though buses run every 45 minutes. $39/$29 ages 5-12, and the ticket is good for 48 hours. http://miamicitysightseeing.com **Harbor cruises** depart from Bayside Marketplace. **Island Queen Cruises** and **Miami AquaTours** are the big operators, and discounts can be had at their web sites: http://www.islandqueencruises.com http://www.miamiaquatours.com.

Nassau
(3- and 4-Night Itineraries—First Port of Call)

One-third of all Disney cruisers visit Nassau on New Providence Island in the Bahamas, one of the cruising world's most fabled ports. If you've heard the song Sloop John B ("Around Nassau town we did roam, drinkin' all night, got into a fight"), you might think twice about stepping ashore, but you can have an enjoyable day in this busy capital city if you do your homework.

A statue of Columbus greets visitors to Government House in Nassau

AMBIENCE

Many cruisers feel uncomfortable walking around Nassau's wharf area, where they're likely to encounter aggressive, enterprising locals intent on their piece of the tourist pie. Hair wrappers, cab drivers, street vendors, and tour hawkers swarm the seedy wharf area—hardly the squeaky-clean welcome Disney crowds prefer. But this large, attractive island boasts a long, British colonial heritage. Historic buildings, large casinos, and attractive beaches await travelers willing to take an excursion or strike out on their own.

HISTORY

Bahamian history starts with the first voyage of Chris Columbus. He called the area "baja mar"—low (shallow) sea—and the name stuck. The Spaniards left in search of gold and the native inhabitants were decimated by disease before the British arrived in the 1600s. Nassau, which was originally called Sayle Island, was a favorite port for fabled pirates like Blackbeard and Anne Bonney, until the islands became a Crown Colony in 1718. Governor Woodes Rogers, a former buccaneer himself, cleaned house and created a town plan that—more or less—remains in effect to this day. The islands became a haven for British loyalists fleeing the American Revolution, and for Southerners during the U.S. Civil War. Trade revived during the Prohibition era, when rum running became a major stock in trade. The islanders voted for and received independence on July 10, 1973, making the Bahamas a member of the British Commonwealth.

FACTS

Size: 21 mi. long (34 km.) x 7 mi. wide (11 km.)	
Climate: Subtropical	**Temperatures**: 70°F (21°C)–90°F (32°C)
Population: 211,000	**Busy Season**: Mid-February to April
Language: English	**Money**: Bahamian Dollar (equal to U.S. $)
Time Zone: Eastern (DST observed)	**Transportation**: Walking, taxis, and ferries
Phones: Dial 1- from U.S., dial 919 for emergencies, dial 916 for information	

Getting Around Nassau

GETTING THERE

Your ship berths at **Prince George Wharf** in the heart of the port. Paradise Island is across the water. A short walk puts you in the heart of town. Disembarkation starts at around 9:30 am (check your *Personal Navigator* for going ashore details), and be sure to bring photo ID—wharfside security is tight these days. Enjoy the view from deck 10 or 12 to note major landmarks before going ashore, including the Water Tower at the top of the hill, the towering Atlantis resort on Paradise Island, and the arching bridge to Paradise Island. Check your *Personal Navigator* for the all-aboard time, usually at 5:00 or 6:00 pm.

GETTING AROUND

Nassau is a **good port for walking**, but several popular attractions, including Paradise Island and Cable Beach, are best reached by taxi, jitney, or water taxi. The taxi stand is to the right as you leave the wharf, beyond the hair braiders stand. • As you leave the pier, you'll pass through a pierside welcome center, with a tourist information booth (get free tourist maps here), post office, ATM, telephone/ Internet facilities, and a small, pleasant shopping mall. • As you leave the wharf, you'll find Woodes Rogers Walk, which parallels the waterfront. One block inland is the main shopping district, Bay Street. To your left, you'll find the grand government buildings near Rawson Square, while a right turn on Bay Street will take you toward the Straw Market. The streets follow a rough grid, and the town is built on a slope. If you get disoriented, just walk downhill to the waterfront. • Small jitneys provide local bus service. The fare is $1 (exact change). Taxi fares are negotiable, but expect to pay $8 for a trip for two to Paradise Island, $12 to Cable Beach, and about $6 for shorter trips. The fare is good for two people, with a $3 surcharge for each extra passenger. Note that the passenger in the front seat may be required to pay the bridge toll. • When crossing streets and if you rent a car or scooter, note that Nassau follows the British tradition of driving on the left-hand side of the road.

STAYING SAFE

Safety is often a state of mind, and that's especially true here. Downtown Nassau is **reasonably safe**, but it can be intimidating, with busy streets near the wharf and many locals hustling aggressively. The streets can be empty a few blocks beyond the wharf, so you'll feel better (and be safer) walking with a companion. You can't hide the fact that you're a tourist, so relax, look self-assured, stay alert, keep valuables out of sight, and use your big city street smarts. Panhandlers may offer their "services" as tour guides. Be firm, and don't get sucked in. Carry a few dollars, just in case you need to tip a guide.

➤

Touring Nassau

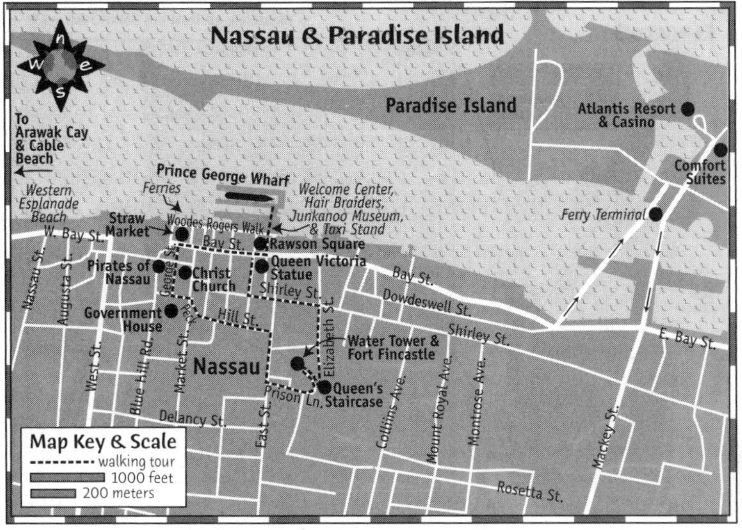

A **self-guided walking tour** around Nassau is a break from the ordinary. Grab one of the free tourist maps distributed on the wharf, play connect-the-dots with your choice of highlighted sights, and trace a route around the perimeter of the downtown district. Allow at least two hours for a nonstop walk or more if you want to spend time exploring. Finish before 5:00 pm, when the streets get empty. Here's our suggested walking tour (highlighted on map above): Leaving Prince George Wharf, turn right onto Bay St. Near the corner of Bay and George St. is the famous (or infamous) Straw Market. Turn left up George St. to continue our tour, or follow Bay St. west to the beaches of Western Esplanade and the seafood vendors of Arawak Cay. On George St., you'll soon pass Christ Church and the Pirates of Nassau attraction. Follow George St. to its end, and peer through the gates of Government House (see photo on page 233). Turn left again, cross Market St., and make your way uphill on winding Peck Slope to Hill St. for a commanding view of the port. Follow Hill St. to its end, turn right on East St. to Prison Lane, and follow the lane up to the Water Tower and Fort Fincastle. Exit via the remarkable Queen's Staircase and follow Elizabeth St. down the hill. Turn left onto Shirley St., then right onto Parliament St. to view the Library (Old Jail) and the statue of Queen Victoria in Parliament Square. From there, it's a short walk back to the wharf.

Playing in Nassau

ACTIVITIES

Bay St. is lined with **shops** offering the typical selection of upscale luxuries and downscale knickknacks, but Nassau is probably best-known for its Straw Market. There was a time when nobody could leave the port without a straw hat, basket, or handbag, but not every visitor is enchanted by the experience. The stalls and crafters of the market fill a city block between Bay St. and the waterfront—its narrow quarters are shaded by a huge, temporary awning.

The soft, white sands of Nassau are a major attraction. The nearest **public beach** to the wharf is Western Esplanade, along West Bay St. Famed Cable Beach, with its hotels, casino, and water sports, is more attractive and just a few miles farther down the road. Paradise Island has many first-class beaches, best visited as part of a shore excursion. Remote South Ocean Beach is a $33 cab fare from the wharf, or rent a car. Its quiet beauty may be worth the journey.

Casino action centers on Paradise Island's fancy Atlantis Casino and the older Crystal Palace Casino on Cable Beach. A day in either spot offers beach lounging, water sports, and similar distractions for those family members too young or disinclined to gamble. Water taxis serve both destinations from Prince George Wharf.

The **Atlantis Resort** offers aquariums and sea life exhibits to go along with the casino, recreation, and dining. All-day admission is $25/adults, $19/kids 3–12, and includes a guided tour, but does not include their water park—for that, you need to do the Atlantis Aquaventure excursion (see page 240) or get a room at Comfort Suites Paradise Island that includes use of the resort's facilities for up to 4 guests/room (http://www.comfortsuites.com, 877-424-6423)

Nassau offers too many scuba, snorkeling, boating, and sea life encounters to list here, but Disney's shore excursions (see next page) offer a good **cross-section** of these activities. Golf, tennis, fishing, and other sporting opportunities abound for those willing to do it on their own. Fortunately, you have a long day in Nassau. For details, visit the Bahamas' official site at http://www.bahamas.com.

"Goombay" and "Junkanoo" have become well-known Bahamian catchwords. Goombay is a local musical style that gets its name from the African term for rhythm. The Bahamas famed Junkanoo parades take place when your ship is out of port, but you can view a Junkanoo exhibit right on Prince George Wharf.

➢

Embarking on Shore Excursions in Nassau

Ardastra Gardens and City Tour [N16] — Rating: 7

Tour
Active
All ages
$42/adult $29/child 3-9
2.5 hours

First visit the jungle gardens of the Ardastra Gardens, Zoo, and Conservation Centre, famous for its marching Caribbean Flamingos. After an hour and a half at the gardens, enjoy a city tour in air-conditioned van. A fair amount of walking is required. Includes a complimentary sparkling soda, and snacks and additional beverages are available for purchase. Note that you must walk 15 minutes to and from the pickup point for this tour. Typical meeting time is 12:45 pm. Cruiser reviews are mostly positive: The excursion offers "variety" and a way to see a lot in a "short amount of time." Kids enjoy the "zoo" and the animals and birds are "great." The tour's worth "depends on your tour guide." Overall, most "enjoyed it" though a few felt it would have been better to "take a taxi" and do "on your own." (On Your Own: Ardastra Gardens at http://www.ardastra.com, 242-323-5806)

Atlantis Beach Day & Discover Atlantis [N07] — Rating: 6

Beach
Active
All ages
$95/adult $59/child 3-9
4-6 hours

Spend the day lolling about on the beach on Paradise Island. The excursion includes a 25-minute bus ride (to and from Paradise Island), a self-guided tour of The Dig aquarium, and a meal/beverage coupon. Upon arrival, enjoy your reserved spot on the beach, complete with chair and towel. You can explore the resort's casino, shops, and aquarium on your own, but this excursion ***does not include access to the Atlantis water park, pools, or slides****. Typical meeting time is 10:30 am. Buses return every 30 min. from 1:30 pm to 4:30 pm. Cruiser reviews are uniform: The bus ride to Paradise Island was "bad" and travelled through a "not-so-nice area of Nassau." The highlight was the "private beach for cruisers," which is "wonderful" with "beautiful" water "so blue" and with "so many fish." The meal coupon left a bit to be desired, as you could only get "certain items" and the food "was not that great." If you want to buy something else, it can be "difficult to pay with cash." And cruisers felt it was unfortunate that they "can't use any of the pools at Atlantis." In sum, the beach is "beautiful" but the rest is just so-so. (On Your Own: Atlantis Resort, http://www.atlantis.com, 888-528-7155)*

Atlantis Dolphin Cay Deep Water & Aquaventure/Observer — Rating: n/a

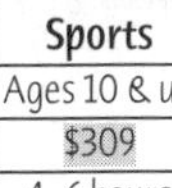

Sports
Ages 10 & up
$309
4-6 hours

*Enjoy the Atlantis Aquaventure (page 240), plus a hands-on, interactive dolphin experience at the 11-acre Dolphin Cay. You'll receive instruction, put on a provided wet suit, and get in waist-high water to meet a dolphin, then ride a dolphin-pushed boogie board. You'll have the opportunity to touch, snorkel and swim with the dolphins. The two-hour Dolphin Cay visit is first, followed by the Aquaventure water park and free time to explore the resort's beaches, shops, and casino. Typical meeting time is 9:10 am. "**Observer**" (no dolphin interaction, but full Aquaventure benefits) is $189/$134, and open to all ages.*

Nassau's Dolphin and Sea Lion Excursions

Every year seems to bring more ways to interact with marine life in Nassau, so many that we've run out of room to list them all! Atlantis now has two versions of most dolphin experiences, with either an Aquaventure water park add-on, or a cheaper version with a tour of the hotel grounds. Blue Lagoon offers tours with either dolphins or sea lions. There are shallow-water "touch" experiences, "swim-with" versions in deeper water, and "observer" experiences... Read the Port Adeventure descriptions carefully!

See page 218 for a key to the shore excursion description charts and their icons.

Embarking on Shore Excursions in Nassau *(continued)*

Caribbean Queen Snorkel Tour [N04] — Rating: 9

Sports
Very active
Ages 6 & up
$37/adult
$27/child 6-9
2-3 hours

Like the Sunshine Glass Bottom Boat excursion on page 241, this trip cruises Nassau Harbour before heading off to Athol Island. Unlike the Sunshine Glass Bottom Boat excursion, you WILL get wet! Snorkel equipment and instruction are provided for your open-water snorkeling adventure. Freshwater showers and a cash bar are available onboard the 72-foot boat. Typical meeting time is 1:45 pm. Cruiser reviews are consistently good: The "great" excursion crew offers some "sightseeing" along the way to the island. Once there, the snorkeling is "awesome" and there was a "great variety of fish." Younger children and "uptight" people may be "a little frightened at first" but the "crew is wonderful at relieving fears." Chips and beverages ("local beer" plus soda and water) are available for sale on the boat. In sum, "it was great" and cruisers would "do it again." (On Your Own: Stuart Cove's Aqua Adventures at http://www.stuartcove.com, 800-879-9832)

Catamaran Sail & Reef Snorkeling [N14] — Rating: 8

Sports
Very active
Ages 5 & up
$49/adult
$34/child 5-9
3.5-4 hours

Set sail on a comfortable, 65-foot catamaran with a large sundeck and shady lounge deck. After a brief tour of Nassau Harbour, you'll sail to a coral reef for snorkeling (equipment provided). Sodas and water are served during the sail, as are snacks and alcoholic beverages after snorkeling. Typical meeting time is 9:15 am. Cruiser comments are mostly positive: The 20-minute sail is "enjoyable" and "relaxing." The snorkeling is "wonderful" though some felt it was in "pretty deep water for beginners" and you cannot "touch bottom." Most report seeing "plenty of fish." Overall, most "loved it!" (On Your Own: Flying Cloud at http://www.flyingcloud.info, 242-363-4430)

Discover Atlantis [N05] — Rating: 6

Tour
Active
All ages
$59/adult
$39/child 3-9
2-4 hours

This excursion begins with a 20-minute bus ride to the Atlantis resort, where you receive a guided tour of the resort and aquarium on Paradise Island. We did this excursion in 2002 and we enjoyed it—be aware that you will do a lot of walking. Typical meeting times are 11:15 am or 1:15 pm. Buses return every half-hour from 1:30 pm to 4:30 pm—don't miss it, or you'll have to pay for a taxi. Cruiser reviews are mixed: This very popular excursion begins with a "capacity-filled" ride to Paradise Island, during which the tour with "very little narrative" could not be "heard or understood over the roar of the engines." Once on the island, you are taken in "smaller groups" to the "stunning" Atlantis Resort, but the walk to it is "boring" because there is "nothing to see." Inside you may "spend a lot of time touring the retail areas," but then are led to the "breathtaking" aquarium. After the aquarium, some felt you were "left somewhere to find your own way back" while others enjoyed the "free time to explore." Expect to "spend the entire tour walking." Overall, some cruisers felt the excursion was "awesome" while others felt it "takes way too much time" and "wasn't interesting at all." (On Your Own: Atlantis Resort, http://www.atlantis.com, 888-877-7525)

Nassau Harbour Cruise — Rating: 5

Tour
Leisurely
All ages
$25/$15 (0-9)
1-1.5 hours

Enjoy a relaxing ride through Nassau Harbour and around Paradise Island on a state-of-the-art, custom-built catamaran (the "Ballyhoo"). You'll need to walk 15 minutes to get to the boat. During your cruise on the yacht, your guide will narrate the sights while you enjoy comfy seats and island music. Note that there are no restrooms available on the yacht. Typical meeting times are 10:15 am and 2:00 pm.

Embarking on Shore Excursions in Nassau *(continued)*

Blue Lagoon Island Dolphin Encounter [N21] Observer [N22] Rating: 9 

Sports
Active
Ages 3 & up
$125/adult
$110/age 3-9
4.5-5 hours

*Despite the hefty price tag, this is the most popular excursion and it typically sells out quickly. Everyone wants the chance to cavort with a friendly dolphin! Guests stand on a platform set at a few feet under the water and play with bottlenose dolphins. (If you want to swim with the dolphins, book the Dolphin Swim excursion—see below.) This excursion includes a cruise to private Blue Lagoon Island (Salt Cay)—a calypso band plays during your ferry trip. Once there, you can swim, sunbathe, and play—water sport rentals are available—in addition to your dolphin encounter. Food and beverages are available for purchase. Complimentary lockers and changing rooms are available, as are wet suits during the colder months. Professional photos of your dolphin encounter are $10-$22/each, packages are $40-$80/each, and movies are $40-$60/each. Collapsible strollers and wheelchairs are allowed, but you must be able to board the boat and enter the water unassisted. Guests age 3-12 must have an accompanying adult booked on the same excursion, while guests age 13-17 may have an accompanying adult booked on the Observer [N22] excursion. (**Blue Lagoon Island Dolphin Observer [N22]** offers the same benefits without dolphin interaction. $40, all ages.) Typical meeting times are 12:45 pm and 2:30 pm. Note that if you have the 12:45 pm departure time, you will return around 5:00 pm, which may mean you can make it to dinner (if you're on the first seating). Cruiser ratings are mostly positive: The excursion starts with a long, "45-minute" ferry ride that some felt was "slow" and "miserable" while others found it "a lot of fun." At the dolphin encounter area, small groups of "10-12" guests stand around a "small pool" and watch a "skit" between the dolphin and "informative handlers." You stand in the "cold" water for about "20 minutes" to "hug, kiss, and dance with" the dolphins, but you only get about "2-3 minutes with a dolphin personally." Cruisers recommend you "wear water shoes" for ease and comfort. All loved the "unbelievably intelligent animal" and the "expertise, friendliness, and humor of the trainers." Some were put off by the "expense" of the photo; others wanted them but "did not know to bring enough money." Overall, most felt it was "exactly as advertised" or "better than expected," though a few felt it was "neat but not worth that much money." (On Your Own: Blue Lagoon Island at http://www.dolphinencounters.com, 866-918-9932)*

Blue Lagoon Dolphin Swim [N41] Rating: n/a

Tour
Active
Ages 6 & up
$199/adult
$199/child
3-5 hours

For all dolphin lovers out there, this excursion gives guests ages 6 & up the opportunity to actually swim with a dolphin! After the same introduction that travelers get in the above excursion (N21), you'll have your chance to play, dance, hug, and kiss your dolphin friend. Then it's time to "swim" across the lagoon as your dolphin propels you forward by pushing your feet (you can see a good video of this at http://www.youtube.com/watch?v=GI10xzcZZiQ). After your swim with the dolphin, you'll be able to visit the sea lions rescued after Hurricane Katrina passed through in 2005. Everything available in the above excursion is also offered in this one.

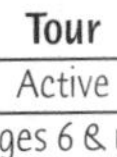

Atlantis Resort Ocean Club Golf Course [N?] Rating: n/a

Sports
Active
Ages 10 & up
$499/guest age 10+
6.5-7 hours

Play 18 holes on this championship, Tom Weisskopf-designed course, home to the Michael Jordan Celebrity Invitational. Transportation, greens fees, cart (shared), clubs and shoes (if needed) are included. Food and beverages are available at extra cost at the clubhouse. Full pro shop. Appropriate attire is required: collared shirts for men, tops with sleeves or collar for the ladies, no denim jeans, no basketball or soccer shorts.

Embarking on Shore Excursions in Nassau *(continued)*

Scuba Dive at Stuart Cove [N20] — Rating: 3

Certified divers receive an exciting look at the coral reefs and marine life that make their home here. Price includes basic dive equipment (regulator, tank, weight belt, buoyancy control device, mask, snorkel, and fins—wet suits are available for an extra fee). Note that guests ages 12–17 must be accompanied by parent or guardian. Typical meeting time is 11:45 am. Cruiser reviews are uniform: The Disney scuba excursion is "OK" but not "great." The dive takes them "windward" and the waters can be "very rough"—rough enough that most cruisers report that they were able to do only "one of the two dives." The excursion does "provide all equipment," but you may only go "10 to 15" feet deep. The best thing about it is that you don't have to worry about "getting there or back" since it was all arranged through Disney. Overall, the dive was "disappointing" and most felt it would be best to "arrange your own scuba dive" through an outfit like Stuart Cove's. (On Your Own: Stuart Cove's Aqua Adventures at http://www.stuartcove.com, 800-879-9832)

Sports
Very active
For certified divers only
Ages 12 & up
$145
5–5.5 hours

Atlantis Aquaventure [N25] — Rating: n/a

Enjoy the 141-acre water park at the famous Atlantis Resort. The excursion begins with a 25-minute bus ride to Paradise Island. Once here, you can explore the aquarium, relax on the many beaches, and dive into the amazing, well-themed water park. The park features nine thrilling water slides that utilize "master blaster" water jet technology, pushing you both uphill and downhill. The water park also has a mile-long "lazy river" with underground tunnels, churning rapids, waterfalls, and conveyors to water slides. Complimentary light lunch, towels, and life jackets included. Lockers and other water rentals are extra. Typical meeting time is 9:15 am. Guests must be at least 48" tall to ride all water slides.

Beach/ Sports
All ages
$169/adult
$115/3–9
4–6 hours

Atlantis Dolphin Cay Shallow Water & Aquaventure/Observer — Rating: n/a

*Take the above Atlantis Aquaventure and add a hands-on, interactive dolphin experience at the 11-acre Dolphin Cay. You'll receive instruction, put on a provided wet suit, and get in waist-high water to meet a dolphin. You'll have the opportunity to touch and play with the dolphin, but this is not a swim with the dolphins experience. The two-hour Dolphin Cay visit is first, followed by the Aquaventure water park access and free time to explore the resort's beaches, shops, and casino. Typical meeting time is 9:10 am. "**Observer**" (no dolphin interaction, but full Aquaventure benefits) is $189/$134, and open to all ages.*

Sports
Ages 3 & up
$259/adult
$229/3–9
4–6 hours

Atlantis Ultimate Trainer for a Day [N02] — Rating: n/a

Ever wonder what it would be like to train dolphins? Now's your chance with this excursion and a hefty chunk of change! You'll begin with a 15-minute bus ride to the Atlantis Resort, then walk 10 minutes to the Dolphin Cay facility where you'll learn about the care and feeding of dolphins during a backstage tour. After a light lunch with a Marine Mammal Specialist, you'll meet the resident sea lions. Then it's time to put on your snorkel gear, hop on a power scooter, and swim alongside the dolphins. You'll also have an opportunity for hands-on interaction with the dolphins. Includes complimentary use of towels, lifejackets, wet suits (when needed), snorkel gear, and lockers. For more information (or to book this on your own), visit http://www.dolphincayatlantis.com/programs/trainer.aspx.

Sports
Active
Ages 10 & up
$459
7–7.5 hours

See page 218 for a key to the shore excursion description charts and their icons.

Embarking on Shore Excursions in Nassau *(continued)*

Sunshine Glass Bottom Boat Tour [N02] — Rating: 3

Tour
Leisurely
All ages
$26/adult
$17/ages 0-9
1.5 hours

Curious about what's under that aquamarine water? Take this excursion and you won't even have to get wet. The 70-foot boat has one sundeck, a covered deck, restrooms, cash bar, and (what else?) a glass bottom. You'll cruise the Nassau Harbour, then head off to the coral reefs—if the weather permits, you see a shipwreck, too. Typical meeting times are 10:45 am and 2:30 pm. Cruiser reviews are mostly negative. It is a "bit of a walk from the ship to the pier" where the glass bottom boat is moored. Once on the boat, the "scratched up" glass bottom was "way too small" and you may have to stand to see. On the other hand, it "wasn't too expensive" and the "kids really enjoyed it." Overall, the experience was a "complete and total" waste of money for some, while others thought it was a "nice little ride."

Blue Lagoon Island Sea Lion Encounter [N40] — Rating: n/a

Sports
Active
Ages 8 & up
$115/$109
4-4.5 hours

Your adventure begins with a 40-minute voyage aboard a high-speed, double-decker catamaran through Nassau Harbour. Once you arrive at Blue Lagoon Island, the sea lion trainers will meet you and introduce you to these fascinating marine mammals. Then it's time to get in the waist-deep water for your hands-on encounter with the friendly sea lions. You'll learn how to communicate with the sea lions, feed them, and offer positive reinforcement. You'll also have the opportunity to get the sea lion version of a kiss, handshake, and hug! Afterward, you'll observe the resident dolphins and have some photo ops. Note that you'll spend about 30 minutes in the water with the sea lions. Guests must be at least 48" tall to participate; guests age 8-12 must be with an accompanying adult on the same excursion, while guests age 13-17 may have an accompanying adult on the Dolphin Observer excursion (N22). Jewelry is not allowed in the water; complimentary lockers and wet suits (during the winter months) are provided. Food is available for purchase. Typical meeting time is 9:30 am.

Nassau Forts and Junkanoo Discovery [N30] — Rating: n/a

Tour
All ages
$41/adult
$31/3-9
3-3.5 hours

This is a cultural highlights tour of Nassau. This excursion starts with a 15-minute walk to the pick-up point, then you'll board an air-conditioned van for a ride to Fort Fincastle with its gorgeous views. You'll also visit the Queen's Staircase, a 65-step, 100-foot-high solid limestone staircase cut into the side of a hill. Your next stop is to a Junkanoo exhibit filled with costumes, photos, and music from this national cultural festival. Your final stop is Fort Charlotte, Nassau's largest fort. Afterward, you can go right back to the ship or get dropped off in the straw market to shop. This excursion is wheelchair and stroller accessible, but both must be collapsible. Wear comfy walking shoes! Typical meeting time is 9:45 am.

See and Sea Island Tour/Seaworld Explorer Semi-Submarine — Rating: n/a

Tour
Moderate
All ages
$55/adult
$39/0-9
2.5-3 hours

*Combine a sealife-viewing tour on the semi-submersible Seaworld Explorer with a short bus tour of Nassau including stops at Fort Fincastle/Queen's Staircase and Fort Charlotte. (**The Seaworld Explorer Semi-Submarine Tour** delivers the "sea" without the "see" for $43/$29 and lasts about 1.5 hours.) A 10-minute boat ride takes you from the cruise pier to Athol Island, home to the Seaworld Explorer, a craft that floats on the surface while passengers view sea life from windows five feet below the surface. The captain delivers a guided tour of the undersea life, including a feeding session to be sure to attract the fish. No wheelchairs. Strollers must be foldable.*

Embarking on Shore Excursions in Nassau *(continued)*

Blue Lagoon Island Beach Day

Rating: n/a

Beach
Leisurely
All ages
$69/adult
$55/0-9
4-7 hours

Take a 30-minute catamaran cruise to Blue Lagoon Island (Salt Cay), for a day of fun and relaxation at this secluded, private island. Light lunch and two soft drinks are included, additional food and beverages at extra cost (bring a credit card). Volleyball, basketball, ping pong and other games are included. Use of floats is also included. Kayaks, water bikes, and paddle boat rentals $10–$15/30 minutes. A 40-minute snorkel tour is $15 (all extras payable on-island), and $30/$20 buys a tour to view the dolphin and sea lion programs. Two return times are selectable, allowing 3.5 or 6.5 hours of island time. On your own http://www.bahamasbluelagoon.com (866-918-993)

Graycliff Escape Nassau [N33]

Rating: n/a 

Tour
Leisurely
All ages
$129/adult
$89/0–9
5.5 hours

The Graycliff is Nassau's most prestigious five-star hotel, offering an elegant environment perfectly suited for a relaxing, Bahamian day. This excursion begins with a 15-minute stroll to the pick-up point, where you'll get a 10-minute ride to the Graycliff in an air-conditioned van. Upon arrival, your adventure starts with a tour of the property which ends at a beautiful garden with two pools. You'll be left alone to lounge about with two complimentary beverages and a full lunch, which can be enjoyed beside the pool or in the lovely dining room. Massages, special wines, and cigars are available for purchase (e-mail dcl.shore.excursions@disney.com for options once booked). Wheelchair and stroller accessible, but both must be collapsible. Typical meeting time is 10:45 am.

Graycliff Hotel Wine Luncheon [N31]

Rating: n/a

Tour
Leisurely
Ages 21 & up
$189
2.5-3 hours

Tour Graycliff Hotel's world-famous wine cellar and enjoy a gourmet luncheon with wine pairings on this special, signature excursion. Like the Graycliff Escape excursion (above), you'll begin with a 15-minute walk and a 10-minute ride to the hotel. After an introductory glass of champagne you'll be met by the Master Sommelier who will give you a tour of the wine cellar and the rest of the hotel. That will be followed by your four-course luncheon, accompanied by appropriate wines from the cellar. After your experience, you can get a ride back to the pier. Wheelchair accessible, no ECVs.Large bags and backpacks are not allowed in the wine cellar. Typical meeting time is 1:15 pm.

Graycliff Hotel Cigar and Rum Experience [N32]

Rating: n/a 

Tour
Leisurely
Ages 21 & up
$189
2 hours

Would you like to try your hand at rolling your own cigar? Now you can! This signature excursion takes you to the Graycliff Hotel (see above excursion for transportation details) where you'll meet a master cigar roller who will teach you how to sort, clean, and roll a cigar. You'll also learn about the fine art of rum appreciation from Graycliff's extensive collection. Guests get to keep the cigar they rolled and a complimentary cigar cutter. After your experience, you can get a ride back to the pier or stay to enjoy a meal in the restaurant at your own expense (if you have a meal, you'll need to take a taxi back on your own dime). Wheelchair accessible, no ECVs. Typical meeting times are 10:45 am and 12:45 pm.

See page 218 for a key to the shore excursion description charts and their icons.

Castaway Cay

(All Bahamas and Most Caribbear

Castaway Cay is Disney's private island, exclusively for the use of Disney Cruise Line guests and crew. It's clean, safe, and well-themed, and lunch is complimentary on the island. We recommend you get up early on your Castaway Cay day—you don't want to miss a minute of the fun! This port is usually the last stop on most cruise itineraries.

Megan and Natalie on Castaway Cay

© Media

AMBIENCE

Castaway Cay (pronounced "Castaway Key") is a **tropical retreat** with white sandy beaches, swaying palm trees, and aquamarine water. What makes it so magical is its theming—it's not unlike visiting one of Disney's excellent water parks, such as Typhoon Lagoon. The island even has its own legend—they say three explorers set sail with their families to the scattered islands of the Bahamas in search of fame and fortune. Their adventures brought them to this island, where they found sunken treasures, the secret of youth, and the skeletal remains of a giant whale. The explorers and their families remained on the beautiful island for years as castaways—you can still see the original structures and artifacts left behind.

HISTORY

Disney may call this out-island Castaway Cay, but in its previous incarnation it was **Gorda Cay**. The island is a part of the Abaco Bahamas island archipelago. Its history is murky. It may have first been inhabited by Lucayan Indians, "discovered" by the Spanish, later used as a harbor for pirates, and was long used by the Abaconians for farming pumpkins and sweet potatoes. In the '70s and '80s, the island was a base for drug operations. Disney leased the island and, over the next 18 months, spent $25 million to fix up 55 acres (only about 5% of the island). 50,000 truckloads of sand were dredged to make the beautiful beaches. Its extensive facilities are the best in the cruise industry. For more history, visit: http://www.disneydispatch.com/content/columns/the-626/2011/04-the-colorful-story-of-castaway-cay/

FACTS

Size: 2 mi. (3.2 km.) x 1.25 mi. (2 km.)	**Distance**: 260 nautical miles from home port
Climate: Subtropical	**Temperatures**: 66°F (19°C) to 88°F (31°C)
Language: English	**Money**: U.S. Dollar/stateroom charge
Time Zone: Eastern (DST observed)	**Transportation**: Walking, bicycles

Reservat | Staterooms | Dining | Activities | Ports of Call | Magic | Index

Making the Most of Castaway Cay

GETTING THERE

Thanks to a deep channel Disney dredged when it acquired the island, **your ship pulls right up to the dock** on Castaway Cay. Typical all-ashore time is 8:30 or 9:30 am, and you have until about 4:30 pm (7–8 hours) to play on this delightful island. When you alight from the ship, proceed down the dock (picking up towels on your way) to the island—it's about a 3-minute walk to the tram. Be aware that when the seas are rough, the ship may be unable to dock at Castaway Cay, and therefore, you'll be unable to visit. This is most likely to happen in January and February, but it can occur at any time.

GETTING AROUND

Castaway Cay is the **easiest port to get around**, thanks to the well-marked paths and convenient trams. As you walk down the dock to the island, you'll pass the Castaway Cay post office on your right and Marge's Barges sea charters dock on your left, after which you'll reach a tram stop—hop aboard the next tram, or simply take the 10-minute walk to the family beach. Once you're at the family beach, you can continue down the path past buildings that house the restrooms, shops, and services. At the far end of the main path—accessible by foot or tram—is the recently expanded family beach, more dining, and private cabanas. A teen's Hide Out is beyond that. An adults-only beach is accessible by another tram (or a long, hot, 25-minute walk down the airstrip) near the end of the main path. All locations are marked on the map on the next page, as well as on the color map Disney provides with your *Personal Navigator*.

DINING

Unlike the other ports, the Disney Cruise Line provides lunch on Castaway Cay. For complete details on Castaway Cay dining, see page 170 (we've repeated some of the same information here for your reference). Everyone can eat at **Cookie's BBQ** and **Cookie's Too** near the family beaches. Cookie's typically serves from 11:30 am to 2:00 pm, and offers the best selection with burgers, BBQ ribs, chicken sandwiches, corn on the cob, fruit, frozen yogurt, and cookies. Food is served buffet-style. Plenty of sheltered seating is nearby. Basic beverages (including sodas) are also provided, or you can buy an alcoholic beverage across the way at the Conched Out Bar. Adults can eat at the **Castaway Cay Air Bar-B-Q** located at Serenity Bay, the adults-only beach, from about 11:00 am to 1:30 pm. Offerings include burgers, salmon, potato salad, fresh fruit, and fat-free frozen yogurt. Alcoholic beverages can be purchased at the bar nearby. If you choose not to visit Castaway Cay, a buffet is served onboard in Parrot Cay/Enchanted Garden, usually from 8:00 am to 1:30 pm.

Exploring Castaway Cay

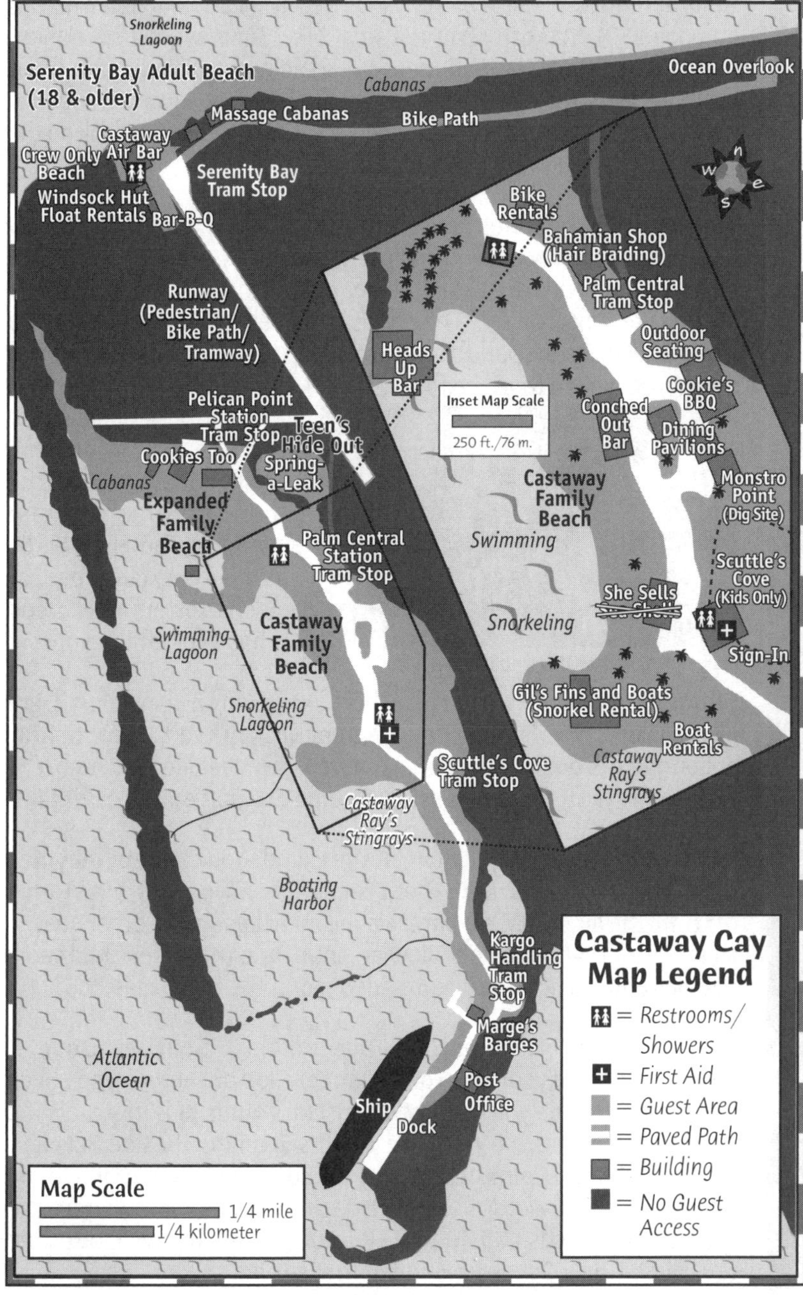

Playing in Castaway Cay

ACTIVITIES

Some **activities** on Castaway Cay require advance booking (see details on page 250). You can reserve floats, bikes, and snorkel equipment rentals in advance, though these are usually available on a walk-up basis. Strollers and beach wheelchairs are free for use on a first-come, first-served basis—while beach wheelchairs are designed to roll on the sand, they are still very hard to push.

The **beautiful beaches** are a big draw at Castaway Cay. The family beaches are the largest and busiest—arrive early to get a good beach chair. Float rentals are available near Gil's Fins snorkel rentals and at the bike rental shack. The adults-only beach—Serenity Bay—is a wonderful place to spend a little grown-up time. The beach there is a little more barren than the family beach. Bring some water shoes as the bottom is coarser and may be uncomfortable. Walk farther down the beach for the most privacy. The Hide Out—which is exclusively for teens—offers music and shade for chilling out.

© MediaMarx, Inc.

A kids' water play area

Stingray encounters, a popular shore excursion on many islands, are also available on Castaway Cay. We think Disney's version of stingray encounters is one of the best, so if you can't decide which port to see stingrays in, choose Castaway Cay! See page 251 for details.

Would you like to see a bit more of the island? You can **rent bicycles** near the family beach at $6/hour for all ages. Two bike trails branch off from the air strip. One parallels the adult beach, the other goes to a large observation tower. Allow an hour for either ride. Child seats can be requested. Water is provided along the bike trails, too.

Kids have their own supervised playground at **Scuttle's Cove**. If you've registered your kids for Oceaneer Club or Lab, you can check them in here while you go play. Counselors guide kids in structured activities, but they do not take them swimming. Beside Scuttle's Cove is Monstro Point, which has a huge whale "skeleton" to dig up! And a 1,200-sq.-ft. soft wet deck area has more water fun! Programming ends at 3:30 pm. Note that kids can check out sand toys at Scuttle's Cove—first come, first served.

Playing in Castaway Cay

Snorkeling is a very popular activity on Castaway Cay, which is an excellent spot for beginners to try out the sport. You can rent equipment at Gil's Fins, and Flippers and Floats, both by the family beach—prices are $25/adult and $10/kid (includes masks, fins, and vest). You can reserve your snorkel rental in advance (see page 250), though they rarely run short. If you reserve, you'll be charged, whether or not you manage to use them. The snorkeling lagoon is extensive—there's plenty of fish and sunken treasure to discover, as well as a submarine from Walt Disney World's "20,000 Leagues Under the Sea." Look for the map that shows the snorkeling course before you get in. Put sunscreen on your back—the water intensifies the sun's rays and you can get badly sunburned. Consider clipping a water bottle to your vest to rinse out your mouth—the saltwater can be bothersome. Note that there is an unofficial snorkeling lagoon at Serenity Bay (it's straight out from the first massage cabana)—rent your equipment at the family beach and tote it over. You can use your own snorkel gear in the lagoons, too. (Disney requires that all snorkelers wear a flotation device—you may need to pay a small fee of $6 for its use.) Some families like to bring their own (better) equipment, or simply purchase cheap snorkel sets for kids and then leave them behind.

Boat rentals are available, appropriately enough, at the Boat Beach. Rent paddle boats ($8 for two-seater, $10 for four-seater), Aqua Trikes ($15), sea kayaks ($8 for one-seater, $10 for two-seater), small Aqua Fins sailboats ($15), and Sun Kat sailboats ($20)—all prices are for a half-hour. No advance reservations are necessary for rentals other than Banana Boats.

Watercraft on Castaway Cay

Family games are available at In Da Shade Game Pavilion (replaced the Grouper Pavilion) near the Family Beach. This shaded patio offers table tennis, foosball, billiards, pin pong, and basketball. This is a great place to getaway when you or a family member need some time out of the sun.

Playing in Castaway Cay

A recent addition are the **rental Beach Cabanas**, sixteen cabanas on the family beach and four more on the adult beach. These private, 325-sq.-ft. cabanas offer a refrigerator stocked with soft drinks, fruit and snacks, lockable storage, outdoor shower, a shaded deck with cushioned chaise lounges, side tables, a dining table, snorkel gear, floats, bike rentals, beach toys, sunscreen, and towels. Cost is $499/day at the family beach, $399/day at the adult beach, for up to 6 guests. Extra guests are $50 each. Reserve online.

Adults can reserve a popular **cabana massage** near Serenity Bay. If you do just one spa treatment, this is the one we recommend. Cabana massages are $147/person—reserve in advance online to avoid disappointment. If you are sensitive to the sun, book a massage for later in the day—the oils make your skin more likely to sunburn. You can bring your own sunscreen and ask to have it applied at the end of the massage.

A massage cabana on Castaway Cay

Shopping is limited to four small shops. She Sells ~~Sea Shells~~ and Buy the Sea Shore are Disney-themed shops with unique Castaway Cay logo items. Visit these shops early, as the crowds are huge later in the day and some items and sizes get gobbled up quickly. Two Bahamian-run retail shops near Peilcan Point sell crafts, shirts, and trinkets—this is also where you can get hair braiding for $1/braid or $2/cornrow—expect to pay about $30 for the whole head (which takes about 3 hours). There is sometimes a merchandise cart at Serenity Bay, too. The shops on the ship are closed while the ship is docked at Castaway Cay.

You can meet your favorite **Disney characters** on Castaway Cay. Check the back of the Disney-provided Castaway Cay map for times. Photo opportunities are available all over the island. Look for ship's photographers near the ship and at the family beach.

Playing in Castaway Cay

While it's not possible to **hike** around the island, you can take a leisurely stroll down the bike path near the adult beach. Water is provided along the trail, and there's a two-story scenic ocean overlook at the end of the hike. If you're looking to see parts of the island that are normally off-limits, we recommend the delightful Walking and Kayak Adventure excursion described on page 252.

If offered on your cruise, the **Pirate Scavenger Hunt** is a fun, free activity—watch your *Personal Navigator* for a "Pirate Scavenger Maps" distribution session the day before your scheduled day in Castaway Cay. At this session, you'll pickup that all-important packet of items that you need for the hunt! Once you dock at Castaway Cay, you're free to begin your scavenger hunt—it will take you over a wide range and call on your keen observation skills. There's no reward for being the fastest to solve the scavenger hunt, and the reward isn't anything valuable, but it is a lot of fun and we really enjoyed it!

Organized sports include a 5k run, a power walk, yoga at the adult beach, and beach volleyball. Check the back of the island map for the schedule. The 5k run route is marked, for solo runs at any time.

Let's not overlook one of our favorite activities on Castaway Cay—**relaxing**! You can do it practically anywhere, but we really like lounging about in hammocks on the family beach or adults-only beach. We've had the best luck finding empty hammocks behind Gil's Fins (the snorkel rental shack). If you find a hammock, please enjoy it, but don't try to save it by leaving your things on it.

Big changes came to this little island in late 2010. In addition to the new rental beach cabanas, the family beach has expanded, there's now a floating water feature with water slides and water cannon called "Pelican's Plunge," a 2,400-sq.-ft. water play area with pop jet fountains and other watery fun called "Spring-A-Leak," a soft wet-deck with fountains in Scuttle's Cove, a new beach bar called "Sand Bar," a new rental location known as "Flippers & Floats," the Teen Hideout pavilion inland behind Spring-A-Leak that replaces the Teen Beach, and an additional shop called "Buy the Sea Shore" featuring Castaway Cay-exclusive merchandise. We've noted these new additions on our map on page 245. Do note, however, that the Flying Dutchman ship from *Pirates of the Caribbean: Dead Man's Chest* is no longer docked at Castaway Cay. But you may still find Captain Jack Sparrow wandering the island!

Advance Rentals & Excursions on Castaway Cay

These rentals are nonrefundable unless your cruise skips Castaway Cay.

Snorkel Lagoon Equipment Rental [C01]

Explore Disney's 12-acre snorkeling lagoon—price includes all-day rental of mask, fins, and vest (light flotation). Beginners can take the Discover Trail; experienced snorkelers may like the longer Explorer Trail. Both trails have lots to see. Pick up your snorkel equipment at Gil's Fins. Note that children under 13 must be with an adult. (On Your Own: Bring your own equipment and use the lagoon!)

Sports | Active | Ages 5 & up | $25/adult | $10/kids 5-9

Float & Tube Rentals [C03]

Enjoy the water with a lounge float or tube. (On Your Own: Purchase inflatable floats from a dollar store at home and bring along on your cruise.) Ages 5 & up.

Beach | $6/each

Bicycle Rental [C04] — Rating: 8

Dozens of bikes in a range of sizes await. Training wheels, child seats, and helmets are available. The biking paths are on flat terrain, and there's plenty of drinking water along the way. Look for the ocean outlook at the end of the bike path! Cruiser reviews are positive: The bikes are "comfortable" and the "trail is beautiful." At the end of the trail is a "very peaceful," "secluded beach."

Sports | Active | All ages | $6/hour

Castaway Cay Getaway Package [C05] — Rating: 7

*This package includes all-day float and snorkel equipment rentals, and a one-hour bike rental, for a savings of $5-6. Very popular—book early. Cruiser reviews are positive: Cruisers enjoyed having the rentals "secured" and felt it is "good deal," though many noted they weren't able to use all three rentals. Note: The **Extreme Getaway Package** ($54/$39) adds a Castaway Ray's session (see next page for details) to everything else mentioned here, saving $3-$6/person.*

Sports | Active | Ages 5 & up | $32/adult | $16/child

Parasailing [C08] — Rating: 9

If you've never tried parasailing, this is a great experience for beginners. You can go solo or tandem, and you'll take off from the boat and land in it when you're done. Expect to be airborne for 5-8 minutes, with 600 feet of rope between you and the boat. Guests must be 90-375 lbs. (40-170 kg.) to parasail. Tandem parasailing is possible if you're both under the maximum weight combined (and may even be required on windy days). Be sure to take a disposable camera for amazing photos while in the air! Cruiser reviews are very positive: "No experience is necessary" to enjoy this "amazing flight" over the water. The "views" are "stunning." It's a "real adrenaline rush" and a "genuine highlight." "Book early" as "spots fill up quickly." Cruisers say "go for it!" May be cancelled due to high winds.

Sports | Active | Ages 8 & up | $79/person | 1 hour

Castaway Cay Island Cruise (Seasonal) [C06] — Rating: 5

Board a catamaran for a scenic cruise all the way around Castaway Cay. Along the way you'll learn about the history and geography of the island and enjoy a complimentary beverage (bottled water or fruit punch). In addition, each child receives a souvenir fish card. The catamaran has both shaded and unshaded seating areas. Typical meeting time is 1:15 pm. Cruiser reviews are lackluster: The cruise was a "vague tie-in to the overall pirate mania." It is "not bad" and a "nice sightseeing diversion," but provides "no behind-the-scenes information." Overall, readers thought it was "okay" but were "not overly impressed."

Tour | Leisurely | All ages | $39/$29 (0-9) | 1.5-2 hours

See page 218 for a key to description charts and their icons.

Embarking on Shore Excursions on Castaway Cay

Castaway Cay Bottom Fishing [C02] — Rating: 9

Fishing
Active
Ages 6 & up
$117/person
2.5-3 hours

Up to six guests can enjoy a ride around the Abaco Islands for bottom fishing (catch and release). Tackle, bait, and beverages (soda and water) are provided. Guests 12 and under must wear life jackets. Typical meeting times are 9:00 am, 9:30 am, and 1:00 pm. Very popular—book early! Cruiser reviews are very positive: The "friendly" captain takes you out to a "beautiful setting" to fish. There are "lots of fish," and "plenty to catch." Cruisers do note that there is no "head" (restroom) on the boat. All cruisers had a "great time" and considered it a "highlight" of their cruise. This excursion may be suspended without notice depending on the season and other conditions.

Castaway Ray's Stingray Adventure [C13] — Rating: 9

Sports
Active
Ages 5 & up
$35/adult
$29/ages 5-9
1 hour

This adventure begins when you check in at the Castaway Ray's Stingray Hut near Gil's Fins and Boats (see Castaway Cay map on page 245). After receiving your snorkel equipment (mask, snorkel, and flotation vest), guests gather under a shelter for a fascinating and educational orientation on the stingrays. This program was developed in partnership with The Seas With Nemo & Friends at Epcot, and cast members from Epcot are often the ones to give you your orientation. Among other things, you will learn that the barbs have been trimmed from the stingrays that live in the lagoon, so you and your family are safe from stings. After your briefing, you wade into the shallow water with the stingrays. A guide accompanies you and encourages the stingrays to come closer so you can view them up close and touch them. You may even have the chance to feed them! Special U-shaped ramps (see photo below) were created and the stingrays are trained to swim up them, giving you an unparalleled look. After this, there's free time to don your snorkel equipment and swim among the stingrays for an underwater look. Note that children under 16 must be accompanied by an adult. A portion of the proceeds from this excursion go to Disney's Wildlife Conservation Fund. Typical meeting times are every hour from 9:00 am to 3:00 pm. Cruiser reviews are very positive: The experience was "enjoyable" as well as "educational." The "innovative" stingray ramps gave cruisers "a better look at the rays" than on other stingray excursions. The stingrays "don't bite" and their "barbs have been removed." Cruisers "did not feel threatened" but the "snorkeling was poor" due to the stirred-up sand. Overall, most cruisers say they want to "do it again" on their next cruise.

Dave meets a stingray at Ray's

Glass Bottom Boat Scenic Voyage [C11] — Rating: 2

Tour
Leisurely
All ages
$35/$25 (0-9)
1 hour

Board a 46-foot trawler with a glass bottom for an hour-long ecotour of the barrier reefs surrounding Castaway Cay. Typical meeting times are 9:45 am, 11:15 am, 12:45 pm, and 2:15 pm. Cruiser reviews are uniform: The "rocky," "overcrowded boat" is filled with people "pushing and shoving" to see out the "cloudy" glass bottom. "Very limited fish" are visible. There are "very few seats," meaning most have to stand the entire time. Overall, cruisers say "don't bother."

See page 218 for a key to description charts and their icons.

Embarking on Shore Excursions on Castaway Cay

Watercraft Ski Adventure (Single and Double) [C12] Rating: 9

Sports
Active
Ages 8 & up
$95 single
$160 double
1 hour

Explore Castaway Cay on a personal watercraft (also known as a "WaveRunner" or "Jet-Ski") with a knowledgeable tour guide accompanying you. Note that you must be 18 years or older to drive the personal watercraft (guests ages 16 and 17 may drive with a parent on the same craft). Max. weight is 375 lb./170 kg. Typical meeting times are 9:45 am, 10:30 am, 11:15 am, 12:00 pm, 1:00 pm, 1:45 pm, and 2:45 pm. Cruiser reviews are very positive: Guests love "riding the WaveRunners" at a "brisk pace" while getting "gorgeous views" of Castaway Cay and the Abacos. Cruisers recommend you "bring watershoes" and a "waterproof camera" as there are "good photo-ops on the tour." Those who've done this excursion remind us that "just hanging on to the WaveRunner for a long time as you navigate through the waves can leave you a bit tired and even a little sore." Parents also point out that kids who ride double with you "just hang on to your waist—there are no buckles or restraints" to keep them from falling into the water. Most cruisers found this an "excellent excursion" and "highly recommend it" to others.

Seahorse Catamaran Snorkel Adventure [C09] Rating: 4

Sports
Active
Ages 5 & up
$52/$36 (5-9)
2-2.5 hours

If the snorkeling lagoon doesn't satisfy your itch to snorkel, this excursion puts you aboard a 63-foot catamaran to sail to a prime snorkeling area. Snorkel gear and instruction provided. Typical meeting times are 9:15 am and 1:15 pm. Cruiser reviews are mixed: The "excellent" catamaran trip was "delightful" for most. The snorkeling proves trickier, however—some enjoyed an "abundance of sea life," while others battled with "wind and currents." Cruisers felt the "open water can be choppy" and this is "not good for those prone to motion sickness or snorkeling beginners."

Walking and Kayak Nature Adventure [C10] Rating: 7

Sports
Very active
Ages 10 & up
$64
2.5-3 hours

Explore areas of Castaway Cay normally off-limits to guests! Start with a 40-min. nature hike to reach your kayak launch site, then enjoy an hour-long kayak trip through mangroves. Afterward, swim at a deserted beach, then take a 20-min. walk back. Typical meeting times are 9:00 am, 9:15 am, and 12:45 pm. We did this ourselves and really enjoyed it—we recommend it to anyone who wants to be active and explore the ecosystem. Wear appropriate footwear. We think it's best for those who've visited the island before. Cruiser reviews are mixed—most think the kayaking is "awesome" but others felt the overall "pace was too slow." Kids were "bored" with the nature aspects and "didn't do much paddling." Cruisers report seeing "lots of wildlife." Other guests recommend you "bring/wear bug repellent" although "bugs aren't too bothersome."

The Wild Side (for Teens Only) [C07] Rating: 9

Sports
Very active
Ages 13-17
$35/teen
4 hours

Retrace the adventures of the first teens on the island—Molly and Seth. There's plenty of action, and you'll get to do some snorkeling, biking, and sea kayaking. Typical meeting time is very early for teens—around 9:00 am. Teen cruiser reviews are overwhelmingly positive: First, "wait until you see who else is going" before you book—this tour "is best when you go with people you know" (but don't wait too long—it can book up). On Castaway Cay, you "do the bike ride first," "kayak for about 20 minutes," then bike back to go "snorkeling." After lunch at Cookies, you "hook up with other teens at the teen beach." Many think this was the "highlight" of their cruise; those who disagree had issues with "other teens," not the excursion.

See page 218 for a key to description charts and their icons.

St. Maarten/St. Martin
(Eastern Caribbean Itineraries)

The Dutch say Sint Maarten, the French say St. Martin, but what's in a name? Where else can you visit **two countries** this easily, dine so lavishly, shop so extravagantly, and sunbathe so beautifully? Two nations share this bit of paradise, but if we must take sides, we'll take the French. Alas, the Disney ships dock on the Dutch side.

© MediaMarx, Inc.

Alexander on the beach in St. Maarten

AMBIENCE

With the Atlantic to the east, the Caribbean to the west and a lagoon in between, St. Maarten's 37 beaches offer **everything** from roaring surf to gentle ripples, and brisk trade winds keep the island cool. Its 37 square miles (96 sq. km.) include tall, luxuriantly green mountains, two capital cities, hundreds of appetizing restaurants, a dizzying array of shops, and a dozen casinos. Philipsburg, the bustling Dutch capital, hosts up to four cruise ships daily, and offers handy, excellent shopping. Picturesque Marigot, the French capital, offers a lot more charm and sophistication for cruisers willing to go the extra distance.

HISTORY

The **history** of this island begins with the Arawaks, seafaring Indians who gathered salt on the island. Later, Columbus named and claimed this island as he sailed past on the Feast of St. Martin. After harassing the Spanish for some years (New Amsterdam's Peter Stuyvesant lost his leg here), the Dutch and French moved in and carved it up in 1647. Relations are friendly now, but the border moved several times during the next 200 years. Sugar cane was the cash crop until slavery was abolished, and sea salt was produced in Philipsburg's Salt Pond, but this was a very quiet place until tourists came to call. And despite this long history, there's still a strong difference in culture and architecture between very French St. Martin and commerce-focused Dutch Sint Maarten.

FACTS

Size: 12 mi. long (19 km.) x 8 mi. wide (13 km.)	
Climate: Subtropical	**Temperatures**: 80°F (27°C) to 85°F (29°C)
Population: 77,000	**Busy Season**: Late December to April
Language: English, French, Dutch	**Money**: Euro or Florin (U.S. dollar accepted)
Time Zone: Atlantic (no DST)	**Transportation**: Taxis and cars
Phones: Dial 011- from U.S., dial 22222 for emergencies	

Making the Most of St. Maarten/St. Martin

GETTING THERE

Your ship docks at the **Captain Hodge Wharf** in Philipsburg in Dutch St. Maarten, at the east end of Great Bay. Taxis and tour buses leave from the wharf, and a water taxi makes two stops along Front Street ($6 buys a pass good for unlimited trips, all day long). A beachfront promenade provides direct access to the beach and the shops, casinos, and restaurants of Front Street. It's about a 10- to 15-minute walk to the near end of Front St., and about a half-mile (0.7 km) from one end of the shopping district to the other. The wharf hosts a tourist information booth. Disembarkation time is typically 7:45 am with an all-aboard time around 6:30 pm.

GETTING AROUND

As with many ports, the real pleasures are found outside of town. Most destinations are within a half-hour drive of Philipsburg, and a **rental car** is the way to get there. Research and book your rental in advance, as rates skyrocket for on-site rentals. All major agencies are represented, but only some have pierside offices. • The island is really two rocky land masses. A pair of sand spits connects the roughly circular main bulk of the island with the small western portion, Terre Basses (the Lowlands). Between the sand spits is Simpson Bay Lagoon. • The French side occupies 21 sq. miles (54 sq. km.) of the northern part of the island, the Dutch 16 sq. miles (41 sq. km.) of the south. A picturesque range of mountains runs north to south, further dividing the island. From Philipsburg, nearly every point of interest, including Marigot, can be reached by driving around the perimeter of the island. • **Taxis** use a government-controlled rate chart. The base fare is for two persons, and each additional person costs about 1/3 the base fare. Sample fares from Philipsburg: Marigot, Orient Beach, Dawn Beach, Maho Resort, all $15; Grand Case, $20. An island tour is $50. • **Public buses** travel between Philipsburg and Marigot. The fare is around $3, U.S. funds are accepted. • Once you're in Philipsburg, Marigot, or any other community, everything will be within walking distance.

STAYING SAFE

There's nothing too unusual about staying safe on "The Friendly Island." No place is crime-free, but St. Maarten does very well. Be wary when carrying parcels, of course. Don't bring valuables to the beach. American and Canadian drivers will be happy, as the island follows U.S. driving practices (right-hand side), but beware of **speed bumps** through towns and resorts. The breeze may fool you into forgetting the sun—be sure to apply plenty of sunblock, especially if you'll be more exposed than usual (if you catch our drift).

Touring St. Maarten/ St. Martin

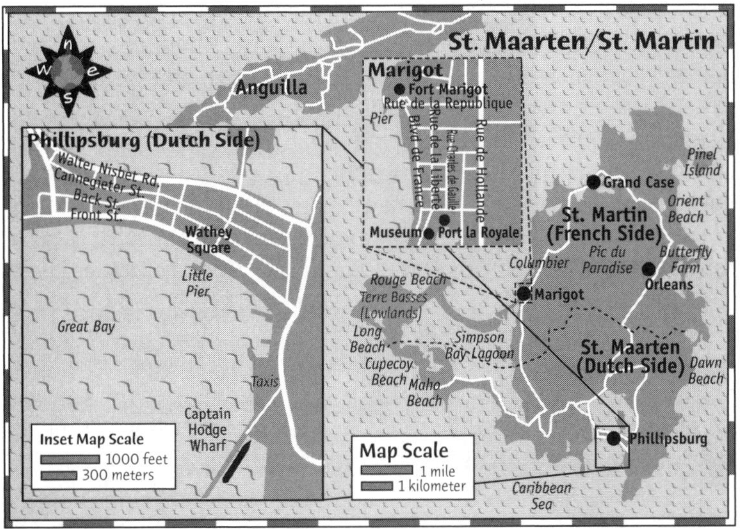

Walking Around in Philipsburg: Philipsburg is a narrow sand spit, just four streets deep and about a mile long (1.6 km.). Front Street runs the length of the town and supplies most of the tourist shopping and dining. If you take the water taxi you'll arrive at old Little Pier, where the cruise ship tenders used to dock. Great Bay Beach is right at hand, as is the beachfront promenade. Leave Little Pier and you'll be in Wathey Square, with its landmark Dutch courthouse. From there, a crafts market is another block inland. (If you walk from the ship, you'll be at the east end of Front Street, and Wathey Square will be about three blocks west.) You'll find shops, restaurants, and casinos no matter which way you turn. Just walk west until you've had your fill, then retrace your steps.

Walking Around in Marigot: The heart of Marigot is a rough rectangle, bordered on the west by the harbor. On the north, Rue de la Republique offers some shopping, with the local pier, crafts market and cafés offering lunch deals at its west end. From the pier, head north to climb to the ruins of Fort Marigot, or head south on restaurant-lined Boulevard de France to the Creole graveyard and small museum at the south end of town. Also on the south side, about a block inland, is Port la Royale, a marina surrounded by restaurants and shops—a perfect spot for lunch. Afterward, head back north on shady Rue de la Liberté or shop-filled Rue Charles de Gaulle.

Playing in St. Maarten/ St. Martin

ACTIVITIES

Great Bay Beach is a short walk from the ship along the beachfront promenade. The surf is gentle, and food and shopping are right behind you on Front Street. To the north, **Orient Beach**, with its long crescent of soft white sand and gentle surf, is called the "French Riviera of the Caribbean," but it achieved fame as the island's official nude beach. Beachfront restaurants and resorts have dressed the place up, but bathers at the south end of the beach are still very undressed (not that you have to be). **Maho Beach**, **Mullet Bay**, **Cupecoy Beach**, and **Long Beach** are way out west by the big resorts, past Juliana Airport (traffic can be brutal, so allow lots of time). All are very pleasant, with Maho offering full resort amenities. Other beaches include remote Rouge Beach (one of Dave's favorites) and Grand Case Beach. Note: With the possible exception of Great Bay Beach, you're likely to encounter European-style beach attire (topless women, men in thongs).

The brisk trade winds make the island very popular for **sailing**. For convenience, take one of several "shore" excursions described below. Excursions are also available near the marina in Philipsburg.

The island is a **diner's paradise**, with fabulous French, Creole, Indian, Vietnamese, and Indonesian restaurants (and KFC). You'll have no trouble finding a meal along Front Street in Philipsburg, but you'll do better in "France." In Marigot, head toward charming Port la Royale Marina, which is encircled by more than a half-dozen bustling bistros. Or choose one of the many spots by the waterfront offering French and Creole specials. Many restaurants automatically include a 15% service charge (tip), so watch that bill carefully before you tip.

Twelve **casinos** dot the Dutch side. Four are within walking distance of the wharf, on Front Street in Philipsburg. The largest (and most elegant) casino is the Princess Casino at Port de Plaisance.

The **luxury goods shops** on both sides of the island present a staggering array of French perfumes and cosmetics, crystal, fine porcelain, jewelry, clothing, liquors, and wines. Philipsburg offers many of the French brands you'll find in Marigot at equal or lower prices, but somehow it feels better to shop in Marigot. The huge Little Switzerland luxury goods chain has shops in Philipsburg and Marigot. Cigar fans can find good Cubans, but be sure to smoke them before you arrive back home.

Embarking on Shore Excursions in St. Maarten/St. Martin

☐ Golden Eagle Catamaran [SM03] — Rating: 9

Sports
Active
Ages 5 & up
$82/$46 (5–9)
4–4.5 hours

Enjoy a half-day jaunt to Tintamarre—a real deserted island—aboard the majestic Golden Eagle. The luxurious, 76-foot catamaran sails at up to 30 knots! The excursion price includes pastries, an open bar, and complimentary use of beach floats and snorkel equipment. Typical meeting times are 7:45 am and 1:00 pm. Cruiser reviews are very positive: The ride over is "fun" and "not too fast for kids to enjoy," while the crew are "friendly and courteous." The "deserted island" is a "great place to snorkel or just relax on the beach." The "beautiful" beach is "scenic" with "very clear" water. There is "music and singing" during the cruise. All cruisers report that they would "do it again," but some would be sure to "take seasickness medicine" first. (On Your Own: Eagle Tours at http://www.sailingsxm.com or 599-542-3323)

☐ Twelve Metre Regatta [SM04] — Rating: 10

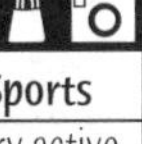

Sports
Very active
Ages 12 & up
$89
3 hours

Become a crew member aboard one of the famous America's Cup yachts, such as "Stars and Stripes." You'll race on a shortened version of the America's Cup course. You may get to "grind a winch" or "trim a sail"—no experience is necessary. Wear soft-soled shoes. Typical meeting time is 8:15 am. Cruiser reviews are overwhelmingly positive: This excursion lets you be "as active" as you like—some cruisers were "captain" while others were "in charge of the beverage chest." The "exciting" race is "great fun" with "friendly competition." Cruisers enjoyed the option to purchase a "great photo" of their team. While the seas are "not rough," this is not for anyone "prone to motion sickness." Overall, this excursion is a "highlight of the cruise" and "a blast!" (On Your Own: America's Cup at http://www.12metre.com at 599-542-0045)

☐ Island Drive & Explorer Cruise [SM05] — Rating: 7

Tour
Leisurely
All ages
$49/$27 (0–9)
4 hours

Drive to Simpson's Bay Lagoon, then board the "Explorer" pleasure boat for a 30-minute cruise to Marigot (the island's French capital). Cash bars onboard. There's time for shopping, dining, and sightseeing before you return to Philipsburg. Typical meeting time is 1:15 pm. (On Your Own: Eagle Tours at http://www.sailingsxm.com or 599-542-3323)

☐ Under Two Flags Island Tour [SM06] — Rating: 7

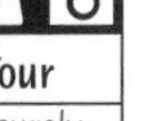

Tour
Leisurely
All ages
$25/$17 (3–9)
3 hours

Board an air-conditioned bus for a scenic, narrated tour of both the French and Dutch sides of the island—you'll see much of the island. The bus makes short 15-minute stops for photos, plus a 45-minute stop in Marigot (the French capital) so you can shop or explore. The tour ends back in Philipsburg. Typical meeting time is 8:45 am. Cruiser reviews are mixed: Most cruisers enjoyed the island drive in a "comfortable, clean bus" with a "friendly driver," though a few did not like to see the "ramshackle houses" along the way. There are several "photo op stops" on "both sides of the island," plus a "French market shopping stop." Most feel this is an "informative," "get acquainted tour" that is "short enough," but some felt the "shopping time is too short" and "kids will be bored out of their skulls." (On Your Own: n/a)

See page 218 for a key to the shore excursion description charts and their icons.

Embarking on Shore Excursions in St. Maarten/St. Martin *(continued)*

French Riviera Beach Rendezvous [SM07] Rating: 8

Beach
Leisurely
All ages
$59/$40 (3-9)
5 hours

Enjoy a beach day at Orient Bay, which has been called the "French Riviera of the Caribbean." You'll receive a guided tour on your way to the beach, where you'll be welcomed with a complimentary beverage and a full-service lunch. Then it's off to your reserved beach chair for relaxation. One end of this beach is clothing-optional. Typical meeting time is 9:15 am. Cruiser reviews are mostly positive: The "20–30 minute" bus ride is informative, filled with "facts regarding the island," though some cruisers were uncomfortable with the "visible poverty" on the island. At Orient Beach, you get a "padded lounge chair" to use and a complimentary "fruit punch" with "optional rum." Lunch is "good" with "ribs, chicken, and fish." Cruisers report "topless" bathers and "full nudity," but "forgot about it" after a while. Most felt this excursion is an "adventure" and a "fun experience." (On Your Own: Just take a taxi to Orient Beach!)

St. Maarten Island & Butterfly Farm Tour [SM09] Rating: 8

Tour
Leisurely
All ages
$38/$28 (3-9)
3-4.5 hours

Board a bus for a narrated tour through Philipsburg to the famous Butterfly Farm on the French side of the island. After the farm you'll stop at Marigot for shopping and exploration. Tip: Wear bright colors and perfume if you want the butterflies to land on you. Typical meeting time is 8:00 am. Cruiser reviews are mostly positive: The "great island tour" with "narration" from the "entertaining driver" gave insight into the "rich history" of St. Maarten. The "best part of the trip" was the Butterfly Farm, which "should not be missed" and is good for "kids under 12." Most had not seen "so many butterflies so close" and were enchanted when they "landed" on them. Most felt this was a "great overall tour," but some said there are "better butterfly farms at zoos." (On Your Own: The Butterfly Farm at http://www.thebutterflyfarm.com or 599-544-3562)

© MediaMarx, Inc.

The Butterfly Farm

See & Sea Island Tour [SM10] Rating: 6

Tour
Leisurely
All ages
$55/$36 (0-9)
3.5 hours

Explore the best of both worlds, with a narrated bus tour to Grand Case and a cruise on the "Seaworld Explorer"—a semi-submarine—for an underwater glimpse of sea life. Afterwards, there's time for shopping and exploring Marigot. Typical meeting times are 8:15 am and 1:15 pm. Cruiser reviews are mixed: The bus driver is "knowledgeable" and "personable," but the ride was "slow" and "harrowing" at times as the roads are very narrow. The "sea portion" aboard the "semi-sub" was "interesting" and "educational," and the "kids really loved seeing the fish." Some reports suggest that "the sea life is minimal." Overall, some cruisers liked seeing "pretty much all" of the "pretty island," while others felt there were "better ways" to see the island. (On Your Own: Seaworld Explorer at http://www.atlantisadventures.com or 866-546-7820)

See page 218 for a key to the shore excursion description charts and their icons.

Embarking on Shore Excursions in St. Maarten/St. Martin *(continued)*

The Ultimate Charter Choice

Rating: n/a 

Tour
Modearate
All ages
$1,899+
4-4.5 hours

Charter a 65-foot catamaran for a private island adventure for up to 10 guests (get quote for 11-20 guests). The Golden Eagle Catamaran and her crew of three are at your disposal for up to 4 hours (additional hours extra) to visit some of the more remote beaches of the south and west shore, snorkel, or explore the Tintamarre Island nature reserve—your choice. Beer, rum punch, soft drinks and sandwiches are included, and more elaborate meals can be arranged in advance. Snorkel gear and a rib boat are included, to aid your explorations. Guests over 330 lbs. and wheelchairs are not allowed. Not recommended for pregnant guests and those with asthma or heart ailments. (On Your Own: Must be booked through cruise line.)

Mountain Top Downhill Rainforest Trek [SM30]

Rating: n/a 

Sports
Very active
Ages 8 & up
$65/$58 (8–9)
3.5–4 hours

Are you ready for a challenging hike on Pic du Paradise, St. Martin's tallest mountain at 1,400 feet (427 m.)? After a 30-minute, air-conditioned bus ride to the Lotterie Farm Hidden Forest, you'll board a 4x4 open-air safari truck for the ascent to the top of Pic du Paradise. Once you've taken in the spectacular views, you'll begin your all-downhill, 2-hour descent on foot along 1 1/4-mile-long wooded trails. A guide accompanies you to point out folklore, history, flora, and fauna. You'll end your hike at Chewbacca Point where you'll be rewarded with a cold rum or fruit punch before the 30-minute bus ride back to the ship. Be sure to bring good walking shoes and comfortable clothing; bottled water and wooden walking sticks will be provided. Typical meeting time is 8:15 am. (On Your Own: Rent a car and drive up yourself, but you'll need to hike both down and back up.)

© MediaMarx, Inc.

Jennifer on Pic du Paradise

Mountain Bike Adventure [SM19]

Rating: n/a 

Sports
Very active
Ages 12 & up
$78
3.5 hours

Need some exercise? This excursion outfits you with a mountain bike and safety gear, then takes you for a bumpy on- and off-road bike tour. You'll ride along the coastline, through the village of Colombier, and encounter at least one steep hill. After your exertions, take 30 minutes to relax and swim at Friar's Bay Beach (under-dress your swim suit). Typical meeting time is 7:45 am. We received no cruiser reviews for this excursion. (On Your Own: n/a)

Rhino Rider and Snorkeling Adventure [SM18]

Rating: 9 

Sports
Very active
Ages 10 & up
$89
3.5 hours

This excursion offers a chance to zoom about on your own, two-person inflatable boat (the "Rhino Rider") in Simpson Bay Lagoon. After your cruise, you'll have the opportunity to snorkel (equipment provided). When your adventure is over, you can relax with a complimentary beverage. Note that each boat holds two people maximum (400 lb. total), and only those 18 or older can drive. Typical meeting times are 7:45 am and 1:45 pm. Cruiser comments are positive: After a bus ride out to Simpson Bay, guests get a "brief explanation" on using the "two-seater mini boats." Take a "30-minute" ride with "great views" to the "good" snorkeling location. Most cruisers agree the excursion is "worth it" and offered a "great time." (On Your Own: Atlantis Adventures at http://www.atlantisadventures.com or 866-546-7820)

See page 218 for a key to the shore excursion description charts and their icons.

Introduction | Reservations | Staterooms | Dining | Activities | Ports of Call | Magic | Index

Embarking on Shore Excursions in St. Maarten/St. Martin *(continued)*

Afternoon Beach Bash Tour [SM23] Rating: n/a

Here's your chance to relax on beautiful Orient Beach. Bask in the sun, swim in the ocean, or explore the coastline. Beverages are included, umbrella and watersport rentals are extra. 2-2.5 hours of beach time. Allow 3.5 to 4 hours.

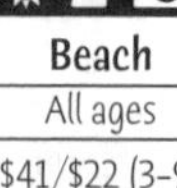

Beach | All ages | $41/$22 (3-9)

St. Maarten Snuba and Snorkel Rating: n/a

Breathe underwater without wearing a tank or scuba certification! A 20-foot air hose connects to a floating air tank on the suface that follows along as you swim. After a short ride from the ship, you'll have a 15-minute briefing, 25 minutes of snuba, a half-hour of snorkeling, then a complimentary beverage at the end. Must be under 250 lbs., and complete a health questionnaire. (On Your Own: St. Maarten Shoretrips at http://www.stmaarten-shoretrips.com

Sports | Active | Ages 10 & up | $85 | 3.5-4 hours

Seaworld Explorer–Coral Reef Exploration [SM27] Rating: n/a

You'll begin with a 30-minute bus ride to Grand Case on the French side, where you'll board the semi-submarine to see beneath the waters. The fully submerged sub ride is 45 minutes long and includes a diver who encourages underwater creatures to move within sight of the sub's windows. You'll enjoy a complimentary glass of fruit punch or rum punch. (On Your Own: Seaworld Explorer at http://www.atlantissubmarines.com, 866-546-7820)

Tour | Leisurely | All ages | $45/$29 | 2.5 hours

See page 218 for a key to the shore excursion description charts and their icons.

St. Maarten On Your Own

Dave's family had a house on Sint Maarten for over 30 years, so we're more familiar with this than any other island. Here are our special tips for on-your-own travelers. Driving and riding in **taxis** on the island gets more frustrating with each passing year, and a late afternoon dash back to the ship is especially perilous (for safety, add at least an extra hour to your travel times). No matter what the authorities do to upgrade the roads, traffic manages to out-pace the improvements. The drawbridge on Airport Road creates miles-long backups several times daily, and passing through either Phillipsburg or Marigot at lunchtime and rush hours is slow and frustrating. Forget about driving Front or Back Streets in Phillipsburg—bypass downtown via Walter Nisbet Road. • **Shoppers**, note that there are native craft markets in both Marigot and Philipsburg. In Philipsburg, walk through Wathey Square and past the old Court House towards Back Street—you can't miss the stalls. In Marigot, head for the waterfront. Again, you can't miss 'em. While the vendors may be locals, we wouldn't bet that the merchandise is locally made. • **Great Bay Beach** in Phillipsburg is a serious alternative to shore excursions—proximity to the ship; the clean, pleasant beach; good food, drink, and shopping; and the long beachfront promenade make this more attractive with each visit.

© VideoVik

Great Bay Beach in Phillipsburg

San Juan, Puerto Rico
(Eastern Caribbean Itineraries)

INTRO

This large, very busy port city is one of the oldest in the New World and one of the busiest ports in the Caribbean trade. You can easily spend your entire day within the ancient walls of Old San Juan or head out to the scenic countryside for rainforest or waterfront eco-delights.

AMBIENCE

Cruise ships dock in Old San Juan, the fortified old city, which was spruced up for Columbus' 500th anniversary and is awaiting its own 500th in 2021. Located on a rocky island at the mouth of San Juan harbor, all points of interest are within walking distance. Dramatic El Morro Fortress supplies the island's best-known landmark (a World Heritage Site). As one of the few walled cities in the Americas, the spirit of the Old World and Spain's colonial heritage is all around, while east of Old San Juan rise the grand beachfront hotels and casinos of the modern city.

HISTORY

Discovered on Columbus' second voyage, Puerto Rico quickly became the headquarters for Spanish rule in the New World and the last stop for treasure ships bound for Spain. San Juan was founded in 1521 by Juan Ponce "Fountain of Youth" de León and was soon a fortified city, fending-off attacks by Spain's many rivals in the New World. Unlike smaller Caribbean islands, Puerto Rico remained a Spanish colony until 1898, when it was ceded to the U.S. after the Spanish American War. Puerto Rico was a U.S. Territory until 1952, when the Commonwealth of Puerto Rico was established—a possession of the U.S. with its own constitution. As throughout the Caribbean, the native peoples didn't last long after "discovery," but hints of native blood lines and traditions survive. The dominant culture and architecture is strongly Spanish Colonial, with African and Caribbean influences. El Yunque forest reserve is one of the New World's oldest, established by Spain in 1876. Now the Caribbean National Forest, it's both the smallest U.S. National Forest (28,000 acres) and the Forest Service's only tropical rainforest (120 in./305 cm. of annual rainfall).

FACTS

Size: 100 miles (161 km.) long by 35 miles (56 km.) wide	
Climate: Subtropical	**Temperatures**: 70°F (22°C) to 89°F (32°C)
Population: 3.89 million	**Busy Season**: Late November to Late March
Language: English & Spanish	**Money**: U.S. Dollar
Time Zone: Atlantic (no DST)	**Transportation**: Taxis, trolleys, cars
Phones: Dial 1- from U.S., dial 911 for emergencies, local pay calls 25 cents	

Making the Most of San Juan

GETTING THERE

The Disney Fantasy is expected to dock at either **Pier 3** or **Pier 4**, the port's largest and most modern, towards the east end of Old San Juan. There are a few shops right at the piers, but the entire old city is close at hand. The tourism information center (La Casita) is about 1/3 mile west along the waterfront, and the ferry to Cataño (Bacardi Distillery) is nearby at Pier 2. A waterfront promenade completed for the Christopher Columbus quint-centennial makes waterfront strolls very pleasant. All-ashore is at 7:45 am, and all-aboard is 4:45 pm.

GETTING AROUND

Old San Juan is **made for walking**, but there's also a free trolley service across the street from the pier that wends its way throughout the old town. We don't recommend a car rental in San Juan unless you're already very familiar with the area. Considering the brief time you'll be ashore, the time spent at the rental agency will be very precious indeed. The narrow, cobblestone streets of Old San Juan are often clogged with traffic and parking is near-impossible, so why add to the frustration? To the east, the beaches and casinos of Condado Beach (3-4 miles) and Isla Verde (6-7 miles) are easy and inexpensive to reach by taxi (see below). If you're interested in the natural wonders of El Yunque or other out-of-town destinations, play it safe and take an official excursion so the ship won't sail without you. Taxi fares are regulated, but be sure to discuss the fare before you hop in. Fixed fares may be offered. Typical rates are approximately: Pier to Old San Juan: $10, Pier to Condado Beach: $12, Pier to Isla Verde: $19. Metered fares start at $3 (all prices in U.S. dollars). There are no extra, per-person fees for up to five passengers.

SAFETY

Personal safety in this metropolitan city should be approached with the **same caution** you'd show in any large urban area. Leave your flashy valuables back in the stateroom safe. Shoulder bags should be hung diagonally across your chest. If you'll be carrying purchases back to the ship, travel with a buddy and stay alert. The free trolley will take you safely from the main shopping district right back to the waterfront. If you're headed for the beach, keep a limited amount of cash and any credit cards in a small, waterproof container so you can carry it at all times. And need we say it, "Sunscreen!" Oh, and if the Pirates of the Caribbean happen to sail into port, hide behind those high, fortified city walls.

Touring San Juan

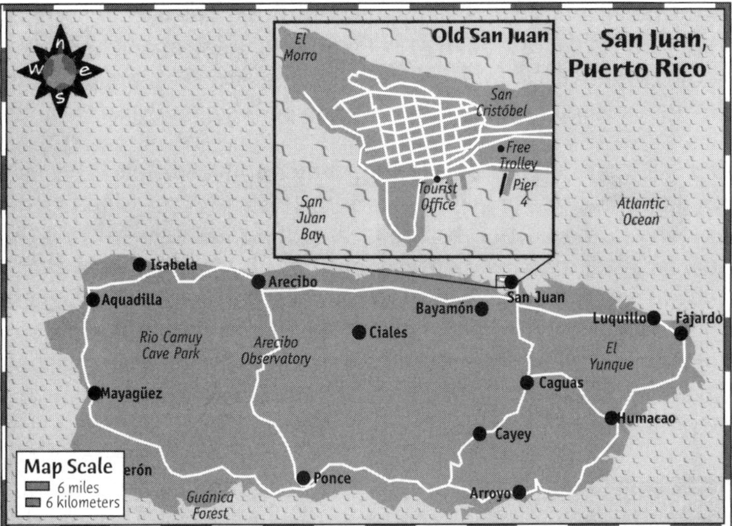

The bulk of **Old San Juan** is contained in an eight-block square area to the north and west of the cruise pier, and there's far more to see than we have space to catalog. Leaving the pier, we suggest you first visit the tourist office, La Casita, for up-to-date info and maps (see location on inset map above). Afterwards, take a free trolley ride to get your bearings—start with a ride all the way to El Morro and the walk back will be downhill. There's a $3 per person per fort fee, or $5 for both (children under 16 are free) to explore El Morro and San Cristóbal fortresses, or use your National Parks Annual Pass (for more information on the fortresses, visit http://www.nps.gov/saju). Several major points of interest are clustered near El Morro, including the Plaza del Quinto Centenario, Casa Blanca (the de León family home), the church of San José, the Museum of San Juan, and the Pablo Casals Museum. From there, head south on Cristo St. to the Cathedral of San Juan and east on San Francisco to Plaza de Armas and San Juan's City Hall. Return to Cristo St. and continue south for serious shopping, and the nearby La Fortaleza, the historic Governor's mansion—tours are available from 9:00 am to 4:00 pm, on the hour. You'll now be near the city's southern wall, which you can follow eastward back towards the cruise piers. This walking tour can take from three hours and up, depending on how much time you spend at the old fortresses and other points of interest.

Playing in San Juan

ACTIVITIES

With the exception of walking, **recreation** of all sorts requires a journey outside this urban port. Eco-tourism is strong here, thanks to the El Yunque rainforest. We suggest booking an excursion to this distant site. Sea kayaking, snorkeling and biking are also options.

Old San Juan offers excellent **shopping opportunities**, especially for those in search of antiques and crafts. Some of the island's most unique and notable crafts are lace-making (descended from the Spanish tradition), hand-carved religious figurines called "santos," and fanciful papier-mâché festival masks. Then there are guayabara shirts, hand-rolled cigars, and rum. The island has a strong fine arts community – paintings and sculpture are also attractive possibilities. Goods purchased in Puerto Rico can be returned to the mainland U.S., duty-free—keep those receipts!

The **Bacardi Rum Distillery** (for tours and free samples) is across the harbor in Cataño. You can take an excursion that includes this stop, or grab a ferry that departs Old San Juan's Pier 2 every half-hour. It's a long walk from the dock in Cataño, or catch a bus.

Beaches in Old San Juan are not the best. For a resort experience, the Condado Beach area is closest to the pier and quite popular with visitors, and slightly farther, the Isla Verde district is also attractive. Situated between the two, the beach at Ocean Park is especially popular with wind surfers. While beachfront hotels dominate Condado and Isla Verde, the public is welcome, and those hotels offer a variety of options for recreation and refreshment.

For **gamblers**, the Sheraton Old San Juan Hotel and Casino is right on the waterfront, nearly opposite the pier. The grander casinos require a journey. Condado Beach is home to the Radisson Ambassador Plaza, Diamond Palace, San Juan Marriott, and Conrad Condado Plaza casinos. These are good choices for beach/casino getaways. Still farther east is Isla Verde, with five more casinos: Courtyard by Marriott, Embassy Suites, InterContinental, Ritz Carlton, and the grandest of all, the El San Juan.

For detailed information on the forts of **Old San Juan**, visit the National Park Service web site: http://www.nps.gov/saju. If you're headed to **El Yunque**, visit the Caribbean National Forest site at http://www.southernregion.fs.fed.us/caribbean.

Embarking on Shore Excursions in San Juan

Disney Cruise Line offers a wide variety of excursions in San Juan. We've chosen to combine descriptions for the sake of space.

New & Old San Juan City Tour

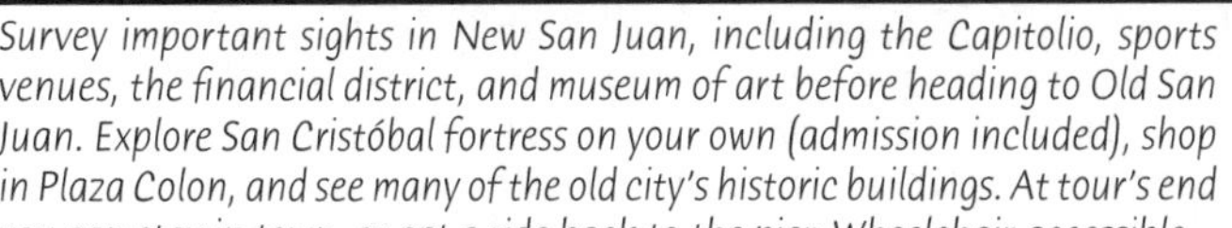

Survey important sights in New San Juan, including the Capitolio, sports venues, the financial district, and museum of art before heading to Old San Juan. Explore San Cristóbal fortress on your own (admission included), shop in Plaza Colon, and see many of the old city's historic buildings. At tour's end you can stay in town, or get a ride back to the pier. Wheelchair accessible.

Tour | Leisurely | All ages | $59/$39 | 4-4.5 hours

Bacardi Rum Distillery Tour/& Old City Tour

Tour the Bacardi Rum distillery, take in the gift shop, and enjoy free samples of Bacardi's wares. (All-ages and adults-only tours are offered.) For an extra $18 ($14 ages 3-9) add a one-hour bus tour of Old San Juan, plus a visit to San Cristóbal Fortress. On your own: Take the Cataño ferry (see page 264).

Tours | Leisurely | $31-$59 | 2.5-5 hours

San Juan Walking, Biking and Segway Tours

Walking ($49/$32 ages 3-9, 2 hours, all ages) and Segway ($105, 2 hours, ages 16-65, 100–260 lbs.) tours guide you through the streets of Old San Juan. The walking tour focuses on Castillo San Cristóbal, involving guests in its 1797 defense. The bike tour ($84, 2.5 hours, ages 16-67) surveys the city from Old San Juan to Condado Lagoon, a 10-mile loop that includes a refreshment stop at a local market.

Tours | Active | $49–$105 | 2-2.5 hours

El Yunque Rainforest Tour & Hike/Rainforest Nature Walk

El Yunque National Forest, 45 miles southeast of San Juan is the site for these very similar tours. Both visit picturesque Yokahú Observation Tower, then their paths diverge. El Yunque Rainforest Tour and Hike ($59/$39 ages 3-9, all ages, moderate, 5-5.5 hours) vists La Coca Falls, a striking sight near the park's entry road, and includes time at the Visitor Center. Rainforest Nature Walk and Waterfall Adventure ($109/$89 ages 6-9, ages 6 and up, active, 6-6.5 hours), the more strenuous tour, follows La Mina River to La Mina Falls, at 0.7 miles the most popular trail in the forest.

Tours | Active | $59-$109 | 5-6 hours

Discover Scuba Tour/San Juan Scuba Tour

These tours based in San Juan's Escambrón Marine Park cater to both first-time and certified divers. Both supply all equipment, an hour of dive time, and a 25-minute walking tour of the park. Discover Scuba Tour ($169) includes basic scuba instruction, but no certification (time spent in open water may count towards future certification). San Juan Scuba Tour ($139) is for certified divers, explores deeper waters, and includes a half-hour of free time on the beach.

Sports | Very active | Ages 12 & up | $139-$169 | 3-3.5 hours

La Marquesa Canopy Adventure/ Campo Rico Zipline & Kayak

There's special appeal to ziplining in a tropical forest, as rainforest researchers put this sport on the map. The La Marquesa tour ($129, ages 8+) emphasizes quiet exploration on their "spylines." The Campo Rico tour ($139, ages 8-68) adds a 15-minute kayak session to the mix.On your own: Campo Rico Ziplining includes pickup at the port: http://www.camporicoziplining.com.

SportsRa | Very active | Ages 8 & up | $129-$139 | 4 hours

See page 218 for a key to the shore excursion description charts and their icons.

Embarking on Shore Excursions in San Juan *(continued)*

Horseback Riding and ATV excursions

A pair of locations offer a chance to explore the countryside on horseback or ATV. The El Yunque Rainforest horseback ($99, ages 9-70) and ATV ($119, ages 16-67) tours last 5 hours and explore private Carabalí Park, in the El Yunque foothillls an hour from San Juan. A post-ride swim is included. Hacienda Campo Rico, just east of San Juan, hosts Horseback Riding Adventure ($89, ages 9 & up) and ATV Excursion ($165, ages 16 & up), which last 3.5 hours. Showers are offered here. The difference in tour length is due to travel time.

Isla Verde Beach Escape/San Juan Family Beach Day

Beach
Leisurely
All ages
$109-$115
4-4.5 hours

This pair of excursions both take you to Isla Verde Beach, out on the east end of San Juan, near the airport. Both excursions provide a soft drink on arrival, a lunch buffet, beach lounges and umbrellas, and last 4 hours. The Isla Verde excursion includes use of the resort pool. Isla Verde Beach Escape ($109/$75 ages 3-9), San Juan Family Beach Day ($115/$89 ages 3-9) .

Catamaran Sail and Snorkel/Nature Lovers Kayak Adventure

Both tours start near Fajardo, an hour from San Juan. Catamaran Sail and Snorkel ($159/$129 ages 5-9, ages 5 & up, 5.5 hrs) visits an offshore islet to snorkel and swim. Snorkel gear, soft drinks, light lunch, and limited open bar included. Nature Lovers Kayak Adventure ($109, ages 10 & up, 6 hrs) visits a mangrove-lined lagoon in 2-person kayaks; A beach break, snack, and bottled water are included.

Caguas-Route to the Heart of Criollo Culture/Hands-On Criollo Cooking

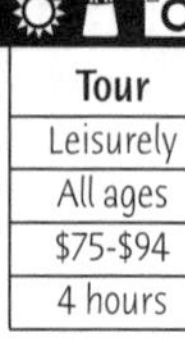

Explore Criollo (Creole) culture, the Caribbean's melding of native, European, and African cultures. The Caguas tour ($75/$55 ages 3-9, all ages, 5 hrs.) visits the island's fifth-largest city to see its museums, botanical garden, and town square. Lunch is not included. Criollo Cooking ($94/$82 ages 2-9, all ages, 4 hrs.) takes you to a San Juan restaurant where you learn to make mofongo (fried plaintains with meat or veggies), eat lunch (adult drink included), and spend 90 minutes exploring Old San Juan. You get to take home the necessary mortar and pestle!

See page 218 for a key to the shore excursion description charts and their icons.

San Juan and Puerto Rico On Your Own

Here's some info for those who want to do it on their own. Please note that we have not used these operators, nor is any mention here an endorsement of their services. Also note that as San Juan is a bustling home port for many cruises, it's best to let your tour operator know that you're a cruise ship passenger and the time you need to be back onboard. **Legends of Puerto Rico** offers several interesting tours, including one that visits the places "where the pirates attacked" and another that explores "exotic" trails. For more information, visit http://www.legendsofpr.com or call 787-605-9060. **Rico Sun Tours** (RST) is a large tour operator offering a variety of excursions, including Camuy Caverns and surfing lessons. For more details, visit http://www.ricosuntours.com or call 787-722-2080. **American Tours of Puerto Rico** offers tours in-town and to El Yunque, Camuy Caverns & Arecibo Observatory, and the city of Ponce. Visit http://www.puerto-rico-tourism.com/americantoursofpuertorico.htm or call 800-250-8971. Another option is to explore the San Juan excursions through ShoreTrips at http://www.shoretrips.com.

St. Thomas & St. John
(Eastern Caribbean Itineraries)

Welcome to pretty St. Thomas, the **busiest cruise ship port** and duty-free shopping haven in the Caribbean! Pirates once roamed freely here, but your visit will be far tamer, thanks to its status as a U.S. Territory. Shopping not your cup of tea? The neighboring island of St. John is a prime, back-to-nature getaway.

© MediaMarx, Inc.

The Disney Magic in St. Thomas (view from Paradise Point)

AMBIENCE

St. Thomas boasts beautiful beaches like many Caribbean islands, but its **rugged mountain terrain** gives it a distinctive look. St. Thomas is shaped like an elongated hourglass and is about 28 square miles (72 sq. km.) in size, making it the second largest island in the U.S. Virgin Islands (St. Croix is the largest). Shoppers throng the narrow lanes and old, stone buildings of St. Thomas' downtown Charlotte Amalie, a duty-free port since the 1700s. The neighboring island of St. John is just a ferry ride away, home to the hiking trails, wildlife, and remote beaches of 7,200-acre Virgin Islands National Park. Your day in port is brief, so a trip to St. John will take most of your day.

HISTORY

Adventurers from many nations visited St. Thomas, but none put down roots until Denmark colonized in the late 1600s. The Danes made the island's prime harbor a **safe haven** for pirates, cashing in on this early "tourist" trade. They also operated sugar plantations, a thriving seaport, and one of the busiest slave markets in the Americas. Charlotte Amalie's waterfront is still lined with old stone buildings from its commercial heyday. The economy crashed after slavery was abolished in the mid-1800s, so by 1917 the Danes were happy to hand the islands to the U.S. for $25 million (it's now a U.S. Territory). Then in 1956, Laurence Rockefeller donated 5,000 acres on St. John to create the Virgin Islands National Park (and not incidentally, to ensure an attractive setting for his Caneel Bay resort).

FACTS

Size: St. Thomas: 13 mi. (21 km.) x 4 mi. (6 km.) /St. John: 7 mi. (11 km.) x 3 mi. (5 km.)	
Climate: Subtropical	**Temperatures**: 77°F (25°C) to 85°F (29°C)
Population: 51,000 & 4,000	**Busy Season**: Late December to April
Language: English	**Money**: U.S. Dollar
Time Zone: Atlantic (no DST)	**Transportation**: Walking, taxis, cars
Phones: Dial 1- from U.S., dial 911 for emergencies	

Making the Most of St. Thomas and St. John

GETTING THERE

Your ship docks near **Charlotte Amalie**, capital of the U.S. Virgin Islands, normally at the West India Company pier in Havensight, 1.15 miles (1.85 km.) east of downtown. Alternately, you may dock at the Crowne Bay Centre pier in Frenchtown, 1.6 miles (2 km) west of downtown, and on rare occassion, you may have to tender in. All ashore is typically at 8:00 am, with all aboard around 5:30 pm. Note: In the past, all guests had to meet with U.S. Immigration officials onboard the ship, regardless of whether they planned to go ashore. This is no longer a requirement, but be sure to watch for any notices placed in your room regarding immigration procedures, just in case. Visitors traveling to St. John should either book a shore excursion, or take a taxi to the Red Hook ferry on the eastern end of the island—round-trip ferry fare is $12/adults, $2/kids (15- to 20-minute ride). There's also a ferry from downtown Charlotte Amalie for $24/ adults, $6/kids, but again you'll have to take a taxi to the ferry.

GETTING AROUND

Plan to take a taxi into town and most destinations, but there is **shopping at both piers**. Havensight Mall offers more than 60 shops, and other malls are nearby, while Crowne Bay Centre has just a handful of shops. • The Paradise Point aerial tram ($21/$10.50 ages 6–12) is a short walk from Havensight pier, and offers panoramic views of the island. • There's far more shopping in downtown Charlotte Amalie. A taxi will cost about $3 (no meters, get the rate in advance). • Car rentals are available at the pier, but taxis and mini-buses are generally a better idea. • Maagens Bay, several miles from Charlotte Amalie on the island's north shore, is a beautiful and well-known beach. Nearby is Mountain Top, famed for its views and banana daiquiris. A half-mile west of Charlotte Amalie is the picturesque fishing village of Frenchtown, known for its eateries. • If you want to visit **St. John**, Disney offers shore excursions to most of St. John's most famous spots, and with the day's tight schedule, they make sense. If you want to explore on your own, Hertz and Avis both have agencies in Cruz Bay, and taxi fares to the major sights are $3–$9. Ferries arrive in Cruz Bay, and the National Park interpretive center is a short walk away. • The beach at Trunk Bay is most popular ($4 day use fee). • History buffs may enjoy the ruins of Annaberg Sugar Plantation.

SAFETY

Pickpockets and beach theft are the most notable crime problems you'll encounter, so **leave your valuables on board**, and safeguard your purse or wallet while shopping. Drinking water is collected in cisterns from rain water, so you may prefer to drink bottled water.

Introduction Reservations Staterooms Dining Activities Ports of Call Magic Index

Touring St. Thomas and St. John

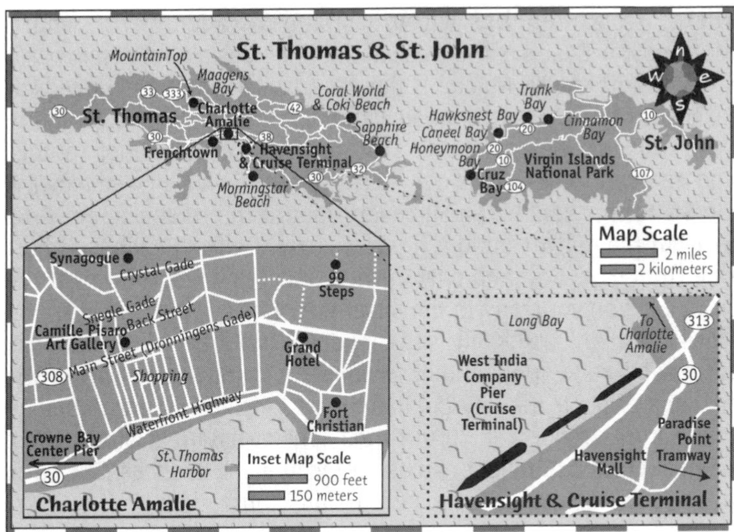

St. Thomas: Charlotte Amalie is a nice place to stroll on steep, narrow streets with Danish names. Most sights are found on the island's many shopping streets, which are within three blocks of the waterfront. Waterfront Highway provides a harborfront promenade. One block inland is Main Street (Dronningens Gade), followed by Back Street, Snegle Gade, and Crystal Gade. More than a dozen Alleys, Gades, Passages, Plazas, and Malls run between Main Street and the waterfront, all lined with shops. Strollers will find historic Fort Christian and the Virgin Islands Museum at the southeast end of downtown. A tourist information center is located nearby, in the former Grand Hotel. One of the New World's oldest Jewish congregations in a charming, 1833 synagogue can be found three blocks inland, near the corner of Crystal Gade and Raadets Gade. Toward the west side of Main Street is the Camille Pissaro Art Gallery, named for the impressionist painter, a St. Thomas native, and featuring works by local artists. Walkers will also enjoy the many brick staircases, including the 99 Steps, that connect the steep streets in the northeast corner of downtown.

St. John's tiny port town of Cruz Bay is good for a short stroll among its cluster of shops and restaurants. The Virgin Islands National Park Visitor Center is a short walk from the dock, and several hiking trails depart from there.

Playing in St. Thomas and St. John

ACTIVITIES

There are no **beaches** within walking distance of the wharf. Morningstar Beach is the closest, and includes all the comforts of the Marriott resort. Maagens Bay ($4/day for adults) is famed for its beauty, but will be thronged with fellow cruise visitors. Sapphire Beach out on the east end offers full, resort-based recreation rentals, and nearby Coki Beach is convenient to Coral World (see below). • On **St. John**, there's a small beach right at the ferry dock in Cruz Bay, but the real attractions are elsewhere. Caneel Beach is a short ride from Cruz Bay, and part of the Caneel Bay resort (stop at the front desk on your way to the beach). Along St. John's north shore, Hawksnest Bay, Trunk Bay, and Cinnamon Bay are easily accessible, offer food, recreation, and other amenities, and are all part of the national park. Trunk Bay ($4/day) is very beautiful, most popular, and features a snorkeling trail. Cinnamon Bay has great windsurfing. • **Snorkeling** equipment can be rented at many beaches. The early departure time makes fishing excursions impractical.

Shopping is St. Thomas' biggest attraction. Shopping is duty-free, sales-tax-free, and is conducted in U.S. dollars. As always, while prices can be excellent, know what you'd pay back home for the same goods. Not everything is a "deal." Some shopkeepers will bargain with you. Just ask, "Is that your final price?" With as many as eight cruise ships in port per day, it takes hundreds of shops to absorb the throngs. We suggest you head into Charlotte Amalie and start exploring. If your time is short, the malls and shops in and around the cruise wharf will be most convenient.

Visitors to St. John will find the **Virgin Islands National Park** web site very helpful, with a detailed map of the island including its 22 hiking trails. Get more info at http://www.nps.gov/viis.

Coral World Marine Park and Undersea Observatory on St. Thomas' east end (adjacent to Coki Beach) offers underwater observation areas, aquariums, exhibits, stingray encounters, nature trails, and the "Sea Trek" adventure where you get to walk the sea bottom ($79/adult and $70/child 8 & up, including park admission). Admission is $19/adults and $10/kids 3–12, or $60 for a family of two adults and up to four kids. Visit http://www.coralworldvi.com or call 888-695-2073.

For one of the most informative and well-laid-out **web sites** for the U.S. Virgin Islands, visit http://www.vinow.com.

Embarking on Shore Excursions on St. Thomas and St. John

St. John Trunk Bay Beach & Snorkel Tour [ST01] — Rating: 6

Sports
Active
Ages 5 & up
$62/$37 (5-9)
4-4.5 hours

Travel by sea and land to Trunk Bay, where you'll have 1.5 hours to swim, snorkel (equipment provided), and relax in this beautiful national park. Typical meeting time is 7:15 am. Cruiser comments are mixed: Most report that the "ferry ride" over was "long" and "boring." Once at Trunk Bay, however, cruisers found it to be "one of the most beautiful" and "breathtaking" beaches. There is a "marked snorkel trail" and some cruisers have seen a "lot of fish," "stingrays," and "sea turtles." Most felt this was the "highlight of their cruise," while some "were not impressed." (On Your Own: Take a taxi to Red Hook, a ferry to St. John, and then a taxi to Trunk Bay)

St. John Island Tour [ST02] — Rating: 9

Tour
Leisurely
All ages
$55/$32 (0-9)
5 hours

Take a boat ride to St. John, then board an open-air safari bus for a guided tour through the unspoiled beauty of this island. Includes a stop at Annaberg Ruins and many stops for photo ops. For all ages. Typical meeting time is 7:15 am. We took this excursion a few years ago and absolutely adored it. Cruiser reviews are uniformly positive: Most enjoyed the "boat ride" to "beautiful" St. John, though it was "long." The "very good driving tour" "makes a lot of stops for pictures" and the driver is both "entertaining" and "knowledgeable." Some of the roads are "very curvy," which could bother some. Overall, the tour is a "great way" to "see a lot" of the island.

© MediaMarx, Inc.

Dave stops for a panoramic photo on St. John

St. John Eco Hike [ST03] — Rating: 8

Sports
Very active
Ages 6 & up
$69/$50 (6-9)
5 hours

Take a ferry to Cruz Bay, where you'll embark on a two-hour guided hike (1.5 miles). You'll stop at Lind Point Lookout and Honeymoon Beach for swimming. Typical meeting time is 7:15 am. Cruiser reviews are positive: This "wonderful way to see this island" starts with "long ferry ride" then a short walk through the city to meet your "knowledgeable guide." The "very easy" hike is "informative," with a look at "local flora and fauna" ("bring bug spray!"). At the end of the "hot" hike, you get 30 min. to "frolic" in Honeymoon Bay ("wear your swimsuit under your clothes").

Tree Limin' Extreme Zipline Adventure — Rating: n/a

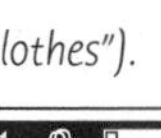

Sports
Active
Ages 8 & up
$125/$115 (8-9)
4-4.5 hours

Would you like your ziplining to come with a panoramic view of Magens Bay and the British Virgin Islands? This new facility has six ziplines, eight platforms, and two sky bridges, including a "yo-yo" zip that goes forwards and back! You'll be met at the pier, weigh-in (must be 75-275 lbs. and no taller than 6.5 ft.), and be transported to St. Peter Mountain. After receiving your gear and a safety talk it's up to the top of the course in a 6-wheel drive Pinzgauer transport. The next 2.5 hours will zip by. You may have time to check-out St. Peter Mountain Greathouse Botanical Gardens. (On Your Own: http://www.ziplinestthomas.com)

See page 218 for a key to the shore excursion description charts and their icons.

Embarking on Shore Excursions on St. Thomas and St. John *(continued)*

Maagens Bay Beach Break [ST27] — Rating: 9

Beach | Leisurely | All ages | $47/$37 (3-9) | 4.5-5 hours

Relax and swim at the beautiful white sandy beaches of Maagens Bay. Take a 25-min. scenic drive, stopping at Drake's Seat along the way for photos and great views. A beach chair and bottled water are included in the price of the excursion. Typical meeting time is 9:00 am. Cruiser reviews are positive: Those visiting Maagens Bay found the beach "wonderful" and "absolutely beautiful." They also "enjoyed the ride from the pier" as "some of the views going over the mountain were absolutely gorgeous." "Restrooms and a snack bar" are available. Most cruisers recommend you "do the excursion on your own" because "it's so easy to do and much cheaper than paying what Disney charges per person for the same thing." (On Your Own: Take a taxi from the pier to Maagens Bay for about $5/person each way, and then pay $4/person admission to the beach.)

Doubloon Turtle Cove Sail & Snorkel [ST08] — Rating: 9

Sports | Active | Ages 5 & up | $58/$35 (5-9) | 3.5 hours

Help hoist the sails of the 65-foot "Doubloon" schooner and cruise to Turtle Cove on Buck Island. Snorkel (equipment provided) and swim. Includes snacks and drinks. Typical meeting time is 7:15 am. Cruiser reviews are positive: This "fun" excursion with a "heavy pirate theme" is fun for "kids and adults alike." While it's not a "major sailing experience," it is "enjoyable" and the "crew is attentive." Snorkeling at Buck Island is "good," though you may not be able to walk on the beach due to "nesting birds." "Rum punch," "beer," and "soda" are served. Overall, most cruisers "recommend it."

Best of St. Thomas Island Tour and Shopping [ST11] — Rating: n/a

Tour | Leisurely | All ages | $39/$24 (3-9)

Take an open-air safari bus tour to St. Peter's Great House, a beautiful botanical garden, and Mountain Top, the highest point on the island. The bus does make some stops for photo opportunities. Optional drop-off downtown for shopping. Typical meeting times are 7:15 am and 12:30 pm. Cruisers visiting Mountain Top on their own claim it is "amazing" how you can "see so much!" Allow 2.5-3 hours.

Caribbean Sea Safari, Snorkel & Beach — Rating: 6

Sports | Ages 5 & up | $55/$29 (5-9) | 4-4.5 hours

Cruise to Buck Island and St. John, check out the beautiful coral formation teeming with exotic fish, snorkel above a sunken ship in a beautiful wildlife refuge, and swim at Honeymoon Beach. Snorkel equipment, vests, and instruction are provided. This excursion is appropriate for both beginners and experienced snorkelers, but you must be able to swim and be in good health. Snacks and beverages are included on the sail back. Typical meeting time is 7:15 am.

Kayak, Hike, and Snorkel of Cas Cay [ST32] — Rating: n/a

Sports | Ages 8 & up | $79/$59 (8-9) | 4-4.5 hours

A 20-minute van ride brings you to the Virgin Islands Eco Tours Marine Sanctuary where the fun begins. There you board a two-person kayak to enjoy a guided tour of Cas Cay. Then hike through the tropical ecosystem to see a marine tidal pool and a blowhole along a coral beach. Now strap on snorkel gear for a guided tour. End with a 15-minute kayak trip. Typical meeting time is 8:00 am.

See page 218 for a key to the shore excursion description charts and their icons.

Embarking on Shore Excursions on St. Thomas and St. John *(continued)*

Coral World Ocean Park & Scenic Drive [ST12] — Rating: 7

Tour
Leisurely
All ages
$39/$29 (3-9)
3.5 hours

Take a guided tour to Coral World in St. Thomas, with a stop at Mountain Top along the way. Cruiser reviews are mostly positive: Coral World is a "wonderful adventure," a bit like "Sea World" but "more science-oriented." "Kids love it," and "see all kinds of sea life" and "pet a shark." The disappointments were the drive which was "not well narrated," and the length of time at Coral World ("only an hour and a half"). Cruisers did enjoy Coral World, but many would "do it on their own" next time. An "Easy" version of tour is available ($10 extra) for guests in wheelchairs or with walking difficulties. (On Your Own: See page 270)

Coral World Ocean Park by Land and Sea [ST34] — Rating: n/a

Tour
Leisurely
All ages
$56/$42 (0-9)
3.5 hours

Enjoy a 25-minute ride in an open-air safari bus to the Coral World Marine Park, where you'll board the Nautilus VI semi-submarine for a 45-minute guided tour. View the marine life and coral gardens from windows eight feet below the surface. After your cruise, you'll have 90 minutes of free time to explore Coral World, including the underwater observation tower, before returning to the ship by bus. Food and beverages are available for an additional cost. Strollers and wheelchairs are allowed, but they must be collapsible.

Coral World and Butterfly Garden — Rating: n/a

Tour
Leisurely
All ages
$46/$36 (3-9)
4 hours

Coral World now operates Butterfly Garden, so you can now book a tour that features colorful, tropical creatures of both sea and air! For full descriptions, see Butterfly Anytime (page 274) and Coral World Ocean Park & Scenic Drive (above). The tour ends at Butterfly Garden, so you can return to the ship on foot when you please. Saves $5 over the price of separate tours. An "Easy" version of tour is available ($8 extra) for guests in wheelchairs or with walking difficulties.

Captain Nautica Mini Boats — Rating: n/a

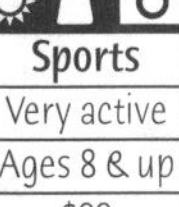

Sports
Very active
Ages 8 & up
$99
3.5 hours

Pilot your own 14-foot rigid inflatable power boat on a 30-minute trip to the waters near Great St. James Island, off the southeast corner of St. Thomas for an hour of snorkeling and exploration (snorkel gear is provided). At excursion's end you can wet your head under a freshwater shower, and wet your whistle with a complimentary fruit punch or rum punch (adults only). The mini-boats have a maximum weight limit of 500 lbs., which can include up to two adults and one child. Must be 18 or older to drive. Life jackets are mandatory.

Castaway Catamaran Sail & Snorkel to Shipwreck Cove — Rating: n/a

Sports
Very active
Ages 5 & up
$52/$32 (5-9)
3 hours

Board your 65-foot catamaran right by the cruise pier and set sail for Shipwreck Cove. After 45 minutes you'll reach your dive site, where you can snorkel above a shipwreck and view coral, fish, and other sea life. There's also plenty of deck space for sunning, and shade as well. After 1.5 hours of snorkeling adventure you'll head back to the pier, enjoying a snack and beverages (including the adult kind) along the way. All snorkel gear is supplied, and complimentary soft drinks are served throughout the cruise. An optional, guided snorkel tour is offered.

See page 218 for a key to the shore excursion description charts and their icons.

Embarking on Shore Excursions on St. Thomas and St. John *(continued)*

Full Day Caribbean Sail & Snorkel — Rating: n/a

Sail the pirate-styled schooner Bones to Turtle Cove at Buck Island National Wildlife Refuge for snorkeling, including instruction and an hour-long guided swim. From there it's on to Water Island's secluded Honeymoon Beach (access by boat only) for relaxation, swimming, and more snorkeling. A BBQ lunch follows, with ribs and chicken for the adults, and hot dogs and chicken tenders for the kids. Lunch, snacks, and soft drinks are included. Wear swimwear and cover-ups. (On your own: http://www.bonesusvi.com or 340-344-6812)

Tour
Active
5 and up
$105/$65 (5-9)
6.5-7 hours

Skyride to Paradise Point [ST23] — Rating: 7

Enjoy a great view (see photo on 267) in this suspended tram. Bird shows are held twice daily. You can do this excursion anytime after 9:00 am. Jennifer tried this and found it a fun diversion with great views, but not a don't-miss. Cruiser reviews are mostly positive: The tramway is an "easy 10- to 15-minute walk" from the pier (but if you tender in, it's a "$3/person taxi from town" instead). The view from the tram is "just amazing" and you get a "great view of the Disney Magic." The "birds are cute" (shows are at "10:30 am and 1:30 pm") and there are some "nice shops" to browse. There is also a quarter-mile "nature walk" and a "little cafe." Most cruisers simply walked over (you can see the tramway from the pier) and purchased tickets on their own, at the same price ($21/$10.50).

Tour
Leisurely
All ages
$21/$10.50 age 6-12 (0-5 free)
1 hour

Captain Nautica's Snorkeling Expedition [ST25] — Rating: 9

Enjoy a speedboat ride to two different snorkeling sites, Buck Island's Turtle Cove, where swimming with turtles is "most likely," and Shipwreck Cove. Price includes snorkeling equipment, snacks, and beverages. Typical meeting times are 7:15 am and noon. Cruiser comments are very positive: The "adventurous" speedboat ride is "pretty fast" and "lots of fun." The crew is "friendly" and "helpful." Snorkeling is "wonderful" with "many colorful fish." The only complaint reported was with the snacks, which "weren't all that great." Overall, cruisers "loved it" and "would do it again." (On Your Own: Not available.)

Sports
Active
Ages 8 & up
$75/$60 (8-9)
3.5 hours

Adventure Snorkel Tour on Sea Blaster — Rating: n/a

A short walk down the pier brings you to Sea Blaster, a 70-foot high speed power boat. Expect to get wet as the boat pounds the waves on the way to your dive site at Fish Island, between St. Thomas and St. John. After 60 minutes of snorkeling (equipment and instruction provided) it's back to Charlotte Amalie, where you can shop or return to the ship. Punch, rum punch, and light snacks provided. Wheelchairs must fold, guests must climb 4 steps. Bring a towel.

Tour
Active
Ages 5 & up
$49/$39 (5-9)
3-3.5 hours

Butterfly Anytime [ST36] — Rating: n/a

Take a three-minute walk from the Havensight pier to the Butterfly Garden for a guided tour through the gardens and a bird show. This excursion is stroller and wheelchair (standard only; no electric chairs) accessible. The Butterfly Garden opens at 9:00 am and you may arrive, stay, and depart when you wish. Note: This tour is not available when the ship docks at Crown Bay or tenders. (On Your Own: http://www.butterflygardenvi.com)

Tour
Leisurely
All ages
$12/$6 (3-9)
Allow 2 hours

See page 218 for a key to the shore excursion description charts and their icons.

Embarking on Shore Excursions on St. Thomas and St. John *(continued)*

Tortola Dolphin Encounter [ST37] — Rating: n/a

Sports
Active
Ages 3 & up
$188/10 & up
$162 (3–9)
8–8.5 hours

Begin with a ferry across the bay to Tortola in the British Virgin Islands, then take a one-hour bus tour of the island before arriving at Dolphin Discovery. There you'll receive an orientation, then wade in waist-deep water for a 30-minute, hands-on "meet and greet" with the dolphins, including an opportunity to touch and kiss a dolphin. A buffet lunch and beverages are included. Note that the excursion includes a 30-minute immigration stop (bring your passport or birth certificate). If you want to simply observe, sign up for the Tortola Dolphin Observer excursion (ST38) for $129/$101. Typical meeting time is 7:00 am.

Tortola Dolphin Observer [ST38] — Rating: n/a

Sports
Active
Ages 3 & up
$129/10 & up
$101 (3–9)
8–8.5 hours

Like the excursion above, you'll begin with a ferry across the bay to Tortola in the British Virgin Islands, then take a one-hour bus tour before arriving at Dolphin Discovery. Once there, you'll join the orientation session, and then watch from a special observation area as your companion(s) participate in the Dolphin Encounter. A buffet lunch of burgers, pasta, chicken wings, fries, salad, juice, and bottled water is included. The excursion includes a 30-minute immigration stop (bring your passport or birth certificate).This excursion should only be booked in conjunction with the above excursion. Typical meeting time is 7:00 am.

Water Island Mountain Bike Adventure [ST13] — Rating: 10

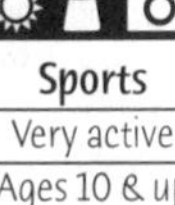

Sports
Very active
Ages 10 & up
$72/10 & up
3.5 hours

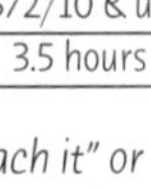

Enjoy a short boat ride to Water Island where you'll explore 5 ½ miles of trail by mountain bike. Includes all necessary equipment. Includes a beach stop. Typical meeting time is 12:15 pm. Cruiser reviews are overwhelmingly positive: Get a ride to Water Island on a "large pontoon boat" and listen to the "history" of the island. Once on the island, you get a "quick how-to" on the bikes, they "fit you for your helmet," and you're off. Most of the ride is "downhill," but it does cover ground with "gravel and loose rocks." After reaching Honeymoon Bay, you can "beach it" or "keep biking" a mostly "uphill trail." Cruisers of "all shapes and sizes" enjoyed this excursion.

Screamin' Eagle Jet Boat [ST28] — Rating: n/a

Sports
Active
Ages 5 & up
$49/10 & up
$39 (5–9)
1 hour

Just a 10-minute walk from the pier and you'll be aboard this 650 horsepower, turbo-charged jet boat known as the Screamin' Eagle. After a brief orientation and a cruise around the harbor with your tour guide, you'll blast into action and race around the coastline at high speeds for 30 minutes. You WILL get wet from the sea water spray! Note that guests must be at least 48" tall to ride. Be sure to wear hats with straps and sunglasses with cords to keep them on you during the ride. Small bags will be provided free of charge to keep your personal items dry. Typical meeting times are 7:45, 10:30, and 11:30 am.

Screamin' Eagle for Teens [ST30] — Rating: n/a

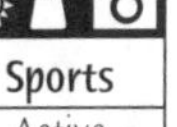

Sports
Active
Ages 13–17
$49

This is the same excursion as ST28 described above but ... it's only for teens! For this special version of the excursion, teens will meet onboard in the teen club and be escorted by Disney Cruise Line youth counselors. Parents or guardians: Note that you must sign a waiver release for your teen to participate.

See page 218 for a key to the shore excursion description charts and their icons.

Embarking on Shore Excursions on St. Thomas and St. John *(continued)*

Sea Trek Helmet Dive at Coral World [ST33] — Rating: n/a

Sports
Active
Ages 10 & up
$89
3.5 hours

Take a 25-minute, open-air safari bus ride to the Coral World Marine Park for your adventure. You will receive a brief safety orientation and be suited up with special water shoes, gloves, and a Sea Trek helmet that allows you to breathe underwater while keeping your face and hair dry. You'll then submerge in the water at depths of up to 20 feet as you hold a handrail, follow your tour guide, and marvel at the marine life. After 45 minutes, you'll dry off and get 90 minutes of free time to explore the park. A complimentary locker is provided; food and beverages are extra. Guests must be at least 80 lbs. to participate, but do not need to have diving or snorkeling experience. Typical meeting time is 7:15 am.

Legendary Kon Tiki Sightseeing and Beach Cruise — Rating: n/a

Tour
Mild
All ages
$49/$29 (0-9)
3.5-4 hours

Tour St. Thomas Harbor on a "legendary" party barge, with a live Calypso band providing a soundtrack for the ride. View the harbor, cruise the waters around nearby Hassel and Water Islands, view coral and sea life from glass-bottomed viewers, and stop for a one-hour beach break (probably Honeymoon Beach on Water Island). There's sun on the upper deck and shade below, dancing, games, and a limbo contest, too. Water and fruit punch provided, bring cash for the snack bar. Wheelchairs OK, no ECVs, and must be able to climb 2 steps.

St. John Champagne Sail & Snorkel [ST21] — Rating: 7

Sports
Active
Ages 5 & up
$85/$59 (5-9)
4.5 hours

After a 20-minute scenic drive in an open-air taxi, you'll board a boat and sail to St. John, where you'll swim, snorkel, and sunbathe. Snacks, snorkel gear, and open bar included. Typical meeting time is 7:45 am. Cruiser reviews are mostly positive: This "great sailing trip" "over and back to St. John" is "excellent." The crew is "terrific" and served "drinks and snacks" both coming and going. Snorkeling at Honeymoon Bay is "very good" with "clear water, lots of fish, and even stingrays," but be aware that if you just want to lounge on the beach you'll need to "swim a short way from the catamaran to the beach." Overall, this excursion is "highly recommended" but a few would "do something else next time."

See page 218 for a key to the shore excursion description charts and their icons.

Stunning St. John, with Tortola on the horizon

Galveston, Texas
(Western Caribbean Itineraries' Special Home Port)

Moody Gardens in Galveston

© CJTravelTips.com

Galveston, near the eastern end of Texas' Gulf Coast, is a **seaside port and resort** city with a storied past and promising future. Now the fourth-largest cruise port in the U.S., the city's beaches, amusements and historic districts draw vacationers from nearby Houston and beyond.

AMBIENCE

Though long a city with a past that was searching for its future, Galveston managed to find its stride by tying that past to its present. With two National Historic Districts, four other historic districts, over 60 buildings on the **National Register of Historic Places**, and its historic seaport, it's easy to feel this town's roots. Yet her modern beach-front hotels, amusement parks, and other attractions means Galveston hardly feels old.

HISTORY

Long inhabited by native peoples, Galveston entered the historical record in 1528, when Explorer Álvar Núñez Cabeza de Vaca was shipwrecked on the "**Isle of Doom**." Later, José de Evia mapped the island as Gálveztown, for Spanish Colonial governor Bernardo de Gálvez y Madrid. Pirates made good use of the natural harbor, until Jean Laffite was evicted by the U.S. Navy in 1821. Its prime natural seaport made Galveston the center of commerce for the young Republic of Texas, and one of America's busiest cotton ports. Prosperity was cut short by the Hurricane of 1900, America's deadliest natural disaster, which killed an estimated 8,000. The city rebuilt behind the 17-foot high, 10-mile long Galveston Seawall, but competition from the new Port of Houston prevented a full return to the city's former glory. Tourism, including a stint as Prohibition Era "Sin City," gradually grew to be a major force in the local economy.

FACTS

Size: Land: 46.1 sq. mi. (119.5 sq. km.) Total: 208.3 sq. mi. (539 sq. km.)	
Climate: Humid Sub-Tropical	**Temperatures**: 50°F (10°C) to 89°F (32°C)
Population: 47,743	**Busy Season**: Summer and holidays
Language: English	**Money**: US Dollar ($)
Time Zone: Central	**Transportation**: car, bus, trolley, walking
Phones: Area codes 409, dial 911 for emergencies	

Introduction | Reservations | Staterooms | Dining | Activities | Ports of Call | Magic | Index

Making the Most of Galveston

GETTING AROUND

Nearly all visitors arrive via I-45 and the Galveston Causeway. Once on the island, traffic is heading northeast on Broadway Street, though visitors headed to Moody Gardens and Seawall Blvd. would exit onto 61st St., southbound. The Disney Magic docks at **Texas Cruise Ship Terminal 2** on the bay side of the island (see next page), with Pier 21 and the Strand District just blocks away. 25th Street runs 1.4 miles south from the cruise terminal to Seawall Blvd. and the Gulf shore, ending at the newly-rebuilt Pleasure Pier. The city's public transit system was devastated by Hurricane Ike, with the trolleys that connected the main tourism districts still out of service at this writing. A special tourist bus that substitutes for the trolley may be in service. Until full trolley service can be restored, the only practical way to travel between the various tourist areas is by private vehicle.

HIGHLIGHTS

Moody Gardens tops the list of Galveston's man-made attractions. Three huge, glass pyramids—a veritable Giza by the Gulf—enclose a rain forest conservatory, aquarium, and discovery museum, plus 3D, 4D, and Ridefilm theaters. Add to that the adjacent hotel, spa, convention center, live theater, golf course, paddlewheel steamer, and during the summer months, beach and lazy river, and you have a multi-day resort destination! A project of the Moody Foundation, this non-profit institution's core is Hope Therapy, a rehab facility for individuals with mental or physical disabilities. Tickets for the individual attractions cost from $10-$22/adults, $8-$18/ages 4-12 and 65+. A single-day Value Pass is $50, and a two-day pass is $65 (all ages). Moody Gardens is open daily, year-round, typically from 10:00 am to 6:00 pm. 1 Hope Blvd. Visit http://www.moodygardens.com or call 800-582-4673.

Next door to Moody Gardens, and among the top 10 water parks in the U.S., **Schlitterbahn Galveston Island** offers both outdoor and indoor play. Ten rides and attractions in the park's Wasserfest area are enclosed and heated for the winter season, and operate weekends and holiday weeks from the end of September through Christmas week, then re-open in March. The outdoor schedule starts up in mid-April and runs to the end of September. One-day Winter season tickets are $28/adults, $23/ages 3-11, with lower rates after 2:00 pm and for two-day tickets. Typical winter hours are 10:00 am - 5:00 pm. 2026 Lockheed Dr., Galveston. Visit http://www.schlitterbahn.com or call 409-770-9283 .

Touring Galveston

GALVESTON MAP

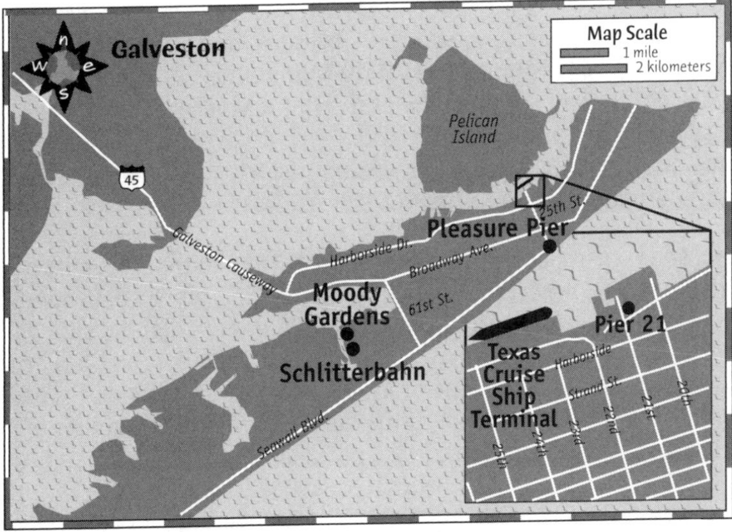

NEARBY ATTRACTIONS

The cruise terminal is a short walk from a variety of attractions, including The Strand historic district. Strand Street is one block inland from Harborside Drive, and covers about 34 square blocks, between 25th St. and 19th St. to the east, and from Harborside Blvd. on the north to Post Office Street to the south. If it's operating, the the trolley system circulates throughout the district (see previous page). The **Galveston Railroad Museum** at Right at 25th St. and Strand is a good starting point for a tour, with 40 pieces of rolling stock, model railroad layouts, and on most Saturdays, short rides on the Harborside Express. $6/$4 ages 4-12. The Galveston Visitors Center is two blocks down on Strand, by 23rd St. and the Galveston County Museum (free) is by 23rd and Market. You'll find shops and restaurants throughout the area, with Postoffice St. noted for its art galleries. Major historic buildings include the 1894 Opera House and the 1861 Custom House, both near Postoffice and 20th. Back on the waterfront, **Pier 21**, just blocks from the cruise terminal, is home to the **Texas Seaport Museum** (including the Tall Ship Elissa), restaurants, and a hotel. Museum admission is $8 adults, $5 ages 5-18. **The Pier 21 Theater** shows films about The Great Storm and pirate Jean Laffite. Each film is $6/5 ages 6-18, or see both for $10/$8. Pier 19 next-door is home to the **Ocean Star Offshore Drilling Rig and Museum**. The floating museum focuses on energy development in the Gulf. Admission is $8/$5 ages 7-18.

More Exploring in Galveston

Galveston is home to several **grand, historic homes**. All are some distance from The Strand, and some may be open for tours, depending on the day and season. Broadway is home to **Moody Mansion** by 26th St., **Ashton Villa** by 23rd (also site of the **Galveston Island Visitors Center**), and **Bishop's Palace** at 14th. All these, and many other historical sites and museums are operated by the Galveston Historical Foundation. Visit http://galvestonhistory.org or call 409-765-7834.

The latest addition to Galveston's entertainment and tourism round-up is **Historic Pleasure Pier**, which opened in May 2012. A project of Landry's, the folks behind Rainforest Cafe and Kemah Boardwalk (Landry's CEO is a Galveston native), the pier revives an old city landmark destroyed by a hurricane. 16 classic amusement rides, midway games, gifts and foods, plus a Bubba Gump Shrimp Company restaurant fill the pier, and four other Landry's restaurants are nearby. Basic pier admission ($10/48" and up, $8/under 48") does *not* include rides. Individual ride tickets are $4 and up, or get an All-Day Ride Pass for $27/$22 that includes pier admission. The amusements are only open for the summer season, but we expect the restaurant and some retail shops will be open in the off-season without a ticket. 2501 Seawall Blvd., Galveston. Visit http://www.pleasurepier.com or call 855.789.7437.

With the Disney Magic sailing from Galveston during the cooler months, **beaches** may not be high on your list. Lifeguards are on duty from Memorial Day to Labor Day, and some beachfront parks close altogether. The Galveston Island Park Board of Trustees operates most Gulf beaches and parks. Visit http://galvestonparkboard.org. • The board also runs **Dellanera RV Park**, offering both day parking and overnight hookups, right on the beachfront, year-round 888-425-4753. • Out west beyond the resorts and historic districts, along the Farm to Market Highway (FM 3005), lies over 20 miles of sandy Gulf beachfront, salt marshes, and bayous, interspersed with residential development. Most of these homes stand on stilts to survive storm waters. This area is a prime refuge for shore and migratory birds. **Galveston Island State Park**, about 8 miles west of town, offers trails, boardwalks and beachfront birding opportunities on the Gulf and Galveston Bay ($5 admission ages 12+, open year-round). • Closer at hand, **Big Reef Nature Park**, on the east end of the island, is another prime birding site, though it's closed from mid-October through February.

For more information on Galveston see our information starting on page 94 of this guide, and visit http://www.galveston.com.

Key West
(Western Caribbean Itinerary)

Casually hanging out at the tip of the fabled Florida Keys, Key West is the southernmost point in the continental U.S., famous for Ernest Hemingway and Jimmy Buffett (and their favorite hangouts), charming homes, sunsets, sport fishing, historic spots, and a way-laid-back lifestyle. You won't be in town long enough to waste away, but you sure can try.

© MediaMarx, Inc.

Key West's Mallory Square at sunset

AMBIENCE

As Florida's southernmost landfall, Americans feel more secure wandering Key West than other ports. The charm of its century-old buildings and the small-town air put you right at ease. Most attractions are a short stroll from the pier, and streets head off in (mostly) straight lines. To visit the sights, just start walking!

HISTORY & CULTURE

Spaniards called this flat, sun-drenched outpost "Cayo Hueso" (Island of Bones). The English (some buccaneers among 'em) were soon mispronouncing it "Key West." The U.S. Navy banished the pirates and has been stationed here ever since. Nearby, treacherous reefs sank countless vessels in the New Orleans trade, making salvage crews fabulously rich. A lighthouse turned that boom into a bust, and the town has been reborn again and again as a capital for spongers, cigar rollers, a President, treasure seekers, wealthy vacationers, artists and writers (James Audubon, Tennessee Williams, Robert Frost, Ernest Hemingway, and Thornton Wilder), and generations of dropouts from the rat race. Islanders declared the Conch Republic in 1982 to protest a federal roadblock that choked access to the Florida Keys. They soon had enough media attention to restore free passage, and though this is the U.S.A., the Conch Republic's flag still flies high.

FACTS

Size: 4 mi. (6.5 km.) wide x 2 mi. (3 km.) long	
Climate: Subtropical	**Temperatures:** 72°F (22°C) to 82°F (28°C)
Population: 24,832	**Busy Season:** Mid-February to April
Language: English	**Money:** U.S. Dollar
Time Zone: Eastern (DST observed)	**Transportation:** Walking, scooters
Phones: Dial 1- from U.S., dial 911 for emergencies	

Introduction
Reservations
Staterooms
Dining
Activities
Ports of Call
Magic
Index

Getting Around Key West

GETTING THERE

Your ship docks around noon right at the **Hilton Marina** (Pier B), which is an easy five-minute walk to Mallory Square and Front Street. Tendering is not necessary, unless the ship is unable to dock (rare). All Ashore time varies between 7:30 am and Noon (check your *Personal Navigator* for going ashore details). The marina is on the northwest corner of the island, looking out to the Gulf of Mexico. For those exploring on foot, most of the major destinations are within easy reach of the marina. Check your *Personal Navigator* for the all-aboard time, usually 3:30 pm to 7:30 pm.

GETTING AROUND

This is one of the **easiest ports to navigate**, thanks to its small size and pedestrian-friendly streets. Most visitors here just **walk**, and even many of the residents don't bother with cars. Almost all of Key West's streets near the docks run on a grid, making it easy to get around with a map. If you'd rather not walk, try one of Key West's famous **tram tours**. The Conch Tour Train (described on page 287) is $32/adults, kids 12 and under free—board the tram near Mallory Square. If you'd rather get off and look around, the Old Town Trolley makes 12 stops (see page 287) for $32/adults, kids 12 and under ride free—board near the dock. Both tours offer discounted tickets online • The Key West **bus system** is less expensive than the trams at just $2/adults and $1/kids and seniors (kids under 6 are free). There are always two buses running—one goes clockwise around the island, the other goes counterclockwise. Call 305-809-3910 for bus info. • **Taxis** are also available—the meter starts at $2.75 and adds 60 cents per one-fifth mile. You can get taxis near the dock—if you need to call for one, try Five 6's Taxi (305-296-6666). • Need your own transportation? Try a **scooter** rental. Adventure Rentals (Cruise Ship Pier B, 305-293-8883, http://keywest-scooter.com) rents scooters for about $50/day for single riders, $70 for a two-seater.

STAYING SAFE

The "key" to **staying safe** in Key West is simple common sense. The biggest potential dangers here are overexposure to sun (bring that sunscreen and hat) and overindulgence at a local bar. Key West is very laid-back—we didn't encounter any street hawkers on our visit and we felt secure walking around. If you rent a scooter, be sure to wear your helmet. If you swim, note the color-coded flags that indicate conditions at the beach: blue = safe, yellow = marginal, red = dangerous and prohibited, and purple = hazardous marine life. If you walk, wear comfortable, well-broken-in walking shoes. And bring a watch so you don't lose track of time and miss the boat!

Touring Key West

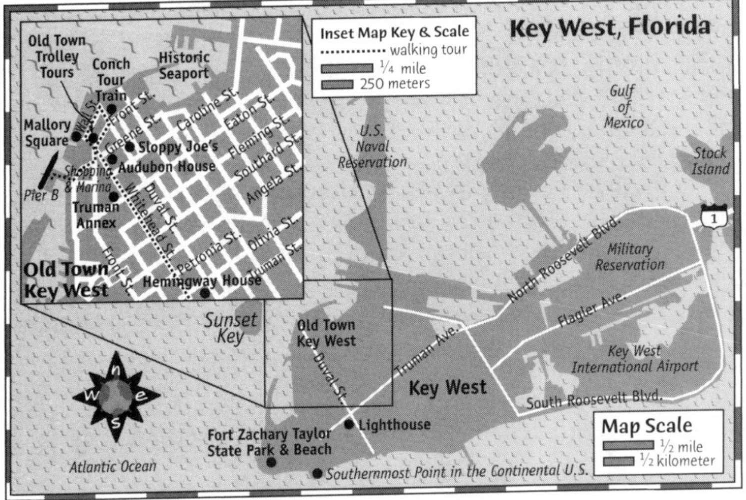

Key West is one of the best ports for a **casual walking tour**. Take along our map or pick one up at the Chamber of Commerce at 510 Greene Street, about five blocks inland from the pier. We've marked a walking tour on the map above. From the pier, you first reach the Truman Annex waterfront shopping area. Near Front and Greene Streets is the brick 1891 Custom House and its Museum of Art and History. Turn left onto Front Street, passing the U.S. Customs House (and Post Office) and the Naval Coal Depot building. At the corner of Front and Whitehead is the Key West Art Center, showcasing local artists. Nearby are the Key West Shipwreck Museum ($16/adult, $7/kids 4–12) with its 60-foot lookout tower, and the Key West Aquarium ($16/adult, $7/kids 4–12), Key West's oldest tourist attraction (save on a Shipwreck Museum/Aquarium combo ticket). Turning onto Wall St. you'll find famous Mallory Square (see next page for sunset viewing tips). Continue along Wall St., rejoining Front St., where you can board the Conch Tour Train (see previous page), or stroll another block along Front to the Historic Seaport boardwalk. Follow Front St. back toward the ship, crossing Duval St. then turn onto Whitehead for its charm and many museums. Stop where you will, but if you're in a walking mood, follow Whitehead nine blocks to the Lighthouse and Hemingway House. When you've had enough, retrace your steps toward the waterfront to explore Duval and nearby side streets, or re-board the ship. For a more directed tour, try the "Presidents, Pirates & Pioneers" shore excursion (see page 288).

Playing in Key West

ACTIVITIES

Sloppy Joe's isn't the original Hemingway hangout; that's Captain Tony's, which used to be Sloppy Joe's. Captain Tony's gave Jimmy Buffett his first place to waste away, but now Jimmy can afford his own Margaritaville. Got all that? Regardless of your choice, these and many other atmospheric bars are a short crawl from the ship.

One of the joys of Key West is its **architecture**. Walk along Whitehead Street and turn down a few of the side streets. The old, clapboard homes, trimmed with Victorian gingerbread and surrounded by flowering foliage and white picket fences, are a delight. Household eaves are painted sky blue to ward off bugs, demons, or some such.

This isn't really a **beach zone**. The rocky bottom isn't bare-feet-friendly. Fort Zachary Taylor State Park offers an attractive, nearby place to sun (enter via the Truman Annex gate on Thomas St.), but be careful of the sharp shells (wear sandals).

Your day in port is too short for an all-day **fishing or diving trip**, but a half-day may work. Plan in advance. Visit the Florida Keys & Key West Visitors Bureau at http://www.fla-keys.com or call 800-FLA-KEYS for information and lists of charter operators.

Want some authentic **Caribbean junk food**? Try hot, greasy, conch fritters for a fair price at the stand by the Aquarium entrance. For seafood and Key Lime Pie, just follow your nose.

The daily **Mallory Square sunset ritual** gathers thousands of revelers to watch the legendary sunset. We surveyed the superb scene from deck 10. Go to http://floridakeyswebcams.tv for web cam previews. Sunset time is printed on the front of your *Personal Navigator*, or visit http://www.earthtools.org.

Key West has too many **museums** for a brief cruise ship visit. Choose just one or two. Whitehead St. is the equivalent of Museum Mile, with nearly every attraction listed here either on the street or a block away. For glimpses inside beautiful historic homes, visit Audubon House, Harry S. Truman Little White House, Hemingway House, and/or Oldest House. All charge admission.

Key West and **t-shirts** seem to go together. Nearly every bar sells its own, Hog's Breath Saloon, Sloppy Joe's, and Margaritaville among 'em. Try the Conch Republic Store for local color. Brand luxuries can be had at U.S. prices, but you'll also find items by local designers.

Embarking on Shore Excursions in Key West

Sail, Kayak, & Snorkel [K01] — Rating: n/a

This is the "smorgasboard" of shore excursions, offering three different adventures in one. You'll start with a sail in a two-masted schooner to mangrove islands. At the islands, you'll hop into kayaks and paddle about the backcountry mangrove creeks for an hour. When you're done, it's time to don snorkeling equipment (provided) and explore underwater for 45-60 minutes. Top it all off with a refreshing snack of fruit, chips, salsa, and beverages back at the pier. Meeting time is typically 12:15 pm. Bring an extra pair of dry shorts for the return trip. Unfortunately, we received no reviews for this excursion, nor could we find anyone who'd experienced it. Most cruisers preferred the Back to Nature Kayak Tour or the Key West Catamaran Sail & Snorkel Tour, described later. (On Your Own: JavaCat Charters at http://www.keywestkayak.com, 305-294-7245)

Sports
Very active
For more experienced snorkelers
Ages 10 & up
$79/person
5-5.5 hours

Key West Butterfly and Nature Conservatory & Aquarium — Rating: 6

Take a trip through a state-of-the-art nature conservatory to observe some of the most exotic creatures the tropics have to offer. See butterflies, birds, and exotic fish. The Key West Aquarium is the next stop and admission is included in the price. Find out what makes up the ecosystem of the Islands of Key West, watch stingrays feed, and if you're lucky, pet a shark! Cruisers think this is a "neat experience" with "butterflies landing on you," and it is "great for families with young kids." Typical meeting time is 12:30 pm.

Tour
Leisurely
All ages
$43/$28 (3-9)
About 3 hours

Key Lime Island Bike Tour — Rating: n/a

Why take a walking tour, when you can cruise around Key West on a bike? After a 10-minute walk from the pier you'll be fitted for your bike and (mandatory) helmet. From there, you'll pedal about Key West for about 2 hours to see the sights, passing some attractions, pausing for photo stops at others, from one end of the island to the other. At the end, you'll stop at Kermit's Key Lime Pie Shoppe for a complimentary tasting. Must be at least 60" tall. (On Your Own: Get a map, rent a bike! Eaton Bike Rentals http://www.eatonbikes.com 305-294-8188)

Tour
Active
Ages 10 & up
$39
3-3.5 hours

White Knuckle Thrill Boat [K17] — Rating: 7

Have the need for speed? Yes? This excursion is for you. A short 20-minute bus ride lands you at the dock. Board a jet boat with 11 other people and hang on for the next half-hour. Sudden stops, sharp power slides, and complete 360° turns are sure to get your heart pumping! Listen as the tour guide gives lessons on the Island of Key West. Typical meeting time is 12:15 and 1:30 pm. Plan to spend two hours.

Sports
Active
Ages 5 & up
$72/$59 (5-9)
2 hours

Champagne Sunset Cruise (schedule permitting) — Rating: n/a

Sail the 65-foot Fury Catamaran for a sunset to remember! Your boat departs right from the cruise pier for a two-hour tour. Champagne, beer, wine, soft drinks and snacks are included. Tour departure depends on local sunset time. Space limited so reserve early. (On Your Own: Watch the sunset from deck 10 or nearby Mallory Square (photos on page 281), or Fury Water Adventures at http://www.furycat.com or 897-994-8898)

Tour
Leisurely
All Ages
$45/$25 (0-9)
2-2.5 hours

See page 218 for a key to the shore excursion description charts and their icons.

Embarking on Shore Excursions in Key West *(continued)*

Back to Nature Kayak Tour [K03] Rating: 8

Sports
Very active
For beginners and all levels
Ages 10 & up
$59
3.5 hours

Looking for wildlife beyond Duval Street? Take a boat to the Key West Wildlife Preserve and paddle around in two-person, stable kayaks. Your tour guide leads you through the protected salt ponds and points out the many species of birds and marine life in their natural habitat. Typical meeting times are 12:45 pm and 1:50 pm. Bring an extra pair of dry shorts for the return trip—cameras and binoculars are a good idea, too. Water and soft drinks are provided. Cruiser comments are positive: You start with a 20-minute boat ride ("board at the pier") to a mangrove wash called "Archer Key." From here you board yet another boat to "receive a short lesson on using the two-person kayaks." You then kayak "beside the mangroves" and down "some passages." The "interesting guide" points out the "local birds and sea life," plus "natural history." The kayaking "is not difficult," except for those cruisers who experienced "stiff winds."

Key West Catamaran Sail & Snorkel Tour [K05] Rating: 6

Sports
Active
For all levels
Ages 5 & up
$49/adult
$28/5-9
3.5 hours

Set sail on a comfortable 65-foot catamaran with large sundecks, shady lounge deck, restrooms, and a fresh-water shower. The catamaran takes you about 6.5 miles (10 km.) south of the harbor to the only living coral reef in the continental U.S. Snorkeling equipment is provided for you to explore the reefs. Bring an underwater camera. Sodas and water are served, as are complimentary beer and white wine after snorkeling. Typical meeting time is 12:30 pm. Cruiser reviews are mixed: The "great crew" motors the "super clean" sailboat out of the harbor, though a few cruisers report "no sailing, just motoring." The snorkeling location "feels like the middle of the ocean" with depths of "20 feet or so." Some cruisers report that "snorkeling is great" with "plenty of coral and fish," while others note that "surge can be strong" and "kids may be afraid to snorkel" in the "bobbing water." Overall, most "enjoyed it" but "probably wouldn't do it again." (On Your Own: Fury Catamarans at http://www.furycat.com, 305-294-8899 or 800-994-8898)

See page 218 for a key to the shore excursion description charts and their icons.

A famous Key West sunset as seen from deck 10 of the Disney Magic

Embarking on Shore Excursions in Key West *(continued)*

Conch Republic Tour & Museum Package [K08] Rating: 4

Tour
Leisurely
All ages
$56/adult
$29/ age 3-9
2-2.5 hours

Yes, you can do this all on your own, but if you'd prefer a more directed tour at a slightly steeper price, this is for you. First take an hour-long tour aboard the Conch Tour Train or the Old Town Trolley (see below). After the tour, you'll disembark at Mallory Square to visit the Aquarium and Shipwreck Museum on your own. Wear comfortable walking shoes and bring a camera. Typical meeting time is 12:40 pm. Cruiser reviews were uniform: The "city tour" is "great," conveying a "lot of info" in a "short amount of time" (good enough that some say it "made them want to visit Key West in the future"). The downfall seemed to be the Shipwreck Historeum, for which you "have to wait outside for the group before entering" and "then listen to a guide" before you are "free to explore on your own." The Aquarium is "ok" but many have "seen better at home." In general, this excursion has "too much waiting around." (On Your Own: See page 283.)

Old Town Trolley or Conch Train Tour [K09] Rating: 6

Tour
All ages
$32/adult
$16/age 3-9
1-1.5 hours

A great way to get an overview of Key West and learn something on the way. The one-hour tour (either the trolley or the train) passes 100 points of interest and your tour guide offers historical and cultural commentary. We've done the Conch Train Tour and recommend it to first-time visitors as a friendly overview of Key West. Bring a camera. Young kids may get bored. Typical meeting time is 1:00 pm. Cruiser reviews are mostly positive: The "informative" tour is a "lot of fun." A complete circuit of the tour route "takes about an hour," which is "good for kids who can sit still long enough." The "friendly tour guide" "driver" provides "plenty of information about the history and architecture" of "Key West." The downfall to booking this excursion through Disney is that "you cannot get on and off it" like you can when you book it yourself (which is useful when you want to use it as transportation as well as a tour). (On Your Own: There's not much reason to book this one with Disney—see page 266 for more information.)

Glass Bottom Boat Tour on the Pride of Key West [K10] Rating: 1

Tour
Leisurely
All ages
$42/age 10+
$25/age 0-9
2.5 hours

If you'd like to see the underwater world of Key West but don't want to get wet, this catamaran is your ticket. The catamaran boasts an air-conditioned viewing area and an upper-level sun deck. Your guide delivers a narrated eco-tour as you visit the continental U.S.'s only living coral reef about 6.5 miles (10 km.) south of Key West. Typical meeting time is 1:15 pm. Cruiser reviews were mostly negative: The boat's "bottom viewing window" is "way too small for everyone to use." And while the viewing area is air-conditioned, the sun deck is "miserably hot" with "no shade." The only refreshments were "sodas for a buck a pop." Some cruisers also report that they did not visit the reef because "the tide was too strong." Overall, most cruisers "were not impressed." (On Your Own: Fury Water Adventures at http://www.furycat.com, 877-994-8998)

See page 218 for a key to the shore excursion description charts and their icons.

Embarking on Shore Excursions in Key West *(continued)*

President Truman's Key West [K23] — Rating: n/a

Tour
Active
All ages
$46/adult
$25/age 3-9
2-2.5 hours

President Truman loved Key West, and you can see where he spent his time while he was here. Your tour starts with a 5-minute walk to the Little White House, where Truman loved to come for relaxation. You'll get a guided tour of this historical building and learn how it continues to play a role in recent political affairs. After your visit, you'll take another 5-minute walk to the Conch Train or Trolley Tour, on which you'll see the Audubon House (Ernest Hemingway's house) and more than 100 other points of interest. This excursion is wheelchair and stroller accessible, but both must be collapsible. You can expect to walk about a half of a mile on this tour. Typical meeting time is 1:00 pm. (On Your Own: You could do this one easily on your own by walking to the Little White House [admission tickets are $16/$5], then walking over to the train/trolley [ride tickets are $32/$16].)

Presidents, Pirates, & Pioneers [K18] — Rating: n/a

Tour
Active
All ages
$38/adult
$23/age 3-9
2 hours

This two-hour walking tour meanders through Old Town, passing Truman's Little White House and the birthplace of Pan Am. Along the way you'll hear history of this remarkable place. The tour concludes in Mallory Square, where you are treated to complimentary conch fritters and bottled water. Afterward, admission to the Shipwreck Historeum is included so you can explore Key West's rich history in wrecking. Wear comfy walking shoes and bring your camera. Typical meeting time is 12:45 pm. (On Your Own: See page 283)

Snuba Key West [K20] — Rating: n/a

Sports
Very active
Ages 10 & up
$109
2.5-3 hours

Snuba is a cross between snorkeling and scuba, and it allows you to go deeper in the water without having to wear a heavy air tank on your back (nor do you have to be a certified scuba diver). This excursion begins with a 15-minute van ride to Garrison Bight Marina, where you'll board a 33-foot catamaran called Miss Sunshine and take a 30-minute cruise to the best snuba spot of the day. After you receive an orientation and your gear, you'll dive off the back of the boat to explore the coral formations and see the marine life (expect about 25 minutes underwater). You'll have a complimentary beverage (water or soda) back onboard before returning to shore. Experience is not required, but you must be comfortable swimming in open water. Typical meeting time is 12:45 pm.

Snorkel, Kayak, and Dolphin-Watching Adventure [K20] — Rating: n/a

Sports
Very active
Ages 5 & up
$95/adult
$85/age 5-9
3.5-4 hours

This jam-packed excursion takes place at the Key West Wildlife Refuge, a 20-minute boat ride from the port. At the refuge, you'll begin by boarding two-person kayaks and paddling through the tropical mangroves, led by your tour guide. Then you'll have an opportunity to snorkel and see fish cavorting about a shipwreck. Then it's back onboard the boat to cruise to the "Dolphin Playground," where about 100 local dolphins live. Keep your eyes peeled and your cameras ready for glimpses of the dolphins jumping and playing nearby. Includes use of life jackets, snorkel gear, kayaks, and a complimentary beverage. Guests must be comfortable swimming in open water. Typical meeting time is 12:45 pm.

See page 218 for a key to the shore excursion description charts and their icons.

Grand Cayman
(Western Caribbean Itinerary)

In these days of corporate scandals, the Cayman Islands have come to symbolize shady dealings hidden by offshore banks. Cruise visitors find a different pleasure waiting offshore; some of the most spectacular coral reefs in the Caribbean. Whether you snorkel, scuba, tour by submarine, or swim with the fishes at Stingray City, Grand Cayman is the perfect island for **watery recreation**.

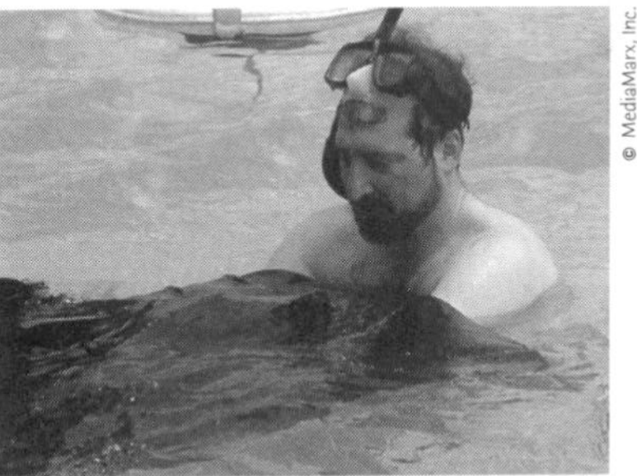

Dave plays with stingrays in Grand Cayman

AMBIENCE

Of all Disney's ports of call, Grand Cayman seems the **quaintest**. Visitors arrive at a small pier, adjoining a relatively modest shopping street. We find scattered, freestanding buildings and several outdoor malls. The real action is taking place offshore, where fleets of excursion boats help visitors enjoy the island's sea life and fabled coral reefs. Alas, Grand Cayman was hit hard by Hurricane Ivan in September 2004, but the island has long been restored—in fact, new buildings and shopping centers have reinvigorated its appearance.

HISTORY & CULTURE

A wayward breeze pushed the Cayman Islands onto the map in 1503, when Columbus stumbled upon these essentially flat outposts. He named them "**Tortugas**," for the plentiful local sea turtles, but soon the islands were renamed the Caimanas, after some other local reptilians (either crocodiles or Blue Iguanas, depending on who you ask). For centuries nobody bothered to settle here, but many ships visited to gather fresh turtle meat for their crews. Famed pirates visited frequently, but eventually the islands were ruled from British Jamaica. Still, with the exception of some mahogany-logging operations, there was little development here until well into the 20th century, and its famous banking industry didn't arrive until the 1950s. When Jamaica voted for independence from Great Britain in 1962, the Cayman Islanders chose to remain a British Crown Colony.

FACTS

Size: 22 mi. (35 km.) long x 8 mi. (13 km.) wide	
Climate: Subtropical	**Temperatures**: 78°F (25°C) to 84°F (29°C)
Population: 37,000	**Busy Season**: Mid-February to April
Language: English	**Money**: Cayman Islands Dollar (= $1.25 US)
Time Zone: Eastern (no DST)	**Transportation**: Walking, taxis, cars
Phones: Dial 1- from U.S., dial 911 for police, or dial 555 for an ambulance	

Making the Most of Grand Cayman

GETTING THERE

Currently, this is the only regular Disney Cruise Line destination that regularly **requires tendering** (a long-delayed, new cruise ship pier will make tenders obsolete). The ship anchors a short distance offshore of George Town, Grand Cayman—capital of the Cayman Islands. Tenders ferry guests to the pier in a matter of minutes, and run continuously throughout the day. Tenders returning to the ship depart from the South Terminal pier. A notice in your stateroom outlines tendering procedures. A taxi stand is just a few steps from the dock, and the island's duty-free shopping district is tightly clustered within several blocks of the pier. The nearest beach is Seven Mile Beach, a short drive north of George Town. The first tender ashore is typically 11:30 am, with the last tender around 4:45 pm.

GETTING AROUND

Grand Cayman is **shaped like a sperm whale**, with its capital of George Town where a whale's "fluke" would be (see map on next page). It's easy to get around on foot in town. • Grand Cayman hardly overflows with sights to see, so while car rentals are available, we don't suggest them. Shore excursions can take you to nearly every sight, and taxis are fine for those who want to tour on their own. Taxis use a rate chart that is posted at the taxi stand by the cruise pier. Most car rental agencies are at the airport. Reserve in advance and arrange to have the car waiting at the pier for you. • Due north of George Town are Seven Mile Beach and the settlement of West Bay, home to the Cayman Turtle Farm and a tourist trap named Hell. Just to the east, kettle-shaped North Sound takes a big bite out of the north shore. A long coral reef guards the entrance to this bay, and just south of the reef, miles from shore, is "Stingray City," where excursion boats gather and guests cavort with the gentle stingrays (see photo on previous page). • The resort-and-beach destination of Rum Point is at the easternmost extreme of North Sound. • A single road follows the perimeter of the island (except for a huge gap between West Bay and Rum Point) connecting the island's many scuba dive destinations. • One of the most famous dive sites is Wreck of the Ten Sails, just beyond the village of East End.

SAFETY

For water-based excursions, **leave your valuables** (and change into your swimwear) on the ship. Lockers aren't easy to come by on the island. Wear cover-ups, as local customs are sedately British, and carry lots of sunscreen. As always, know your prices before you shop, and agree to taxi fares in advance (fares are posted at the pier's taxi stand).

Touring Grand Cayman

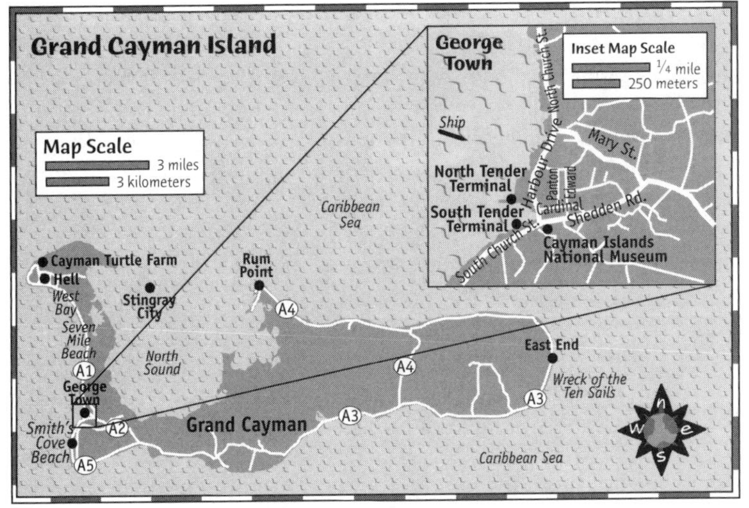

There are **many shops** but few sights to see in George Town. After several hours of walking and shopping you'll be ready to head back to the ship. Your tender arrives at South Terminal pier, a few steps from a tourist information center, the taxi stand, and tour bus loading area. North Terminal pier is just across the tiny harbor. A single road, known alternately as North Church St., Harbour Drive, and South Church St., lines the waterfront. As you face inland, North Church will be to your left, and South Church to your right. Cardinal Ave., opposite North Terminal, heads directly inland from the waterfront into the heart of the shopping district. Shops and malls line Cardinal and wrap around onto Panton St. and Edward St. You'll find the Post Office at the corner of Cardinal and Edward. The shops of Anchorage Centre can be reached from Cardinal or Harbour Drive, directly across from the docks. The worthy Cayman Islands National Museum ($5 U.S./adults, $3/children) is across from the terminal, at the corner of South Church and Shedden Rd. Follow Harbour Drive a block northward to reach Blackbeard's Rum Cake shop, and two blocks beyond, Cayman Auto Rentals and the Nautilus undersea tours. Follow South Church southward to reach Atlantis Submarines and a cluster of shops and restaurants including the local Hard Rock Cafe, Blue Mountain Cyber Cafe, and the Tortuga Rum Cake Bakery. A long walk or short cab ride along South Church brings you to small Smith's Cove Public Beach, the closest sunning spot to the pier.

GRAND CAYMAN ISLAND MAP

WALKING TOUR

Playing in Grand Cayman

ACTIVITIES

The **shopping** is passable in this duty-free port, offering the usual selection of jewelry, luxury goods, and island wares. Serious shoppers report less-than-wonderful experiences, but if you know your prices and can cut a bargain, you may do fine. The principal "native" item is rum cake (yo ho, yo ho). Many visitors stock up on small sampler packages, perfect for gift-giving. Turtle and coral-based items cannot be brought into the U.S., so don't buy them!

Certified scuba divers may be tempted to bring their own gear on the cruise and make their own dive arrangements. The Cayman Islands Department of Tourism at http://www.divecayman.ky has a useful online guide. Several shore excursions also exist for divers who don't want hassles. Snorkeling excursions are a good choice for those lacking scuba credentials.

While several **beaches** can be found around the perimeter of the island, we suggest you take an excursion to either Seven Mile Beach or Rum Point. Seven Mile Beach starts a short cab drive north of the port, with most of its length dominated by resorts and condos. A public beach with restrooms is found toward the beach's north end. Small Smith's Cove Beach at the south end of George Town also has restrooms, and is a long walk or short cab ride from the pier.

Unless the island's legendary coral reefs draw you elsewhere, you may want to consider an excursion that includes **Stingray City**, a submerged sand bar out in the middle of a huge bay. Guests climb from the boat right into the waist-high water for an encounter with friendly stingrays. We were instructed to "Stingray Shuffle" (shuffle your feet in the sand—the rays only sting if you step on them), and members of the crew introduced us to their aquatic protégé. While the rays are wild creatures, they've become willing partners in this enterprise—anything for a free handout (think pigeons in the park). On the ride to the sandbar, one of our crew members spent his time cutting bait (frozen squid). The rays will swim right up to (or even into) a wader's arms for a snack, and the boat's crew showed us how to snuggle up with the rays (see photo on page 289). Silky-soft rays swim among the guests, brushing past legs, sucking bait out of loosely closed hands, and tolerating all sorts of petting zoo behavior. While the squeamish need some time to get used to the activity, eventually everyone becomes captivated by this up-close and personal encounter with these very gentle, odd creatures.

Embarking on Shore Excursions on Grand Cayman

Grand Cayman's shore excursions offer jaunts to less-than-sterling tourist sights and several attractive water-based activities.

☐ Grand Cayman Golf [G29] — Rating: n/a

Sports
Active
Ages 10 & up
$189
5-5.5 hours

Enjoy an 18-hole round of golf at Grand Cayman's best golf course, North Sound Club. Your adventure begins with a 10-minute drive to the course, where you'll discover a 6605-yard, par-71 course with gorgeous views and an abundance of wildlife. The course has well-groomed fairways, large greens, white sand bunkers, and plenty of little ponds and lakes, all overlooking the Caribbean Sea. Greens fees and a shared cart are included, but the Nike club rental is an extra $50. You must wear appropriate golf attire. The return trip to the port is included. (On Your Own: http://www.northsoundclub.com or 345-947-GOLF).

☐ Two-Tank Dive Tour [G03] — Rating: 9

Sports
Very active
Ages 12 & up
$135
4 hours

Certified scuba divers can take this two-tank dive. The first dive will be along the Cayman Wall, followed by a shallow dive of 50 ft. (15 m.) or less. All equipment is provided, though wet suits (if desired) are extra. This excursion is very popular (Grand Cayman is an excellent diving spot) and has been known to fill up more than 30 days in advance. If you find this excursion is full, here are some other scuba operators used by Disney cruisers: Bob Soto's Reef Divers at 800-262-7686 (from the U.S.) or 345-949-2022 • Abanks Scuba Diving Diving Center, http://caymanislandsdiscounts.com/AbanksDiveCenter.htm, 345-946-6444 • Don Foster's Dive Cayman at http://www.donfosters.com, 800-833-4837 (from the U.S.) or 345-949-5679. Note that Red Sail Sports (http://www.redsailcayman.com) is the exclusive dive operator for Disney Cruise Line, but they prefer you do not book directly with them.

☐ Nautilus Undersea Tour and Reef Snorkel [G07] — Rating: 8

Beach
Leisurely
Ages 5 & up
$52/$43 (5-9)
2 hours

Board a semi-submarine for a peek at shipwrecks and the Cheese Burger Reef, then spend some time snorkeling from the boat (equipment included). Cruiser reviews are positive: This excursion is "great if you have both snorkelers and non-snorkelers in your group." The "tour is short" and "you stay close to the shore." Snorkeling is "great" and "views are phenomenal," with "fish," "plants," and a "wreck." (On Your Own: http://www.nautilus.ky or 345-945-1355)

☐ Sea Trek Helmet Dive - Grand Cayman [G24] — Rating: 9

Sports
Active
Ages 10 & up
$89

Using a specially designed diving oxygen helmet, you'll be up close and personal with tropical fish. But don't worry—you'll receive full instructions before donning your helmet. Once outfitted and instructed, you are submerged into the water for a 30-minute guided underwater tour. No swimming skills are needed. The helmet even keeps your hair dry! Typical meeting times are 8:30 am and 1:15 pm. (On Your Own: http://www.seatrekcayman.com or 345-949-0008)

☐ Seven Mile Beach Break/Family Beach Day at Tiki Beach — Rating: 7

Beach
Leisurely
All ages
$36/$26 (3-9)

Both excursions take you to Seven Mile Beach for loads of relaxation in the warm Caribbean sun. Stretch out on a beach chair and sip on a complimentary island beverage. If you are so inclined, go for a swim in the waters just a few feet from your chair. Food and recreational rentals extra. Allow 3-4 hours.

See page 218 for a key to the shore excursion description charts and their icons.

Embarking on Shore Excursions on Grand Cayman *(continued)*

Stingray City Snorkel Tour/Deluxe Stingray City Sandbar Snorkel — Rating: 9

Sports
Active
Ages 5 & up
$45-$49
2.5 - 3.5 hours

These two excursions are much the same, varying mostly by length and watercraft (why one is "deluxe" is beyond us). Stingray City Snorkel Tour ($49/$38 ages 5-9, ages 5 and up, 3.5 hours) is the "classic," with a 45-minute cruise to reach the stingrays. Deluxe Stingray City Sandbar Snorkel ($45/$35, ages 5-9, ages 5 and up, 2.5 hours) features a 25-minute cruise in a specially-built boat. Both feature snorkeling with stingrays in 3 to 6 feet of water (tide dependant) along a natural sandbar (see photo on page 289). All gear is supplied and water is served. If you want to see stingrays, these are the excursions we recommend. Cruiser reviews are very positive: The cruise to Stingray City is "fun," with "great scenery." The stingrays are "amazing," but be aware that "some kids may be afraid at first" and the "water may be over their heads" if it's "high tide." Overall, this "unique" excursion is one "the whole family can participate in." (On Your Own: Captain Marvin's—see page 296)

Seaworld Explorer Semi-Submarine [G10] — Rating: 9

Tour
Leisurely
All ages
$43/$31 (0-9)
1.5-2 hours

Take a ride on this semi-submarine to discover shipwrecks and sea life. A marine expert is on board to provide narration and answer your questions. Note that this excursion is very similar to the Nautilus Undersea Tour (see below). Cruiser reviews are very positive: This "short" excursion takes you down "five feet below the water" to view "Cheese Burger Reef" and two "shipwrecks," with "coral reefs" and "many fish." The "viewing windows" are "generous" and "clear." Overall, a "fun time for the whole family!" Typical meeting times are 8:30 am and 10:30 am. (On Your Own: Atlantis Adventures at http://www.caymanislandssubmarines.com or 800-887-8571, but note that it may not be possible to book this on your own anymore.)

Atlantis Submarine Expedition [G11] — Rating: 6

Tour
Leisurely
Ages 4 & up
$99/$57 (4-9)
2.5 hours

This submarine dives down to 90 feet (27 m.). Guests must be at least 36 in./91 cm. tall). Typical meeting times are 9:15 am and 1:15 pm. Cruiser reviews are mixed, though more positive than similar excursions elsewhere, thanks to the better views and visible sea life. (On Your Own: https://www.caymanislandssubmarines.com or 800-887-8571)

Nautilus Undersea Tour [G12] — Rating: 8

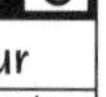

Tour
Leisurely
All ages
$43/$31 (0-9)
2 hours

Cruise on a semi-submarine with a marine expert. The Nautilus glides like a boat and never entirely submerges. This excursion is very similar to the Seaworld Explorer described earlier, except that your craft does not go down as deep (which one you choose to do may depend on your comfort level). Typical meeting time is 9:15 am. Cruiser comments are positive: The "view is phenomenal" and cruisers loved seeing "actual wrecks," "sea creatures," and "water plants." The "friendly" crew identified the wrecks and sealife. The "comfortable" boat was "a lot of fun." (On Your Own: http://www.nautilus.ky or 345-945-1355)

Rum Point Beach Adventure [G13] — Rating: 6

Beach
Leisurely
All ages
$59/$49 (0-9)
5 hours

Enjoy a relaxing half-day at a secluded beach. Includes lunch and a soft drink. Watersport rentals available for extra fee. Cruiser reviews are mixed: Take a "long journey" (first a bus then a 45-min. ferry) to reach the "nice" but "small" beach. Cruisers suggest you "try to secure beach chairs as soon as you arrive." Lunch is "good" with a "variety of food." Overall, some cruisers enjoyed "being able to relax" while others felt "herded like cattle." Typical meeting time is 8:20 am.

Embarking on Shore Excursions on Grand Cayman *(continued)*

Rum Point Beach Adventure & Stingray City Tour [G14] Rating: 7

Add a visit with the stingrays to the previous excursion for $33-$36 more. After playing at the beach, you'll board a glass bottom boat and cruise out to Stingray City to snorkel. Cruiser reviews were mixed but very similar to those for Rum Point Beach Adventure and Stingray City tours on the previous page—basically the big winner is the stingrays. Typical meeting time is 8:20 am.

Sports
Active
Ages 5 & up
$95/$82 (5-9)
5 hours

Shipwreck & Reef Snorkeling/Catamaran, Reef & Kittiwake Rating: 9

These excursions each visit a shipwreck and a reef. Shipwreck and Reef Snorkeling ($39/$31 ages 5-9, ages 5 & up, 2.5 hrs.) visits the wreck of the schooner "Cali." Catamaran, Reef and Kittiwake Snorkel Sail ($72/$55 ages 5-9, 3.5 hrs.) uses a catamaran and visits the USS Kittiwake, sunk in 2010 to make an artificial reef. Both include snorkel gear, water and lemonade. Cruiser reviews are very positive: This "great" excursion is "good for beginners." Some cruisers report snorkeling "within sight of the Disney ship," where they explored the "way cool" "shipwreck" which rests in about "15 to 20 feet of water." Then move about a "quarter mile" down to snorkel among "protected reefs" and see "awesome" sea "critters." Overall, cruisers "loved" this "fun excursion."

Sports
Active
Ages 5 & up
$39-$72 adult
$31-$55 (5-9)
2.5-3.5 hours

Island Tour & Snorkeling With Stingrays [G19] Rating: 7

Take in the island's sights by bus—you'll stop and visit the Cayman Turtle Farm and Hell (a prehistoric rock formation). Then head out to sea on a 45-minute boat ride to meet the stingrays at the Stingray City sandbar. Equipment and instruction is provided so you can swim with the stingrays in 3-6 feet deep water. Only stingrays—and no fish—will be seen. See the cruiser reviews on the island tour portion below.

© MediaMarx, Inc.

Turtles at the Cayman Turtle Farm

Tour
Leisurely
Ages 5 & up
$72/adults
$56/ages 5-9
4.5 hours

Grand Cayman Island Tour [G17] Rating: 7

Your bus tours the streets of George Town, past the Gingerbread House, on through Hell, and to the Cayman Turtle Farm. This is very touristy—we felt it was mostly a tour of souvenir shops, but cruiser reviews are mostly positive: A "nice overview" of the island ." The tour guide is "informative" and "friendly." The turtle farm is "the best part" and "fun for the kids" (ask if you can "hold a turtle"), though some may be "appalled by the crowding of the turtles in the tanks." Hell "didn't impress" most cruisers, however. Overall, most cruisers felt it "worth their time" even though is "isn't a sophisticated" excursion.

Tour
Leisurely
All ages
$39/ $29 (3-9)
2 hours

Grand Cayman Duck Boat Tour Rating: n/a

Tour land and sea without leaving your seat. After a half-hour touring around downtown Georgetown and nearby Seven Mile Beach, your amphibious craft takes to the water to view coral reefs, sea life, and shipwrecks. No glass bottom here; undersea views are from the duck's underwater cameras, seen on six monitors. A roof and open sides provide both breeze and shelter from the rain.

Tour
Leisurely
All ages
$45/$30 (0-9)
1-1.5 hours

See page 218 for a key to the shore excursion description charts and their icons.

Embarking on Shore Excursions on Grand Cayman *(continued)*

☐ Stingray City Reef Sail and Snorkel [G09] — Rating: 8

Yet another stingray excursion, this one featuring a nice, seven-mile sail in a 65-foot catamaran. For details on the stingray experience, see related excursions on the previous pages. Includes snorkel equipment and beverages (water and lemonade). Typical meeting time is 12:40 pm. 3.5 hours.

Sports
Active
Ages 5 & up
$60/$47 (5-9)

☐ Aquaboat & Snorkel Adventure [G20] — Rating: 9

Here's an excursion with an exciting twist—piloting (or riding) in your own, two-person inflatable motorboat. You'll cruise along Grand Cayman's shores, then explore an uninhabited island (Sandy Cove). Then it's off to Smith's Cove to swim and snorkel (equipment provided). On your way back, you'll stop at the Cali shipwreck. When it's all done, you may stop for a complimentary beverage (fruit or rum punch) at Rackams Bar on the dock. Guests must be 18 or older to pilot a boat.

Sports
Active
Ages 6 & up
$84
3 hours

☐ Boatswain's Beach Adventure Marine Park [G26] — Rating: n/a

Take an air-conditioned mini-bus ride to the 23-acre Boatswain's Beach (pronounced "Bo-suns Beach"), which contains the famous turtle farm. Snorkel equipment is provided to explore a 1.3-million-gallon lagoon filled with tropical fish. Typical meeting time is 9:20 am. 4.5-5 hours.

Sports
Active
All ages
$92/$72 (3-9)

☐ Discover Native Cayman & the Saltwater Forest — Rating: n/a

Your mini-bus whisks you from the pier for a photo op at Seven Mile Beach, then stop in West Bay to view traditional Caymanian cottages and watch artisans at work (and shop). You'll board a boat to explore a saltwater mangrove marsh, gliding amidst overhanging trees. Children under 3 are free, but must have a ticket.

Tour
Leisurely
All ages
$62/$45(3-9)

☐ Dolphin Encounter/Extreme Swim/Observer and Turtle Farm — Rating: n/a

Take a 30-minute bus ride to meet the dolphins at Discovery Dolphin Cayman. The 30-minute "Encounter" takes place in 3 feet of water where you can touch, play, feed, shake "hands," and kiss the creatures. This is followed by 45 minutes of free time to explore the center, then a visit to the Cayman Turtle Farm. An Observer version of this is available for $39/$29, as well as an "Extreme Swim" (where you get a dolphin "belly ride") for $125/$115. (On Your Own: http://www.dolphindiscovery.com/grand-cayman or 866-393-5158)

Sports
Active
Ages 3 & up
$95/$89 (3-9)
3.5-4 hours

See page 218 for a key to the shore excursion description charts and their icons.

Grand Cayman On Your Own

Grand Cayman is another port where you find cruisers going on non-Disney excursions. Here are some popular options, though please note that we have no experience with these tour operators: **Captain Marvin's Watersports** is a very popular and well-liked outfit that offers snorkeling, island tours, and fishing charters at great prices, fewer crowds, and excellent service—visit http://www.captainmarvins.com or 866-978-6364. Another option, also popular, is **Native Way Water Sports**—they have excursions to Seven Mile Beach and Coral Gardens in addition to Stingray City. Visit http://www.nativewaywatersports.com or 345-916-5027.

Cozumel
(Western Caribbean and Panama Canal

Welcome to **Mexico**! The island of Cozumel, just off the northeastern tip of Mexico's Yucatan peninsula and a bit south of Cancun, offers the Disney Cruise Line's primary taste of the Caribbean's Hispanic heritage. You can stay on the island, or visit the Mayan ruins on the mainland. Cozumel offers a wide range of enticing activities and Mexican handcrafted goods.

© MediaMarx, Inc.

Relaxing on the beach on Cozumel

AMBIENCE

Cozumel is a **destination of contrasts**. For some, it's a crowded shopping port, intimidatingly foreign to some, exciting for others. It can be a jumping-off point for a visit to ancient ruins, or a gateway to some of the world's greatest reef diving. A unique nature park offers underwater and jungle adventure, and white, powdery beaches offer sheltered, resort/upscale experiences on the western shore, or remote, raucous rolling surf on the eastern shore.

HISTORY & CULTURE

With a history as a **religious destination** dating back to Mayan pre-history (the name Cozumel derives from the Mayan for *island of swallows*), this is one port where you can visit ruins that actually pre-date Christopher what's-his-name. The island's substantial population was destroyed after the Conquistadores' brutal arrival, and its many coves and inlets served as hideouts for pirates such as Jean Lafitte and Henry Morgan. Settlers returned in the mid-1800s and cultivation of rubber here and on the mainland made this once again a trading center. The island's beautiful beaches made it part of the State of Quintana Roo's "Mexican Riviera." Undersea explorer Jacques Cousteau really put the island on the tourism map in the 1960s, thanks to the island's prime coral reefs, part of the second-largest coral reef formation in the world.

FACTS

Size: 30 mi. (48 km.) long x 9 mi. (16 km.) wide	
Climate: Subtropical	**Temperatures**: 75°F (24°C) to 90°F (32°C)
Population: 65,000	**Busy Season**: Mid-February to April
Language: Spanish, English	**Money**: Nuevo Peso ($10 Pesos = $1 U.S.)
Time Zone: Central (DST observed)	**Transportation**: Walking, taxis, scooters
Phones: Dial 011- from U.S., dial 060 for emergencies, dial 20092 for police	

Making the Most of Cozumel

GETTING THERE

Your ship docks at the **Punta Langosta** pier in the city of San Miguel de Cozumel, on the island's western shore. Tendering is not required. You can see Playa del Carmen on the mainland—the channel is just two miles (3 km.) wide. The typical all-ashore time is 7:15 or 8:30 am, with all aboard at 3:45 or 5:30 pm. A tourist information office is at the end of the pier, as is the glitzy Punta Langosta shopping plaza. The plaza is reached via a pedestrian bridge over Avenida (Avenue) Rafael Melgar, and provides a convenient, secure shopping and dining destination. There is no beach within walking distance.

GETTING AROUND

You disembark the ship near the **center of town**, about five blocks south of Muelle Fiscal, the city's central plaza and ferryboat dock (ferries to the mainland). Several miles to the south are the International and Puerta Maya piers, in the resort hotel district. The waterfront road, Avenida Rafael Melgar, goes right past the pier, and leads to most of the sights in town and on the island's west shore. Just five blocks north you'll find Avenida Benito Juarez, which heads directly to the San Gervasio ruins and the beaches of the eastern shore. Drive south on Avenida Rafael Melgar to reach Chankanaab National Park, San Francisco Beach, Playa Del Sol, and Palancar Reef. • Car and scooter rentals are advisable for those who wish to set off on their own, but taxis ($4 for up to four passengers) are more convenient for in-town travel. Four wheel drive vehicles are especially useful if you head for the eastern beaches. Alamo Car Rental (888-826-6893) is located in the Punta Langosta Mall, and several other agencies are nearby. Note that cars are driven on the same side of the road as in the United States.

STAYING SAFE

Safety is always, in part, a **state of mind**. Certainly the crowds of sprawling San Miguel will put most travelers on the defensive, as may the dominant, Spanish language (though most shop owners speak some English). Take typical big-city precautions, then try to relax and enjoy. A polite, friendly attitude toward the locals will ease your way—it always helps to treat your host with respect. "Do you speak English?" is a good way to start your conversations. Drinking water and food safety are a classic concern for visits to Mexico. Be sensible. Drink bottled water and commercially prepared beverages, and think twice about dining from street vendors. However, most restaurants will be well up to stateside health standards. As always, sunblock is a must. Dress according to your planned activities—changing rooms are hard to find at the beach.

Touring Cozumel

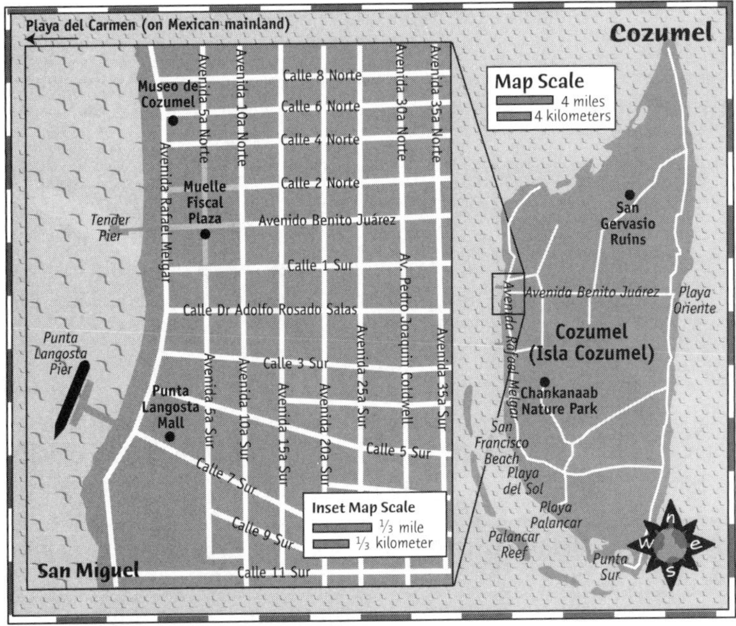

There's not much to see on a **walking tour** other than Punta Langosta Mall. Just across the street from the cruise pier, the mall has stylish architecture reminiscent of fashionable stateside malls (it reminds us a bit of Downtown Disney in Orlando). You'll find upscale souvenir and luxury shops, the popular bars Carlos 'n' Charlie's and Señor Frog's, and a Burger King. While the Punta Langosta Mall offers a secure experience, you'll get a better taste of the town by taking a short stroll or cab ride five blocks north to Muelle Fiscal, the town's central plaza. A six-block area has been converted to a pedestrian mall, featuring many restaurants, shops, and a large souvenir and crafts market. Three blocks farther north on Avenida Rafael Melgar is the island's museum, Museo de la Isla de Cozumel ($3 admission), which features two floors filled with archaeological and ecological exhibits and a very popular rooftop restaurant (Del Museo), which is open until 1:30 pm. Most tourist-oriented restaurants and shops are clustered along a ten-block stretch of Avenida Rafael Melgar between Punta Langosta on the south and the museum on the north. However, if you're bargain-hunting, the shops on the side streets and a block inland may offer better deals.

Playing in Cozumel

ACTIVITIES

The best of the island's and mainland's **play spots** and attractions are featured in shore excursions on the next six pages, which we recommend for most visitors. Many are day-long experiences. Serious divers may prefer to make their own arrangements.

The island does not produce much in the way of local crafts, but you can find a wide range of silver, carved wood and stone, and other Mexican specialties, imported from the mainland. **Shops** near the cruise pier will tend to be the most expensive. Know your prices, and be prepared to bargain. Silver items are typically sold by weight, and black coral cannot be brought back into the United States.

White, powder-soft sands and clear, turquoise waters make the island's **beaches** very attractive. The strong undertow found on the east coast beaches, such as Playa Oriente, can be perilous for swimmers, but the big surf, dunes, stretches of rocky coastline, and small crowds are very tempting. Playa Oriente is at the far eastern end of the central, cross-island road, and others can be found by turning right and following the paved road southward. Several of these beaches offer restaurants and watersport rentals. The safe, gentle beaches on the sheltered west side of the island are generally built up, offering a wide variety of recreational and dining opportunities. Top picks (all south of San Miguel) include San Francisco Beach, Playa del Sol, Playa Francesa, and Playa Palancar.

Palancar Reef, at the island's southwest corner, is probably at the top of most serious divers' list, but dozens more **dive sites** dot the map. Visit http://www.travelnotes.cc/cozumel/links/scuba.html for a good introduction to Cozumel diving, listings, and reviews.

Chankanaab Park offers first-rate snorkel, nature, and wildlife encounter opportunities. • On the mainland, the **Xcaret** Eco-Archaeological Park offers many unusual opportunities (book an excursion for either of these). The island's archaeological sites are quite minor, with the most developed at San Gervasio, near the island's center. Archaeology buffs should book an excursion to Tulum Ruins, about 80 miles (128 km.) away on the mainland. Alas, famed Chichen Itza is a bit too far for a day trip.

Your schedule may allow for both **lunch and dinner** ashore. Carlos 'n Charlie's is a town fixture, relocated to Punta Langosta Mall. In the center of town, Casa Denis and La Choza offer regional specialties.

Embarking on Shore Excursions on Cozumel

Cozumel Golf Excursion [CZ01] — Rating: n/a

Play a round at the Cozumel Country Club on a course designed by the Nicklaus Group. Includes greens fees, golf cart, golf balls, and your taxi ride. Lunch and club/shoe rentals are additional. Golf attire required. Typical meeting time is 9:45 am. We received no cruiser reviews for this excursion. (On Your Own: Cozumel Country Club, http://www.cozumelcountryclub.com.mx, 987-872-9570)

Sports
Active
Ages 10 & up
$165
5-5.5 hours

Certified Scuba Tour [CZ02] — Rating: 9

Certified divers enjoy two dives–first to Palancar Reef (70–80 ft. or 21–24 m.) and then to a shallower dive (50–60 ft. or 15–18 m.). Includes equipment, fruit, and drinks. Typical meeting time is 9:45 am. Cruiser reviews are positive: Two "drift dives" offer the opportunity to see more "unique underwater life" than in many other ports. Palancar Reef is "phenomenal" and the reef wall is "very deep" with "lots to see." Visibility is "incredible." (On Your Own: Eagle Ray Divers, http://www.eagleraydivers.com, 866-465-1616)

Sports
Very active
Ages 12 & up
$99
4.5 hours

Dolphin Discovery Cozumel [CZ04] — Rating: 7

This popular excursion takes you to Chankanaab National Park, where you'll encounter dolphins in waist-deep water. Afterward, stay and enjoy the park. If you want to swim with the dolphins, you will need to book that separately. Typical meeting times are 9:45 am, 10:45 am, 11:45 am, and 12:45 pm. Cruiser comments were mixed: Listen to a "brief training session," don "bulky life jackets," then enter one of five "water areas" where you stand in the water. Several cruisers report that the "waist-high" water was in fact "chest-high" or even "chin-high" instead, and that it could be over the heads of guests under 7. Most cruisers loved being able to "touch and interact" with the "amazing" dolphins. Cruisers note that you cannot wear "water shoes." Some feel this excursion isn't really great for cruisers "under 12" due to the depth of the water.

Encounter
Leisurely
Ages 3 & up
$112/$89
3-3.5 hours

Dolphin Discovery Observer [CZ25] — Rating: 6

This excursion is for those with friends or family on the Dolphin Discovery Cozumel excursion who wish to observe and not interact with the dolphins. While your friend or family member is getting their orientation and interaction, you'll be observing from an unshaded area approximately 50 feet away. Also note that the taxi ride to and from the facility is in a non-air-conditioned vehicle. Observers may stay to enjoy the park, which includes a beach. Typical meeting times are 9:45 am, 10:45 am, 11:45 am, and 12:45 pm.

Tour
Leisurely
All ages
$49
3-3.5 hours

Mayan Frontier Horseback Riding Tour [CZ05] — Rating: 5

Giddyup! Mosey on down a Mayan trail on horseback, passing ruins on your way. Afterward, visit a ranch. Must wear closed toe shoes and long pants. Maximum weight is 240 lbs. Typical meeting time is 10:15 am. Cruiser reviews were mediocre: The "very friendly staff" are "helpful," but the "saddles are old and unpadded." The horses are also "over the hill" (which could be a good thing as they are more sedate than younger horses). Cruisers also note that some of the "ruins and artifacts" are "not real." Younger guests "enjoyed it," but most cruisers were "not impressed."

Sports
Very active
Ages 12–65
$89
4 hours

See page 218 for a key to the shore excursion description charts and their icons.

Introduction
Reservations
Staterooms
Dining
Activities
Ports of Call
Magic
Index

Embarking on Shore Excursions on Cozumel *(continued)*

Cozumel Ruins & Beach Tour [CZ19] — Rating: 3

Tour the San Gervasio Ruins, then off to Playa Mia for an hour and a half of beach relaxation. Includes soft drinks (food is extra). Watersports available for extra fee. Typical meeting time is noon. Cruiser reviews were mostly negative: While the "water is beautiful," there "wasn't enough time" at the beach and food "didn't seem fresh." Most time is spent at the "ancient sites" which are "interesting," but not "spectacular." "Bring bug spray!" Overall, cruisers "do not recommend it."

Tour/Beach
Leisurely
All ages
$52/$35 (3-9)
4-4.5 hours

Speed Boat Beach Escape [CZ32] — Rating: n/a

Power off to a tropical getaway in your very own mini speedboat! Take a short 20-minute ride to the instruction center. You're given a briefing on speedboat safety and operating instructions, then handed the keys. Once aboard, cruise through the beautiful Cozumel waters for an hour, then stay around to enjoy the beach. Light buffet and beverages included. Must be 18 to drive.

Sports
Active
Ages 10 & up
$88
4 hours

Jeep Exploration [CZ09] — Rating: 7

Drive a four-person, standard-shift, 4x4 vehicle through the "tropical" scrub. After bump-bump-bumping along the dirt roads, enjoy a yummy lunch on the beach and explore some low-key ruins. If you're a party of two, you'll share a vehicle with another couple and take turns driving. Cruiser reviews are mostly positive: After a "long walk," you get into your "open air" vehicle ("no air conditioning") and "take a fun drive" through town. Once on the dirt roads, it's "very bumpy and dusty" but "adventuresome." Lunch at a "beautiful beach" is "very good," though the ruins are "unimpressive." Overall, most cruisers enjoyed the "entertaining tour guides" and "had a good time." We tried it and enjoyed it! Must be 18 to drive.

Tour
Active
Ages 8 & up
$85/$75 (8-9)
4.5 hours

© MediaMarx, Inc.

Our Jeep safari

Xcaret Eco-Archaeological Park [CZ10] — Rating: 9

This mainland park is a favorite—it's like a natural water park. Swim, visit an aquarium, and see ruins. Includes transportation, lunch, and entrance fee. Bring cash to buy souvenirs. Regular sunscreen is not allowed; you will be provided with environmentally friendly sunscreen upon arrival. Cruiser reviews are very positive: While the "travel time is long" (about "1.5 hours"), the "beautiful nature park" is "well worth the journey." A favorite feature is the "unique underground fresh water river" that you "float through" (but beware that it is "cold water"). There are also "good spots for snorkeling" with "lots of fish." Many cruisers feel this excursion is the "highlight of their trip."

Tour
Active
All ages
$119/$89 (0-9)
7-7.5 hours

Dune Buggy & Beach Snorkel Combo [CZ23] — Rating: n/a

Drive a dune buggy along the eastern coast of Cozumel, see where the locals live in San Miguel, and drive through the busy hotel district. Upon reaching your destination, play in the sand and snorkel to your heart's content. Beach umbrellas, blankets, chairs, showers, unlimited soft drinks, and a snack including nachos, guacamole and fruit is included. Then pile back into the dune buggy and make your way back to town. Must be at least 18 years of age and have a license to drive.

Sports
Active
Ages 8 & up
$92/$80 (8-9)
4-4.5 hours

Embarking on Shore Excursions on Cozumel *(continued)*

Fury Catamaran Sail, Snorkel, & Beach Party [CZ12] — Rating: 10

Sports
Active
Ages 5 & up
$58/$31 (5-9)
3-3.5 hours

Board a 65-foot catamaran and cruise out to snorkel in 3–20 ft. (1–6 m.) of water. Afterward, party on the beach with free soft drinks, margaritas, and beer. Cruiser reviews are overwhelmingly positive: Enjoy a 35-minute sail on a "large," "unexpectedly smooth" catamaran with an "exceptional" crew. Then snorkel for 45 minutes in a "beautiful" area with "many fish and coral." Hop aboard for "short," "20-minute" sail to a "gorgeous beach" with "plenty of shady areas." The food served at the beach is "very good" (about "$8/person"). Then it's back onboard for a "30- to 45-minute" sail back, with "music" and "dancing." "Plenty of free drinks." "Bring cash" for food and tips. Note that you "do need to be mobile to exit and reenter the catamaran at sea." Overall, cruisers had a "great time" and would "do it again." (On Your Own: Fury Catamaran at http://furycat.com, 987-872-5145)

Clear Kayak & Beach Snorkel Combo [CZ24] — Rating: n/a

Sports
Active
Ages 10 & up
$68
2.5-3 hours

Paddle in transparent kayaks over the unspoiled beauty of coral reef formations, watching tropical fish swim right under your kayak. Afterward, don the provided snorkel equipment to get an even closer look at the underwater world. Then relax on Uvas Beach. Weight limit of 425 lbs. per two-person kayak. Includes fruit and two complimentary drinks (soda, water, beer, margaritas, or daiquiris). Bring biodegradable sunblock. Typical meeting time is 11:45 am.

Cozumel Beach Break [CZ15] — Rating: 8

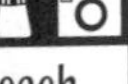

Beach
Leisurely
All ages
$79/$65 (3-9)
4.5-5 hours

Bum around Playa Mia beach. Price includes bus transfers to and from the beach, admission, use of pools and beach, open bar (mixed drinks, beer, soda, and juice), water toys, recreation, entertainment, kid's club, and lunch buffet. Typical meeting time is 10:10 am. Cruiser comments were mostly positive: The beach has a "family party atmosphere" with "lots to do," including "water trampolines" and "a climbing iceberg" (though these are "pretty far out in the water"). Keep in mind that while the drinks may be free, they are also "watered down." Lunch is "good" by most accounts, though you have to "contend with vendors" to get to the food area. (On Your Own: Playa Mia at http://www.playamiacozumel.com, or Mr. Sanchos—see end of section)

Atlantis Submarine Expedition [CZ20] — Rating: 6

Tour
Leisurely
Ages 4 & up
$99/$57 (4-9)
2.5 hours

Board the "Atlantis" submarine and dive up to 110 ft. (33 m.), viewing tropical fish and 30 ft. (9 m.) coral heads. Includes beverages. Height restriction of 36 in./91 cm. minimum. Typical meeting times are 10:45 am and 12:45 pm. Cruiser reviews are very similar to those on same excursion in St. Thomas, but it gets a slightly higher rating thanks to the better views and visible sea life.

Ocean View Explorer Tour [CZ22] — Rating: 5

Tour
Leisurely
All ages
$46/$35 (0-9)
2 hours

Explore the coral of Paradise Reef in this semi-submersible. Typical meeting time is 10:45 am. Cruiser reviews on this excursion are limited, but those we received were mixed: Some felt it was a good "compromise" between the Atlantis sub and a snorkeling excursion, while others felt it was "boring" and would not do it again. Compared to the Atlantis, it is less expensive and allows kids 0–3. (On Your Own: AquaWorld at http://www.aquaworld.com.mx)

See page 218 for a key to the shore excursion description charts and their icons.

Introduction
Reservations
Staterooms
Dining
Activities
Ports of Call
Magic
Index

Embarking on Shore Excursions on Cozumel *(continued)*

Tulum Ruins [CZ06] — Rating: 9

An all-day adventure to the mainland for a visit to the sacred ruins. Includes a beach visit, drinks, and sandwiches. Note that there is an extra fee if you bring a camcorder. Typical meeting time is 9:15 am. Cruiser reviews are positive: The "boat to Mexico" is "large and comfortable," though a "little bouncy." The "fantastic" tour guides are "knowledgeable," making the ruins "way more interesting than you'd expect." The "beautiful" beach is "perfect," but be aware there are "no changing rooms." Overall, a "worthy" and "fun" excursion.

Sports
Active
Ages 5 & up
$99/adult
$75 (5-9)
7-7.5 hours

Mexican Cuisine Workshop and Tasting [CZ33] — Rating: n/a

After a 25-minute ride to Playa Mia Grand Beach Park, you are met by a chef who introduces you to authentic Mexican cuisine. You'll prepare a full-course meal together during the next two hours, then enjoy your fine food with a glass of good wine. After the meal, you'll have time to enjoy the private beach. Cooking utensils and ingredients are provided. Guests must be 21 or older to consume alcohol. Typical meeting time is 10:45 am.

Workshop
Leisurely
Ages 14 & up
$89
5-5.5 hours

Eco-Park & Snorkel [CZ34] — Rating: n/a

Take a 35-minute ride in an open-air ATV to Punta Sur Ecological Park at the southernmost point of the island. At the park, you'll take in its wild beauty, traveling the unpaved roads alongside the sea and through the jungle. Along the way you'll stop at Columbia Lagoon filled with salt-water crocodiles, a small Mayan temple ruin ("El Caracol"), and the Punta Sur Lighthouse Museum. Be sure to climb the lighthouse tower to take in the magnificent view. After the tour, you'll have the chance to relax on a white-sand beach—sunbathe, swim, or snorkel! Snorkel equipment is provided, as are beverages. Note that guests must be at least 8 years of age to snorkel. Typical meeting time is 10:45 am. (On Your Own: You could take a taxi for about $50–$60 roundtrip and pay $10/person admission to the park, known locally as Parque Punta Sur, but the Disney excursion is about the same price and more convenient.)

Sports
Active
All ages
$62/$40 (3-9)
4.25 hours

Xplor Park/The Secret River and Playa Del Carmen — Rating: n/a

Swim or float through the area's stalctite-filled limestone caves. Xplor Park ($195, ages 12 & up, 7 hrs.) is a high adventure trip combining 13 ziplines (some with water splash-downs), ATV riding through jungle and cave (must be 18 to drive), plus swim/float cave exploration in 75°(F)/24°(C) water. Buffet lunch and fruit drinks are included. The Secret River and Playa Del Carmen ($109/$99 ages 6-9, ages 6 & up, 7 hrs.) combines a 90-minute guided walking and floating cave tour (wet suits provided for the 64°F/18°C water) snack and beverage, and 90 minutes of free time in Playa del Carmen for beach or shopping.

Sports
Active
Ages 12/6 & up
$195/$105
7 hours

Snuba Cozumel [CZ45] — Rating: n/a

Explore the turquoise waters of Cozumel without being a certified diver! Snuba is a method of underwater swimming in which you use fins, a mask, weights, and a breathing apparatus like that used in scuba diving, but the air tanks remain on the water's surface. A certified dive master leads your group down to depths of about 15-20 feet to view tropical fish and colorful coral formations. You'll spend about 25 minutes in the water. Bottled water is included. Guests must fill out a medical questionnaire before participating.

Sports
Active
Ages 10 & up
$69
2-2.5 hours

Embarking on Shore Excursions on Cozumel *(continued)*

Dolphin Swim at Dolphinaris [CZ38] — Rating: n/a

A mere five-minute ride from the pier is Dolphinaris, a dolphin facility created with families in mind. Cruisers who book the Dolphin Swim begin with a short dolphin presentation to learn about their behavior, then don a life jacket and proceed to a waist-deep submerged platform to get a closer look at the dolphins and their anatomy. After this, you'll head out to deeper waters to touch and kiss the dolphins and enjoy a belly ride with a dolphin! You'll then have 40 minutes to swim freely among the dolphins (snorkel mask is provided). Minimum height is 48 in. (122 cm.), though smaller children can be held by a parent in the water. Guests 5-11 must be accompanied by an adult booked on this excursion. 12-17 must be accompanied by an adult on this or the Dolphin Observer excursion (below). Cameras, jewelry, and sunscreen are not permitted in the pool areas. (On Your Own: Dolphinaris at http://www.dolphinaris.com)

Sports
Active
Ages 5 & up
$146/$117 (5-9)
3 hours

Dolphin Push, Pull, and Swim [CZ50] — Rating: n/a

In this less-expensive variation on the above excursion, you'll spend a bit less time in the water with the dolphins but you'll have a lot of hands-on interaction. After a briefing, you'll move to deeper waters where a dolphin will push you (while you are on a boogie board) and pull you (with its pectoral fins) through the water. After the experience, enjoy the beach and attractions at Chankanaab National Park. A taxi (included) will return you to the ship when you want. All guests under the age of 18 must be accompanied by a parent or guardian on the same tour. Guests under 42 in. (106 cm.) have a modified experience involving a parent. (On Your Own: Dolphin Discovery at http://www.dolphindiscovery.

Sports
Active
Ages 5 & up
$132/$109 (ages 5-9)
3.5-4 hours

Dolphin Kids @ Dolphinaris [CZ39] — Rating: n/a

A special dolphin interaction program just for kids ages 4-9 is offered at Dolphinaris (see Dolphin Swim description). This excursion is similar to the one above, but there is no swim time with the dolphins, just touch. 40 minutes of in-water time with the dolphins. A parent or guardian must accompany a child as a Dolphin Observer (see the excursion below),and be dressed to enter the water if their child needs support. Note also that kids must be able to swim.

Sports
Active
Ages 4-9
$105
3 hours

Dolphin Trainer for a Day in Cozumel [CZ40] — Rating: n/a

Live your dream job and work alongside the dolphin trainers at Dolphinaris! Your day begins with a 50-minute orientation, then a snack. You'll then put on a snorkel and mask to explore the ocean cove. Next, assist the Dolphinaris trainers in every aspect of their work including feeding and behavioral training techniques. You can expect kisses and rides, too! Finish with a complimentary lunch at the Dolphinaris restaurant before heading back. Guests under 18 must be accompanied by an adult booked on the same excursion.

Sports
Active
Ages 10 & up
$285
5.5 hours

Dolphin Observer at Dolphinaris [CZ41] — Rating: n/a

This excursion is for those with friends or family on a Dolphinaris excursion (see above) who wish to observe and not interact with the dolphins. While your friend or family member is getting their orientation and interaction, you'll be observing from a scenic area with some tables.

Tour
Leisurely
All ages
$25/(3 & up)

See page 218 for a key to the shore excursion description charts and their icons.

Introduction | Reservations | Staterooms | Dining | Activities | Ports of Call | Magic | Index

Embarking on Shore Excursions on Cozumel *(continued)*

Cozumel Highlights and Mayan Ruins [CZ42] — Rating: n/a

Tour
Active
All ages
$52/$39 (3-9)
4.5 hours

Take a 10-minute stroll to your air-conditioned bus where you'll enjoy a 20-minute drive to the recently excavated ruins of San Gervasio. Here you'll receive a 90-minute guided tour of the fascinating centuries old structures. Then you'll hop on the bus again for a 20-minute drive to the eastern side of the island, stopping at a tequila distillery and El Mirador, for photos of the stunning vista, and then on to El Cedral, the ancient site of Cozumel's first Catholic Mass (and the very spot that Spanish settlers landed on in 1518). You'll have the chance to shop for souvenirs here as well. The drive back to the port is 30 minutes. A complimentary bottle of water is included. Note that you will need to walk a total of two miles during this excursion, so be sure to bring comfortable clothing. The excursion is stroller accessible (though you may need to fold it in places), but wheelchairs are not permitted.

Adventure Park (Zip Line, & Snorkel Combo) [CZ43] — Rating: 7

Sports
Very active
Ages 10 & up
$75
3-6 hours

A 15-minute taxi ride gets you to Cozumel's Adventure Park, well-known for its thrills. After a safety orientation, you'll be fitted with a harness, helmet, and climbing shoes and then zip-line from tower to tower (50 feet total) at a height of about 25 feet over the ground. After your zip-line adventure, you'll cross suspension bridges and climb one or more of the six climbing structures in the park. Then you get to rappel down to the ground! And if that wasn't enough, you also get the opportunity to snorkel in the Caribbean sea, explore a hidden ocean cavern, and sunbathe on the beach. A beverage is included, and food and drinks are available for purchase. Maximum zip-line weight is 300 lbs. All necessary equipment is included in the price of the excursion. Preview at http://www.youtube.com/watch?v=8UKtW9628VQ.

Three Reef Snorkel [CZ46] — Rating: n/a

Sports
Active
Ages 8 & up
$49/$39 (8-9)
3.5-4 hours

Love to snorkel? This is the excursion for you! Your pilot and crew will choose the three best snorkel spots of the day and you'll cruise from one to the other in a special snorkeling boat. Snorkel gear and safety briefing are included. You'll have about 30 minutes at each reef to discover the tropical fish and coral formations. You'll also receive a complimentary boxed snack (chips, cookies, fruit, and beverage) onboard the boat after your snorkeling adventure. Please note that you need to be comfortable swimming in open water and all guests must be mobile to participate (wheelchairs are not permitted). Possible snorkeling destinations include Paraiso Bajo, Paraiso Profundo, and Dzul Ha, all spots within Cozumel's protected marine park which is reserved just for small tour groups.

Cozumel On Your Own

Want to set out on your own? There are other popular tour operators and destinations preferred by Disney cruisers. While we haven't tried this one ourselves, we offer the information here for your reference: **Mr. Sancho's Cozumel Beach Club** is a nice alternative to the Cozumel Beach Break excursion—just take a taxi to Mr. Sancho's and enjoy a less expensive day at the beach with plenty of amenities should you wish to use them. For more information, visit http://www.mrsanchos.com.

Charming Cozumel

Costa Maya
(Special 7-Night Western Caribbean Itinerary)

Ruins and coral and beach, oh my! The port of Costa Maya isn't even on most maps. Development in this **quiet corner** of Mexico's Yucatan coast began in 2000, headed by the same group that made Cancun what it is. The nearby village of Majahual is dwarfed by this, the first Mexican port created for the cruise industry.

© Corel

Costa Maya's port complex

AMBIENCE

The port of Costa Maya and its "**Mayan Pavilion Park**" are more like Disney's Castaway Cay and Downtown Disney than a traditional port. That can be reassuring—virtually no signs of poverty, no uncomfortable encounters with the locals—just shopping mall-style commerce; clean, safe swimming; free entertainment; and excursions to exciting Mayan ruins. It has everything a Western Caribbean vacationer can expect of a 10-hour port visit, including a dolphin encounter. If "adventure" calls, a short walk brings you to the beachfront village of Majahual.

HISTORY & CULTURE

Native American empires have risen and fallen in the southeast corner of Mexico's Yucatan, but all has been quiet for many centuries. The 80-mile-long "**Costa Maya**" **(Mayan Coast)** is dotted by some 800 historical sites (mostly unexcavated) and small villages peopled by Mayan descendants. Such was the village of Majahual (population 200) until the year 2000, when developers seized on the area as the next big thing. To the north is the huge Sian Kaán Biosphere Park, which buffers this region from Cozumel and Cancun. Scant miles to the south is the ecotourism-friendly nation of Belize. Promised to be eco- as well as tourist-friendly, Costa Maya has become a popular stop for most major cruise lines, providing "private island" conveniences on the Mexican mainland. Costa Maya has been a convenient, alternate cruise port after hurricanes elsewhere in the region, but was briefly out of commission itself in 2007, after Hurricane Dean.

FACTS

Size: 1 mile long by 1/2 mile wide	
Climate: Subtropical	**Temperatures:** 80°F (26°C) to 87°F (30.5°C)
Population: 2,000	**Busy Season:** Mid-December to April
Language: Spanish	**Money:** Mexican Peso (10.50 Pesos = $1 U.S.)
Time Zone: Central (DST observed)	**Transportation:** Walking, taxis
Phones: Dial 011- from U.S., dial 060 for emergencies, dial 20092 for police	

Making the Most of Costa Maya

GETTING THERE

Costa Maya's pier can berth three large cruise ships (even huge Oasis-class ships dock here). Visitors are shuttled down the long quay in Disney-style trams, directly to the **modern port complex** (see photo on previous page). From there, it's a short walk to your tour bus, or you can "hang" in a complex that includes 70,000 sq. ft./6,500 sq. m. of shopping, a crafts market, two salt water pools, live entertainment, cultural presentations, and several restaurants. The swimming, lounge chairs, and entertainment are all free, included in the port fees paid by Disney Cruise Line. Water sport rentals are available, too. Independent tour operators can be found just outside the complex's gates. The "New" Majahual, a planned town with a target population of 20,000, is growing just beyond the pier facilities, and the village of Majahual is about a half mile to the south (left as you leave the port). The Disney ships typically dock around mid-day and depart at 5:30 pm. The relatively brief time in port can affect the availability of some shore excursions.

GETTING AROUND

Until recently, only a rutted, dirt road served Majahual and nearby villages. With planned development comes a few paved roads, but we strongly recommend that you **stick to the shore excursions** if you want to venture far afield. A local excursion company, Toucan of Costa Maya (http://www.tucancostamaya.com) offers van and jeep hires, with or without driver and guide. The nearby airport has been under development, but service is slim, so if you're stranded when the boat leaves, you may have an adventure on your hands. The Uvero Beach excursion includes unlimited use of shuttle buses that depart every 35 minutes. If you have the urge to abandon tourist heaven and find the "real" Majahual fishing village, it's about a half mile south of the pier area. Taxis and shuttles are available for $2–$3 per person each way, or you can walk.

STAYING SAFE

Costa Maya is about as **safe as any port can be**. Access to the port area facilities are well guarded, and let's face it, anyone who doesn't belong is going to be pretty conspicuous. Much the same can be said for all the shore excursion destinations. Still, leave valuables on board and take advantage of the port facilities to shuttle purchases back to your room. As always, sunscreen is a must, and insect repellent is a very good idea, especially on excursions that venture near the jungle or visit ruins.

Touring Costa Maya

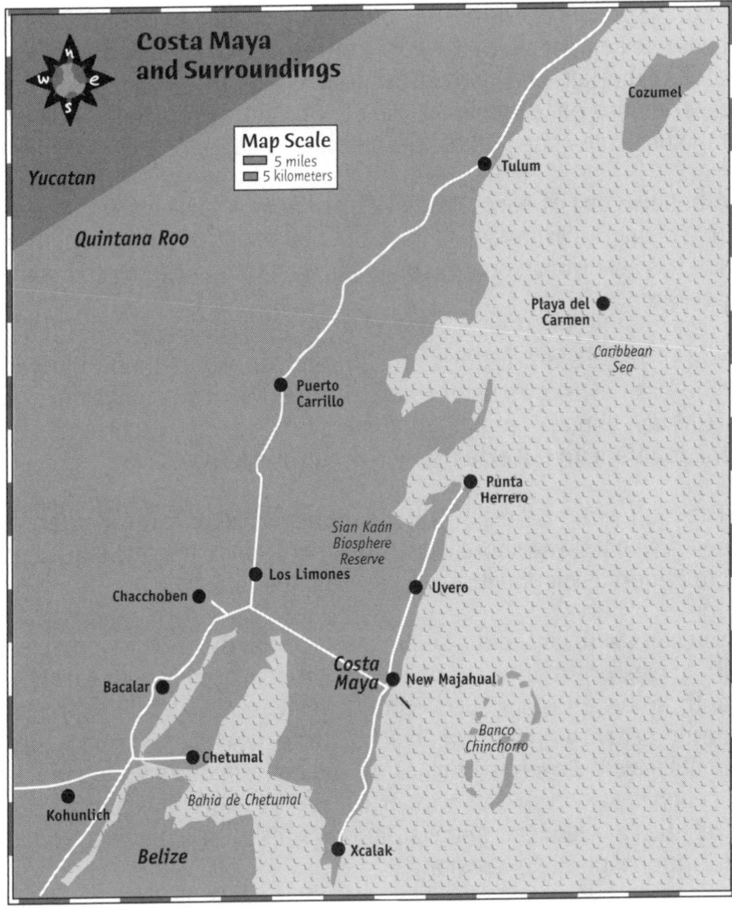

Costa Maya **stretches along the coastline** from Punta Herrero to Xcalak, as shown in the map above. You can see how close it is to Belize—it's not even all that far from Cozumel. You'll want to use organized excursions to do any venturing outside of the port area, however, as roads are not well maintained and rental cars aren't easy to come by, as we've already mentioned. The port's shopping and recreation complex is about a 300-400 yard walk down the long pier from where the cruise ships dock.

Playing in Costa Maya

ACTIVITIES

With the growth of cruise ship tourism, the **village of Majahual** has begun to compete with the port's offerings. Parasailing, jetskiing, scuba, snorkel, and fishing excursions are all available without reservations once you leave the confines of the Costa Maya port facilities (see page 308 for tips on how to do this).

A **beachfront of sorts** has developed near the village, with water sports operators, restaurants, bars, and shops popping up, but it still has small-town charm and is far less "touristy" than the main port area.

So far, there's not a Carlos 'n Charlie's in sight, though Señor Frog has now set up shop (these are the Mexican equivalents of TGIFridays and Bennigan's). Cruisers report happy experiences at the **locally run eateries**, which focus on fresh seafood.

There are also no sites of significant historical or cultural interest near the port. The shore excursions take you to historic sites that are under development to serve Costa Maya.

You can **swim** within the secure arms of the Costa Maya complex in a free-form salt water pool, but the nearby coastline is rocky, and the beach is for sunning only. "Downtown" Majahual has a better beach, with part roped off to protect swimmers from power boats. Uvero Beach is 15 miles up the coast and is a very popular "beach break" excursion with cruisers. The beach is beautiful, the facilities are modern, and water sports rentals are plentiful. Food is optional on the excursion.

Scuba and snorkel are popular activities, thanks to the same huge barrier reef that makes Cozumel so famous. Banco Chinchorro, 18 miles off shore, is the Northern Hemisphere's largest coral atoll. No organized excursions go there (it's an hour each way by boat), but you can make arrangements on your own, either on the spot or from several dive operators that are listed on the web.

Embarking on Shore Excursions in Costa Maya

Adventure by Jeep — Rating: n/a

Drive (or ride in) a Jeep through the fishing village of Majahual and the Mexican jungle to a remote beach. The drive is 75 minutes each way and the road is sometimes bumpy. You'll have about 80 minutes of beach time, which includes a lunch/snack. Drivers must be 21 years of age, able to drive stick shift, and have a valid driver's license. Traveling parties may be combined or split up in order to fill every seat.	**Tour** Moderate Ages 8 & up $99 adult $79/ages 8-9 3.5-4 hours

Off Road ATV & Beach Adventure — Rating: n/a

Ride 20 minutes in a Kodiak truck, receive a briefing, then you're off on a 60-minute ride through winding coastal paths on your single-seat all terrain vehicle (ATV). Your destination is a beach where you can swim or join a snorkel trip for an hour and a half. Snack and beverage are no longer included, so bring some cash. Guests must wear closed-toe shoes. This excursion is not recommended for pregnant women or guests with back problems.	**Tour** Active Age 16 & up $99 3-3.5 hours

Costa Maya Beach Snorkel — Rating: n/a

Beginner and intermediate snorkelers can explore an ecosystem with parrotfish, butterfly fish, and angelfish visible at depths from 3 to 15 feet. Your adventure starts from the beach, so you can snorkel at the depth that is most comfortable for you. Equipment and basic snorkel instruction is included, food and drink are extra. Snorkel time is one hour, you'll have about 50 minutes of free time on the beach, and travel to and from the beach is 50 minutes each way.	**Sports** Active Ages 5 & up $46/adult $38/ages 7-9 4-4.5 hours

Bike & Clear-Bottom Kayak — Rating: n/a

Explore the Costa Mayan coastline in two ways—by bike and kayak. After donning safety gear and adjusting your bike, you're off on a 30-minute ride along a dirt road to the village of Majahual. Next, board two-person kayaks and paddle along the reef. After kayaking, you bike back to Costa Maya along a different route. This excursion is not recommended for guests over 6 feet tall due to the size of the bikes. Guests must weigh 240 lbs. or less.	**Sports** Very active Ages 10 & up $59/person 3-3.5 hours

Catamaran & Snorkel — Rating: n/a

Hop aboard a catamaran at Fisherman's Pier for a delightful cruise on the Mayan Wind Catamaran along the virgin coast of Costa Maya. Mid-point through the cruise, the catamaran will drop anchor so you can snorkel for about 45 minutes. Equipment (mask, fins, and float jacket) and instruction are provided. Transportation to the pier and a soft drink or beer is provided with the excursion. Time to shop is provided back at the pier.	**Sports** Active Ages 8 & up $54/adult $39/child 3-3.5 hours

Chaccohoben Mayan Ruins (adult-only tour available) — Rating: n/a

Board a motorcoach to explore the Mayan ruins of Chacchoben deep in the jungle near Belize. Chacchoben, which means "the place of red corn," is believed to have been settled around 200 B.C. The 10-acre site is mostly unexcavated, but there is a grand pyramid and several temples. A lot of walking over uneven ground is required during this tour, as well as stair climbing. $5 government fee for video cameras, special permit and fee needed for tripods.	**Tour** Active All ages $75/adult $59/ages 3-9 4-4.5 hours

See page 218 for a key to description charts and their icons.

Embarking on Shore Excursions in Costa Maya

Beach Power Snorkel — Rating: n/a

Snorkel the Gulf's crystal waters with a power-assist from a Sea Doo Scooter. The hand-held aqua scooter propels you along faster than you could swim during your 50-minute dive so you can see more, with less effort. After your dive return to the beach for an hour of free time. Full instruction and equipment are provided. Food and beverages are extra (cash-only). Guests must weigh 240 lbs. or less to participate.

Sports | Active | Ages 12 & up | $55 | 4-4.5 hours

Costa Maya Highlights & Beach Combo — Rating: n/a

Tour the Mexican jungle and seashore in an air-conditioned bus, on your 45 minute ride to a remote beach, where you can swim and enjoy the sun. Hammocks, kayaks, and volleyball are included, as is a light snack of fruit, chips, and salsa, plus a soft drink or beer. Then it's back on the bus for a ride to the village of Majahaul for an hour of shopping and exploration. You can then board the bus for the short ride back to the pier, or return to the ship later on your own.

Tour | Leisurely | All ages | $69/adult | $45/ages 3-9 | 4-4.5 hours

Dune Buggy, Jungle & Beach Safari — Rating: n/a

If a Jeep doeen't push your buttons, how about a four-person, customized dune buggy convertible? Bump along dirt roads as a driver or a rider. Enjoy the beach halfway through your drive. Light snacks and a soft drink are included. Drivers must be 21 years of age and have a valid driver's license. The ride is bumpy, and we do not recommend it for guests who have back or neck problems or who are pregnant. Parties will be broken up or combined to fill empty seats.

Tour | Active | Ages 8 & up | $86/adults | $76/ages 8-9 | 3.5-4 hours

Costa Maya Salsa & Salsa — Rating: n/a

Learn to make three kinds of salsa in the kitchen, and another on the dance floor at a nearby beachfront restaurant. Adults also learn how to make margaritas (up to 3 drinks are included), and kids and grownups alike can take a whack at a piñata. Party potential is high as you dance, drink, and dip chips, and if you need to cool off, take a dip in the sea right outside—a 75-minute beach break is included.

Tour | moderate | Ages 6 & up | $65/adults | $45/ages 6-9 | 2.5-3 hours

Jungle Beach Break — Rating: n/a

Board a bus for a 40-minute trip to Uvero Beach, a popular beach with white, powdery sand, palm trees, and plenty of beach activities. Beach chairs, floats, and kayaks are included, as are kids activities, salsa lessons, and beverages. The beach can get crowded, but if you venture farther down the beach, you can find quiet spots. Food and shopping is nearby. Board a shuttle back to the ship when you've had enough.

Beach | Leisurely | All ages | $39/adult | $29/ages 3-9 | 3-4.5 hours

Kohunlich Mayan Ruins (full-day port visits only) — Rating: n/a

Travel two hours by air-conditioned bus to a secluded jungle near the border of Belize to reach these famous ruins. A broad range of architectural styles in a naturally beautiful setting await you, including the Temple of the Large Masks. A box lunch is served onboard the bus. The tour includes a lot of walking on uneven terrain and stair climbing. No flash, professional cameras, or tripods allowed, $5-$8 fee for video cameras. An adults-only tour is also offered.

Tour | Active | All ages | $89/adult | $69/ages 3-9 | 6-6.5 hours

Embarking on Shore Excursions in Costa Maya

Discover Scuba Dive — Rating: n/a

Learn the basics of scuba and take your first one-tank dive on this no-certification-required adventure. PADI-certified instructors deliver a 45-minute lesson, and then you head out to Mesoamerican Barrier Reef for your first dive. All equipment is provided. A medical questionnaire and release form is required, and guests with heart and back conditions need a doctor's note. Guests must be less than 300 lbs., in good health, and able to swim.	**Sports** Moderate Ages 12 & up $125 3.5-4 hours

Dolphin Encounter — Rating: n/a

Costa Maya's Dolphin Discovery Center is right at the end of the cruise pier! After a brief orientation, your 30-minute touch encounter with the dolphins begins. Stand in 37 in.-deep water as you touch and play with these amazing creatures. This is **not** *a swim-with-dolphins experience. Children 3-12 must be accompanied in-water by a paying adult. A parent/adult guardian must escort ages 13-17 to the session. Observers can attend at no charge (quite a deal!).*	**Sports** Moderate Age 3 & up $89/adults $74/ages 3-9 1-1.5 hours

Dolphin Swim — Rating: n/a

Much like the Dolphin Encounter (above), participants will have a 30-minute touch encounter with the dolphins at Dolphin Discovery Cener. Afterwards, the adventure moves to deeper water, where participants can swim and be pulled through the water while holding on to the dolphins' fins. Children 8-12 must be accompanied in-water by a paying adult. A parent/adult guardian must escort ages 13-17 to the session. Observers can attend at no charge!	**Sports** Moderate Ages 8 & up $119/adult $99/ages 8-9 1-1.5 hours

Dzibanché & Kohunlich Ruins (full-day port visits only) — Rating: n/a

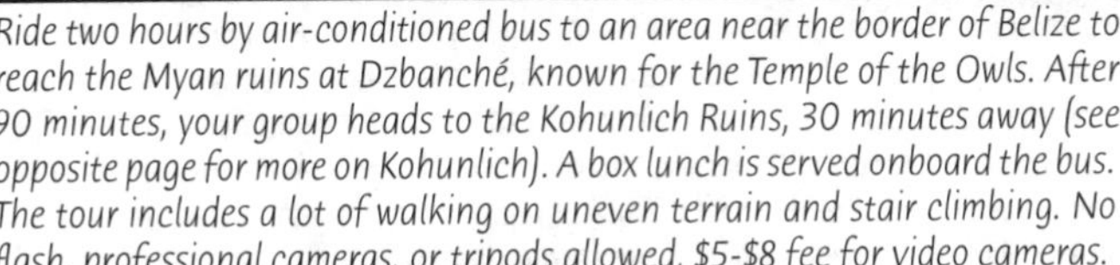

Ride two hours by air-conditioned bus to an area near the border of Belize to reach the Myan ruins at Dzbanché, known for the Temple of the Owls. After 90 minutes, your group heads to the Kohunlich Ruins, 30 minutes away (see opposite page for more on Kohunlich). A box lunch is served onboard the bus. The tour includes a lot of walking on uneven terrain and stair climbing. No flash, professional cameras, or tripods allowed, $5-$8 fee for video cameras.	**Tour** Active All ages $98/adult $75/ages 3-9 8-8.5 hours

Glass-Bottom Boat & Snorkel (November-April only) — Rating: n/a

View the coral and colorful sea life of the Caribbean from a glass-bottom boat, then don mask and fins to explore the waters close-up. A brief transfer takes you from the cruise pier to the village of Majahual, where you'll board the glass-bottom boat for a cruise to a tropical reef and a 45-minute, small-group guided snorkel tour of the reef. All equipment is supplied, plus two soft drinks. Guests must be able to swim and meet health requirements.	**Sports** Active Ages 5 & up $65/adult $45/ages 5-9 2.5-3 hours

Mini-Jeep Adventure — Rating: n/a

After a short transfer in a Kodiak truck, drive (or ride in) a 2-seat all-terrain vehicle along the Costa Maya beachfront and on rustic trails! 75 minutes later you'll reach your beach for an hour of swimming, relaxation, and a light snack, before your 75-minute return trip. Drivers must be 21 years of age and have a valid driver's license. Traveling parties may be combined or split up in order to fill every seat. Helmets and goggles are supplied, and are mandatory.	**Tour** Moderate Ages 6 & up $99/ages 10 & up 3.5-4 hours

See page 218 for a key to description charts and their icons.

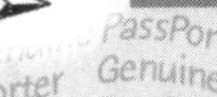

Introduction | Reservations | Staterooms | Dining | Activities | Ports of Call | Magic | Index

Embarking on Shore Excursions in Costa Maya

Sea Trek Pod

Rating: n/a 

Explore the ocean bottom wearing a Sea Trek Pod, a space-age diving helmet connected to the surface by air hose. Walk on the sea floor, breathe freely, and even wear your own eyeglasses! You'll ride 50 minutes to your dive site in a Kodiak truck, and after a briefing, you're off on a 30-minute, guided, undersea walk. Afterwards, you'll have an hour to enjoy the beach before it's time to return to the ship. Guests must be between 90 and 350 lbs. to participate.

Sports | Moderate | Ages 10 &up | $99 | 4-4.5 hours

Segway Adventure & Beach Break

Rating: n/a 

Learn to ride a 2-wheeled Segway personal transporter (one-on-one training included), ride along the beachfront, explore the village of Majahual, and maybe do some shopping. After about 90 minutes with your Segway, your route ends at a beachfront resort, where you can relax for an hour before a taxi (included) takes you back to the ship. Guests must weigh between 100 and 250 lbs., and must wear close-toed shoes. Helmets are provided and are mandatory.

Tour | Moderate | Ages 12-65 | $85/person | 3-3.5 hours

Snuba Adventure

Rating: n/a 

Swim, explore, and breathe scuba-style beneath the waves, while connected by air hose to an air tank floating on the surface that follows you as you swim. Certification is **not** *required. Your adventure begins with a 50-minute ride to a remote private beach in a Kodiak truck. After a brief class you'll have 40 minutes of Snuba time, followed by a 50-minute beach break. Then, it's back to the ship. Guests must weigh 240 lbs. or less to participate.*

Sports | Active | Ages 12 & up | $82/person | 4-4.5 hours

The Mayans Through the Ages

Rating: n/a

Mayan temples may be in ruins, but the Mayan people are still here on the Yuccatan Penninsula, eager to share their culture and cuisine with visitors. Drive 45 minutes to a Mayan village, explore a ruin at the village's center, and then visit a Mayan home for a 90-minute introduction to the Mayan way of life, including an authentic lunch of Pibil chicken, guacamole, salsas, and handmade tortillas. Two soft drinks or beers are also included.

Tour | Mild | All ages | $85/adults | $65 ages 3-9 | 4-4.5 hours

Two-Reef Snorkel

Rating: n/a

Explore not one, but two of Costa Maya's beautiful coral reefs! After a brief transfer from the ship, you'll receive a safety briefing and all necessary gear. Then, it's off by boat to your first dive site. After 35 minutes beneath the waves you'll take a break and sip some soft drinks while the boat moves on to your next dive site, for another 35 minutes of exploration. Guests will enter the water from the boat and must be comfortable snorkeling in open water.

Sports | Moderate | Ages 6 & up | $68/adult | $55/ages 6-9 | 2.5-3 hours

Two-Tank Certified Dive

Rating: n/a

Certified scuba divers can explore the Mesoamerican Barrier Reef under the auspices of a PADI 5-Star Dive Center. All gear, including wet suits, is included. Guests must present a valid dive certification and photo ID on board the ship and on the day of the dive, and it's recommended that you've completed at least one dive in the past 12 months. Guests must be under 300 lbs., in good physical condition, and complete a medical questionnaire.

Sports | Active | Ages 12 & up | $139 | 4-4.5 hours

Falmouth, Jamaica
(Western Caribbean Itineraries)

Few islands conjure more mystique than this, the Caribbean's third-largest isle. Harry Belefonte's "Jamaica Farewell" and the reggae beat of Bob Marley, Rasta, and dreadlocks, the unmistakable patois, terraced waterfalls and pristine beaches, rum, coffee, savory jerk chicken, Olympic athletes... a **large island** that looms even larger in our minds!

© Yannick Lyn Fatt

Dunn's River Falls in Jamaica

AMBIENCE

Jamaica has **many faces**, from upscale beach resorts and stately remnants of a plantation-based aristocracy to the poverty of the countryside; from a pristine cruise pier marketplace to dusty local streets (within just a few blocks). Any Caribbean island can boast sea and sand, but few add river-running, from a tranquil float on a bamboo raft to modest whitewater in a rubber raft. The north coast's ample rainfall dissolves the underlying limestone, spawning waterfalls, caverns, and the unique hollows and conical hills of Cockpit Country, an area that protected rebellious ex-slaves and gave birth to Reggae's superstar. All this is within easy reach of Falmouth, whose bygone prosperity left it with a remarkable collection of Georgian-era buildings.

HISTORY

Before Columbus stepped ashore in 1494, Jamaica was inhabited by Arawak tribes. The British ended Spanish rule in 1655, and built a **slave-based plantation economy**. Jamaica became a top sugar producer, but harsh treatment of the slave population by planters, and the planters' refusal to change, were key factors leading to Britain's abolition of slavery in 1838. The economic crash that followed had a long-lasting effect on islanders. In 1957 Jamaica went from Crown Colony to self-governing member of the West Indies Federation, and in 1962 islanders voted to leave the Federation and received full independence from Great Britain.

FACTS

Size: Parish: 337 sq. mi. (874 sq. km.) Island: 4,244 sq. mi. (10,991 sq. km.)	
Climate: Tropical	**Temperatures:** 72°F (22°C) to 88°F (31°C)
Population: 2,889,187	**Busy Season:** December to April
Language: English/Jamaican Patois	**Money:** Jamaican Dollar (J$100 ≈ $1 US)
Time Zone: Eastern (no DST)	**Transportation:** taxi, bus
Phones Area Code 876 from US	Dial 119 for emergencies

Making the Most of Jamaica

GETTING THERE

On the north coast of Jamaica between Montego Bay and Ocho Rios, the **little port of Falmouth** opened to cruise ships in 2011. Built to berth two of Royal Caribbean's Oasis-class cruise ships at a time (currently the world's largest), the pier is bringing new life to a port that was once one of Jamaica's busiest. You'll find shops, restaurants, tourist information, and ground transportation within the 32-acre pier complex, with downtown businesses and sights just a short walk away. The Disney Magic visits Falmouth on Tuesdays in 2013, docks at Berth 1, and on most visits will be the only cruise ship in *any* Jamaican port. All-ashore time is 7:45 am, all-aboard is at 5:45 pm.

GETTING AROUND

Jamaica is a **large, mountainous island**, with over 9,320 mi./1,500 km of paved roads. Cars drive on the left-hand side, British-style. While car rentals are available from most agencies for pickup/dropoff in Falmouth, we don't recommend it. **Taxis** are plentiful. They may or may not have meters, but fares should be posted. As always, discuss the fare before you depart. Jamaican Tourist Board-licensed taxis have a JTB sticker on the windshield, and the drivers carry photo ID. "Route Taxis" have red license plates and lower, flat fares, but they can stop and pick up other passengers en route. Falmouth is under rapid re-development. While you can certainly walk around the compact town, you may prefer an organized walking or tram tour, or perhaps even a horse-drawn surrey, all of which can be found at the pier.

SAFETY

Jamaica has a reputation for its **high crime rate**, although it has been dropping. Crime is centered in the far distant Kingston area. Tourist areas are less affected, so regular precautions are advised; be alert (especially if carrying parcels), have a companion (or more), leave valuables in your stateroom (especially if headed to the beach), and don't forget your sun screen. The island is very well known for marijuana, both production and consumption. Note that posession and use of "ganja" is illegal, and cruise tourist or not, if arrested expect you'll go to jail. Vendors of legal goods and services tend to be aggressive. Be friendly but firm if you're not interested. Have some Jamaican currency in small denominations ($50 & $100 Jamaican), available at the pier and in town. While U.S. dollars are usually welcome, you may get Jamaican dollars as change. At the least, have plenty of small U.S. bills so you don't have to break a large one. While not exactly a safety tip, many Jamaicans do not want to be photographed. Please ask first!

Touring Jamaica

Falmouth is a small town with a prosperous past. Once a key port in the sugar trade, many 19th-century buildings survive, preserved because there was little economic activity since then. Its collection of historic buildings is one of the largest in the Caribbean. Seat of Trelawny Parish, the Barretts (of Wimple St. fame) were once the principal landowners. Water Square commemorates a municipal running water system that pre-dates New York City's!

Montego Bay 22 mi./36 km. west of Falmouth, has the island's busiest airport and biggest tourist trade. Known for its waterfront Hip Strip, quiet Cornwall Beach, and hoppin' Doctor's Bay Beach, "Mobay" is the jumping-off spot for most snorkel and scuba excursions.

Ocho Rios 45 mi./73 km. east of Falmouth, is one of Jamaica's top destinations. Attractions include oft-photographed Dunn's River Falls, excellent beaches, and scenic gardens. Mystic Mountain has a scenic chair lift, zip line, and bobsled adventure. Dolphin Cove offers dolphin experiences, animal exhibits, and "Little Port Royal" for pirate fans.

Negril: 68 mi./110 km., is nearly a two-hour drive. This resort area is widely known for its beaches, but it's not the most practical choice.

River-based fun: The Martha Brae River flows into Falmouth. You've seen the photos of bamboo rafts being poled down a narrow stream while passengers sit in straight-backed chairs? That's the place! Other streams, including Rio Bravo and White River, offer mild whtewater journeys by tube, raft, and inflatable kayak.

Great Houses: These estate houses record plantation life of years past. Good Hope Great House shows off its estate, serves-up food-focused experiences, and hosts a long list of adventure excursions. Greenwood displays its collection of antiques. Rose Hall, haunted by the White Witch, is inside a large resort. Croyden focuses on agriculture.

Beaches: There are no beaches within walking distance of the pier. Beautiful Burwood Beach is closest, 3.5 mi./5.7 km by cab. Facilities have been few, but things are changing fast. Beach excursions boasting a 10-minute ride from Falmouth come here or nearby Duncans. Several hotels offer beach breaks with full amenities, nearly every trip to Montego Bay includes a beach, and Shaw Beach is a stop on many Ocho Rios trips. Expect to pay admission to most, if you're not with a tour.

Embarking on Shore Excursions in Falmouth, Jamaica

At this writing, Disney Cruise Line has yet to release information about its shore excursions. **Here are our recommendations**, based on typical offerings:

Low Budget: It doesn't get cheaper than a walking or tram tour of "downtown" or a bare bones beach excursion, all are $25-$30. If offered, $70 to visit both Dunn's River Falls and Green Grotto Caves is a deal; a falls-only tour may cost the same. You may see similar low-priced add-ons to a Dunn's visit. $100 for a 7-hour tour that includes lunch is a deal, the catch is a trip to Bob Marley's Nine-Mile has you on the bus for 3-4 of those hours.

Big Budget: We expect Disney to offer tours in private vehicles, perhaps a helicopter flight or two ($100–$300), and probably several gourmet meal experiences at Good Hope Great House ($190–$300). If offered, the Iberostar Beach excursion will cost around $140 (the buffet had better be good)! Compared to some other Caribbean courses, $160 to golf at White Witch seems a bargain. Rainforest Adventures Mystic Mountain: You thought Disney parks were expensive? The skyride offers great views of Ocho Rios, and basic admission includes the pool and water slide. If you add the zipline and bobsled (just one ride on each), it'll cost around $140.

Nature: Dunn's River Falls is nearly a must-see; 25% of all excursions stop there. While it can get quite crowded when several large ships are in port, things should be quieter when Disney visits. If you head this way, pick an excursion that adds other activities, they'll be a much better value. Most nature excursions are fairly active (see below), but either Coyaba Gardens or Shaw Gardens may appeal to the less-energetic.

Active: This may be zip line paradise—we count five zip line operators in the area. It's hard to pick favorites, as many are bundled with other activities ($100 and up). We're partial to whitewater, so it's hard to resist a Rio Bravo or White River trip, on whatever float that suits your fancy ($80 and up). And there's something about horseback riding in the surf... ($100).

Armchair: What's more armchair than an armchair affixed to a bamboo raft on the Martha Brae River($70)? A tour to Appleton Rum Plantation ($140) takes you for a long drive through the Jamaican countryside.

On Your Own: Chukka operates a wide range of well-regarded tours—visit http://chukkacaribbean.com. Real Tours Jamaica is a transportation company organizing private tours to many popular attractions—visit http://www.realtoursjamaica.com. Jaital offers tours from many operator at competitive prices—visit http://www.jaital.com.

Cartagena
(Repositioning Itineraries)

Whether the name Cartagena conjures images of "Romancing the Stone" with Michael Douglas and Kathleen Turner, marauding pirates chasing Spanish gold, or less romantic images of drug cartel-related crime, Cartagena's popular image does not match the port city's reality. Upscale beach resorts, a glittering, high-rise skyline, and a beautifully preserved **old city** that has earned UNESCO World Heritage Site status will be more than enough to fill your eight hours ashore.

© Lobo

Castillo San Felipe de Barajas

AMBIENCE

This is a **vibrant, cosmopolitan city** with deep colonial roots and an optimistic future, as well as Colombia's number one tourist destination. Cartagena has a large harbor protected by barrier islands; a well-preserved Spanish Colonial old city; ancient fortresses; glamorous, densely packed beachfront high-rises; and glitzy shopping districts, yet pristine beaches and nature areas are a short drive (or sail) away.

HISTORY & CULTURE

When the Spanish Conquistadors plundered Peru and Colombia of its gold, it was hoarded and then loaded onto galleons in Cartagena. This appealing fact was not lost on privateers like Francis Drake, and even military forces from France and England. For years the marauders came and fortifications rose to defend the thriving port. Certainly, Walt Disney's **Pirates of the Caribbean** could have been inspired by Cartagena. Alas, the locals don't forgive or forget the actions of the British and French, or the American politicians who managed to wrest Panama from Colombia so the canal could be built without local involvement. Warfare has dominated recent Colombian history, although Cartagena was affected less than many other areas. Former President Alvaro Uribe receives credit for reducing violence and spurring the growth of the local economy, leading to Cartagena's return to the ranks of popular tourist destinations.

FACTS

Size: 235 sq. mi./609 sq. km.	
Climate: Tropical	**Temperatures**: 87°F (30°C) to 90°F (32°C)
Population: 895,000	**Busy Season**: November to March
Language: Spanish	**Money**: Colombian Peso (1,935 Pesos = $1 U.S.)
Time Zone: Eastern (DST observed)	**Transportation**: Walking, taxis, buses
Phones: Dial 112 for police, 132 for Red Cross, 113 for tourist info	

Making the Most of Cartagena

GETTING THERE

Your ship docks in the busy port's **Manga district**, in a modern container ship facility and close to an upscale neighborhood of luxury high-rise residences and yacht basins. You're a short drive from the old, walled city that will be visited by most excursions. All ashore is at 6:30 or 8:30 am, all aboard at 2:30 or 4:30 pm.

We generally recommend you **book a Disney shore excursion**, which takes care of all your transportation needs. If you want to venture out on your own, a **taxi tour** is popular. Know that taxis are not metered, but operate on a zone system. The minimum fare is around $2; a one-hour drive may cost $8. A taxi to the old city should cost about $5 one way. You will see several taxi drivers at the pier, but if you walk past them and out to the port gates, you'll find more taxis at better rates. Car rentals? Forget about it!

© Lobo

Cartagena bus

STAYING SAFE

All of Colombia is on the U.S. State Department's watch list, but violent crime isn't the problem movies and TV might lead you to believe. **Fleecing tourists**, on the other hand, appears to be high art. Colombian "emeralds," "Cuban" cigars, "Pre-Colombian" art and gold, money changing, picked pockets, swiped handbags, drug purchase shakedowns ... you name it, there seems to be a scam built around it. Naturally, the upscale, higher-priced shops are far more reputable, and you undoubtedly pay for the peace of mind. Look for "recommended" shops in your Shopping in Paradise guide. While limited to advertisers, at least the publisher's shopping guarantee offers some recourse. Note that you need an export permit for Pre-Colombian goods of any sort, but reputable dealers should explain that. Fakes, of course, don't require a permit—just make sure you paid a low, low price. Definitely carry only small bills of U.S. currency—getting change will be either expensive or mark you as a juicy target. Despite that, Cartagena is a very popular vacation destination. Fortunately, since you'll be on your way out of town before dark, will most likely be taking a guided excursion, won't talk to or make eye contact with hustlers or beggars, and won't be going off the beaten track (right?), you should be able to avoid major trouble.

Touring Cartagena

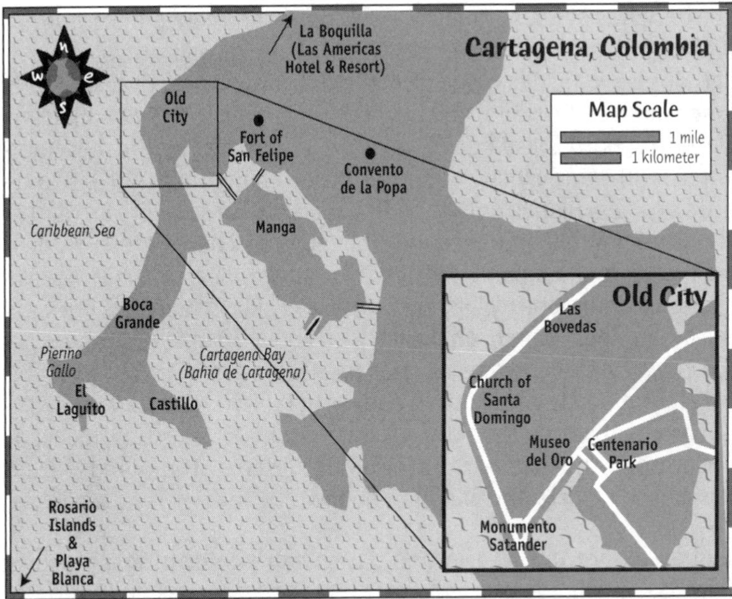

Popular spots visited by official shore excursions include the old city, with four neighborhoods packed within massive city walls; El Centro, with the greatest concentration of historic sites—its Plaza de Bolívar alone can keep you busy for hours, surrounded as it is by the Palace of the Inquisition, the Gold Museum, the Cathedral (Basilica Menor), and La Gobierno, seat of the State of Bolivar. The well-known Clock Tower and the Church and Monastery of San Pedro Claver are also here. Other districts are San Diego, La Matuna, and the oldest, Getsemani, with its large Parque del Centenario. La Popa Hill rises about 500 feet/150 meters above the city in a wooded setting, just a mile from El Centro and beachfront areas. Views from the hilltop Convent la Popa are quite dramatic. Between the walled city and la Popa looms massive Castillo San Felipe de Barajas (see photo on page 319), the largest Spanish fortress in the New World.

For **more information**, visit http://www.cartagenainfo.net, http://www.cartagenacaribe.com/en and http://gosouthamerica.about.com/od/cartagena/Cartagena_Colombia.htm—these are all useful sites for additional information on the city.

Playing in Cartagena

ACTIVITIES

The **beaches** of Bocagrande are well known and convenient, but not necessarily the best of the best. You'll have to visit on your own—perhaps a two-mile taxi ride from the ship. In-town beach excursions take you to La Boquilla, just beyond the airport to the northeast of El Centro. Both these beach areas are dominated by the adjoining hotels, with more elbow room to be had at La Boquilla. A trip to out-of-town Playa Blanca or Islas de Rosario promise far more attractive surroundings, but greatly reduce the time you'll have to tour in-town sights. La Boquilla (Las Americas Hotel) is the beach most offered as shore excursions by Disney Cruise Line. Playa Blanca is perhaps the area's finest beach, on Baru Island about 20 miles southwest of the city, often reached by a water taxi leaving from the edge of the old city (opposite the modern convention center). Islas de Rosario is a group of lightly developed islands about 20 miles southwest of El Centro, just offshore from larger Baru Island. The islands host a number of resorts and vacation homes.

Two areas are big on the one-day-visitor's **shopping map**: Las Bóvedas, an arcade of handcraft shops and galleries built into the north corner of the old city's walls in the San Diego district, and the Pierino Gallo shopping mall in Laguito at the far south end of Bocagrande—both are common tour group stops. Leather goods, jewelry, crafts, and antique shops are scattered about the old city for those with time to browse, and a budget-busting combination of high-end leather, fashion, and jewelry shops (emeralds and silver and gold, oh my!) lines Avenida San Martín in Bocagrande and the Pierino Gallo mall.

Popular tourist **destinations** include Manga, a large island in the harbor that is home to upscale residential development, historic forts, yacht clubs, and a modern container port (and the Wonder's moorings). Bocagrande (also, Boca Grande) is a long, beachfront peninsula directly to the southwest of El Centro, known for its hotels, shopping, dining, and waterfront promenade. Tierra Bomba is a large, mostly undeveloped island in the mouth of Bahía de Cartagena (Cartagena Bay), south of Bocagrande. The Fort of San Jose de Bocachica is situated on a small island just offshore of Tierra Bomba. Cienaga de la Virgen, a destination for eco-excursions, is a large lagoon just behind a strip of barrier-beach hotels, about a half-mile from the airport in the northwest corner of the city.

Introduction Reservations Staterooms Dining Activities Ports of Call Magic Index

Embarking on Shore Excursions in Cartagena

Best of Cartagena [CT01]

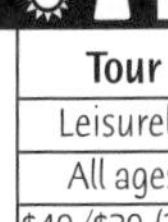

Travel to the center of Cartagena by motorcoach and marvel at the lush vegetation and hillsides that surround you. The first stop will be at Convento de la Popa, a 400-year-old monastery used as a meeting place by local Indians and runaway slaves. After 25 minutes, you'll travel to the largest Spanish fort built in the New World. Fort of San Felipe de Barajas was built in the 17th century with towering walls and sprawling grounds. Next explore the dungeons of Las Bovedas—originally built for storage, they are now occupied by vendors selling handcrafts and jewelry. You'll also visit San Pedro Claver Church and the Navy Museum of the Caribbean. Finish the excursion by traveling to Pierino Gallo mall for some sightseeing and shopping before traveling back to the ship.

Tour
Leisurely
All ages
$49/$39 (3-9)
4.5-5 hours

City Drive, Shopping, and La Popa [CT02]

Learn about the historical and cultural values of Cartagena as you travel by motorcoach to the city center. After the guided tour, stop at Convento de la Popa and marvel at the 400-year-old architecture and well-kept grounds. Next, walk to the dungeons of Las Bovedas filled with vendors selling handmade goods and crafts. Board the motorcoach again and view many colonial buildings and the new modern neighborhood of Bocagrande. Finally, stop at the Pierino Gallo shopping center for some shopping featuring gold, emeralds, and handcrafts, then enjoy the trip back to the ship.

Tour
Leisurely
All ages
$45/$35 (3-9)
3.5 hours

Deluxe Cartagena and Folkloric Show [CT03]

A short 20-minute drive will take you to the historic Convento de la Popa monastery. This 400-year-old structure was built on La Popa hill and acted as sanctuary for both local Indians and slaves. Next board the motorcoach and an experienced guide will point out different points of interest. You'll also visit the largest fort built by Spain in the New World, Fort of San Felipe de Barajas, the dungeons of Las Bovedas, and the Navy Museum of the Caribbean. You'll then be treated to a Colombian folklore show with traditional dances and songs. Finally, travel to Pierino Gallo shopping mall for shopping before returning to the ship.

Tour
Leisurely
All ages
$49/$32 (3-9)
5-5.5 hours

Historic Cartagena and Old City Walking Tour [CT04]

Start out by taking a 20-minute motorcoach ride to the center of Cartagena for a walking tour of the city's historic centers. See Plaza de Bolivar, a tree-lined square with statues representing Colombia's past. See Palaciao de la Inquisicion, housing torture chambers and jails used during the Spanish Inquisition. Visit Museo de Oro, or the Gold Museum, displaying over 600 pre-Colombian gold treasures. Visit the Church of Santo Domingo, Plaza de la Aduana, Plaza de la Proclamation, Plaza de la San Pedro Claver, and the dungeons of Las Bovedas, too.

Tour
Active
All ages
$39/$29 (3-9)
4.5-5 hours

Mangrove Caves Eco Tour [CT05]

Board an air-conditioned motorcoach for a scenic, 30-minute trip to Las Americas Hotel and Resort. Upon your arrival at the resort, you'll climb into a six-person canoe and glide among the swamps and mangroves of the Cienaga de la Virgen. Your guide will point out flora and fauna during your one-hour trip; the bird-watching is especially good. After the cruise, relax and enjoy a complimentary beverage before boarding the bus for the return trip, which includes 30 minutes of sight-seeing. Note that guests do not paddle the canoe.

Tour
Leisurely
All ages
$52/$42 (0-9)

Embarking on Shore Excursions in Cartagena *(continued)*

Tour of the Rosario Islands [CT06]

Take a speedboat ride past the beauty of the Colombian coast to the Rosario Islands to enjoy all that the Islands have to offer. Designated a National Natural Park, the Rosario Islands are made up of 27 islands boasting activities ranging from sightseeing to snorkeling. If you wish to snorkel, a small boat can take you to a nearby reef that is teeming with tropical fish and stunning coral formations. If snorkeling is not your thing, beaches are plentiful for swimming or relaxing in a cozy beach chair. Lunch and beverages are included.

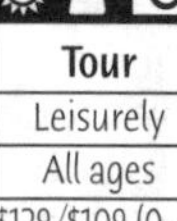

Tour
Leisurely
All ages
$129/$109 (0-9)
6-6.5 hours

Chiva Bus Panoramic Tour (Ages 21 and up)

Enjoy a festive tour in a brightly painted open-air Chiva bus and sing along with the live band on board! Snacks, beer, and soft drinks are served. You'll stop at historic San Filipe Fortress, and see the sights of the walled city and all around town. You'll stop for an hour at Santa Calatina's Bastion where the band will play (dance if you dare), you can enjoy local entertainers, or shop the Las Bovedas Artisan Center. Then it's back on the bus for another half-hour of touring before you return to the pier.

Tour
Leisurely
Ages 21 & up
$45
3-3.5 hours

Cartagena by Horse Carriage

Combine a bus tour of Cartagena with a one-hour carriage ride through the cobblestone streets of the walled city! Your motor coach will take you to San Felipe Fortress for a photo stop at one of the most important Spanish fortifications in the New World, then it's off again to see more of the city before arriving at Plaza Santa Theresa for your carriage ride. At ride's end you can shop at Las Bovedas before boarding the bus for the last half-hour of your tour. Note: Parties will be combined to fill each 4-passenger carriage.

Tour
Leisurely
All ages
49/$39 (0-9)
3.5-4 hours

Los Americas Pool and Beach Getaway [CT10]

Take a motorcoach through neighborhoods of elaborate mansions and old world architecture as you make your way to Las Americas Hotel and Resort. Once at the resort, enjoy a beverage and explore the grounds. Take a dip in the Atlantic Ocean or relax in a beach chair. If the ocean is not for you, swim in one of the resort's three pools, play a round of miniature golf, or enjoy a folkloric show. Then enjoy a mouth-watering buffet lunch consisting of grilled chicken, steak, fish, salad, dessert, and more. After lunch, rest a while before returning to the ship.

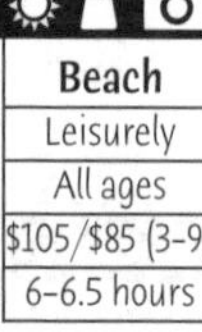

Beach
Leisurely
All ages
$105/$85 (3-9)
6-6.5 hours

Mangroves, Show, and Lunch [CT11]

As you travel by motorcoach to Las Americas Hotel and Resort, view the tropical landscapes that surround Cartagena. Once at the resort, board a canoe and follow your guide through the mangroves of Cienaga de la Virgen. View the canopies of trees, and as you glide through them smell the sweet scent of the flowers. Returning to the resort, you'll enjoy a buffet lunch and 3 hours of free time to enjoy the resort's beach and pools (see above). Your adventure concludes with a show featuring the folklore of Colombia's past before returning to the ship.

Tour
Leisurely
All ages
$129/$109 (0-9)
6.5-7 hours

See page 218 for a key to the shore excursion description charts and their icons.

Panama Canal
(Repositioning Itineraries)

Welcome to one of the great, **man-made wonders** of the world. While Disney Cruise passengers won't be debarking in Panama, the roughly eight hours spent traversing this fabled passage may be more eventful and fascinating than any other port along this grand voyage, with the possible exception of Los Angeles.

© MediaMarx, Inc.
Disney Magic transversing the Panama Canal

AMBIENCE

To a large extent, the tale of Panama is the **tale of the canal**, and you'll be witnessing it first-hand as your ship passes through its massive locks and cruises across man-made lakes and through a towering, man-made gorge. You'll follow in the footsteps of Spanish explorers, American railroaders, French canal-builders, and the most "bully" of American Presidents. You can only begin to imagine what the canal has meant to world growth and commerce as you contemplate the ships that had to sail 'round the Horn of South America in the era before the canal. And you can watch it all from the comfort of your verandah or from the height of deck 10.

HISTORY

The **notion for a canal** (and a route very close to today's actual path) goes back to the early days of Spanish rule. The explorer Vasco Nuñez de Balboa was the first to cross Panama (and "discover" the Pacific) in 1513. By 1534, King Carlos V of Spain commissioned a survey to plan a canal, which concluded that current technology wasn't up to the task. Gold from Peru and other Pacific Coast Spanish holdings crossed the isthmus by mule train instead. In the wake of the California Gold Rush of 1849, U.S. interests built a railroad across the narrow isthmus, so for the first time, transcontinental cargoes could bypass the long route around South America. However, passing goods from ship to rail and back to ship again wasn't the easiest or cheapest way to get things done.

Continued on next page

FACTS

Size: 50 miles/80 km. long	
Transit Time: 8 hours (with waiting time prior to entry, 24 hours)	
Gain in Altitude: 85 feet/26 meters	
Narrowest Channel: 630 feet/192 meters (in Gaillard Cut)	
Climate: Tropical	**Temperatures**: 79°F (26°C) to 84°F (34°C)
Time Zone: Eastern (DST not observed)	

Discovering the History of the Panama Canal

HISTORY (continued)

The **notion of a canal across Panama** was studied by the U.S. in the 1870s, but it was the French who moved it forward, fresh from their triumphal success building the Suez Canal and flush with the machinery and optimism of the Industrial Revolution. The same Ferdinand de Lesseps who led the construction of Suez leapt to the challenge of Panama, and Alexandre Gustave Eiffel (yes, the fellow responsible for the structural supports for the Statue of Liberty and the tower that bears his name) was among the French engineers involved. Alas, de Lesseps was overconfident and under-equipped—he originally aimed to build a sea-level canal, similar to the one he built in Egypt, with no locks at all, just a deep trench all the way across the isthmus. French investors poured huge sums into the 20-year project, but Panama's landslide-prone hillsides consumed all the money, while accidents and tropical diseases consumed the lives of more than 20,000 construction workers who had been recruited by the French from throughout the Caribbean basin. Confident from its military success in the Spanish American War and now a global power, the United States was more than eager to see the project finished for its military and commercial benefits. President Theodore Roosevelt led the charge. The government of Colombia, which then controlled the isthmus, wasn't well-inclined to let the U.S. follow in France's footsteps. So the U.S. lent its support to the local Panamanian independence movement and received the 50-mile-long, 10-mile-wide Panama Canal Zone as a thank you from the new nation. The U.S. paid the French $40 million to take ownership of the project, and placed the U.S. military in charge of construction. Learning from French mistakes, the Army engineers brought massive, innovative machinery to the task and chose to build a canal with locks and man-made lakes, rather than try to dig all the way down to sea level. At about the same time, Army surgeon Walter Reed (then stationed in Cuba), learned that mosquitoes were responsible for both Yellow Fever and Malaria. The canal project was among the first places this knowledge was applied, through a Herculean effort at controlling the insects' habitat and propagation. Without the improved health conditions, the canal may never have been finished. Although it's hard to believe, this huge government project actually came in under budget and six months ahead of schedule, opening with little fanfare (thanks to the start of World War I) on August 15, 1914, ten years after the U.S. started construction. Proving to be a masterwork of design and construction, the Panama Canal continued to operate under U.S. ownership until December 31, 1999, when the U.S. ceded the canal and the Canal Zone to the government of Panama.

Enjoying the Sights of the Panama Canal

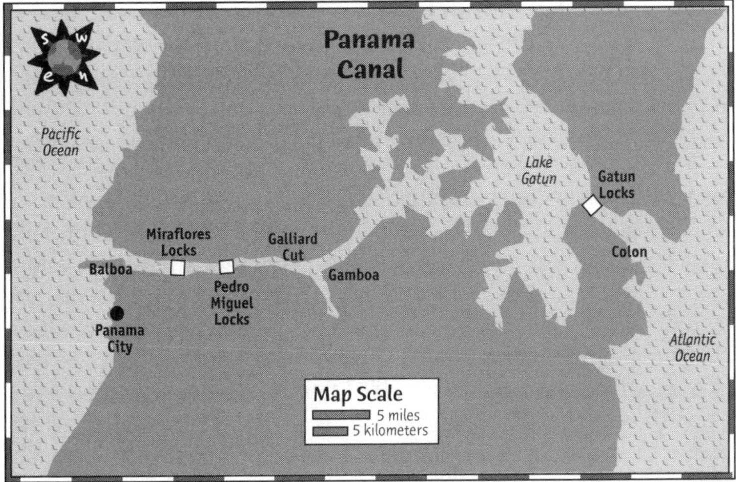

Whether your eyes are fixed on verdant hillsides or the mechanical marvels of the canal's locks, you'll be **viewing it all from the comfort of the ship**. The lower decks offer the most intimate view of your passage through the locks. Outside staterooms on decks 1 and 2, and public areas on deck 3, have an ultra-close-up view of the walls of the locks, until the ship rises above them. You can even catch some of the action from the windows in Parrot Cay during breakfast or lunch. Diversions on deck 3 forward, and the big portholes in Route 66, are also comfy viewing spots. Otherwise, we highly recommend heading to the promenade on deck 4. For those preferring a bird's-eye view, deck 10 has its advantages, and lunch on the deck behind Beach Blanket Buffet (deck 9 aft) is particularly scenic. Cruisers do crowd deck 10 forward, so consider abandoning that deck for a lower deck to see the action at the locks. In 2005, the Panama Canal Authority provided a tour guide on the Disney Magic as she passed through the canal, giving us all expert commentary over the ship's public address system.

Geographical Facts—Though we may casually imagine that the canal runs east/west between the Caribbean and Pacific, thanks to a little kink of geography, it actually runs from the Caribbean on the north to the Pacific on the south! The flood-prone Chagres River provides much of the water for the canal. A large dam and reservoir controls the river's flow into Gatun Lake, and from there, the river's waters flow into both the Caribbean and Pacific.

Knowing the Most About the Panama Canal

TIPS AND TRIVIA

When constructed, **Gatun Lake** was the largest man-made lake in the world, its dam the largest earthen dam on Earth, and the canal's locks were the largest structures ever built of concrete. More than 900,000 vessels have passed through the canal since it opened. More than 5% of the world's trade goods pass through every year.

No water pumps are required to fill and drain the lock chambers (66 million "gallons per flush"/250 million liters). Electrically controlled valves are opened and closed, and gravity does the rest in about eight minutes. Each chamber's water requirements are met by 18-foot/5.5-m. diameter water tunnels. • Up to eight custom-built electric locomotives help guide ships through each lock. • Electricity to operate the canal's locks and locomotives is generated by dams along the canal. • The Panama Canal is a two-lane "highway," with a pair of side-by-side lock chambers at every elevation. • The largest of the steel lock gates are 65 feet/19.8 m. wide, 82 feet/25 m. tall, and 7 feet/2.13 m. thick and weigh more than 662 tons/600 metric tons. • Each lock chamber is 1,000 feet/305 m. long and 110 feet/35 m. wide—the Magic Class ships are just 36 feet /11 m. shorter, and 6 feet/1.8 m. narrower than the locks.

What do we save by going through the Panama Canal instead of the **old route around the "horn" (southern tip) of South America**? More than 9,000 nautical miles/16,668 km., greater than the distance from Los Angeles to Hong Kong! Port Canaveral to Los Angeles 'round the Horn is approx. 14,500 mi./26,850 km. To look at it another way, the earth's circumference at the equator is 21,600 nautical miles/40,000 km. At her cruising speed of 21.5 knots (and ignoring stops at such fabled ports-of-call as Caracas, Rio de Janeiro, Montevideo, Santiago, and Lima), your ship would be at sea at least 20 more days. Not that more time on a Disney ship would be such a tragedy, but we'd also have to cope with some of the worst oceangoing weather on Earth. And since it'd be the depths of winter down at Cape Horn... no, we wouldn't want to go there!

The Magic Class ships' beam (width) and length are at the canal's (current) maximum size. That makes them **"Panamax" vessels**. There's now an entire class of "Post-Panamax" cruise ships, including the Disney Dream and Disney Fantasy, that can't fit through the canal at all. That will change in 2015, when the canal's huge expansion program is done.

Passing Through the Panama Canal

POINTS OF INTEREST

Here's a step-by-step description of the **canal's major points of interest**, in Caribbean-to-Pacific (westbound)order. Just work your way up from the bottom if you're on an eastbound sailing.

Colon—The second-largest city guards the canal's Caribbean entrance. Canal-bound ships pass the long Cristobal breakwater and one of the most extensive port facilities in the Caribbean.

Gatun Locks—Three successive lock chambers take ships from the Caribbean Sea to the canal's maximum altitude of 85 feet/26 m. All together, the lock complex is about a mile long, and each lock lifts the ship between 27 and 30 feet.

Gatun Lake—This was the world's largest man-made lake when built, at 163 mi. sq./422 km. sq. The water used to operate the canal is stored here and in a smaller lake and dam on the Chagres River. Various improvements have added an extra 2.5 ft. to the lake's depth, and dredging for the canal expansion project have substantially increased the canal's cargo capacity.

Gaillard Cut (Culebra Cut)—This 8.75-mi./14-km. man-made passage cuts through the ridge of hills that marks the Continental Divide. The cut runs from Gamboa on the north to the town of Pedro Miguel on the south. To cross the Continental Divide, a gap was punched through the lowest point (333.5 feet/102.26 m.) on the ridge connecting Gold Hill (587 feet/179 m.) on the east and Contractors Hill on the west. Landslides were a constant problem during construction and are still a concern today. Contractors Hill, named in honor of the companies that worked on the project, was originally 377 feet/115 m. tall, but it has been cut down to reduce the risk of landslides. Originally named for the nearby village of Culebra, the passage was renamed in honor of the engineer who led the American construction of this section of the canal. The channel has been enlarged several times during the canal's history. Two Panamax-sized ships can now pass in the night (or any other time). With more than a third of all ships passing through the canal Panamaxed-out, easy two-way traffic is critical to the efficient use of the canal.

Pedro Miguel Locks—One lock chamber moves ships in a single, 31-foot step between the canal's maximum elevation in the Gaillard Cut and Gatun Lake and the intermediate level of Miraflores Lake.

Passing Through the Panama Canal (cont.)

POINTS OF INTEREST

Miraflores Lake—This mile-long man-made lake is 45 feet above sea level and exists to connect the Pedro Miguel and Miraflores locks.

Miraflores Locks—Two lock chambers move ships in 27-foot steps between Miraflores Lake and the Pacific Ocean. The lower chamber of the two has the tallest gates on the canal, necessary to accommodate the Pacific's tidal variations. This is also the site of the canal's visitor center (not that we'll be landing to pay it a visit).

Balboa and Panama City—You're through the locks and headed to the Pacific! Dramatic Centennial Bridge crosses the channel, connecting Balboa to the west with Panama City to the east. Other sights include the Amador Causeway, a 3.25-mile-long breakwater built with rock from the construction of the Gaillard Cut, and the canal's Administration Building on a hill overlooking the canal.

Expansion Project—There's no missing the enormous construction underway so that larger ships can transit the canal. When done, a set of new locks will open a third lane for ships up to 1,200 ft./366 m. long, 160.7 ft./49 m. wide, and 50 ft./15.2 m draft. That's 235 ft. longer, 54.7 ft. wider, and 10.4 ft. deeper than before. The Dream Class ships are "merely" 1115 ft. long, 121 ft. wide, and 27 ft. draft.

COOL STUFF

You can get a **preview** of your Panama Canal crossing at the official Panama Canal web site at http://www.pancanal.com.

Wondering how we can get through the locks without bumping the sides when the ship is a mere 6 feet narrower than the locks themselves? While your ship moves under its own propulsion, four to eight small **railroad engines called "mules"** run along tracks on either side of the locks to keep the ship centered using attached cables. The mules can also help with towing and braking.

© MediaMarx, Inc.

A "mule" alongside the Disney Magic

From 2008 to 2010 the Disney Magic held the record for highest toll paid to pass through the Panama Canal, $331,200! And you thought the tolls on the New Jersey Turnpike were high!

Port of San Pedro (Los Angeles)

(West Coast Itineraries)

If you are anything like us, you may stay in San Pedro (also known as the Port of Los Angeles) for a day or so before or after your West Coast cruise. If you don't head up to Disneyland, you can stay in this convenient port town and partake of its **museums, shops, and eateries**.

San Pedro's Thomas Bridge and S.S. Lane Victory

AMBIENCE

Thanks to the natural harbor, the bustling port, and a revitalized downtown, San Pedro is the classic **port town**. Add to this its location at the edge of the Palos Verdes Peninsula with its majestic ocean vistas and cliffs, and you've got a scenic town that enjoys excellent weather year-round. In fact, San Pedro is a popular movie set location—"Pearl Harbor" was filmed here in 2001.

HISTORY & CULTURE

Before the arrival of the Portuguese, the San Pedro area was a **hunting ground for Indians**. When Juan Rodriguez Cabrillo arrived in 1542 and saw the smoke from Indians rising over the hillsides, he named the natural harbor here "Bahia de los Fumos" (Bay of Smokes). The area remained quiet until 1769, when the Spanish arrived to exploit the coastline and natural resources. San Pedro Bay prospered as a result of cargo shipping, though most of the cargo the ships carried was being smuggled. In 1848, the Americans stepped in to boost the cargo capacity of the harbor to meet the growing needs of Los Angeles. In fact, the San Pedro port is credited with bringing in most of the products needed to build Los Angeles. San Pedro continued to enjoy a booming trade until the Depression. World War II brought the port back to life as ship and aircraft builders manufactured more than 15 million tons of war equipment. Since the war, the Port of Los Angeles has grown into the largest cargo port in the U.S., handling both containers and passengers.

FACTS

Size: 7.7 sq. mi. (20 sq. km.) (water area is 18.5 sq. mi./47.8 sq. km.)	
Climate: Mediterranean	**Temperatures**: 66°F (19°C) to 76°F (24°C)
Population: 72,000	**Busy Season**: Summer
Language: English	**Money**: U.S. Dollar
Time Zone: Pacific (DST observed)	**Transportation**: Walking, cars, taxis
Phones: Dial 911 for emergencies; local phone call = 35 cents	

Exploring San Pedro

GETTING AROUND

You may be surprised to learn there's a fair amount to see and do in San Pedro. And whether or not you have a rental car, you should check out the **Red Car** trolley, which makes stops along the length of Harbor Blvd. These replica trolley cars resurrect a part of the original Pacific Electric San Pedro Line that took passengers to the piers. Movie fans may recall the Red Car from "Who Framed Roger Rabbit." The cars now make four stops on their 1.5-mile run—the cruise terminal, downtown, Ports O' Call Village, and the marina. An unlimited, one-day pass is $1.00 for ages 7+ (you'll need exact change as you board). The cars operate from Noon to 9:30 pm, Friday through Sunday (and other days when cruise ships are in port). Details are at http://www.sanpedro.com/spcom/redcar.htm or phone 310-732-3473.

HIGHLIGHTS

Downtown San Pedro fills a rectangle bounded by 6th Street and 7th Street, Harbor Blvd. and Pacific Ave. Here you'll find a variety of restaurants and shops. Highlights include The Whale & Ale Pub and Williams' Book Store (founded in 1909). On the waterfront at the base of 6th Street is the **Los Angeles Maritime Museum**. The 75,000 sq. ft. museum focuses on the maritime history of coastal California, featuring more than 700 ships, boat models, and equipment. It's open every day except Monday, from 10:00 am to 5:00 pm. Adults are $3, teens and seniors are $1, and kids are free http://www.lamaritimemuseum.org. Next door is **Fire Station #112**, which houses a classic, 99-foot-long fireboat and various fireboat-related exhibits. Admission is free. • New to San Pedro is the battleship USS Iowa. She's docked right next to the cruise terminal and is open daily from 9:00 am to 5:00 pm. Tours, interactive exhibits, and "virtual battle" experiences are on the menu. Admission is $18 for adults, $10 for ages 6-17. http://www.pacificbattleship.com • The **Ports O' Call Village** is a New England-style seaside mall with shops and restaurants, which are spread out over 15 acres. There's a boardwalk along the waterfront, with one seafood restaurant after another, many with outdoor seating overlooking the ship channel. The area has seen better days, but hopes of renovation lie just around the corner. • **The Korean Bell of Friendship** in Angels Gate Park is a worthwhile stop if you have some time. The huge bronze bell in its open air pavilion is surrounded by formal gardens and expansive, hilltop views of the Pacific, the harbor, and the rugged coastline. • For more information, visit http://www.sanpedro.com.

Exploring San Pedro
(continued)

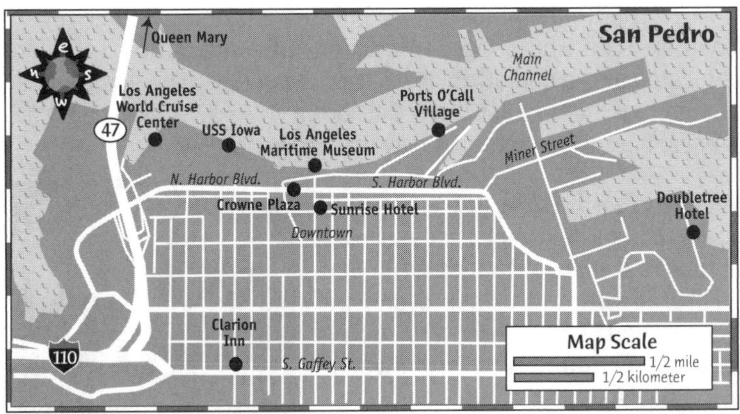

SAN PEDRO MAP

WALKING TOUR

San Pedro is a great place for a walking/trolley tour! We suggest you **begin your tour downtown**—drive or take a Red Car to the downtown stop and begin walking west along 7th St. Stop for coffee and pastry (or even goulash) at Mishi's Strudel (309 W. 7th). When you get to Pacific Ave., turn north (right) and walk one block to 6th St. and turn right again. Right here at the corner is the Warner Grand Theatre, a restored performing arts and film center. At the bottom of 6th St. is the U.S.S. Los Angeles Naval Memorial with a mast and anchors from the battleship/cruiser U.S.S. Los Angeles. Next door is the Maritime Museum, described on the previous page. Turn left and walk north along Harbor Blvd. passing several statues and memorials, to the USS Iowa. Retrace your steps to 6th St., hop on the Red Car and take it north to the end of the line, by the cruise terminal. Enjoy Fanfare at San Pedro Gateway, a beautiful fountain, music, and light show, and walk over to the SS Lane Victory, a World War II cargo ship/museum. Get back on the trolley and take it south to Ports O' Call Village. Pick a nice spot for lunch or an early dinner, browse the shops, and soak up the atmosphere. When you're done, you can reboard the Red Car if you like. If you have the time, head to the **Cabrillo Marine Aquarium** in Cabrillo Coastal Park (shuttles may be available from the 22nd St. Red Car stop).The park includes a beach, fishing pier, and preserved natural habitats. The compact aquarium features local marine animals in 38 saltwater displays, including a "touch tank." The aquarium is open daily from noon to 5:00 pm (open at 10:00 am on weekends). Admission is free (but they ask for a donation of $5); parking is $1/hour (max $15/day). For details, visit http://www.cabrilloaq.org.

Beyond San Pedro

ATTRACTIONS

One of the great things about San Pedro is that virtually every Southern California attraction is within a **30-mile radius**. San Pedro is located at the end of the Harbor Freeway (110) and affords easy access to the entire Southern California Freeway system. Here are some places we expect you may want to visit:

Disneyland Resort—We know many of you will pay Disneyland a visit—it's a mere 20 miles from San Pedro. If you don't have a car, we suggest you use a shuttle service (see page 99). You'll find our award-winning *PassPorter's Disneyland Resort and Southern California Attractions* guidebook very helpful in making travel, hotel, and touring plans. For official Disneyland information, visit http://www.disneyland.com or call 714-781-4565.

© MediaMarx, Inc.

Sleeping Beauty Castle at Disneyland Park

RMS Queen Mary—This famous cruise ship is permanently berthed in Long Beach, San Pedro's next door neighbor (take Hwy. 47 east). You can take guided "shipwalk" tours, explore historical exhibits, have a meal, and even sleep aboard this historic, Art Deco ocean liner. Hotel rates begin at $139/night for an inside stateroom up to $700+/night for a Royalty Suite. For more information, see our detailed description on page 101.

Catalina Island—You can catch the Catalina Express (800-481-3470, http://www.catalinaexpress.com), for a 1 hour and 15 minute boat trip to the beautiful, 76 sq. mi. Catalina Island. There's plenty to explore here, including The Casino (not a gambling casino, but rather a museum and art gallery), plus diving, golf, eco-tours, parasailing, snorkeling, and swimming. For more information, visit http://www.visitcatalina.org.

What else is within a **reasonable distance**? Knott's Berry Farm, Universal Studios, Venice, Malibu, Beverly Hills, Hollywood, the Los Angeles Convention Center, the Rose Bowl, and Dodger Stadium. All are described in more detail in *PassPorter's Disneyland Resort and Southern California Attractions* guidebook (see page 489).

Introduction Reservations Staterooms Dining Activities Ports of Call Magic Index

Puerto Vallarta
(Repositioning Itineraries)

© Corel

The town clock in Puerto Vallarta

The romance of the Mexican Riviera awaits you in sun-drenched Puerto Vallarta, the quintessential Mexican beach resort town. As the sixth most popular travel destination in the world, it boasts world-class resorts, palm-fringed beaches, lush tropical vegetation, and the Sierra Madre mountains. Despite its popularity and size, it manages to retain the **charm of Old Mexico** with cobblestone streets, white-walled houses, wrought-iron balconies, and red tiled roofs.

AMBIENCE

Puerto Vallarta is nestled along the shores of the second largest bay on the North American continent, Bahia de Banderas. It enjoys more than 300 days of sunny weather each year, offering visitors an array of activities along its **100 miles of coastline** and around the majestic Sierra Madre Mountains. The romance of Puerto Vallarta is realized with a stroll down The Malecón, a mile-long oceanfront boardwalk—it begins near the first hotel built in the 1940s and ends at "Los Arcos," an open-air theater.

HISTORY & CULTURE

Unlike many other ports with long, rich histories, Puerto Vallarta's recorded history goes back only as far as 1850 when Guadalupe Sanchez began farming here. It was known as "Puerto las Peñas" until 1918 when it was officially designated as a municipality and named after Don Ignacio Vallarta, a state governor. For the next 30 years, it remained a **sleepy little fishing village** without any inroads—the only access was by boat or air. After World War II, American G.I.s relocated to the area, setting up businesses or retiring. But it was Hollywood that put Puerto Vallarta on the map when John Huston filmed "The Night of the Iguana" with Ava Gardner and Richard Burton in nearby Mismaloya Beach in 1963. After the movie, tourism dollars poured in and first-class hotels were constructed. Today, the city sees more than two millions tourists each year.

FACTS

Size: 670 sq. miles/1735 sq. km.	
Climate: Semi-tropical	**Temperatures:** 71°F (22°C) to 83°F (28°C)
Population: 350,000	**Busy Season:** November to May
Language: Spanish, English	**Money:** Mexican Peso (12 Pesos = $1 U.S.)
Time Zone: Central (DST observed)	**Transportation:** Walking, taxis, buses
Phones: Dial 011- from U.S.; dial 060 for emergencies; dial 2220123 for police	

Making the Most of Puerto Vallarta

GETTING THERE

Your ship docks at the **Terminal Maritima** (Maritime Terminal) three miles north of downtown. The Disney Wonder pulls right up to the pier. Cruises are scheduled to arrive at 7:30 am and depart at 5:30 pm. There's not much you can do right at the pier other than shop or board excursion boats. There's a fairly large, tourist-focused flea market at the terminal's south end, and believe it or not, Wal-Mart and Sam's Club are right across the street if you need to pick up some familiar essentials.

GETTING AROUND

Taxis charge about $2/person for the 15-minute ride to downtown Puerto Vallarta. You can also rent a car—a Dollar Rental Car agency is right at the port. Buses are the least expensive way to move around, and they are really quite easy. A bus ride is just 4 pesos (50 cents) and drivers accept American currency. You can catch a bus going to "Centro" (downtown) at the stop just outside the port entrance. Buses are owned by individuals rather than a company, so don't be surprised to encounter some quirky but amusing bus decor. The Puerto Vallarta region encompasses a large area—much too large to show on our map. Pick up a regional map at a tourist information center once you're off the ship. Beyond downtown, popular spots to visit include Mismaloya (John Huston's film site and spectacular views) and Old Vallarta (also known as the Romantic Zone, it evokes that ol' Mexican charm)—these are both within taxi distance, though you may feel more comfortable booking one of the many excursions.

STAYING SAFE

Crime in Mexico has been rising in recent years. Take the same precautions you would in any large U.S. city, keeping valuables out of sight and your money secure. You may be accosted by kids selling "Chiclets" (gum) or other items. Don't buy from them or give them money. Support programs are in place for these children to help get them off the street. There are **bilingual tourist police in the downtown and resort areas**—they are dressed in white and wear pith helmets or black baseball caps. Don't hesitate to approach them if you need assistance. The drinking water in Puerto Vallarta consistently exceeds World Health Organization's criteria, but bottled water is also plentiful. Observe warning flags on beaches—if black flags are up, don't go in the water. Jellyfish can be a problem during the warmest summer months, but the Wonder's schedule means you'll probably miss them. Still, if you know you or a family member are allergic, take appropriate precautions.

Touring Puerto Vallarta

PUERTO VALLARTA MAP

WALKING TOUR

You can begin a good walking tour of "**Viejo Vallarta**" (old downtown Vallarta) by taking a taxi or bus into town and starting at Hotel Rosita, Puerto Vallarta's first hotel. The Malecón boardwalk (which, interestingly, has no boards) begins here—follow it to enjoy the beautiful ocean views and shops lined up across the street. Along the boardwalk are some famous sculptures, including "La Nostalgia" (a sculpture of a man and woman gazing off toward the ocean) and "The Seahorse." At the end of the Malecón you'll find Los Arcos, an outdoor amphitheater with four arches. Turn left here and cross the street to the "Plaza Principal" (Main Square)—you'll see City Hall on one side, banks and shops on the other, and a large gazebo where you can sit and listen to the Mariachi musicians who hang out at the square. From the square, walk one block east to Hidalgo, where you can see the gorgeous Church of Our Lady of Guadalupe—from here, turn left onto steep Zaragoza and climb up to Casa Kimberley at Zaragoza 446, the house Richard Burton bought for Elizabeth Taylor (check out the bridge!). This area is known as Gringo Gulch because it's where many foreigners settled in the "old" days post-World War II. Keep walking along Zaragoza to Miramar, then walk one block to Libertad to find the "Mercado Municipal" (City Flea Market) with plenty of t-shirts, silver, and trinkets. When you're done shopping, walk back along Miramar, turn left on Guerror (lots of shops here), then left again onto Hidalgo. The street becomes Guadalupe Sanchez—several landmarks are here, including the Café des Artistes restaurant and Casa de la Torre. Turn left at Allende, walk two blocks, and you'll be back at the Malecón. Walk back along the Malecón or take a taxi back to the pier.

Playing in Puerto Vallarta

ACTIVITIES

Wondering about those **famous golden beaches**? There are more than a dozen sandy beaches fringed with palm trees bordering Banderas Bay. The closest beach to the pier is Playa de Oro, which is a wide sandy beach with a few rocky areas—it's popular with both locals and tourists. Puerto Vallarta's most popular beach is Playa de los Muertos, south of the downtown area in "Zona Romantica" (Romantic Zone). There are plenty of services here, including restaurants, shops, and tube and toy rentals. While you're here, walk to the east end of Calle Pulpito for a lookout over the bay.

There are seven **golf courses** within 18 miles of the city—the closest course to the pier is Marina Vallarta Club de Golf (221-0073). There's also the new Vista Vallarta Golf Club about 10–15 minutes away, with courses by Jack Nicklaus and Tom Weiskopf. For more information, visit http://www.golfinvallarta.com.

You can do some good **deep-sea sportfishing** for marlin, snapper, and sailfish. Fishing boat charters can be hired at most beaches, or take an excursion.

Whale watching season runs from December 15 through March 15 (see page 343).

Diving is also available in Banderas Bay and in the Marietas Islands wildlife reserves. We recommend you take the Disney excursion or go through Vallarta Adventures (see description on page 340).

We hear that **shopping** isn't quite as good here as in other ports, but it certainly is available nonetheless. Beyond the beach vendors, there's the City Flea Market (see previous page) and plenty of little shops downtown and along the Malecón. The galleries in Puerto Vallarta are particularly good, and the local artists are plentiful.

If you're looking for a **good lunch or early dinner**, try Trio Cafe (Mediterranean, 222-2196) in downtown Puerto Vallarta. And yes, there is a Hard Rock Cafe (222-2230) and Planet Hollywood (223-2710) in town as well.

To explore Puerto Vallarta **on your own**, we suggest you visit http://www.puertovallarta.net. There are even fun webcams at http://www.puertovallarta.net/interactive/webcam/index.php

Embarking on Shore Excursions in Puerto Vallarta

Disney offered the following shore excursions at press time:

Tropical Rainforest by Horseback [PV02]

Become a "charro" (cowboy)! Travel 45 minutes to a working ranch and saddle up a horse suited to your size and ability (even beginners). After orientation, you'll ride on horseback (wooden saddle) through orchards and jungles to a 60-foot waterfall, where you can swim and rest. You'll then ride back and enjoy a lunch with free soft drinks. Guests must be in good physical condition and weigh no more than 250 lbs. Closed-toe shoes and long pants are recommended. Riding helmets are provided. Wear swimwear under clothes. Typical meeting time is 9:15 am.

Sports
Very active
Ages 12 & up
$95
6.25 hours

Paradise Beach Adventure [PV03]

Visit the Paradise Village Beach Resort in Nuevo Vallarta for relaxing, swimming, playing beach volleyball, and exploring underwater caves, Mayan-style pyramids, and a small zoo. The included buffet lunch features fajitas, burgers, chicken, seafood, three beverages (including beer), lounge chair, umbrella, and the use of an ocean kayak is included. The resort offers a swimming pool with two water slides. Complimentary lockers (deposit required). 20-minute ride to and from the resort. Typical meeting times are 7:40 am and 12:40 pm.

Beach
Leisurely
All ages
$69/$34 (3-9)
5-5.5 hours

Puerto Vallarta City Tour [PV04]

Enjoy a walking tour of Puerto Vallarta. After a 20-minute scenic ride, your tour begins in the center of town and you'll visit the Malecón (seawall), historic buildings, and Our Lady of Guadalupe cathedral. You'll then take a 30-minute ride to an eatery for complimentary drinks and snacks—local crafts are on display, and there's a piñata party for the kids. After the tour, you can choose to stay downtown to shop or explore (if you do stay, you'll need to find your own way back to the dock). Typical meeting times are 8:40 am and 12:50 pm.

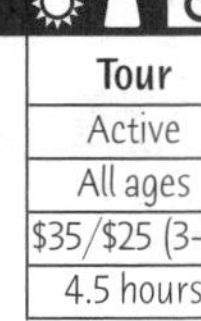

Tour
Active
All ages
$35/$25 (3-9)
4.5 hours

Discover Scuba at Las Caletas

Beginners, get a full-day taste of scuba diving with PADI-certified instructors! A scenic catamaran cruise takes you to Las Caletas Cove for land- and pool-based training (all equipment provided), followed by a one-tank dive in the cove (does not qualify for PADI certification). Afterwards you'll have a BBQ lunch with soft drinks and alcoholic beverages (included) and time to enjoy the beach at Las Caletas before sailing back to the ship. Medical form required, maximum weight 250 lbs. (On Your Own: http://www.vallarta-adventures.com)

Sports
Very active
Ages 12 & up
$129
7-7.5 hours

Historic Towns and Tequila Making [PV07]

Want to see the more traditional side of Mexico? This van tour takes you to the village of Mezcales to visit a tequila refinery that still makes its liquor by hand. Cruisers 21 and over can sample tequila and try their hand at agave-mashing. Then it's over to Porvenir to sample tortillas. From there you go to San Juan to see the village's church and plaza. You'll also visit El Valle before driving to a restaurant for a complimentary lunch. Your last stop will be a woodcarving studio before the 40-minute ride back to the ship. Typical meeting time is 9:20 am.

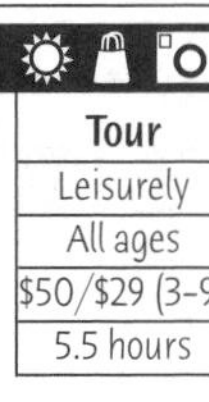

Tour
Leisurely
All ages
$50/$29 (3-9)
5.5 hours

See page 218 for a key to the shore excursion description charts and their icons.

Embarking on Shore Excursions in Puerto Vallarta *(continued)*

Extreme Canopy Adventure [PV08]

Sports
Very active
Ages 8 & up
$129
5.5-6 hours

You can make-believe you're Tarzan on this unique excursion. A 5-minute boat ride and 50-minute bus ride get you to a rainforest with a series of 90-foot high platforms and zip lines. After safety instructions and equipment are received, you'll zip from platform to platform along the cables to marvel at the rainforest wonders below. There are 14 observation platforms, 8 horizontal traverses, a "Tarzan" swing, hanging bridges, and vertical descents (rappel). That's not enough? Ride the jungle waterslide or take a Polaris ATV around the jungle course (drivers must be 18 and licensed). Afterwards you'll receive complimentary snacks. This is for guests at least 48 in./122 cm. tall and under 250 pounds who are physically fit; you must wear closed-toe shoes and long shorts/pants. If you bring a bag, it should be a backpack. (On Your Own: Vallarta Adventures, http://www.vallarta-adventures.com)

Marietas Islands Snorkel and Kayak Tour [PV09]

Sports
Very active
Ages 8 & up
$75/adults
$40/ages 8-9
7-7.5 hours

Enjoy a 90-minute catamaran ride through Banderas Bay to the Marietas Islands, a national wildlife preserve. At the reserve you'll embark on a guided bird-watching trip (by boat), after which it is time to explore by kayak and snorkel. All necessary equipment and instruction is provided. A complimentary light breakfast and deli-style lunch are served, including beverages. After lunch visit a secluded beach, where you can relax, swim, and take a guided nature walk. Available March 15–December 15. Typical meeting time is 8:15 am.

Scuba Dive Marietas Islands for Certified Divers Only [PV10]

Sports
Very active
Ages 12 & up
$115
7-7.5 hours

Take the same 90-minute catamaran ride described above to the Marietas Islands for some of the best in Mexican diving. All equipment (including wet suit) is provided for this 40-minute dive down to 60 feet. Afterwards, the group moves to another site for snorkeling. Complimentary light breakfast, deli-style lunch, and beverages are served. Afterwards, relax on a secluded beach before your journey back. Must show certification and have logged a dive in the last year. Maximum weight 250 lbs. Typical meeting time is 8:15 am.

Dolphin Encounter [PV10]

Sports
Active
Ages 3 & up
$125/adults
$105/ages 3-9
3-3.5 hours

This is your chance for a hands-on encounter with a dolphin! You'll take a 25-minute ride to Nuevo Vallarta Marina where you'll learn about dolphins and stand in waist-deep water to meet Pacific Bottlenose dolphins. Your 20-minute encounter will include a dolphin kiss! Includes lunch and soda. Guests must be at least 53 in./135 cm. tall or held by a parent. No sunscreen, jewelry or cameras in the pool. Children under 12 must be accompanied by a parent booked on the same excursion. Typical meeting times are 9:00 am, 11:00 am,

Dolphin Kids [PV12]

Sports
Active
Ages 4-8
$105
3-3.5 hours

This is the same excursion as described above but geared towards kids ages 4–8 who are accompanied by a parent (parents are required to purchase the Dolphin Observer excursion—see next page). Kids will be in knee-deep water and will have a chance to feed, pet, hug, and dance with the dolphins. Kids must not wear sunscreen or jewelry or take cameras into the pools. Includes lunch and sparkling soda. Typical meeting times are 9:00 am and 11:00 am.

See page 218 for a key to the shore excursion description charts and their icons.

Embarking on Shore Excursions in Puerto Vallarta *(continued)*

Dolphin Swim Experience [PV13]

This is similar to the Dolphin Encounter on the previous page, but in-water time is 30 minutes and includes a belly ride with a dolphin (lifejackets are provided on request). Includes lunch and sparkling soda. No cameras in the pool, but photos are allowed from the observation deck. Guests must be at least 53 in./135 cm. tall or held by a parent. No sunscreen, jewelry or cameras in the pool. Includes lunch and soda. Children under 12 must be accompanied by a parent booked on the same excursion. Typical meeting times are 9:00 am, 11:00 am, noon, and 3:00 pm.

Sports
Active
Ages 5 & up
$175/ $155 (5-9)
3-3.5 hours

Dolphin Trainer For a Day [PV23]

This is a unique opportunity to learn the basics of training dolphins and sea lions at the Dolphin Adventure Center. Upon arrival you will change into a trainer's uniform and follow the dolphin training team as they perform their daily activities. You will visit the food preparation facility and life support systems. Then, it's on to the Sea Lion Encounter (see below). Afterwards, you'll meet with the on-site vet for some dolphin anatomy lessons, followed by a 45-minute in-water session with the baby dolphins and a 40-minute, one-of-a-kind dolphin swim. In this swim, you will get one-on-one experience with dolphins as they swim and "dance" around you. Includes an authentic Mexican lunch. Guests under 18 must be accompanied by a parent on this or the Dolphin Observer excursion.

Sports
Active
Ages 12 & up
$325
6.5-7 hours

Sea Lion Encounter [PV26]

Located at the Dolphin Adventure Center in Nuevo Vallarta is a special sea lion encounter experience you won't soon forget. You first meet with a marine mammal trainer who goes over the basic anatomy and physiology of sea lions. Then with the assistance of the trainer, you are taken to a shallow pool, where you have 20 minutes to pet and touch sea lions. Afterwards, you will be served a buffet lunch. Guests must be at least 53 in./135 cm. tall or held by a parent. No sunscreen, jewelry or cameras in the pool. Includes lunch and soda. Children under 12 must be accompanied by a parent booked on the same excursion.

Sports
Active
Ages 5 & up
$89/$79 (5-9)
3-3.5 hours

Dolphin & Sea Lion Observer [PV14]

If you want to accompany your friends or family on one of the dolphin or sea lion excursions previously mentioned, but don't want to get in the water or just want to watch, this is the one for you. You can ride with them to and from the marina and watch them interact in the water with the dolphins or sea lions from a distance. Includes lunch and sparkling soda. (On Your Own: Dolphin Adventure, http://www.dolphin-adventure.com, 866-256-2739)

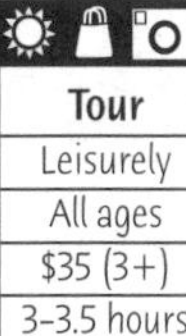

Tour
Leisurely
All ages
$35 (3+)
3-3.5 hours

Dolphin Signature Swim

This is similar to the Dolphin Swim Experience above, but in-water time is 40 minutes, there's an added dorsal tow swim, and a reduced dolphin-to-guest ratio. Includes lunch and sparkling soda. No cameras in the pool, but photos are allowed from the observation deck. Guests must be at least 53 in./135 cm. tall or held by a parent. No sunscreen, jewelry or cameras in the pool. Includes lunch and soda. Children under 12 must be accompanied by a parent booked on the same excursion.

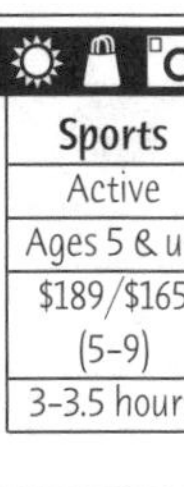

Sports
Active
Ages 5 & up
$189/$165 (5-9)
3-3.5 hours

See page 218 for a key to the shore excursion description charts and their icons.

Embarking on Shore Excursions in Puerto Vallarta *(continued)*

☐ Las Caletas Hideaway [PV15]

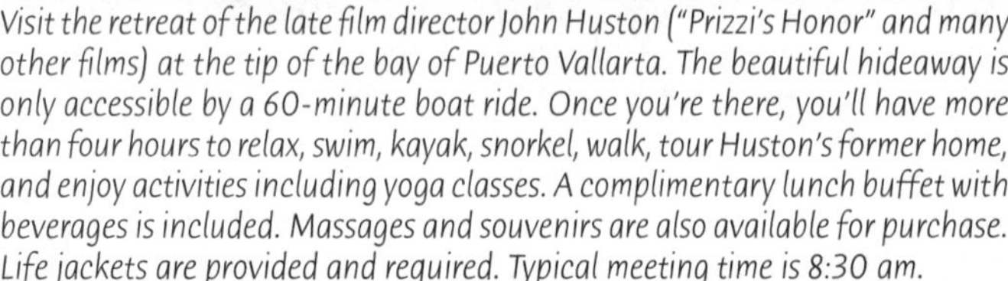

Visit the retreat of the late film director John Huston ("Prizzi's Honor" and many other films) at the tip of the bay of Puerto Vallarta. The beautiful hideaway is only accessible by a 60-minute boat ride. Once you're there, you'll have more than four hours to relax, swim, kayak, snorkel, walk, tour Huston's former home, and enjoy activities including yoga classes. A complimentary lunch buffet with beverages is included. Massages and souvenirs are also available for purchase. Life jackets are provided and required. Typical meeting time is 8:30 am.

- Beach/Tour
- Leisurely
- All ages up
- $95/$65 (0-9)
- 7-7.5 hours

☐ Banderas Bay Private Sailing Charter [PV16]

Learn the basics of sailing on a private charter, monohull, single-mast sailboat (50- or 47-foot). Your captain and first mate will sail you north while you relax and enjoy complimentary beverages and fresh fruit. You'll arrive at a secluded beach where you can relax, swim, or snorkel for two hours. After a gourmet-style deli lunch served onboard, you'll sail back to the ship. Humpback whale sightings are common December 15–March 15. Everyone has the chance to help sail the craft. 16 guests maximum. Typical meeting time is 9:55 am. Note that you must download and submit a special request form from Disney's web site.

- Sports
- Active
- Ages 5 & up
- $1,899/boat
- 6-6.5 hours

☒ Pirate Boat Sail and Snorkel Adventure [PV19]

Here be pirates! Board the pirate ship "Marigalante" for a rousing good time. Your wacky pirate Captain Crispin and his friendly crew will treat you to breakfast, dancing, pirate contests, and surprises during the two-hour cruise to Majahuitas Beach. On dry land, you'll have two hours to swim, snorkel, kayak, and relax (equipment is provided). Volleyball, beach games, and a sand sculpture contest are held at the beach, too. Back onboard you'll enjoy a BBQ lunch, a pirate show, and a fiesta during the two-hour cruise back to the dock. Typical meeting time is 8:00 am. (On Your Own: Marigalante Pirate Ship, http://www.marigalante.com.mx, 322-223-0309)

- **Sports**
- Active
- All ages
- $85/$65 (0-9)
- 6.5-7 hours

☐ Yelapa & Majahuitas [PV28]

Snorkeling and sightseeing is in store for you on this excursion. First, enjoy a scenic 75-minute catamaran cruise along the coast of Banderas Bay. You will see Las Caletas, the famed marine geyser. You'll drop anchor in a secluded cove in Majahuitas for a 45-minute guided snorkel tour and kayaking (equipment included). Afterward, you will visit the seaside village of Yelapa for a guided, jungle hike to the magnificent Cola de Caballo waterfalls. You will have about 2.5 hours in Yelapa before returning to the catamaran for lunch during the journey back to the ship. Guests must be at least 8 years of age to participate in snorkeling.

- **Tour/Sports**
- Active
- Ages 5 & up
- $75/$39 (5-9)
- 7-7.5 hours

☐ Sea Safari: Horseback Riding, Snorkeling, and Paradise Beaches

Enjoy a 45-minute powerboat ride along the Mexican coastline to Quimixto. Once here, you will venture on a guided horseback ride through the jungle to the 100-foot-high waterfalls in Tecomata. Then you'll travel by sea to the small seaside village of Pizota, where you can swim, snorkel, and kayak (equipment provided). If you don't want to get in the water, there is a hiking trail that will lead you through a tropical forest. By now you've worked up an appetite, and a buffet lunch is provided for you before the cruise back to the ship.

- **Tour/Sports**
- Active
- Ages 12 & up
- $110
- 6.5-7 hours

➢

Embarking on Shore Excursions in Puerto Vallarta *(continued)*

Banderas Bay Snorkeling Treasure Hunt [PV31]

Board a 68-foot schooner and sail along the coastline of Puerto Vallarta to reach a large rock formation known as Los Arcos. In one of Mexico's best snorkeling areas, you will snorkel past expansive coral formations as you look for underwater clues to help you with your treasure hunt. Back on board the schooner, scores will be tabulated and awards will be given to those who found the hidden treasure. On the journey back to the ship, snacks and beverages will be served.

Sports | Moderate | Ages 5 & up | $69/$59 (10-11) | 4-4.5 hours

Outdoor Adventure [PV24]

A short speedboat ride across Banderas Bay will take you to the shores of Boca de Tomatlan. Here, you will board an all-terrain, 4x4 Unimog and travel 2,000 feet above sea level to the heart of the Sierra Madre jungle. From there, you'll ride mules to the mountain top for a zip line experience. You will go from canyon side to canyon side via a zip line network 250 feet above the ground. Afterwards, you'll hike on a jungle path, rappel to a waterfall, and splash your way through streams and pools back to base camp, where you will be treated to light refreshments before returning to the ship. 250 lb. maximum weight, 48" minimum height for zip line.

Sports | Active | Ages 10 & up | $129 | 5.5-6 hours

Whale Photo Safari (seasonal)

Available December 15-March 15. Cruise Bandaras Bay in an inflatable powerboat for a 3.5 hour guided expedition to view and photograph humpback whales in their winter breeding grounds. The bay is one of North America's top whale-watching sites during the winter season. A light snack of fresh fruit and cookies is provided, and bottled water is available throughout the cruise. There's no restroom on board. Life jackets are required for all guests.

Tour | Mild | Ages 10 & up | $99 | 4-4.5 hours

Mexican Cooking Experience [PV32]

Take a 50-minute motorcoach to a private ranch in the Sierra Madre. At the ranch, you'll be led to the on-site kitchen, where you'll meet your chef instructor for the day. You will learn how to make some of Mexico's best-loved dishes, such as salsas, guacamole, and stuffed peppers ... and then you get to try them all! After lunch (soft drinks and wine included), you can wander the ranch, swim in the pool, or take pictures of the panoramic views. Then sit back and relax on the journey back to the ship. Wheelchair accessible (no ECVs).

Tour | Leisurely | All ages | $39/$29 (3-9) | 5-5.5 hours

Whale Watching, Snorkeling, and Kayaking at Marietas Islands

(Seasonal - Available December 15-March 15) Cruise two hours towards the Marietas Islands on a comfortable catamaran while you watch for humpback whales and dolphins. Once you arrive, embark on a 45-minute, wildlife-filled guided snorkel session, where you're likely to see dolphins, manta rays, and colorful tropical fish.Your snorkel experience is followed by a 30-minute kayak tour, where you can explore caverns and archways along the rocky sea coast.A beach stop is also included. A light breakfast and a deli-style buffet lunch are included, with complimentary alcoholic beverages served after the snorkeling and kayaking. Snorkel and kayak equipment is provided. (On Your Own: Vallarta Adventures–http://www.vallarta-adventures.com, 888-526-2238)

Sports | Moderate | Ages 10 & up | $79 | 7-7.5 hours

See page 218 for a key to the shore excursion description charts and their icons.

Embarking on Shore Excursions in Puerto Vallarta *(continued)*

Private Vans - Puerto Vallarta

See Puerto Vallarta at your own pace and on your own itinerary in the comfort of a private van or SUV. Your vehicle includes an English-speaking driver/guide, who will take you on a tour of the sights that interest you. Your driver will meet you at the pier in Puerto Vallarta and the tour lasts either 4 or 8 hours. Download and submit a Private Vehicle Request Form through the Disney web site for pricing and availability. Up to 12 guests per vehicle. A beverage is included.

Tour
Leisurely
All ages
$325 & up
4 or 8 hours

See page 218 for a key to the shore excursion description charts and their icons.

Puerto Vallarta On Your Own

For those who want to get a head start on their excursion plans, or just want to do it on their own, here is some information on tour operators in Puerto Vallarta. Please note that we have not used these operators, nor is any mention here an endorsement of their services. For a huge variety of excursions, check out **Vallarta Adventures**, which seems to offer a version of almost every Disney excursion available and then some. You can get loads of information on their excursions at http://www.vallarta-adventures.com, or call toll-free at 888-526-2238. If the canopy tours through the jungle intrigue you, you can book this on your own through **Canopy Tours de Los Veranos**, about which we've heard very good things. For more information, visit http://www.canopytours-vallarta.com, or call 800-396-9168.

Whale Watching on the West Coast

Each year, migrating whales swim up and down North America's west coast between winter breeding grounds in Southern California and Mexico and their summer feeding grounds in Alaska. Disney's 2013 and 2014 cruise schedules are out of sync with the Mexico/California whale watching season,which happens during the winter. But Alaskan cruisers are in luck, as the whales are up north during the summer. Puerto Vallarta's Bay of Banderas is one of North America's premier humpback whale watching sites. In mid-December humpback whales begin to arrive from Alaska to breed and raise their young. By mid-March adults and young alike are ready to swim nearly 6,000 miles northward, back to Alaska's seafood-rich summer waters. Whale watching during this period is not limited to Mexico. San Diego and San Pedro, California are prime spots for watching a wide variety of migrating whale species. Gray whales, sperm whales, blue whales, Orcas, Minke, and humpbacks are among the regular visitors at various times of the year, along with a wide range of dolphins and porpoises. The Cabrillo Marine Aquarium in San Pedro (web: http://www.cabrillomarineaquarium.org–see page 333) and Long Beach's Aquarium of the Pacific (web: http://www.aquariumofpacific.org) offer frequent whale watching cruises. In San Diego, the season runs from December-April, and you can even watch from shore from spots like the the Birch Aquarium, Torrey Pines State Reserve, and Cabrillo National Monument!

Cabo San Lucas
(Repositioning Itineraries)

Perched on the southern tip of the **Baja California** peninsula, Cabo (Cape) San Lucas and its sister-town, San José de Cabo are pleasure destinations, pure and simple. Pleasant bars, pleasant beaches, pleasant shopping, and some of the best sport fishing you'll find anywhere. These towns were barely on the map until wealthy sportsmen started flying in after World War II.

Lands End in Cabo San Lucas

AMBIENCE

This is a **Lifestyles of the Rich and Famous** destination, and the restaurants, hotels, and shops cater to this upscale market. You won't find many bargain-rate tourists driving in here—it's more than 1000 miles from anywhere else, over a highway that's short on fuel, water, and other services. The town is compact, although resort development stretches along the 20 miles of coast between Cabo San Lucas and neighboring San José de Cabo (together, these towns are known as Los Cabos). Picturesque beaches are scattered along the rocky coastline, and the sea beckons fishermen, scuba divers, and surfers alike.

HISTORY & CULTURE

Dry and mountainous, Baja was always **sparsely populated**. It's thought that the indigenous people may have migrated here across the Pacific—there's no evidence that Mexico's major civilizations ever put down roots here. Spanish missionaries didn't get to Baja's deserts, mountains, and rocky coast until the late 1600s. Most missionaries moved on, leaving little behind of either historical or archaeological interest in Cabo San Lucas. On the other hand, San José de Cabo has a historic Spanish mission, tales of visits by buccaneers, and an attractive downtown district. After World War II, high-end fishing resorts were soon hooking wealthy fishermen. Mexico completed the Transpeninsular Highway in the early '70s, and realizing Cabo's popularity, started making major investments in the '80s.

FACTS

Size: 14 mi. (23 km.) long x 11 mi. (18 km.) wide	
Climate: Tropical	**Temperatures**: 81°F (27°C) to 87°F (31°C)
Population: 68,000	**Busy Season**: November to April
Language: Spanish, English	**Money**: Mexican Peso (12 Pesos = $1 U.S.)
Time Zone: Atlantic (no DST)	**Transportation**: Walking, taxis, scooters
Phones: Dial 33-977 or 119 for emergencies	

➤

Introduction Reservations Staterooms Dining Activities Ports of Call Magic Index

Making the Most of Cabo San Lucas

GETTING THERE

Although there have been rumors of a full-fledged cruise ship pier under development, for the foreseeable future, expect to be **tendered** into the small inner harbor of Cabo San Lucas. From the small ferry terminal, the town is easily explored on foot, with the town square, restaurants, and shopping just a few blocks distant. A waterfront boardwalk makes for a pleasant stroll, and if your interest is game fishing, you'll find charter boats close by the pier. San José de Cabo is 20 miles to the east, along Highway 1. Beaches along this route are marked, if you want to stop and explore. But if you stray outside of Cabo San Lucas, hurry back! All aboard" is 7:00 pm and 1:30 pm, respectively, 14 hours altogether. This is the last port before Los Angeles, and it's a long haul (36 hours at full speed), so the Wonder can't stay for cocktail hour. The 14-night Panama Canal cruise stops here for just over five hours.

GETTING AROUND

Car rentals are available in downtown Cabo San Lucas from most major agencies, including Alamo, Avis, Budget, Dollar, Hertz, and National (reserve in advance), but you should only rent if you have an out-of-town destination in mind. Taxis are plentiful, but are only really necessary to get to the beaches. Everything else is **within walking distance**. As nearly all points of interest are visited by shore excursions, they remain, as always, your safest bet—you don't want to miss your ship's departure! Due south of the inner harbor is Lands End (see photo on previous page), the southernmost point of Baja, where the Sea of Cortez meets the Pacific Ocean (you'll get a great view of this as you tender into shore). The entire area has been set aside as a natural preserve. Scuba diving is popular, as are sightseeing cruises. Los Arcos is an oft-photographed natural stone arch at Lands End, and next door is beautiful and isolated Lover's Beach, which can only be reached by sea (water taxis operate from the inner harbor and Playa El Médano across the bay).

SAFETY

Cabo is **safer than most tourist ports**, so no special warnings apply—just use standard cautions and procedures. And just one word for you, just one... sunblock!

© Corel.

Charter fishing boats

For **swimming and recreation**,

Touring Cabo San Lucas

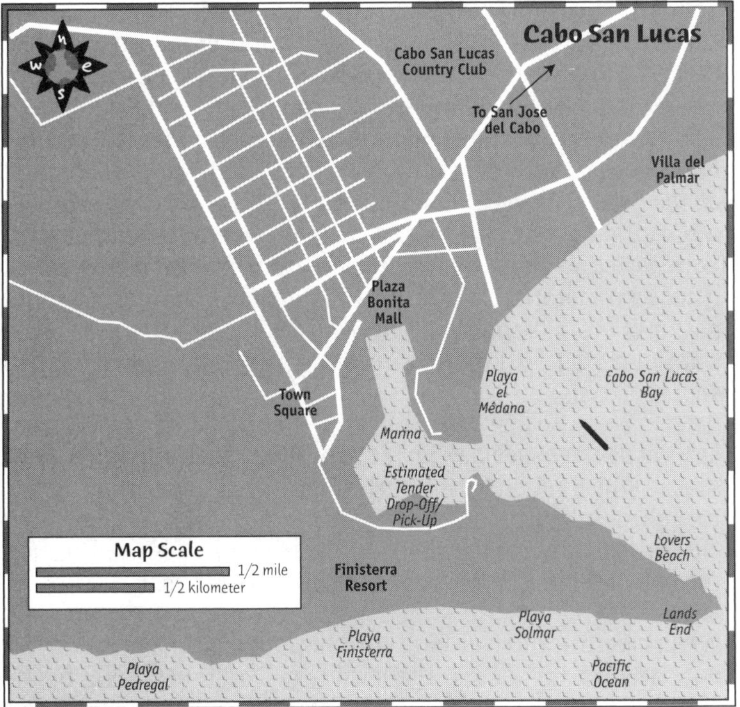

Playa El Médano is the place, just east of the inner harbor's entry. You'll find every sort of water sport rental and beach amenity on this broad beach with modest surf and numerous resort hotels. While it's just across the bay from the pier, a short cab ride is probably the best way to get there. Previously mentioned, Lover's Beach is a short boat ride away. It's reputed to be one of the most picturesque beaches anywhere, but swimming is dangerous. Attractive Solmar Beach is also a short cab ride from the pier and guarded by resort hotels, but it, too, is not suitable for swimming. Most other area beaches are also too dangerous for swimming, although several along the road to San Jose de Cabo attract scuba divers, snorkeling, or surfers (see next page). Of those, Playa Chileno, with its offshore reef, offers the best swimming opportunities. None of the beaches have safety patrols, so you're on your own. If you want to book your own excursions, consider Cabo San Lucas Tours at http://www.cabosanlucastours.net or 866-348-6286.

Playing in Cabo San Lucas

ACTIVITIES

Scuba diving, snorkeling, and surfing are all popular activities at beaches scattered across more than 20 miles of rugged coastline. Prime surfing beaches are just west of San Jose de Cabo. A good rundown is at http://www.surfline.com. There's fine scuba and snorkel action at Lands End, so you don't have to stray very far. But if you must venture out, Playa Palmilla (17 mi./ 27 km. east of town) and Playa Chileno (9 mi.,/14 km. east of town) both offer top-notch diving, snorkeling, and general beach facilities. Both have dive shops. Playa Chileno has the added advantage of being a no-motorized-watersports area. Golf is another attractive pastime here, although you'll need an awfully early tee time if you want to get back to the ship in time—play it safe and book that shore excursion!

Los Cabos are especially famous for **blue marlin fishing** (peak season June through November). There's always something biting, though, check http://www.mexfish.com/cbsl/cbsl/cbslseasons/cbslseasons.htm for a calendar. The fishing pier is right next to the ferry terminal if you want to snag a charter boat.

While plentiful and pleasant, the **shopping** in Cabo San Lucas is not particularly exciting. The jewelry and craft boutiques of San Jose de Cabo, apparently, are another matter. The quality is said to be high and the prices fair.

Hungry and/or thirsty? Cabo lacks a Carlos 'n Charlies, but there's now a Senõr Frogs (both are run by the same chain). **Two local spots are legendary**. El Squid Roe Bar & Grill has a rockin', party reputation. Cabo Wabo Cantina has the added allure of being owned by Van Halen's Sammy Hagar—a party spot, that has been cloned in Vegas and Tahoe! You'll find these and many more a short walk away in the harbor area. You'll also not lack for lunch choices if you head for Playa El Médano or San Jose de Cabo.

For something a bit out of the ordinary, the **Vitrofusion Y Arte** glass works is located on the outskirts of Cabo San Lucas (take a cab). You can watch the artisans produce functional mouth-blown glassware and art glass (hand-blown doesn't seem to be the right term), and naturally, there's a retail shop on premises, too. You'll also find Vitrofusion goods on sale at some downtown shops.

Embarking on Shore Excursions in Cabo San Lucas

Land's End Coastal Cruise & Beach Break

Combine two popular Cabo activities! First, see Land's End and Los Arcos from a double-decked power catamaran, while you sip a complimentary beverage and hear the tour narration. Once back at the pier you'll be off by bus to a nearby beach club for 2.5 hours of sun, sand, a light lunch, and another complimentary drink. Loungers and beach umbrella are included, recreational equipment is extra.	Tour/Beach Leisurely All ages $55/$39 (0-9) 4-4.5 hours

Cabo del Sol Golf [CL02]

Play the Desert Course at Cabo del Sol, about 30 minutes from the ship. The par-72, 7,097-yard course was designed by Tom Weiskopf. A cart and bottled water are provided; you can rent clubs if you didn't bring your own. About 6.5-7 hours.	Sports Active Ages 10 & up $299

Certified Two-Tank Dive Adventure

Open-water certified scuba divers can explore the area around San Lucas Bay with two 45-minute, one-tank dives near the stone arch and Lovers Beach. Complimentary bottled water and a snack are served. All necessary equipment is provided. Divers must have completed a logged, certified dive in the last year, and present certification. A parent must accompany guests under 18.	Sports Very active Ages 12 & up $115 3-3.5 hours

Cabo San Lucas Sportfishing [CL04]

Board a 6-person cabin cruiser for a 35-minute cruise to a prime fishing site. Guests take turns to fight and reel in fish from the fishing chair. A boxed lunch and three beverages are included in the price. Note that catch-and-release of all billfish is mandatory. Boat, skipper, mate, tackle, and Mexican fishing license are included in the price.	Sports Active Ages 10 & up $199 5.5-6 hours

Pacific Side Horseback Riding [CL05]

Ride to a seaside ranch, then it's off to explore the shoreline of the Sea of Cortez for an hour. After the sedate ride you'll have 15 minutes to relax at the ranch. You can then get a ride back to the pier or be dropped off downtown. Bottled water included. Maximum rider weight is 240 lbs. Long pants and closed-toe shoes are recommended.Suitable for all levels of experience.	Sports Active Ages 12-65 $79 3.5-4 hours

Harbor Cruise and Scenic Stop [CL06]

Begin with a 40-minute catamaran trip to the tip of the Baja peninsula to see Lands End and Los Arcos. Along the way, you'll hear a narration by Cousteau and enjoy a complimentary beverage. Then it's time for a 20-minute drive to Giorgio's clifftop restaurant for a drink and the view. Get a ride back to the pier or be dropped off downtown.	Tour Leisurely All ages $45/$29 (0-9) 3-3.5 hours

Chileno Bay Snorkeling Adventure [CL07]

Board the "Tropicat," a 65-foot catamaran—it even has a water slide! You'll cruise by many points of interest, including Lover's Beach, the arch at Lands End, and the sea lion colony on the 45-minute trip. You'll then drop anchor at Chileno Bay for snorkeling; equipment is provided. You'll also receive complimentary snacks and drinks on the way back.	Sports Active Ages 5 & up $75/$45 (5-9) 4-4.5 hours

See page 218 for a key to the shore excursion description charts and their icons.

Embarking on Shore Excursions in Cabo San Lucas *(continued)*

Cabo Whale Photo Adventure (seasonal)

Cruise the Sea of Cortez in an inflatable watercraft to view and photograph humpback whales, gray whales, orcas, native sea birds, and many of Cabo's most famous sights, including Los Arcos. A professional photographer and marine mammal expert will be on hand to enrich the experience. Bottled water and a snack are included. Operates December 15-April 15.

Tour
Active
Ages 6 & up
$89/$59 (6-9)
3-3.5 hours

Coastal Highlights Tour [CL10]

Enjoy a scenic bus tour to various Cabo San Lucas highlights, including a glassblowing shop, the town of San Jose del Cabo, and the clifftop restaurant of Cabo Bello (plus a complimentary beer or soda). Afterward, return to the pier, or visit downtown Cabo San Lucas and then take the 20 min. stroll back to the ship.

Tour
Leisurely
All ages
$49/$35 (3-9)
4-4.5 hours

Santa Maria Snorkel & Sail [CL11]

Sail aboard a catamaran to Santa Maria Cove, passing by Lover's Beach, the sea lion colony, and Lands End along the way. At the cove, you'll get your snorkeling equipment to explore the reefs (or just swim) for an hour. Life vests are provided and required. Back onboard, you'll enjoy beverages and snacks during the return.

Sports
Active
Ages 5 & up
$69/$39 (5-9)
4-4.5 hours

Cabo Resort Pool Getaway

Take a 10-minute ride to a five-star resort to lounge by the resort's pool, soak in the hot tub, play volleyball or soccer, stroll on the beach (ocean swimming not allowed due to currents), and enjoy a buffet lunch with included beverages. Beach chair and umbrellas included. Use of pool by children in diapers is prohibited.

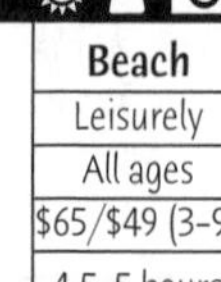

Beach
Leisurely
All ages
$65/$49 (3-9)
4.5-5 hours

Snorkel & Sea Adventure

Ride an APEX inflatable watercraft past Land's End, Los Arcos, and Lover's Beach for swimming, power-snorkeling, and kayaking in a beautiful cove. Your guide will point out wildlife that may include sea turtles, rays, and dolphins. Your 75 minutes at the cove will be divided between the three activities, so expect you'll have a limited time for each. Guests enter and exit the water directly from the boat, so you should be comfortable swimming in open waters. Bottled water and a light snack are included.

Sports
Active
Ages 6 & up
$75/$65 (6-9)
3-3.5 hours

Deluxe Villa Escape

Enjoy Cabo from the privacy of your own villa overlooking the Sea of Cortez and the Pacific Ocean. An air-conditioned van ride will take you to the elegant Villas La Estancia. Includes a private chef (and lunch). Max 10 guests. Download and submit a request form on Disney's site.

Special
Leisurely
All Ages
$1,500 & up

Embarking on Shore Excursions in Cabo San Lucas

Cabo Dolphin Encounter

Walk 5 minutes to the Cabo Dolphin Center. After a presentation by the trainers, guests enter the pool for a 25-minute session where they'll learn to communicate with the dolphins and have a chance to pet them and share a farewell kiss and handshake (guest-to-dolphin ratio 10:1). Kids under 8 must be accompanied in-water by an adult on the same excursion. One observer is free with each paid ticket.

Sports
Active
Ages 3 & up
$125/$105 (3-9)
1-1.5 hours

Cabo Dolphin Trainer Program

Cabo's deluxe dolphin experience. "Trainers" prepare the dolphin's food (and humans get a deli lunch, too). Spend 30 minutes swimming, touching, and interacting with the dolphins, and at the end, receive a belly ride or dorsal push (guest to dolphin ratio 5:1). Receive a diploma, DVD, photo, and keep your "uniform." Under 18s must be with an adult booked on a dolphin excursion.

Sports
Active
Ages 12 & up
$345
4.5-5 hours

Cabo Dolphin Kids

You and your child will set out on a short 5-minute walk to the Cabo Dolphin Center, where your child will meet with dolphin trainers. The trainers will teach the basics of dolphins and their care. After the information session, your child will get a 25-minute shallow-water session with a Pacific Bottlenose dolphin under the direct supervision of a trainer (guest-to-dolphin ratio 10:1). Kids have a chance to pet, hug, feed, and kiss the dolphin. Note that this is a not a "swim with the dolphins" experience. A bottle of water is provided. An adult observer is required, but there's no extra charge. No cameras allowed.

Sports
Mild
Ages 4-9
$105
1.5 hours

Cabo Dolphin Swim

Take a short 5-minute walk to the Cabo Dolphin Center for a one-of-a-kind dolphin experience. Your guide will educate you on dolphin anatomy and physiology, along with the daily activities of the dolphin trainers. Then, get into the water with Pacific Bottlenose dolphins where you can swim, touch, and interact with them (guest-to-dolphin ratio 8:1), capped off by a ride across the pool by dorsal push or belly ride. After your 40-minute swim, enjoy a complimentary bottle of water. Kids under 11 must be accompanied in-water by an adult on the same excursion. One observer is free with each paid ticket.

Sports
Active
Ages 5 & up
$175/$155 (5-9)
1-1.5 hours

Teen Surfin' Safari [CL28]

Designed exclusively for teens, this excursion combines surfing and sun for an unforgettable day. A private van will take you on a 30-minute drive to a prime surfing beach, Playa Costa Azul. After a brief meeting with your instructor, you will be assigned a surfboard and gear for the afternoon. You will then go with your instructor into the water for an hour-long training session. After this, you will be turned loose to catch some waves and splash with your friends. Afterward, enjoy a complimentary beverage before heading back to the ship. Maximum surfboard weight is 220 lbs. Wet suits and life vests are provided.

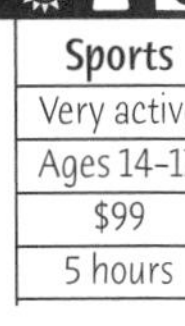

Sports
Very active
Ages 14-17
$99
5 hours

See page 218 for a key to the shore excursion description charts and their icons.

Embarking on Shore Excursions in Cabo San Lucas *(continued)*

Mexican Fiesta & Folkloric Show

Lunch on traditional Mexican specialties, watch as hand-made tortillas are prepared, and enjoy refreshing beverages (fresh-squeezed lemonade, beer, or margaritas). Then enjoy a performance of Mexican folk dance, mariachi music, and Aztec-Pre-Hispanic dancers, and feel free to sing and dance right along with the show! Afterwards, take a short bus ride back to the ship, or walk through town. Wheelchair accessible, no ECVs.

Tour | Mild | All ages | $85/$59 (3-9) | 2.5-3 hours

Cabo Resort Beach Getaway

Take a 10-minute ride to a five-star resort on Medano Beach to lounge by the resort's pool, play on the beach, and enjoy a buffet lunch with unlimited soft drinks and adult beverages (for those 21 and over). Families can enjoy a treasure hunt and sandcastle-building. Lounge chairs and umbrellas are included, water activities like boogie boards, sailboats, and parasailing are extra.

Beach | Leisurely | All ages | $79/$55 (3-9) | 4.5-5 hours

Discover Scuba

Dive into scuba with this introductory course. 50 minutes of classroom instruction and a 50-minute pool session prepare you for your first open water, one-tank dive (45 minutes), accompanied by a PADI-certified instructor (does not count towards a PADI open water certificate). All gear, bottled water, and snack included. Guests under 18 must be accompanied by an adult.

Sports | Very active | Ages 12 & up | $125 | 3-3.5 hours

Camel & Mexican Outback Adventure

Traverse desert canyons in a Unimog military-style transport enroute to your coastal ranch getaway. Once there, take a guided nature walk, soak-in the wildlife and scenery, take a 15-minute camel ride, participate in optional tortilla-making and tequilla-tasting workshops, and enjoy a Mexican lunch featuring items like chicken Mole. 48 in./1.2 m minimum height.

Tour | Moderate | Ages 6 & up | $119/$99 (6-9) | 4-4.5 hours

San Jose City Tour

Drive for 30 scenic coastal miles to San José del Cabo, for a taste of the area's arts and history. Visit the arts district, the historic Spanish mission, and the city square, and stop for an hour of shopping in Plaza Artesanos. Cold drink included. Guests planning to visit the mission church should have shoulders and knees covered. Wheelchairs not allowed.

Tour | Leisurely | All ages | $49/$35 (3-9) | 3.5-4 hours

See page 218 for a key to the shore excursion description charts and their icons.

Embarking on Shore Excursions in Cabo San Lucas

Salsa & Salsa

Learn to make 7 salsas and margaritas with your "dancing chef instructors." Then the chefs trade their aprons for dance shoes to teach you one more salsa (dance). Snack away on salsas, chips, chicken taquitos, and cheese quesadillas, and wash them down with unlimited margaritas and soft drinks (herbal tea and water). 45 minutes of free time included, to lounge by the pool or stroll the beach.

Tour	Mild	All ages	$89/$59 (3-9)	3.5-4 hours

Whale Watching & Deluxe Coastal Cruise (seasonal)

Search for gray, humpback, blue, sperm, and finback whales in their winter home. A double-decked catamaran with on-board naturalist will take you on your two-hour cruise. Be sure your camera is ready for action! Chips, salsa, and unlimited drinks included. Available December 15 to March 15. Wheelchair accessible, but no ECVs. Must be able to board unassisted.

Tour	Leisurely	All ages	$65/$40 (0-9)	2-2.5 hours

Cabo My Way - Private Vehicles

Do you want to visit Cabo, but none of the other excursions pique your interest? Then this one is for you. You can arrange to have a private van with a driver/guide to cater to you and your interests. Four suggested itineraries are supplied, but you're free to plan your own. Tours typically are four hours in duration, but you can reserve additional hours if needed. Up to 11 guests per vehicle (specify group size). Beverage (bottled water, soda, beer) included. You will need to download and submit a Request Form through the Disney Cruise Line web site at least 7 days prior for pricing and availability.

Tour	Leisurely	All ages	$325 & up	4 hours

Cabo Canopy Adventure

An air-conditioned van will take you through countryside surrounding Cabo and bring you to Boca de la Sierra, a protected site in the High Sierras. Here you will meet with your guide and then travel across the canyons by a network of pulley systems. You will speed across a zip line and fly through the treetops. You will also get to do a bit of rock climbing and then rappel 90 feet down the canyon wall. Finally, climb onto another zip line and sail over 800 feet back to the base camp. In camp, enjoy a bottle of water and a snack (fruit, sandwich, chips). Max. weight is 250 lbs. Min. height is 48 in./122 cm.

Sports	Very active	Ages 8 & up	$99	5-5.5 hours

4X4 Mini Jeep Adventure

Take a ride on a scenic drive through the Mexican countryside to a coastal ranch. Here you will meet your guide, who will cover operating and safety protocols for your two-person Yamaha Rhino or Honda Big Red 4x4. Then you're off, across Baja's rugged terrain. After your 90-minute drive, head back to the ranch for 15 minutes of free time. Then, return to the pier or be dropped-off in town. Must wear close-toed shoes. Drivers must be 21 and licensed.

Sports	Active	Ages 10 & up	$99	4-4.5 hours

Exploring Cabo San Lucas

Cabo San Lucas On Your Own

For those who want to get a head start on their excursion plans, or just want to do it on their own, here is some information on tour operators in Los Cabos. Please note that we have not used these operators, nor is any mention here an endorsement of their services. Cabo San Lucas Tours by Johann & Sandra offers something close to one-stop shopping (more choices than the cruise line), and sometimes, excellent discounts from cruise line pricing. This is a travel agency that specializes in shore excursions, and represents many tour operators (web: http://www.cabosanlucastours.net, 866-348-6286). The same company operates similar sites for Puerto Vallarta on the Mexican Riviera, as well as Cozumel in the Mexican Caribbean. One of the largest tour operators in Cabo is Cabo Adventures (web: http://www.cabo-adventures.com, 888-526-2238). They operate the Cabo Dolphin Center, and many of their other excursions will seem awfully familiar when compared to Disney's offerings. Discounts are sometimes available, but compare regular prices carefully—prices are not always better than Disney's, especially for kids. The same company also operates Vallarta Adventures (web: http://www.vallarta-adventures.com, 888-526-2238). There are more fishing charters than you can shake a pole at, but Redrum Charters is particularly popular (web: http://www.redrumcabo.com, 760-481-7667). The company has a fleet of 9 boats, from 28 ft. to 53 ft.

Vancouver, Canada

(Alaska Itineraries' Home Port)

Vancouver is a cosmopolitan, great city nestled amidst the **natural grandeur of the Pacific Northwest**. Canada's third-largest metropolis is a first-class tourist destination and one of the great jumping-off spots for cruises. The ethnically diverse city is a center of commerce, culture, and education.

© MediaMarx, Inc.

Vancouver's waterfront

AMBIENCE

Resembling both Seattle and San Francisco, Vancouver is considered one of the world's most livable cities. The highrises of downtown gaze north across Burrard Inlet, the city's deepwater harbor, to the steep slopes of cloud-shrouded Grouse and Cypress mountains, with suburban North Vancouver at their feet. The green span of Lion's Gate Bridge echoes the Golden Gate as it guards the harbor's mouth, with 1,000-acre Stanley Park at it's south end. A diverse immigrant population, great universities, and thriving arts and film communities add to the **rich tapestry of city life**.

HISTORY

Vancouver's recorded history is brief compared to many great cities, but **native tribes have lived here for some 10,000 years**, enjoying the rich fishing and moderate winter climate. The region was first visited by Europeans, including British explorer George Vancouver, in 1791-1792. The excellent, natural harbor and stands of giant timber perfect for sailing ships attracted commerce from the start. European settlements in the area were rough, gritty places dependent on lumbering until the Canadian Pacific Railway was completed, connecting both coasts and the Canadian interior in 1886. The population of newly re-named Vancouver ("Granville" seemed insufficiently grand) was just 5,000 at the time. The metro area population grew to 1.2 million over the next century.

FACTS

Size: City: 44.3 sq. mi. (114 sq. km.) Metro: 1,111 sq. mi. (2878 sq. km.)	
Climate: Oceanic West Coast	**Temperatures**: 43°F (6°C) to 72°F (22°C)
Population: 2,116,000 (metro)	**Busy Season**: Year-round
Language: English	**Money**: Canadian Dollar ($)
Time Zone: Pacific	**Transportation**: Walking, bus, SkyTrain
Phones: Area codes 604 & 778, dial 911 for emergencies	

Making the Most of Vancouver

GETTING THERE

The Disney Wonder docks at the **Canada Place Pier**, with much of downtown Vancouver within ten blocks walking distance. Once established in your hotel, public transportation is an excellent choice. The area's ultra-modern buses, subway ("SkyTrain") and ferry ("SeaBus") can get you nearly everywhere quickly, pleasantly, and at low cost. Public transit tickets are good on SkyTrain, bus, and SeaBus, and offer unlimited transfers within the zone(s) purchased. (Detailed Vancouver travel and lodging information starts on page 104.)

GETTING AROUND

Canada Place is home to the cruise pier, convention center, and luxury, highrise hotels. Stroll the promenade around the pier, soak in the views, and, in bad weather, consider the IMAX theater right at the pier. The **Tourism Vancouver** office nearby at 200 Burrard St. is a must-visit, and includes a half-price theater ticket booth (visit http://www.tourismvancouver.com). Canada Place is part of the **Coal Harbour** waterfront, with parks, hotels, luxury highrises, a marina, and a seaplane port. Just beyond to the west is **Stanley Park** (see next page). Gastown is just east of Canada Place, and grew up around the original Canadian Pacific Railway station. Its old, brick buildings house boutiques, bistros, pubs, and dance clubs cater to students from the neighborhood's colleges. If skies are clear, the **Vancouver Lookout** observation deck in Harbour Centre offers breathtaking views just a few blocks from Canada Place at 555 Hastings St. Gastown's neighbor to the southeast is **Chinatown**, North America's third-largest, but it's a bit remote and isolated (take a taxi). The **center of downtown** is six to ten blocks south (inland) of Canada Place. The area between Burrard and Granville Streets is its heart, home to a lively theater district, department stores, hotels, museums, and restaurants. **Yaletown** is just south of downtown. Hotels are plentiful, the theater district is a reasonable walk, and Granville Island (see next page) is a water taxi ride away, across False Creek. **West End** is a mixed hotel and upscale residential neighborhood with nice shopping and restaurants, and is a bit quieter than downtown proper.

SAFETY

Staying safe in Vancouver is **not too difficult** so long as you're not lulled into a false sense of security. Stay alert and take normal precautions. Downtown streets that are lively during the day become quiet at night, though the Granville St. area remains comfortably busy. Marijuana is officially illegal, but the police do not arrest casual users. You may encounter an occasional, funky spot where it's openly used.

Touring Vancouver

VANCOUVER MAP

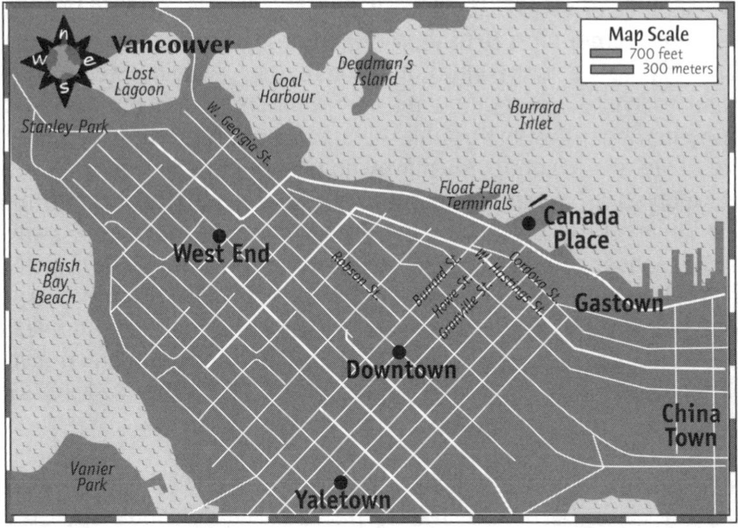

OTHER ATTRACTIONS

Stanley Park is 1,000 acres of thick timberland, gardens, and waterfront, just west of downtown. Like New York's Central Park, there are scenic drives and several restaurants in picturesque spots, and it's home to the Vancouver Aquarium, Canada's largest, offering shows, exhibits, and animal encounter programs (http://www.visitvanaqua.org). Bicycle rentals are popular, especially for the 5.5 mi. (8.8 km) ride around the sea wall. Spokes Bicycle Rental is near the park entrance, at 1798 Georgia St. West 604-688-5141. **Granville Island** is a converted industrial zone south of downtown. It houses the city's wonderful Public Market, "Kids Market," restaurants, galleries, theaters, art studios, and a college of art and design. The goods offered for sale, edible or not, are mouth watering (http://www.granvilleisland.com). A bit farther afield, south and west of downtown, the **University of British Columbia** area includes woodlands, a fine botanical garden, Japanese gardens, Totem Park, and the Museum of Anthropology.

Vancouverites eat very well! Seafood, of course, is first-rate, from fish and chips to sushi. If you see a Japa Dog cart, queue up for Japanese-garnished hot dogs. On Granville Island, Go Fish is a casual shack serving great fish sandwiches and fish and chips, the Public Market is a gourmet feast, and The Sandbar is a satisfying seafood restaurant. Near Canada Place, The Mill Marine Bistro in Harbour Green Park has a gorgeous view, but the pub/bistro fare is average.

Introduction
Reservations
Staterooms
Dining
Activities
Ports of Call
Magic
Index

Exploring Nature in North Vancouver

Most cruise lines offer pre-/post-cruise excursions featuring a visit to the **Capilano Suspension Bridge**, a 15-acre tourist attraction in North Vancouver that has been operating since the 1880s. A swaying, steel cable-supported footbridge crosses the Capilano River gorge, connecting visitors to a network of boardwalks through the lush, temperate rainforest, and an Ewok Village-style "canopy" walkway going from tree to tree. Exhibits include totem-carving and native culture, and guided nature walks are included. While offering a lot of bang in a small space, it's not the best way to enjoy Vancouver's natural world. Admission ranges from $31.95 CDN (adults) to $12 (ages 6–12), and under 6 are free. 20% discount for entry after 5:00 pm. The 236 bus will take you here from the SeaBus terminal at Lonsdale Quay, and free shuttles serve Canada Place and other downtown spots. Information at http://www.capbridge.com / 877-985-7474 / 3735 Capilano Road, North Vancouver.

Grouse Mountain Tramway, just up the road, competes head-to-head with Capilano for tourist dollars. The ski area, an Olympic venue, operates a wealth of summertime attractions, most included with your tram ticket, including a lumberjack show (see it here and save time and money in Ketchikan), movies, chairlifts, a birds of prey show, grizzly bears and wolves, and guided nature walks. Views are breathtaking when/if the clouds lift. For an extra fee there's a zipline (adds $69) and a tour of their mountaintop wind turbine (with an observation deck atop the tower) adds $15. General admission is $39.95 adults, $23.95 ages 13–18, $13.95 ages 5–12, 4 and under are free. Locals reach the mountaintop at a much lower price on the Grouse Grind, the challenging hike up the mountain ($5 for the tram ride back down). Parking is $5, and the 236 bus will take you here from the SeaBus terminal. Visit http://www.grousemountain.com 604-980-9311 / 6400 Nancy Greene Way, North Vancouver.

A favorite with locals is **Lynn Canyon Park**, a North Vancouver nature park with its own high, swaying footbridge and an extensive trail network through the rainforest. If hiking's your thing, this beats Capilano hands down, and you can't beat the price (free).There's also a nice cafe in the park. Located at the end of a suburban street, the 228 or 229 bus will take you there from the SeaBus terminal. Visit http://www.dnv.org/ecology.

The famed **Whistler** ski area is 85 mi./137 km north of Vancouver via Highway 99 (Sea to Sky Highway), about a two-hour drive. Float plane trips are possible from the Coal Harbour airport, and bus service is also available. Details at http://www.whistler.com.

Tracy Arm, Alaska
(Alaskan Itineraries)

Watching icebergs shear off the face of a massive glacier from the deck of a cruise ship is an **enduring symbol** of the Alaskan itinerary. For the Disney Wonder, the visit to Tracy Arm Fjord will be your only chance to experience that wonder (conditions permitting).

© MediaMarx, Inc.

A cruise ship dwarfed by Tracy Arm

AMBIENCE

Just 40 mi./64 km. south of Juneau, the Tracy Arm Fjord does **resemble an arm with bent elbow**. The sea reaches 23 mi./37 km. inland, from Stephens Passage to the fjord's end at the Sawyer Glacier. Steep, ice-polished granite walls plunge into 1,000 ft./305 m. deep waters that are tinted a vivid blue-green by suspended minerals, the passage often little more than .5 mi./.8 km wide. The softly rounded shapes of the gorge and its surrounding mountains resemble California's Yosemite and the White Mountains of New Hampshire, with just a few jagged peaks tall enough to escape the glacial grindstone. Elevations are deceptive—the fjord walls rise between 2,000 and 3,000 feet (600 and 900 m.) and nearby peaks may be 5,500 ft. (1,600 m.) or more. Only when you see another Panamax-sized cruise ship pass by, resembling a tiny toy boat at the bottom of a near-empty bathtub, may you get a true sense of scale.

ACTIVITIES

You may want to **start your day before sunrise**, as those first magical hours of daylight can be superb, both in the open waters of Stephens Passage and as you enter Tracy Arm; just be sure to dress warmly! The cruise line provides narration by an expert guide via the ship's public address system, and interpretive talks and films are available indoors. One thing that cannot be promised is a view of the Sawyer Glaciers. Floating ice may be too thick to allow a close approach, and even a distant glimpse may be impossible if you can't pass the last bends in the channel. That was the case on our research trip, but the visit was still glorious. There's much to be said for viewing your passage from the bow of the ship, but the Wonder doesn't provide a lot of forward observation space. Expect the Outlook Lounge and the Wide World of Sports Deck to be packed. Joggers on the Vista Spa's treadmills should get a real eyeful!

Making the Most of Tracy Arm

GETTING THERE

The Disney Wonder visits Tracy Arm on Wednesday afternoons in 2013, and most weeks shares the fjord with two other cruise ships, though they'll be exiting the fjord as the Wonder is entering. Disney Cruise Line **does not offer shore excursions** during its visit to Tracy Arm, although other cruise lines have been known to offer a "nature, up close" excursion by small boat. You'll have to be content with watching the spectacle outside slide past as you glide majestically through on the ship.

GLACIERS

The southern panhandle of Alaska and coastal British Columbia are **home to thousands of glaciers**. Some of these "rivers of ice," built-up by years of mountain snows, dwarf all but a few of earth's liquid rivers in breadth and power, as they slowly slide downhill. Others appear to be mere mountainside patches of snow, their identity only sure after careful examination. Regardless of size, glaciers are natural wonders that are steadily disappearing as the earth's climate shifts. When naturalist John Muir explored this region in 1879 and 1880 and "discovered" Glacier Bay, he estimated that the entire bay had been ice-filled a century earlier, and therefore, not identified by explorer George Vancouver. The bay was even new to Muir's native guides. The world was then exiting the "Little Ice Age," and most of Alaska's glaciers have been receding ever since. Glaciers like those in Glacier Bay and Tracy Arm, which still calve icebergs directly into the sea, are becoming increasingly rare, while the faces of other glaciers, such as Juneau's Mendenhall Glacier, have receded miles inland. Glaciers scour mountainsides, capturing huge amounts of rock and gravel. Clean ice may hide beneath a dingy, gray crust resembling a dry river bed. Often, the glacier's surface fractures and erodes into a forest of jagged ice towers, "seracs," which display dazzling shades of white and ice-blue in bright sunlight. After visits to both Tracy Arm and Glacier Bay, we can say that both are distinctive. Glacier Bay offers broad vistas of mountain, sea, and sinuously flowing ice fields, with numerous fjords snaking back from the bay. When weather permits, the blindingly white, pyramid-peak of Mount Fairweather (15,325 ft./4,671 m.) is a sight to behold. Tracy Arm holds more mystery, its steep walls often deep in shadow, new vistas appearing as the ship rounds another bend.

Introduction | Reservations | Staterooms | Dining | Activities | Ports of Call | Magic | Index

Skagway, Alaska
(Alaskan Itineraries)

Skagway is a direct route into the days of the Klondike Gold Rush of 1897, guarding the ends of the White Pass and Chilkoot trails, the **best routes** into the Yukon. Photos of prospectors queued-up heel-to-toe in the snow as they climbed the pass have made an indelible mark on our imaginations.

© MediaMarx, Inc.

Historic Skagway

AMBIENCE

Set in a **deep valley surrounded by dramatic peaks**, Skagway has the feel of a small ski resort, only at sea level. While its port and the road and railway through White Pass have been in constant commercial use since gold rush days, tourism dominates today. Up to five large cruise ships visit daily, their passengers wandering the streets heedless of traffic. Historic buildings have been moved to prime downtown locations to enhance the ambience and populate the national historical park. The town sometimes borders on tourist trap, but there's enough charm that you probably won't mind. The year-round population is less than 900, and once the tourist hoards depart, a fair number go back to creating the fine art objects that fill local shops and galleries.

HISTORY

Tlingit people have lived here for thousands of years, but recorded history starts in 1887 when William Moore, a surveyor sure that gold would be discovered in the Yukon, built a homestead and dock at this promising deepwater port. The **prospectors** arrived 10 years later. Despite his foresight, Moore didn't prosper as well as he'd hoped, but the town did, for a short while. "Hell on Earth" to the Royal Canadian Mounted Police, the town celebrates the memory of its one shoot-out, which ended the lives of crime boss "Soapy" Smith and vigilante Frank Reid. By the time the White Pass & Yukon Railroad was finished in 1900, the Gold Rush and events of major historical interest were already near their end.

FACTS

Size: 464 sq. mi. (1,200 sq. km.)	
Climate: Temperate Oceanic	**Temperatures**: 40°F (4°C) to 68°F (20°C)
Population: 862	**Busy Season**: Summer
Language: English	**Money**: U.S. Dollar ($)
Time Zone: Alaska (Pacific -1)	**Transportation**: Walking, tour bus, train
Phones: Area code 907, dial 911 for emergencies	

Making the Most of Skagway, Alaska

GETTING THERE

Welcome to the **northernmost ice-free deep water port in the U.S.**, at the north end of the Lynn Canal (actually, a long, straight fjord). Skagway's docks—Railroad, Broadway, and Ore—can berth five large cruise ships, but on Thursdays in 2013, just two or three will be docked beside the Wonder. Passengers can walk into downtown from any of the piers, tour buses and even trains may be waiting dockside, and the main White Pass & Yukon Railway depot is at the edge of the waterfront. All ashore time is 7:15 am and all aboard is 7:30 pm. As you cleared U.S. Customs in Vancouver, there will be no customs here, but you will need your passport if your excursion crosses into Canada.

GETTING AROUND

Skagway is a small, very walkable town sandwiched into the long, narrow Skagway River valley, with most tourist areas within a half mile of the piers. The main tourist street is Broadway, a pleasant row of low-rise Victorian-era buildings housing shops, restaurants, and galleries. You'll find both the **Klondike Gold Rush National Historical Park Visitor Center** and the **White Pass & Yukon Railroad Depot** on Second Street just as you enter town, and by about Eighth St. you'll have run out of shops. The **Skagway Visitor Center** is in very picturesque Arctic Brotherhood Hall (marked "AB") between Second and Third Streets. While you don't want to ignore the side streets, you'll find that the shops and cafes peter-out about a block either side of Broadway. A city bus service offers rides around town, but if you hope to get out of town, it's a very long drive up the Yukon Highway to the next human outpost—take a bus or a train! Still, there is an Avis car rental office at Second and Spring.

SAFETY

Skagway's tiny population and remote location add up to **small town safety**. The biggest risk may be falling for some of the town's pricier *objets d'art*. If you go hiking, be prepared for wildlife encounters, including black bears, and dress for changeable weather with warm layers and suitable rain gear.

SHOPPING

If you need **cuddly outerwear**, you'll find many shops offering good deals. For high quality native goods and works by local artisans, both Kirmse's and Corrington's are worthy stops, on opposite sides of Broadway by Fifth. Red Onion Saloon has a limited bar food menu and lots of brews and local root beer on tap. By Railroad Dock, Skagway Fish Company serves excellent fish and chips and chowder. Broadway Bazaar between 5th and 6th is a pleasant courtyard with shops offering chowder, crepes, reindeer sausage, and gelato.

........➤

Touring Skagway

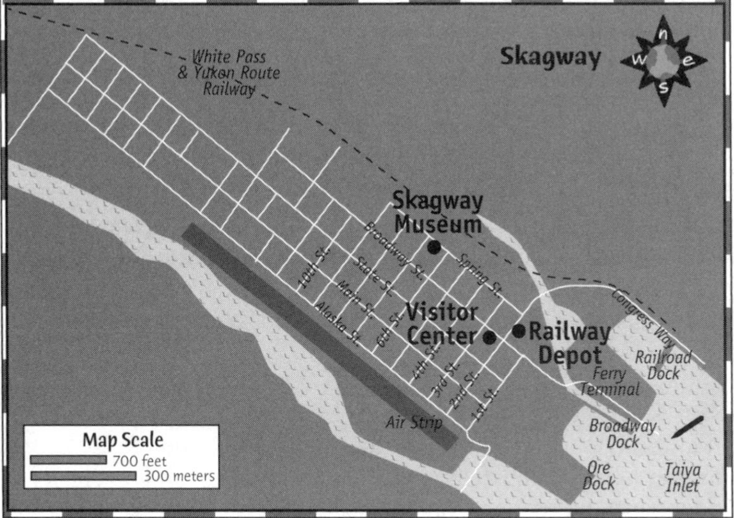

SKAGWAY MAP

ON YOUR OWN

You have a long day in Skagway, so you can enjoy a shore excursion and still have time to explore in town. There are many tour offices on Broadway, and savings are good if you book your own. We highly recommend a ride on the **White Pass & Yukon Route Railroad**, which follows the path of the gold rush up to and beyond Fraser, B.C. Reserve in advance, as the cruise lines gobble up a lot of seats (http://www.wypr.com, 800-343-7373). Our rail excursion included a return trip by bus, with a stop at Liarsville. This spot on the edge of Skagway was jumping-off point for the prospectors, and provides just modest entertainment. Back in town, the **Days of '98** show is more satisfying, a professionally-acted melodrama about the town's famous shoot-out. Tickets are easy to get at the box office, with several shows daily. The Red Onion Saloon offers hourly **Brothel Tours** for $5 (which is what "it" cost, back in the day). The young female guides make the slightly spicy tour worthwhile. More serious-minded walking tours are available at the National Park headquarters nearby. Hikers can explore the local Dewey Lake trail network, departing near the intersection of 3rd St. and Spring St. Or, walk about two miles up State St. to the Gold Rush Cemetery and Reid Falls. The railway will drop hikers off at higher elevations. None of the museums are worth more than a half-hour of your time, including the Skagway Museum at 7th and Spring, and various National Park exhibits. The Corrington Museum in the shop of the same name is worthwhile and free.

Embarking on Port Adventures in Skagway, Alaska

Of the 46 excursions offered by Disney Cruise Line at press time, here are our **recommended port adventures** for visitors to Skagway:

Low Budget: The cheapest excursions, as always, are the city tours - best budget tip? Save your money and tour the town on foot, on your own! The Yukon Suspension Bridge and Klondike Explorer bus tour ($69/$35 age 3–9, under age 3, no charge, 3–3.5 hours) gives you much of the scenery of the railway ride, at a much lower price. While we have misgivings, Liarsville Gold Rush Trail Camp and Salmon Bake Featuring Exclusive Disney Character Experience ($89/$49 ages 3–9, under age 3, no charge, 2.5–3 hours) has been rescued by Disney's "plussing" of an otherwise mediocre tourist attraction.

Big Budget: Dog Sledding and Glacier Flightseeing ($562/$499 ages 2–9, age 5 and up recommended) hits all the high altitude notes. Dogs and sleds on snow rather than wheels, walking on a glacier, and a helicopter ride through amazing scenery. Sign us up! And at just 2–2.5 hours, think of all the money you can spend during the rest of the day on a second excursion and/or shopping in Skagway.

Nature: So many choices! We're tempted to cruise down Lynn Canal to Haines, for any one of several excursions: Eagle Preserve Float Adventure and Lynn Fjord Cruise ($198, ages 10 and up only), Haines Wilderness River Adventure ($199/$127 ages 5–9, ages 5 and up only) and Glacier Point Wilderness Safari ($229, ages 10 and up only), since they include sea life, bald eagles, and a good bit of ice, in varying manners. Choose the one that best matches your interests. Each of these excursions lasts 6 to 6.5 hours.

Active: Laughton Glacier Wilderness Hike and Rail Adventure ($225, ages 9 and up, 9-9.5 hours) or Laughton Glacier Snowshoe Hike and Rail Adventure ($275, ages 9 and up, 9-9.5 hours). You get a taste of the railroad and a serious hike in a gorgeous location, wearing snowshoes when conditions dictate. Then again, bicycle fans may enjoy testing their brakes on the long, 15-mile downhill run included in the budget-priced Klondike Bicycle Tour ($87, ages 13 and up only, 2.5–3 hours) or add the train ride with White Pass Train and Bike Tour ($199, ages 13 and up only, 4–4.5 hours).

Armchair Travelers: Any ride on the White Pass & Yukon Railroad is worthy, but only some offer round-trips on the train. Others may bus you for half the trip, but include additional attractions.

Juneau, Alaska
(Alaskan Itineraries)

Juneau is Alaska's capital, and the only state capital that **cannot be reached by road**. Located between Skagway and Tracy Arm on the Gastineau Channel, and surrounded by the Tongass National Forest, the only ways in or out are by sea or air.

© MediaMarx, Inc.
Tramway above Juneau

AMBIENCE

More like a **county seat** than the capital of the largest U.S. state, downtown Juneau occupies a small plot of land between the water and steep mountains. Suburban Douglas is just across the channel, and other neighborhoods are several miles to the north, along the road to the airport and Mendenhall Glacier. The low-rise clapboard and brick buildings and the cruise ships berthed along the shore quickly give way to the steep, forested slopes of Mounts Roberts (3,819 ft./1,164 m.) and Juneau (3,576 ft./ 1,090 m.), and while tourism-focused shops dominate the south end of town, a short walk takes you into more sedate districts near the statehouse. All this gives way to expansive natural vistas when you visit Mendenhall Glacier, ride the Mount Roberts Tramway, or helicopter over to the huge Juneau Icefield.

HISTORY

The **Auke and Taku tribes of the Tlingit people** have hunted and fished this area for millennia. The first Europeans arrived in 1794 with George Vancouver's expedition, which bypassed the ice-choked channel. Settlement began in 1880, after the U.S. purchase of Alaska and the subsequent Juneau Gold Rush. Mining continued in downtown Juneau into the 1940s. The territorial capital was moved here from Sitka in 1906, and outside of the everyday business of government, gold, and fishing, some of the most noteworthy historical moments have been the attempts to move the capital elsewhere, which have yet to succeed.

FACTS

Size: 12 sq. mi. (31 sq. km.) (urban) / 3,255 sq. mi. (8,430 sq. km.) (total)	
Climate: Temperate Oceanic	**Temperatures:** 40°F (4°C) to 64°F (18°C)
Population: 17,311/30,988	**Busy Season:** Summer
Language: English, Tlingit	**Money:** U.S. Dollar ($)
Time Zone: Alaska (Pacific -1)	**Transportation:** Walking, buses, taxi
Phones: Area code 907, dial 911 for emergencies	

Introduction Reservations Staterooms Dining Activities Ports of Call Magic Index

Making the Most of Juneau, Alaska

GETTING THERE

The Wonder berths on **Juneau's waterfront** on Fridays in 2013, sharing the port with up to three other ships, depending on the week. Most ships dock parallel to the shore along Franklin St. A shuttle bus serves most-remote AJ Dock ($3 for unlimited rides), but the trip is just .75 mi./1.2 km. The other piers are all very walkable. The Mount Roberts Tramway is right at the docks, and a Juneau visitor center office is in the tramway parking lot; stop by for a map. Tours and shuttles often leave from the tramway parking lot. Shopping and dining begins right at the piers along Franklin Street, which will lead you north into town. All ashore time is 6:15 am; all aboard is at 4:30 pm.

GETTING AROUND

The streets of downtown Juneau are **easy to navigate**, as you can only go about 8–12 blocks in any direction. With only 41 miles of major roads to roam, car rentals won't take you very far, and the rental offices are out at the airport—arrange a pickup at the pier. Tour buses, shuttles, taxis, and walking are the best choices for cruise passengers. **Mendenhall Glacier** is 12 miles to the north, and the ways there are many. For a basic ride, the MGT "Blue Bus" shuttle runs every half-hour to and from the glacier's visitor center for $16 round-trip. Taxis are metered, at city-set rates: $3.40 initial fare, $2.20 per mile, $0.75 additional persons. A trip from the pier to Mendenhall Glacier will be about $35 each way. Evergreen Taxi, 907-586-2121; Juneau Taxi and Tours, 907-586-1111; and Glacier Taxi Tours, 907-796-2300 serve the area, and also offer tours by car and van, in the range of $55 per hour, per vehicle.

SAFETY

Safety warnings in Southeast Alaskan ports tend to be about the wildlife, weather, and outdoor safety. **Don't approach or feed the wildlife!** Trail hikes may lead to encounters with black bear, so consider an experienced guide. This is temperate rainforest, and conditions can change quickly. Be prepared for damp and chill, dress in layers and have proper rain gear. Folks in these parts don't play around with umbrellas.

SHOPPING

Shopping is concentrated along **Franklin Street**—just keep walking. Furs, jewelry, and native crafts are the headliners. On the dock, The Twisted Fish is a bustling, satisfying casual eatery. Next door, Taku Smokeries offers edible souvenirs (and free samples). An alley just north of the piers hosts casual food kiosks, including Tracy's King Crab Shack. Their crab bisque is an affordable treat, with pricier temptations for crab lovers. Red Dog Saloon is impossible to miss, plays the Gold Rush to the hilt, and sells lots of souvenirs.

Touring Juneau, Alaska

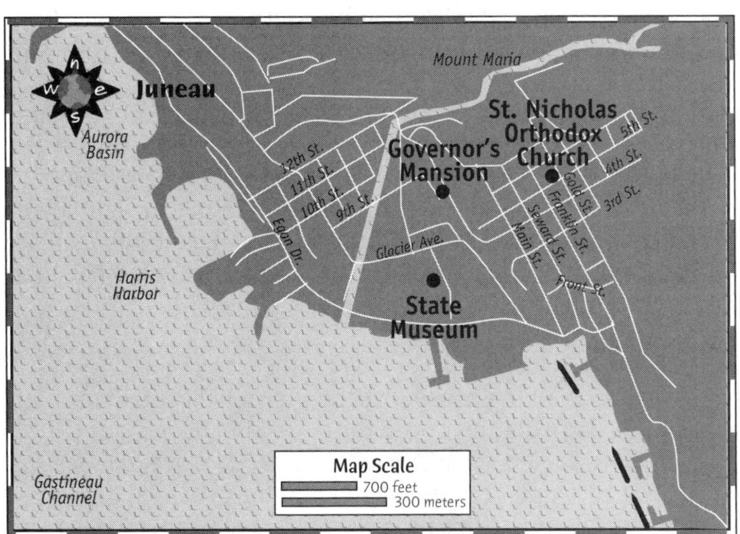

Juneau offers a wide variety of attractions, from glacier walks and sled dogs to museums. The **Mount Roberts Tramway**, owned and operated by Alaska natives, is the most popular in-town attraction. The views are spectacular, and allow time to walk the trails and enjoy the exhibits, including wildlife, a film, and artisans at their crafts. The gift shops are above-average. Adults $31/$15.50 ages 6–12, 5 and under free. The **Alaska State Museum** on Whittier St. offers the most extensive exhibits on history, native culture, and wildlife. **St. Nicholas Orthodox Church** is a tiny, wooden Russian church on 5th near Franklin that's on the National Register of Historic Sites. **Last Chance Mining Museum**, about a mile out of town, shows the remains of Juneau's gold mining past. **Macaulay Salmon Hatchery** is about three miles north of downtown, and offers a fascinating look at Alaska's commercial fisheries. Adults $3.25/$1.75 ages 2–12–http://www.dipac.net. By far the most popular destination is **Mendenhall Glacier**, the focus of many tours. The National Forest Visitor Center is jumping-off spot for free ranger-guided and self-guided hikes of various lengths. The longest is East Glacier Loop, a two-hour walk that brings you closest to the glacier, ending at thundering Nugget Falls. Most tour groups only visit for an hour. Visit on your own and spend more time! Tickets for the Blue Bus shuttle (see previous page) can be bought online at http://mightygreattrips.com or at the dock.

Introduction Reservations Staterooms Dining Activities Ports of Call Magic Index

Embarking on Port Adventures in Juneau, Alaska

Of the 49 excursions offered by Disney Cruise Line at press time, here are our **recommended port adventures** for first-time visitors to Juneau:

Low Budget: Mount Roberts Tramway – At Leisure ($29/$14.50 ages 6–9/under 6 free, allow 1–2 hours). The tramway departs right from the pier, the views (on a clear day) are fabulous, and there's plenty more to explore. The price is higher at the ticket counter, so take advantage of the deal and book ahead. Best value? Take the Blue Bus to Mendenhall Glacier on your own ($16 round trip), pay the visitor center fee ($3), and spend all the time you want hiking and exploring the park.

Big Budget: Disney Exclusive Glacier Dog Musher for a Day ($709/$499 ages 5–9) Combine the breathtaking scenery of a helicopter ride with the maximum sled dog experience, add the cost of taking the kids (who'd never forgive you if you left them behind), and say goodbye to those spa treatments! Every helicopter excursion promises breathtaking views, and this is the port for 'choppers (it's float planes in Ketchikan). The biggest cost factor is the flight, so spend a bit extra for more time on the glacier.

Nature: Mendenhall Glacier and Whale Quest ($165/$94 ages 0–9, 5.5–6 hours) This combines the top two nature activities in Juneau, so what can be bad? Your time at the glacier is just an hour. You could take a whale-watch-only excursion, and spend several hours at the glacier on your own (see Low Budget, above).

Active: This category hosts some of the most inexpensive and expensive adventures. Mendenhall Glacier Adventure Hike ($89/$49 ages 8–9, 4.5–5 hours) takes you out into the wooded hills for spectacular views. On the big-budget side, why walk to look at the glacier, when you can take an Extended Helicopter Glacier Trek ($535 age 15 and up, 5–5.5 hours) *on* a glacier? If hiking doesn't do it for you, Alaska's Ultimate Rainforest Canopy & Zipline Adventure ($184 age 10 and up, 3–3.5 hours) may, but Ketchikan offers ziplining, too, with no glaciers to compete.

Armchair: Perhaps the ultimate sight-seeing trip is Enchanted Taku Glacier Lodge Flight and 5-Glacier Seaplane Discovery ($309/$265 ages 2–9, free under 2, but recommended for ages 5 and up, 3.5–4 hours). An hour of glacier flight-seeing time, a remote lodge in a spectacular setting, and an intimate grilled salmon meal. If this pushes your buttons, reserve asap, it books-up fast! There's no shortage of ways to go whale watching, a very worthy pursuit—combine it with your choice of additional sights. If not whales, head out to Mendenhall Glacier in whatever way you wish.

Ketchikan, Alaska
(Alaskan Itineraries)

© MediaMarx, Inc.

Downtown Ketchikan

Ketchikan, **Alaska's "First City,"** and self-styled "Salmon Capital of the World," is more firmly rooted in fishing and logging than its fellow ports of call. Barely beyond the city limits, the Misty Fjords National Monument is a stunning destination for seaplane flights.

AMBIENCE

Similar in scale to downtown Juneau, Ketchikan's downtown is just across the street from the piers. Low-rise brick and wood-frame buildings dominate downtown, houses cling to steep, wooded hillsides, and farther north the waterfront evolves into seafood processing plants and fishing wharfs. Creek Street preserves the city's red light district, its rickety wood shacks hanging over the creek. The world's largest collection of **standing totem poles** is here, brought together from around the area to aid preservation. The town sits on Revillagigedo Island near the south end of Misty Fjords National Monument. Moist, northern rainforest, glacier-polished granite peaks, and rugged shorelines pierced by deep inlets and fjords afford captivating vistas outside of town. Whether the weather in the fjords is wet (most likely) or dry (it can happen), visitors will be captivated.

HISTORY

Tlingit people have fished and dwelled here for thousands of years. Europeans settled in 1883, with fishing and fish processing the first industries. The early 1900s brought both mining and timber to town, and a pulp mill operated until 1997. The city's most recent mark on history is the **now-canceled "Bridge to Nowhere,"** which would have connected the communities on the east side of Tongass Narrows to the airport (and nothing else) across the water. How many international airports can only be reached by ferry?

FACTS

Size: 4.1 sq. mi. (8.8 sq. km.) (city)/ 1,754 sq. mi. (4,543 sq. km.) (borough)	
Climate: Temperate Oceanic	**Temperatures**: 55°F (15°C) to 65°F (31°C)
Population: 7,368/14,070	**Busy Season**: Summer
Language: English, Tlingit	**Money**: U.S. Dollar ($)
Time Zone: Alaska (Pacific -1)	**Transportation**: Walking, buses, taxi
Phones: Area code 907, dial 911 for emergencies	

Making the Most of Ketchikan, Alaska

GETTING THERE

The Wonder visits Ketchikan on Saturdays in 2013, and sometimes all of the port's four large ship berths will be occupied. The berths run parallel to the **waterfront** along Front St./Water St., with the Wonder assigned to southernmost Berth 1 every week (see map). (In 2011 she was sometimes tied-up at Berth 4.) From Berth 1 downtown is just across the street, but from Berth 4 it's a 1/3 mile walk. A free shuttle bus stops at Berth 4 (see below). The main Visitor Information Center, with its well-known Liquid Sunshine Gauge, is near Berth 2, but there's also information and restrooms near Berth 4. All ashore time is 11:15 am, all aboard time is at 7:30 pm.

GETTING AROUND

For cruise ship passengers, Ketchikan is a very compact place. Downtown and the historic Creek St. district cover a five-block by five-block area, and the longest drive anywhere is less than 20 miles. After that, you run out of road. Totem Bight Park is a nine mile drive to the north, Saxman Indian Village is three miles to the south. **Walking** is the main mode of transportation, with highly-promoted attractions like the lumberjack show just a couple of blocks from the pier. In most cases, **taxis** won't be necessary, but fares are $3.70 drop, and $3.50/mile, and they can usually be found by the Visitor Information Center. A **free shuttle bus** circulates in the downtown area on a 20-minute route, including stops at Berth 4. **Car rentals** are possible, but hardly necessary. Budget and EZ operate by the airport along with local Alaska Smart Rentals 907-225-1753. Ask if they'll pick you up at the pier. **Float plane tours** are very popular, with at least a half-dozen tour operators, both large and small. We got a walk-up booking with mom-and-pop operation SeaWind Aviation (877-225-1203) at their desk in the Visitor Information Center. There are several other tour desks in the center, so if you haven't booked ahead (which is a good idea for discounts and better selection of flight times), you may still be able to bargain hunt, especially if they have empty seats to fill on short notice.

SAFETY

Thanks to its remote location, Ketchikan, like its fellow Alaskan ports of call, is a **pretty safe place**. Normal precautions always apply. City streets are not particularly busy, but don't be lulled into a false sense of security. Stay on the sidewalks, and keep aware of traffic. It's not likely you'll be headed into the forest on your own, but if you do, black and brown bear are an important consideration, as are all regular backcountry hiking safety rules.

Touring Ketchikan, Alaska

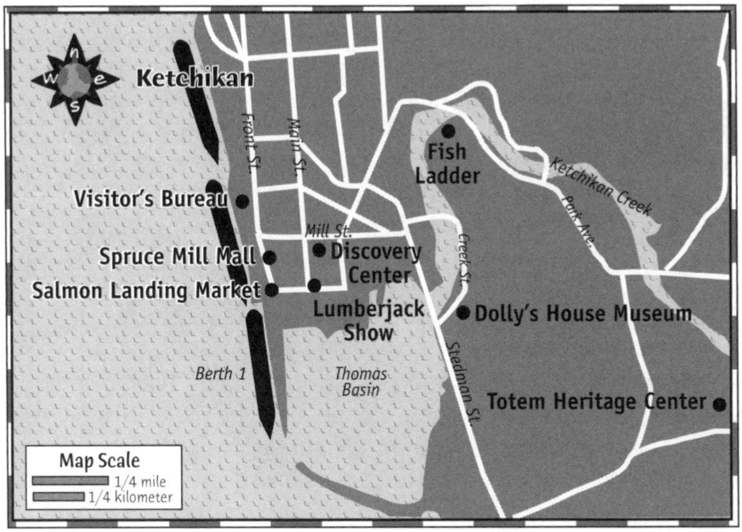

Ketchikan doesn't have many major, in-town attractions. The more enticing out-of-town tours are often fully-booked by the cruise lines. If you want to do a particular tour on your own, book far in advance. The **Visitor Information Center** has many tour sales desks, but choices may be slim. A good walking tour map is readily available and covers anything you can possibly see in town. Fish fans will love the fish and chips stands right at the docks. The Great Alaskan Lumberjack Show is the top in-town attraction, just three blocks from the Berth 1 pier. The 60-minute shows are $38 adults/$17.50 children 3-12, under 3 free. Walk-up tickets may be available, but don't count on it. Advance tickets are only sold by the cruise lines. Right across the street, Southeast Alaska Discovery Center is a U.S. Forest Service facility with native culture and natural history exhibits ($5 adults, ages 0-15, free). Trace Ketchikan Creek upstream through the Creek St. red light district and onward, to follow the salmon swimming up fish ladders to the Deer Mountain Hatchery and Eagle Center. Tour this hatchery and animal rescue center for $12, $5 ages 12 and under. Totem Heritage Center, a short distance from the hatchery, hosts a large collection of 19th-century totems ($5). Totem Bight State Park is a beautiful waterfront spot 9 miles to the north, and admission is free. Three miles south of town, Saxman Native Village has totems, craftsmen, and interpretive tours. Walk-up tours ($35/$18) may be available, but they ask cruisers to book through the cruise line.

Introduction Reservations Staterooms Dining Activities Ports of Call Magic Index

Embarking on Port Adventures in Ketchikan, Alaska

Of the 42 excursions offered by Disney Cruise Line at press time, here are our recommended port adventures for first-time visitors to Ketchikan:

Low Budget: Saxman Native Village & Exclusive Lumberjack Show ($103/$45 ages 3–9, allow 4 hours) gives better bang for the buck than most other inexpensive tours. If you want more nature in the mix, Rainforest Wildlife Sanctuary, Raptor Center and Totems ($82/$45 3–9, under 3 free, 2.5 hours) takes you to out-of-town sights, unlike the City Highlights tour, which lists similar-sounding attractions. City Highlights, Totems and Creek Street by Trolley is very low-priced, but all sights can be covered on a self-guided walking tour (get the very good free map).

Big Budget: This is the town for flightseeing in seaplanes. Every excursion promises breathtaking views (and they really are) and the thrill of watery take-offs and landings. Flight time and additional activities are responsible for price variations. You pay similar rates for a mid-distance airline flight. To save a bit or get more flight time, book early, directly with the excursion operators. The only other big-ticket excursions are the private charters (boats, planes, and Hummer), but if you fill the vehicle to capacity, the per-person cost is little different than a regular excursion.

Nature: Bering Sea Crab Fishermen's Tour ($185/$105 ages 5–9, 3.5 hours) is ultra-cool. If you want to hook 'em yourself, take your pick of fishing excursions (this is the Salmon Capitol). If you can fill the boat, the private boat excursions cost nearly the same per person. Neets Bay Bear Watch by Floatplane ($365/ages 2-9, 3 hours) isn't always available, but it takes you deep into the Misty Fjords outback like no other excursion.

Active: Rain Forest Canoe Adventure and Nature Trail ($112/$69 ages 5–9, 3.5–4 hours) should get the adrenaline pumping. Mountain Point Snorkeling Adventure ($109/$99 ages 8–9, 3–3.5 hours) should be on the list for novelty alone (and when else can you swim on this cruise?) Both ziplining excursions offer something that's available in every port, but Ketchikan offers the fewest competing active excursions. The kayak adventure here could be better, as on-water time is quite brief.

Armchair: The best "armchair" may be a seat in a Dehavilland float plane (see Big Budget, above). Wilderness Exploration and Crab Feast ($155/$99 ages 0–9, 4–4.5 hours) gets you out on the water and puts something yummy in your tummy, Misty Fjords and Wilderness Explorer ($185/$109 ages 0–9, 4–4.5 hours) gives you the most on-water time in the fjords. A visit to Saxman Native Village is better than Totem Bight for native culture.

San Francisco, California
(West Coast Itineraries)

© MediaMarx, Inc.

Famous cable cars of San Francisco

AMBIENCE

The City by the Bay. Grand bridges shrouded in fog, cable cars scaling storied hills, exotic neighborhoods nurturing poets, painters, writers, and musicians; great food, fine wines, constant innovation and strong traditions... San Francisco is a city and legend unto itself.

This is the second most densely populated major U.S. city, heart of one of the nation's largest and most prosperous metro areas, with a **cultural footprint far greater than its size**. But where to begin? Perhaps the cool breezes, dramatic views, and bright sunshine that greet your arrival? The nearby Golden Gate, Alcatraz, Telegraph Hill, and the towers of downtown? Legendary Chinatown, North Beach, Fisherman's Wharf, and the Presidio? The universities in Berkeley and Stanford? Napa Valley to the north? Silicon Valley to the south? All have made their mark on this very remarkable place.

HISTORY

Archaeological evidence of San Francisco's popularity dates back over 5,000 years, though recorded history began with explorer Don Gaspar de Portolà in 1769. Within seven years, a mission dedicated to St. Francis of Assisi and the military base known as The Presido had been raised. Despite her natural attributes, this was a sleepy outpost until the **1849 California Gold Rush** filled the harbor with ships. The transcontinental railroad arrived 20 years later, so when the Great San Francisco Earthquake hit in 1906, 400,000 called the city home. That setback was so brief, the economy so strong, that both of the city's great bridges were built at the height of the Great Depression. World War II's Pacific headquarters found new life post-war as a center for progressive culture, technology, and tourism.

FACTS

Size: City: 231.89 sq. mi. (600.6 sq. km.) Metro: 3,524.4 sq. mi. (9,128 sq. km.)	
Climate: Mediterranean	**Temperatures**: 46°F (8°C) to 71°F (22°C)
Population: 805,235/4,335,391	**Busy Season**: Year-round
Language: English	**Money**: U.S. Dollar ($)
Time Zone: Pacific	**Transportation**: Walking, bus, subway
Phones: Area Code 415, dial 911 for emergencies	

Making the Most of San Francisco

GETTING THERE

The Wonder docks at **Pier 35 on San Francisco's Embarcadero**, the waterfront boulevard. There's a very long list of great places to visit within walking distance, and all sorts of public transit is at hand, starting with the F-Line streetcars that travel the waterfront (see below). It's a great jumping-off spot, no matter where you're headed. Disney's port visits here are usually two-day affairs. The 2013 Los Angeles/ Vancouver repositioning cruise will be in port Monday, September 9 from 8:00 am to 9:30 pm.

GETTING AROUND

San Franciscans love their **mass transit**. Regular, one-way fares on the F Line and other Muni System buses and subways is $2 (have exact change or buy multi-ride passes). Free transfers are available on most lines, so the fare can take you a long way. The famed **cable cars** cost $6 per trip. A one-day, unlimited-ride **Muni Passport** is $14, available at selected locations in San Francisco (it's also included in CityPASS, see next page). The pass covers bus, subway, cable car, the waterfront F-Line, plus rush-hour use of the Presidio Shuttle (see below). For more info on public transit, visit the San Francisco Municipal Transportation Agency web site at http://www.sfmta.com. With so much time in port, and attractions like the wine country and the Monterey Peninsula within reach, a **car rental** is a practical choice. Budget has the closest office to the pier, at 5 Embarcadero, near Market St. Most other major agencies have offices closer to the heart of downtown. **Taxis** cost $3.50 for the first 1/5 mile, $0.55 for each additional 1/5. Licensed cabs have "San Francisco Taxi" written on the side and rear of the vehicle, and there will be a small, metal license plate (taxi medallion) on the dashboard. Towncar/limo rides must be pre-arranged. Want a **free ride to the Walt Disney Family Museum**? The Presidio operates shuttle buses from downtown near the waterfront to the Presidio Transit Center, which is just a short walk to the museum. The downtown shuttles are free between 9:30 am and 4:30 pm, use a Muni Passport at other times. Shuttles also circulate throughout the Presidio, from 6:30 am to 8:00 pm, and are free at all times.

SAFETY

San Francisco is one of the U.S.' largest cities, and **personal safety** should always be on your mind. Take all customary precautions, and be especially careful when using ATM machines and carrying bags and parcels.

Touring San Francisco

SAN FRANCISCO MAP

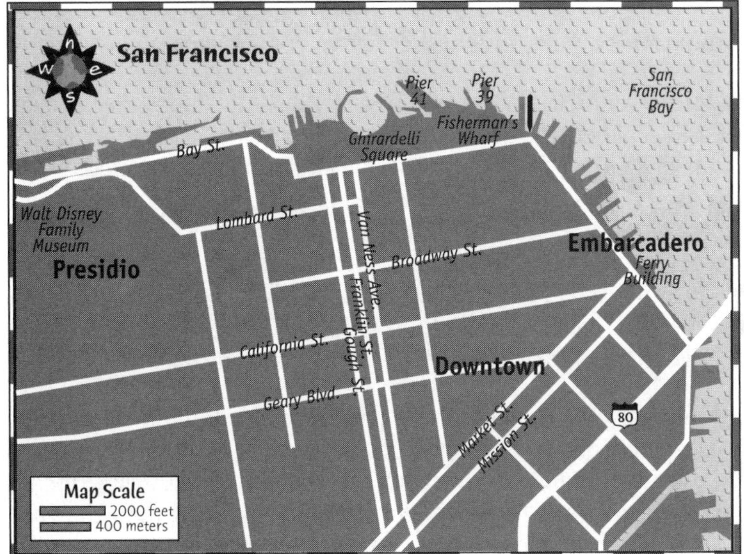

COVERING THE WATERFRONT

The sights of the Bay Area are too numerous to cover here, so we'll focus on the Embarcadero and the Walt Disney Family Museum.

Sights along the waterfront can easily fill a full day. The cruise pier is centrally located on the Embarcadero, one mile to **Ghirardelli Square** in one direction, and a mile to the the **Ferry Building and Market St.** in the other. Walk towards the Golden Gate and you'll quickly reach **Pier 39**, which is full of shops, restaurants, the Aquarium of the Bay, a museum of mechanical arcade games, and a World War II sub. Next is Pier 41, home to the **Blue & Gold Fleet**, for tours and the ferry to Sausalito ($22/$13.50 child, round-trip, http://www.blueandgold.com). A bit beyond that is **Fisherman's Wharf**, with even more places to eat, and then the **National Maritime Historical Park** on the Hyde St. Pier, filled with historic ships. Two more blocks and you're at **Ghirardelli Square** for food and shopping. Turn right exiting the cruise pier, and the **Alcatraz Ferry** will be right next door. Book ahead, as walk-up tickets may be hard to get (http://www.alcatrazcruises.com). Unless you plan a casual lunch at Pier 23 Restaurant, consider riding the F-Line trolley to the **Ferry Building** at the base of Market St., which is a foodie heaven filled with food shops and restaurants, plus **Tuesdays Farmer's Market** (10:00 am–2:00 pm) • The **Walt Disney Family Museum** is about three miles from the pier, in the Presidio. The museum's excellent, interactive exhibits are a must-do for serious Disney fans. The 2-3 hour visits on shore excursions are too brief for enthusiasts–visit on your own. $20/$12 ages 6-17. Closed Tuesdays! Visit http://www.waltdisney.com for more information. While there, **tour the Presidio** on the park's free shuttles (see previous page). Visit http://www.presidio.gov • Consider **CityPASS**, which includes Muni transit and cable car passes, a harbor or Alcatraz cruise, and admission to three museums ($69/$39 ages 5-12, http://www.citypass.com).

Embarking on Port Adventures in San Francisco

Of the 17 excursions listed by Disney Cruise Line at press time, here are our **recommended port adventures** for visitors to San Francisco:

Low Budget: We find the Walt Disney Family Museum tours over-priced, and it's easily reached on your own (Museum admission is $20, but adding a two-hour museum visit to the Views of San Francisco tour adds $40). Muir Woods & Sausalito ($65/$39 ages 0-9) take you farther afield, to some great locations. Views of San Francisco ($59/39 ages 0-9)is attractive for the number of sights seen, and, if the weather is good, Chinatown Walking Tour & San Francisco at Night ($59 ages 10 and up) can be enchanting. Remarkably, Wax Museum and Aquarium of the Bay - At Leisure ($27/$13 ages 3-9) is cheaper than buying the combo ticket at the attraction!

Big Budget: Lasseter Family Winery ($325 ages 21 and up) has to lead the list. How can you top fine wine, good food, a beautiful location, and Disney-Pixar royalty? In the same vein, Napa Valley Wine, Art & Culinary Experience ($299 ages 21 and up) comes a close second (and the food may be even better). If the Lasseter Family connection isn't important to you ("Who's John Lasseter?"), it's a better value, too.

Nature: Though there are no nature-focused excursions, San Francisco is surrounded by natural beauty and several tours take you there. Monterey & Carmel ($179/$159 ages 3-9) is an 11-hour journey. Though the sights and towns are memorable, it'll be a very long day. Muir Woods and Sausalito ($65/$39 ages 3-9) takes you to a breathtaking redwood forest and a picturesque town, and leaves time for in-town exploration. Sonoma Wine Country ($179 ages 21 and up) is the affordable wine country choice.

Active: There's no heavy exertion on the list here, unless you count some walking (and we don't).The Presidio is nearby and offers many recreational opportunities, from hiking to golf (http://www.presidio.gov).

Food and Beverage: There are four tours that qualify, and two are covered in Big Budget, above. If you say "dim sum" we're usually there in a flash (we've had some great Chinese feasts in San Francisco), but we figure you're paying $30 for the food on San Francisco City Tour With Dim Sum Lunch ($85/$49 ages 0-9), and you can feed two for that price.

Armchair: While nearly all tours include some walking, Monterey & Carmel (above) and Views of San Francisco (also above) deliver a large helping of sights and a minimum of exertion. Consider a harbor cruise on the Blue & Gold Fleet (see previous page).

Madeira, Portugal
(Transatlantic Repositioning Itineraries)

Soaring mountains, lush gardens, and fresh air beckon travelers to this **little island paradise** they call Madeira. You'll find much to do here, whether it's watch dolphins, explore scenic villages, sample the local wines, or just lay back and enjoy the warm breezes and sunshine.

© Terri Sellers

Funchal, Madeira from the deck of the Disney Magic

AMBIENCE

Madeira's archipelago lies far out in the Atlantic Ocean, more than 600 miles from Portugal itself. The capital city, Funchal, is nestled in the south within a **natural amphitheater** formed by dramatic mountains on one side and the warm Gulf Stream waters on the other. Rich volcanic soil produces gorgeous flowers and lush agriculture, forming gardens nearly everywhere you look. The tiny island's mild weather and crystal clear waters draw visitors from around the world to sample its wines, view its flowers, and admire its embroideries.

HISTORY

The island of Madeira was officially "discovered" in 1419 by João Gonçalves Zarco and Tristão Vaz Teixeira, two Portuguese sea captains bent on exploration. It was quickly settled by the Portuguese and they began growing grains and sugarcane, creating the world's first sugarcane plantation and mechanical sugar mill. Wine production also grew, and Madeira became famous for its excellent wines and ports. At one point, **Christopher Columbus** (Cristofõm Colon) himself lived here before embarking on his historic voyage to the Americas. Tourists arrived in the 19th century, and eventually became the island's prime source of revenue. More recently, Madeira has become known for Cristiano Ronaldo, a world-famous football (or soccer, as we Americans call it) player.

FACTS

Size: 13 mi. (21 km.) wide and 35 mi. (56 km.) long / 320 sq. mi. (828 sq. km.)	
Climate: Mediterranean	**Temperatures**: 64°F (18°C) to 76°F (24°C)
Population: 250,000	**Busy Season**: July to October
Language: Portuguese	**Money**: Euro (€)
Time Zone: Western European	**Transportation**: Walking, taxis
Phones: Dial 011-351 from U.S., dial 112 for emergencies	

Making the Most of Madeira, Portugal

GETTING THERE

The Disney Magic ship docks at the **Molhe da Pontinha** breakwater in the heart of Funchal. The dock offers delightful views of the bay and city, and even the approach to the dock is considered to be one of the most beautiful vistas you'll see on your cruise. If you plan to walk into town, factor in at least 10 minutes to walk along the berth. Taxis are also available if you prefer not to walk. There's just one visit here in 2013, on the Eastbound Transatlantic Repostioning. All-ashore time is 10:30 am with an all-aboard time of 6:45 pm. Cruisers on the eastbound repositioning will arrive on a Tuesday.

GETTING AROUND

The simplest and cheapest way to get around is simply to **walk** off the ship and wander into Funchal. You'll be able to see the ship from nearly any point in Funchal, so there's not much fear of getting lost. • If you prefer a **taxi**, they are available near the dock, and can provide island tours (see http://www.danielmadeirataxis.com for more information). Taxis are easy to spot as they are bright yellow with a blue stripe down the side. You should pay no more than **€10** for a taxi ride around Funchal. • A fun thing to do in Madeira is to take a *cable car* up to Monte (€10/adult, €5/child 4–14) for lovely views, and then take a **guided wicker toboggan** down (€12,50/person + €10/person for a taxi to get the rest of the way down). • Look for the Open Top Bus, a hop-on, hop-off bus that covers all of Funchal—there are plenty of departure points around the dock and marina area (€12/person). • You can **rent cars** in Funchal—most roads are paved and safe, though some of the narrower, steeper, and scarier roads still exist, so be careful.

SAFETY

Madeira has **very little crime** and is considered to be very safe, perhaps the safest port you'll visit on your cruise. But, as always, be aware of your surroundings and keep your valuables out of sight, or better yet, back on the ship. Take extra caution if you go off the beaten path, as this is a mountainous area with many cliffs, and some walks can be hazardous.

SHOPPING

The **closest shopping boulevard** from the ship in Funchal is the Avenida Arriaga, just opposite the marina. You'll find several shops and eateries here, as well as the Madeira Wine Company. You'll also find plenty of stores along the backstreets, so don't be afraid to explore. Note that while many of Madeira's flowers are for sale, you will not be able to bring them back onto the ship. Instead, seek out the famous wine, honey cakes, and embroidered goods.

➢

Touring Madeira, Portugal

MADEIRA MAP

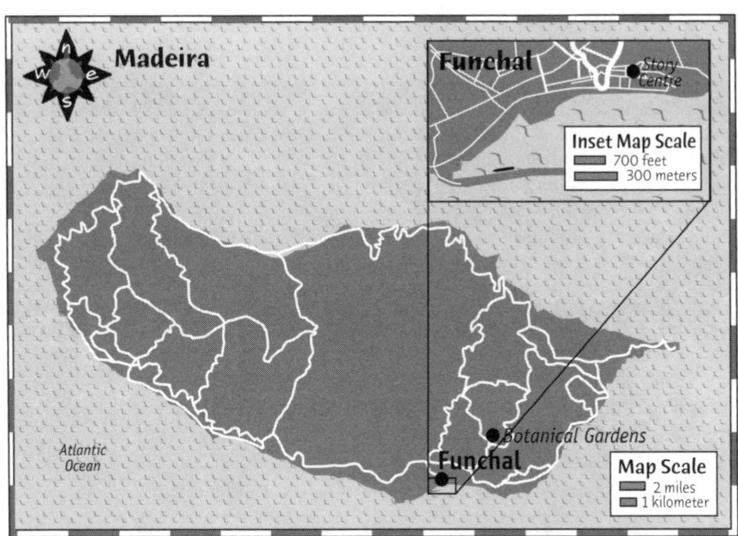

ACTIVITIES

Madeira offers plenty to see and do, from surfing and scuba diving to aqua and theme parks. If you'd like to try something more involved, visit http://www.madeira-web.com for excellent details on activities, as well as gorgeous photos! If you just want to check out Funchal on foot, you can easily take a half-day and see many sights. As you walk into town, look out for the old fort, the Santa Maria replica ship, and plenty of public parks and gardens. Consider a visit to one of the **many excellent museums** here, such as the Madeira Story Centre, where you can take a virtual, interactive journey into the island's history and culture (€9.90/adult, €4.95/child 4-14, see more information at http://www.storycentre.com). Stop by the Catarina Park to see the Christopher Columbus statue. The Botanical Garden is another very lovely place to visit. A combo ticket that includes the cable car is (€21/adult, €18 ages 15-18/€9.75 ages 7–14.

© Leo Seta

Cable car over Funchal

If you'd like to see what Funchal looks like before you arrive, check out http://www.madeira-web.com/camera/cam-01.html for **several live web cams**!

Embarking on Port Adventures in Madeira, Portugal

Of the 13 excursions offered by Disney Cruise Line at press time, here are our **recommended port adventures** for first-time visitors to Madeira:

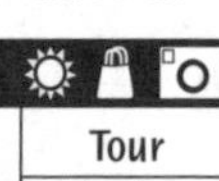

View and Parks

This excursion offers an excellent overview at an affordable price. You begin your tour bus excursion by driving along the high cliffs of the west coast, finding your way to the village of Camara de Lobos. You'll enjoy 40 minutes of free time in the village before driving to Santa Catarina, a beautiful park overlooking the Bay of Funchal. You then take a walk into town to sample Madeira wine (non-alcoholic beverages provided for those under age 21).

Tour
Active
Ages 12 & up
$35/12+
4-4.5 hours

Catamaran Whale and Dolphin Watching

Climb aboard a catamaran for a 3-hour cruise along the south coast of Madeira, the best place to spot whales and dolphins! The ocean floor drops sharply just a few miles off the coast of Madeira, making it possible for cruisers to spot whales and dolphins in their natural habitat. Afterward, the vessel will drop anchor at the base of a sea cliff so you can cool off in the ocean. Be sure to wear your swimsuit under your clothes so you can sunbathe or swim.

Tour
Active
Ages 5 & up
$69/$49 (5-9)
4-4.5 hours

Santa Maria Columbus Galleon

Would you like to see—and board—a replica of Christopher Columbus' Santa Maria sailing ship? This is your opportunity! Board this 15th century replica nearby where the Disney Magic docks and set sail on a cruise along Madeira's southern coast. Along the way you'll witness the galleon ship crew as they go about their daily routine. You'll also learn the folklore of seagoing explorers, and kids can participate in a scavenger hunt! Be sure to keep an eye out for dolphins! The ship has both a bar and restrooms aboard as well. Honey cakes and Madeira wine (or non-alcoholic beverages) are served during your voyage.

Tour
Leisurely
All ages
$95/$75 (0-9)
4-4.5 hours

See page 210 for a key to the shore excursion description charts and their icons.

Beyond these three recommended excursions, other port options (at press time) include a beach day in the town of Calheta ($105/$75. all ages), an exploration of Madeira caves and the north coast ($105/$69, all ages), a tour bus excursion to West Madeira ($99/$59, all ages), a cultural and historical tour which includes a cable car and a toboggan ride ($155/$115, all ages), a 4x4 Landrover expedition into the island's interior plain ($99, ages 12+), a 9-mile bicycle tour of Funchal ($95, ages 12+), a hiking and rapelling adventure through Ribeiro Frio ($175, ages 14+), a 6-mile hike through the Valley of Rabaçal ($89, ages 12+), and a wide selection of 4- and 8-hour Funchal by Private Vehicle tours (with driver) in your choice of sedan (2-3 guests) or minibus (6 guests) and with or without a tour guide ($245-$775).

© Terri Sellars

Funchal Fort

Gibraltar
(Repositioning Itineraries)

We've all heard of the solid "Rock of Gibraltar." But did you know that while Gibraltar is at the southern tip of Spain, it's actually a **British overseas territory**? This tiny, densely populated region stands sentry over the Strait of Gibraltar, which links the Atlantic Ocean to the Mediterranean.

© Photodisc

The famous Rock of Gibraltar

AMBIENCE

"The Rock," a **gray limestone monolith** nearly two miles (three km.) long and 1,396 ft. (426 m.) high, dominates Gibraltar's scenery. Miles of tunnels and 140 natural caves riddle the soft limestone, making the solid "Rock" almost hollow! The top slopes are the Upper Rock Nature Reserve, home to Europe's remaining wild monkey, the Barbary macaque. The eastern side offers small beaches nestled against sheer cliffs, while the western side harbors the town and its residents. Impressive fortress walls and a Moorish castle enclose the town, and its bay is a well-known spot for dolphin watching and diving. The southernmost tip of Gibraltar is Europa Point, from which you can see the North African coast 14 miles away.

HISTORY

Gibraltar is firmly rooted in the bedrock of history. The ancients alternately feared and revered it, thanks not only to its magnificent geography but also its position at the entrance to the Atlantic Ocean. The Greeks named the Gibraltar promontory one of the two **Pillars of Hercules**, which formerly marked the end of the world. Its vantage point meant it was much sought after as a defensive point—it has been besieged 15 times—and occupied by the Visigoths, the Arabs, the Spanish, and eventually the British, in whose hands it has been since 1713. Today, Gibraltar's economy is based on financial services and tourism.

FACTS

Size: 2.5 sq. mi. (6.5 sq. km.)	
Climate: Mediterranean	**Temperatures**: 71°F (21°C) to 82°F (28°C)
Population: 28,000	**Busy Season**: Winter
Language: English, Spanish	**Money**: Pound Sterling (£)
Time Zone: Central European	**Transportation**: Walking, taxis, cable car
Phones: Dial 011-350 from U.S., dial 999 for emergencies	

Making the Most of Gibraltar

GETTING THERE

The Disney Magic docks at the **Port of Gibraltar**, located on the western side of the Gibraltar peninsula. Your ship berths alongside the port's cruise terminal, which offers visitors a cafeteria, local handicrafts store, and a tourist information desk. More information on the port is at http://www.gibraltarport.com. A taxi stand and excursion tour buses are a short walk away. It's also quite possible to walk into town from the pier. Disembarkation time is typically 7:30 am with an all-aboard time of 6:00 pm. Cruisers on the 2013 eastbound repositioning will visit on a Thursday.

GETTING AROUND

If you're just interested in shopping, it's an **easy walk** (less than a mile) from the cruise terminal to Main Street (see map on next page). Other sights, such as the Moorish castle, are within walking distance. • **Taxis** are popular and plentiful here—ask a driver for a "Rock Tour" for about £18-25/person. The tour encircles the Rock and takes in most of the major sights in about 90 minutes. For more information, visit http://www.gibtaxi.com. Do note, however, that if you want to cross the border and visit Spain, Gibraltar taxis are not allowed into Spain—you'll have to get dropped off at the border, walk across, and hail another taxi. • If you're not on an excursion, you can get to the top of the Rock via **cable car** (round-trip £11.75/£7.00)—the station is next to the Alameda Botanical Gardens (see map). • We do not suggest you **rent a car** in Gibraltar—roads are very narrow and parking spaces are severely limited.

SAFETY

Safety in Gibraltar isn't difficult. Crime rates are very low. Pickpocketing is a concern, albeit to a lesser extent than other Mediterranean ports. Humans aren't the only creatures to remain alert around; Gibraltar's famous Barbary apes have been known to pickpocket, too. Perhaps more importantly, the apes can bite and scratch, so we discourage you from feeding or touching them.

SHOPPING

Gibraltar's **Main Street** is the focus of shopping here—its main pedestrianized thoroughfare runs almost the entire length of the town (see map). You'll find luxury goods (leather, jewelry, watches, and perfume) and electronics for sale in both chain stores and small boutiques. And let's not overlook the plethora of toy monkeys, a popular souvenir. Prices are usually given in pounds as well as Euros at most stores—if you use Euros to pay, however, your exchange rate may not be favorable.

➤

Touring Gibraltar

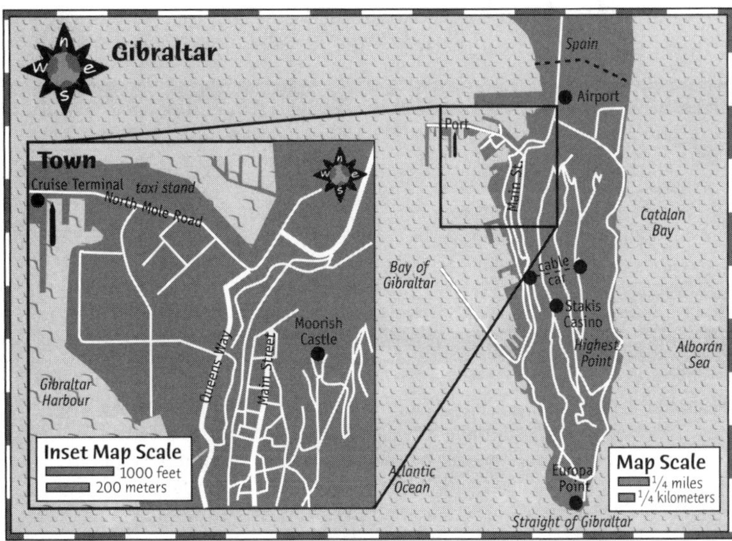

A visit to the Rock is the main draw for tourists in Gibraltar, but there are several other interesting sights as well. Here are details:

The Rock—View it from afar (you can see it from the cruise dock) or get up close on an excursion or with the cable car (see previous page). Consider also a visit to upper St. Michael's Cave—this extensive cave system has enough room for a concert auditorium! Entry to the cave is free with a cable car ticket. The cable car also gets you up to the Apes' Den to see the fascinating monkeys.

The Bay—The Gibraltar bay is home to three species of dolphin as well as whales, turtles, and flying fish. "Dolphin safaris" are available to attempt to spot these creatures (http://www.dolphinsafari.gi). Diving is also popular in the bay, which has several shipwreck sites and plenty of marine life (http://www.divegib.gi).

The Food—With most excursions lasting less than half your day, consider finding yourself a decent lunch spot. Gibraltar food is known for two things—its unique cuisine and its British pub fare. For a taste of Gibraltar, look for eateries serving *calentita* and *panissa*—baked chickpea dishes. You'll find tapas bars around, too. Feeling British? Look for pubs—we hear The Clipper is particularly good. You'll also find some Moroccan cuisine in Gibraltar.

Embarking on Port Adventures in Gibraltar

Of the 9 excursions offered by Disney Cruise Line at press time, here are our **recommended port adventures** for first-time visitors to Gibraltar:

Panoramic Gibraltar and Afternoon Tea

This driving tour shows you all of the important sites of Gibraltar, albeit in a condensed version. As your bus tour starts out, you'll pass the American War Memorial and the British naval headquarters stationed in Gibraltar. Next, your tour bus drives to the Europa Point for photo opportunities of the Strait of Gibraltar, the Spanish mainland, and, if it's a clear day, Africa. From there, you travel to the Caleta Hotel where you'll partake of an English-style afternoon tea with a magnificent view of the Mediterranean.

Tour
Leisurely
All ages
$52/$42
2-2.5 hours

Rock Tour

You'll be hard pressed to get a better experience of Gibraltar than on foot. Your guided tour begins with a visit to Gibraltar's military fortifications with its beautiful floral gardens and spectacular views. Next, take the cable car to the top of the Rock, where you'll be able to view Catalán Bay before walking a wooded footpath to St. Michael's Cave. After seeing the cave, you'll be shuttled to Apes' Den, home of the Barbary apes. See the Great Siege Tunnels and then walk pass the Moorish Castle before walking back into town for some shopping. From the shopping area, it's only a short walk back to the pier. Wear comfortable shoes.

Tour
Moderate
All ages
$49/$39
1.5-2 hours

Dolphin World

Your tour begins with a water taxi at the ferry terminal to the Bay of Gibraltar. If for some reason no dolphins are spotted here, your boat continues on to the Strait of Gibraltar. After viewing the dolphins, the water taxi passes the western face of Gibraltar while the onboard guide provides facts and history. After you return to the ferry terminal, you can choose to go back to the ship or take a shuttle into town for some shopping.

Tour
Leisurely
All ages
$59/$49 (0-9)
1.5-2 hours

See page 218 for a key to the shore excursion description charts and their icons.

© Terri Sellers

The Disney Magic in Gibraltar

Tip: Look for the camera symbol throughout the text to indicate when additional photos are available online along with our trip report at http://www.passporter.com/dcl/mediterranean.asp

Barcelona

(Mediterranean Itineraries' Home Port)

See pages 108–113 for details on flying into Barcelona, terminal information, and more

Mention Barcelona and you may think of delicious *paella* and *tapas*, or its delightful climate and sunny beaches. Did you know it's also the **second largest city in Spain**, and the capital of Catalonia? Steeped in more than 2,000 years of history, Barcelona is a cultural and commercial center of world significance.

© MediaMarx, Inc.

Barcelona's Christopher Columbus Monument

AMBIENCE

Basking in the glow of the Mediterranean sun, Barcelona is a vibrant city with a **balance of old world charm and modern enterprise**. The stylish city offers eccentric and modern architecture, culinary treats, trendy shopping, and impressive art collections. The rounded top of Mt. Tibidabo provides a backdrop to the picturesque city, which is located on a plateau along the southeast corner of the Iberian peninsula, bounded by the Collserola mountain range, the Llobregat and Besós rivers, and the sea.

HISTORY

Believed to be **founded around 250 B.C.**, the Barcelona region began as small villages settled by Carthaginians. The villages grew into a city, which the inhabitants called Barcino. The Romans arrived by the first century A.D., leaving its architectural legacy behind for us to enjoy. Several more invasions arrived—Visigoths, Muslims, Franks—thanks to its desirable location. Barcelona eventually became one of the most powerful trade cities in the Mediterranean, becoming the seat of the Spanish monarchy until it shifted to Madrid in the 15th century. The region suffered in the 16th and 17th centuries, enduring revolts and repression. The industrial boom of the 19th century brought good things to Barcelona, including several international exhibitions. In 1992, Barcelona hosted the Olympic Games, which revitalized the city even further.

FACTS

Size: 188 sq. mi. (487 sq. km.)	
Climate: Mediterranean	**Temperatures**: 68°F (20°C) to 82°F (28°C)
Population: 1,500,000 (city)	**Busy Season**: Summer
Language: Catalan and Spanish	**Money**: Euro (€)
Time Zone: Central European	**Transportation**: Walking, taxis, subway
Phones: Dial 011-34 from U.S., dial 112 for emergencies	

Making the Most of Barcelona

GETTING THERE

The Disney Magic docks at the **Moll D'Adossat Terminal**, a large port facility on Barcelona's coast. Taxis and tour buses leave from the pier. The ship leaves port at 4:00 pm and returns at 7:00 am on each of the 2013 itineraries that include Barcelona (4-, 7-, and 12-night cruises). You can catch a shuttle bus (€1,50) from the dock to Monument de Colom, which is at the southern end of Las Ramblas pedestrian promenade. Taxis are also available in this area if you wish to go farther afield.

GETTING AROUND

Unlike so many other Mediterranean ports, downtown Barcelona is within easy distance of the dock. Barcelona **taxis** are black and yellow, and plentiful. Look for a green light atop a taxi that indicates it's available for hire. Prices are posted inside the taxi, and a meter shows the final price (though do expect an extra fee if you're going to the airport and/or have luggage with you). Plan to tip about 5–10% of the fare. • If you'll be in town for a while, consider Barcelona's excellent public transportation system, the **Metro**, with six subway lines crisscrossing the city. A subway or bus ride is €2, a 2-day pass €13.40. For Metro routes, visit http://www.tmb.net (L4 route is the closest to the port). If you're going to a nearby town, the FGC (Ferrocarrils de la Generalitat de Catalunya at http://www.fgc.es) commuter line has routes at the same price as a subway ride. • While **rental cars** are available, we don't think they are necessary for most of our readers. If you're in the minority, Hertz, Avis, National Atesa, and Europcar all have agencies at the airport. • Plan to do a lot of **walking** in Barcelona—most of the city center is pedestrian-friendly.

STAYING SAFE

Despite its charm, Barcelona has a bad reputation for **petty crime**. Dave lost his wallet in Barcelona, and while we can't be sure, we suspect his pocket was picked in a subway elevator. Your best bet is to avoid looking like a tourist (keep those maps and books tucked away) and secure your wallet and purse. Avoid tourist dress (i.e., shorts) and wear fitted, earthtone clothes. Be wary of anyone attempting to sell you a trinket, beg, or even help you clean up bird droppings—they may be hoping to distract you long enough to pick your pocket. Carry the absolute minimum in cash and ID, too (thankfully, Dave followed this advice). We also suggest you avoid the southern end of Las Ramblas in the late evening, as it can get rather seedy. If you'll be spending some time in Barcelona, visit this site with tips on avoiding problems: http://www.barcelona-tourist-guide.com/barcelona-safety.html

Touring Barcelona

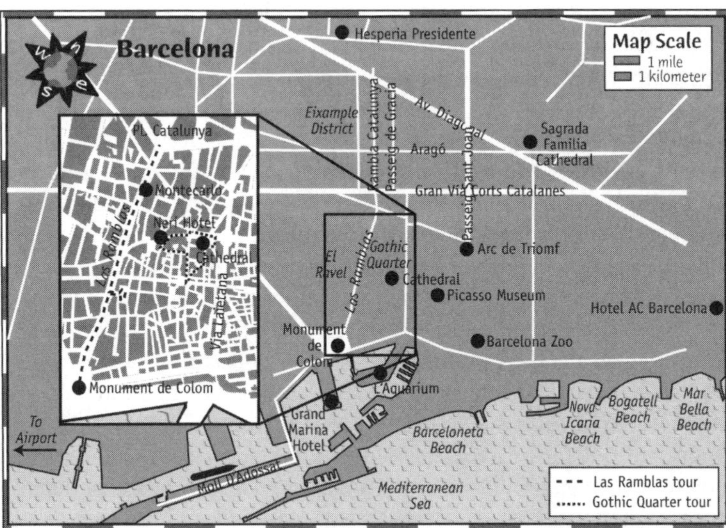

Walking Las Ramblas: Starting from Monument de Colom, walk north along Las Ramblas 📷. Your first stop will be the Reials Dressanes (medieval dockyards) and the Museum Maritime. The Wax Museum comes along next, followed by Plaça Reial, a gorgeous square with an iron fountain. As you continue on, look for the mosaic in the walkway by Joan Miro. Next is the Sant Josep (Boqueria Market) which houses popular food stalls. Walking on, look for the Palau de la Virreina, a lavish 18th-century rococo building. As you come to Carme street, look for Iglesia de Belén, an ancient Jesuit church with a Gothic interior. You'll finish at the Font de Canaletes 📷, a 19th-century iron fountain, near the Placa de Catalunya. Allow about 3–4 hours.

Walking Around the Gothic Quarter: Begin at Plaça Nova 📷 with one of the Roman gates to the old city. Here you'll see the 12th-century Palau Episcopal (Bishop's Palace). A street opposite the palace leads to the Cathedral, which you may enter by the main door (wear respectful clothing—no shorts or tank tops). Leave the cathedral by way of the cloisters and enter Plaça Garigia i Bachs—cross the square to Plaça Sant Felip Neri. Nearby is a shoe museum. Exit to Carrer del Bisbe and walk south to the Placa Sant Jaume, the heart of the city. You can walk north through the same way, or wander down the enchanting streets. Allow 3–4 hours. Note: Look for signs showing the route 📷 of an alternate walking tour, too.

Playing in Barcelona

ACTIVITIES

Barcelona has so many attractions you'll find it hard to decide. That's why we spent several extra days in Barcelona. Here are the attractions we found most interesting during our visit:

The Gothic Quarter (Barri Gotic) is a must-see and one of our favorite sights. Try our walking tour detailed on the previous page. This is the "old town Barcelona," dating back to the Roman era with ancient fortified walls, Roman palaces, and narrow cobblestone streets. Picasso lived and worked here. The Gothic Quarter is very near Las Ramblas (see next page) if you want to combine visits.

L'Aquarium de Barcelona is a large, popular aquarium at the port. Over 11,000 sea creatures (450 different species) make their home here in the 20 tanks and displays. The walk-through shark tunnel (262 ft./80 m. long) is a visual treat. There's also an interactive, hands-on area where you explore three marine ecosystems. An IMAX theater is next door, but you can visit one at home, right? The aquarium opens every day from 9:30 am to 9:00 pm (open a little later on summer weekends). Tickets are €19/adults, €15/seniors 65+, €14 ages 5-10, and €10/ages 3-4. Phone: 93 221 74 74. http://www.aquariumbcn.com

Montjuic is a huge, hilltop park, home to the 1992 Olympics, many museums (including Poble Espanyol—see next page), and great city views. It's easily reached by city transit and aerial tramway from Barceloneta.

Sagrada Familia is a huge, ornate temple that has been a work in progress since 1882 (and still has at least 20 years to go). The church—which happens to be Barcelona's #1 tourist attraction—is open 9:00 am to 8:00 pm. Admission €13.50/€11.50, add a tour for €4.5/€3.50 . http://www.sagradafamilia.org

Montserrat is a breathtaking mountain with a monastery perched atop it. It's located about 35 miles northwest of Barcelona, so consider a tour operator or excursion. You can go inside the cathedral to view the 12th century "Black Madonna." Try to time your visit to catch the Escolonia boy choir at 5:00 pm. We also had a nice, inexpensive meal at L'Arsa La Cafeteria. http://www.abadiamontserrat.net

Atop Montserrat

Shopping and Relaxing in Barcelona

SHOPPING

The world-famous **Las Ramblas** is a 3-km.-long, tree-lined boulevard with a pedestrian promenade down the middle and shops and restaurants along the sides. ("Las Ramblas" actually means "dry riverbed" in Arabic.) You'll find designer boutiques (Versace, Giorgio Armani) as well as department stores and street vendors. You'll also find several tourist museums, including a maritime museum, wax museum, art museum, and a museum of erotica. You can walk here from the port–see the map on page 387. The Barcelona Transport bus (€7.25 for an all-day card) runs along Las Ramblas from 7:30 am to 9:45 pm weekdays and 9:00 am to 9:20 pm Saturdays (the line does not run on Sundays, as nearly all the shops are closed). This is a very busy area and prime for pickpockets; guard your valuables.

Poble Espanyol de Montjuic, the "Spanish Village," sits atop Montjuic Mountain and displays architecture and culture from different parts of Spain (we think of it as the "World Showcase" of Spain). More than 50 vendors, craftspeople, and workshops create traditional Spanish goods here among the squares and streets. This is the home of El Tablao de Carmen restaurant and flamenco show–see next page. The village is open 9:00 am to midnight or later, though most cafes and shops close earlier. Admission is €11 for adults, €6.25 for kids 4–12 (kids under 4 are free). Phone: 93 50 86 300. http://www.poble-espanyol.com

RELAXING ON BEACHES

What better way to relax than on a sunny Spanish beach? Barcelona has **four main beaches**. Barcelona's beaches are generally clean and most have lifeguards. The closest large beach to the port is Barceloneta, a wide but crowded beach lined with a boardwalk and several American-style eateries, as well as the yummy Can Majó paella eatery (see next page). Beyond that is Nova Icaria, which offers several beach bars and restaurants on its broad, golden sand. Adjoining Nova Icaria is Bogatell–it features a paved path for cycling and jogging. A bit farther down is Mar Bella, the city's only "naturalist" (nude) beach. If none of the city beaches appeals to you, consider Casteldefells beach with five kilometers of wide sand and many eateries–it's a 15-minute train ride south from the city to the nearby station of Platja de Casteldefells. If you want a beach off the beaten path, hop on a train going north to Ocata–here you'll find a long, golden beach with space to breathe. Remember to bring your sunscreen and wear your swimsuit under your clothing on your way to and from the beach–swimwear is only appropriate attire on the beaches in Spain.

Dining in Barcelona

If you're into food, be sure to get into one (or several) of Barcelona's eateries. Widely regarded as **Europe's latest culinary capital**, Barcelona offers its own unique twist on traditional Catalan food. You'll want to try the *paella*, of course, but also look for *tapas* (tasty little appetizers), *zarzuela* (fish stew), and *meti i mató* (soft cheese and honey).

Traditional lunch hour is 2:00–4:00 pm. Dinner is taken late between 9:00 and 11:30 pm. Locals generally make lunch their main meal of the day.

Most restaurants serve a **fixed-price meal at lunchtime**, consisting of an appetizer, an entree, dessert, and a drink. This meal, called *menú del dia*, is usually an excellent bargain (around €8–12).

In January 2011, Spain banned **indoor smoking** in bars and restaurants.

Legal drinking age is 16. Bars and lounges are everywhere. Do consider ordering *una jarra de sangria* (one pint of sangria). Mmmmm!

Plan to **tip about 5–10%** of your total—leave your tip in cash. A 7% sales tax will also appear on your bill.

Here are the restaurants we **tried and enjoyed during our stay**, plus a few we haven't tried but have heard good things about:

Taller de Tapas —Excellent tapas restaurant with English menus and English-speaking staff. They also serve breakfast. Get a seat outside to watch the Gothic Quarter strollers. This was our favorite dining experience in Barcelona—highly recommended! Address: Plaça Sant Josep Oriol 9. Phone: 93 301 80 20. Web: http://www.tallerdetapas.com

Café de L' Academia—A charming old town restaurant with an enchanting outdoor terrace, complete with an old, bubbling fountain. Affordable prices. Address: Lledó 1 Plaza San Just, Barri Gotic. Phone: 93 315 00 26. Open Monday–Friday (closed most of August).

Can Majó —This popular waterfront restaurant serves up excellent seafood, paella, and fideuas (paella with noodles instead of rice). Try for a table on the terrace. You'll want to make reservations, especially on a weekend. Address: Almirante Aixada 23 (on the Barceloneta beach). Phone: 93 221 54 55. http://www.canmajo.es/en

Barceloneta —If you can't get into Can Majó, walk farther down the beach to Barceloneta for great paella and fisherman's rice (€21.95 each). Address: L'Escar 22, Moll dels Pescadors (near the Barceloneta beach). Phone: 93 221 21 11. Web: http://www.rte-barceloneta.com

El Tablao de Carmen—Yes, this is a tourist destination, but what fun! The set menus are a bit pricey at €39 (drink-only)–€77 (dinner), but the price includes the 75-minute flamenco show. Reservations should be made in advance at their web site. Address: Poble Espanyol (see previous page). Phone: 93 325 68 95. Web: http://www.tablaodecarmen.com

Lodging in Barcelona

If you decide to extend your stay in Barcelona but opt not to book one of Disney's pricey pre- or post-cruise hotels (see pages 110–111), here is a list of more moderately priced and special hotels. We haven't checked these out ourselves, but we hear good things about them. Keep in mind that Barcelona hotels are quite popular and enjoy an 85% occupancy rate, so availability can be hard to come by unless you book in advance. Tip: If you can manage it, we suggest you plan to stay in Barcelona before your cruise—this gives you time to acclimate to the time zone before your cruise starts.

Catalonia Plaza Catalunya (Duques de Bergara)—Would you like to sleep in a duke's townhouse? This renovated 1898 home built for the Duke of Bergara has 149 guest rooms with marble bath. Rates start at €99. Address: Bergara 11, Ciutat Vella. Phone: 93 301 51 51. Web: http://www.hoteles-catalonia.com

Hotel Constanza—A trendy boutique hotel of just 46 rooms within easy walking distance of shops and La Ribera. Breakfast buffet. Rooms start at about €80. Address: Bruc 33, L'Eixample. Phone: 93 270 19 10. Web: http://www.hotelconstanza.com

Neri Hotel—Another boutique, 22-room hotel, this one in the Gothic Quarter near the cathedral. Its focus is on romance—check out its terrace and rooftop garden. Rooms start at €250. Address: Sant Sever 5, Barri Gotic. Phone: 93 304 06 55. Web: http://www.hotelneri.com

Montecarlo—Situated right on Las Ramblas, this 200-year-old building features an ornate facade and rooms with adjustable beds and jetted tubs. Rates start at about €150. Address: Las Ramblas 124. Phone: 93 412 04 04. Web: http://www.montecarlobcn.com

Vincci Marítimo Hotel—If sunbathing on beaches is your thing, consider this modern hotel near the Barceloneta beach. The hotel even has a communal Japanese garden to relax in. Rates start at €140. Address: Llull 340, Poble Nou. Phone: 93 356 26 00. Web: http://www.vinccihoteles.com

Learning More About Barcelona

- Recommended web sites about Barcelona:
  - http://www.barcelona-tourist-guide.com
  - http://www.aboutbarcelona.com
  - http://www.timeout.com/barcelona
- Recommended guidebook: *Insight Guide Barcelona* (ISBN: 978-1780050553).
- Our trip report: http://www.passporter.com/dcl/mediterranean.asp.

Disneyland Paris

Thinking about taking a side trip to Disneyland Paris? You're not alone—several of our readers asked us to research this possibility. We haven't made a visit there when we've been to the Mediterranean , but we did visit Disneyland Paris some years ago with our son Alexander. And we now offer an entire guidebook, *PassPorter's Disneyland Paris* by Sabine Rautenberg—get more details at http://www.passporter.com/disneyland-paris.asp.

First things first—**how do you get to Disneyland Paris** from Barcelona? Your best bet is to take the "Trainhotel" on the RENFE (Spanish National Railway Network). The Trainhotel leaves from the Barcelona Franca station in the evening and arrives in Gare de Paris-Austerlitz the following morning. Prices start at about €200 per person, round-trip. For more details, see http://www.seat61.com or http://www.raileurope.com. Once you reach Paris, take a taxi—it's about 30–45 min. to the park and about €70 (bring cash). It is possible to take a train to Disneyland Paris, but it requires switching lines several times—we don't recommend it.

Disneyland Paris itself could be blitzed in a day (not counting your transportation to and from Barcelona, of course), though we spent three days here in order to really enjoy it. Keep in mind that there are now two parks at the resort as well as **several resort hotels**. We splurged on the Disneyland Hotel, a grand Victorian hotel right at the entrance to the Disneyland park. Our large, first-floor room had high ceilings and a four-poster bed—quite enchanting and very French. Room rates here start at €390. If you're more budget-minded, consider Disney's Davy Crockett's Ranch at €195/night. More Disney resort hotel options exist between these two rates, as well as several non-Disney hotels that begin at about €180/night. (All of the rates we mention are per adult, based on double occupancy, and include park admission.)

The parks themselves—**Disneyland Park and Walt Disney Studios**—are within walking distance of each other. Admission is €61/adult and €56/child age 3-11 for a one-day/one-park ticket. Park hoppers are available—one-day hopper (€74/€66), two-day (€129/€116), and three-day (€159/€144). You can tour the park attractions and eateries before you arrive at http://www.disneylandparis.com. One attraction you should not miss is CinéMagique at Walt Disney Studios—it's a delightful journey through 100 years of movies with Martin Short!

© MediaMarx, Inc.
Sleeping Beauty Castle

Tip: Look for the camera symbol throughout the text to indicate when additional photos are available online along with our trip report at http://www.passporter.com/dcl/mediterranean.asp

Villefranche and Cannes
(Mediterranean Itineraries)

Ahhh, the **French Riviera**! Its azure waters, terraced hills, and sun-bleached buildings are what many of us picture when we imagine the Mediterranean. The charming, small town of Villefranche is the gateway to the jet-set glitter of Monaco and Monte Carlo, the big city of Nice, and the sunny beaches of Cannes.

© MediaMarx, Inc.

The enchanting Villefranche waterfront

AMBIENCE

Villefranche is nestled in a **natural harbor** between Nice and Monaco. It's famous for its warm, luminous light, which we experienced on our visit. The three "Corniches" (the main roads between Nice and Italy, just beyond Monaco) pass through Villefranche. For our friends who enjoy the "Impressions de France" film at Epcot: Do you recall the waterfront scene of Villefranche or the sunbathers and Bugatti race cars in Cannes? You can see these magical vistas through your own eyes near this port!

HISTORY

Villefranche (pronounced Veal-fransh) literally means "town without taxes," so named in the 13th century when King Charles II gave the town **tax-free status** to encourage the villagers from the hills to live in the town. The area's history begins long before this with prehistoric settlements. Farming communities sprouted up in the surrounding hills. The Greeks and Romans valued the deep-water harbor. Fast-forward to the 14th century and we find the area in a tug-of-war between the Holy Roman Empire and France. Franco-Turkish armies occupied the city in 1543, prompting the construction of the large Citadel. The area changed hands several times, belonging to Savoy, then France, then Sardinia. In 1860, it returned to the French and became a favored spot for the wealthy to winter. Today it is France's most popular cruise ship port.

FACTS

Size: 2 sq. mi. (5 sq. km.)	
Climate: Mediterranean	**Temperatures**: 67°F (19°C) to 80°F (27°C)
Population: 8,000 (island)	**Busy Season**: Summer
Language: French	**Money**: Euro (€)
Time Zone: Central European	**Transportation:** Walking, taxis
Phones: Dial 011-34 from U.S., dial 112 for emergencies	

Introduction | Reservations | Staterooms | Dining | Activities | Ports of Call | Magic | Index

Making the Most of Villefranche and Cannes

GETTING THERE

Itineraries that stop at Villefranche dock in the **Bay de Villefranche** while itineraries that stop in Cannes arrive at **Degrad des Cannes**—either will have you tender ashore in boats (expect a boat ride of about 15 minutes). In Villefranche, you arrive at a very nice terminal that has an information booth and restrooms—the wharf is also an excellent spot to take a picture of Villefranche as we did (see photo on previous page). From here you can walk to just about anywhere in Villefranche or take the nearby train to Nice (see below for details). Disembarkation time is typically 8:00 am with an all-aboard time of 7:00 pm. The 7-night itinerary stops here on a Monday, while the 4-night and 5-night itineraries stop on Wednesday.

GETTING AROUND

Villefranche is one of those happy ports you can explore without booking a shore excursion. It's not large and it's best to **walk** through the picturesque town to see its charm (see our walking tour on the next page). This is a very hilly area, however, so wear your most comfortable shoes. • Another option is the **Little Tourist Train**, which takes you around Villefranche. Cost is €5 for a 25-minute tour in the morning, or €6,50 for an hour tour in the afternoon. Get more information at the terminal's information booth. • If you want to visit Nice or Monaco, there's a convenient **train** going in both directions. You can see the red train station (*Gare SNCF*) a 15-minute walk from the wharf—just follow the harbor around to the beach area (the stairs to the station are just beyond the Carpaccio restaurant). Purchase your tickets before you board—a round-trip to either Nice or Monaco is about €5. The train makes several stops in Nice—you'll want the "Nice-Ville" stop. Tip: The terminal's information desk has the train schedule. • **Taxis** are available—expect to pay about €25 for a one-way trip to Nice. • A **rental car** agency is available at the cruise terminal if you're feeling up to exploring the area on your own. There's also a Hertz agency in nearby Beaulieu-Sur-Mer (a 20-minute walk away).

STAYING SAFE

Of all the ports on your Mediterranean cruise, Villefranche/Cannes may be the **safest**. That said, if you exercise the same precautions you would in any other tourist area, you can feel secure in walking about here. If you do decide to rent a car, keep your doors locked and your windows rolled up—"traffic light muggers" are infamous in Nice and Cannes, according to the U.S. Department of State. But for the most part, your biggest worries will probably be avoiding blisters with all the walking, and keeping sunscreen on your skin.

Touring Villefranche and Cannes

VILLEFRANCHE MAP

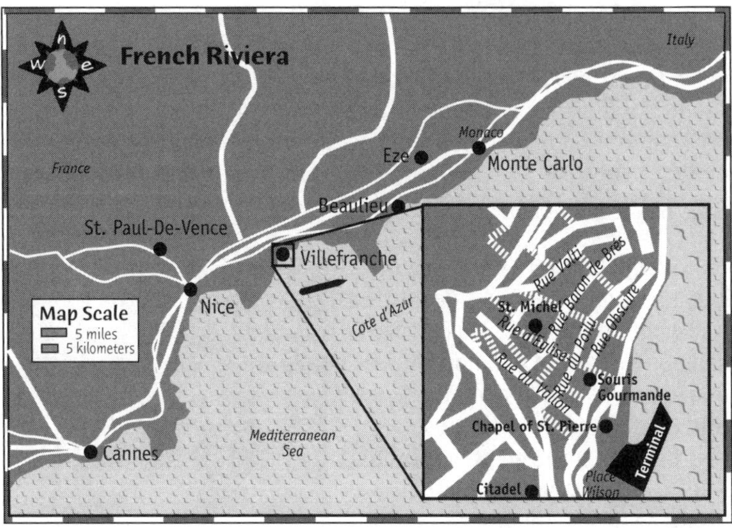

WALKING TOURS

Walking Around Villefranche (Old Town): Start by heading toward the Citadel 📷, the massive stone fortress. Inside the Citadel is the town hall, a chapel, and several free museums, including the Musée Volti 📷 and the Goetz Boumeester Museum. Walk along the ramparts and look for the open-air theatre. Head back to the village passing through Place Philibert and walking north past the Jardin des Chasseurs. Continue along the Rue du Poilu, turning left on the Rue de l'Eglise to pass the St. Michel church 📷. Turn right on Rue de May and left back onto Rue du Poilu. At the end of this street, turn right and right again to reach Rue Obscure 📷, a delightful "covered" street that has a "Phantom of the Opera" feel to it. Turn left to get back to Rue de l'Eglise and a view of the waterfront and pier. Continue south and you'll arrive at the Chapel of St. Pierre 📷, a charming church decorated with frescoes by Jean Cocteau (€2 to enter). If you're hungry, look nearby for the Souris Gourmande sidewalk café 📷—excellent food and prices! Also consider the seaside walkway 📷 that goes under the Citadel, leading to the yacht harbor. It's a particularly romantic walk with much atmosphere, especially at twilight. You can walk along the waterfront in the other direction, toward Beaulieu-sur-Mer—it offers many colorful vistas to enjoy. If you'd like a guided walking tour, the Tourist Office offers one for a nominal charge—book in advance through http://www.villefranche-sur-mer.com or e-mail ot@villefranche-sur-mer.com.

Playing in Villefranche and Cannes

ACTIVITIES

Cannes—Southwest of Nice is Cannes (pronounced "kahn"), home to the most famous film festival in the world. It's also supposedly the place that the "suntan" trend started (by Coco Chanel), a testament to the popularity of its beaches. Miles of beaches are the big draw here—people come to see and be seen on these beaches. Most beaches are private, but there are public beaches as well. Web: http://www.cannes.fr

Nice and Eze 📷—Nice (sounds like "nees" or "niece") is a delightful city brimming with sidewalk cafés, art museums, and a famous flower market. Despite its relative size (Nice is France's fifth largest city), the city is eminently walkable. Must-see attractions include the Promenade des Anglais, Castle Hill, the Russian Cathedral, and several museums, including the Chagall Museum (€5,50) and the Matisse Museum (€4). Eze is just east of both Nice and Villefranche. The main attraction in Eze is its picturesque, medieval village perched high atop a cliff. The village is so pretty you may think you've stepped onto a movie set, or perhaps the newest "land" at Walt Disney World. In Eze, be sure to visit the gardens (Jardins d'Eze), the chateau (Eze Chateau), and the church. If you can see beyond the tourists here, you'll enjoy the magnificent views.

© MediaMarx, Inc.

The Promenade in Nice

Monaco and Monte Carlo 📷—The second smallest independent country in the world is a 45-minute drive from Villefranche, making it a popular spot to visit. This principality is a mere 1.95 sq. km. (482 acres, or smaller than Disney's Animal Kingdom), but it's full of interesting things to see and do. The Prince's Palace (€6, 9:30 am–6:00 pm) is delightful, and the Monaco Cathedral (free admission) houses the tombs of the former princes of Monaco, as well as Grace Kelly. The famous Monte-Carlo Casino is not your daddy's casino—it's absolutely gorgeous inside with soaring ceilings and onyx columns. If you want to visit the casino outside of a tour, be aware that it opens in the afternoon, you'll need to be 18, show your passport, pay admission (€10), and wear proper dress (no jeans or tennis shoes). Web: http://www.visitmonaco.com

Embarking on Port Adventures in Villefranche and Cannes

Of the 14 excursions offered by Disney Cruise Line at press time, here are our **recommended port adventures** for visitors to Villefranche/Cannes:

Cannes, Grasse, and St. Paul

Tour
Moderate
All ages
$145/$95
8.5-9 hours

While being bused along the coast, you'll pass through the town of Nice, before stopping in Cannes, the French town famous for its annual international film festival. You'll be able to walk along the Cannes charming seafront, La Croisette. Next it's on to the village of Grasse, where you'll tour a perfume manufacturer to see firsthand how perfumes are created. After a brief stop for lunch (included in the price), you'll travel to the town of St. Paul-de-Vence. Since the 16th century, this town has intrigued visitors with its ancient walls and medieval stone buildings. Along its many narrow walkways, you'll find shops featuring craft shops and art galleries. The tour bus will then take you on a scenic drive back to the ship.

Monaco, the Marina, and the Little Train

Tour
Leisurely
All ages
$89/$49
4-4.5 hours

Board a tour bus for a drive to Monaco along the famous Grande Corniche, a road that was originally built by Napoleon. Once in Monaco, you'll begin a 45-minute guided walking tour of portions of old Monaco. You'll see the Oceanographic Museum, the 19th-century Romanesque cathedral, and the Prince's Palace. Note that if you want to enter the cathedral, your shoulders and knees must be covered. Next, you'll board a little, open-air "train" tram for a 30-minute ride through Monaco, viewing the harbor and the Grand Prix circuit. After you're done here, you'll have a refreshment and one hour of free time before the tour bus takes you back to the ship.

Monaco, Monte Carlo, and Eze — Rating: 9

Tour
Moderate
All ages
$165/$89
8-8.5 hours

Experience the city of Monaco in all its glory. From Villefranche, you'll be driven along the St. Jean Cap Ferrat peninsula enroute to Monaco. In Monaco, you'll visit the Rock of Monaco and begin your guided walking tour through the old quarter. Along your tour, you'll see the prince's palace and the 19th-century cathedral that is the resting place of the Princess of Monaco, Grace Kelly. As you leave Monaco, the tour bus drives along portions of the Grand Prix Motor Circuit on your way to Monte Carlo. A stop at the Grand Casino (for guests ages 18 and over) gives you time to explore the casino and the areas surrounding. Note that while a passport is not required to enter the casino as you're with a tour, you will need a passport to collect any gaming winnings. Additionally, beachwear, jeans, and tennis shoes are not allowed in the casino. You'll then re-board the bus for a 30-minute drive to Eze, where you'll have a 30-minute guided walking tour. The tour bus returns you to the ship. Dave took a version of this shore excursion and really enjoyed it. He observed: "The layer cake that is Monaco is fascinating—built up, built down, parking garages for tour buses, roofed over by public gardens. Elevators up, elevators down, tunnels under, layer after layer." For more details on his excursion experiences, visit our trip report at http://www.passporter.com/dcl/mediterranean.asp.

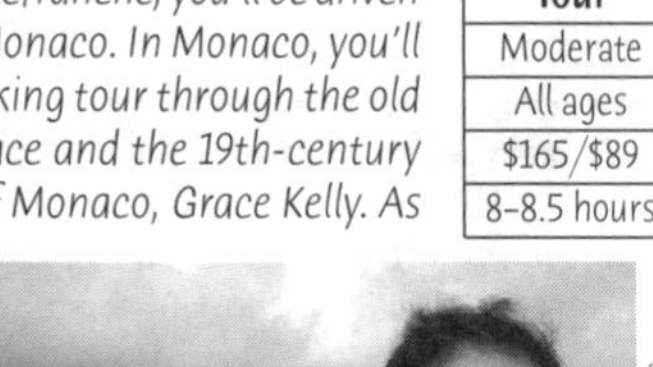

© MediaMarx, Inc.

Overlooking Monaco

Embarking on Port Adventures in Villefranche and Cannes *(continued)*

Nice and Eze with Wine and Cheese — Rating: 8

Tour
Leisurely
All ages
$85/$42
4-4.5 hours

Board a tour bus for a drive along the Middle Corniche Road to the village of Eze. Eze offers a look back to simpler times with its cobblestone streets and many small shops. This medieval village is only accessible by foot, and it is a long uphill walk to the town proper. After your guided tour, you'll re-board the bus to make your way to the city of Nice. There you'll drive along the Park Imperial, a sophisticated section of Nice dotted with many large, old houses. You'll see the Franciscan Monastery, its gardens, and an old Roman arena. Moving on, take in locations of the Old City by bus and on foot. Take a walk along the Promenade des Anglais. This picturesque street stretches for more than three miles along the Baie des Anges. Before you return to the ship, you'll stop at a vintage wine cellar for a tasting of local cheeses and wines. Jennifer and Alexander took a version of this excursion and recommend it for those who don't want to spend a full day. Look for the old double-decker carousel (€2) in a park along the promenade in Nice. Eze was very charming, although the shops were pricey. Eze is perfect for photos!

© MediaMarx, Inc.

The view from Eze

Nice and Monaco

Tour
Leisurely
All ages
$169/$125
8-8.5 hours

Your tour begins along the Corniche Road, where you'll pass small medieval villages and million-dollar yachts. You'll stop for an hour in Nice, where you can visit the Old City and take a stroll on the Cours Saleya. You'll then visit the medieval village of Eze, where you'll have a three-course lunch (included). Next stop is Monaco for a guided tour of the exteriors of the Prince's Palace, the Oceanographic Museum, and the Monaco Cathedral. You'll also see part of the Grand Prix Race Circuit and Casino Square before enjoying refreshments on the patio of Cafe de Paris, followed by 45 minutes of free time.

Nice and Train Tour

Tour
Leisurely
All ages
$72/$35
4-4.5 hours

This half-day excursion starts in Nice, which you'll reach by tour bus. You'll pass many of the major tourist destinations in Nice—Promenade des Anglais, Negresco Hotel, Regina Hotel, Franciscan Monastery—before boarding an open-air tram that looks like an antique train. Onboard the train, you'll travel the narrow streets of Old Town, past the Flower Market, and up to the Castle Hill Park for amazing views. You'll get 75 minutes of free time to explore the Old Town before reboarding the bus and returning to the pier.

Scenic French Riviera

Tour
Leisurely
All ages
$59/$29 (3-9)
3.5-4 hours

One of the most beautiful drives in the French Riviera is yours as you travel along the Lower Corniche Road, passing through Beaulieu, Eze Sur Mer, Cap d'All, and Monaco. You'll stop near the Vista Palace for photo opportunities. At this stop, from a 1,600-ft. vantage point, you can enjoy spectacular views of Italy, Cap Martin, and Monaco. Next you'll stop in Eze, a charming village 1,400 feet above the Mediterranean. You'll have about 45 minutes to explore Eze and its shops, and sample a piece of Socca (a local delicacy). Then it's back on the bus for a tour of Nice before returning to the ship.

See page 218 for a key to the shore excursion description charts and their icons.

Tip: Look for the camera symbol throughout the text to indicate when additional photos are available online along with our trip report at http://www.passporter.com/dcl/mediterranean.asp

Florence and Pisa (La Spezia)
(Mediterranean Itineraries)

With the possible exception of Rome, no other port on Disney's Mediterranean itineraries offers **more bewildering choices** than La Spezia, gateway to the Renaissance art and architecture of Florence and Pisa, the luscious Tuscan countryside, the charming villages and rugged coastline of Cinque Terre, and a hint of the glamorous Italian Riviera.

© MediaMarx, Inc.

The famous Ponte Vecchio bridge in Florence

AMBIENCE

Travelers may visit Rome, but they dream of settling down in a rural villa in this region elevated by the Renaissance's greatest artists and architects and nourished by some of Italy's most prized agricultural bounty. The **rolling Tuscan countryside** with its vineyards, fields, and olive groves divided by ancient stone walls and winding roads, makes way for small cities that seem little changed in 500 years (although they're undoubtedly more tourist-friendly). Galileo, Dante, Michelangelo, Machiavelli, Bruneleschi, Medici, Savanarola, Rossini ... The never-ending roll call of cultural giants is staggering, enhanced by expatriate British luminaries like Byron and Shelley.

HISTORY

This home to the **ancient Etruscans** is located astride the key land route between both Imperial and Papal Rome and the rest of Europe. Sprinkle in medieval sea power and productive agricultural lands. Trade brought great riches and the Medici princes brought enlightened leadership—enough fuel to fire an artistic and intellectual Renaissance that spread throughout Europe. Pasta? With pesto, of course. Pizza (the rhyme with Pisa notwithstanding)? That's another Italy, but foccacia will certainly do! This region's agricultural bounty dishes up red wine (Chianti and Brunello), grilled steaks, and golden olive oil. Just slightly more distant, the cities of Parma and Modena add fabulous cured ham and balsamic vinegar to the feast.

FACTS

Size: 9216 sq. mi. (23871 sq. km.)	
Climate: Temperate	**Temperatures**: 74°F (23°C) to 87°F (31°C)
Population: 3,750,000	**Busy Season**: Summer
Language: Italian	**Money**: Euro (€)
Time Zone: Central European	**Transportation**: Walking, taxis
Phones: Dial 011-39 from U.S., dial 112 for emergencies	

Making the Most of Florence and Pisa

GETTING THERE

The Disney Magic docks in the commercial and naval port of La Spezia, the southeastern corner of the coastal province of Liguria. The long, narrow, **Molo Italia pier** mostly serves ferries and excursion boats, and has few (if any) amenities. You should expect to take a tender to and from the shore at this port. All ashore is at 7:30 am, all aboard at 6:30 pm. You'll be in port on a Monday for a 7-night itinerary. You should be aware that it is a bit unusual for a cruise ship to dock in La Spezia when visiting Florence and Pisa; normally a cruise ship docks in Livorno 📷, 50 miles to the south.

GETTING AROUND

Nearly everyone will board **tour buses** to inland destinations or tour boats to nearby Cinque Terre. • The **rail station** is about a half-mile inland, offering alternate transit to the Cinque Terre. • A **stroll** around the port area may yield attractive neighborhoods, a nearby park, and waterfront promenade. If you plan a do-it-yourself walking tour, add a few more guidebooks to your collection. Inexpensive "on your own" bus excursions will get you to Florence, Pisa, and (perhaps) Lucca if you'd rather not be guided. The city centers are mostly pedestrian-only. Footing (and wheeling) on cobblestone streets can be a challenge, and there are often stairs to climb. Parking is on the periphery, with the preference going to buses over cars. Admission tickets are needed for many sights and, when possible, is best pre-arranged (this is one of the advantages of the guided tours). • Most major **car rental agencies** are present, but not pierside—we do not recommend you rent a car. • **Taxis** are ill-advised due to the distances involved, but a car hire with driver/guide may be an excellent alternative to shore excursions or rental-only. The official tourism web site at http://www.turismoprovincia.laspezia.it/en includes a search engine for registered private tour guides. Driving distances: Florence is 90 mi. (85 min.), Pisa is 53 mi. (55 min.), Lucca is 50 mi. (50 min.), Portofino is 55 mi. (1 hr.), Parma is 80 mi. (80 min.), and Siena is 130 mi. (2 hrs.) Want to drive to a winery? Bring a designated driver!

SAFETY

Sharp operators have been **fleecing tourists** here for well over 2,000 years. In crowded tourist towns, take standard pickpocket precautions: sturdy straps on shoulder bags, slung diagonally, with the bag under your arm. Wallets are safer in front pants pockets. Be discrete when opening wallets, and guard purchases carefully. Carry the absolute minimum, in case the worst happens.

➤

Touring Florence and Pisa

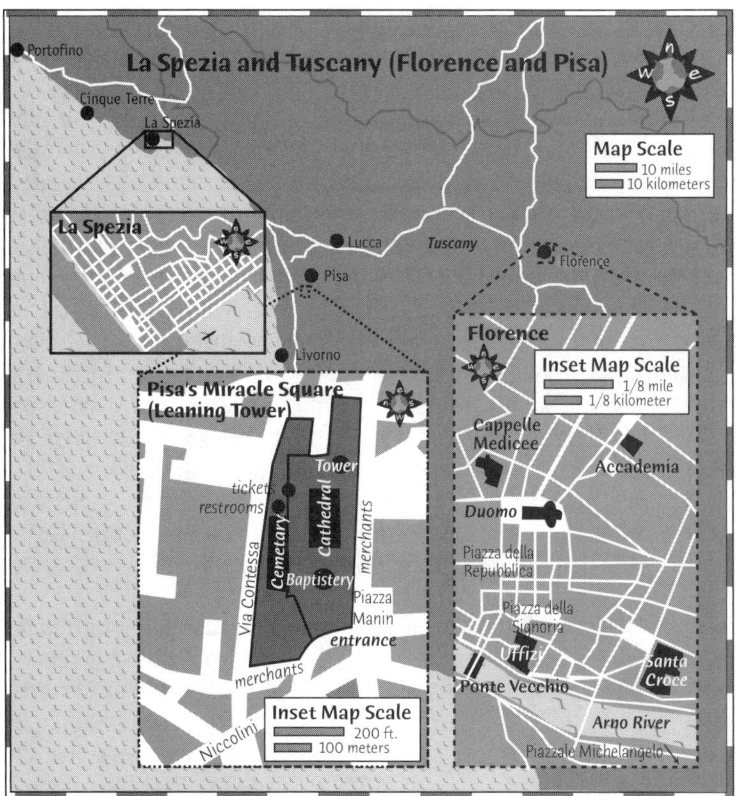

Decisions, decisions.... Almost everyone agrees that first-timers **must visit Florence** 📷. Pisa 📷 is an easy stopover along the way, but other than roaming that town's plaza with its famous tower, hard-core art buffs will do better to skip that stop in favor of Florence. If you've been there, done that (or really don't relish the idea of viewing old buildings and trekking through museums), a visit to the more manageable town of Lucca (Siena, alas, is more than a two-hour drive from La Spezia), a winery tour, or a jaunt to Cinque Terre or Portofino offer further, hard choices.

Disney promises to offer **beach excursions** to nearby Cinque Terre, with watersport rentals available. Cinque Terre is also perfect for hikers, with its five villages and hillside vistas connected by footpath. A hiking permit is required (see page 404). There is no beach in La Spezia.

Exploring Florence

ACTIVITIES

Florence (Firenze) is the capital city of Tuscany and capital of the Italian Renaissance. Florence is a must for lovers of art and architecture, and for shoppers in search of fine jewelry, antiques, and leather goods. Even if art and architecture normally bores you silly, famous sights like the Ponte Vecchio, Michelangelo's David, and the famed Duomo (cathedral) are on everyone's list. Guided tours may seem uncool, but with admission required at nearly every turn, a tour guide can whisk you into more places with less hassle than you can manage on your own. If you want to savor your visit, pick just a few choice destinations and tour on your own. Tour buses will undoubtedly deposit you near the heart of the city, by the Duomo (cathedral). Brunelleschi's famous dome is a work of architectural and engineering genius. Tours of the dome are offered (€6), but most day visitors don't bother to go inside (free). The cathedral's museum (€6) houses a worthy collection of religious art by the great masters. Next to the Duomo is the Battistero (baptistry), noted for its history, glorious interior decorations, and Ghiberti's bronze doors (€3 to enter). Web: http://www.duomofirenze.it/index-eng.htm.

A couple of blocks southwest of the Duomo, **Piazza della Repubblica**, the center of Roman Florence, has all the cafes you could ever enjoy. For lovers of religious art, the Medici Chapels (€4), just a block north of the Duomo, and Santa Croce cathedral, on the southeast side of town (burial place of just about everybody), are worthy stops. Of the many galleries, the Uffizi (€6,50) tops the list. Due south of the Duomo on the banks of the Arno, the gallery was first opened to the public in 1591 and houses an unbelievable collection of paintings. The Bargello (€4), north of the Ufizzi, has a fabled sculpture collection, and the Accademia Museum (€6,50), at the far north end of town, ranks third, mostly due to Michelangelo's David and other sculptures by that master. Right outside the Ufizzi is Piazza della Signoria. This plaza has enough sculpture and fountains to satisfy most casual sightseers. From there, Ponte Vecchio is just a stone's throw away. This "new bridge," built in 1345, is lined from end to end with gold and jewelry shops. Cross the Ponte Vecchio for Boboli Gardens—as glorious a formal garden as you'll see on this cruise (€8).

Tip: The State Museums of Florence web site located at http://www.polomuseale.firenze.it covers **nearly every museum** mentioned above. Admission to the Ufizzi and Accademia museums is a challenge. Phone in advance at 39 055294883.

Exploring Pisa and Lucca

© MediaMarx, Inc.

The famous leaning tower of Pisa (and Alexander's leaning bottle of water!)

ACTIVITIES

Pisa 📷—We have our own slant on this famous town. The fact that shore excursions to Pisa last four hours, with two of those dedicated to driving, should give you a hint. Pisa offers similar architectural glories as Florence, at a far more relaxed pace. If Florence is a cup of espresso, then Pisa is café misto (latte). Most visits begin and end in Pisa's "Miracle Square," 📷 the open expanse that houses the Duomo (cathedral), Baptistry, and the famed Leaning Tower. These go hand in hand with Camposanto cemetery, the Duomo's museum, and a tour of the city walls. Admission is charged for all, from €2 for the walls, to €15 to climb the Leaning Tower (yes, since recent work to prevent the tower's fall, you can climb to its top, but you must secure tickets early as they are quite limited). Online booking of Tower tickets (€17) up to 45 days in advance is available at http://www.opapisa.it. Note: Jennifer and Alexander took a half-day excursion to Pisa, but were disappointed by how most of the time was spent riding on a tour bus through boring terrain. If you do Pisa, we recommend you make it part of a longer excursion.

Lucca—The attraction here is the central fortress city. While not world-class in any one aspect, it's a very attractive and manageably sane cross-section of Tuscan culture. Walk, bicycle, or picnic on the tree-shaded ramparts—a full circuit is about 3 mi./5 km. Piazza del Anfiteatro Romano, built over the Roman amphitheater, is lined with cafes and shops. Climb to the top of Torre Guinigi—it doesn't lean, but the view is still worth it. If that's not enough, visit the Duomo, several other churches (San Frediano features the mummified remains of St. Zita and closes at noon), or the Villa Guinigi Museum. Lucchese olive oil is famous (buy a bottle or two), soup may include emmer, a barley-like grain, and rabbit finds its way into several stews and sauces. (Did we mention that lunch should be part of your plans?) Tourist information offices are found in Piazzale Verdi and Piazza Santa Maria. Web: http://www.welcometuscany.it/tuscany/lucca/lucca.htm.

Exploring Cinque Terre and Portofino

ACTIVITIES

© Photodisc

Cinque Terre

Cinque Terre—Just around a coastal bend from La Spezia, this UNESCO World Heritage Site and National Park preserves tiny villages perched between sea and cliff, hidden beaches and grottoes, impossible mountainside vineyards, and breathtaking vistas. Easy access by rail and tour boat make this a busy spot during the summer, but by all reports, it's still quite worthwhile. Hikers in for the day can "roll their own" by catching a train in La Spezia, which stops at all five villages. The necessary hiking permit plus unlimited day rail fare and shuttle bus service within the reserve is included in a Cinque Terre Card (€6) available at any station, which also comes with a map, rail and ferry timetables, and tourist guide. The same card with ferry (within the reserve only) is €15. Boat service from La Spezia is €21–23. Most of these boats stop en route in Portovenere, a favored haunt of Lord Byron. The coastal hiking path is most practical for the day, stitching together all five villages if you have the time and stamina (the full distance is 8 mi./13 km.). The steepest portion is the climb up to the village of Corniglia, but you can take a short shuttle bus ride instead (included in the Cinque Terre Card). Of course, you may just linger at one of the villages when the mood strikes. The most practical beach is at Monterosso, at the far end of the district (small fee). Learn much more at http://www.parconazionale5terre.it (including links to train timetables) and the official tourism site at http://www.cinqueterre.it.

Portofino—About an hour up the coastal highway A12 (or the even more picturesque route S1, which may be crowded with summer traffic), Portofino is the quintessential "rich and famous" destination. Small, picturesque, with a yacht-filled harbor, it is said to be the cleanest town in Italy. You'll have to drive (no direct rail service), and once here, it's a place to stroll, dine, and shop. If your stop in Monte Carlo isn't enough to sate your Grace Kelly/James Bond-in-a-sports-car appetite, this trip may do the trick. Walk up the hill to medieval Castello (castle) di San Giorgio and stroll out to the lighthouse on Punta Portofino for a fine view, and you'll have covered most of the sights. Dining and shopping will not be bargain-priced, but if you have to ask, you can't afford it, right?

Embarking on Port Adventures in Florence and Pisa

Of the 15 excursions offered by Disney Cruise Line at press time, here are our **recommended port adventures** for visitors to Florence and Pisa:

☐ Discovering Florence — Rating: 9

Tour
Moderate
All ages
$179/$149
10–10.5 hours

A 2½-hour shuttle ride to Florence will start your 3-hour walking tour. You'll see Piazza del Duomo, home of the Cathedral with Brunelleschi's landmark dome, Giotto's Bell Tower, and the Baptistry with Ghiberti's breathtaking bronze doors. Moving on, you'll visit the city's largest town square, the Piazza della Signoria, famous for its copy of Michelangelo's "David" and the Loggia dei Lanzi, a sheltered collection of impressive statuary. You can window shop for gold and jewels on the famous Ponte Vecchio and visit the church of Santa Croce, where Italian greats are buried. Its white, green, and pink marble facade is a beautiful example of Florentine Gothic style. Lunch is included, as well as 45 minutes to shop and explore. Dave did a version of this excursion called Historical Florence that also visited the Accademia Museum, home of the original "David" statue and other Michelangelos. With all the copies around town it's hard to believe the original can still be breathtaking, but it is! Dave's tour also included a stop at Piazzale Michelangelo, a hilltop overlook with a fantastic view of the city. Despite the fact that this tour and others like it generally don't take you inside the city's famed galleries and museums, a first-time visitor will still feel the day was very well spent. Recommended!

Dave and "David" in Piazza del Signoria

☐ Lerici's Castle and Dinosaurs

Tour
Moderate
All ages
$105/$89
5–5.5 hours

Take a 30-minute bus ride along the coast to Lerici, a pretty town with a very old stone castle guarding the waterway. You'll then begin a 90-minute walking tour through the castle, discovering that the thick stone walls hold prehistoric remains of Triassic-period dinosaurs and a fascinating geological history. Kids get to make a plaster mold of a shell fossil, see a dinosaur skeleton, and enjoy interactive exhibits. You'll also get a 30-minute tour of Lerici's town center, along with 60 minutes of free time and a beverage/snack.

☐ Cinque Terre Scenic Boat Ride

Tour
Leisurely
All ages
$129/$109
4.5–5 hours

Begin your tour with a 60-minute scenic boat cruise and admire the beautiful views of the coast and the island of Palmaria before arriving at the protected area of Cinque Terre. Cinque Terre is a national park featuring steep slopes with vine-covered terraces. Sheer cliffs rise from the sea, with small creeks and enchanting beaches squeezed among the rocks. The first stop is Vernazza, a seaside village with elaborate architecture. You'll then visit Monterosso al Mare to explore the historical center, browse the tiny shops, and peek into the local eateries. You'll then have 30 minutes of free time to look around and have a bit to eat (but note that lunch is not included), before the cruise back to La Spezia.

See page 218 for a key to the shore excursion description charts and their icons.

Embarking on Port Adventures in Florence and Pisa *(continued)*

Pisa

Rating: 3

Tour
Leisurely
All ages
$89/$75
4–4.5 hours

A 75-minute bus ride to Pisa begins the excursion. Upon reaching Pisa, you'll walk about 15 minutes to the walled "Miracle Square" of Pisa. Inside you'll receive a brief guided tour of the Leaning Tower, cathedral, and baptistry, but your admission to actually go into these buildings is not included in the excursion. You can purchase admission to the buildings (other than the Tower) for €5 (one building), €6 (two buildings), or €8 (three buildings). Tower admission is €15 on-site (but it's really unlikely you'd be able to do this on such a short excursion) or €17 in advance online at http://www.opapisa.it. While the square is beautiful, it is also crowded with both tourists and merchants selling questionable goods. In fact, you'll need to "run the gauntlet" on the way in and out of the square by passing through a relatively narrow alley filled with slightly seedy merchants pushing fake Gucci handbags. Jennifer and Alexander did this excursion and did not feel it was worth the time or money. The best part of the excursion was the 15 minutes we had to relax on the lawn. If you want to see Pisa, do it as part of another excursion—many excursions include Pisa on their itineraries.

© MediaMarx, Inc.

Making the most of the Miracle Square

Florence on Your Own

Rating: n/a

Tour
Leisurely
All ages
$85/$64
10–10.5 hours

This is an excellent excursion for those of you who have already been to Florence, or who just want something a little less structured. A tour bus to Florence starts the day as you are dropped off at Lungarno dell Zecca, from which an escort takes you to Santa Croce Square. You'll be given about five hours to explore and grab lunch (not included in excursion price). You'll return to the ship via tour bus (2.5-hour return trip).

Explore Lucca and Pisa

Tour
Moderate
All ages
$189/$139
9.5–10 hours

Take a drive through the Tuscan countryside by bus to Lucca. Start your two-hour walking tour by learning the town's history. See Piazza San Michel, the Via Fillilungo, Torre delle Ore, Piazza Dell'Anfiteatro, and the Duomo. Lucca's Cathedral dates from the 12th century and features a facade with elaborate reliefs and columns. After the tour, you'll have lunch at a local cafe (lunch included in price of excursion), then you'll drive to Pisa for about 90 minutes of free time to explore, shop, or relax. When you're done, you'll meet your bus driver and make the 2 ½-hour drive back to La Spezia.

Portofino and Santa Margherita

Tour
Leisurely
All ages
$125/$109
8–8.5 hours

Drive 75 minutes to Santa Margherita, passing along the Via Aurelia ("Golden Sun Road") on your way. Once in town, you'll hop aboard a boat for a 15-minute cruise to Portofino, where you'll enjoy a 1.5-mile walking tour. You'll also have 30 minutes of free time. Back on the boat, you'll return to Santa Margherita for a pizza party (included in the price of the excursion), featuring many different types of pizza (plus Nutella Pizza for dessert!). Another 75 minutes of free time is offered before making the journey back to La Spezia.

See page 218 for a key to the shore excursion description charts and their icons.

Tip: Look for the camera symbol throughout the text to indicate when additional photos are available online along with our trip report at http://www.passporter.com/dcl/mediterranean.asp

Rome (Civitavecchia)
(Mediterranean Itineraries)

Your brief day in Rome can only **scratch the surface** of one of the world's greatest cities. Plan to spend your entire day on an intensive tour—the extra effort and expense will be more than worthwhile. And by all means, toss coins in the Trevi Fountain—you will return!

Rome's Colosseum

AMBIENCE

There's nothing else quite like the **power and glory of Rome**, a city where "awe" takes on a whole new meaning, whether looking skyward inside the dome of St. Peter's or deep into the earth at the Roman Forum. Pagan temples are converted to churches, palaces of all eras greet you at every turn, and a single snapshot can capture monuments from every age. Ancient columns and pediments are recycled for newer building facades, and all but the recently restored sights are covered by the everyday grime of a thriving metropolis. This is a city of landmarks, history, and faith, and if none of that excites you at the moment, your mood will change once you arrive.

HISTORY

Rome, founded by Romulus and Remus (or so goes the legend), was capital of the Roman Republic and the Empire that followed. When Rome fell, the **capital of the Roman Catholic Church** rose from its ashes. The power and wealth of the church attracted the greatest architects and artists of the Renaissance and as the capital of the modern Italian state, a century's worth of newer monumental works lies layer upon layer with more than 2,500 years of history. This is Rome, described (accurately) by countless clichés, a city that put its imperial and ecclesiastical stamp so firmly on its conquests that even today its language, culture, architecture, and intellectual impact dominates half of all world culture. This is the city where it all happened and continues to happen on a daily basis.

FACTS

Size: 496 sq. mi. (1285 sq. km.)	
Climate: Mediterranean	**Temperatures**: 72°F (22°C) to 84°F (29°C)
Population: 2.55 million	**Busy Season**: Summer
Language: Italian	**Money**: Euro (€)
Time Zone: Central European	**Transportation**: Walking, taxis
Phones: Dial 011-34 from U.S., dial 112 for emergencies	

Making the Most of Rome

GETTING THERE

Your ship docks in **Civitavecchia**, an ancient port 90 minutes from the heart of Rome by bus (longer in rush hour traffic). Fortunately, that long trip is fairly picturesque, following the coast for some distance before heading inland. Cruise ship facilities pierside are minimal, little more than tents at the moment. It's unclear if a new terminal is being built at this time, but no new building can hold a candle to older port facilities you can see across the harbor, designed by the likes of Michelangelo and Bernini. There will undoubtedly be some shopping available in the new terminal. Otherwise, just expect a lineup of taxis and tour guides for hire, and a parking lot full of tour buses. There are no recreational or tourist facilities within walking distance. The 7-night cruises visit on Tuesdays. All ashore is at 7:45 am and all aboard is 9:00 pm.

GETTING AROUND

Tour buses are your principal option, with private tour guides providing a pricey but rational alternative if you've got the right-sized group. Research and book a guide in advance, rather than taking your risk at the dock. Tour guides are licensed, but that hardly narrows your choices. For do-it-yourselfers, look for a shore excursion option that supplies basic transportation into and out of Rome. • **Taxis** are easy to come by if you get one from the cruise terminal or a taxi stand. Taxis in Rome are white with a "Taxi" sign on the roof, a sign on the door, and a meter. Plan to pay your fare in Euros and expect to tip about 5–10% of the fare. • There are currently no **car rental agencies** at the dock—you may need a taxi to pick up a car, and as we've said several times regarding European ports, we really don't recommend driving on your own unless you've got plenty of driving experience in the area.

© MediaMarx, Inc.

A typical Rome taxi and tour bus near St. Peter's Square

STAYING SAFE

Rome is busy, Rome's tourist sites are crowded, and you'll be more than a little bit distracted by everything around you. Pickpockets are undoubtedly the greatest risk, so try to be alert. Queues in spots like St. Peter's Square are long and crowded, so stay securely within your group or be **especially watchful**. When you shop for souvenirs, consider buying only very compact items that can be stowed out of sight in your day pack. Overall, try to travel very light—the more you carry, the more distracted and the more of a target you'll be.

Touring Rome

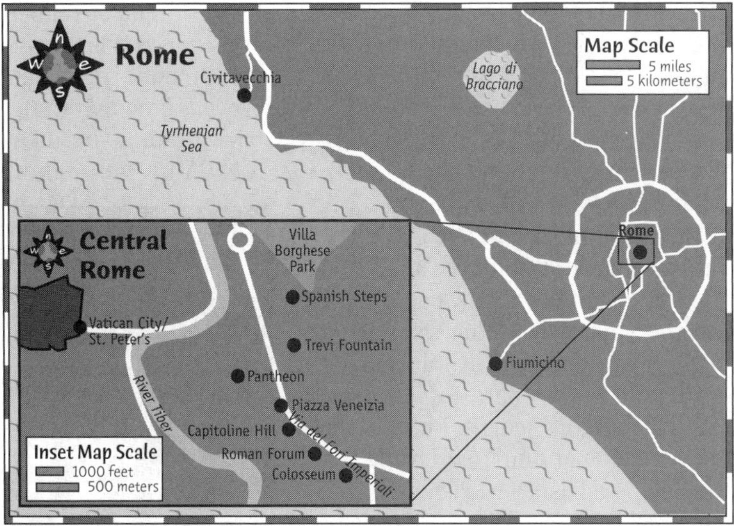

Central Rome is just large enough that one walking tour just won't do. You'll need transportation—a taxi ride will do it. **Vatican City** 📷 doesn't need so much of a planned walking tour as a visit (with itinerary). A more structured plan is needed for the sprawling **Roman Forum** 📷, where there are more sites than you can visit in a day (we'll focus on the most practical choices). These are the top two visitor destinations, and your choice of activities at either will determine if you can spend much time at the other. Rule of thumb—if you include a museum in your plans, expect to spend two-thirds of your day at either the Vatican or Forum. The Spanish Steps and nearby shopping district are more for wandering than touring—take a taxi. Adjacent to the Spanish Steps is the Villa Borghese (park) and its famed museum. The museum is a long way from the Steps, though—you'll want a taxi. Reservations are required for the museum. Stranded between these three major destinations are two sights that are on everyone's must-see list—the Pantheon, the remarkable domed temple to the gods, and the cascading waters of the Trevi Fountain 📷. The two are separated by about eight city blocks, and are roughly eight blocks from either the Forum or the Spanish Steps. If you want to visit everything, all in the same day, hope you can book a tour that visits them all. Your guide gets you past most of the ticket lines and queues, you'll have the needed transportation, and no time will be lost studying your map.

Playing in Rome

VATICAN

The Vatican—If your heart yearns for the heart of religious Rome, spend most of your day here. St. Peter's Square is immense and amazing, and the interior of the basilica is breathtaking, regardless of your faith. The Vatican museums are an art-lover's dream. Entrance to St. Peter's Basilica is free, but the Vatican Museums—including the Sistine Chapel and the Vatican Historical Museum—require admission (€12/€8 available only at the door, audio guide €5,50). The Vatican Gardens tour (€13,50/€9) must be reserved in advance by fax. See the Vatican Museum web site at http://mv.Vatican.va for information on this and other hard-to-get tours. Add the museums and that'll be the bulk of your day. Everything will be open on the days the Disney Magic is in port, but Papal Audiences are Wednesdays, so you're out of luck on that. Be sure to check the Vatican web site for the museum schedule—it's typically closed a couple of weekdays every month. Dress for the occasion—bare shoulders and/or bare knees will keep you from entering the basilica and museums.

© MediaMarx, Inc.

The Vatican's Swiss Guard

© MediaMarx, Inc.

St. Peter's Square teems with humanity

Playing in Rome

Ancient Rome—The heart of ancient Rome is a fairly compact rectangle, roughly ¾ mile square. You can spend days exploring the sights. An optional walk to the Pantheon and/or the Trevi Fountain adds another half mile or so to the tour. We suggest you start at one end, and work your way to the other end to minimize backtracking. There are many more sights than can be covered in this guide—a comprehensive Rome or Italy guidebook or a visit to the official web site (http://www.capitolium.org) in advance of your visit is a must. The web site includes an interactive map of the entire area, which will greatly aid your plans. At the northwest corner, Piazza Venezia is an expansive crossroads dominated by the monument to Victor Emmanuel II, who united modern Italy. The broad Via dei Fori Imperiali (Street of the Imperial Forums) heads southeast from here, skirting the edge of the excavated Foro Romano (Roman Forum) on the right, leading to the Colosseum at its far end. Five additional forums line this road, added as the empire outgrew the original. As you walk this way, look back toward the Victor Emmanuel monument. It's the "topper" to an amazing wedding cake of buildings and ruins piled one above the other that span the millennia.

© MediaMarx, Inc.

Victor Emmanuel monument at Piazza Venizia

Halfway between Piazza Venezia and the Colosseum is the entrance to the Foro Romano/**Roman Forum** (free admission), where you can descend into its deep vale. The visitor center offers audio tours (€4), live tours, maps, and other resources. Down in the heart of the Forum you'll find the Arch of Severus, the famous triple columns of the Temple of Castor and Polux, the Temple of Vesta, Caesar's Senate, streets trampled by countless armies and statesmen, and the Arch of Titus with its depictions of the sack of Jerusalem's temple, among many other sights.

Playing in Rome

Ancient Rome (continued)—Across the street from the Roman Forum entrance is Trajan's Forum and Market (€6,20), including what is perhaps the first multistory urban shopping mall. It's worth a quick walk-by, even if you don't enter. Overlooking the Foro Romano on the northwest is Capitoline Hill, noteworthy today for its museums (€6,20, closed Mondays) and the plaza and steps designed by Michelangelo. To the southwest of the valley is Palatine Hill (included with Colosseum admission of €10), ancient Rome's answer to 1600 Pennsylvania Avenue, Versailles, and Buckingham Palace, combined. Beyond that to the far southwest is the Circus Maximus (free), where the charioteers raced. The Colosseum (€10) is in the southeast, and the attractive Arch of Constantine is nearby. Lines for the Colosseum are long, even if you reserve tickets in advance, but you can't not venture inside for the sheer spectacle, even though the curtain rang down 1,600 years ago. Across the road to the northeast is the Domus Aurea, which hides the amazing buried chambers of the palace of Nero (€5) and nearby Baths of Caracalla (€5). These are probably too much to include in a one-day visit.

© MediaMarx, Inc.

The Forum and Palatine Hill

Tickets—There's no central ticket source, but http://www.pierreci.it comes closest. It's a cultural/ticket agency that represents many cultural institutions and provides phone numbers for many others. The site also offers the Roma Pass, which supplies admission to the first two participating sites visited, discounts on other sites visited subsequently, and free public transit, all for €18. The Colosseum, Capitoline Museums, Baths of Caracalla, Trajan's Forum, and the Villa Borghese museum are all included. It's good for three days, but you can easily break even in one day if used wisely, and an advance purchase will save you a lot of time in queues.

Embarking on Port Adventures in Rome

Of the 13 excursions offered by Disney Cruise Line at press time, here are our **recommended port adventures** for visitors to Rome:

Panoramic Rome — Rating: 3

Tour
Leisurely
All ages
$129/$109
7-7.5 hours

A 90-minute tour bus ride to Rome passes through the Etruscan countryside. Upon reaching Rome, you'll see the Vatican walls, which encompass Vatican City. You'll also glimpse the old Roman walls, the famous Villa Borghese, and Porta Pinciana. A short drive takes you by Via Veneto, Piazza Venezia, the Arch of Constantine, the Circus Maximus, and the Colosseum. A stop at St. Peter's Basilica offers a short time to explore on your own before returning to the ship. Jennifer and Alexander took this excursion because it was really the only half-day excursion offered. Alas, it was quite disappointing. Most of the time was spent getting to or from Rome, and in Rome, we whizzed by the sights so fast that we would have missed them if we blinked. Also, we were supposed to have a fair amount of time at St. Peter's Basilica, but instead were only given 25 minutes—barely enough time to get off the bus, walk down to the square, and get back. Frankly, we think it's best to book a full-day excursion rather than shortchange yourself with this fly-by tour.

© MediaMarx, Inc.

The Fly-By Bus Tour

Rome on Your Own

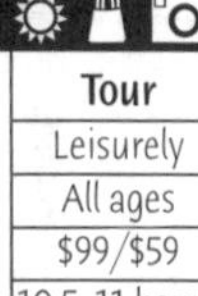

Tour
Leisurely
All ages
$99/$59
10.5-11 hours

The perfect excursion for those who have visited Rome in the past or just want to see Rome without so much structure. A 90-minute tour bus ride to Rome sets you on your way. Upon reaching Rome, you'll have seven hours to spend as you wish (we recommend you get yourself a good Rome guidebook if you plan to spend the day here on your own). Remember your bus pickup location and time—if you miss the bus, your transportation back will be your own responsibility. This tour does not include lunch or entrance fees.

Classical Rome — Rating: 9

Tour
Leisurely
All ages
$219/$189
11-11.5 hours

Your first stop is the Vatican Museum, which contains thousands of amazing treasures and pieces of art collected by popes over the centuries. As there are time restraints, you will only see a small portion of the museum before heading off to the Sistine Chapel. The Sistine Chapel contains famous works of art by Michelangelo, including the "Last Judgment." Next stop is the largest church in the world, St. Peter's Basilica. This church is home to Michelangelo's work, "Pieta," and the beautiful Bernini Pulpit. After a three-course lunch (included in excursion price) and before returning to the ship, your tour bus will drive past the Colosseum. Please note that a strict dress code is enforced at the Vatican Museum, the Sistine Chapel, and St. Peter's Basilica—shorts, tank tops, and revealing clothing are not permitted. You may be required to check large bags and backpacks, video cameras, and water bottles at security checkpoints. Dave took an excursion similar to this one and felt it was well worth his time. While there's still just too much to see in Rome in one day, it did provide a satisfying overview of this magnificent city.

© MediaMarx, Inc.

Embarking on Port Adventures in Rome *(continued)*

Taste of Rome

Tour
Active
All ages
$100/$90
10 hours

Upon arriving in Rome, you're greeted by your group's official Roman tour guide and set out together on a walking tour of the most popular and important sights. The tour visits the famous Trevi Fountain and then walks through the ruins of the Roman Forum, actually passing through the ancient arches and wandering among the pillars. You'll then continue on to The Colosseum before boarding a bus to visit St. Peter's Square in Vatican City, where you'll have two hours of free time to explore or have lunch (lunch is not included in the price of this excursion, though you will receive a voucher for some Italian gelato). Note that the walking tour includes about two miles of walking, some of which is on uneven terrain and uphill.

The Best of Rome

Tour
Leisurely
All ages
$329/$289
11.5-12 hours

A stop at St. Peter's Basilica is first on the list for this deluxe, small group, full-day excursion. St. Peter's Basilica, the largest church in the world, rests on 800 pillars and took more than 100 years to build. You'll then move on to the Vatican Museum and the Sistine Chapel. The chapel is home to the ceiling painting by Michelangelo titled "Creation of the World." Enjoy a five-star lunch (included in the price). You'll also visit the beautiful Trevi Fountain and toss in a coin or two. The tour bus will proceed through Rome seeing Circus Maximus, the Colosseum, and many more sights before returning to the ship.

Highlights of Rome for Families

Tour
Moderate
All ages
$229/$189
11-11.5 hours

A full-day excursion to Rome is a lot for kids to take in, but this special tour takes kids' interests to heart! Sure, you have the 90-minute drive to Rome, the guided tour of St. Peter's Basilica (and some free time to grab a souvenir), the obligatory visit to Trevi Fountain (kids will love throwing in a coin), and a nice, Italian lunch at a local restaurant (price of lunch included in excursion). But then you drive to Villa Borghese where a very quaint, very Italian puppet show is staged for the kids! Disney Cruise Line youth counselors are also along to hang with the kids, meaning parents can wander off on their own to sightsee or shop. Then it's back on the bus to check out the Colosseum before the 90-minute drive back to the ship. Had this excursion been an option when Jennifer and Alexander visited Rome, they would have jumped at the chance to participate!

Italian Countryside and Olive Oil

Tour
Moderate
All ages
$49/$49
4.5-5 hours

Looking for something different and a little less time consuming? Take a tour bus ride to the ancient city of Tarquinia, just north of Civitavecchia, for a guided walking tour. Your first stop will be at the church of San Francesco—it's known for its extravagant arches and is the largest church in Tarquinia. Next you'll see Palazzo dei Priori, a massive urban fortification built in the first half of the 15th century by Cardinal Vitelleschi, who was a supreme strategist of the Roman Curia. You'll get 30 minutes of free time to explore the medieval village. Everyone ends up at a farmhouse to explore the history of olive oil production and enjoy the sampling of two different types of the olive oils produced here with bruschetta. Take some time to relax and take in the culture before heading back to the ship.

See page 218 for a key to the shore excursion description charts and their icons.

Tip: Look for the camera symbol throughout the text to indicate when additional photos are available online along with our trip report at http://www.passporter.com/dcl/mediterranean.asp

Naples
(Mediterranean Itineraries)

Exuberant, chaotic, and a little shaggy around the edges is the best way to describe Naples, the largest city in Southern Italy. This **historically rich**, gastronomically famous, and incredibly crowded urban center is a gateway to ancient wonders and inspiring beauty.

© MediaMarx, Inc.

The ever-present Mt. Vesuvius

AMBIENCE

Located halfway between the Vesuvius and Campi Flegrei volcanoes, the legendary city of Naples lies on the Mediterranean coast, tucked away in a natural bay. Its **majestic scenery** has inspired art throughout the ages. The city is rife with underground layers and catacombs beneath its Greco-Roman avenues. There are hotels and spas there that have been operating for thousands of years; you can feel the history seep into you as you walk along the streets. Yet, thanks to Naples' dense population, frenetic pace, and slightly grimy appearance, we predict you'll either love it or hate it.

HISTORY

Naples, or *Napoli* in Italian (NA-po-lee), means **new city**. It was founded between the 7th and 6th centuries B.C. by the Greeks, not far from the older town of Partenope. The original city center was located on the site of Castel dell'Ovo (see page 417). Greek culture reigned early on, even during the Roman Empire's domination of the city. This period was followed by an influx of Spaniards, Byzantines, Goths, and Normans. Eventually the King of Sicily added Naples to his territory in 1139, and shortly thereafter it became the capital. The city flourished and prospered, creating the University of Naples in 1224. After a period of rule by both the Spaniards and the Austrians, Naples became autonomous in the 18th century. Today the city is a commercial and cultural center with an active port.

FACTS

Size: 45 sq. mi. (117 sq. km.)	
Climate: Mediterranean	**Temperatures**: 72°F (22°C) to 85°F (29°C)
Population: 1,000,000 (city)	**Busy Season**: Summer
Language: Italian, Neapolitan	**Money**: Euro (€)
Time Zone: Central European	**Transportation**: Walking, taxis
Phones: Dial 011-39 from U.S., dial 112 for emergencies	

Introduction
Reservations
Staterooms
Dining
Activities
Ports of Call
Magic
Index

Making the Most of Naples

GETTING THERE

Your ship docks in **Molo Angionio at Maritime Station** (Stazione Marittima) in Naples, smack dab in the center of the city's bustling waterfront. From the pier, Naples' city center is about ½ mile away, so while you can walk you may also prefer to take a taxi or tour bus. You can get a taxi outside the large cruise terminal building, which houses a few souvenir shops and an information booth. (Tip: There are several elevators here, but they are tucked out of the way—look for signs indicating the *ascensore*.) For more information on the port, visit http://www.porto.napoli.it/en. Disembarkation time is typically 8:30 am with an all-aboard time around 9:00 pm.

GETTING AROUND

If you're not doing an excursion, which we strongly recommend in Naples, you'll probably take a taxi into the city or to another location. **Taxis** are plentiful, but do try to get an "official" licensed taxi (white with the Naples symbol on their front doors, a taxi number, and a meter) by using a taxi stand found in most piazzas. Be aware that Naples traffic is crazy, so your trip may take longer than you expect. Tip: If your driver tries to tell you the taxi's meter is not working, ask that they switch it on anyway and don't rely on their guesstimate, which will undoubtedly be higher than necessary. • If you're exploring the city on your own, consider a **funicular** (as in the famous "Funiculi-Funicula" song), a cable car that goes up the steep hill of Vómero. You can catch one at the Piazetta Duca d'Aosta—just make sure you leave enough time to get down and back to the ship. • Right next to the cruise pier is Molo Beverello, where you can board **ferries and hydrofoils** to Capri, Sorrento, and Amalfi. • Hoping to **rent a car or moped** (a la "Roman Holiday")? Don't bother. The traffic is not conducive to pleasure driving, and mopeds shouldn't be rented. Buses are available (most leave from Piazza Garibaldi—not a nice area), but they aren't convenient or very clean.

STAYING SAFE

Naples is a dense, highly populated urban area and **pickpocketing** is a serious issue. Keep those valuables back on the ship in your safe, carry minimal cash, and keep the cash in a wallet secured in a front pocket or under your clothing. Try to travel in groups when possible, like on a Disney shore excursion. If you've got an expensive camera, keep it under wraps when not in use and don't carry it around your neck or arm. Be wary of gypsies and grifters, and watch out for suspicious behavior. Women, ignore "flirtatious" men altogether. It's best to just not make eye contact at all with questionable characters.

Touring Naples

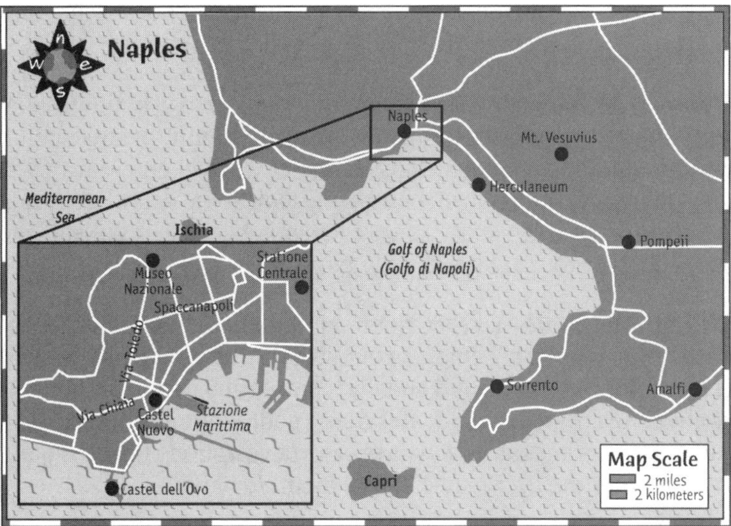

Normally we devote this space to a **"do it yourself" walking tour**. In the case of Naples, we really don't recommend it—the city is chaotic, dirty, and not particularly easy to get around. If you're feeling adventuresome, however, your best bet is to take a taxi to Spaccanapoli for the best representation of Naples. If you're interested in shopping, you can take a 10-minute walk from Stazione Marittima north to the pedestrian shopping street of Via Chiaia.

Museo Archeologico Nazionale—If one of the world's most extensive collections of Roman and Greek artifacts interests you, make a beeline for this huge museum. You'll find many items from Pompeii and Herculaneum here. Admission is €6,50. Address: Piazza Museo 19, Spaccanapoli. Web: http://www.archeobo.arti.beniculturali.it.

Castel Nuovo 📷—This gloomy, colossal castle is considered one of the best works of Renaissance honorary architecture. Inside are 14th- and 15th-century sculptures and frescoes. Admission is €5. Address: Piazza Municipio. Phone: 081 795 5877.

Castel dell'Ovo (Castle of the Egg)—A 12th-century fortress built directly over the ruins of an ancient Roman villa, overlooking the harbor. Free admission. Address: Santa Lucia Waterfront, Via Partenope. Phone: 081 240 0055.

Playing in Naples

ACTIVITIES

You're most likely to see these attractions while on shore excursions, but we include them to give you additional background.

Pompeii 📷—Lost for 1,600 years under volcanic ash, this Roman city offers extraordinary insight into the height of civilization during the Roman Empire. Most of the city has been excavated at this point, and offers an awe-inspiring look at the doomed city and its occupants. Dave chose to visit Pompeii because it's one of the most popular tourist attractions near Naples.

Herculaneum 📷—Like Pompeii, Herculaneum was a victim of Mt. Vesuvius. This Roman resort was buried under 75 feet of superheated volcanic mud and lava, protecting and preserving its architecture, wood, fabric, and even food! Jennifer chose to visit Herculaneum because the nature of its devastation offers a unique glimpse into the everyday life of ancient Romans.

Mt. Vesuvius (Mons Vesuvio) 📷—This famous stratovolcano is about 6 mi. (9 km.) east of Naples. In addition to its famous eruption on August 24, 79 A.D., which covered Pompeii and Herculaneum, Vesuvius has erupted three more times—its most recent eruption was in 1913 and 1914. There are no current signs of volcanic unrest. Even if you don't visit this historic volcano up close, you can see it from most everywhere in Naples.

Capri 📷—The isle of Capri is a celebrated resort near Sorrento about 40 minutes from Naples by boat. It is a charming town of narrow streets and elegant villas clinging to limestone cliffs.

Sorrento and the Amalfi Coast 📷—The stunning, rocky coastline of Amalfi leads to the resort town of Sorrento, filled with museums and churches. Sorrento is famous for Limoncello, an apertif.

Pizza Margherita—This taste of Naples is indeed a top attraction for many visitors. Naples is the birthplace of pizza, specifically *pizza margherita,* which is made with just tomatoes, garlic, olive oil, basil, and mozzarella on the crust. Famous places to sample this yummy treat include Da Michele (Via Cesare Sersale 1/3), Trianon (Via P. Colletta 46), and Di Matteo (Via del Tribunali 94). If these are too far off your path, just look for a pizzeria with a wood-burning oven for the most authentic flavor.

Embarking on Port Adventures in Naples

Of the 17 excursions offered by Disney Cruise Line at press time, here are our **recommended port adventures** for first-time visitors to Naples:

Pompeii - Half Day

Tour
Moderate
All ages
$75/$65 (3-9)
4-4.5 hours

As you travel to the famous city of Pompeii by tour bus, you'll see Mt. Vesuvius in the distance. When Vesuvius erupted in 79 A.D., it covered Pompeii in 30 feet of volcanic ash and pumice stone. The town has since been excavated and provides a look into how the original inhabitants of Pompeii lived. See the many mansions, temples, and porticoes. Note that you must be able to walk 1.5 miles over cobblestones, as well as climb 20-25 steps. You'll stop at a cameo factory for about 20 minutes along the way, where you'll be treated to an Italian gelato.

The Ruins of Herculaneum

Rating: 10

Tour
Moderate
All ages
$89/$69 (3-9)
4.5-5 hours

This excursion takes you to Herculaneum and back, and stopping at a cameo factory along the way. Herculaneum is a fascinating alternative to Pompeii—you'll find fewer crowds here and a more complete look at life in Roman times thanks to Herculaneum's better preservation. Jennifer and Alexander went on this half-day excursion and feel it was the best shore excursion of the entire cruise. Walking amidst the ruins, knowing that you were walking on the same paving stones as people nearly 2,000 years ago, was simply mind-blowing. We were able to go into many of the structures, where we marvelled at what the little rooms may have been used for. We did have a tour guide with us who led our group around and explained the function of many of the buildings, but halfway through, we set off on our own to explore. We could easily have spent the entire day here, completely fascinated. Our best recommendations are to do some research into Herculaneum or pick up a book with good descriptions so you can better appreciate the visit. Also, while this is not a wheelchair- or stroller-friendly place, there is a ramp into Herculaneum and Jennifer was able to push a sleeping Alexander in his stroller by sticking to the "sidewalks," but it wasn't easy. We highly recommend this excursion!

Seaside Herculaneum

Treasures of Naples

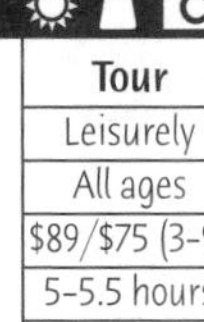

Tour
Leisurely
All ages
$89/$75 (3-9)
5-5.5 hours

This excursion takes you to the Museum of the Treasury of Saint Gennaro, a vast collection of precious objects, silver, jewels, and paintings collected over the centuries. You'll also have the opportunity to explore a 13th century Gothic Cathedral, home to the oldest church in Naples (all guests who wish to visit the church must wear clothing that covers your shoulders and knees). A short tour around Naples will highlight the notable sights of the city. Visit Castel Nuovo, San Carlo Opera House, Villa Comunale Park, Piazza Plebiscito, and Piazza Municipio. Before heading back to the pier, your tour bus will stop at a Neapolitan pizzeria for a pizza lunch in the land where it was born (lunch included in price of excursion).

See page 218 for a key to the shore excursion description charts and their icons.

Introduction Reservations Staterooms Dining Activities Ports of Call Magic Index

Embarking on Port Adventures in Naples *(continued)*

Mt. Vesuvius by 4x4, Hike, Wine Tasting & Pompeii

Tour
Very active
Ages 10 & up
$179
8–8.5 hours

A short bus drive to the west coast marks the beginning of your trek. At the National Park of Mt. Vesuvius, you'll board a special 4x4 coach to drive up this natural wonder, enjoying breathtaking views of Naples and its bays on the way. At 3,000 feet, you'll continue on foot up to the crater's rim. Then it's back onto the coach to drive down to a winery for a sample of five different wines, along with a light lunch. You'll also get a two-hour guided tour of the ancient city of Pompeii. This excursion requires strenuous up and down climbing and hiking over several miles. Guests should wear comfortable shoes and be in good health.

Timeless Pompeii and the Flavor of Sorrento

Tour
Moderate
All ages
$149/$125
8.5–9 hours

Travel 75 minutes by bus to the seaside town of Sorrento, where you'll get a guided tour of the town's historical center. After 60 minutes of free time to explore Corso Italia (scenic main street of town) or Correal Museum (antique furniture, porcelain, and Neapolitan paintings), you'll go to a local farmhouse to learn the process of producing mozzarella cheese (and get a sample, of course!). After a break for lunch (included in the price of your excursion), you'll take an hour-long drive to Pompeii for a 90-minute guided walking tour of this amazing place (wear comfortable shoes and be prepared for uneven terrain and some steps). Then it's just a 30-minute drive back to Naples. Note: The order of tour stops may vary.

Capri, Sorrento, and Pompeii

Rating: 9

Tour
Moderate
All ages
$269/$229
10–10.5 hours

Travel the scenic Amalfi coast eastward to Pompeii. Your group may visit a cameo factory, or a rustic farm to observe olive oil and cheese production (and maybe nibble some samples). That's followed by a guided tour of Pompeii to see its many restored buildings and architecture once covered by 30 feet of volcanic ash. You'll then take a coastal drive to nearby Sorrento where you can explore the streets of Sorrento, shop in its quaint stores, and dine at one of the outdoor cafes (lunch is included). After lunch, walk to the marina and hop aboard a hydrofoil boat for a 25-minute ride to the isle of Capri. In Capri you'll take the funicular up to the town for spectacular views and upscale shopping among the picturesque, narrow streets. Dave took this full-day excursion and thoroughly enjoyed himself. This excursion seems unbelievably ambitious at first glance. However, by the time you deduct the time you spend traveling and waiting, you've got about 3.5 hours of "meat" in this excursion, including lunch. It's still quite efficient. There's no retracing steps. You'll travel either by boat from Naples to Capri across the full expanse of the Bay of Naples, boat from Capri to nearby Sorrento, bus northeast along the scenic coastline to Pompeii, and bus back to Naples, or vice versa. Half the excursion groups go one way, half the other, to ensure that the bus and boats are filled going both ways. Dave has written a much longer review of this shore excursion at http://www.passporter.com/dcl/mediterranean.asp.

© MediaMarx, Inc.

Pompeii and the looming Vesuvius

See page 218 for a key to the shore excursion description charts and their icons.

Valletta, Malta
(Mediterranean Itineraries)

Malta evokes images of Medieval knights and dry, rocky landscapes, valiant battles and long history. Visitors to Valletta enter a **World Heritage Site** that has been a strategic port since Roman times, overflowing with churches, fortresses, museums, and monuments.

© foxypar4

Fort St. Elmo in Valletta, Malta

AMBIENCE

To British Prime Minister Benjamin Disraeli, Valletta was a city "built **by gentlemen, for gentlemen**." The Knights of Malta controlled Mediterranean maritime commerce for centuries, so this is an apt description. The knights' many residence halls (auberges) are just part of that legacy—many historic buildings are still in use by the modern government. With religion so close to the heart of these former Crusaders, their churches are richly decorated in Baroque style. If you venture beyond Valletta you may encounter the island's brightly-painted wooden fishing boats (decorated with a protective seeing-eye), the world's oldest surviving stone monuments, noteworthy churches, and deep grottoes carved into the rugged seacoast.

HISTORY

This **mid-Mediterranean crossroads** has been inhabited for at least 7,000 years. Some of the world's earliest surviving monuments are here, and the Maltese language is the sole survivor of Sicilian-Arabic. There's not room here to recount the many occupants and conquerors, including Phoenicians, Greeks, Romans, Byzantine Christians, Muslim Arabs, those famous Knights of Malta, Italians, French, and British. During World War II Malta, like Gibraltar, successfully resisted Axis invasion. The nation is now a member of the British Commonwealth and the European Union. Valletta was founded by the Knights of Malta in 1566 on the tip of an easily-defended small peninsula in the seaport.

FACTS

Size: 121 sq. mi. (316 sq. km.) (Malta) / 0.3 sq. mi. (0.8 sq. km.) (Valletta)	
Climate: Mediterranean	**Temperatures**: 59°F (15°C) to 87°F (31°C)
Population: 413,609/6,098	**Busy Season**: Summer
Language: Maltese, English	**Money**: Euro (€)
Time Zone: Central European	**Transportation**: Walking, taxis, buses
Phones: Dial 011-356 from U.S., dial 112 for emergencies	

Making the Most of Valletta, Malta

GETTING THERE

The Magic berths at Valletta's cruise pier on the **Grand Harbor**, overseen by the fortress city's battlements. A long row of restored stone buildings line the waterfront at the base of the city wall, housing shops and restaurants. A short way across the harbor are more battlements, on sister cities Senglea and Vittoriosa. From the pier you can catch a taxi or take a carriage ride, or walk uphill into town for shopping and sightseeing. All ashore time is around 8:30 am and all aboard is around 6:00 pm. As Malta is a European Union nation, there will be no customs clearances.

GETTING AROUND

The nation is actually **three inhabited islands**, Malta (where you berth), more rustic Gozo, and tiny Comino. Ferries to them leave from Cirkewwa, 12 miles distant, so a shore excursion is a safer bet. **Valletta** is a town designed for **walking**, if you can manage the climb from sea level to the city's hilltop location. The far side of the narrow peninsula is just a 1/2 mile away, and the extreme tip is 1 mile distant, so all of the important sights are within walking distance. Unusual for a city of this age, the streets are laid out on an easy-to-navigate grid. • "CT" **Taxis** are small, two-passenger electric cabs that can be hailed. Fares start at €2 per person. White Taxis are conventional cabs. Agree on the fare before departing. • A romantic transportation option is **horse-drawn carriages**, or *karozzin*, which are common in tourist areas. Rates are negotiated - some feel they're a great value, other think they're a tourist trap. Thinking about **renting a car**? Don't do it—the Valletta area has bad traffic and very little parking. • **Buses** depart Valletta for nearly every point of interest on the island (the terminal is about a half-mile from the pier), and are a reliable, cost-effective option http://www.atp.com.mt. An all-day, all routes ticket is €3.49, available from the driver. Individual, short trips are around €0.50! Route 198 connects the pier with the rest of Valletta (saves that hill climb), and circles around Valletta.

STAYING SAFE

Valletta offers many shopping opportunities, including its famous silver filigree, so **keep your purchases safe** and beware pickpockets on the crowded, narrow streets. For cash, depend on Euros—the U.S. Dollar is not always favored here. While not safety-related, many churches require modest garb—no bare shoulders, spike heels (as if you'd trek around in those), and no shorts. Still, the sun is hot, so sun hats and airy fabrics are a great idea. If you do rent a car, driving is British-style, on the left.

➢

Touring Valletta, Malta

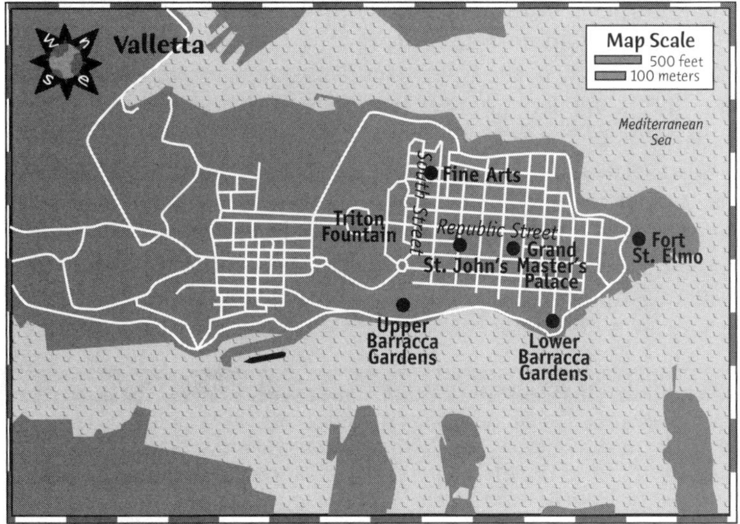

VALLETTA MAP

WALKING TOUR

Walking Around Valletta: Republic Street is the heart of the city—it forms the "backbone" for this tour, and offers plenty of dining and shopping, too. There's more here than you can do, and lots more that we haven't listed, so, good luck! Starting near the pier, pass through the City Gate.Two blocks beyond is South St., where the National Museum of Fine Arts is on the left, three blocks down. Back on Republic for one block, to the National Museum of Archaeology. Another block beyond is St. John Street. To the right is the Cathedral of St. John, with a must-see Baroque interior and Carravagio's *Beheading of St. John*. Back to Republic to Palace Square, where the Grand Masters Palace houses the Palace Armoury and State Rooms (€10) and Malta's legislature. To the left off the square is Old Theatre St. and Manoel Theatre Museum, domed Carmelite Church, and St. Paul's Anglican Church, with its oft-photographed tower. Retrace your steps, cross Republic and go two more blocks to the city market (open until Noon). Turn right on St. Paul Street a half-block to Parish Church of St. Paul's Shipwreck. Back on Republic, two more blocks yields the Toy Museum and Casa Rocca Piccola Museum. The street ends four blocks later at Fort St. Elmo and the War Museum. On your way back, Merchant St. is prime shopping territory, running parallel to Republic St., one block over. Slightly off the grid along the southeast battlements are Upper and Lower Barracca Gardens, with choice views of the Grand Harbor (see the map).

Embarking on Port Adventures in Valletta, Malta

Of the 17 excursions offered by Disney Cruise Line at press time, here are our **recommended port adventures** for first-time visitors to Malta. Now, we do find many of the other excursions quite worthy. As lovers of scavenger hunts, we might opt for the Valletta Treasure Hunt, and most of the bus tours of the island also appeal—pick and choose, based on the round-up of destinations. And, since most are half-day tours, there's still time for Valletta on your own (see the previous page). If you crave a theme park-style family day on this voyage, then what could be better than Popeye's Sweetheart Village? Finally, there's the visit to Malta's sister-island, Gozo, which would probably make you the Adventurers of the Day at your dinner table.

Highlights of Malta

Tour
Active
All ages
$119/$69 3-9
8.5 hours

This is our choice for an all-day, see-the-most, all-day tour. Start your day with a walking tour of Valletta, including visits to the Grand Master's Palace's State Rooms and St. John's Cathedral, two of our top picks (see previous page). You'll then head out of town for a taste of the rest of Malta. You'll visit Medina, another great historical city, and its Baroque cathedral. Then on to a religious site of another color, the Tarxien Temple ruins, which pre-date many far more famous ancient temples. A seafood lunch follows (included in the price, non-fish alternatives available) and the day wraps up with a visit to Marsaxlokk, the quintessential small Maltan fishing village, for strolling and shopping. Wheelchairs not permitted. Over two miles of walking, sometimes on cobblestones. Modest apparel. Limited availability, so book early.

Blue Grotto Boat Trip and Fishing Village

Tour
Moderate
Age 5 and up
$52/$32 5-9
4-4.5 hours

Sun-baked cities and historic and religious sites not for you? Head out of town for a 40-minute bus ride to the south side of the island to view the dramatic coastline and cruise in small boats to the Blue Grotto. This cluster of sea-carved caverns is famous for its breathtakingly beautiful blue waters. From there, it's off to Marsaxlokk, Malta's model small fishing village, for gazing and shopping. Lifejackets are mandatory on the boat ride, and the boat ride may be replaced, in the case of bad weather, by a bus tour. Wheelchairs are not permitted. Limited availability.

Three Historic Cities and Dghajsa Boat Ride

Tour
Moderate
Age 5 and up
$39/$19 5-9
4- 4.5 hours

When you're berthed in Valletta, ancient battlements beckon from across the water. Here's a way to check them out, and still have time to venture into Valletta (or at least the waterfront shops by the pier). And you can't beat the price! Your bus takes you to Senglea, one of Valletta's fortress sister-cities across the bay, for a walking tour and dramatic views of Valletta. Then it's on to the other "sister," Vittoriosa, for another walking tour. Cool off in the sea breezes as you explore the historic harbor in a small, wooden, brightly painted dghajsa boat (keep your camera handy!). Finally, head out of town to the fishing village of Marsaxlokk for shopping and more boat ogling. Wheelchairs not permitted. Bad weather may require substituting a stop in Valletta for the boat ride. Limited availability.

See page 218 for a key to the shore excursion description charts and their icons.

Palma, Mallorca
(Mediterranean Itineraries)

When many Europeans think, "**Island getaway**," Mallorca is "it." This beautiful Spanish island 105 miles south of Barcelona draws nearly 25 million visitors annually. While sun may be on most minds, the island's capital, Palma, offers the joys and mysteries of a Medieval city.

© Vix_B

The Palma harbour

AMBIENCE

Palma follows the classic European hub-and-spoke plan, her historic core encircled by **tree-shaded ramblas and boulevards**, Plaza Major anchoring dead center, while the glorious Gothic cathedral, la Seu, and the Moorish royal palace sit on her rim, at harbor's edge. Narrow streets wander in all directions, sunlight rarely penetrating, until the traveler steps into a sunny intersection or plaza. Outside La Ciutat ("The City," as the locals call it), a steep and rocky coastline rings the island, the hard stone punctuated by bays and coves sheltering soft crescents of sand. The rugged northern mountains climb to 4,741 ft.(1,445 m.), while to their south, much of the island is rolling farmland, though these days the farmhouse is likely to be a vacation villa.

HISTORY

As with most Mediterranean islands, Mallorca has been settled since the Stone Age, and over 270 stone structures, Talaiot, survive from the Bronze Age. Modern Palma was **founded by the Romans** in 123 BC, atop one of those Bronze Age settlements, though only a few hints of Rome or the Moors that followed exist today. The Vandals sacked the island in 426 AD, and it remained under their rule until the Byzantine conquest in 524. Moorish rule began in 902, though Christian forces sacked the city in 1115 to suppress piracy. Construction began on the city's cathedral in 1229, the year Christian Spaniards evicted the Moors, which is also when the city was re-named Palma.

FACTS

Size: 1,405 sq. mi. (3,640 sq. km.) (Mallorca) / 80 sq. mi. (208 sq. km.) (Palma)	
Climate: Mediterranean	**Temperatures**: 59°F (15°C) to 85°F (30°C)
Population: 869,067/401,270	**Busy Season**: Summer
Language: Catalan, Spanish, English	**Money**: Euro (€)
Time Zone: Central European	**Transportation**: Walking, taxis, buses
Phones: Dial 011-34-971 from U.S., dial 112 for emergencies	

Making the Most of Palma, Mallorca

GETTING THERE

The Magic may berth at one of two piers in **Palma's harbor**, both southwest of the city center. Most likely, it will be the modern cruise ship terminal. An alternate pier is just to the southwest of the terminal. Shuttles and taxis will be on hand to take you into town, or you can walk two (or three) miles along a waterfront lined with marinas. There's no tourist-focused shopping or dining near the piers, but a modern mall, Porto Pí, is nearby, on Ave. Joan Miro (take a cab). You'll be in Palma on Friday. All ashore time is around 7:45 am and all aboard is around 6:00 pm. As Spain is a European Union nation, there will be no customs inspection.

GETTING AROUND

Walking is nearly your only choice if you're touring the old town, but the walk there from the piers is 2 or 3 miles, depending on the pier. There is one beach, Cala Major, about a mile southwest from the piers. Either way, consider a cab! • Taxis are metered and reasonably priced. Initial "drop" is €1.95, plus €0.80/km. Some cabs offer "Taxi Tours" of 1, 2, and 3 hours, at €30 per hour, with pre-recorded narration. Look for the sign on the cab.• City Bus Route 1 stops at both piers and heads for the old town. Exit as soon as it reaches the Cathedral area, as it's headed elsewhere afterwards. Tickets are €2. See the next page for the #50 tour bus. • Thinking about renting a car? Highways are good here, so for those adventuresome enough to try, EuroRent (http://www.eurorent.es) has an office at the cruise terminal, and other agencies are in the area. • While not exactly modern mass transit, the Sóller Train will take you out of the city on a glorious ride through the countryside and into the Tramuntana Mountains on 100 year-old rail cars, behind a unique, electric locomotive. The ride to the town of Sóller takes 50 minutes each way, and costs €11 round-trip. The 10:10 am, 10:50 am, 12:50 pm and 1:05 pm trains are practical, and leave from Palma's Plaça d'Espanya rail station, on the far side of the old town (take a cab). Once in Sóller, a historic trolley will take you down into the scenic Port of Sóller for €2 each way.

STAYING SAFE

Palma and other shore excursion destinations offer many shopping opportunities. **Keep your purchases safe**. Beware of pickpockets on the crowded, narrow streets and especially in popular spots like the cathedral. You're there in the height of tourist season, when the jostling crowds make picking especially easy. Leave valuables on board. For cash, depend on Euros. Sun hats, sunscreen, and airy fabrics are a great idea. While not safety-related, the churches require modest garb—no bare shoulders and no shorts.

Touring Palma, Mallorca

PALMA MAP

ON YOUR OWN

First, note that **siesta is widely observed**. Many shops, restaurants, and museums close around 1:30-2:00 pm and don't re-open until 5:00 pm. Plan accordingly. An exploration of the old town starts right at the waterfront. Almudaina Palace and the glorious cathedral, La Seu are there, side by side. East of the cathedral, Banys Arabs is the Moorish-era public baths, one of the only surviving structures from that era. Passeig de Born is the place to stroll, sit at a cafe, or window shop, like Barcelona's Las Ramblas. It's one block beyond the Aludaina Palace, via Ave. de Antoni Maura. Outside the old town but within a mile of the pier, Poble Espanyol (Spanish Village) contains reproductions of 22 famous buildings from around Spain, similar to the attraction of the same name in Barcelona. On a hill overlooking the pier, Castelle de Bellver is an impressive 13th century fortress with a history museum and, as the name implies, excellent views. The #50 city bus is a hop-on/hop-off tour bus that makes 16 stops, including right at the pier. Narration (headphones provided) in 8 languages. Service starts at 10:00 am, every 20 minutes thereafter, the complete tour is 80 minutes. €13/€6.50 ages 0-15. Beaches and Mallorca tend to go together, but you're visiting at the height of tourist season, so big crowds should be assumed. The web site http://www.mallorca-beaches.com is an excellent resource, and there are plenty of excellent choices within 7–10 miles of the pier. Cala Major is closest, but you can do better.

Introduction | Reservations | Staterooms | Dining | Activities | Ports of Call | Magic | Index

Embarking on Port Adventures in Palma, Mallorca

Of the 13 shore excursions offered by Disney Cruise Line, here are our recommendations for your visit to Palma Mallorca:

Low Budget: Every excursion offered is under $100, so how low can you go? At the rock bottom, Scenic Palma & Valldemossa ($39/$25 ages 0-9, 4 hours) gives the best bang for those bucks. Worst value? The beach break. That excursion for one is about the same cost as a round-trip cab fare from the pier, so two or more travelers come out way ahead by cab (you'll need those savings to rent a chaise lounge). Want to save even more? The nearest beach, Cala Major, is just a mile from the pier.

Big Budget: Apparently, Mallorcans (and the cruise line) haven't discovered a legal way to extract large sums from day visitors. That's OK, you probably went over-budget in Florence or Rome, anyway. If you must, hire a car with driver for the day and go beach-hopping, or up into the mountains. Yes, $99 isn't exactly big budget, but Valldemossa, Deia & Soller ($99/$69 ages 0-9, all ages, 8 hours) is pushing our buttons. The road trip alone may be worth the price, plus they toss in lunch (they'd better, on an 8-hour trip). The drive, much of it along narrow, steep, and winding mountain roads overlooking the sea, is breathtaking, and the villages visited are quite picturesque.

Nature: We're not sure that an aquatic theme park would be our first choice, but the kids may feel differently. Marine Turtle Recovery Hospital and Sea Life ($79/$59 ages 3-9, ages 3 and up, 4 hours) has a lot to offer to sea animal-lovers. While a hike in the mountains or sea kayaking the coast would be very appealing, the cruise lines don't offer those options. We do like the idea of Drach Caves and Porto Cristo ($59/$40 ages 0-9, all ages, 4.5 hours). While only the underground portion of the excursion fits this category, the caves are one of the island's most popular attractions. And chamber musicians boating by on an underground lake? Hat's off to whoever came up with that!

Active: Not only is it the only "active" choice, but Bike Ride through Palma de Mallorca ($79, ages 12+ only, 3.5 hours) is a great way to see the city. We figure you're paying over $10/hour for the bike rental and $10/hour for the tour guide, but what the heck?

Armchair: Take the Soller Train Ride ($70/$55 ages 3-9, ages 3 and up, 4 hours). Read about it in our Getting Around section on page 426. Either do it with the cruise line, or do it on your own. The official excursion takes you by bus in one direction, by train in the other, though the bus portion follows the same route. Decisions, decisions!

Venice, Italy
(Special Mediterranean Itinerary)

"The Floating City" is one of the **most romantic places** in Europe. Perched off the northeastern coast of Italy, Venice is famous for it's art, music, and architecture which weaves through the city's history like the gondolas and water taxis along the city's canals.

© Arian Zwegers
Venice from the Ponte di Rialto

AMBIENCE

The city is built upon an **archipelago of 117 small islands**, which are linked by 409 bridges over 177 canals in a shallow lagoon. The canals serve the same function as roads in the older areas, and the main methods of transportation are by water or on foot. Venezia, as it is called by the locals, is characterized by an elegant sort of decay that only attracts, not detracts, from a visit. The city retains its charm as a monument to the Renaissance, from the gondoliers gliding down the canals and little shops tucked into corners and crevices to the majestic palaces and belltowers soaring overhead. In the evenings, Venice really shines, making it perfect for romantic strolls along the quiet canals, the only sounds the lapping of the water at the ancient walls around you.

HISTORY

Venice is the stuff of legends. The name itself comes from the ancient *Veneti* people who lived in the area about 3000 years ago. Refugees from nearby Roman cities later congregated here, and the first church was founded in the year 421. Geography and politics combined to isolate Venice, and the city gained increasing autonomy. Charlemagne attempted to conquer the city, but failed when the soldiers contracted diseases from local swamps. Venice emerged as a city state of military and commercial power, becoming the **most prosperous European city** by the 13th century. Venice lost her independence when Napoleon conquered the city in 1797.

FACTS

Size: 160 sq. mi. (414.5 sq. km.)	
Climate: Humid subtropical	**Temperatures**: 42°F (5.8°C) to 81.5°F (27.5°C)
Population: 270,000	**Busy Season**: May, June, September, October
Language: English	**Money**: Euro (€)
Time Zone: CET (UTC+1)	**Transportation**: Walking, boats, buses
Phones: Area Code 041, dial 113 for police, or 800-355-920 for tourism issues	

Making the Most of Venice

GETTING THERE

The Disney Magic enjoys an overnight visit to Venice in 2013 and 2014, and berths at the **Venice Cruise Terminal** (*Marittima*) on the far west side of the city. You'll arrive at Piazzale Roma, which is right on the Grand Canal. The nearest *vaporetto* (water bus) stop is S. Marta. The train station is also nearby, north of Piazelle Roma, which leads to the mainland. You can easily walk from the cruise terminal right into the city if you wish. All ashore time is 1:00 pm; all aboard is at 5:00 pm the following day.

GETTING AROUND

Venice is a **confusing network** of canals, pathways, and bridges. If you're moving about the city on your own, get a good, detailed map (the shopping flyer available as you disembark usually has a decent map). Venice is the original and oldest pedestrian city, so you can get everywhere on foot. But it's typically faster, and more scenic, to take a boat. ***Vaporetto*** (large water buses) have regular routes along the Grand Canal. The #1 *vaporetto* route stops at every stop along the Grand Canal, making it the best choice for sightseeing. Price is €7 for 75 minutes of travel time. Another option are the ***traghetti***, which are largish, undecorated gondola used to ferry pedestrians across points in the canals without bridges—price is just €1-2 per crossing, a bargain! Finally, we would be remiss without mentioning the famous ***gondola***, which should really be considered an attraction rather than a valid method of transportation because it is very pricey—official prices per gondola are €80-100 for 40 minutes, with each additional 20 minutes costing €40-50. If you're with friends or a group, go together and split the cost—most gondolas hold 6 passengers. And beware of gondoliers who may try to get more from you—negotiate the price upfront (feel free to haggle).

SAFETY

Your biggest challenge in Venice will be to **avoid getting lost**. Bring a good map and pay attention to official signs. Beyond that, Venice is pretty safe. If you're walking at night, choose well-lit areas for safety (and to avoid falling into the water). Don't touch the water—untreated sewage is released directly into the canals.

SHOPPING

Venice has **many shops** selling masks, costumes, Venetian glass, and the usual designer Italian brands (Gucci, Prada, etc.) The Rialto market is another shopping destination, as is the touristy Piazza San Marco. Note that most shop hours are 9:00 am to 12:30 pm and 3:00 pm to 7:30 pm, Monday-Saturday. Just keep your receipts in case questioned (law requires customers keep receipts).

Touring Venice

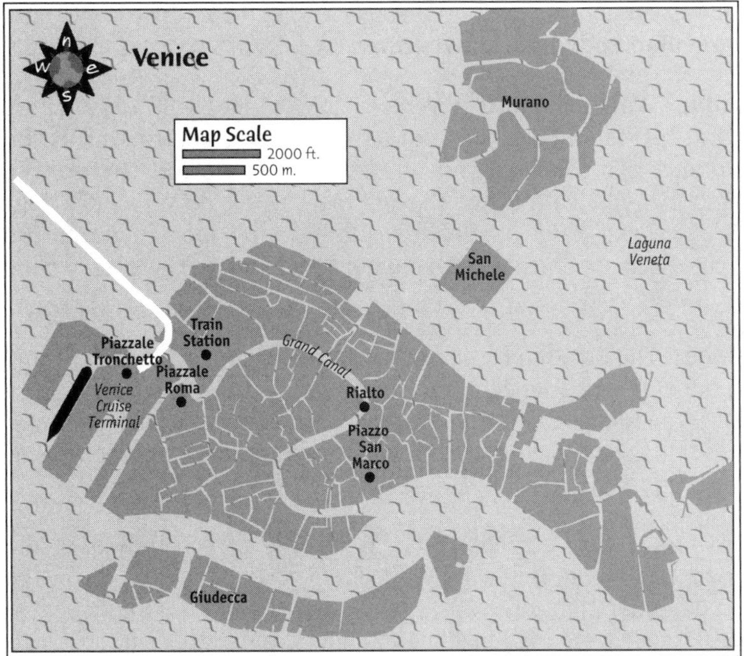

Venice has many famous sights to see. **Doge's Palace** in Piazza San Marco will be familiar to anyone who's seen Epcot's Italy pavilion—ask about the Secret Itinerary guided tour (€16) which shows, among other things, Casanova's jail. The nearby **Bell Tower of St. Mark** offers excellent views of the city and lagoon for €8. **St. Mark's Basilica** is something to behold and right in Piazza San Marco—you can go in for free (or pay €1,50 to reserve official tickets online), but you must be dressed appropriate (no short skirts or bare shoulders) and photography/filming is forbidden. There's also a museum upstairs (€5) and the opportunity to view the high altar and treasury (€2). **Galleria dell'Accademia di Venezia** (€6,50) is one of Venice's most important art museums. If you're looking for something to do in the evenings beyond a gondola ride, you can simply wander about Piazza San Marco or enjoy a meal at nearby place like **Restaurant la Caravella**, where you can eat in a traditional courtyard (http://www.restaurantlacaravella.com). If you want to drink, head over to Erbaria on the west side of the Rialto Bridge. For more details on Venice attractions as well as web cams, visit the Official City of Venice page at http://www.comune.venezia.it.

Embarking on Port Adventures in Venice

Of the 24 excursions offered by Disney Cruise Line at press time, here our are **recommended port adventures** for first-time visitors to Venice:

Low Budget: We like the Taste of Venice ($59/$49 ages 3–9), which offers a moderate 110-minute walking tour of the city, down narrow alleys and across bridges. This walking tour utilizes a headset so you can hear the guide better. If you want to see the San Marco area, do Venice On Your Own ($49/$39 ages 3–9) with private motor boat transportation from the pier to the plaza and back again—you get three hours of time to explore Venice on your own.

Big Budget: The Cooking Lesson at a Venetian Home ($599 ages 21 and up) is a signature experience and the opportunity to visit the 16th century home of a Venetian. You'll meet Countess Lelia Passi, who will teach you Italian cooking secrets, after which you'll enjoy an elegant lunch in her stately dining room.

Active: Grand Canal by Dragon Boat ($299/$279 ages 8–9) takes you to the Canottieri Bucintoro Rowing Club where you'll learn how to row the dragon boat for 90 minutes with up to 19 other rowers. The Gondolier for a Day ($379 ages 16 and up) teaches you how to punt the traditional, flat-bottomed gondola, then you get to propel your craft for about 60 minutes! Be sure to bring hats, sunglasses, and sunscreen for these adventures!

Kids: The Mask Workshop, St. Mark's Square and Doge's Palace ($319/$299 ages 5–9) gives kids the opportunity to make their own mask at a local Venetian mask shop while their parents can do some shopping or sightseeing nearby. The tour also includes a walking tour of nearby attractions and a visit to Doge's Palace for all participants.

Armchair: Venetian Panoramic Cruise ($52/$42 ages 3–9) is perfect—the only walking is from the pier to the loading zone. Boat tours like this are certainly scenic, but isolate you from the real charm of the city.

Beyond Venice: The Murano Glass and Burano Lace excursion ($65/$49 ages 3–9) starts with a 45 minute boat ride to Murano, where you can witness glassblowers at work. You'll then visit the island of Burano, once renown for the finest lace in Europe. This tour packs a lot of sightseeing (4–4.5 hours) into its relatively low price.

Dubrovnik, Croatia
(Special Mediterranean Itinerary)

Located on the Dalmatian coast on the southwest tip of Croatia, the centuries-old city of Dubrovnik is a charming Mediterranean port and has been called the "Pearl of the Adriatic." Dubrovnik is a **UNESCO World Heritage** site rich in culture and history, complete with a walled city.

© Michael Cavén

Old City of Dubrovnik

AMBIENCE

The pace of Dubrovnik is considerably slower than other Mediterranean ports, making this a delightful place to relax. This **medieval walled city** allows you to actually stroll along its one-mile-long city wall for amazing views of the town and the harbor. Walk the old, narrow alleyways made of smooth marble. Enjoy the sun at one of the well known beaches. Or explore one of the many museums, cathedrals, or churches that fill this little port town.

HISTORY

Dubrovnik began as a **maritime trading port** in the Middle Ages in the 7th century A.D. thanks to its excellent position along the coast. The port was originally known by its Greek name—Raugia or Ragousa—and was part of the Republic of Ragusa in the Middle Ages (together with Venice, Genoa, Pisa, and Amalfi). The city's huge fleet of merchant ships traveled the waters freely, traveling as far as India and America. Interestingly, Dubrovnik helped the American Revolution by entering into a trade agreement with the American colonies, as it realized the economic potential of the new world. And despite the fact that Dubrovnik was demilitarized during Croatian's war for independence in the '90s, the city was still attacked and sustained heavy shell damage. The city was repaired according to UNESCO guidelines, but if you look close you can still see some bullet holes in buildings.

FACTS

Size: 8.2 sq. mi. (21.3 sq. km.)	
Climate: Humid Subtropical	**Temperatures**: 50°F (10°C) to 78.4°F (26°C)
Population: 43,000	**Busy Season**: July and August
Language: Croatian	**Money**: Kuna and Euro (7.3 Kuna = 1 Euro)
Time Zone: CET	**Transportation**: Walking, bus, taxi
Phones (city): Area code +385-20; dial 112 for emergencies	

Introduction | Reservations | Staterooms | Dining | Activities | Ports of Call | Magic | Index

Making the Most of Dubrovnik

GETTING THERE

The Disney Magic docks at the **Gruž Harbor**, which is just under two miles northwest from Dubrovnik's famous Old City. Tendering should not be necessary, but that does depend a bit on weather and other ship traffic (there is room for just one ship to dock in the port). You can get information on the cruise terminal at http://www.portdubrovnik.hr. From here you can take a 10-minute taxi or bus to the city gate. The Disney Magic is currently scheduled to arrive in Dubrovnik on Friday, July 5, 2013 and Monday, June 23, 2014. All ashore is 11:15 am, all aboard is 7:00 pm.

GETTING AROUND

Most visitors not on a shore adventure will likely want to make their way to the Old City. You can take a **bus** (there's a bus stop very close to where your ship docks) for about 15 Kuna (2 Euro)—take bus 1, 1a, or 3 to reach the Old City. Buses are frequent. Alternately, you can take a **taxi** for about 80 Kuna (11 Euro). Once in the Old City, you'll be **walking**—this is a pedestrian-only place. Wear comfortable shoes that have a non-slip sole, as the marbled streets can be slippery when wet. For that reason, we do not recommend you rent a car unless you intend to visit destinations other than Dubrovnik (and if you do, be sure to bring your passport as Dubrovnik is isolated from the rest of Croatia and you will need to pass through Bosnia to reach it—we do not recommend this).

SAFETY

Like other tourist destinations, Dubrovnik has its **share of dangers** to avoid. We hear pickpockets can target busy tourist areas, so keep your valuables tucked away and don't put anything in your back pockets. Be careful of the high walls you can walk along, which do not always have fences. Similarly, there are a lot of steps/stairs, so use caution. Use the restroom on the ship before disembarking, as reports indicate there is just one public restroom at the Pile gate entrance. If you go swimming, keep an eye out for sea urchins (black, spiky creatures)—stepping on one will cause pain and possible infection.

SHOPPING

Plenty of little **shops and boutiques** can be found in the Old City. Dubrovnik is well known for its lavender, olive oil, wine, and Rakia (a hard liquor like brandy). Intricately painted eggs are another local favorite. And while you'll see women crocheting doilies (which you can buy), crocheting isn't an old-world art; opt instead for Poprsnica (Konavie embroidery), which is counted thread needlework made with silk threads.

Touring Dubrovnik

© Jennifer Boyer

Walking the Walls of Old Town

Your "don't miss" attraction for Dubrovnik is a walk along the city's 80-foot-high fortified walls, which were built between the 13th and 16th centuries. The best entrance to the walls is immediately to the left of the Pile Gate (city gate) when you enter the Old City, but you can also enter at the Dominican Monastery (Dominikanski Samostan) and near the Aquarium on Kneza Damjana Jude. Entrance fee is 70 Kuna/adult and 30 Kuna/child—bring Kuna, as Euros are not accepted. You can walk the perimeter of the entire Old City in just 1.25 miles, which takes just about an hour at a steady pace (or up to two hours at a relaxed pace). Bring water, hats, and sunscreen, as you won't find much shade here. We recommend you walk the walls first thing in the day, when crowds are thinner and the sun is a little less hot—plus it gives you an excellent overview of the Old City. There are some cafes and shops along the walls.

Introduction
Reservations
Staterooms
Dining
Activities
Ports of Call
Magic
Index

Embarking on Port Adventures in Dubrovnik

Of the 27 excursions offered by Disney Cruise Line at press time, here our are **recommended port adventures** for first-time visitors to Dubrovnik:

Low Budget: The Folkloric Show, Old Town City Tour, and Panoramic Dubrovnik adventure ($69/$49 ages 3 to 9/$0 ages 0 to 2) is a good deal! The four hour tour takes you to Park Orsula to overlook the city, then to Pile Gate for a 90-minute walking tour of the Old City, and then to a theater for a 45-minute show feature Croatian dance groups. You also get an hour of free time to explore Old City.

Overview: The Dubrovnik Scenic Cruise and Old Town City Tour ($79/$39 ages 3 to 9/$39 ages 0 to 2) is an excellent overview of Dubrovnik. You get to board a galleon-style wooden boat for a 60-minute cruise to the Old Town where you'll have a 45-minute walking tour and an hour of free time. You'll get back on the galleon to explore the scenic Adriatic and enjoy some ice cream before returning to the port.

Active: If you want to get out and do something, consider Kayaking the Dubrovnik Coastline ($129 ages 10 and up/$99 ages 8 and 9). This 4-hour excursion has you board two-person kayaks and cruise the Adriatic Sea, exploring caves, hidden beaches, and Lokrum Island. You'll also have the opportunity to swim and snorkel.

Kids: Croatia's Silk Heritage Featuring Exclusive Family Activity ($129/$99 ages 3–9) takes you to the village of Gruda where you'll meet artist Antonia Ruskovic in her workshop. You'll learn all about silk, from production to usage. You will actually get to produce your own silk thread, which will be used to embroider new Croatian costumes to replace those lost in the war. You'll then have the opportunity to create a Christmas ornament to take home. Before the end of the adventure, you'll take a trip to the Old City where you'll have an hour to explore.

Beyond Dubrovnik: If you'd like to relax, consider the Dalmatian Coastline and Wine Tasting excursion ($99/$75 ages 3 to 9/$0 ages 0 to 2). You'll board a bus and travel 30 minutes to the village of Orasac, where you'll visit an historic house and learn the old way of making olive oil. Then back on the bus for another 45 minutes to the town of Ston, which is known as the "oyster capital" of Croatia. You'll then continue on to the village of Ponifvke to visit a local winery, where adults can taste the famous "Peljesac" wines.

Athens, Greece (Piraeus)

(Special Eastern Mediterranean Itinerary)

One of the **world's oldest cities**, Athens is widely proclaimed to be the cradle of Western civilization. It's historical heritage is significant, and still evident in its monuments and arts. As the capital of Greece, Athens is the focal point for cultural, industrial, financial and economic matters in the country.

© Roger Salz

Hadrian's Arch in Athens

AMBIENCE

Unlike some of the other Mediterranean ports on your itinerary, Athens is a **bustling metropolitan city that is forever changing**. The city is really a collection of neighborhoods, from the City Center with the 2,400-year-old Acropolis temple and Plaka which dates back to 5th century B.C., to Kolonaki with its museums, restaurants, and shops and Varrakios' Kotsa Plaza and markets. The recent Olympics hosted here have helped to spruce things up and create a more tourist- and pedestrian-friendly place.

HISTORY

Athens has been continuously inhabited for at least 7000 years, meaning it dates back to the Stone Age. It was the capital of Mycenaean civilization of Ancient Greece, from which we get much of the ancient Greek literature and myths. In the 6th century B.C., Athens entered into its Golden Age of Athenian democracy, creating the foundations of Western civilization that echo throughout the world today. In the Middle Ages, Athens was conquered by the Ottoman Empire, only achieving her independence in 1834. The first modern Olympics were hosted in Athens in 1896, and the city began to grow and expand in size and population. Today Athens is a center for archaeological research, a hub for the performing arts, and a long-standing destination for tourists.

FACTS

Size: Municipal: 15 sq. mi. (39 sq. km.)/Metro: 1,131 sq. mi. (2982 sq. km.)	
Climate: Subtropical	**Temperatures**: 54°F (12°C) to 92°F (33°C)
Population: 665,000/3,750,000	**Busy Season**: Summer
Language: Greek	**Money**: Euro (€)
Time Zone: EET	**Transportation**: Walking, buses, taxis
Phones: Area code 21; dial 112 for emergencies and 171 for the tourist police	

Making the Most of Athens

GETTING THERE

The **Disney Magic docks in Piraeus**, the largest passenger seaport in Europe with a long history of seafaring dating back to ancient Greece. You should not need to tender, and can walk right off the ship and explore the city of Piraeus if you wish—plenty of shops and eateries are nearby. Athens itself is about seven miles from the port. The Disney Magic will visit Athens on Friday, June 21, 2013, Sunday, June 29, 2014, Thursday, July 17, 2014, and Friday, August 1, 2014. Disembarkation time is typically 7:15–8:15 am with an all-aboard time of 6:30–6:45 pm.

GETTING AROUND

If you'd like to go to Athens on your own, just sign up for the Explore Athens On Your Own **port adventure** ($39/$29 ages 3 to 9/$0 ages 0 to 2) and avoid the transportation hassles. If you don't remember to sign up for this, we recommend you **take the train**. Walk to the train station about one mile away, buy a ticket, then board the green line to Monastiraki, change to the blue line (Syntagma)—cost is only about 70 cents (€), though you will need to validate your ticket in the orange canceling machines. If you're willing to brave the wilds, you can take a **taxi** into Athens, but be prepared to negotiate the price in advance down to something reasonable—€10–15 is a reasonable price (that's per vehicle, not per person). Avoid the taxi drivers who want to give you a "tour" and ward yourself against aggressive tactics. If necessary, call the tourist police (dial 171). Once in Athens, you can (and should) **walk**—it's a great city for pedestrians. We do not recommend you rent a car here.

SAFETY

Staying safe in Athens is mostly common sense. **Pickpocketing** is real and, sadly, common in both Piraeus and Athens—keep your money and valuables stashed safely. Better yet, bring no valuables at all and carry just the bare necessities stashed in a travel wallet tucked inside your shirt or jacket. Avoid the taxis—we hear nothing but bad things about them. Also, Athens can get very, very hot in the summer—carry and drink water, rest often in shade, and stay cool when you can.

SHOPPING

So you'd like to go shopping in Athens? It's important to keep shop hours in mind—hours are typically 9:00 am to 2:30 pm and 5:00 to 8:30 pm (they **close for a siesta** in the mid-afternoon). Note that shops are closed on Sundays. Not sure where to go? The Plaka district is a good shopping spot, and easy to get around thanks to its pedestrian-only avenues. Plaka has both touristy souvenir shops as well as arts and crafts local to the area.

Touring Athens

© Arian Zwegers

The Acropolis

The Acropolis is really the big highlight of a visit to Athens, and it deserves some background and information. Located on a rocky hilltop 490 feet above sea level, the Acropolis is the location of several ancient buildings, including the famous **Parthenon**. Evidence suggests construction began in the 5th century B.C. with the Parthenon, the Propylaia gateway, the Erechtheion temple, and the Athena Nike temple. The Parthenon is a temple dedicated to Athena, whom the Athenians considered their patron deity. Also of note are the Odeon of Herodes Atticus, the Theatre of Dionysus Eleuthereus, and the Odeon of Pericles, which are theaters—some of which still offer concerts and performances.

If you visit the Acropolis outside of a port adventure, it's easy to reach from many spots, including Plaka and Monastiraki. Admission is €12 . Operating hours are 8:00 am–7:00 pm (Sundays are 8:00 am–3:00 pm). We recommend you visit earlier when it is less crowded. Bring water and comfortable walking shoes, as there are plenty of steps and uneven ground to contend with. Licensed tour guides are available near the entrance for about €50.

The official Acropolis web site is http://www.acropolisofathens.gr.

Embarking on Port Adventures in Athens

Of the 21 excursions offered by Disney Cruise Line at press time, here our are **recommended port adventures** for first-time visitors to Athens:

Low Budget: The cheapest option is the Explore Athens On Your Own (mentioned two pages prior), which is nothing more than transportation to and from Athens. If you're looking for more substance, we recommend the Highlights of Athens—A Panoramic Drive ($39/$26 ages 3 to 9/$0 ages 0 to 2) which offers a 75-minute ride aboard an air-conditioned bus past various notable spots, including the Temple of Olympian Zeus and Hadrian's Arch, and then stops at the bottom of the Acropolis for a 45 minute shopping visit.

Big Budget: If you've got money to burn, why not do the Athens by Private Vehicle for 8 hours with a driver? It's only $999 and accommodates up to 3 guests. If that's too rich for you, there's a 4-hour option for $699. Have more than three people? You can get a Mini Bus with a driver and a guide for $1199—this tour accommodates up to 16 guests, so it's a much better deal. There are other configurations, too.

Active: If you want to get out and do something, we recommend one of two port adventures. The first is Games at Panathenaic Stadium ($49/$39 ages 3 to 9/$0 ages 0 to 2) which takes you to the Panathenaic Stadium (where the first modern Olympics were held) where you get a guided tour and the chance to run and race on the same track as the Olympians have. The second option is the Walking Tour of Athens ($79/$49 ages 3 to 9, $0 ages 0 to 2) which features a 135-minute walking tour that visits Pnyka Hill, Ancient Agora, and Plaka.

Family: Acropolis Sightseeing and Family Archaeological Excavation ($129/$89 ages 5 to 9) offers not only a trip to the Acropolis aboard an air-conditioned bus, but you then visit a cultural center where you get a snack (sandwich, fruit, and juice) and then participate in a one-hour excavation for ancient artifacts. Families will work together to excavate and catalog their findings. The only down side we see to this excursion is the length at 5.5 to 6 hours.

Full Day: Want the full Athens experience? Do the Athens Sightseeing, Acropolis, and New Acropolis Museum with Lunch adventure ($199/$129 ages 3 to 9/$0 ages 0 to 2) to visit the major highlights—the Acropolis, Plaka (where you'll have a Greek lunch), and the New Acropolis Museum with a huge collection of artifacts. This tour is 8–8.5 hours long.

Ephesus, Turkey (Kusadası)
(Special Eastern Mediterranean Itinerary)

The old town of Kusadasi rests on the west coast of Turkey (known as the "**Turkish Riviera**"). As a center for art and culture, this resort town attracts visitors with its close proximity to the Ephesus outpost. Ephesus itself was an ancient Greek city, and now an archaeological site.

© Esther Lee

Library of Celsus in Ephesus

AMBIENCE

Kusadasi is **perched on a bay**, sticking out into the Aegean Sea. Outdoor cafes serving thick coffee, Turkish baths, carpet and rug shops, and a modern European style are easily found in the town. The real draw here is nearby Ephesus, arguably the best-preserved ancient city in the Eastern Mediterranean, housing one of the seven wonders of the Old World. A visit to these ruins is like taking a step back in time to a place where both the Virgin Mary and Alexander the Great strolled, the great library housed thousands of scrolls, and St. Paul the Apostle lived and wrote.

HISTORY

Ephesus and the surrounding area has been inhabited from about 6000 BC. In the 10th century it became an Attic-Ionion colony, later joining the Ionion League. Alexander the Great later liberated the town in the Battle of Granicus. During the Roman period, Ephesus became capital of Asia Minor—second only in importance to Rome—and grew very prosperous. The city built the Temple of Artemis, the Library of Celsus, and the Theater, which could hold 25,000 spectators for **performances and gladiatorial contests**. Sadly, the city was destroyed by the Goths in 263 AD and the harbor was slowly silted up. The Turkish era of the city began in 1304 and it began to flourish again, only to be completely abandoned in the 15th century.

FACTS

Size: 87 sq. mi. (224.6 sq. km.)	
Climate: Humid subtropical	**Temperatures**: 7°F (7°C) to 72°F (33°C)
Population: 70,000	**Busy Season**: May to October
Language: Turkish	**Money**: New Turkish Lira (1 = $0.54 US)
Time Zone: EET	**Transportation**: Walking, taxis, buses
Phones: Area code 90-0256, dial 155 or 112 for emergencies	

Making the Most of Ephesus

GETTING THERE

The Magic docks at Kusadasi Port, which extends out into the harbor and accommodates four large cruise ships. You can step right off the ship (no tendering necessary), stroll along the dock, and walk into the Grand Bazaar in a matter of minutes, if you wish. There are plenty of places to shop and eat—even a bookstore—right beyond the port gate. The Magic is scheduled to dock in Kusadasi on Saturday, June 22, 2013, Saturday, July 2, 2014, and Friday, July 18, 2014. All ashore is 7:15–8:00 am, all aboard is 6:30–6:45 pm.

GETTING AROUND

In Kusadasi, it's easiest to simply **walk** around the town. Grab a map on your way off the ship, or pick one up from the Kusadasi Tourist Information Office across the street from the harbor. You can easily reach the "old" section of Kusadasi by walking north along the main street until you get to the top—you're looking for the ancient Kaleici neighborhood with tiny streets and even Turkish baths. **Taxis** and minibuses are also available, but they're really only necessary if you're going somewhere like Ephesus (14 miles away from port) or the House of Virgin Mary (10 miles away from port) on your own (but we really don't recommend that). As is usual with taxis in tourist areas, be sure you confirm the price in advance. Getting around when you're at **Ephesus**, which is a very large place, will require a great deal of walking and climbing. If you go as part of a port adventure, be aware that your pickup and drop-off may be a different points (i.e., drop-off at Magnesia Gate, pick-up at north end), so be sure you know.

SAFETY

This resort town is **remarkably safe** compared to others on your cruise itinerary. Your biggest dangers are likely to be sunburn, dehydration, and possibly a bad deal on a souvenir. Just use common sense and stay aware.

SHOPPING

Looking for a little **Turkish delight**? You'll find this confection for sale, along with many other local items, including dark honey, traditional coffee and tea service, carpets and rugs (kilim), leather coats, copper trays, and gold and silver jewelry. If you are tempted to buy something called zultanite, check for authenticity. It's fine to haggle in the marketplaces—in fact, we'd say it's all part of the experience of shopping in a Turkish marketplace! Feel free to start at $^1/_3$ to $^1/_2$ of the offered price and work from there.

Touring Ephesus

© QuartierLatin1968

The Great Theater in Ephesus is still used for concerts today.

Most cruisers who go ashore are likely to be heading to the great **Ephesus**, which deserves a bit more attention. First, be sure to bring your warm weather gear (hat, sunscreen, and water), patience (for the crowds), and a sense of adventure. The main sites are the Library of Celsus (it once held 12,000 scrolls), the Temple of Artemis (one of the Seven Wonders of the Ancient World), the Great Theater (largest outdoor theater in the old world), the Odeon (a smaller theater that once had a roof), the Temple of Hadrian (reconstruction from fragments), the Temple of Domitian (largest temple in the city), the Fountain of Pollio, and two Agoras (assembly halls). Also here are the Terrace Houses, where the powerful and wealthy lived during the Roman period—among the six residential units you'll find detailed frescos and mosaics, courtyards, and evidence of clay pipes that provided heat and running water. You'll want to have a guide of some sort when visiting—there aren't many signs. If you're on your own, you can buy a tourbook on site or hire a local guide for a decent price. The entrance fee is 25 Lira, with the Terrace Houses an additional fee of 15 Lira. There's also a museum you can visit for 8 Lira.

Embarking on Port Adventures in Ephesus

Of the 28 excursions offered by Disney Cruise Line at press time, here are our **recommended port adventures** for visitors to Kusadasi/Ephesus:

See It All: The Best of Ephesus tour ($99/$68 ages 3 to 9/$0 ages 0 to 2) gives you a full-day experience where you get guided tours of all the major historical sites: House of the Virgin Mary, Ephesus, and St. John's Basilica. You even get lunch and a chance to visit Kusadasi. Best bang for your buck!

Signature: The Exclusive Ephesus and Terrace Houses with Archeologist Encounter ($129/$79 ages 3 to 9/$0 ages 0 to 2) gets you to Ephesus and the Terrace Houses, as well as the opportunity to meet with a local archaeologist for 30 minutes to discuss the recent findings and techniques.

Immersive: The Ephesian Modus Vivandi excursion $149/$119 ages 3 to 9/$0 ages 0 to 2) takes you to Ephesus, the Terrace Houses, and St. John's Basilica, and then gives you the opportunity to don period outfits and join a Roman feast with "Romans and Ephesians of Ancient Times." Fun!

Spa: Try the Turkish Bath Experience ($55 ages 18 and up) for a visit to a traditional "hamam" (Turkish bathhouse) where you'll get to experience a cleansing ritual in the communal area–attendants will provide scrubbing and foam baths. An optional olive oil massage is available afterward for 20–25 Euro per person.

Family: The Ephesus and Sirince Village Featuring Exclusive Youth Activity ($139/$79 ages 5 to 9) offers a 105-minute guided walking tour of Ephesus followed by a visit to the village of Sirince where kids get the opportunity to make a Turkish bracelet. An al fresco buffet lunch is included. If you want something more active, consider the Ephesus and Aquapark excursion ($110/$75 ages 3 to 9/$0 ages 0 to 2) which includes a tour of Ephesus and a 4-hour visit to a waterpark with 12 slides, a wave pool, and a lazy river.

Armchair: The Easy Ephesus tour (no price listed) is a bus tour to the Gate of Ephesus, a stop at the Statue of the Virgin Mary, a drive down to the lower gate of Ephesus, and then a stop at the Temple of Artemis. This 3–3.5-hour tour is designed for guests who have difficulty walking and is wheelchair friendly. The bus has an access ramp.

Mykonos, Greece
(Special Eastern Mediterranean Itinerary)

Legend has it that Zeus and the **Titans battled** on the island of Mykonos. These days, the small resort island is more likely to attract celebrities and tourists than a primeval race of deities. The golden beaches, stylish shops and eateries, and picturesque streets draw visitors far and wide.

© Richard Martin

A vista of Mykonos

AMBIENCE

This small Greek island in the middle of the Aegean Sea is part of the Cyclades, known as the pearls of the Greek isles. The idyllic landscape is covered in **whitewashed dwellings**, packed into a labyrinthine maze of tiny streets and alleys. Hot, dry air and little rain makes for a sunbaked experience, mitigated only by the constant wind. Beaches ring the island and sunbathers—many who consider clothing optional—throng the shores. Mykonos is the quintessential "Greek Island Getaway" and is very popular (and crowded) as a result.

HISTORY

Like so many places in the Mediterranean, Mykonos' roots go back a long way. The island has been inhabited since 3000 B.C., and the Ionians settled here in the 11th century B.C. Delos, a holy sanctuary, is less than two miles away and this made Mykonos a convenient supply stop as well as destination for the Delians. The island flourished as a **crossroads for shipping** during the reign of Julius Caesar. In the Middle Ages, Mykonos was ruled by the Venetians, and fell victim to the Saracens and Turks. Thousands of islanders were taken from their homes as slaves. Pirates and buccaneers also used Mykonos for dealings. Finally, in 1830, the Greek War of Independence liberated the island. Tourism began in the 1950s and it soon became a popular spot for the rich and famous, thanks to its beautiful architecture, gorgeous views, and relative seclusion.

FACTS

Size: 40.6 sq. mi. (105 sq. km.)	
Climate: Hot subtropical	**Temperatures**: 57°F (14°C) to 82°F (28°C)
Population: 10,000	**Busy Season**: July and August
Language: Greek	**Money**: Euro (€)
Time Zone: EET	**Transportation**: Walking, taxis, buses
Phones: Area code +30-22890, dial 112 for emergencies	

Introduction Reservations Staterooms Dining Activities Ports of Call Magic Index

Making the Most of Mykonos

GETTING THERE

The Magic docks at **Tourlos**, which is 1.2 miles north of the town of Hora (the capital of Mykonos). Shuttles are available at the port to take you into town (3 min. ride), as are taxis at the Taxi Square on the Mykonos waterfront (central square). If you prefer to walk, plan for a 30 minute journey. The Magic is scheduled to arrive in Mykonos on Sunday, June 23, 2013, Monday, June 21, 2014, and Sunday, July 3, 2014. All ashore is 7:15–7:30 am, all aboard is 6:30–6:45 pm.

GETTING AROUND

Mykonos is the sort of town you'll want to **walk** about. It's small, maze-like streets are much easier to deal with on foot! If you want to move greater distances than your feet will allow, taxis and buses are both available. As expected, **taxis** are expensive—rates are fixed (no meters) and posted at the Taxi Square (which is the best place to find a taxi). Due to the island's small size, there are only about 30 taxis, so don't be surprised if you have to wait awhile. If your pocketbook prefers a **bus**, note that there are two main bus stations—the North station is behind the archaeological museum, and the South station is in Fabrika square. Bus tickets are usually less than €2. We do not recommend you rent a car or scooter because this is a very congested island. It's also possible to take a boat to Delos—daily excursions from the pier at the west side of the harbor leave at 9:00, 10:00, and 11:00 am—cost is €17.

SAFETY

The best way to stay safe and happy in Mykonos is to follow this advice: wear sunscreen and a hat, drink water, do not rent a car or scooter, and bring a map (if you get lost, look for the water to get your bearings). Also, if you or someone you're with is uncomfortable with nudity and/or partying, avoid beaches like Paradise or Super Paradise. Finally, if you have issues with **seasickness**, the wind can make any boat rides (like to Delos) very choppy—plan accordingly.

SHOPPING

Shopping is fun in Mykonos, with all its little boutiques amongst the narrow alleys. Look for jewelry, trendy clothes, and art galleries—Mykonos is home to a **thriving art colony**. Traditionally woven scarves, rugs, and tablecloths are also available here.

If you want to hit the **beaches**, Omos and Agios Stefanos are both family friendly spots. Psarou and Agia Anna are both small and pretty. If you're looking for the "party," go to Paradise or Super Paradise. Beaches where nudity may be encountered include Elia, Paranga, Agrari, Agois, Kapari, Paradise, and Super Paradise.

Touring Mykonos

© Alex Healing

The Temple of Isis in Delos

Delos is a "must see" for a visit to Mykonos. The Ancient Greeks considered Delos to be the birthplace of the twin gods Apollo and Artemis, and was thus considered a sacred place. If you visit, lookout for the Sacred Lake (now in a circular bowl and left dry), the Minoan Fountain (rectangular public well), the Temple of the Delians, the Terrace of the Lions (with seven marble lion statues), the Stoivadeion (either side of the platform supports giant phallus statues, the symbol of Dionysus), the Doric Temple of Isis (built on a hill), the Temple of Hera the House of Dionysus (great floor mosaics), the House of the Dolphins (more mosaics), and the Delos Synagogue (which happens to be the oldest synagogue known today). If you're up to it, you can climb the 368-foot high Mt. Kynthos' summit for amazing views of Delos. There is no shade or food/drink on this tiny, rocky island—bring proper sun protection and water. Also be aware that the ground is strewn with small rocks, so be careful of your footing.

Embarking on Port Adventures in Mykonos

Of the 17 excursions offered by Disney Cruise Line at press time, here are our **recommended port adventures** for visitors to Mykonos:

Low Budget: Kalafatis Beach ($34/$24 ages 3 to 9/$0 ages 0 to 2) offers bus transportation to the Kalafatis Beach, which is a public beach where you can rent chairs and umbrellas for an additional fee.

Big Budget: The Mykonos In Style Resort Stay ($699-$999) offers a private car and driver and a private room at the Mykonian Imperial Resort & Villas (accommodates up to 3 guests, or 4 guests if two are 12 and under) to enjoy the luxury and amenities of this seaside resort.

Archaeological: Delos Island ($85/$49 ages 0 to 9) is a boat ride and 135-minute walking tour of the Delos sanctuary. There's also an adults-only offering of this excursion ($85).

Beach: Besides the Kalafatis Beach adventure, you may want to consider the Elia Beach ($79/$49 ages 3 to 9/$0 ages 0 to 2) adventure, which offers bus transportation to the pretty Elia Beach. Here you'll enjoy a lounge chair, shared umbrella, and a light Greek lunch.

Family: Delos Island Featuring Exclusive Youth Activity ($179/$139 ages 5 to 9) offers a walking tour of Delos as well as a mosaic workshop for the kids in Mykonos.

Armchair: The Island Drive and Ano Mera Village ($79/$45 ages 3 to 9/$0 ages 0 to 2) gives you a scenic and air-conditioned motorcoach ride to the village of Ano Mera to visit the small monastery Panagia Tourliani, after which you'll taste ouzo and a Greek appetizer in the village square.

© Glen Scarborough

Elia Beach on Mykonos

➤

Port Activity Worksheet

Electronic, interactive worksheet available– see 492

Use this worksheet to keep track of the activities and shore excursions you want to do most on your cruise. List your activities in order of preference–when booking shore excursions with Disney, you'll be more likely to get an excursion if you list a second and third choice along with the first. When you're ready to book your shore excursions through Disney, reserve online or call 877-566-0968 no later than two days in advance of your sail date (see page 217). Note that you cannot make excursion reservations until Disney has received the final payment for your cruise. Check off any excursions you've booked with a notation in the "Reserved?" column. Once you know your excursions are confirmed, circle them and cross off the others.

My sail date: ________ less 60 days = ________ (*first reservation date*)

Activity/Excursion	Location	Time	Cost	Reserved?	Notes
Port:		Date:			
1.					
2.					
3.					
Port:		Date:			
1.					
2.					
3.					
Port:		Date:			
1.					
2.					
3.					
Port:		Date:			
1.					
2.					
3.					
Port:		Date:			
1.					
2.					
3.					

Notes:

Introduction
Reservations
Staterooms
Dining
Activities
Ports of Call
Magic
Index

Cavorting in Port

We predict that some of your favorite cruise memories will be made at your ports of call! Below are tips to help you get the most out of your jaunts, as well as port memories to get you in the mood.

- You can mail a **postcard home from the Castaway Cay post office** and get your stamp canceled with a cool Castaway Cay postmark (see page 20). Be sure to bring some cash to purchase your stamps as you can't use your shipboard charge here. Small bills and change are best, as it can be difficult for the staff to break large bills.

- The **sun** can be brutal. Be sure to wear sunscreen on your visits to the shore—you are likely to be in the sun more often than the shade. Sunglasses also come in handy against the glare of the bright sun off sidewalks and water. And don't forget hats—you'll find a soft fabric, crushable hat with a chin strap is invaluable!

- "Wear a **waterproof watch**. Even though we are on vacation, all the rest of the world is on a schedule. On a Disney Cruise ship, there is a clock in the Lobby Atrium, in your stateroom, and that's it! A watch keeps you on track for all the events of your vacation, especially your shore excursions!" – contributed by Disney cruiser Jody Williams

Magical Memory

- *"What began as a simple activity on our Castaway Cay day has become a much-anticipated tradition. My 8-year-old son Alexander is very much into pirates and treasure chests. Five years ago I decided to improvise a little 'treasure hunt' on Castaway Cay for him. I bought a plastic treasure chest—filled with 'booty'—from Mickey's Mates onboard ($20). Then on the morning of our day at Castaway Cay, I marked a big, bold 'X' on the Disney-provided map of Castaway Cay and presented it to Alexander as a treasure map. He noticed the 'X' immediately and was quite excited. He got out his 'telescope' and a nice big shovel for digging up treasure. On Castaway Cay, we walked to the end of the family beach and Alexander's dad distracted him while I buried the treasure chest and marked an 'X' in the sand over it. Then Alexander came running over, having spotted the 'X.' He began digging for that treasure chest excitedly, happy beyond belief. He was so proud of himself! He proudly showed his treasure chest to Donald Duck before re-boarding the ship. We repeated this little adventure on our next four cruises. He still believes in the magic of buried treasure!"*

  ...as told by author and proud mom Jennifer Marx

- *"I was on Castaway Cay for just one hour during the Dream's Christening Cruise (had to get back on board for more press briefings). On the island, I took a tour conducted by Jim Durham, a Walt Disney Imagineering VP who's worked on Castaway Cay from Day One. Besides sharing all sorts of useful information, Joe told us that Heads Up Bar was named by the island's construction team, who quickly learned to beware of the pelicans flying overhead (yes, you may want to wear a hat)."*

  ...as told by author Dave Marx

Making Magic and Wonder

TAKE the best cruise photos

BE WELL healthy, and happy on your cruise

Is your mind still filled with nagging little questions? This chapter may just banish the last of those concerns. Among other topics, we'll discuss toddler care, special occasions, seasickness, meeting Disney characters, clearing U.S. Customs, how much to tip, and what happens when you arrive back in the U.S.A. (for those cruises that do). These are some of the little (and not so little) things that can make the difference between an ordinary vacation and a trip filled with magic and wonder.

Is your tot too small for the regular children's programs? We tour the ships' nurseries; Flounder's Reef (Magic and Wonder), and It's a Small World (Dream and Fantasy). Children of all ages can get the lowdown on meeting Disney characters. Learn how to preserve fond memories with your own photographs and glossies from the ship's photographers. Do you have money left after shopping in port? We describe all the stores and shopping opportunities on board, too.

While modern cruises aren't the fancy dress extravaganzas they used to be, every cruise includes opportunities to dress up. In fact, the seven-night and longer sailings include officially designated formal and semi-formal nights (at least one of each). Here's where we button-down all the details on appropriate attire, tuxedo rentals, and other dress-up options. We describe special and celebrity cruises, and deliver tips for creating your own special celebrations on board, whether you're tying the knot or want to give a loved one an extra-special send-off.

Next, there's the business of staying healthy and avoiding that curse of the deep, *mal de mer* (seasickness). Plus, a few tips on keeping up-to-date with your business back home.

It's also time to set your feet back on shore after your cruise. Nobody likes this part, but now is the perfect time to explore the mysteries of "customary gratuities" (tipping), the rules and regulations of U.S. Customs, and the rituals of debarkation. We've had a great time cruising with you! Alas, that it had to end so soon. Bon voyage!

Cruising With Kids

Disney cruises and kids go together like peanut butter and jelly! We've had the pleasure of cruising with kids many times, with our son Alexander (at 4 mo., 11 mo., 1, 1½, 2, 3, 4, 5, 6, and 7), our daughter Allie (at 9 and 12), our nieces Megan (at 3, 5, and 8) and Natalie (at 2, 4, and 7), our nieces Kayleigh (at 13 and 16), Melanie (at 11 and 14), and Nina (at 10 and 13), and Dave's second cousins Bradley (2) and Andrea (1). So we've been "around the deck," so to speak. Here are our tips for happy cruising with kids, along with tips from Jennifer's sister Kim Larner, mother of Megan and Natalie.

Introduce kids to Disney cruising before you go. Order the free DVD, have a family showing, and encourage your child(ren) to watch it on their own. It builds excitement and also breeds familiarity, which is important to kids. If you have a child with an interest in pirates and treasures, draw a treasure map showing your journey from your home to the ship and review the map in the weeks and days leading up to your cruise.

Your stateroom choice depends on your budget, but spring for an **outside stateroom** if possible. The natural light helps kids stay on their regular sleep cycles. Kim says, "The split-bathroom units were very convenient and the large porthole made the room feel very open." These are all big pluses when cruising with kids.

Kids absolutely love **swimming**, and the pools onboard are lots of fun. They also tend to be very crowded, however, and "you'll need to keep an eagle eye on your kids in the pools," according to Kim. She also suggests you make time to go swimming in the ocean at Castaway Cay—"the kids loved the warm water and found crabs and starfish." Keep in mind that diaper-age kids can only use the designated splash areas onboard (see page 147).

The **Oceaneer Club and Lab**, both of which are now open to ages 3-12, tend to be big hits with most kids, though there can be downfalls. Alexander loved the idea at 3, but really wanted mom to stay with him. Megan fell in love with the Oceaneer Club at age 3, she had a "potty accident" due to the exciting and unfamiliar environment, and wasn't allowed back in to the Club for a while. Certainly let the kids know about the Oceaneer Club and Lab before you go, but don't build it up too much in the event there are disappointments. Kim also suggests you "put your kid(s) in the Club/Lab for at least one of your meals to allow you the chance to really enjoy the dinner."

Speaking of meals, **early seating** tends to work much better than late seating for kids, especially young kids. Kim says, "the kids enjoyed the start and end of the meal, but were impatient during the middle." We suggest you bring an activity or two with you to dinner to keep the kids entertained after they've grown tired of coloring their menus, such as sticker books or doodle pads. Older kids like Allie also get impatient—consider letting older kids go to Oceaneer Club/Lab, Edge or Vibe, as appropriate. The **Dine and Play program** (for ages 3-12) can really help with the impatient kid syndrome—see page 171 for details!

© MediaMarx, Inc.

Natalie, Megan, and Alexander coloring in Parrot Cay

© MediaMarx, Inc.
Alexander asleep at the end of a show

The **stage shows** are popular with kids, though very young kids may find it hard to sit through one of these hour-long shows. We suggest you arrive early enough to either sit close (the proximity tends to better engage the child in the show), sit on an aisle (so you can make a convenient escape), or bring along whatever you need to help your child sleep through the show (bottles/sippy cups, pacifiers, and/or blankie). On-stage characters can present difficulties, too. Kim says that "both Megan and Natalie wanted to go up to the stage and give the characters a hug, and Natalie cried for some time about not being able to do it."

Of all the **cruise activities**, it's most common for kids to love swimming and Castaway Cay the best. You may want to take at least two swimsuits so you always have a dry one. We also recommend some water shoes and a bathrobe, for comfortable trips to and from the pool (the air conditioning inside the ship can be quite chilly when you've got nothing on but a wet swimsuit).

The Disney Cruise photographers can capture some **amazing shots of your children** in the pool, in the Club/Lab, and on Castaway Cay—be sure to check Shutters Photo Studio (see page 456) for images of your kids. A Disney cruise is also a great opportunity to get professional photographs of your family or just your kids. To have the best selection of backdrops and characters, and to minimize waits for young kids, plan to arrive in the Lobby Atrium (deck 3) at least an hour before your dinner begins.

Give serious thought to giving your child a "night out" in Flounder's Reef/It's a Small World Nursery or at Oceaneer Club and Lab, thereby giving you at least one **adults-only evening**. The facilities are excellent (much better than other, non-Disney ships on which we've cruised) and the crew members that staff them are very good with kids. Having time alone is as good for your kid(s) as for you.

That said, we also suggest you **savor the time** you spend with your kids on this cruise. You'll have the opportunity for special moments and new discoveries together. Be sure to plan time together every day, whether it's to do a scheduled activity or just hang together as a family. We've found our cruise time with Alexander provided some of our most treasured moments, including the night we passed through the Panama Canal and he took his very first independent steps, and the times on Castaway Cay when we devised treasure hunts for him with real treasure chests buried in the sand under a big "X."

© MediaMarx, Inc.
Sara Varney and her son Ryan with his "Dumbo ears"

Overall, we've observed that a Disney cruise is **better than a Walt Disney World vacation** when you're with young kids. There's less walking, less overstimulation, less exhaustion, and just as much magic. On every Disney vacation we've gone on with young kids (under 5), the kids (and their parents) were much happier on the ship than at the parks. Kim says, "The cruise was the best part of our vacation."

Introduction Reservations Staterooms Dining Activities Ports of Call Magic Index

When the Disney Magic returns from drydock in late 2013, Flounder's Reef Nursery will become It's a Small World Nursery, with decor based on the famous Disney theme park attraction. This is the same theme as the nurseries on the Dream Class ships.

Childcare

Yes, parents, this is your vacation, too! While family time spent together is golden, Disney makes sure there's plenty of time and space for adults-only relaxation and fun. So what do the kids do while the grownups play? They're having a party of their own, in some of the **best childcare** programs you'll find on land or sea.

Kids at least three years of age and potty-trained can enjoy supervised play at the Oceaneer Club and Lab (see page 149). If your child is between twelve weeks and three years old, or not yet toilet-trained, you can use the **Flounder's Reef/ It's a Small World Nursery**. This is the ships' full-service childcare center located on deck 5, the same deck as the Oceaneer Club/Lab. The nursery is equipped with a playroom filled with age-appropriate toys, Disney movies, baby bouncers, and rocking chairs, and a sleeping room with cribs for infants and mats for toddlers. Separate areas are dedicated to changing tables.

Reservations are required for the nursery, and you can make them in advance online (see page 141). If you don't reserve in advance, do it very soon after boarding, because it's a popular place. Only a limited number of spaces are available, to maintain a child/counselor ratio of 4:1 (infants) and 6:1 (toddlers). You can make reservations for the nursery on embarkation day, typically from 12:30 pm to 3:15 pm and again from 4:30 pm to 5:30 pm, or by phoning from your stateroom (if no one answers, leave a message with your name, child's name, stateroom, and date and time requested). You will receive confirmation via your stateroom phone or Wave Phone. Disney initially limits you to ten total reserved hours. After the initial reservation period, services are offered on a space-available basis, and you can request more sessions anytime during your cruise. If you are planning to dine at Palo or Remy, we recommend you reserve Palo and/or Remy first, then do your nursery booking. The nursery staff will work with you when they know you have a meal reservation.

Unlike the Oceaneer Club and Lab, which are included in your fare, the nursery has an **hourly fee**—they charge $6/hour for the first child and $5/hour for each additional sibling. There is a two-hour minimum. Reservations must be canceled four hours prior to your reserved time, or you will be charged a cancellation fee equal to 50% of your scheduled time. The nursery is open daily, typically from 9:00 am to 1:00 or 2:00 pm and again from 5:30 pm to midnight, though times may vary for at-sea days and some port days may offer extended hours to accommodate guests going on shore excursions. The portable Wave Phones found in your stateroom (see page 147) are used by the childcare staff to reach parents. Please also be aware that the nursery is unable to accept children who show symptoms of fever, vomiting, diarrhea, or unexplained skin rash, or any child who has other contagious diseases or illnesses. Crew members are unable to administer any medication. If your child has any special needs at all, be sure to mention them so they can accommodate your child.

The Flounder's Reef Nursery crew members are friendly and attentive

When you **check in** your young cruisers to the nursery, bring diapers/pull-ups, wipes, an extra set of clothing/pajamas, and anything else that may be needed, such as premade bottles, sippy cups, baby food in jars, pacifiers, and security items (such as a blanket). The nursery does not provide meals and the official policy states that no outside food is permitted due to allergies. For this reason, we always fed Alexander before bringing him to the nursery. In practice, however, if you have packaged baby food in your diaper bag, the nursery crew may feed it to your baby. We always kept baby/toddler food in our diaper bag as a rule, and we were surprised to learn that the crew had fed it to him when we picked him up at the end of a session (as we assumed they would not). And while the rules state that no meals are provided, on baby Alexander's last visit the crew informed us that they gave him some saltine crackers and apple juice during his session. We're sure experiences with food vary from ship to ship and cruise to cruise, but you should be aware of the range of possibilities. Our advice is to assume "no food" and then ask the crew upon your arrival.

If you are **nursing your infant**, you can return to the nursery in mid-session to nurse—when Jennifer visited with baby Alexander, the crew moved a rocking chair into the back room for privacy. A reader recently wrote that she encountered resistance from the crew to this on her cruise—the crew did not allow her to enter the nursery itself due to separation anxiety issues with other children in their care. If you encounter such resistance, ask to speak to their superior crew member immediately. When our reader wrote Disney regarding the situation after her cruise, Disney apologized for the miscommunication and stated, "Nursing mothers are allowed to breast feed in the back room."

© MediaMarx, Inc.

The back of Flounder's Reef Nursery

© MediaMarx, Inc.

Age-appropriate toys are provided.

If you have a **three-year-old who is not yet potty trained** (and therefore unable to be left at Oceaneer Club and Lab), you may use the nursery. The price and other rules are the same as those for kids under 3. Some three-year-olds are okay with this, while others are not (the room is really geared for younger children). If you're considering this, be sure to visit with your child during their open house on embarkation day to see if your child finds the room interesting.

Helpful Tips for Parents:

✔ If you are dropping your child off in the evening, put him/her in **pajamas**—it will make the transition back to your stateroom (and to bed) that much easier.

✔ For a **Palo or Remy dinner**, reserve at least three hours in the nursery with the starting time about 15 minutes before your dinner reservation.

✔ Your **Wave Phone** won't work off the ship, except at Castaway Cay.

✔ Parents **traveling with infants** can request a high chair in the dining room, as well as a pack & play crib and a Diaper Genie in the stateroom.

✔ No need to lug an extra suitcase full of diapers! You can now pre-order more than 1000 brand-name **baby supplies** and have them waiting for you onboard—read more and order at http://www.babiestravellite.com/?AFFIL=DCL or phone 888-450-5483. You can order up to six months in advance, but be sure to order at least two weeks before sailing.

Photographs

Say cheese! Whether you're taking your own photos or letting a ship's photographer snap the shot, a Disney cruise is the perfect photo op!

Bring your own camera and batteries. Should you forget this essential bit of cruising equipment, you can buy Pentax and Olympus cameras ($200+), Kodak single-use cameras, film, memory cards, and batteries onboard. We use a digital camera, which allows us to take as many photos as we like and not bother with film. Camcorders are also very popular—if you bring yours, be aware that the high humidity can be a problem. To keep moisture out of your camcorder, keep it in the shade whenever possible and allow at least 30 minutes to adjust to different environments (such as from your air-conditioned room to outside).

Onboard photo processing is offered in **Shutters Photo Studio** (deck 4 aft/mid). Drop off your film before 11:00 am and it'll be ready the same day by 5:00 pm—otherwise your photos are ready the next day. For every roll of film you develop at Shutters, you get a free photo of the ship and a trading pin (as of press time). Developing costs are about $5 for 12 4x6 prints or $10 for 24 (double prints are 35 cents). Shutters processes regular 35mm film and Advantix film, as well as prints from underwater, single-use, and digital cameras. Tip: You can have your digital photos downloaded to a CD for $14.95.

Ship's photographers are everywhere. The moment you board the ship, you'll be asked to pose for a portrait. Candid and posed photos are snapped throughout the cruise—just swing by Shutters or the electronic kiosks found in public spaces around the ship to see the photos (on the Dream Class ships, they can also be viewed on your stateroom TV). Photos taken during the day are typically available in the evening, while photos taken after 5:00 pm or so are displayed the next day. Printed photos on the Magic Class ships are posted in Shutters, while photos on the Dream Class are collected for you in a folio at Shutters. Not all shots are printed, check the kiosks/stateroom TV for more. On the Magic Class, if you aren't sure which photos you want to buy, collect all your photos and stack them behind one another on the display to keep them together. Save your receipts to use for quantity discounts, and wait until the end of the cruise to decide on photo packages. If you need photo reprints after your cruise, images may be archived for up to ten weeks—call 800-772-3470 ext. 11.

Dave poses for a portrait in the atrium

The **professional photos** at Shutters come in two sizes: 6 x 8 prints are $10 each (10 for $89, 20 for $149, or 30 for $199); 8 x 10 prints are $20 each (5 for $89, 10 for $149, or 15 for $199). A photo CD with all shots is $299 for 2 to 5-night cruises, and $399 for longer cruises. Formal portraits and some other shots only come in 8 x 10. Photos are copyrighted and you can be fined up to $500 for unauthorized duplication—visit http://www.image.com/html/guest-postcruiseCopyrightReleaseForm.cfm to download a copyright release waiver. Tip: Shutters can turn your family portrait into greeting cards with lots of "character!"

Shutters is **open** all day on at-sea days, and from about 5:00 pm to 11:00 pm on port days. Note that Shutters is also open debarkation morning from 6:45 am to 8:30 am. We recommend you avoid the last night and morning, as they are incredibly busy.

Shopping Onboard

The Magic and Wonder sport a 5,500-square-foot shopping area, and the Dream and Fantasy have even more! Combine that with extra shopping opportunities aboard and great shopping in port (see chapter 6), and you'll find it easy to shop 'til you drop anchor. Prices are a bit on the high side, but the quality is excellent.

Due to U.S. Customs regulations, the onboard shops **cannot be open while in port**. Check your *Personal Navigator* for shop operating hours, and keep in mind that the last night of your cruise is your last opportunity to shop. And before you splurge on that big-ticket item, see page 468 for details on customs allowances.

Mickey's Mates (deck 4 midship on Magic & Wonder)/**Mickey's Mainsail** (deck 3 midship on Dream and Fantasy) is the Disney character and logo shop, filled with stuffed animals, souvenirs, logowear, trading pins, postcards, etc.

Treasure Ketch (deck 4 midship on Magic & Wonder)/**Sea Treasures** (deck 3 midship on Dream and Fantasy) is near Mickey's and offers more upscale and practical merchandise, such as resort wear, jewelry (including loose gemstones and "gold by the inch"), collectibles, toiletries, film, batteries, books, and magazines. Collectors, check your *Personal Navigator* for Captain's signings—he'll sign posters, hats, T-shirts, pins, and ship models for free.

The Dream Class ships add a third shop, **Whitecaps** (deck 3 midship) with designer goods and duty-free merchandise, such as fragrances, watches, and sunglasses. Guests on the Magic Class ships will find tax-free items in Treasure Ketch, as well as duty-free liquor in **Up Beat/Radar Trap** (deck 3 forward). Up Beat/Radar Trap stock liquor (50+ brands), fragrances (60+ brands), cigars (25+ brands), and cigarettes, as well as snacks, candy bars, cameras, film, batteries, first aid and personal hygiene items. Note that duty-free orders are delivered to your stateroom on the last night of your cruise—you cannot consume them while you're onboard. The shop is typically open evenings until midnight. The Dream Class ships also have **Whozits & Whatzits** in the deck 11 mid elevator lobby, selling a small selection of sun-and-fun items, and **Quacks**, a kiosk on deck 11 selling pirate wear.

Preludes Snacks/Hollywood and Wine (deck 4/3 fwd) are small bars that sell packaged snacks such as candy bars, chips, and popcorn, typically open around show times.

Shutters (deck 4 aft/mid) sells cameras, frames, and photos. See previous page.

Vista Gallery (deck 4 forward/mid) features Disney fine art and collectible Disney Cruise Line items. See page 137 for all the details.

Pin Trading Station (deck 3 or 4 midship) opens nightly on the port side of the Atrium Lobby, typically from 7:30 pm to 8:30 pm. This is a great place for limited edition pins.

A poolside merchandise cart may be parked near the **family pool** on certain days.

Let's not forget the **onboard gift brochure** you receive with your cruise documentation before you embark—any items ordered from this brochure or at the Disney Cruise Line web site's Planning Center will be waiting for you in your stateroom when you board.

Check your *Personal Navigator* for daily specials, featured items, and operating hours.

Shops are **busiest** from 7:00 pm to 10:00 pm, so you may want to go earlier or later.

Formal and Semi-Formal Occasions

What is it about a cruise that brings out our Fred Astaire and Ginger Rogers? It may be passé ashore, but a formal night at sea is still magical!

On **3- to 6-night** cruises, there are no official formal nights. Instead, there's a "dress-up night." On your Lumière's/Triton's/Royal Palace/Royal Court night, you might wear dressy attire, such as a jacket for men and a dress or pantsuit for women, but it isn't required. Always wear dressy attire for Palo and Remy. The other nights are casual or tropical/pirate.

On the **7-night** cruises, you have one formal night—day 2 on Eastern Caribbean itineraries and day 3 on Western Caribbean itineraries—and one semi-formal night on day 6 of both itineraries. (Longer cruises have 1–2 more formal and semi-formal occasions.) Formal night is "black tie optional." Many men wear tuxedos or suits and women typically wear evening gowns, but semi-formalwear is fine, too. During the formal and semi-formal nights, the photographers set up backdrops and take formal portraits (see page 456). In addition, you might wear dressier attire when you eat dinner in Lumière's/Triton's/Royal Palace/Royal Court.

Men's Formalwear: Fortunately, you don't have to rent a tuxedo and haul it across the country and back. Cruise Line Formalwear supplies men's formalwear on the Disney Cruise Line, and cruise-long rentals range from $85 to $160 (this price includes everything but the shoes), plus accessories ($5 to $20). Order at least two weeks before you cruise with the order form in your cruise documents, online at http://www.cruiselineformal.com or on the phone at 800-551-5091. You can also view the tuxedos and accessories on their web site. When you order a tuxedo from them, it'll arrive in your stateroom on your first day aboard (try it on right away to see if it needs any alterations). When the cruise ends, just leave it in your room. Note that Cruise Line Formal does keep extra inventory onboard for exchanges and last-minute rentals. Another option is to buy a tuxedo (try a local tux rental shop or http://www.ebay.com). Perhaps you'd like a Disney-themed vest and tie set to go with your own tux? If so, check on the Internet at http://www.tuxedosdirect.com.

© MediaMarx, Inc.

Jennifer and Dave decked out at Palo

Women's Formalwear: If you don't happen to have an evening gown or old bridesmaid's gown hanging in your closet, you can make do with a nice dress on both semi-formal and formal evenings. A "little black dress" is a popular choice. Feel free to wear your dress more than once on your cruise—accessorize to change the look. Consider adding a wrap for chilly dining rooms. Formal evenings see most women in long evening gowns—try shopping the department stores (such as J.C.Penney's) for good deals. You could also try Chadwick's (http://www.chadwicks.com) and Victoria's Secret (http://www.victoriassecret.com).

Kids' Formalwear: Dressing the boys in slacks and a button-down shirt is just fine. If your boy really wants to dress up like Dad in a tux, special order rentals are available through Cruise Line Formalwear. You can also look for a good deal at http://www.ebay.com or at http://www.tinytux.com.The girls look great in sun dresses, and this is the perfect opportunity to wear Disney princess dresses (available beforehand at the Disney Store and onboard in Mickey's Mates/Mickey's Mainsail). You'll find gorgeous formalwear for girls at http://www.woodensoldier.com. Of course, that's if they even dine with you. Some kids prefer the company of their peers and have dinner at the Club/Lab.

Special/Celebrity Cruises

Looking for something a bit special on your next cruise? Disney plans many special cruises each year—some are once-in-a-lifetime events, while others just feature celebrity guests. Here are some past and upcoming events to give you an idea of what to expect:

Inaugural Cruises—The first sailing of a new ship, or the first sailing of a ship on a new itinerary is a big deal. On the up side, you get the thrill of being "the first" to sail, and you may get a few extra treats—on the Western Caribbean Inaugural Cruise in May 2002, we were treated to a Mexican mariachi band before embarking, given special "fans" to wave as we set sail, and presented with complimentary champagne glasses. We were aboard for the Dream's Christening Cruise, January 19-21, 2011 (an invitation-only event), and Jennifer returned on January 26 for the Dream's Inaugural Cruise, which was available to the general public. There were commemorative gifts, special merchandise, and the premieres of a new stage show and a revised Pirates in the Caribbean Night, among many notable events. While any early sailing on a new ship may exhibit some glitches, we've encountered very few, and the excitement of being "first" more than makes up for the kinds of disappointments we've encountered. First-time visits to new ports of call may be honored with a small ceremony and debarking cruisers may receive a special welcome.

Celebrity Cruises—Many cruises have at least a minor celebrity or notable speaker, while others feature bigger names. For example, for some years, Roger Ebert and Richard Roeper held a Film Festival at Sea, and the 2012 California Coast itineraries highlighted Pixar animation. Most celebrity guests have some connection with Disney, and include actors, artisans, and authors–guests have included Ernie Sabella (voice of "Pumbaa" in Disney's The Lion King—see photo below), Leslie Iwerks (granddaughter of Ub Iwerks), Raven, and former presidents George H.W. Bush and Jimmy Carter. Disney rarely announces their celebrities or speakers ahead of time, but you can call 888-DCL-2500 to inquire.

Holiday Cruises—If your cruise coincides with a major holiday, you can bet Disney has something special planned. Halloween cruises have costume contests, Thanksgiving cruises offer traditional dinners, all December cruises feature magical holiday decorations and special holiday events, and so on. Special Holiday itineraries encompassing Christmas and/or New Year's Eve are very, very popular—book early if you're interested. Note also that religious holidays (Ash Wednesday, Easter, Passover, Hanukkah, Christmas, etc.) have clergy onboard for observances.

Fan Cruises—Disney fans love to cruise together, and usually one group or another is organizing a group cruise. Check with your favorite community to see what plans they have in store!

Other Cruises—Keep an ear out for more special cruises, such as pin trading cruises and Disney Vacation Club cruises. And it's always fun to be on board whenever a major Disney movie premieres.

Ernie Sabella and Dave at Castaway Cay

Celebrating Special Occasions

We firmly believe there's always something to celebrate ... even if it's just the fact that you're going on a cruise! And, of course, there are always birthdays, anniversaries, and holidays to remember. If you are celebrating a special occasion while you're onboard, be sure to let your Disney reservation agent or travel agent know when you book your cruise, or at least three weeks before you sail.

Bon Voyage Celebrations—Why not throw a party before you depart for your cruise? Invite your friends and family and make 'em jealous! Or if you happen to know someone going on a cruise, surprise them with a send-off party or a gift in their stateroom (see sidebar below). And don't forget about a celebratory drink when you board! Note: Only passengers are allowed on board or in the terminal, so parties with non-cruisers must take place before your arrival at the cruise terminal.

Birthdays—Let Disney know about your celebration in advance, and you'll be serenaded by your serving team (no more cakes at dinner, though). You may also get a birthday pin!

Honeymoons—The Disney Cruise Line is popular with honeymooning couples, although Disney no longer offers "romance" packages for the celebration as they did in years past. But be sure to let Disney know about your honeymoon!

Anniversaries—We celebrated Dave's parents' 50th wedding anniversary aboard the Wonder in 2001—it was magical! Again, tell Disney about your celebration ahead of time and you may get a surprise.

Holidays—Disney does the holidays in grand style, particularly on Christmas and New Year's Eve—look for Santa Goofy, a three-deck-tall tree, holiday feasts, a New Year's Eve party, and a New Year's Day tailgate party.

Tip: **Decorate your stateroom** and/or stateroom door in honor of your celebration! You can order basic stateroom decorations from Disney (see "Stateroom Gifts" below) and they'll put them up before you arrive. Or bring your own decorations from home. Another fun idea is to buy (or make) magnets with which to decorate your metal stateroom door (see photo)—please note that only magnets are allowed on the doors (no tape or glue).

Door decorations for Dave's "Who Wants to Be a Millionaire —Play It!" winning cruise

Stateroom Gifts

Disney Cruise Line offers a variety of gifts that you can order ahead of time and have waiting for you in your stateroom (or that of a friend or family member). Check the brochure that comes with your cruise documents, visit the Planning Center at http://www.disneycruise.com, or call 800-601-8455. If you're looking for something extra special, a Cape Canaveral-based company, The Perfect Gift, delivers delightful cruise baskets at good prices to your stateroom—you can even custom design your gift baskets. Call 800-950-4559 or visit http://www.theperfectgift.cc for more information.

Reunions and Group Cruises

A Disney cruise is ideal for a reunion or group event. Unlike a gathering on land, say at Walt Disney World, the Disney cruise allows groups to stay within close proximity of one another, offers a number of built-in activities and meals, and offers fun reunion packages. We've planned a number of reunions and group cruises over the years—here are our tips for a successful gathering:

Pick the best dates. Consult with the members of your group to find the dates that work best for their schedules and wallets. While spring and summer breaks may be best for groups with kids, those are among the priciest and may prevent some from joining you. Whenever possible, go for the less-expensive seasons, such as January, February, May, or early December.

If you're cruising as a family or small group, it may be possible to select staterooms in **close proximity** to one another, which facilitates communications and meetings. But if you cannot, don't fret—the ship isn't that big of a place. You may also be able to switch to rooms in closer proximity around final payment time (75 days before), when other cruisers cancel.

Keep in **close communication** with your group both before and during your cruise. Simple notes or newsletters, via e-mail or on paper, can be very helpful for educating and notifying them of events. Once onboard, you can use your Wave Phones (see page 147) or leave voice mail and notes on stateroom doors.

When you book your cruise, let Disney know that you're traveling as a group and ask them to **link the reservations together** so you can dine in close proximity to one another. The dining room tables usually hold up to eight guests—on one of our family reunion cruises, we had a family of 16, and we were seated at two tables of eight, end to end. We've found that having this time together at dinner is very important to the success of a group cruise. Keep in mind, however, that everyone in your party needs to be on the same dinner seating—discuss early vs. late seating with your group before making a unilateral decision.

If your group wants to **dine at Palo and/or Remy**, make your reservations online as early as possible! Large groups are hard to accommodate and space goes quickly. Several small tables may be a better idea. Note: If your group's reservations are linked in Disney's system and you book a Palo table large enough to accommodate your group, be aware that other members of your group may not be able to make their own, separate Palo reservations.

Don't expect or try to do everything together. The beauty of a Disney cruise is that you don't have to hang together all the time to enjoy your group. You'll inevitably do some activities together during the day, bump into one another during free moments, and then enjoy quality time together at dinner.

Group reservations start at eight staterooms or more. Specifically, a minimum of 16 adult fare guests (based on double occupancy) occupying a minimum of 8 staterooms constitutes a group in Disney's eyes (third through fifth berths do not count toward meeting minimum group size). Disney will also throw in special amenities like private parties, depending on the size of the group. Phone Group Reservations at 800-511-6333 (Monday through Friday, 8:00 am to 10:00 pm EST). A trusted travel agent will be a big help if you want to make a group booking and to coordinate stateroom selection, payments, dining arrangements, and the like.

Weddings and Vow Renewals

Ah, what is more romantic (or simple) than getting married or renewing your vows aboard a cruise ship? Disney Cruise Line makes it very easy to do both, and when compared to a land-based wedding, the prices are a good value, too!

First, if you're interested in either a wedding or vow renewal ceremony onboard a Disney ship, be aware that this isn't something you can arrange on your own. You'll need Disney's assistance, and you'll need to purchase their wedding or vow renewal package. Visit http://disneycruise.disney.go.com/cruises-destinations/packages/wedding-vow-renewal, for information on the "Weddings at Sea" package and the "Vow Renewal" packages. This is where you'll find prices and package details. You can also call 321-939-4610 for information.

When you're **ready to book**, call a professional Disney wedding consultant at 321-939-4610 or contact your travel agent. You can book a wedding or vow renewal up to 12 months in advance, though it is not necessary to book it so early—you can plan a cruise wedding or vow renewal in as little as a month or two (based on availability).

Ceremony locations vary. Many wedding ceremonies are held outdoors at the Head's Up Bar on Castaway Cay—the lagoon and ship provide a beautiful backdrop. You can also get married in either Sessions (Magic) or Cadillac Lounge (Wonder) on deck 3 forward, or Outlook, the Dream & Fantasy's private party space on deck 14. The lounges and Palo are also the typical spots for Vow Renewal ceremonies. Other locations may be possible under certain circumstances—inquire with your Disney wedding consultant. Ceremonies can be arranged on most itineraries, including on the West Coast and European sailings. On Castaway Cay, weddings are performed by a Bahamian official. The Captain or another officer presides at vow renewals.

Those getting married should note that you'll have a **private, legal ceremony** in the cruise terminal before your ship leaves port. This means you're technically married for your entire voyage, even though your public marriage ceremony happens later in the cruise.

Want to know more? Check out **PassPorter's Disney Weddings & Honeymoons guide** by author Carrie Hayward. The book covers weddings and honeymoons at Walt Disney World and on the Disney Cruise in delightful detail and lovely photos. It's available in both print and e-book formats. For information, the table of contents, and a sample page, visit http://www.passporter.com/weddings.asp.

© Disney

A Castaway Cay wedding

➢

Preventing Seasickness

Seasickness—just the thought of it can make some of us a little queasy. And if you actually have it ... no, let's not think about it. Let's think about how fortunate we are to be sailing on a large, modern cruise ship on some of the calmest waters in the world. Two huge stabilizer fins take the bite out of the worst wave action, and modern medicine has provided more than one helpful remedy. If you're looking for that ounce of prevention, read on!

✔ **Purely Natural**—Go topside, take deep breaths, get some fresh air, and look at the horizon. The worst thing you can do is stay in your stateroom. Seasickness is caused by the confusion between what your inner ear senses and what your eyes see. If you can look at something steady, it helps your brain synchronize these. Eventually your brain gets used to the motion and you get your "sea legs," but that can take a day or two. Drink lots of water and have some mild food, such as saltine crackers—avoid fatty and salty foods, and eat lightly.

✔ **Herbs**—Ginger is reported to help reduce seasickness. It comes in pill and cookie form—even ginger ale can help. It's best to begin taking this in advance of feeling sick.

✔ **Bonine, or "Dramamine Less Drowsy Formula"**—These are brand names of Meclizine, which has far fewer side effects than its older cousin Dramamine (which we don't recommend). Try it at home before your cruise to check for side effects, then take it a few hours before departure for maximum effectiveness. Note: For kids ages 6 to 12, look for "Bonine for Kids," or use regular Dramamine. Tip: The onboard medical facility (discussed on the next page) provides free chewable Meclizine tablets (25 mg.) from a dispenser next to its door on deck 1 forward. Guest Services (on deck 3 midship) may also have some Meclizine if you can't make it down to deck 1.

✔ **Sea-Bands**—These are elastic wrist bands that operate by applying pressure to the Nei Kuan acupressure point on each wrist by means of a plastic stud, thereby preventing seasickness. Some people swear by them; some say that they don't work. Either way, they are inexpensive (unless you buy them on the ship) and have no medical side effects. They don't yet come in designer colors to match your formal evening gown, however.

✔ **Scopolamine Transdermal Patch**—Available by prescription only. It is the most effective preventative with the least drowsiness, but it also comes with the most side effects, such as dry mouth and dizziness. For more information about scopolamine, speak to your doctor and visit http://www.transdermscop.com.

✔ **Ship Location**—A low deck, midship stateroom is generally considered to be the location on a ship where you'll feel the least movement, and midship is better than forward (worst) or aft (second-best). This fact is reflected in the higher price for a midship stateroom. If you know you're prone to seasickness, consider requesting a stateroom on decks 1–2, midship. But once you're onboard and you find yourself feeling seasick, the best thing to do is get out of your stateroom, go to deck 4 midship, and lie down in one of the padded deck chairs—then use the tips noted in "Purely Natural" above.

✔ **Choose Excursions Wisely**—Those prone to motion sickness may want to avoid shore excursions that rely heavily on smaller boats such as ferries and sailboats, and glass-bottom boats and subs. Read the excursion descriptions in chapter 6 carefully for mentions of motion sickness or rough seas. If you don't want to miss out on anything, begin taking your preferred seasickness remedy well in advance of the excursion.

Staying Healthy

Staying healthy is easy with some preparation and knowledge. Folks who are already healthy may only have to worry about getting seasick (see the previous page) or picking up a virus. Here's what you can do to prevent illness:

Getting a virus is less likely than seasickness, but still possible—any time you get people together for more than two or three days at a time, you're going to have some percentage become ill. Cruise ships are significantly less vulnerable than schools, hotels, nursing homes, and restaurants, contrary to the media attention the Norwalk-like virus received some years back—cruise ships account for 10% of the outbreaks, while restaurants, nursing homes, and schools account for more than 70%. The Centers for Disease Control (CDC) report that normally 1–2% of a cruise population gets sick on a regular basis; during the Norwalk-like virus epidemics, this number may only rise to 2–4%. Nonetheless, Disney takes many precautions to avoid illness on its ships, including thoroughly disinfecting surfaces that are touched, encouraging hand-washing, providing hand wipes or hand sanitizer at the entrances to restaurants, and refusing passage to visibly ill passengers to reduce the risk of transmitting a virus to others.

To avoid catching a bug, get a full night's sleep before you embark, eat well, drink lots of water, and wash your hands thoroughly and frequently. Hand-washing cannot be emphasized enough. Wash your hands for at least 15 seconds after using the bathroom, after changing a diaper, and before handling, preparing, or consuming food. Regular soap and water does the trick—there's no need for antibacterial soaps (in fact, the Centers for Disease Control suggest that antibacterial soaps may contribute to the problem and suggests you do not use them). Alcohol-based hand sanitizer can be used as a supplement in between times hands are washed, but it should not replace soap and water and isn't effective after using the bathroom, after changing diapers, or before handling food. There's no need to bring your own Lysol either—all surfaces are disinfected before you board as well as while you're underway (besides, Lysol does nothing to stop the Norwalk-like virus). Tip: To make sure both you and your kids wash your hands for long enough, try singing or humming the "Happy Birthday" song slowly while washing your hands—when the song ends, your hands are clean.

If you get sick, be aware that reporting illness to the cruise staff is taken seriously—the cruise line is required to report any onboard cases of gastrointestinal illness to the CDC. You may be required to visit the medical facility onboard (see below), and if you're found to have a gastrointestinal illness, you may be restricted to your stateroom to avoid passing the illness to others. And if you're sick when you check in at the terminal, you may need to visit a medical professional before boarding—you may even be refused passage. If you're prone to stomach ailments, bring your own remedies—none are sold onboard.

Viruses aside, there's one medical problem that far too many cruisers contract during their cruise—**sunburn**. Bring that sunscreen (SPF of 30 or higher) and use it. And wear hats and cover-ups whenever possible. Don't take your chances with a sunburn.

As much as we don't like to think about it, accidents happen and guests get sick. Knowing that this is unavoidable, Disney has put a well-equipped **medical facility** aboard—it's equipped with modern medical equipment such as cardiac life support equipment, ventilators, and an X-ray machine. Two doctors and three registered nurses are on staff. The care, we hear, is excellent and the fees are reasonable. Any medical care you receive is billed to your stateroom account and you bill your insurance company separately.

Doing Business Onboard

We know, we know ... "work" is a four-letter word on a cruise. If you can avoid your work entirely on the cruise, we heartily recommend it! Alas, we know better than anyone that sometimes your business doesn't take a vacation just because you do. If you need to keep up with work while you're cruising, here are our tried-and-true tips:

Phone Calls—You have four options when making phone calls: use Disney's ship-to-shore phone system (the phone in your stateroom) for $6.95/minute, use your cellular phone in your stateroom (see page 151), use your cell phone when in port or sailing past islands with cell roaming service, or use a pay phone in port (most cruise terminals have pay phones available). Your stateroom phone system is detailed on page 147. If you opt to bring a cell phone, call your wireless provider to inquire about international roaming.

Laptop Computers—We always bring along our laptop, and now that we can connect to the Internet with it via wireless access onboard (both in public areas and in our stateroom), doing business is much easier. Typically, we use the laptop to download photos from the digital camera, but on one cruise we did some printing (with a portable printer hooked up to our laptop) and faxing through Guest Services. Be sure to bring all necessary cables!

Internet Access—We've devoted two full pages to Internet Access starting on page 145. If you're relying on Internet access to keep up with work, keep in mind that the Internet Cafe is the least busy earlier in the day and late at night. Note also that the Internet Cafe may not open on debarkation morning, though recently it has stayed open. We noticed no pattern to the occasional and short downtime experienced with wireless access onboard.

Faxes—You can send and receive faxes from the Guest Services desk (deck 3 midship). Cost is the same as ship-to-shore phone calls—$6.95/minute. We faxed several sheets during a 4-night cruise and found that each page takes about one minute to fax, though fax transmission time does depend on the density of the page.

Copies—The Guest Services desk is also the place to have copies made.

Meeting Space—All Disney ships have public spaces and a/v equipment that may be rented, and the Dream has conference rooms. See http://www.disneymeetings.com for details.

Tip: If your work is portable, take it outside to one of the patio tables behind Topsider's/Beach Blanket Buffet/Cabanas (deck 9/11 aft), near the Quiet Cove pool, or enjoy the solitude of the small area on deck 7 aft on the Magic and Wonder.

Joining the Ship's Crew

Ever thought of working on a Disney ship? If you are at least 21 years old, there are job opportunities. From what we understand, it takes a huge time commitment (you typically sign a six-month contract and work about 70–80 hours a week) and it's difficult to be away from home for the long stretches required. On the flip side, Disney does offer several perks, such as crew-only areas (including a beach on Castaway Cay and an onboard pool), free theme park admission, and so on. If you'd like to learn more, call the job line at 407-566-SHIP or visit http://www.dcljobs.com.

Disney Characters

One of the benefits of a Disney cruise is the opportunity to meet your favorite Disney characters—you won't find them on any other cruise in the world. Typically, the Disney celebrities joining you on your cruise include Mickey, Minnie, Goofy, Pluto, Donald, Chip, Dale, and Stitch (often in tropical attire) as well as appearances from special "face" characters like Cinderella, Snow White, and Alice. Here's where to meet your Disney friends onboard:

Character Appearances—The Lobby Atrium (both decks 3 and 4) is a popular gathering place for Disney friends, typically in the evenings for photo opportunities. If you forget your camera, there are often ship's photographers to snap a shot. You'll also find characters in the terminal before you board, at deck parties, the kids' clubs, and near the Mickey Pool. For schedules, check your *Personal Navigator*, or the character appearance display in the Lobby Atrium (or outside Shutters), or call 7-PALS on your stateroom phone.

Character Autographs: Bring a notebook or autograph book to the character meets—you can buy them in Mickey's Mates/Mickey's Mainsail, or just make one at home before you board (see photo on right). Take a photo of the Disney character autographing the book and you can later attach a copy of the picture to each autographed page—this makes a great keepsake!

A homemade autograph book

Character Breakfasts—Guests on the seven-night and longer cruises on the Magic Class ships get the opportunity to mingle with Mickey, Minnie, Goofy, Pluto, Chip and Dale at a character breakfast in Parrot Cay. For more details, see page 162.

Tea With Wendy—This is a special character event on the seven-night (and longer) cruises. Check your *Personal Navigator* for the day and time to pick up tickets (at no extra charge) and arrive early—this is a popular event and tickets go quickly. The half-hour "tea" is held in Studio Sea/D Lounge (deck 4 midship) on some afternoons. As you might have guessed, the tea is hosted by Wendy Darling (from Disney's Peter Pan), who demonstrates the proper way to serve tea, and tells a story. Chocolate chip cookies and iced tea are served. The event is attended predominantly by young girls, but everyone is welcome—young or old, male or female. After tea, guests may greet Wendy personally and get a photograph with her. Tip: Crew members select two boys from the audience to play John and Michael, Wendy's brothers.

Character Parties—In addition to the Disney character appearances at the deck parties, there is another special character party for which to check your Personal Navigator. 'Til We Meet Again is a farewell party in the Lobby Atrium held on your last evening (usually at 10:00 or 10:15 pm)—most of the characters come out to bid everyone a special goodbye.

Enchanted Art/Mickey's Midship Detective Agency—New technology on the Disney Dream and Fantasy brings Disney character artwork to life in the public areas! You can also spot characters in the "virtual porthole" of an inside stateroom (see page 142).

Introduction · Reservations · Staterooms · Dining · Activities · Ports of Call · Magic · Index

Tipping and Feedback

Tipping is your way of thanking the crew for their fine service. Here are Disney's recommended gratuities for each guest, regardless of age:

Crew Member/Service	Per Night	3-Night	4-Night	5-Night	7-Night	10-Night
Dining Room Server	$4	$12	$16	$20	$28	$40
Dining Room Asst. Server	$3	$9	$12	$15	$21	$30
Dining Room Head Server	$1	$3	$4	$5	$7	$10
Stateroom Host/Hostess	$4	$12	$16	$20	$28	$40
Palo/Remy Server	Your discretion (on top of the service charge)					
Bartender/Lounge Server	If no tip was automatically added, 10% to 15%					
Room Service	Your discretion (usually $1 to $2/person)					
Kids' Counselors	Not necessary, but do reward good service					
Shore Excursion Tour Guide	$1 to $2/person					
Baggage Porters (at terminal)	$1 to $2/bag					

Need help calculating your tips? See page 492 for details on how to get an interactive worksheet that does the calculations for you!

Disney's tipping guidelines are **not etched in stone**. Exceptional service deserves an exceptional tip, and substandard service should earn a lesser reward. But don't save all your compliments for cruise end—people thrive on appreciation.

Disney Cruise Line has changed to an "**auto pre-paid gratuities**" system. If you have not pre-paid gratuities prior to the cruise, the standard recommended gratuities for dining room staff and stateroom host/hostess (above) will be automatically charged to your stateroom account (a letter will be given to you at check-in, explaining the charges). The final gratuity is still up to you, just visit Guest Services on deck 3 to make adjustments. Tip: You can prepay your gratuities up to three days before you leave home at the Disney Cruise Line web site!

Tipping is a form of feedback for services received, but you can give **additional feedback** on your experience. Neither we nor Disney Cruise Line would be where we are today without your feedback. For instance, did you know that those obstructed-view category 7 staterooms we mentioned on page 137 were reclassified (and reduced in price) based on cruiser feedback? And even with PassPorter, our depth of detail is a direct reader request.

The night before you disembark, a **questionnaire** is placed in your stateroom. Fill it out and deposit it in the collection boxes at breakfast or on the gangway. If you had problems, there is a small section to describe what happened—if you need to communicate more, read on.

To send **detailed comments** (complaints or compliments) to Disney once you return home, write a letter and mail it to: DCL Guest Communications, P.O. Box 10238, Lake Buena Vista, FL 32830. You can also send e-mail to dcl.guest.communications@disneycruise.com or visit http://disney.go.com/mail/disneycruiseline. Disney is typically very responsive to guest feedback, and you should hear back from them within six weeks.

Contacting us at **PassPorter Travel Press** is even easier. E-mail feedback@passporter.com or send a letter to P.O. Box 3880, Ann Arbor, MI 48106. We also recommend you visit http://www.passporter.com/register.asp to register your copy, which is another perfect opportunity to tell us what you think. When you register, you get book updates and immediate access to coupons good for discounts on future PassPorters and accessories!

Customs Allowances

Ah, U.S. Customs. While we dreaded customs on our first cruise, we quickly found that the rules aren't hard to understand, and the process is smooth if you pay attention. If you feel unsure about customs and debarkation in general, attend the debarkation talk on the afternoon of the day before disembarkation (or catch it on TV in your stateroom later that evening).

You are required to declare everything that you purchased or were given as a gift on the ship, in your foreign ports of call, and on Castaway Cay. Fill out the **U.S. Customs Declaration Form** left in your stateroom on your last night (extra forms are available at Guest Services) Fill it in and sign and date the form—you will hand it to customs during debarkation.

Each guest is allowed a **total duty-free allowance** of $800 (3-, 4- and 5-night cruises, 7-night Western Caribbean) or $1,600 (7-night Eastern Caribbean cruises). Liquor and tobacco have special limits. One liter of liquor per person over 21 years of age is exempt from duties (Eastern Caribbean cruisers are allowed four more liters from the Virgin Islands). One carton of cigarettes and 100 cigars (other than Cuban cigars, which are not allowed at all) are exempt (Eastern Caribbean cruisers can add four more cartons of cigarettes if purchased in St. Thomas). If you exceed the customs allowances, you must report to the Customs Inspector before you debark the ship—check the debarkation sheet left in your stateroom. If you exceed your customs allowances, you will need to have cash on hand to pay your duties—no checks, traveler's checks, or credit cards are accepted.

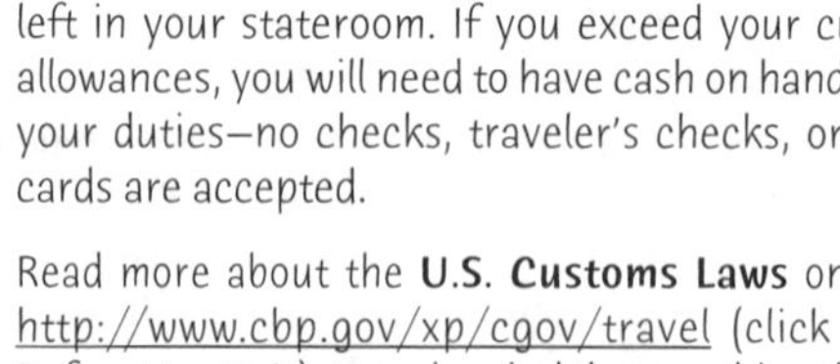

© MediaMarx, Inc.

Fruit taken off the ship

Read more about the **U.S. Customs Laws** online at http://www.cbp.gov/xp/cgov/travel (click "Know Before You Go!"). Keep in mind that anything that you don't declare is considered smuggled—don't forget any items you won onboard. The duties on declared items are low, but the penalties for smuggled items are high. And don't try to carry off items that aren't allowed, such as fresh fruit or flowers—you can face a stiff fine. You'd be surprised how many try to "smuggle" a banana unwittingly (see photo).

Immigration and International Guests

Immigration procedures are in flux right now, as we've mentioned earlier in this guidebook. In the past, international guests had to yield their passports before boarding the ship, but this is no longer the case. Additionally, guests on the 7-night Eastern Caribbean cruise had to get up early for an immigration inspection, but this was discontinued in early 2009. At press time, immigration procedures for international guests were simple and straightforward. If any special immigration procedures are required for your cruise, a note will be placed in your stateroom the evening before with clear directions on what to do. Region-specific information is also available at the Disney Cruise Line web site in the Planning Center.

Debarkation

Yes, your cruise is really over. Wouldn't it be nice if you could just stay onboard and sail forever? Even when it's time to go, nobody gets you to the exit more smoothly than Disney. This is the company that made crowd control a science. There's no waiting in line to depart, nobody calls out your name, and things seem to just flow. Here's the drill:

First, you need to **settle your onboard account**. If you put a credit card on your account at check-in, you're all set. Otherwise, visit Guest Services (deck 3 midship) to check and pay the total with credit card, traveler's checks, or cash. Do this the day before you debark. On the Dream Class ships you can check the status of your onboard account ("folio") on your stateroom TV.

On your **last night aboard**, pack your bags, remove old cruise tags, and attach the new tags provided (more tags are at Guest Services if you need them). Don't forget to fill out the tags and make a note of the tag color. When you're ready, place your tagged luggage in the passageway by 11:00 pm–you will not see it again until you're off the ship. Thus, it's crucial that you pack a small day bag to hold your toiletries, nightclothes, and valuables. And don't forget to keep out an outfit (and shoes) to wear the next morning! Tip: If you're dining at Palo or Remy on your last night and need some extra time to get your luggage out, you can stop at Guest Services and ask for a later pickup time for your luggage so you don't have to rush as much. If you're hoping to get off the ship quickly the next morning, consider keeping your luggage with you and carrying it off the ship yourself–it's not as convenient, but a bit quicker. This is a good time to fill out the customs forms placed in your stateroom (see previous page). Also, make sure your Wave Phones are all accounted for, to avoid the stiff fee for loss.

On **debarkation morning**, take your day bags and go to breakfast in the same restaurant in which you dined the previous evening (unless you ate at Palo or Remy, in which case you go to the restaurant you would have been in). Guests with early seating eat at 6:45 am, while late seating guests eat at 8:00 am. If you prefer, you can get "early bird" coffee and Danish pastries at 6:00 am to 6:30 am at the Beverage Station (deck 9/11 aft) or a continental breakfast from 6:30 am to 8:00 am at Topsider's/Beach Blanket Buffet/Cabanas (deck 9/11 aft). Be aware that guests must vacate their staterooms by 8:00 am. Shutters is open from 7:00 am to 8:30 am (expect crowds!), but all other shops are closed. Drop off your questionnaire (see page 467) at breakfast or as you debark. Typically the first guest debarks at 7:45 am and the last guest debarks at 9:45 am.

Now it's time to **say goodbye** to all your "family." After breakfast, go to the gangway (deck 3 midship), stroll off the ship with your day bags, and head off to customs. Keep your passport or other valid photo identification handy. At the customs area, claim your checked baggage in the color-coded area. Photography is not allowed in the customs area–keep your camera down to avoid complications. Pass through customs (usually you just present your customs forms and walk right through) and you're soon in your Disney motorcoach, car, or limousine. Porters are available to help you–don't forget to tip them. If you're flying out of Orlando International Airport, several airlines give you the option of checking your bags on the ship (see "Disney's Onboard Airline Check-In Program" on page 73).

Now that you've cruised, you belong to Disney's **Castaway Club**! Turn the page to learn more about the club and its benefits.

Castaway Club

Once you've got a Disney cruise under your belt, you're an automatic member of Disney's Castaway Club cruiser loyalty program. As a Castaway Club member, you get **special, member-only perks** for future cruises, such as exclusive insider information, a special toll-free number, special check-in area, and a free "welcome back" gift in your stateroom. In October 2009, the Castaway Club was enhanced with even more benefits for cruisers with multiple sailings!

Castaway Club membership is organized into **three tiers** based on the number of Disney cruises you've completed—Silver (1–4 cruises), Gold (5–9 cruises), and Platinum (10+ cruises). Benefits for each tier are below, and explanations of each benefit on are the next page.

Benefit	Silver Castaway (1-4 cruises sailed)	Gold Castaway (5-9 cruises sailed)	Platinum Castaway (10+ cruises sailed)
Insider Exclusives	✔	✔	✔
Early activity booking	90 days prior to sailing	105 days prior to sailing	120 days prior to sailing
Toll-free number	✔	✔	✔
Early itinerary booking		✔	✔
Special check-in	✔	✔	✔
Stateroom gift	✔	✔	✔
Onboard booking offer	✔	✔	✔
Onboard reception		✔	✔
Merchandise offers		✔	✔
Priority check-in			✔
Exclusive experiences			✔
Palo dinner			✔

Membership is automatic once you complete your first Disney cruise. You can **lookup your Castaway Club membership level**, past cruises, and program information at http://www.disneycruise.com/castaway-club, or call 888-DCL-2500.

When you **book your next cruise**, be sure that Disney or your travel agent knows you are a Castaway Club member—don't just assume they have this information. It's important that your reservations be properly linked with your Castaway Club account so you get credit for them!

When guests with different Castaway Club membership levels cruise together in the same stateroom, all guests in that stateroom are **treated as if they are at same level** as the highest-level guest in the stateroom. This means that everyone in the stateroom is invited to any special receptions or experiences, everyone gets the same color lanyard, etc. This courtesy does not apply to linked staterooms, however.

Castaway Club Benefits

Insider Exclusives—All Castaway Club members get access to the Compass Newsletter, webcasts, information, news, and tips. This information is available at the Castaway Club web site noted on the previous page.

Early Activity Booking—Yes, you get early online access to book Palo, Remy, and parasailing—and many other amenities and shore excursions—before non-members! If you're not sure of the exact day you can start your early online booking, go the Castaway Club web site and click on your cruise—it'll tell you the exact day your early access begins! Note that you must have your cruise paid in full before you can book activities online.

Toll-Free Number—You have a dedicated phone number: 800-449-3380.

Early Itinerary Booking—Gold and Platinum members can be among the first to book Disney's newest itineraries and ships before others. Dates for early booking are announced online and through travel agents.

Special Check-In—All Castaway Club members can use the exclusive, members-only check-in counters at the cruise terminal! This typically means faster service, plus it's fun to be in the members-only line! You will receive a special lanyard, color-coded to your membership level, too! The Key to the World card you receive at check-in also distinguishes you as a Castaway Club member—your card will have Goofy on it (unless you're in Concierge, then it depicts Mickey; first-time cruisers get Donald Duck).

Stateroom Gift—All members get a special gift in their stateroom to welcome them back! Past gifts have included tote bags, lithographs, and towels. Gifts are one per stateroom, regardless of the number of guests in the room, but the gift type is based on the highest level Castaway Club member in the stateroom. Platinum members receive an extra set of gifts on the first night of their cruise, which have included a leather document case, chocolate truffles, luggage straps, and complementary snacks or beverages.

Onboard Reception—Gold and Platinum members on 4-night and longer cruises get an invitation in their stateroom to attend an exclusive Castaway Club reception onboard. At the reception are snacks and complementary beverages, as well as crew and officers—and often a visit from the Captain! Tip: Look for your family's name on the monitors!

Merchandise Offers—Gold and Platinum members can take advantage of special onboard shopping opportunities, such as great deals or early access to special collectibles. A typical offer is when you spend $100 or more in one purchase at one of the onboard gift shops, you get a $25 credit back.

Priority Check-In—Platinum members get concierge priority boarding check-in at the cruise terminal. You get a boarding pass that allows you to board with group one (the first group to board the ship!), and at Port Canaveral, use of a special pre-boarding area.

Exclusive Experiences—Platinum members receive invitations to special cruise activities. Recent Platinum cruisers have received invitations for a backstage theater tour onboard or an inside look at the Castaway Cay animal program.

Palo Dinner—Platinum members ages 18 and older (and their guests staying in the same stateroom) get the Palo dining service fee ($20) complimentary for one dinner.

Additionally, some Platinum cruisers report that when they book another cruise while onboard, they have received larger onboard credits!

Magical and Wonderful Tips

Creating a "magical" and "wonderful" cruise takes a dash of planning, a pinch of knowledge, and a bit of pixie dust! Here are some more tips:

- "**Shopping onboard** the Disney Cruise Line ships can be a daunting task. Between all of the different items to choose from and the crowds coveting the same thing you have had your eye on, shopping can make one's head spin! A few tips to make shopping at the onboard shops a bit more fun! First, if you see something you absolutely must have, purchase it early on in your cruise. Oftentimes items are not replenished until the ship returns to its home port. If it is a popular item, you may be out of luck heading to the ship's shops the last evening of your cruise. On the other hand, if you are unsure you really need that extra notepaper cube, give yourself some time to think about it. Browsing the shops onboard a bit further may uncover an even bigger treasure. In addition, Castaway Cay has plenty of cute items, often dedicated to the island only! Lastly, consider visiting the onboard shops at an "off-time." Heading to Mickey's Mates right after the evening show in the Walt Disney Theatre has let out can mean wall-to-wall people inside the shops. Visiting the shops during a down-time allows you to meander at your own pace ... and gives you more elbow room to work with! Happy Shopping!" *– contributed by Disney vacationer Cindy Seaburn*

- "While flying home from our first Disney Cruise, I made a corrected packing list for our **next cruise** which we had booked onboard. This was the perfect time to consider what could be left behind next time, and what I wanted to be certain to bring. Now my list is filed in my PassPorter binder, ready for next year!" *– contributed by Disney vacationer Kathleen David-Bajar*

- Please **share your memories and tips**. If we publish them, we'll credit you by name and send you a free copy when they're published! Visit http://www.passporter.com/customs/tipsandstories.asp.

Magical Memory

"The use of facial recognition software on the Disney Dream really tickles the techie in me. When you board, the ship's photographer takes your portrait and swipes your Key to the World card. From then on, the computer remembers your faces and stateroom number, and finds your face in any photo taken by the ship's photographers. Touch your key card to a photo kiosk's card reader, and your photos are automatically displayed. Photos that have been printed (not all are), are gathered together for you in a folio (again, a touch of your key card to the card reader to learn where your folio is on the shelves). And you can view them on your stateroom TV! If you've ever spent hours searching through the photos displayed on the photo shop's walls, you'll appreciate just how magical an improvement this is!"

...as told by author Dave Marx

Glossary of Terms

While this guide isn't exactly overflowing with salty terms, we thought a brief glossary could be useful, and a bit of fun.

Aft–Towards the rear. The *after* section of the ship. Also *abaft*.
All Aboard– The latest time a passenger may board in a port.
All Ashore–The earliest time a passenger may disembark in a port.
Amidships–The center of the ship, between fore and aft. Also *midship*.
Assistant Server–The crew member who assists your server, typically by looking after drinks, clearing the table, and carrying trays to and from the kitchen. On the Disney Cruise Line, a single assistant server attends your needs throughout your voyage.
Beam–The widest portion of a watercraft.
Berth–Any bed on a ship, but more commonly, the fold-down or fold-out beds in a stateroom.
Boat–A small watercraft, sometimes carried onboard a ship.
Bow–The forwardmost section of the ship, pronounced *bough*.
Bridge–The location from which a ship is steered and speed is controlled.
Bulkhead–A vertical wall or partition.
Captain–Ship's officer responsible for the operation and safety of the vessel. See *Master*.
Cast Member–An employee at Disney's land-based theme parks and resorts.
Castaway Club–Disney's free club for past Disney cruisers.
Catamaran–A very stable, fast watercraft with two parallel, widely spaced hulls joined by a broad deck.
Crew Member–A shipboard employee.
Cruise Director–Officer in charge of all passenger entertainment and recreational activities, including shore excursions. "Is everybody having a good time?"
DCL–Abbreviation for the Disney Cruise Line.
Deck–The covering over a vessel's hull, or any floor on a ship.
Diesel Electric–Propulsion system used by ships of the Disney Cruise Line. Diesel generators provide electricity to operate the ship's propulsion motors and other systems.
Displacement–Weight of the water displaced by a vessel, equivalent to the vessel's weight.
Dock–To come alongside a pier. See also *pier*.
Draft–The depth of the submerged portion of a watercraft.
Fathom–A measure of depth. One fathom is equivalent to 6 feet/1.8288 m.
Fender–A device for padding the side of a watercraft or pier to prevent damage.
Fore–Forward. Toward the front. Also, a golfer's warning call.
Gangway–A location on the side of a vessel where passengers and crew can board and disembark. Also, *a retractable walkway broader than a gangplank, connecting ship to shore.*
Guest Relations–Disney's term for a hotel's front desk operations. On the Disney Cruise Line, equivalent to the Purser's Office. Located on deck 3, adjacent to the Atrium Lobby.
Hawser–Long, thick mooring lines for fastening a ship to a pier.
Head Server–The crew member who supervises dining room servers and assistant servers. A single head server attends your needs throughout your voyage.
Hotel Manager–Ship's officer in charge of all passenger-related operations, including accommodations, housekeeping, food and beverages, and entertainment.
Hull–The main body of a watercraft. From Middle English for *husk*.
Keel–One of the main structural members of a vessel to which frames are fastened.
Key to the World Card–Your personal room key, admission, identification, and charge account. Each member of your party has his/her own Key to the World card.

Introduction Reservations Staterooms Dining Activities Ports of Call Magic Index

Glossary *(continued)*

Knot–A measure of speed equal to Nautical Miles Per Hour (6,076 feet/1,852 meters). Also, an undesired tangling of hair.
Latitude–Position north or south of the equator, expressed in degrees.
League–20,000 Leagues = 60,000 miles = 96,560 kilometers
Leeward–Away from, or sheltered from, the wind.
Line–Rope and cord used on a watercraft, or a tall tale told at a bar.
Longitude–Position east or west of Greenwich, England, expressed in degrees.
Mal de Mer–(French) Seasickness. Popular English language euphemism, akin to "green around the gills."
Master–*Master Mariner*, the license held by merchant ship captains.
PFD–Personal Flotation Device. Life jacket. Sometimes known as a Mae West, for the pulchritude (physical appeal) added to those who wear it.
Pier–A platform extending from shore for mooring and loading watercraft.
Pitch–The rising and falling of the bow and stern. See *Roll*. Also, black, tar-like substance used for waterproofing wooden vessels.
Port–The left side of the watercraft when facing Forward. Also, harbor. Also, a fortified wine named for the Portuguese port town of Oporto.
Porthole–An opening in the hull of a vessel. A round window.
Porthos–One of Alexandre Dumas' Three Musketeers.
Propeller–A rotary fan-like device connected to the ship's engines. When it turns, the ship moves. When stationary, the ship is at rest.
Purser–The ship's officer responsible for banking, payroll, and passenger records. See Guest Relations.
Roll–Side-to-side, rocking motion of a vessel. In extremes, this can lead to capsizing.
Rudder–A flat, submerged surface at the stern, used to steer a vessel while underway.
Server–The crew member who attends your table in the dining room, takes food and beverage orders, and supervises the assistant server. Similar to a restaurant waiter. On the Disney Cruise Line, the same server attends your needs throughout your voyage.
Ship–A large watercraft, typically oceangoing, too dignified to be called a boat and big enough to carry boats of its own.
Shorex–Cruise industry abbreviation for Shore Excursion.
Stabilizer–Horizontal, mechanized, submerged flaps that can be extended from a vessel to reduce rolling motion.
Staff Captain–A ship's second-in-command, responsible for crew discipline and ship's maintenance. Also known as "Number One."
Starboard–The right-hand side of the vessel when facing Forward.
Stateroom Host/Hostess–The crew member responsible for your stateroom's housekeeping, baggage pickup/delivery, and your housekeeping-related requests. Sometimes known as a Stateroom Attendant or Steward.
Stem–The part of the bow that is farthest forward.
Stern–The rearmost section of the ship. Also, humorless.
Tender–A watercraft used to convey passengers and cargo from a ship to the shore. Also, easily chewed, as in Filet Mignon.
Tonnage–A measure of the size or cargo capacity of a ship. Also, what you may think you will weigh after a long cruise.
Thruster–A propeller positioned to move the ship laterally while docking and at other times when the ship has little or no forward motion.
Waterline–A line painted on the hull of a watercraft to indicate its typical draft when properly loaded.
Whorf–A character on "Star Trek the Next Generation." See *Pier*.
Windward–Travel into the wind.

Index

We feel that a comprehensive index is very important to a successful travel guide. Too many times we've tried to look something up in other books only to find there was no entry at all, forcing us to flip through pages and waste valuable time. When you're on the phone with a reservation agent and looking for that little detail, time is of the essence.

You'll find the PassPorter index is complete and detailed. Whenever we reference more than one page for a given topic, the major topic is in **bold** to help you home in on exactly what you need. For those times you want to find everything there is to be had, we include all the minor references. We have plenty of cross-references, too, just in case you don't look it up under the name we use.

P.S. This isn't the end of the book. The Web Site Index begins on page 482.

A

B

I

J

K

L

M

Web Site Index

(continued on next page)

Web Site Index *(continued from previous page)*

Site Name	Page	Address (URL)
John Wayne/Orange County Airport	92	http://www.ocair.com
Kayak	73, 102	http://www.kayak.com
Kennedy Space Center	215	http://www.kennedyspacecenter.com
Key West Adventure Scooter	269	http://keywest-scooter.com
Key West Golf	273	http://www.keywestgolf.com
Key West Hunt	269	http://www.keywesthunt.com
Key West Kayak	269	http://www.keywestkayak.com
Key West Scooter	266	http://keywest-scooter.com
Key West Sunrise/Sunset Times	268	http://www.earthtools.org
Key West Visitors Bureau	278	http://www.fla-keys.com
Key West Web Cams	268	http://floridakeyswebcams.tv
La Quinta Inn & Suites North	80	http://www.laquinta.com
LAX Shuttle and Limo	93	http://www.laxshuttlelimo.com
Long Beach Airport	92	http://www.lgb.org
Los Angeles International Airport	92	http://www.lawa.org
Magic For Less Travel	65	http://www.themagicforless.com
Magical Disney Cruise Guide	36	http://allears.net/cruise/cruise.htm
Mahogany Run Golf Course	253	http://www.mahoganyrungolf.com
Mariners Guide	203	http://www.marinersguide.com
MEI-Travel	15	http://www.mei-travel.com
Merritt Island National Refuge	216	http://merrittisland.fws.gov
Meyer Werft Shipywards	37-39	http://www.meyerwerft.de
Monaco Tourism	408	http://www.visitmonaco.com
Motel 6 Cocoa Beach	87	http://www.motel6.com
MouseEarVacations.com	15, 34	http://www.mouseearvacations.com
Mouse Fan Travel	15, 34	http://www.mousefantravel.com
MouseForLess, The	34	http://www.themouseforless.com
MousePlanet	15, 40	http://www.mouseplanet.com
MouseSavers.com	1, 34, 82	http://www.mousesavers.com
Mr. Sanchos (Cozumel)	292	http://www.mrsanchos.com
Nassau Dolphin Encounter	225	http://www.dolphinencounters.com
Native Way Water Sports	280, 282	http://www.nativewaywatersports.com
Nautilus Undersea Tour	279	http://www.nautilus.ky
North Sound Club (Grand Cayman)	279	http://www.northsoundclub.com
Ocean Weather Temperatures	57	http://www.oceanweather.com/data
The Omelet Station	217	http://www.theomeletstation.com
Onboard Media	212	http://www.onboard.com
Orange County Airport	92	http://www.ocair.com
Orbitz.com	65, 73	http://www.orbitz.com
Orlando Airport Marriott	79	http://marriott.com/property/propertypage/MCOAP
Orlando International Airport	74	http://www.orlandoairports.net
Orlando Sanford Airport	76	http://www.orlandosanfordairport.com
Passport Offices	71	http://travel.state.gov
Paradise Point Tramway	254	http://paradisepointtramway.com
Perfect Gift, The	428	http://www.theperfectgift.cc
Photo Copyright Release Waiver	424	http://www.image.com/guest-postcruise.htm
Platinum Castaway Club	15, 36	http://www.castawayclub.com

Web Site Index *(continued from previous page)*

Site Name	Page	Address (URL)
Wave Height Forecasts	57	http://www.lajollasurf.org/nata.html
Wooden Soldier	426	http://www.woodensoldier.com
World Cruise Center	96	http://www.pcsterminals.com
YouTube.com	40	http://www.youtube.com

PassPorter Sites	Page	Address (URL)
PassPorter Main Page	19	http://www.passporter.com
PassPorter's Club	492	http://www.passporter.com/club
PassPorter's Disney Cruise Line	2, 19, 36	http://www.passporter.com/dcl
PassPorter's Deck Plans	5–9	http://www.passporter.com/dcl/deckplans.htm
PassPorter Book Updates	488	http://www.passporter.com/customs/bookupdates.htm
PassPorter PassHolder Pouch	493	http://www.passporterstore.com/store/passholder.aspx
PassPorter Photos	488	http://www.passporter.com/photos
PassPorter Registration	488	http://www.passporter.com/register.asp
PassPorter Message Boards	15	http://www.passporterboards.com/forums
PassPorter Newsletter	464	http://www.passporter.com/news
PassPorter Store	493	http://www.passporterstore.com/store
PassPorter E-Books	490	http://www.passporterstore.com/store/ebooks.aspx

My Favorite Web Sites

Site Name	Page	Address (URL)

PassPorter Online

A wonderful way to get the most from your PassPorter is to visit our active web site at http://www.passporter.com/dcl. We serve up valuable PassPorter updates, plus useful Disney Cruise information and advice we couldn't jam into our book. You can swap tales (that's t-a-l-e-s, Mickey!) with fellow Disney fans, enter contests, find links to other sites, get plenty of details, and ask us questions. You can also order PassPorters and shop for PassPorter accessories! The latest information on new PassPorters to other destinations is available on our web site as well. To go directly to our latest list of page-by-page PassPorter updates, visit http://www.passporter.com/customs/bookupdates.htm.

Register this guidebook and get more discounts

We are **very** interested to learn how your vacation went and what you think of PassPorter, how it worked (or didn't work) for you, and your opinion on how we could improve it! We encourage you to register your copy of PassPorter with us—in return for your feedback, we'll send you coupons good for discounts on PassPorters and gear when purchased directly from us. Register your copy of PassPorter at http://www.passporter.com/register.asp.

Get weekly updates delivered to your e-mailbox

We publish a free, weekly newsletter filled with feature articles about Disney Cruise Line, Walt Disney World, Disneyland, and travel in general, as well as recent news, reader tips, contests, answers to reader questions, and specials on PassPorter guidebooks and gear. To subscribe, visit http://www.passporter.com/news.htm.

View our cruise photos online before you go

Would you like to see photos from Disney cruises and ports of call in lovely, full color? The PassPorter Photo Archive is a large (and free) collection of more than 45,000 photos from Disney cruises, Walt Disney World, Disneyland, and beyond! The archive is fully searchable and each photo carries a description and date. Supersized versions of all our photos are also available to PassPorter's Club passholders (see page 492). Visit http://www.passporter.com/photos.

PassPorter Guidebooks

Deluxe Cruise Edition

Design first-class cruises with this loose-leaf ring-bound edition. Our popular Deluxe Edition features the same great content as this guidebook, plus fourteen of our famous organizer "PassPockets" to plan and record your trip. Special features of the Deluxe Edition include ten interior storage slots in the binder to hold maps, ID cards, and a pen (included). The Deluxe binder makes it easy to add, remove, and rearrange pages ... you can even download, print, and add updates and supplemental pages from our web site or worksheets from the PassPorter's Club (see page 492). Refill pages and pockets are available for purchase. Learn more and order a copy at http://www.passporter.com/wdw/deluxe.htm. The Deluxe Edition is also available through bookstores by special order—just give your favorite bookstore the ISBN code for the 11th Deluxe Edition (ISBN-13: 978-1-58771-121-3).

PassPorter's Walt Disney World

Our best-selling Walt Disney World guidebook covers everything you need to plan a practically perfect vacation, including fold-out park maps, resort room layout diagrams, KidTips, descriptions, reviews, and ratings for the resorts, parks, attractions, and restaurants, and much more! Printed in full color on glossy paper to really let the magic of Disney shine through! Learn more and order at http://www.passporter.com/wdw or get a copy at your favorite bookstore. The 2013 Edition is available in a spiral-bound edition (ISBN-13: 978-1-58771-082-7) and a Deluxe Edition (ISBN-13: 978-1-58771-083-4).

PassPorter's Disneyland Resort and S. California Attractions

PassPorter tours the park that started it all! California's Disneyland Park, Disney's California Adventure, and Downtown Disney get PassPorter's expert treatment, and we throw in Universal Studios Hollywood, Knott's Berry Farm, Hollywood and Downtown Los Angeles, San Diego, SeaWorld, the San Diego Zoo and Wild Animal Park, LEGOLAND, and Six Flags Magic Mountain. Learn more and order a copy at http://www.passporter.com/dl, or pick it up at your favorite bookstore (ISBN-13: 978-1-58771-004-9).

PassPorter's Disney Cruise Clues

Are you looking for tips to save money and time while still having a MAGICAL vacation on the Disney Cruise Line? Wouldn't it be nice to get these tips without having to wade through lots of web sites and message boards? You're in luck! This low-cost book is packed with 250 REAL tips from fellow cruisers—each tip has been hand-picked, sorted, categorized, and edited by Jennifer Marx, the bestselling author of more than 50 books, including the popular "PassPorter's Disney Cruise Line" guidebook. Learn more about this fun book at http://www.passporter.com/dcl/cruiseclues.asp . Available now as an e-book at the PassPorter Store (ISBN-13:9781587710353) and soon, at other e-book retailers. Soon available, also, in a print edition (ISBN-13: 978-1-58771-096-4).

To order any of our guidebooks, visit http://www.passporterstore.com/store or call toll-free 877-929-3273. PassPorter books are also available at your favorite bookstore.

PassPorter E-Books

Looking for more in-depth coverage on specific topics? Look no further than PassPorter E-Books! Our e-books are inexpensive (from $5.95–$9.95) and available immediately as a download (Adobe PDF format). And unlike most e-books, ours are fully formatted just like a regular PassPorter print book. A PassPorter e-book will even fit into a Deluxe PassPorter Binder,. We offer fifteen e-books at press time, and have plans for many, many more!

PassPorter's Disney 500: ***Fast Tips for Walt Disney World Trips***
Our most popular e-book has more than 500 time-tested Walt Disney World tips—all categorized and coded! We chose the best of our reader-submitted tips over a six-year period and each has been edited by author Jennifer Marx. For more details, a list of tips, and a sample page, visit http://www.passporter.com/wdw/disney500.asp. ***Also in print!***

PassPorter's Cruise Clues: ***First-Class Tips for Disney Cruise Trips***
Get the best tips for the Disney Cruise Line—all categorized and coded—as well as cruise line comparisons, a teen perspective, and ultimate packing lists! This popular e-book is packed with 250 cruiser-tested tips—all edited by award-winning author Jennifer Marx. For more details, visit http://www.passporter.com/dcl/cruiseclues.asp.

PassPorter's Disney Character Yearbook
A 268-page compendium of all the live Disney characters you can find at Walt Disney World, Disneyland, and on the Disney Cruise Line. Also includes tips on finding, meeting, photographing, and getting autographs, plus a customizable autograph book to print! For more details, visit http://www.passporter.com/disney-character-yearbook.asp.

PassPorter's Disney Speed Planner: ***The Easy Ten-Step Program***
A fast, easy method for planning practically perfect vacations—great for busy people or those who don't have lots of time to plan. Follow this simple, ten-step plan to help you get your vacation planned in short order so you can get on with your life. For more details, visit http://www.passporter.com/wdw/speedplanner.asp.

PassPorter's Free-Book
A Guide to Free and Low-Cost Activities at Walt Disney World
It's hard to believe anything is free at Walt Disney World, but there are actually a number of things you can get or do for little to no cost. More than 150 free or cheap things to do before you go and after you arrive. Visit http://www.passporter.com/wdw/free-book.asp. ***Also in print!***

PassPorter's Sidekick for the Walt Disney World Guidebook
This is a customizable companion to our general Walt Disney World guidebook—you can personalize worksheets, journals, luggage tags, and charts, plus click links to all the URLs in the guidebook! Details at http://www.passporter.com/wdw/sidekick.asp.

PassPorter's Festivals and Celebrations
at Walt Disney World
Get in on all the fun in this updated 78-page overview of all the wonderful and magical festivals, celebrations, parties, and holidays at Walt Disney World. Included are beautiful color photos and tips on maximizing your experience at the festivals and celebrations. Read more at http://www.passporter.com/wdw/festivals-celebrations.asp. ***Also in print!***

PassPorter's Answer Book
Get answers to the most popular topics asked about Walt Disney World, Disneyland, Disney Cruise Line, and general travel. You've asked it, we've answered it! The e-book's questions and answers are sorted geographically and topically. The e-book is authored by our amazing PassPorter Guide Team, who have heaps of experience at answering your questions! Details at http://www.passporter.com/answer-book.asp.

PassPorter's Disney Weddings & Honeymoons
This is both a guidebook and a bridal organizer tailored to the unique requirements of planning a wedding, vow renewal, or commitment ceremony at Walt Disney World or on the Disney Cruise Line. Walks you through the entire process, outlines your options, offers valuable tips, organizes your information, and helps you plan down to the last detail! Details at http://www.passporter.com/weddings.asp. ***Also in print!***

PassPorter's Disney Vacation Club Guide
A 170-page in-depth guide to all aspects of the Disney Vacation Club, from deciding whether to join to deciding where and when to use your points. Included are beautiful color photos and tips on maximizing your experience. If you've ever wondered what the club is all about or wanted to learn more, this is the perfect introduction. Get more details at http://www.passporter.com/disney-vacation-club.asp. ***Also in print!***

PassPorter's Walt Disney World for Brit Holidaymakers
Brits, you can get super in-depth information for your Walt Disney World vacation from fellow Brit and PassPorter feature columnist Cheryl Pendry. This e-book is more than 250 pages long and filled with amazing detail on both Walt Disney World as well as other Orlando-area attractions. Learn more at http://www.passporter.com/wdw/brits.asp. ***Also in print!***

PassPorter's Disneyland Paris
This comprehensive, 204-page book covers every aspect of visiting Disneyland Paris, including traveling to France from the United States and the United Kingdom. We provide all the information you need to get the most out of your stay! Read more and see a sample page at http://www.passporter.com/disneyland-paris.asp.

Learn more about these and other titles and order e-books at:
http://www.passporterstore.com/store/ebooks.aspx

Introduction
Reservations
Staterooms
Dining
Activities
Ports of Call
Magic
Index

Do you want more help planning your Disney cruise vacation? Join the PassPorter's Club and get all these benefits:

- ✔ "All-you-can-read" access to EVERY e-book we publish (see current list on the previous pages). PassPorter's Club passholders also get early access to these e-books before the general public. New e-books are added on a regular basis, too.
- ✔ Interactive, customizable "e-worksheets" to help make your trip planning easier, faster, and smoother. These are the electronic, interactive worksheets we've been mentioning throughout this book. The worksheets are in PDF format and can be printed for a truly personalized approach! We have more than 50 worksheets, with more on the way. You can see a sample e-worksheet to the right—this one calculates your cruise gratuities for you!

Cruise Gratuities Budget Worksheet
personalized for me!

- ✔ Access to super-sized "e-photos" in the PassPorter Photo Archives—photos can be zoomed in up to 25 times larger than standard web photos. You can use these e-photos to see detail as if you're actually standing there—or use them for desktop wallpaper, scrapbooking, whatever!
- ✔ Our best discount on print guidebooks ... 35% off!

There's more features, too! For a full list of features and current e-books, e-worksheets, and e-photos, visit http://www.passporter.com/club. You can also take a peek inside the Club's Gallery at http://www.passporterboards.com/forums/passporters-club-gallery. The Gallery is open to everyone—it contains two FREE interactive e-worksheets to try out!

Price: A PassPorter's Club pass is currently $4.95/month (the cost of just one e-book) or $44.95/annual (an annual pass gives you access to all our big Online Editions, too!)

How to Get Your Pass to the PassPorter's Club

Step 1. Get a free community account. Register simply and quickly at http://www.passporterboards.com/forums/register.php.

Step 2. Log in at http://www.passporterboards.com/forums/login.php using the Member Name and password you created in step 1.

Step 3. Get your pass. Select the type of pass you'd like and follow the directions to activate it immediately. We currently offer monthly and annual passes. (Annual passes save 25% and get extra perks!)

Questions? Assistance? We're here to help! Please send e-mail to club@passporter.com.

You may also find many of your questions answered in our FAQ (Frequently Asked Questions) in the Gallery forum (see link above).

PassPorter Goodies

PassPorter was born out of the necessity for more planning, organization, and a way to preserve the memories of a great vacation! Along the way we've found other things that either help us use the PassPorter better, appreciate our vacation more, or just make our journey a little more comfortable. Others have asked us about them, so we thought we'd share them with you. Order online at http://www.passporterstore.com/store or use the order form below.

PassPorter® PassHolder is a small, lightweight nylon pouch that holds your Key to the World card, passes, ID cards, passports, money, and pens. Wear it around your neck to keep your card with you at all times, and for easy access at the airport. The front features a clear compartment, a zippered pocket, and a velcro pocket; the back has a small pocket and two pen slots. In fact, the Waves Phones actually fit in the small pocket on the back of the pouch, or you can put them inside the velcro pocket! Adjustable cord. Royal blue. 4 7/8" x 6 1/2"

Quantity:
____ x $8.95

PassPorter® Badge personalized with your name! Go around the "World" in style with our lemon yellow oval pin. Price includes personalization with your name, shipping, and handling. Please indicate badge name(s) with your order.

Quantity:
___ x $4.00

Name(s): ________

To order, visit http://www.passporterstore.com/store, call 877-929-3273, or send back the form below.

Please ship my PassPorter Goodies to:

Name ....

Address ....

City, State, Zip ....

Daytime Phone ....

Payment: ❑ check (to "MediaMarx") ❑ charge card

❑ MasterCard ❑ Visa ❑ American Express ❑ Discover

Card number .... Exp. Date. ....

Signature ....

Sub-Total:

Tax*:

Shipping**:

Total:

** Please include sales tax if you live in Michigan.*
***Shipping costs are:*
$5 for totals up to $9
$6 for totals up to $19
$7 for totals up to $29
$8 for totals up to $39
Delivery takes 1-2 weeks.

Send your order form to P.O. Box 3880, Ann Arbor, MI 48106 or order online http://www.passporterstore.com/store.

My Important Numbers

Enter your important numbers in the boxes below. Once you obtain your park passes, write down the number on the back in the appropriate places below—you will need this number if your passes are ever lost. Consider using a personal code to conceal sensitive information.

Personal Information:

Driver's License number(s):

Passport number(s):

Frequent Flyer number(s):

Insurance number(s):

Other number(s):

Financial Information:

Voucher number(s):

Gift card number(s):

Traveler check number(s):

Other number(s):